# THE THEORY OF FINANCIAL DECISIONS

## McGraw-Hill Series in Finance

**Professor Charles A. D'Ambrosio**
*University of Washington*
*Consulting Editor*

**Christy and Clendenin:** *Introduction to Investments*
**Coates:** *Investment Strategy*
**Committe:** *Managerial Finance for the Seventies*
**Curran:** *Principles of Financial Management*
**Dobrovolsky:** *The Economics of Corporation Finance*
**Francis:** *Investments: Analysis and Management*
**Haley and Schall:** *The Theory of Financial Decisions*
**Hastings and Mietus:** *Personal Finance*
**Henning, Pigott, and Scott:** *International Financial Management*
**Lang and Gillespie:** *Strategy for Personal Finance*
**Robinson and Wrightsman:** *Financial Markets: The Accumulation and Allocation of Wealth*
**Schall and Haley:** *Introduction to Financial Management*
**Sharpe:** *Portfolio Theory and Capital Markets*
**Stevenson:** *Fundamentals of Finance*
**Troelstrup and Hall:** *The Consumer in American Society: Personal and Family Finance*

# THE THEORY OF FINANCIAL DECISIONS

## Second Edition

**Charles W. Haley**
**Lawrence D. Schall**

*Department of Finance, Business Economics,*
*and Quantitative Methods*
*University of Washington*

**McGraw-Hill Book Company**

New York St. Louis San Francisco Auckland Bogotá Düsseldorf
Johannesburg London Madrid Mexico Montreal New Delhi
Panama Paris São Paulo Singapore Sydney Tokyo Toronto

THE THEORY OF FINANCIAL DECISIONS



34567890FGFG 83210

This book was set in Times Roman by Bi-Comp, Incorporated.
The editors were Bonnie E. Lieberman and M. Susan Norton;
the cover was designed by John Hite;
the production supervisor was Dennis J. Conroy.
Fairfield Graphics was printer and binder.

**Library of Congress Cataloging in Publication Data**

Haley, Charles W
The theory of financial decisions.

(McGraw-Hill series in finance)
Bibliography: p.
Includes index.
1. Business enterprises—Finance. I. Schall, Lawrence D., joint author. II. Title.
HG4011.H27 1979 658.1'5 78-23426
ISBN 0-07-025568-7

To Don, Lee, Lillian, and Norma

# CONTENTS

# PREFACE

The primary objective of this book is the same as that of the first edition. We wish to provide a rigorous, consistent development of the theory of finance and its implications for managerial decisions. The first edition found widespread use at the graduate level, often in introductory course sequences. It frequently served as a unifying text for graduate seminars and for advanced undergraduate classes. The changes made in this revision are designed to enhance these applications. We have reviewed the entire text and made changes to improve its clarity and readability. A substantial amount of new material has been added to extend our basic analysis in some areas and to reflect recent work in the field. As before, our emphasis is on theory rather than practice; therefore, empirical work is not discussed in depth.

The first three chapters introduce the basic concepts under assumptions of perfect capital markets and certainty. Chapter 4 provides a review of subjective probabilities and mathematical statistics. Chapter 5 examines individual choice under uncertainty and develops the concept of utility functions of the Von-Neuman and Morgenstern type. New in this edition is an appendix to Chapter 5 which covers the mathematical properties of utility functions and the measures of risk aversion for an individual. Chapter 6 is an introduction to portfolio theory, and Chapters 7 and 8 discuss the single-period mean-variance model of capital market equilibrium and its implications for financial decisions. A new appendix to Chapter 8 examines alternative specifications of the required rate of return (discount rate) for firm investment decisions. Most of the changes in these first eight chapters are of an editorial nature. The only exceptions are the new appendixes to Chapters 5 and 8 and a change made in Chapter 3. The project analysis approach of Chapter 3 was revised in response to problems faced by students regarding the definitions of alternatives within a project. Users of the first edition please take note.

The remaining chapters of the book have been substantially revised and reorganized. Chapter 9 introduces the problem of multiperiod valuation under uncertainty in discrete time. We have added a new section containing a multiperiod extension of the mean-variance model. Appendix 9A is now a formal presentation of the time-state preference model that is introduced in the text of Chapter 9. (Material from Appendix 9A of the first edition dealing with the firm's objective is now part of Chapter 17.) Chapter 10 and Appendix 10A are entirely new in this edition. We provide here an introduction to continuous time valuation and the option pricing model of Black and Scholes. The chapter itself is a general presentation without extensive mathematics, and the appendix provides the basics of stochastic calculus and a derivation of the Black-Scholes model. Chapters 11, 12, and 13 examine the financing and investment decisions of firms under assumptions of perfect markets. These chapters reflect only modest revisions from their counterparts, Chapters 10, 12, and 13 of the first edition.

Chapters 14 through 17 examine financial decisions under imperfect markets. Almost all this material is new to the book. Chapter 14 is an introduction to problems posed by departures from the perfect market assumptions used in the book to that point. This chapter also summarizes much of the material found in the subsequent chapters. Many instructors may find Chapter 14 a suitable point to stop. Chapter 15 presents a theoretical analysis of the impact of agency costs, bankruptcy costs, personal taxes, and other imperfections on the financing and investment decisions of the firm. Chapter 16 examines issues regarding leasing and merger decisions under both perfect and imperfect markets. Chapter 17 concerns the theory of firm objectives. Although Chapter 17 and the appendix to Chapter 15 are directed primarily to doctoral students, we have tried to present issues and concepts in a manner appropriate for MBA students majoring in finance and for exceptional undergraduates. This material reflects the state of the art in finance and deals with difficult problems. It therefore relies more heavily on mathematical logic than do other parts of the book. Throughout we attempt to achieve a compromise between the requirements of general, rigorous proofs and an objective readability and intuitive understanding.

A one-quarter course for students lacking prior preparation in financial theory can be built around Chapters 1 through 8. An alternative, somewhat more difficult sequence for the same students is Chapters 1 to 3, Chapter 9, and Chapters 12 to 14. If students have the requisite background, the instructor has much more latitude in the selection of material to be covered.

Our reorganization of the book reflects our views of the proper sequencing of material; however, it is possible to skip over some chapters in order to cover later ones. Chapters 1 to 3 serve as a general introduction, but students can proceed rapidly through them if their previous course work includes some financial theory. Chapters 4 to 8 may be omitted without serious problem. The section in Chapter 9 on the multiperiod mean-variance model assumes knowledge of the single-period model developed in Chapter 7, but otherwise the discussions in Chapters 9 to 17 do not rely on Chapters 4 to 8. Chapters 4 to 7 can serve as a quick review for students with a background in portfolio theory so that it is possible for these students to move rapidly to the analysis of firm financial decisions in Chapter 8.

Chapter 9 serves as the keystone of the remainder of the book and is a prerequisite for Chapters 10 to 17. Chapter 10 may be omitted or included as desired. To a degree, the Chapter 10 continuous time framework is a contrast to the Chapter 9 valuation models, but it also relies on the time-state model presented in Appendix 9A. Although it is certainly not required, we feel that if Chapter 10 is to be used, it would best be assigned immediately following Chapter 9. Chapters 11, 12, and 13 are designed to be covered in that sequence; however, Chapter 13 may be omitted at the option of the instructor. Chapter 14 relies on the development of Chapters 11 and 12 and, somewhat, of Chapter 13. Chapter 14 is an essential prerequisite to Chapter 15 and helpful for Chapters 16 and 17. Chapter 15 is not needed for an understanding of Chapter 16 and may be skipped in order to move directly from Chapter 14 to Chapter 16. The primary prerequisite to Chapter 17 is Chapter 9, although coverage of Chapters 11, 12, and 14, and 15 prior to Chapter 17 is recommended.

College algebra remains the only mathematical prerequisite for the main portion of the text. Many of the appendixes and some special sections denoted by a † require calculus. A background in mathematical programming is recommended for the section in Chapter 15 concerning investment decisions.

We have been greatly helped by many of our students and colleagues in the profession in writing both this and the first edition. The original contributions of Robert Hamada and Robert Winkler remain in this edition. We are also indebted to three of our University of Washington colleagues who reviewed sections of the manuscript and provided many valuable comments—Ritchie Campbell, Richard Castanias, and Harry DeAngelo. G. O. Bierwag, John J. McConnell, and David A. Umstead deserve special thanks for very carefully reviewing the manuscript before its final stage. Our appreciation also goes to one of our students, Linda Lashlee, who saved us some embarrassment and readers considerable confusion by reviewing and proofreading all new material in the text. And we thank the numerous other people who have, over the years, offered us both encouragement and constructive criticism.

Some of the discussion and proofs presented here appeared in articles in *The Journal of Business, The Journal of Finance, The Journal of Financial and Quantitative Analysis,* and *The Review of Economics and Statistics.* We thank these journals for allowing us to draw on such works in preparing the material presented here.

*Charles W. Haley*
*Lawrence D. Schall*

# FREQUENTLY USED SYMBOLS

The table provides the generic definitions of symbols which are frequently used in the text. Generally, those variables which are found in only one chapter are not included. The page references are to a more complete discussion of the meaning of the variable. The variables may appear with special subscripts to indicate the use of the variable in some particular sense; for example $X_t$, the value of $X$ at time $t$. The symbols appear in boldface in later chapters of the text to indicate that they are vectors; see the discussion at the beginning of Chapter 9 on this notation. A tilde over a symbol is used to indicate that the variable takes on its values according to a probability distribution. A "bar" indicates the expected value of the variable.

| *Symbol* | *Definition* | *Pages on which defined* |
|---|---|---|
| English letter symbols: | | |
| $B$ | Value of the firm's bonds (debt) | 282 |
| $B^N$ | The value of new bonds issued to finance investment | 304 |
| $B^{O'}$ and $B^O$ | The zero investment and postinvestment values of the firm's old bonds | 304 |
| cov[,] | Covariance between two variables enclosed by the brackets | 82 |
| $D$ | Dividends paid by the firm | 23 |
| $D_0'$ and $D_0$ | Current (time 0) dividends to old shares with zero investment and with the investment budget, respectively | 304 |
| $DP$ | Depreciation | 215 |
| $E[\ ]$ | Expected value of the terms enclosed by the brackets | 76 |
| $F$ | The costs of financial distress | 446 |

| *Symbol* | *Definition* | *Pages on which defined* |
|---|---|---|
| $i$ | Riskless rate of interest | 18, 144 |
| $k$ | Equilibrium rate of return | 199, 227 |
| $I$ | Firm investment | 209 |
| $r$ | Rate of return* | 145, 191 |
| $R$ | Interest payments to bonds | 215 |
| $R^O$ | Interest to the firm's old bonds | 292 |
| $S$ | Value of the firm's shares | 282 |
| $S^N$ | The value of new shares issued to finance current investment | 304 |
| $S^{O'}$ and $S^O$ | The zero investment and postinvestment values of the firm's old shares | 303 |
| $V$ | The value of the firm, where $V = S + B$† | 282 |
| $V'$ | The value of the firm with zero investment | 303 |
| $V[\ ]$ | Market value of the term in brackets, e.g., $V[\tilde{Y}]$ is the market value of income stream $\tilde{Y}$ | 218 |
| var[ ] | Variance of the terms enclosed by the brackets | 77 |
| $W_S$ | Wealth of the firm's old shareholders provided by their ownership of the firm | 304 |
| $X$ | Firm cash income (revenues less expenses) | 209 |
| $Y$ | Net cash flow paid to owners of the firm's securities ($= Y^B + Y^S$)†† | 210 |
| $Y'$ | Zero investment net cash flow paid to owners of the firm's securities | 307 |
| $Y^B$ | Net cash flow paid to all bonds of the firm | 210 |
| $Y^{BO}$ | Net cash flow paid to old bonds | 213, 291 |
| $Y^S$ | Net cash flow paid to all shares of the firm | 210 |
| $Y^{SO}$ | Net cash flow paid to old shares | 213 |
| $Z$ | The net cash flow generated by project $Z$ | 317 |
| Greek letter symbols: | | |
| $\gamma$ | The proportion of investment financed with debt | 329 |
| $\theta$ | Ratio of outstanding bonds to the total value of the firm | 337 |
| $\lambda'$ | Slope of the capital market line ($\lambda = \lambda'/\sigma_M$) | 147 |
| $\rho$ | Correlation coefficient | 82 |
| $\sigma$, $\sigma^2$ | Standard deviation; variance | 78 |
| $\tau$ | Tax rate (the firm tax rate if no subscript or superscript; personal tax rates have subscripts or superscripts) | 215 |
| $\phi$ | The proportion of current investment financed by new stock or new bonds, i.e., $\phi = (S^N + B^N)/I_0$ | 304 |

* This is referred to as the "internal rate of return" in Chap. 3.

† This also signifies the value of the firm given the capital budget that is adopted; see page 303.

†† In Chap. 2, $Y$ is used to signify any income stream received by an individual.

# THE THEORY OF FINANCIAL DECISIONS

CHAPTER

# ONE

# INTRODUCTION

The topic of this book is the theory of financial decisions of individuals and business firms. All theory involves abstraction from the complexities of actual experience. In this initial chapter we present the fundamental abstractions from reality that form the basis of our discussion in later chapters. We are primarily interested in individual decisions as they affect firm decisions. Therefore, the theoretical development of individual decisions is less extensive than that of firm decisions. Nevertheless, substantial analysis will be devoted to the problems of individuals. Our first concern must be the nature of financial decisions and the objectives of the decision maker.

## FINANCIAL DECISIONS IN GENERAL

People are making decisions all the time. Some decisions involve relationships with other people; some decisions involve purchases of goods and services; some decisions involve the commitment of time to activities. Financial decisions may be broadly characterized by three factors: money, time, and risk. The theory of finance is concerned with the problem of evaluating alternative future monetary flows or values. Since the future is in general uncertain, the problem becomes one of evaluating risky monetary flows or values over time.[1]

[1] We shall use the words "risk" and "uncertainty" as meaning the same thing. This usage differs from that of some authors who distinguish between the two. See chap. 4 for additional discussion.

For the present discussion, the risk factor will be ignored, as it will be our major concern beginning with Chap. 4. Let us therefore look at the problems posed by money and time.

First, our view of the world must be organized into a form that is convenient for analysis. We assume that there are three components to the world which are important to financial decisions—individuals, firms, and financial markets.[2] Individuals own the firms and purchase the goods and services provided by them. Firms are devices for the production of goods and services (including financial services) that are managed by people who make decisions with respect to their operation. We therefore have two kinds of people: individuals and managers. Individuals are consumers and owners of firms' securities; managers are people who operate firms. The financial markets are most conveniently thought of as a place where transfers of securities occur. In the real world, of course, the financial markets are anywhere such transfers occur. The term "financial markets" really refers to the existence of an undefined means of effecting transfers of securities. This is consistent with the general use of the concept of a "market" in economics.

## Individual Financial Decisions

An individual's financial decisions are made within the confines of two constraints: wealth and opportunities. An individual's wealth consists of two components—nonhuman assets and human assets. The latter is the value of labor income, which results from the individual's employment as a producer of goods and services. We shall assume throughout that the characteristics of basic labor income are given and that the individual's financial decisions do not affect this income. The individual's human assets are assumed to be nontradable and given, whereas the nonhuman assets are assumed to be tradable in the market. Of course, the attributes of labor income very much affect the individual's financial decisions. Nonhuman assets in general can be divided into several types—money, securities, and physical assets. To keep our analysis of individual decisions simple we shall assume that individuals do not have physical assets.[3] Physical assets will be assumed to be held by firms. We shall use the

[2] Governments will also be assumed to exist in considering tax effects. The existence of government securities (bonds) is also assumed. However, the investment and other expenditure activities of governments will be ignored.

[3] Assets refer to possessions yielding future benefits. The physical assets an individual might hold include "consumer durables," which yield future services (and therefore have current value), and physical assets held for investment. Inclusion of these assets into the analysis of individual decisions would substantially increase the discussion required without adding appreciably to the main topic of this book, the theory of firm decisions. In analyzing *firm* financial decisions, no restriction is imposed on the nature of individual asset holdings; i.e., individuals may hold consumer durables or producers' goods.

term "cash" instead of "money" to refer to spendable funds (currency, coin, demand deposits) and shall assume that an individual's cash balances are held only to pay for current consumption (more about this later). The remaining asset is securities—"paper" claims against the future income of firms. Therefore, we can consider an individual's wealth position to be determined by the individual's total income (labor income plus income from securities) and cash balances.

An individual's opportunities consist of consumption over time, purchase or sale of financial securities, and issuing personal financial securities (claims against future income). *We shall assume that the fundamental problem for the individual is how to allocate consumption over time given the individual's wealth and opportunities.* In analyzing the choices an individual might make, we assume that individuals are rational in the sense that they do the best they can in achieving the maximum satisfaction from their consumption patterns. The financial decisions an individual must make in achieving this objective are:

1. The amount of consumption in each period over time (consumption)
2. The amount and type of securities to be held in each period (investment)
3. The amount and type of claims to be issued in each period (financing)

Much of the subsequent analysis in this book is devoted to developing theories of how individuals might make such decisions. Note that the choice of which goods and services to consume in each period is not included in the list above. This decision, although clearly related to the individual's financial decisions, is not considered here. Of interest here is the total outlay for consumption and not the allocation of that outlay to particular commodities. A more detailed analysis of the consumption decision is beyond the scope of this text.

### Firm Financial Decisions

Perhaps the fundamental economic and financial decision of the firm is that of determining the level and composition of its investment. Firms can invest in either physical assets or financial assets (securities). Such investment decisions determine the firm's future income. The returns from investment are influenced by factors that are either out of the control of management (conditions in the markets for the firm's products or services) or, in the case of operating decisions, excluded from the analysis.

A firm must make two additional and related financial decisions: first, how much of its current income to pay out to the owners of the firm (the dividend decision), and second, the amount and type of financial securities to issue (the financial structure decision). These constitute the financing decisions of the firm. Therefore, firms are considered to make two general types of financial decisions: *investment decisions* and *financing decisions*. These are the principal subjects of this text.

## MANAGERIAL OBJECTIVES AND THE AGENCY RELATIONSHIP

Although we shall continually refer to "firm decisions," firms in fact do not make decisions, managers do. Some firms are managed by their owners; other firms have managers hired directly or indirectly by their owners. The fact that a great deal of economic activity is carried on by firms whose management is hired only indirectly by the owners presents a basic problem. The owners of a firm are individuals who are concerned with achieving their desired patterns of consumption over time. The managers may or may not have direct knowledge of the preferences of the owners and in any case may have considerable freedom to pursue a variety of objectives. Three problems result:

1. *Should* managers seek to act in the best interests of the owners?
2. *Do* managers seek to act in the best interests of the owners?
3. *If* management is to act in the best interests of the owners, what criteria should management use in making financial decisions?

In this text we focus primarily on the third problem. We usually assume that management is attempting to promote the welfare of the firm's owners in making financial decisions or, at least, is concerned as to the impact of financial decisions on the firm's owners. Therefore, we wish to specify precisely how financial decisions should be made so as to benefit the owners of the firm. The first two problems, although interesting and important, are only in part within the theory of finance and enter into other realms of economic and social theory.[4] Even so, some comments regarding these issues are appropriate here, and aspects of these two problems will be examined in future chapters.

The question of whose objectives should be pursued by management raises issues of public policy and economic organization. The objectives of at least five groups might be considered: the managers themselves, the firm's owners (stockholders), the owners plus all people holding financial claims issued by the firm, all parties involved in the firm's operations including workers and the firm's customers, and the total society. Under classical capitalism, maximum social welfare is assumed to be achieved through private ownership of firms which are operated to benefit the owners. In socialistic societies, ownership is vested in the government, and managers are presumed to act more directly to benefit the total society. In both cases managers are considered to be agents of the owners—everyone under socialism and a subset of society (capitalists) under capitalism. Regardless of the form of ownership, there are divergent views as to the "social responsibility" of management. Many people in

[4] For a more comprehensive discussion of some of the issues here, see Solomon, "The Theory of Financial Management," chap. 2, and Jensen and Meckling, "Theory of the Firm: Managerial Behavior, Agency Costs, and Ownership Structure" (both works are listed in the Suggested Readings at the end of this chapter).

capitalistic societies believe that the managers of large firms should be directly concerned with the welfare of society, not merely the owners or other participants in the firm. Many people in socialistic societies believe that managers should concern themselves with efficient operation of their enterprises and leave the social policy questions for government officials to resolve. These broad issues are clearly outside the scope of finance.

More narrowly, in this text we might examine the interests of those parties who have a direct financial stake in the success or failure of the firm. We can divide this group into two classes—creditors and owners. The creditor group consists of all parties that hold fixed financial claims against the firm. Such claims include pension liabilities, trade accounts payable, wages and salaries payable, liabilities to customers under warranties on prepaid purchases, various forms of debt (leases, notes, mortgages, bonds, etc.), and other securities issued by the firm such as preferred stock. The owners of the firm (common stockholders) have the rights to residual income and assets after creditor claims have been met. The interests of creditors need not coincide with the interests of owners, and we consider the problems posed by this lack of coincidental interests later, especially in Chap. 17. Here we note only that, under conditions assumed throughout most of the book, the interests of the owners are served by acting in ways that benefit both owners and creditors. This topic definitely falls within the scope of finance and is becoming an important issue in the theoretical literature.

The first problem noted above is, largely, a theoretical and philosophical issue; the second one considers how managers behave in practice. Do managers generally act to promote the owner's welfare, or do they serve one of the other groups? A possibility of concern since the time of Adam Smith (1776) is that managers act in their own personal interests and pursue objectives that may or may not contribute to the welfare of owners, of other participants in the firm's activities, or of society at large.

Managers can be viewed as agents of the owners, hired to operate the firm for the owners' benefit. If the firm is owned and managed by the same person, there is no possible conflict in objectives. This is one extreme case. At the other end of the spectrum, the firm's management has no ownership interest in the firm or, in a socialist society, only a minute portion as members of the total society. Thus managers may be owners or purely agents of the owners or anywhere in between. Suppose we assume that managers operate to serve their own best interests. Will their best interests coincide with those of the owners? To the extent that there is a divergence in interests, the owners are less well off than would be so if no divergence existed. The owners' losses are costs of the agency relationship.

Are such agency costs large? The answer is not clear at present, but there are some theoretical arguments that suggest that they are not great. Under idealized conditions (perfect markets), managers have no choice but to strive to maximize the welfare of the owners. Otherwise they would be fired. This is so whenever information as to the firm's performance is freely and costlessly available to the owners. If information is costly, the maximum agency cost cannot be much greater than the costs of information; otherwise it would be worthwhile for the owners to incur those costs to find out what has been going on. Much of the analysis in this book assumes costless information; in that analysis, it is appropriate to assume managers will act in the owners' interests.

Under more realistic conditions, agency costs may be larger; however, they are always limited by the possibility that a present or potential owner may guess or discover management's failure to act in the owner's interests and seize control of the firm to force compliance. Hence managers cannot completely ignore owner preferences or can do so only at a considerable risk to their jobs.

Beyond the threat posed by an owner's discovery of lack of performance, there are two other factors encouraging management to pursue owner objectives. Many actions that are not consistent with owner welfare maximization are illegal, and the legal penalties for committing such acts are ordinarily an effective discouragement. Second, actions that are legal but unethical in that they violate the spirit of the agency relationship are, in many cases, discouraged by management's sense of professionalism. If managers believe that their primary responsibility is to the owners, then their own ethical standards may induce managers to act accordingly. That is, management's interests may include "managing well," and they may pursue owner-oriented objectives, not because they are forced to, but because they want to. Such managerial attitudes, in our opinion, are a major factor in mitigating potential conflicts between management and owners.

The economic and social mechanisms described above limit the degree to which the agency contract is violated in practice. However, we feel that these mechanisms are not completely effective and that agency costs are sufficiently great that the agency relationship is a useful topic of research. Of course, the magnitude of the problem is an empirical matter, and this aspect of the question is as important as are the theoretical principles that are involved.

Given the separation of ownership of the firm from management and given that the objective of management is to act in the best interests of the owners, one might inquire as to how management is to know what those best interests are. Answering this question is the focus of our discussion of individual financial decisions. We assume that the only relationships between management and owners that affect the owners' welfare are the stream of payments (dividends) paid to the owners and the value of the claims held by the owners against the future payments of the firm. In other words, the only way management can affect the welfare of the owners is through the present and future payments to them. Our concern throughout the book will be the impact of management's decisions on this stream and the impact of those decisions on the owners' welfare.

## MARKET EQUILIBRIUM, VALUATION, AND FINANCIAL DECISIONS

We shall see later on that the market value of the firm may be an appropriate measure of the impact of firm financial decisions on the owners' welfare. We shall therefore spend some time on two related issues:

1. How is the value of the firm determined in the capital markets?
2. How do the financial decisions of the firm affect its value?

In order to develop a theory of valuation we shall generally be concerned with equilibrium conditions in the capital markets. Essentially we shall argue that it is difficult if not impossible to determine how firm financial decisions affect the value of the firm when the market is not in equilibrium. This is the main reason for the stress on equilibrium. Moreover, we shall largely be concerned with the equilibrium properties of *perfect markets*. The characteristics of such markets will be discussed in Chap. 2. For the present, it should be noted that the concept of perfect markets is a significant abstraction from reality although a very useful one. This abstraction enables us to deal with the fundamental variables of individual and firm decisions without being snarled up in the myriad of details that characterize real markets. It may be that real markets are approximately perfect or imperfect in ways that have obvious and easily handled solutions. In other words, we consider the theory as developed in terms of equilibrium in perfect markets to provide the foundation for the firm's decisions. The analysis of perfect markets is also helpful in examining imperfect markets and related firm financial decisions in Chaps. 14 through 17.

Two additional comments relating to the discussion of perfect markets are appropriate here. First, we do not assume that the firm's products or factors of production are necessarily traded in perfect equilibrium markets. In fact, implied in our discussion of firm investment decisions is the assumption that profitable opportunities do exist, which would not be the case if product and factor markets were perfect. In our opinion the capital market is the closest thing to a perfect, competitive market that exists in real economies. Therefore, even though perfection in the capital markets may be a reasonable approximation, there is no reason to believe that all markets are nearly perfect. Thus, for example, the market for General Motors' stock is probably closer to perfection than the market for General Motors' cars.

Second, it will be assumed throughout most of the book that individuals and firms are "price takers" with respect to their decisions relating to capital market variables. In other words, when particular individuals or firms buy or sell securities, no appreciable change in equilibrium conditions in the market occurs. The market rates of interest are assumed to be "given" as far as the decision makers are concerned. This, of course, is the standard assumption in discussions of competitive markets in economic analysis.

## TIME AND TIMING

We remarked earlier that one of the important characteristics of financial decisions is the time factor. Most financial decisions by both individuals and firms are affected by the timing of the cash flows resulting from alternative actions. Time is a continuum. We organize time into "periods" which are based on the physical behavior of our planet in space. Some decisions may be viewed as "now-later" problems. That is, the only information of concern to the decision maker is the results "one period from now" (or "later") from an action "now." The definition of "period" is arbitrary. "Now" is well defined as the point in time at which the decision is being made. "One period from now" may be any point in future time—one minute, one year, one century—from now. In other decisions, however, the events that occur between now and later are important. Such situations involve a "horizon" problem. The decision maker here is faced with a multiperiod problem with an ending point—the horizon. Finally, there are situations in which the ending point is indefinite. That is, the stream of payments from a firm may have no particular ending point when viewed from now. We can describe such cases as "infinite horizon" problems.

From this discussion it should be apparent that any definition of period is either arbitrary or dependent on the particular problem. Generally in our examples we shall use the year as the period, recognizing, however, that this choice is not necessary—other definitions could serve as well. Basically, the definition of the appropriate period should follow from the timing of the events that are relevant to the decision maker in the situation. If the stream of dividends is the important event and dividends occur only at 3-month intervals, then perhaps the appropriate period should be 3 months.

In our analysis we shall assume that events occur over regular intervals (periods) in time. Unless otherwise indicated, events will be assumed to occur at the end of the period. Figure 1-1 illustrates this assumption. We are now at time 0. Period 1 extends from time 0 to time 1; period 2 extends from time 1 to time 2; etc. For simplicity, it will be assumed that events for period 1 occur at time 1. Events for period 2 occur at time 2. Nothing of interest occurs during the period. This way of organizing time and the assumptions about the timing of events differs somewhat from the way we usually look at economic variables. In particular, the difference between "stock" variables (e.g., balance sheet items) and "flow" variables (e.g., income statement items) becomes fuzzy. This point requires further discussion.

## STOCKS AND FLOWS

It is customary in economic analysis to distinguish between stocks and flows. A stock variable is thought of as the quantity of something at a particular *point* in time, for example, the cash in your pocket at 2:00 A.M. on January 1, 1979. A

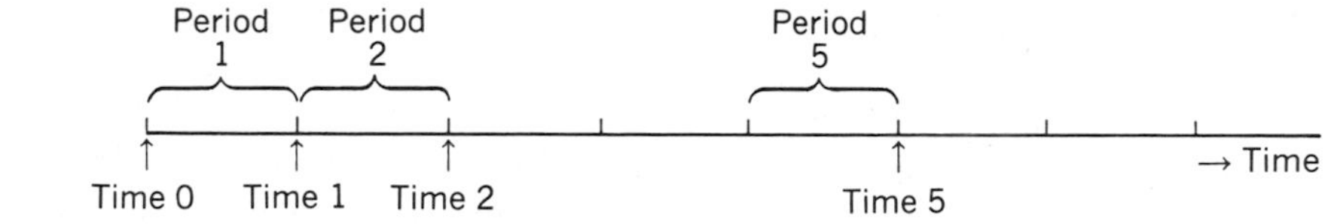


**figure 1-1**

flow variable represents the rate of change in the stock over an *interval* of time; for example your net cash outflow (decrease in cash stock) between 1:00 A.M. and 2:00 A.M. on January 1, 1979. In this book we assume that all flows occur at a point in time, and that they occur only at the end of regular intervals; that is, the interval over which the flow occurs is infinitesimal and is at the end of the associated period. In the example here, assuming that the relevant period is one hour, we would view all payments between 1:00 A.M. and 2:00 A.M. as being made at 2:00 A.M. This is a useful assumption and, we would argue, does not in any essential way affect our analysis since the intervals can be made as short as needed.[5] However, it does introducc the possibility of confusion unless clearly understood. We shall remind the reader of this assumption at critical stages in the analysis. We shall generally refer to flow variables as occurring "during period $t$" (i.e., at time $t$) and to stock variables as measured "at time $t$." However, to emphasize the timing assumption made here we shall also on occasion refer to flow variables as occurring at time $t$.

## FIRM INCOME AND INVESTMENT

The income and investment concepts we shall use differ somewhat from both the economic definitions and the accounting definitions of these items. The purpose of this section is to explain the differences.[6] To understand the approach here, the distinction between four variables must be clarified; these are *cash income, cash flow, economic income,* and *accounting income.*

All firm variables will be measured here on a *cash* basis. The *cash revenues* are cash receipts that result from the sale of goods and services excluding any sales of "productive" assets (e.g., plant and equipment) of the firm during the

[5] An alternative to the discrete time model we are using is to assume that flows occur continuously. The continuous model is used in app. 2B, chap. 2 to examine the degree of approximation involved in the discrete time assumption. Chapter 10 provides an introduction to continuous time models under uncertainty.

[6] The reader is assumed to be familiar with accounting practices. For a review and analysis of the issues, see Jaedicke and Sprouse, "Accounting Flows: Income, Funds, and Cash" (listed in the Suggested Readings at the end of this chapter).

period. *Cash expenses* are the cash payments made by the firm during the period for goods and services purchased to provide *current* revenues. Expenses as defined here do *not* include interest on debt; this will become clear from the discussion below and in subsequent chapters. *Investment* outlays are the *cash* outlays during the period for goods and services purchased during the period to provide *future* cash income; sale of productive assets and the distribution of the proceeds to owners is disinvestment.[7] The distinction between "cash expenses" and "investment" is therefore dependent on the purpose of the cash payments involved. Cash expenses are those payments made to generate current revenues; investment outlays are those cash commitments made to generate future revenues. The *cash income* of a firm equals cash revenues less cash expenses.[8] The *cash flow* of the firm equals cash income less cash investment during the period. As explained below, cash flow is the cash payment during the period to the equity and debt holders of the firm.

The reasons firm variables are defined in this fashion will be made more apparent in Chap. 2. For the present it is sufficient to note that we shall find this the most useful way to analyze financial decisions. In addition it should be clear that cash provides individuals and firms with command over goods and services. We have assumed that the basic welfare of the individual depends on consumption (goods and services consumed); since cash is the basic measure of the individual's ability to command the means of consumption, it is ultimately cash flow to the individual that affects the individual's welfare.

The definition of the *economic income* of an individual was aptly stated by Hicks. Hicks defined an individual's income as "the maximum value which he can consume during a week and still be as well off at the end of the week as he was at the beginning."[9] The critical component of this definition is "be as well off." This clearly refers to the wealth of an individual as borne out by subsequent discussion. Hence the economic definition of income can be viewed as being synonymous with "changes in wealth." The problem then is how to determine "wealth" for individuals and how to relate this concept to the affairs of firms. As we shall see, the notions of "wealth" and "value" are closely related and both these factors are directly related to cash flow.

The definition of firm *accounting income* is closely related to both economic income and the cash flow concepts described above but generally does not equal economic income, cash income, or cash flow. Essentially the accountants

[7] Investment includes all outlays to enhance future revenues including investments in other firms' securities, in bank deposits, in government bonds, etc. In considering dividend policy in chaps. 2 and 11, however, a distinction is made between investment in the firm's productive assets (signified by $I$) and in lending in the market at the existing market rate (the amount loaned signified by $F$ when $F < 0$; see Chap. 2, p. 24. Also, as discussed in this chapter below, firm-held cash is defined here as a productive asset; this implies a particular meaning to firm investment and disinvestment. See pp. 12 and 13.

[8] With firm taxes, cash income equals cash revenues less cash expenses less cash outlay for taxes.

[9] J. R. Hicks, "Value and Capital," 2d ed., p. 172, Oxford University Press, London, 1946.

can be thought of as trying to measure the change in shareholders' wealth resulting from the activities of the firm. Since they deal with real rather than abstract firms, the income measurement rules developed by the accounting profession must of necessity be directly applicable to firms and produce numbers in a reasonably objective fashion.[10] Accounting definitions of income therefore suffer from the same problems as the economic definitions plus the difficulties that arise in making abstract concepts operational.

A simple example will illustrate the differences between accounting income, economic income, cash income, and cash flow. Suppose a firm uses some of its revenues to purchase an asset for cash at time 1 and sells it for cash at time 2. The cash-flow measurement system will treat the purchase of the asset as an investment outlay at time 1, and the investment will therefore not affect *cash income* but will reduce *cash flow* for period 1. The receipts from sale do not affect cash income but do affect cash flow for period 2. The accounting measurement will depend on the characteristics of the asset. Suppose the asset is an "inventory" item that is sold at time 2 at a price greater than its initial cost. The accounting statements will show no effect on period 1 *accounting income;* however, there will be an increase in revenues for period 2 equal to the selling price of the asset and an increase in expenses (cost of goods sold) for period 2 equal to the original (period 1) cost of the asset. Hence accounting income for period 2 will increase by the difference between the two values. The rationale for the accounting treatment of this transaction is essentially that wealth remained unchanged by the period 1 purchase of the asset since cash (an asset) was merely transformed into inventory (another asset). During period 2, there was an increase in wealth since the inventory asset was transformed into a greater amount of cash than was originally used to acquire it.

The effect of the transaction on the *economic income* of periods 1 and 2 will depend on how investors value the firm during these periods. If the asset's sale in period 2 is anticipated in period 1, the value of the firm may rise in period 1, producing an increment of wealth (economic income) for the firm's owners. Of course, this may not occur and the wealth increment may occur in period 2. The point is that economic income depends on the value investors place on the present and future returns to them (cash flow) generated by the firm, and this may or may not equal the accounting income or cash income in any period.

In this book, great attention will be directed to firm cash-flow variables rather than to firm income as defined by accountants. In Chap. 2 and particularly in Chap. 9 firm cash-flow variables are discussed in detail. The term "income" will here refer to "cash income" as defined earlier (cash revenues less cash expenses). In contrast to the accountants' use of the term "cash flow," cash flow will here refer to cash income less investment.[11] As explained

[10] See Jaedicke and Sprouse, *op. cit.*, pp. 30–32, for a more extensive discussion of the issues.

[11] For a discussion of the accountants' definition of "cash flow," see Jaedicke and Sprouse, *op. cit.*, pp. 108–134.

below, cash held by the firm is here viewed as a form of investment. It follows that cash flow as used here is the amount paid by the firm to investors (as dividends to shareholders or interest and principal to creditors).[12] It is this cash-flow stream that is valued by investors in the market. An investor's income (in the Hicksian sense) in any period is therefore *the cash received from the firm plus the changes in the market value of the firm's prospective cash-flow stream to be received from the investor's claims (equity or debt) on the firm.* Thus the accountants' measure of income really has no place in the analysis here, although there is no fundamental inconsistency between that approach and the one used here. In this book, economic (Hicksian) income is received by the investor as cash from the firm and as capital gains on securities. The firm provides this income by generating a cash flow that is received by investors and is valued in the market.

## Cash Balances of the Firm

One confusion that may arise from the concept of cash income is the treatment of cash held by the firm (a stock variable). In our view a firm's cash balances are best thought of as a productive asset, just like any other asset. The only reason a firm holds cash is for the benefits derived from this investment; otherwise the cash would be either provided to the owners or invested in other assets. In short, cash balances, like other investments, are presumed to provide increased cash income to the firm in the future (e.g., by reducing transaction costs).

One way to see the issues involved is to imagine the deposit of a customer's check by the firm in its bank. This is part of cash income. If the firm keeps its cash balance at the new, higher level we say that it has "invested cash in cash balances." Why would the firm do this? Presumably because of some benefit that will result from having this higher balance; for example, it may be an alternative means of compensating the bank for services rendered. If the firm did not keep the higher balance, it would have to pay the bank directly for those services. In this example the benefit derived from the higher balance is a reduction in future payments to the bank for services.

When the definition of a period is reasonably long (a month or more), then our usage is quite consistent with normal business practice. Management does make decisions as to what the firm's average cash balances should be, and most financial managers are very much aware that those average balances should be

[12] In chap. 9 we shall see that, in addition to dividends, interest, and principal, the cash flow paid to investors also includes money paid by the firm in purchasing its own stock and bonds in the market (treasury stock and bonds); from these payments to investors during a period will be subtracted funds received from new investors for new shares and bonds issued. This net amount paid out by the firm equals cash income less investment, or firm cash flow.

carefully determined. No more cash should be held than is economically justified.

In the discussion above of firm income and investment, investment was defined as a cash commitment for assets producing future period benefits. Since such productive assets include cash, an increase in cash during the period is an investment. If the firm reduces its cash holdings during the period to purchase another asset (e.g., a building), this is not net investment; it is an exchange of one asset (cash) for another (a building). Furthermore, if the firm sells a noncash asset (e.g., a building) for cash, this is not disinvestment; it is the exchange of one asset (a building) for another (cash). Under the cash concept of investment used here, net investment occurs when the firm commits *new* cash to increase its holdings of cash or of noncash assets. Disinvestment occurs when the firm reduces its cash plus noncash assets either by reducing firm-held cash by paying cash to firm owners or creditors or by selling noncash assets and paying the proceeds to firm owners or creditors.

An example may help clarify the preceding points. Assume that at the beginning of the period the firm owned 10 machines and had $250,000 in cash; the firm had cash revenues of $200,000 and cash expenses of $100,000 during the period and therefore a *cash income* of $100,000 ($200,000 − $100,000). The firm also purchased one new machine for $50,000 and reduced firm cash to $220,000, using $20,000 of firm income and $30,000 of firm cash to purchase the $50,000 machine. Assume no taxes. The firm's *investment* during the period was therefore $20,000, the new cash committed to raise noncash assets ($50,000) less the decline in firm cash ($30,000). *Cash flow* is $80,000 ($100,000 − $20,000), which is paid to the firm's stockholders and bondholders. Suppose instead that the firm purchases no assets and sells a machine for $10,000. Investment would be zero if the firm held the cash (increased firm cash to $260,000) and would be minus $10,000 (disinvestment) if the firm paid the cash to stockholders and bondholders; cash flow would be $100,000 in the former case and $110,000 in the latter.

It should be pointed out here that an exchange of firm cash for a noncash asset, although involving no net investment, does involve an investment decision. Use of the investment rules presented in later chapters is fully appropriate here as in the case of a nonzero level of investment. This will become clearer in the forthcoming discussion.

The topic of firm cash flow is treated in detail at the end of Chap. 9. A general understanding of the points presented thus far should provide the reader with an adequate background for the material in Chaps. 2 through 9.

## A NOTE ON NOTATION

Symbolic notation for variables and mathematical proofs is a necessary evil in a book of this type. There are some general rules that will be followed throughout the development, and an awareness of them should aid in comprehension. The symbolic definitions of frequently used variables are summarized at the front of the book with a page reference to the place they are originally defined. The general rules for naming variables are summarized below:

1. Capital, italic English letters refer to variables that have money values. For example, $X$ is used to denote cash income of the firm. The only exception to this rule ($T$) is noted in rule (2) below.
2. Lowercase, italic English letters are used for miscellaneous variables and constants, interest rates, time, proportions, etc. An exception is $T$ for a particular future time as compared with $t$ for time in general. For example, the statement $t = 1, 2, \ldots, T$ indicates that we are discussing events which begin at time 1 and end at time $T$.
3. Greek letters are infrequently used; their definition will be stated when introduced.
4. Subscripts and superscripts are used in three ways: (*a*) to identify particular values of the variable, especially at different points in time, for example, $I_0$ is investment at time 0 or $I_t$ is investment at time $t$; (*b*) to distinguish among different versions or modifications of the same general variable, for example, $Y^S$ is cash flow to shareholders and $Y^B$ is cash flow to bondholders; and (*c*) to identify different entities, for example, firm $i$'s value $V_i$ or the proportion of the firm's stock owned by investor $j$, $\alpha_j$.
5. Once a variable has been given a symbol, that symbol will be used throughout the remainder of the book for that variable. The notation is consistent.

## SUGGESTED READINGS

Bodenhorn, Diran: A Cash Flow Concept of Profit, *Journal of Finance,* vol. 19, pp. 16–31, March 1964, reprinted in Archer, Stephen H. and Charles A. D'Ambrosio: "The Theory of Business Finance," 2d ed., The Macmillan Company, New York, 1976.

Jaedicke, Robert K., and Robert T. Sprouse: "Accounting Flows: Income, Funds, and Cash," pp. 1–28, Prentice-Hall, Inc., Englewood Cliffs, N.J., 1965.

Jensen, Michael C. and William H. Meckling: Theory of the Firm: Managerial Behavior, Agency Costs and Ownership Structure, *Journal of Financial Economics,* vol. 3, pp. 305–360, December 1976. (Reading suggested is pp. 305–333; the entire article is suggested reading for chap. 15.)

Solomon, Ezra: "The Theory of Financial Management," pp. 1–26, Columbia University Press, New York, 1963.

Williamson, Oliver E.: Managerial Discretion and Business Behavior, *American Economic Review,* vol. 53, pp. 1032–1057, December 1963.

CHAPTER

# TWO

# DECISIONS UNDER CERTAINTY WITH PERFECT CAPITAL MARKETS

This chapter will begin by developing the theory of individual and firm financial decisions under the assumptions of certainty and perfect capital markets. Certainty means that everyone knows the consequences of every decision for all time. In perfect capital markets there is complete and costless information available to everyone, no individual or firm is large enough to affect prices (interest rates), and there are no transaction costs.[1] The most important characteristic of perfect capital markets is that all individuals and firms can borrow or lend on the same terms. With certainty this implies that individuals and firms can borrow and lend at the riskless rate. In this chapter and in Chap. 3 we also assume the absence of taxes.

As was remarked in Chap. 1, we shall treat individuals as having only one fundamental problem, that of allocating their consumption over time. In this chapter the opportunities available to them are investing at the riskless rate of interest and borrowing at that rate of interest. Individuals are assumed to have given endowed or basic income streams that can be altered through the use of market opportunities (borrowing and lending) to achieve their preferred consumption patterns. It is assumed initially that the only income the individual has is this basic income and that the individual's wealth is entirely represented by the value of that income stream. The only assumption made with respect to preferences for consumption is that each person prefers more consumption to less at any given time.

[1] A complete discussion of the perfect market assumptions is presented in chap. 9.

The analysis will begin with a discussion of an individual's wealth-allocation problem over a single time period. Then we extend the results of that analysis to the multiperiod case. This will provide us with a criterion for firm decisions, assuming that the firm acts in the best interests of its owners. The criterion is then used to analyze the financial decisions of the firm, thereby completing the theoretical development under the assumptions of certainty and perfect markets.

## INDIVIDUAL FINANCIAL DECISIONS

### One-Period Analysis

Suppose Mr. G is planning his consumption pattern over a single period; he will consume some now and some later. This is a one-period situation in the sense that events (consumption, borrowing, lending) occur at time 0 (now) and time 1 (later), and between these two points in time is a single period. G's problem is to choose from among alternative combinations of total consumption at times 0 and 1. For convenience we shall identify the period of time between now and later as 1 year and measure the amount of goods consumed in dollars. The only knowledge of G's consumption preferences we assume is the choice of more consumption rather than less at any given time. That is, if G were given the choice between consuming \$100 now and \$100 later or consuming \$101 now and \$100 later, the latter alternative would be preferred. G, of course, is limited in the amount that can be consumed by income and the available terms under which one can transfer income between now and later. In our world of certainty, individuals know precisely what their basic income will be (for example, \$100 now and \$100 later).

It is assumed that the entire wealth of the individual is represented by the individual's basic income stream. The terms under which the individual can transfer income from one point in time to another are given by the rate of interest. We assume that one can *lend* (invest) in the capital market up to the total amount of current income. Suppose the rate of interest is 6%/year. If so, G can transfer through lending part of his current income to a year from now, and for every dollar lent now he will receive \$1.06 later (which will be used for consumption at that time). In addition, he can *borrow* against his future income up to the total amount of that income at the same rate. Since for every dollar he borrows he must pay back \$1.06, the maximum amount he could borrow for consumption now on a future income of \$100 is \$100/1.06 = \$94.34. Given G's basic income and the rate at which he can borrow and lend, his available consumption alternatives are completely specified. The choices open to him can be represented by a graph as in Fig. 2-1.

The line *AB* contains all the income-consumption alternatives open to G. (He, of course, could choose any point below the line *AB* by throwing away some of his income, but that would be inconsistent with our assumption that more

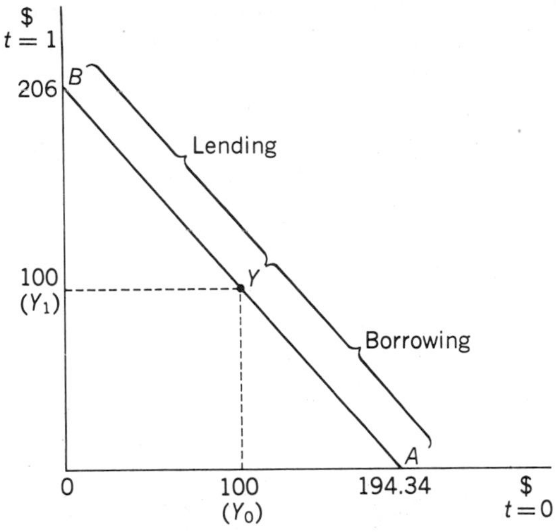


**figure 2-1**

consumption is preferred to less.) That line indicates the set of choices provided by the capital market given G's basic income *Y*.[2] Point *A* is the maximum amount that he could consume now, if he were willing to consume nothing later. The value *A* = \$194.34 is found by adding G's current income of \$100 to the maximum he could borrow against his future income of \$100; that is, \$94.34. He can achieve any point between *Y* and *A* by borrowing the appropriate amount. Similarly, point *B* is the maximum amount that could be consumed one year from now, provided that he lent the full amount of his current income. The value at *B*, \$206, is determined by adding G's future income of \$100 to the return from lending his current income of \$100 to yield \$106. Any point between *Y* and *B* can be achieved by lending the required amount.

The most important feature of the situation shown by Fig. 2-1 is that all income streams which lie on line *AB* are *equivalent*. That is, one will be indifferent between any two income streams on the line; for example, as between the income represented by point *A* and the income represented by point *Y*. This is so because any income stream on line *AB* can be transformed into any other stream on *AB* by the right amount of borrowing or lending. This does *not* mean that all consumption patterns on the line are equivalent from the viewpoint of G. G. is almost sure to prefer particular consumption patterns over others; for example, it would be a rare person who preferred consumption levels *A* or *B*

[2] As noted in the text below, the rate of interest $i$ and the individual's income $Y$ are sufficient to completely specify the set of choices open to the individual. The slope of the line is equal to $-(1 + i)$ in general or $-1.06$ in this particular case. That is, an *increase* in current consumption of \$1 results in a *reduction* in future consumption of $\$(1 + i)$.

to some more even distribution of consumption; G is likely to prefer consuming some now and some later instead of all now ($A$) or all later ($B$).

Since we can consider all points on the line as income equivalents, it is convenient to characterize the line by the value at point $A$. For a given rate of interest that is common to everyone, the value of $A$ determines the set of available consumption choices open to all individuals whose incomes lie on the line. Point $A$ is called the *present value* of income or, alternatively, the individual's *wealth*. Everyone with the same wealth is equally well off; any two income streams with the same present value are equivalent since one can be transformed (through borrowing or lending) into the other. We can express the present value of income $V_Y$ as a function of current income $Y_0$, next year's income $Y_1$, and the rate of interest $i$:

$$V_Y = Y_0 + \frac{Y_1}{1 + i} \tag{2-1}$$

From the preceding discussion it should be clear that the rate of transformation of current and future consumption along line $AB$ in Fig. 2-1 is equal to $(1 + i)$. That is, future consumption can be increased by $(1 + i)$ if current consumption is reduced by one unit; or present consumption can be increased by one unit if future consumption is decreased by $(1 + i)$. Thus the line representing the consumption opportunities available to the individual is determined by the individual's basic income endowment and the market rate of interest at which one can borrow and lend. All streams with the same present value lie on the same present-value line, e.g., on $AB$. Different income endowments with different present values will lie on different present-value lines, for example, $Y$ and $Y'$, which lie on different present-value lines in Fig. 2-2. The present

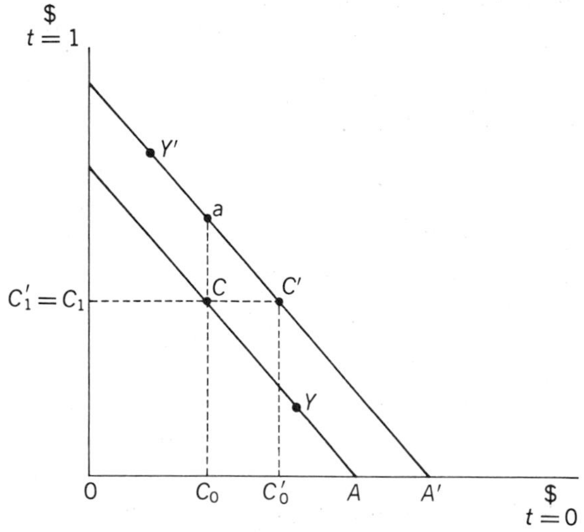


**figure 2-2**

values of $Y$ and $Y'$ are $A$ and $A'$, respectively. The present-value lines through those points both have a slope of $-(1 + i)$ and are therefore parallel.

From the preceding discussion and our prior assumption that more consumption at a given time is preferred to less, we see that the individual always prefers more wealth to less. In other words, a higher present value is preferred to a lower one. This is so because a higher present value always provides the individual with an option of consuming more at one time while consuming the same amount at the other time. This is shown in Fig. 2-2. Suppose someone were offered the chance to trade his or her original income stream $Y$ for a new one $Y'$. The old income stream had a present value of $A$ and the individual planned to consume $C_0$ and $C_1$ at point $C$. The new income stream has a present value of $A'$, which is greater than $A$. It offers the possibility of consuming more at time 0 ($C_0'$ is greater than $C_0$) while retaining the same consumption ($C_1' = C_1$) at time 1. Indeed, at all points on segment $aC'$ more is consumed at either or both points in time than at $C$. At a given interest rate (which implies all present-value lines are parallel), it is obvious that the higher the present value, the better off the individual will be.

To summarize this section, we have shown that, given the availability of borrowing and lending at equal rates, the individual is indifferent to the *time pattern* of his or her income stream and is concerned only with its *present value*. This is so because the individual can transform any given stream into any other stream that has the same present value by borrowing or lending in the market. Two different streams with the same present value provide identical consumption opportunitites. As a consequence the individual will always prefer the income stream with the highest present value since it permits the greatest consumption at one or both points in time and no less consumption in either.

## Multiperiod Analysis

The extension of the analysis to several periods is fairly straightforward. We shall develop the individual's problem in some detail for two periods from which the generalization to $n$ periods follows readily.

**The two-period case.** The individual has an income stream to be received at $t = 0$, $t = 1$, and $t = 2$ of amounts $Y_0$, $Y_1$, and $Y_2$, respectively. The market rate of interest in effect between $t = 0$ and $t = 1$ (period 1) is $i_1$ and the rate between $t = 1$ and $t = 2$ (period 2) is $i_2$. The individual is assumed to be able to borrow and lend freely at those rates. The individual's opportunities for consumption under these conditions can be represented by a plane in space as shown in Fig. 2-3. Point $A$, the point where the plane crosses the $t = 0$ axis, indicates the maximum amount available for consumption at time 0 if nothing is left for times 1 or 2. The value at point $A$ is the present value of the income stream $(Y_0,Y_1,Y_2)$. Similarly, points $B$ and $C$ show the maximum attainable consumption at times 1 and 2 respectively. The values at these points are referred to as $A$, $B$, and $C$ and are determined as follows:

$C$: $Y_0$ is loaned in the market at a rate of $i_1$ to yield $Y_0(1 + i_1)$ at time 1. The amount available at time 1 is $Y_1 + Y_0(1 + i_1)$, which is then invested at $i_2$ to yield $(1 + i_2)[Y_1 + Y_0(1 + i_1)]$ at time 2. The maximum amount available at time 2 is therefore

$$C = Y_0(1 + i_1)(1 + i_2) + Y_1(1 + i_2) + Y_2$$

$B$: $Y_0$ is loaned at $i_1$ to yield $Y_0(1 + i_1)$ at time 1. $Y_2/(1 + i_2)$ is borrowed at time 1. The maximum amount available at time 1 is therefore

$$B = Y_0(1 + i_1) + Y_1 + \frac{Y_2}{(1 + i_2)}$$

$A$: Amounts $Y_1/(1 + i_1)$ and $Y_2/(1 + i_1)(1 + i_2)$ are borrowed at time 0. The maximum amount available at time 0 is therefore

$$A = Y_0 + \frac{Y_1}{(1 + i_1)} + \frac{Y_2}{(1 + i_1)(1 + i_2)}$$

The three intercepts $A$, $B$, and $C$ are completely determined using only the income stream $(Y_0, Y_1, Y_2)$ and the interest rates $i_1$ and $i_2$. In other words, we know all the consumption alternatives available to the individual if we know one point on the opportunity plane (income) and the market interest rates. Therefore, if we know *any* point on the plane (such as point $A$) and the interest rates, we know all the alternatives. Accordingly, using an argument directly comparable to the one presented in the single-period case, the larger the pre-

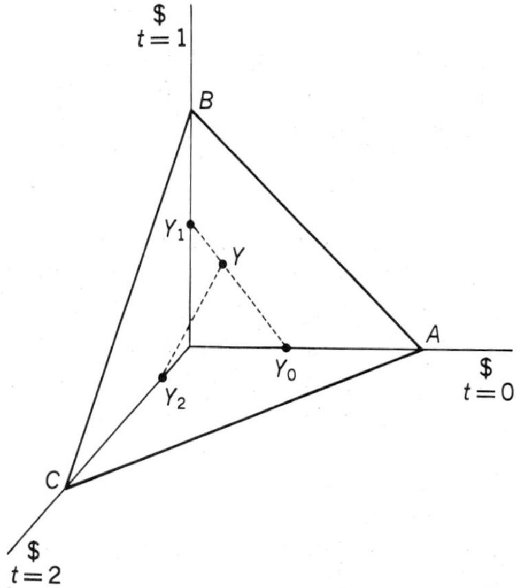


**figure 2-3**

sent value ($V_Y = A$) the better off the individual is in terms of the amounts of consumption available.

### The $n$-Period Case

This line of reasoning extends directly to the $n$-period case. The present value of the individual's income stream, $V_Y$, is

$$V_Y = Y_0 + \frac{Y_1}{(1+i_1)} + \frac{Y_2}{(1+i_1)(1+i_2)} + \frac{Y_3}{(1+i_1)(1+i_2)(1+i_3)} + \cdots + \frac{Y_n}{(1+i_1)(1+i_2)\cdots(1+i_n)} \tag{2-2}$$

Rather than write out all $n$ terms we can use a compact notation for $V_Y$ by defining two mathematical operators: first, there is $\Sigma_{t=0}^{n}$, which means add the included terms as $t$ goes from 0 to $n$; second, there is $\Pi_{j=0}^{t}$, which means multiply terms as $j$ goes from 0 to $t$.[3]

$$V_Y = Y_0 + \sum_{t=1}^{n} \frac{Y_t}{\prod_{j=1}^{t}(1+i_j)} \tag{2-3}$$

where $Y_t$ is the income at time $t$ and $i_j$ is the interest rate in period $j$, which runs from time $j - 1$ to time $j$.

In general, then, we can say that any two income streams with the same present value are equivalent since they each provide the same consumption alternatives to the individual. This is so because the individual can borrow and lend freely at the market rates of interest to transform one stream into the other. This is why we also refer to the present value as wealth, since two people with the same wealth are assumed to have the same consumption opportunities even though they may have very different tastes (preferences).[4]

We now know how to evaluate alternative decisions from the individual's viewpoint: we should seek to provide the individual with that income stream which has the highest present value. Given that we have this objective for the individual, we can determine how the firm should behave if it is to act in the best interests of its owners.

[3] $\Sigma$ is the capital Greek letter sigma used to stand for "sum"; $\Pi$ is the capital Greek letter pi used to stand for "product."

[4] The thoughtful reader will recognize that the assumption made here implies that the same goods and prices are available to everyone with the same wealth. Reflection on this point will lead to a better understanding of both the strengths and limitations of this analysis. However, even if people differ in their situations with respect to goods and prices, for any given person a higher present value provides greater (better) opportunities.

## FIRM FINANCIAL DECISIONS

Business firms are organized to produce goods and services. They may be directly managed by their owners or they may have hired management. In any case, we assume that management will act in the best interests of the firm's owners (stockholders). In many circumstances, as we shall see later, the "best interests" of the stockholders is an ambiguous objective; that is, it may not be clear what those best interests are.[5] However, for the case of perfect capital markets and certainty, we shall show that there is no ambiguity.

The owners of the firm will be referred to as stockholders or shareholders and the income provided to them by the firm as dividends. In a world of certainty, perfect markets, and no taxes, the owners could just as well be viewed as bondholders and their income as interest. When uncertainty is introduced in later chapters, the distinction between stockholders and bondholders will become significant.

There are two basic financial decisions confronting the firm in a world of certainty and perfect markets: what investments to undertake and how those investments should be financed. We shall treat the investment problem as being composed of two parts. In this chapter, the overall objective of investment policy will be determined. In Chap. 3 we shall consider the problem of evaluating different types of specific investment opportunities so that the overall objectives are met. The problem of financing is to determine, for a given amount of total investment, how much to finance through retained earnings as opposed to raising new money in the market (issuing shares or borrowing).[6] Since any income of the firm that is not retained must be paid to its owners, we shall refer to this financing problem as the *dividend policy* problem.[7] That is, we shall ask the question of how much should be paid out to the owners given the amount of investment to be undertaken, keeping in mind that paying out more implies an associated decision to raise more money in the market. These points will become clearer as the analysis proceeds.

### Stockholder and Firm Objectives

Let us begin by looking at the situation faced by a single stockholder who has an income of $Y$ from all sources *other than* his or her ownership interest in the firm. The present value of $Y$ is $V_Y$. The stockholder owns a fraction $s$ of the

[5] What may be "best" in the view of some shareholders may not be as desirable as an alternative action in the view of other shareholders. For example, some shareholders may prefer the firm to pay out all current earnings as dividends although others may prefer the firm to retain and invest those earnings. See the Suggested Readings in chap. 1.

[6] Borrowing and selling new shares are the same thing under perfect markets, certainty, and no taxes, since all capital must provide a return equal to the riskless rate of interest in the market.

[7] Under the assumptions here, the distinction between "dividend policy" and "financing policy" is irrelevant. Later (with uncertainty) it becomes important.

firm's shares and will therefore receive from those shares an income that depends on the dividends paid by the firm to its shareholders. Let us define the present value of the individual's ownership interest as $sV$, where $V$ is the value of the firm. The current wealth ($W$) of the individual is therefore

$$W = V_Y + sV \tag{2-4}$$

Earlier we saw that attainment of the individual's consumption objective requires the maximization of current wealth $W$. For a given income external to the firm ($Y$), and given the proportion of the firm owned ($s$), it follows that $W$ is maximized by maximizing $V$. Therefore, maximization of $V$ is the goal of the firm.

The question remains as to how the current value of the firm ($V$) is determined. Keep in mind that we are assuming that the firm has outstanding only the type of security which we refer to as stock (shares). *V is the present value of the payments on the currently outstanding shares.* Since there may be additional shares ("new" shares) issued in the future, we must be careful to distinguish between the *total* dividends paid by the firm and the amount that will be paid to current owners of currently outstanding shares ("old" shares). It is the present value of the amount which will be paid on currently outstanding shares that determines the value of *those* shares; and it is the total value of currently outstanding shares that equals the current value of the firm. The following example should clarify the point.

At time 0 there are 10 shares of the firm outstanding and it pays out \$10 (\$1 per share). A person owning 20% of the firm at time 0 (two shares) would receive \$2. Now suppose that between times 0 and 1 the firm raises some new money by selling 10 new shares and then at time 1 pays out \$30 (\$1.50 per share). The individual owning 20% of the firm at time 0 would receive \$3 at time 1 from the ownership of two old shares, not 20% of the \$30 of total dividends. The current ($t = 0$) shares in aggregate receive \$10 at $t = 0$ and \$15 at $t = 1$ while the dividends of the firm were \$10 and \$30. The value of the firm *at time 0* is not based on the total dividends of the firm, \$10 and \$30, but on the payments on the old shares, that is, \$10 and \$15.

Since we already know how to evaluate the present value of an income stream, the value of the firm to its current owners is the present value of the dividends that will be paid on the *old* shares (signified $D_t$):

$$V = D_0 + \sum_{t=1}^{T} \frac{D_t}{\prod_{j=1}^{t} (1 + i_j)} \tag{2-5}$$

$T$ is some future period after which all dividends are zero ($T$ may approach infinity). The goal of the firm is to maximize the present value of the dividends on its currently outstanding shares and that value is determined by Eq. (2-5).

Now that we know in general the objective of the firm, we can investigate the impact of dividend policy and investment policy.

## The One-Period Case

Consider a situation in which the firm will be liquidated one period from now and the proceeds from the sale of all its assets will be distributed to the owners. Dividends on the currently outstanding shares will be $D_0$ at time 0 and $D_1$ at time 1. Similarly, the income (revenues less expenses as defined in Chap. 1) of the firm is $X_0$ and $X_1$, where $X_1$ includes the money the firm receives from selling its assets at time 1. We assume that total investment of amount $I_0$ is to be undertaken at time 0. We shall consider the investment budget $I_0$ in more detail after we look at the dividend problem. Income $X_1$ at time 1 includes the returns from investment of $I_0$ plus the proceeds from liquidating all other assets of the firm. Now the value of the firm at time 0 is

$$V = D_0 + \frac{D_1}{1 + i_1} \qquad (2\text{-}6)$$

from Eq. (2-5) above. We now ask whether it makes any difference to our current shareholders if we alter the *pattern* (relative amounts) of the dividends to them *given* $X_0$, $I_0$, and $X_1$. In other words, for a given investment policy does dividend policy affect the value of the firm?

**Dividend policy.** To determine the impact of dividend policy on the value of the firm we must consider the financing implied by the choice of alternative dividend policies. Paying a dividend of $D_0$ at time 0 reduces the funds available to the firm by that amount. We know that the firm has an income of $X_0$ and a commitment of $I_0$ for investment. In order to maintain an equality between money received and money paid out, the firm may have to use additional financing of amount $F_0$. Thus, at time 0 the cash-flow equation for the firm is

$$\underset{\text{(Inflow)}}{X_0 + F_0} = \underset{\text{(Outflow)}}{D_0 + I_0} \qquad (2\text{-}7)$$

Consider this equation in the light of the earlier discussion of the relationship between dividend policy and financing policy. Given the income of the firm and its investment budget, paying an additional dollar of dividends requires it to raise another dollar in the market. To look at the problem primarily as one of financing, we could write (2-7) as

$$(X_0 - D_0) + F_0 = I_0 \qquad (2\text{-}8)$$

where $(X_0 - D_0)$ is retained earnings. The problem then is to determine how much of $I_0$ should be financed with "new money" $F_0$ and how much with retained earnings.[8] To consider the situation in terms of divided policy we can

[8] Notice that, if $X_0 > I_0$, the firm may lend in the market at rate $i$, in which case $F_0 < 0$; that is, the amount loaned equals $-F_0$. This lending reduces $D_0$ by $-F_0$ but increases $D_1$ by $(1 + i)(-F_0)$. All the discussion applies to this case as well as to firm borrowing ($F_0 > 0$). The chapters treating uncertainty will include firm lending (see footnote 7, p. 10). Also, it need not be specified whether the firm is "borrowing" or "issuing new shares" since, as remarked earlier, the two are equivalent here. See app. 2A for a more extensive development.

express (2-7) as

$$D_0 = X_0 - I_0 + F_0 \tag{2-9}$$

Now it is obvious that the more money raised by the firm $F_0$, the greater is $D_0$, given income and investment. Let us continue with our evaluation as we look at what happens at time 1. The cash-flow equation is

$$X_1 = D_1 + (1 + i_1)F_0 \tag{2-10}$$

The firm is being liquidated at time 1; there is no new financing nor any investment at time 1. Income $X_1$ includes all proceeds from selling the firm's assets; $X_1$ will be distributed in part to the owners of the firm at time 0 (as $D_1$) and in part to the new owners who supplied $F_0$. The new owners require payment of $(1 + i_1)F_0$—no more and no less—since $i_1$ is the market rate of interest on all securities. At time 1 the dividend to the original owners is

$$D_1 = X_1 - (1 + i_1)F_0 \tag{2-11}$$

From (2-9) and (2-11) we see that the decision to pay a given amount $D_0$ determines what can be paid at time 1 to the *original* owners. Suppose we substitute the expressions for $D_0$ and $D_1$ [Eqs. (2-9) and (2-11)] into the valuation relationship (2-6). Simplifying, we get

$$V = X_0 - I_0 + \frac{X_1}{1 + i_1} \tag{2-12}$$

and since none of the variables in (2-12) is affected by the dividend-financing decision, that decision does not affect the value of the firm. In other words, dividend policy is irrelevant, even though the value of the firm is solely a function of dividends and the market rate of interest!

This result may seem counter to common sense, but all that is happening is the following. An increase of, say, \$100 in current dividends means that an additional \$100 must be raised in the market to finance investment. Future dividends on the initial shares will therefore be reduced by \$100 $(1 + i_1)$, which is a loss in present value of \$100 since the initial shareholders have the same opportunities in the market as the firm. Thus the gain of \$100 is exactly offset by a loss of future dividends worth \$100. In other words, there is no advantage in the firm's raising money to pay current dividends at the expense of future dividends if the shareholders can borrow against those future dividends themselves should they wish to do so.

**Cash flows and firm value.** Equation (2-11) has significance beyond its implication that dividend policy is irrelevant; namely, that the value of the firm is determined by the cash flow provided to capital suppliers. In this view the firm is a "money pump" and its value is determined by its output of money. To see this point more clearly we can rewrite Eq. (2-7) as

$$X_0 - I_0 = D_0 - F_0 \tag{2-13}$$

$D_0 - F_0$ is the net cash receipts of *all* owners of the firm; some are receiving $D_0$, but others are paying in $F_0$. Equation (2-10) above is a similar relationship. The net cash payment of the firm is $X_1$, which equals $D_1$ paid to the original owners and $(1 + i)F_0$ paid to the people who supplied $F_0$. By writing Eq. (2-12) as we have, we are simply expressing the value of the firm in terms of the total payments to capital.[9]

**Investment policy.** The second major financial decision of the firm concerns investment policy. We wish to determine a criterion for optimal investment decisions. In this chapter we are concerned with the total investment budget $I_0$. We shall look at the characteristics it must have in order to maximize the value of the firm. In Chap. 3 we shall consider the selection of the particular projects that constitute the total budget.

To begin, define $X_1'$ as the income the firm would earn at time 1 if no investment were undertaken ($I_0 = 0$). This amount includes the time 1 liquidating value of the firm's assets, assuming $I_0 = 0$. The effect on the net cash receipts (income) of the firm from any particular capital budget $I_0$ at time 1 is $\Delta X_1$. Amount $\Delta X_1$ includes the increase in the firm's time 1 liquidating value due to $I_0$. The income of the firm at time 1 is therefore $X_1 = X_1' + \Delta X_1$. Substituting into the derived valuation expression (2-12), we have the value of the firm as a function of the investment undertaken at time 0 and its consequences:

$$\begin{aligned} V &= X_0 - I_0 + \frac{X_1' + \Delta X_1}{1 + i_1} \\ &= X_0 + \frac{X_1'}{1 + i_1} + \frac{\Delta X_1}{1 + i_1} - I_0 \end{aligned}$$

Both $X_0$ and $X_1'$ are independent of the investment decision; therefore, to maximize the value of the firm $V$, we should seek to maximize:

$$\Delta V = \left[\frac{\Delta X_1}{1 + i_1} - I_0\right] \tag{2-14}$$

The quantity to be maximized is nothing but the present value of the cash flow resulting from investing $I_0$. Moreover, as shown above, this is the appropriate rule, no matter how the investment is financed.[10] Maximization is achieved by

[9] It should be clear from the discussion that there is no inconsistency between the argument presented earlier that the current (time 0) value of the firm equals the present value of dividends to the *current* shares of the firm and the present argument that it equals the present value of the payments to all capital suppliers over time. Both present values equal that in eq. (2-12). The two present values are equal since an increase (decrease) in dividends on current shares means a compensating (same present value) decrease (increase) in future payments to new shares.

[10] This analysis implies Fisher's separation theorem, which states that in perfect markets the consumption decisions and investment decisions can be made separately. The firm need only maximize the present value of its cash flows and need not concern itself with how that value is converted into the desired consumption pattern of its shareholders. A more detailed example and development are shown in app. 2A.

selecting from among the possible "packages" of investment projects the one with the highest present value.

**An illustration.** To clarify the preceding points an example may be helpful. Assume a firm for which

$$X_0 = 250$$
$$X_1' = 200$$
$$i = 10\%$$

$$\Delta X_1: \begin{array}{ll} \Delta X_1 = 200 & \text{if } I_0 = 150 \\ \Delta X_1 = 300 & \text{if } I_0 = 200 \end{array}$$

Assume no other investment opportunities.

Since $X_1 = X_1' + \Delta X_1$,

$$\begin{array}{ll} X_1 = 400 & \text{if } I_0 = 150 \\ X_1 = 500 & \text{if } I_0 = 200 \end{array}$$

First, let us show that for any given investment policy ($I_0 = 0, I_0 = 150$, or $I_0 = 200$) the value of the firm is unaffected by dividend policy. Assume that the firm decides to invest 150. By Eq. (2-9)

$$\begin{aligned} D_0 &= X_0 - I_0 + F_0 \\ &= 250 - 150 + F_0 \\ &= 100 + F_0 \end{aligned} \tag{2-15}$$

By Eq. (2-11) and since $X_1 = 400$ if $I_0 = 150$,

$$\begin{aligned} D_1 &= X_1 - (1 + i)F_0 \\ &= 400 - 1.1F_0 \end{aligned} \tag{2-16}$$

where $(1 + i) = 1.1$ since $i = 10\%$.

From (2-15), $D_0$ can be increased by borrowing amount $\Delta F_0$; but this decreases $D_1$ in (2-16) by $(1 + i)$ times $\Delta F_0$. The present value of any such increase in dividends of $\Delta D_0 = \Delta F_0$ is zero since

$$\Delta D_0 + \frac{\Delta D_1}{1 + i} = \Delta F_0 + \frac{-1.1\ \Delta F_0}{1.1} = 0 \tag{2-17}$$

Or, stating the same point differently, using Eqs. (2-15) and (2-16) with (2-6), the present value of the firm's dividends equals

$$\begin{aligned} V &= D_0 + \frac{D_1}{1 + i} = 100 + F_0 + \frac{400 - 1.1F_0}{1.1} \\ &= 100 + \frac{400}{1.1} = 463.63 \end{aligned} \tag{2-18}$$

Thus the value of the firm is 463.63 regardless of $F_0$ as long as investment $I_0$ equals 150. Of course, the value of the firm also equals the term in (2-12); that is,

$$V = X_0 - I_0 + \frac{X_1}{1+i}$$
$$= 250 - 150 + \frac{400}{1.1} = 463.63$$

Like reasoning implies the irrelevancy of dividend policy if $I_0 = 0$ or $I_0 = 200$.

To see that the policy which maximizes $V$ is that which dictates maximizing the present value of the incremental cash flow from investment $I_0$ [see relation (2-14)], let us calculate this "incremental present value" and firm present value for $I_0 = 0$, $I_0 = 150$, and $I_0 = 200$. These calculations are shown in Table 2-1.

Value $V$ is computed from Eq. (2-12), which was shown to be equal to $V$ in Eq. (2-6). Notice from Table 2-1 that by selecting the investment budget with the highest incremental present value the firm's present value is maximized (maximum value is achieved at $I_0 = 200$).

†**A more complex illustration.** Assume as before that

$$X_0 = 250$$
$$X_1' = 200$$
$$i = 10\%$$

Assume also that

$$\Delta X_1 = 600 I_0 - I_0^2 \qquad \text{for } 0 \le I_0 \le 300$$
$$\Delta X_1 = 90{,}000 \qquad \text{for } I_0 \ge 300 \tag{2-19}$$

The total return $\Delta X_1$ from $I_0$ is assumed to be a continuous function of $I_0$, increasing with $I_0$ at a decreasing rate. Differentiating (2-19), the marginal (added) return from increments to $I_0$ equals

$$\frac{d\,\Delta X_1}{dI_0} = 600 - 2I_0 \tag{2-20}$$

Thus marginal return is positive (for all $I_0 < 300$) but falling with increases in $I_0$. Equation (2-20) indicates the addition to $\Delta X_1$ (and therefore to $X_1$) from a dollar

**table 2-1**

| *Investment:* $I_0$ | *Incremental present value:* $\frac{\Delta X_1}{(1+i)} - I_0$ | *Firm value:* $V$ |
|---|---|---|
| 0 | $\frac{0}{1.1} - 0 = 0$ | 431.81 |
| 150 | $\frac{200}{1.1} - 150 = 32.82$ | 463.63 |
| 200 | $\frac{300}{1.1} - 200 = 72.73$ | 504.54 |

increase in $I_0$. The results showing that value is necessarily independent of $D_0$ and $F_0$ for any given $I_0$ follow just as before; that is, Eq. (2-12) follows from Eq. (2-6) regardless of the functional relationship of $X_1$ to $I_0$. The arguments will not be repeated here.

To see how the firm-value maximizing level of investment is determined, note that the objective is to maximize $V$ in Eq. (2-12). But, as shown in establishing (2-14) above, this is equivalent to maximizing

$$\left[\frac{\Delta X_1}{1+i} - I_0\right] \tag{2-21}$$

Substituting the $\Delta X_1$ of (2-19) into (2-21), the goal is to maximize

$$\frac{600I_0 - I_0^2}{1 + .10} - I_0 \tag{2-22}$$

Differentiating (2-22) with respect to $I_0$ and setting the derivative at zero for a maximum,

$$\frac{600 - 2I_0}{1.1} - 1 = 0$$

and therefore,

$$I_0 = 299.45 \tag{2-23}$$

at a maximum of (2-21).[11] That is, to maximize firm value, $I_0 = 299.45$.

Notice two points. First, since $X_0 = 250$, in order that $I_0 = 299.45$ the firm will have to borrow at least an amount $F_0 = 299.45 - 250 = 49.45$ even if $D_0 = 0$ in (2-9). Of course, the firm could borrow more than 49.45 and pay positive dividends at time 0; however, as we have seen, no advantage to borrowing more than 49.45 will result, since for any given investment budget (here equal to 299.45) dividend payout is irrelevant.

Second, notice that at a maximum present value

$$\frac{d}{dI_0}\left[\frac{\Delta X_1}{1+i} - I_0\right] = 0$$

which implies that

$$\frac{d\,\Delta X_1}{dI_0} = 1 + i \tag{2-24}$$

Equation (2-24) states that, at the level of investment which maximizes firm value, the additional inflow at time 1 per dollar of additional investment is equal to one plus the interest rate. As long as $\Delta X_1$ [and therefore $X_1$ in Eq. (2-12)] increases by an amount greater than $(1 + i)$ as $I_0$ increases by a unit, $V$ [in Eq.

[11] To see that the same result occurs by using $V$ in eq. (2-12), maximize $V$ by substituting $X_1 = X_1' + \Delta X_1 = 200 + [600I_0 - I_0^2]$ for $X_1$ in (2-12). Maximize $V$ with respect to $I_0$, and (2-23) results.

(2-12)] also increases. That is, the present value of dividends rises. On the other hand, if $\Delta X_1$ (and $X_1$) increases by less than $(1 + i)$ as $I_0$ rises, $V$ is falling. This is perfectly reasonable since it is clear that the firm should not invest additional sums if it can earn more on those additional sums by lending in the market at rate $i$. By lending any added $I_0$ at rate $i$, $\Delta X_1$ rises by $(1 + i)$ for an incremental unit of $I_0$ loaned. This will, by Eq. (2-12), produce no change in $V$. Such lending is obviously preferable to investing at a rate of return less than $i$ which would lower firm value. Define $r^m$ as the rate of return on an incremental unit of investment. That is,

$$\frac{d\,\Delta X_1}{dI_0} = 1 + r^m \tag{2-25}$$

For example, if an added dollar ($dI_0 = \$1$) of investment produces an added inflow at time 1 of \$1.15 ($d\,\Delta X_1 = \$1.15$), then the marginal rate of return is 15% (the added net profit of 15 cents divided by the added investment of \$1). Using this definition of $r^m$ and substituting into (2-24), at a firm value maximum

$$1 + r^m = 1 + i$$

or

$$r^m = i \tag{2-26}$$

To see that Eq. (2-26) produces the same level of investment as determined earlier, note that, given the definition of $r^m$ in Eq. (2-24) and the value of $d\,\Delta X_1/dI_0$ in Eq. (2-20), Eq. (2-26) implies that

$$r^m = (600 - 2I_0) - 1 = .1$$

which implies that

$$I_0 = 299.45$$

This is the result derived earlier.

Equation (2-26) states that, at a firm value maximum, the marginal rate of return on investment will equal the market rate of interest. As long as the firm can invest additional (marginal) dollars and earn more than the market rate it should do so, since it adds an inflow at time 1 with a present value greater than the present value of the added sacrifice of a dollar now (equal to a dollar). If added investment yields a marginal rate of return less than the market rate, the present value of the proceeds will be less than the dollar sacrificed; in such a case, it would be better for the firm to lend its marginal dollars at rate $i$ in the market (or pay out those dollars in current dividends).

## The Multiperiod Case

It was shown that the goal of the firm is to maximize its current value and that this value is the discounted stream of all future dividend payments on its currently outstanding shares [Eq. (2-5)]. The proposition that dividend policy is irrelevant in the multiperiod case can be provided by a straightforward extension of the argument used for a single period, and will not be developed here.

Proof of the proposition is in Appendix 2A. The extended valuation formula comparable to (2-12) and independent of dividend-financing policy is

$$V = X_0 - I_0 + \sum_{t=1}^{T} \frac{X_t - I_t}{\prod_{j=1}^{t} (1 + i_j)} \tag{2-27}$$

Investment policy in the multiperiod case is not quite as straightforward as the dividend policy problem and is worth examining in somewhat more detail. We begin as before by defining an income stream $X'$ for the firm, which it would have if all investment $I_t$ were equal to zero for all $t$. Now consider the $\Delta X_t$, the increment to income resulting from *all prior investment,* i.e., from the $I_j, j = 0 \cdot \cdot \cdot t - 1$. Then $X_t = X'_t + \Delta X_t$, and substituting into (2-27) we have

$$V = X_0 - I_0 + \sum_{t=1}^{T} \frac{X'_t}{\prod_{j=1}^{t} (1 + i_j)} + \sum_{t=1}^{T} \frac{\Delta X_t - I_t}{\prod_{j=1}^{t} (1 + i_j)} \tag{2-28}$$

Time 0 income $X_0$ and future "zero investment" incomes $X'_t, t = 1, \ldots, T$, are independent of investment policy, and therefore maximization of the firm's value requires us to choose those budgets that maximize:

$$\Delta V = -I_0 + \sum_{t=1}^{T} \frac{\Delta X_t - I_t}{\prod_{j=1}^{t} (1 + i_j)} \tag{2-29}$$

So far, the development is directly comparable to the single-period problem. However, the expression above has not been written in terms of a capital budget for just a single period and its related cash flows but in terms of all present and future investment budgets and their incremental returns in aggregate. How, then, can we properly evaluate the impact of a particular period's investment, for example, $I_0$? The answer is that we must consider *all* the consequences of our investing $I_0$, including the impact on any *future* investment alternatives. In general, we are required to consider all possible investment strategies and choose the one with the highest present value. It turns out that this is not as difficult as it sounds; a workable procedure is developed in Chap. 3.

## A COMMENT ON EQUILIBRIUM

The problems in this chapter were treated under the assumption that the market rates of interest (over time) were given to the individual and firm. The question of how such rates are determined was ignored. However, the ideas in the preceding discussion relate closely to the analysis of how such an equilibrium set of rates is attained. Given any set of market rates (which by the perfect market assumption a single individual or firm cannot significantly alter), the borrowing and lending described above are conducted by a large number of individuals and firms. This borrowing and lending in the market cause rates to vary. At equilibrium, market rates are such that planned savings and planned investments are equalized for the economy and all wish to retain their existing claims on present and future income streams. Individuals maximize their utilities from consumption, through borrowing and lending given their wealth constraints. Firms maximize shareholder wealth through investment. It is the aggregate effect of all these individuals and firms that determines the equilibrium of the system.

## SUMMARY

Under conditions of certainty and perfect capital markets, the individual is able to achieve a preferred consumption pattern for a given present value of wealth. This is so regardless of the pattern of the individual's income stream. Two income streams with the same present value provide identical consumption opportunities. Assuming that more consumption is preferred to less, the individual prefers a higher to a lower present value of income; i.e., the individual's objective is to maximize his or her current wealth. Firms seek to act in the best interests of their owners; therefore, the objective of the firm is to maximize the present value of the income stream provided to its current stockholders. However, the pattern of the income distributed does not affect the firm's value—dividend policy is irrelevant. The objective of investment policy is to maximize the present value of all incremental cash flow resulting from investment; however, doing so will likely involve evaluation of opportunities in more than one period. The determination of the optimal capital budget at any single time cannot, in general, be considered independent of the budgets at other times.

APPENDIX

# TWO A

# MULTIPERIOD DIVIDEND POLICY AND FIRM VALUATION

This appendix discusses two related issues. The first is dividend policy and why dividend policy is irrelevant under certainty and perfect markets. The second issue is firm valuation and what firm variables determine that value. It will be shown that with certainty and perfect markets, firm value can be expressed as the present value of dividends, the present value of firm net cash flow, and the present value of adjusted earnings.

## DIVIDEND POLICY

There are several ways to show that dividend policy is irrelevant under certainty and perfect markets. The best known of such proofs, that by Miller and Modigliani,[12] uses a moderately complex set of variables. The proof shown here is a straightforward extension of the single-period case presented in the body of the chapter.

As we have noted, the individual desires a maximum present value of wealth, regardless of the number of time periods involved. The pattern of income is irrelevant since the investor can transform a given income stream into any other income stream with the same present value. The maximization of firm value is therefore the goal of the firm's management. It will be shown that in the multiperiod case dividend policy does not alter firm value. The value of the firm depends on its net cash flow over time, and maximization of firm value is achieved by maximizing the present value of that cash flow.

[12] Miller and Modigliani, Dividend Policy, Growth, and the Valuation of Shares (listed in the Suggested Readings at the end of this chapter).

Assume that the firm's investment policy is determined separately from dividend policy. It will now be shown that for any given investment policy, dividend policy is irrelevant. Only for the purpose of simplifying the algebra, assume that dividends, income, investment, and financing all occur at the very beginning of the period. Recall that period $t$ extends from time $t - 1$ to time $t$. Assume the following definitions:

$D_t$ = the total dividends paid at time $t$ to shares outstanding at time 0.[13]
$i_j$ = the market rate of interest in period $j$.
$F_t$ = the amount of external funds raised at time $t$.

Other variables are as defined for the single-period case.

The value of the firm at time 0 is the discounted stream of all present and future dividends paid on the current shares; therefore

$$V = D_0 + \sum_{t=1}^{T} \frac{D_t}{\prod_{j=1}^{t} (1 + i_j)} \tag{2A-1}$$

which corresponds directly to the single-period case. Equation (2A-1) assumes that in some indefinite future period $T$ (which could be $T \to \infty$) the firm ceases to exist and a liquidating dividend is paid. Let us now look at the dividend-financing problem at some time $t$. The cash flow relationship assumed is

$$X_0 + F_0 = D_0 + I_0 \tag{2A-2a}$$

$$X_t + F_t = D_t + I_t + (1 + i_t)F_{t-1} \tag{2A-2b}$$

We are valuing the firm from the perspective of the "old" time 0 security holders (i.e., excluding any new security holders acquiring stock at time 0 for $F_0$); since payments on any new securities issued at time 0 or thereafter (for amounts $F_t$) reduce the dividends on the old time 0 securities, we deduct those payments (payments $(1 + i_t(F_{t-1})$ in computing $D_t$. For convenience we assume that the financing for period $t$ ($F_{t-1}$ is financing at the beginning of period $t$, at time $t - 1$) is repaid at the end of the period just before new financing takes place.[14] Alternative financing methods could be used, but they would compli-

[13] If $d_t$ is the dividend per share at time $t$ and $n_0$ is the number of shares outstanding at time 0, the $D_t = d_t n_0$, which in general is not equal to the total dividend payment of the firm. Given that new financing results in additional shares being issued, then total dividends would be $n_t d_t$, where $n_t$ is the shares outstanding at time $t$. See Miller and Modigliani, *ibid*.

[14] The financing method used is somewhat more general than may be apparent. We could rewrite (2A-2b) as

$$X_t + (F_t - F_{t-1}) = D_t + I_t + i_t F_{t-1}$$

We interpret $F_t$ as the value of existing external financing at time $t$, and $F_t - F_{t-1}$ is therefore new financing done at time $t$. Quantity $i_t F_{t-1}$ is the cost of external financing for period $t$.

cate the analysis without affecting the results.[15] The assumed financing method is an extension of that used in the single-period case.

From Eqs. (2A-2a) and (2A-2b) we know that

$$D_o = X_o + F_o - I_o \tag{2A-3a}$$

$$D_t = X_t + F_t - I_t - (1 + i_t)F_{t-1} \tag{2A-3b}$$

Substituting for $D_t$ in the valuation Eq. (2A-1) we have

$$V = X_0 + F_0 - I_0 + \sum_{t=1}^{T} \frac{X_t + F_t - I_t - (1 + i_t)F_{t-1}}{\prod_{j=1}^{t} (1 + i_j)} \tag{2A-4}$$

Suppose we separate out the first term of the summation (in 2A-4) and simplify:

$$\begin{aligned} V &= X_0 + F_0 - I_0 + \frac{X_1 + F_1 - I_1 - (1 + i_1)F_0}{1 + i_1} + \sum_{t=2}^{T} \cdots \\ &= X_0 - I_0 + \frac{X_1 + F_1 - I_1}{1 + i_1} + \sum_{t=2}^{T} \cdots \end{aligned} \tag{2A-5}$$

$F_0$ has canceled out of the valuation relationship. Suppose we look now at the term for time 2:

$$V = X_0 - I_0 + \frac{X_1 + F_1 - I_1}{1 + i_1} + \frac{X_2 + F_2 - I_2 - (1 + i_2)F_1}{(1 + i_1)(1 + i_2)} + \sum_{t=3}^{T} \cdots \tag{2A-6}$$

We can simplify (2A-6) to delete $F_1$; we can continue deleting the $F_t$ in this fashion for all future periods to arrive at

$$V = X_0 - I_0 + \sum_{t=1}^{T} \frac{X_t - I_t}{\prod_{j=1}^{t} (1 + i_j)} \tag{2A-7}$$

Equation (2A-7) expresses the current value of the firm as the discounted sum of all cash payments to capital suppliers. $V$ is independent of dividend policy

[15] One such alternative could be issuing securities with the repayment scheme of a bond. The interest rate $r$ on such a security issued at time $t - 1$ would be

$$(1 + r_t)^n = \prod_{j=t}^{n+t} (1 + i_j)$$

where $n$ is the number of periods to maturity. See any introduction to the term structure of interest rates for a discussion, for example, J. W. Conard, "An Introduction to the Theory of Interest," University of California Press, Berkeley, 1959.

because neither the $i_j$, which are market rates, nor future income $X_t$ and investment $I_t$ are affected by dividend policy. $X_t$ is determined by past investment policy, and investment policy is independent of dividend policy by assumption.[16]

In the preceding discussion $F_t$ was assumed to represent firm borrowing, that is, $F_t \geq 0$. If the firm were assumed to lend in the market at rate $i$, then $F_t < 0$ and all the arguments above follow similarly. The equations are identical. That is, firm borrowing (to increase current dividends and reduce future dividends) or firm lending (to increase future dividends and reduce current dividends) will have no effect on the firm's value so long as the firm's investment in productive assets $I$ and therefore income $X$ are given for each period.[17]

## FIRM VALUATION

Assume that the firm has outstanding only one class of securities, which we shall call shares (or stock) and assume certainty, perfect markets, and no taxes. We observed above that under these assumptions the value of the firm's current shares and of the firm (since only shares are outstanding) can be expressed as the present value of the dividends paid on those shares.

The dividend valuation equation is Eq. (2A-1). It was shown that firm value can also be expressed as the present value of the firm's net cash flow, $X_t - I_t$, all $t$; this cash-flow valuation equation is (2A-7). A third valuation equation, one which involves the valuation of the firm's earnings, is also valid. Earnings equal revenues less expenses less depreciation (decline in value of existing assets) during the period. To express earnings in equation form, let $DP_t$ equal the time $t$ depreciation. Define $E_t$ as earnings for period $t$ where

$$E_t = X_t - DP_t \tag{2A-8}$$

Term $DP_t$, for purposes here, can be accounting depreciation (i.e., depreciation recorded on the firm's books) or economic depreciation (the real decline in the value of the assets). As we shall see, before earnings can be valued they must be "adjusted," and consequently the definition of $DP_t$ in (2A-8) is irrelevant. Note also that even if accounting depreciation is used, $E_t$ will differ from accounting earnings because $X_t$ is cash revenues less cash expenses, and firms ordinarily use an accrual rather than a cash-basis method of accounting for revenues and expenses.

Can we simply discount $E_t$ to compute value? The answer is no, because $E_t$

[16] Note that the proof does *not* require constant future interest rates. Also note that if for some reason *investment policy* is dependent upon dividend policy then dividend policy will affect the value of the firm. These notes are relevant to the controversy over dividend policy. See Myron J. Gordon, Optimal Investment and Dividend Policy, *Journal of Finance*, vol. 18, pp. 264–272, May 1963.

[17] See footnote on page 10 on the definition of firm investment.

does not represent the true net firm benefits during the period; we must deduct not simply $DP_t$ from $X_t$ but also any investment in addition to that required to cover depreciation, i.e., in addition to $DP_t$. To clarify this, define $N_t$ as "net investment" for period $t$, where

$$N_t = I_t - DP_t \tag{2A-9}$$

$N_t$ is net cash investment in new assets in period $t$ less the decline in existing assets represented by $DP_t$. Define "adjusted earnings" $E_t^a$ as

$$E_t^a = E_t - N_t \tag{2A-10}$$

$E_t^a$ is earnings less the additional net investment during the period that is made in the firm. But notice that

$$\begin{aligned} E_t^a &= E_t - N_t \\ &= (X_t - DP_t) - (I_t - DP_t) \\ &= X_t - I_t \end{aligned} \tag{2A-11}$$

$E_t^a$ is exactly equal to cash flow, and therefore we can represent firm value using $E_t^a$ instead of $X_t - I_t$; that is,

$$V = E_0^a + \sum_{t=1}^{T} \frac{E_t^a}{\prod_{j=1}^{t} (1 + i_j)} \tag{2A-12}$$

Relation (2A-12) is the third firm valuation equation. Now observe that using (2A-10) and (2A-12), we can also express value as

$$V = (E_0 - N_0) + \sum_{t=1}^{T} \frac{E_t - N_t}{\prod_{j=1}^{t} (1 + i_j)} \tag{2A-13}$$

Equations (2A-12) and (2A-13) indicate that the firm's value is not simply its discounted earnings; discounted earnings represent an overestimate of firm value if net investment $N_t$ is being made, i.e., if $N_t = (I_t - DP_t)$ is positive (which means that capital outlays exceed the amount necessary to just cover depreciation $DP_t$). The reason that $N_t$ must be deducted from $E_t$ is that any net investment $N_t$ that must be made to sustain future earnings has to be deducted at time $t$ as a real cost to the firm, just like any other cost. $N_t$ is a capital expenditure made at time $t$ to raise future periods' (after $t$) cash flow; $N_t$ is a "sacrifice" made at time $t$ to produce benefits in future periods. Put slightly differently, $DP_t$ in (2A-10) understates the true outlay (sacrifice) that is being made by the firm to sustain earnings in later periods. The real sacrifice is $I_t$, and $N_t$ adjusts $DP_t$ in (2A-11) so as to fully account for that sacrifice. Recall that we stated earlier that it does not matter which definition of $DP_t$ is used. The reason is that $N_t$ is always that amount necessary to adjust $DP_t$ so that [using (2A-9)] $DP_t + N_t = I_t$; that is, so that $E_t^a = X_t - I_t$. If $DP_t$ is understated or overstated,

$N_t$ will make up the difference. Also, interestingly, note that if $N_t < 0$ (i.e., if $I_t < DP_t$), then earnings $E_t$ understate the net flow of benefits in period $t$, i.e., $DP_t$ overstates the real sacrifice made to maintain future (after $t$) earnings; in this case, discounting earnings $E_t$ would understate firm value.

In summary, we have three equivalent firm valuation equations:[18]

$$V = D_0 + \sum_{t=1}^{\infty} \frac{D_t}{\prod_{j=1}^{t} (1 + i_j)} \tag{2A-1}$$

$$V = X_0 - I_0 + \sum_{t=1}^{\infty} \frac{X_t - I_t}{\prod_{j=1}^{t} (1 + i_j)} \tag{2A-7}$$

$$V = E_0^a + \sum_{t=1}^{\infty} \frac{E_t^a}{\prod_{j=1}^{t} (1 + i_j)} \tag{2A-12}$$

[18] With certainty and no taxes (2A-1), (2A-7), and (2A-12) define share values and total firm value (since all the firm's securities are shares in such a world, i.e., there is no distinction between stock and debt). With certainty and corporate taxes (with interest on debt tax deductible), (2A-1) defines share values (excluding the value of firm debt), whereas (2A-7) and (2A-12) are total firm value (value of shares and bonds); with debt, $E_t^a$ in (2A-12) is adjusted earnings in period $t$ before deducting debt interest.

APPENDIX

# TWO B

## VALUATION OF CONTINUOUS STREAMS

Whenever discounting models are presented in this text (except for Chapter 10), we assume that funds flow in and out in "chunks" (i.e., in discrete quantities) and that such flows take place only at the beginning and ending of periods—at time 0, time 1, etc. A moment's reflection will make it clear that this assumption is not always a very good one. Some flows take place almost continuously: receipts from sale of goods, for example. If a year is defined as the basic period, then there are many kinds of flows that do not take place at the beginning and end of the year. At best the assumption is an approximation of the real behavior of the flows. One way to deal with the problem that is sometimes convenient in theoretical models is to assume continuous compounding-discounting. This concept is illustrated and compared with discrete compounding-discounting (which was used in the body of Chap. 2) in the following example.

Suppose \$10.00 is invested in a security that will return \$10.60 at the end of 1 year. The interest rate on this investment is 6%/year. Now suppose we plan to reinvest at the same rate for another year. For the second year we would begin with \$10.60 and end up with \$10.60 (1.06) = \$11.24. In this situation we are assuming *annual* compounding; that is, we do not earn anything on our *interest* for a given year until the next year. Suppose, however, that the compound interval is 6 months. At the end of 6 months \$10.00 will be worth \$10.30. Since the *nominal annual* interest rate is 6%, the rate for $\frac{1}{2}$ year is equal to 3%. If we reinvest \$10.30, we shall have \$10.30 (1.03) = \$10.61 at the end of the first year. The *effective* rate for the year is therefore 6.1%. Imagine now that the compounding interval is made smaller and smaller until interest is being compounded every instant. This is called continuous compounding. To determine the value of the investment of \$10.00 at the end of the year, a different mathematical concept must be used.

Note first that the value at the end of the year for an arbitrary number of compounding intervals $m$ can be expressed as

$$V_1 = V_0(1 + i/m)^m \tag{2B-1}$$

For a 6-month compounding interval $m = 2$ and $V_1 = \$10(1.03)^2 = \$10.61$ as above. Now let the number of intervals get very large ($m \to \infty$):

$$\begin{aligned} \lim_{m\to\infty}[V_1] &= \lim_{m\to\infty}[V_0(1 + i/m)^m] \\ &= V_0 \lim_{m\to\infty}[(1 + i/m)^m] \\ V_1 &= V_0 e^i \end{aligned} \tag{2B-2}$$

The proof of Eq. (2B-2) is beyond the scope of this text; but this relationship is sufficient to derive all subsequent results.[19] If $i$ is 6% and $V_0 = \$10$, then with continuous compounding $V_1 = 10e^{.06} = \$10.62$. The effective rate of interest with continuous compounding is therefore 6.2%. Although reducing the compounding interval increases the effective rate, the difference is not large even when the compounding interval is infinitesimal (continuous compounding). This concept generalizes readily to the following:

If we measure time $t$ in years, and the annual rate of interest is the same value $i$ for all $t$,

$$V_t = V_0 e^{it} \tag{2B-3}$$

where $V_0$ = amount initially invested
$V_t$ = value after $t$ years

One useful point about this relationship is that $t$ can be in fractions of a year, such as 2.5 (2 years, 6 months) or 0.083 ($\frac{1}{12}$ year—one month). The equivalent expression for discrete compounding is

$$V_t = V_0(1 + i)^t \tag{2B-4}$$

but $t$ must be an integer in (2B-4) to be consistent with the discrete compounding assumption of equal discrete periods (the periods can be of any length—one month, one year, etc.).

If we now look at the *present value* of a sum of money paid $t$ years from now with continuous discounting, from Eq. (2B-3) we have

$$\begin{aligned} V_0 &= \frac{V_t}{e^{it}} \\ &= V_t e^{-it} \end{aligned} \tag{2B-5}$$

Finally, if the cash flow from an investment is a continuous stream $X(t)$, the present value for a stream ending at time $T$ is

[19] For the proof of Eq. (2B-2), see R. G. D. Allen, "Mathematical Analysis for Economists," pp. 230–231, St. Martin's Press, Inc., New York, 1938.

$$V_0 = \int_0^T X(t)e^{-it}\,dt \tag{2B-6}$$

There are two special cases for $X(t)$ that are of interest—$X(t) = X$, a constant; and $X(t) = X_0e^{gt}$, where $g$ is a constant rate of growth:

1. $X(t) = X$

$$\begin{aligned} V_0 &= \int_0^T Xe^{-it}\,dt \\ &= \frac{X}{i}(1 - e^{-iT}) \end{aligned} \tag{2B-7}$$

When $X$ is a perpetuity ($T \to \infty$), then Eq. (2B-7) is

$$\lim_{T\to\infty}[V_0] = \lim_{T\to\infty}\left[\frac{X}{i}(1 - e^{-iT})\right]$$

$$V_0 = \frac{X}{i} \tag{2B-8}$$

2. $X(t) = X_0e^{gt}$

$$\begin{aligned} V_0 &= \int_0^T X_0e^{gt}e^{-it}\,dt \\ &= X_0\int_0^T e^{-(i-g)t}\,dt \end{aligned}$$

$$V_0 = \frac{X_0}{i - g}[1 - e^{-(i-g)T}] \tag{2B-9}$$

When the stream $X(t)$ continues forever ($T \to \infty$), then $V_0$ approaches a finite value if and only if $i - g > 0$ or $i > g$. Assuming that this condition does hold, then

$$\lim_{T\to\infty}[V_0] = \lim_{T\to\infty}\left[\frac{X_0}{i - g}(1 - e^{-(i-g)T})\right]$$

$$V_0 = \frac{X_0}{i - g} \tag{2B-10}$$

Equation (2B-10) is often used in empirical and theoretical studies, and is sometimes referred to as the Gordon model when $X(t)$ is a stream of dividends and $V_0$ is the current value of the firm's shares.[20]

[20] Myron J. Gordon and Eli Shapiro, Capital Equipment Analysis: The Required Rate of Profit, *Management Science*, vol. 3, pp. 102–110, October 1956.

## SUGGESTED READINGS

Bodenhorn, Diran: On the Problem of Capital Budgeting, *Journal of Finance,* vol. 14, pp. 473–492, December 1959, reprinted in Archer, Stephen H. and Charles A. D'Ambrosio: "The Theory of Business Finance," 2d ed., The Macmillan Company, New York, 1976.

Fisher, Irving: "The Theory of Interest," reprinted from the 1930 ed. Augustus M. Kelly, Publishers, New York, 1965.

Miller, Merton K. and Franco Modigliani: Dividend Policy, Growth, and the Valuation of Shares, *Journal of Business,* vol. 34, pp. 411–433, October 1961; reprinted in Archer and D'Ambrosio, *ibid.*

Samuelson, Paul: Some Aspects of the Pure Theory of Capital, *Quarterly Journal of Economics,* vol. 51, pp. 469–496, May 1937.

CHAPTER

# THREE

# CAPITAL BUDGETING IN PERFECT MARKETS

This chapter concerns the evaluation and selection of the specific investment opportunities that form the total investment budget of the firm. Although the procedures developed here are based on assumptions of certainty and perfect markets, in later chapters the analysis will be shown to apply to some extent under uncertainty and in some types of imperfect markets. The treatment here is theoretical, since a complete discussion of the application of the analysis to practical problems is available elsewhere. The references at the end of the chapter, particularly the excellent work by Grant and Ireson,[1] are recommended for those interested in the practical application of the principles discussed here.

## INVESTMENT STRATEGY AND THE OPTIMAL CAPITAL BUDGET

In Chap. 2 the objective of firm investment policy was derived. That objective is to maximize the present value of the net cash flow from all investment undertaken by the firm [expression (2-29)], given the market rates of interest in effect in all future periods. For the remainder of this chapter we assume that the rates of interest are equal for all future periods,[2] and therefore we can speak of *the* rate of interest or discount rate $i$. The term "discount rate" refers to that

[1] Grant and Ireson, "Principles of Engineering Economy" (listed in the Suggested Readings at the end of this chapter).

[2] As we shall see, this assumption is primarily a matter of convenience, although some methods of evaluating alternatives require it. This limitation on the use of such methods will be noted at the point where the methods are discussed.

rate used by individuals and firms to discount an income stream in order to determine its present value; this rate equals the market interest rate as we saw in Chap. 2. In this case our general objective, from expression (2-29), is to

$$\text{Maximize } \Delta V = -I_0 + \sum_{t=1}^{T} \frac{\Delta X_t - I_t}{(1 + i)^t} \tag{3-1}$$

Recall that $\Delta X_t$ is the time $t$ income resulting from investment outlays from time 0 to time $t - 1$; that is, $\Delta X_t$ is the increase in time $t$ firm income relative to what it would be if the firm's investment were zero from time 0 to time $t - 1$. Expression (3-1) can be considered the *strategic* objective of investment policy. It calls for the firm to consider all possible present and *future* investment opportunities and to select that set of options which maximizes the firm's value. The options that are to be undertaken in a particular period constitute the investment *budget* for that period. Quantity $I_t$ is, of course, the dollar amount of the budget for time $t$. Under *certainty*, once the optimum investment strategy has been chosen, the firm's management never has to concern itself with investment policy again. The budgets for each future period are determined. As we shall see, there is a large computational problem in arriving at the optimal strategy, but that is the *only* problem under certainty. Under uncertainty, management has at best only a rough idea of the future investment opportunities that may arise and therefore can specify only one budget at a time. The strategic objective becomes primarily a matter for managerial judgment.

Although the assumption of certainty is maintained in this chapter, we shall discuss the problem in terms of the development of an optimal single current budget. That is, we shall specify how the firm should go about determining that current (time 0) budget which is required to meet the strategic objective. In this way we can both obtain the theoretical requirements for such budgets and maintain some comparability to capital budgeting problems as they appear in practice under uncertainty.

The current capital budget consists of all investment opportunities that will be undertaken in the current period. For simplicity we usually assume that the funds are spent at time 0. The problem is to select that set of opportunities which provides the maximum increment to the value of the firm. In principle, we could evaluate all possible sets of opportunities and simply choose the one with maximum value. If there were no costs in the process of evaluation and computation, there would be no reason to go further. However, such costs do exist, if only because of the managerial and computer time required. Consequently we are interested in an *efficient* method of determining the optimal budget. To provide some motivation for the need to be efficient, consider the following situation.

Suppose there are only three investment *opportunities* under consideration for inclusion in the current budget: $A$, $B$, and $C$. In general there are eight alternative budgets (combinations of $A$, $B$, and $C$) that must be evaluated:

| | | |
|---|---|---|
| $A$ | $B$ | $C$ |
| $A$ and $B$ | $B$ and $C$ | $A$ and $C$ |
| $A$, $B$, and $C$ | | None |

If the firm has $n$ possible opportunities there will be $2^n$ different budgets. If $n = 10$, $2^{10} = 1{,}024$ alternative budgets. Even a very small firm might have 10 opportunities. A large firm could have 1,000. And $2^{1{,}000}$ is a very large number! Anything that can be done to reduce this job is worthwhile. Fortunately we can be much more efficient than this by exploiting some of the characteristics of investment opportunities.

## THE CHARACTERISTICS OF INVESTMENT OPPORTUNITIES

An investment *opportunity* is simply the option available to the firm to take a particular action involving a payment of cash now to realize some future cash return. Any pair of opportunities must be either economically independent or economically dependent. *Two opportunities are economically dependent if the adoption of one of the opportunities affects the cash flow of the other opportunity*. If the adoption of an opportunity in no way affects or is affected by any other opportunity of the firm, then it can be referred to as an *independent opportunity*. For example, suppose a real estate developer has two adjacent plots of land. If what is built on one will affect the cash flows of what is built on the other, then the investment options for both plots are dependent. The effects may be either beneficial or adverse. A gas station on one plot would be benefited by a shopping center on the other; but single-family homes on one would probably be adversely affected by a shopping center on the other. Suppose, however, that the two plots were several miles apart: what the developer does with one would be independent of what is done with the other.[3]

It should be noted that the types of dependence and independence of concern here are *economic*; i.e., they refer to interdependencies of costs or revenues (and therefore profitabilities) between opportunities. Later, when we consider uncertainty, a second type of dependence, *stochastic* dependence, will be introduced. In this chapter we are assuming certainty; therefore, stochastic processes are not relevant. Throughout this chapter the modifier "economic" will frequently be dropped, since only economic dependencies are considered at this point.

[3] In fact there may be slight dependencies in this case. For example, it may be slightly cheaper to build the same thing on both plots because of economies of scale in labor force usage, materials purchasing, selling costs, or whatever. In general, absolute independence may be difficult to come by. Management must judge whether the dependencies are important enough to warrant inclusion in the analysis. Hence, *approximate* independence is really what is being assumed.

A particular and very important type of dependence is *mutual exclusivity*. Two opporunities are mutually exclusive if the adoption of one precludes the adoption of the other. If all the land of a plot is used for a gas station, one is prevented from building anything else on it. Thus a hotel occupying the entire plot of land would be mutually exclusive of the gas station.

A formal definition of the economic independence of any set of $n$ opportunities is that, for *all* subsets of the $n$ opportunities, the subset made up of $m$ opportunities, $2 \leq m \leq n$, at every point in time $t$, the sum of the individual time $t$ cash flows of the $m$ opportunities equals the total time $t$ cash flow of the opportunities if they were instead adopted together. Thus, if opportunities $A$, $B$, and $C$ are independent, then for all $t$ (including time 0)

$$CF_t^{AB} = CF_t^A + CF_t^B$$

$$CF_t^{BC} = CF_t^B + CF_t^C$$

$$CF_t^{AC} = CF_t^A + CF_t^C$$

$$CF_t^{ABC} = CF_t^A + CF_t^B + CF_t^C$$

Stated mathematically, if we define $C$ as any combination of two or more opportunities from a set of $n$ opportunities, where $C$ is comprised of opportunities $i = 1, \ldots, q$, the $n$ opportunities are economically independent if, and only if, for *all* possible combinations $C$,

$$CF_t^c = \sum_{i=1}^{q} CF_t^i \qquad \text{all } t$$

where $CF_t^c$ is the total time $t$ cash flow from combination $C$ (from all opportunities comprising $C$ if all are adopted) and $CF_t^i$ is the time $t$ cash flow from *only* opportunity $i$ assuming that none of the remaining $(q\text{-}1)$ opportunities that comprise $C$ are adopted.

The useful aspect of the concept of economic independence is illustrated by the following proposition. If an opportunity is independent of all other opportunities, then the only decision that must be made is whether to accept or reject the opportunity. In other words, such opportunities can be evaluated solely in terms of their incremental impact on the cash flows of the firm without considering any other opportunities available. *Independent opportunities can be evaluated independently*. The decision rule for such independent investments is: accept all independent opportunities whose present values are positive; reject all independent opportunities whose present values are negative.[4] The present value of an opportunity is the discounted sum of all cash flows attributable to accepting it, including the initial investment.

[4] If the present value is zero, the firm is indifferent between acceptance and rejection. The reader may assume acceptance or rejection. In some sections of this book, the project-selection criterion will be to accept only if the firm benefits from the investment, implying rejection if there is indifference or loss; the criterion could, of course, just as well indicate acceptance with benefit or indifference.

The concept of independence is important because it is the basis for an efficient method of determining the optimal capital budget. In the example above the firm had three investment options ($A$, $B$, and $C$) and therefore had to consider $2^3 = 8$ different possible budgets. If those three opportunities were independent, then the optimal budget could be obtained by evaluating each one separately; i.e., by making three accept-reject decisions. The result of those decisions would be the optimal budget. A reduction from considering 8 budgets to making 3 decisions does not seem so large, but consider the case of 10 options. If they were all independent, only 10 decisions would have to be made as compared to an evaluation of 1,024 ($2^{10}$) different budgets. This is an appreciable reduction by any standard. As a consequence management should identify the independent options at the outset of the analysis, thereby reducing as much as possible the number of alternatives that must be evaluated.

## PROJECT ANALYSIS AND THE OPTIMAL BUDGET

From the preceding discussion we see that the key to efficient organization and analysis of the capital budgeting problem is the identification of independent opportunities. In this section we shall discuss a way to approach the problem built on the definition of a particular type of investment called a "project." A project is a set of one or more investment opportunities with the following characteristics:

1. Each opportunity included in a project is independent of all opportunities not included within that project.
2. The acceptance of any opportunity included in a project is conditional on the acceptance of the project itself.
3. Every opportunity is included in some project.[5]

Condition (1) means that if any two opportunities are dependent, they must be in the same project. Condition (2) is definitional; i.e., the "acceptance" of an opportunity means by definition that the project with which that opportunity is associated is also accepted. Thus a project is rejected only if all opportunities in that project are rejected; i.e., if the alternative of doing nothing is accepted. Condition (3) merely ensures that all opportunities of the firm are defined as being part of a project. A project may comprise only one opportunity *if* that opportunity is independent of all other opportunities available to the firm [the "if" follows from condition (1)].

Notice that there is nothing in the definition of the term "project" that prevents a project from being made up of other projects. Indeed, the totality of opportunities provided to the firm comprises a project. As will be explained, the efficient approach to investment analysis is to break opportunities into the

[5] No opportunity can belong to more than one project or else condition (1) would not hold.

maximum number of projects. This implies that efficient analysis will involve dividing opportunities so that no single project itself contains smaller projects. Given the definition of a project, we can state the criterion for the optimal capital budget:

> The optimal capital budget consists of all projects with positive present values and contains no projects with negative present values.

Now let us explore in detail what projects are, how they are analyzed, and why project analysis is an efficient way to go about determining the optimal budget.

Beginning with the last issue, sorting the opportunities into the *maximum* number of projects is efficient because we thereby maximize the number of *independent* decisions that can be made. Therefore, we *minimize* the number of alternatives that must be considered. The easiest way to show this is by an example. If the firm had 10 opportunities, we noted that in general 1,024 different budgets would have to be evaluated. We also pointed out that if each opportunity were independent of the other nine, there would instead be only 10 accept-reject decisions. According to the definition of the optimal capital budget stated above, if the opportunities were independent, each would be considered a project and all accepted opportunities would be included in the optimal budget.

Now suppose instead that there exist some dependencies among the opportunities such as the following, where $O_i$ is the $i$th opportunity:

> $O_1$, $O_2$, and $O_3$ are dependent on each other but independent of $O_4$ through $O_{10}$. $O_4$ is independent of all others.
> $O_5$, $O_6$, and $O_7$ are dependent on each other but independent of $O_1$ through $O_4$ and $O_8$ through $O_{10}$.
> $O_8$, $O_9$, and $O_{10}$ are mutually exclusive options but independent of $O_1$ through $O_7$.

In the proposed procedure we can think of having four projects available:

Project $A$: $O_1$, $O_2$, and $O_3$
Project $B$: $O_4$
Project $C$: $O_5$, $O_6$, and $O_7$
Project $D$: $O_8$, $O_9$, and $O_{10}$

Each of the projects can be analyzed separately. In general, project $A$ would require consideration of $2^3 = 8$ mutually exclusive alternatives, the best of which would then be included in the budget.[6] The same would be true of project $C$. Project $B$ can be accepted or rejected as is. Project $D$ requires a comparison of four alternatives—$O_8$, $O_9$, $O_{10}$, and none—the best of which

[6] The "best" alternative may be to undertake none of the opportunities. This alternative has a present value of zero.

would then be accepted or rejected as project *D*. We reduce the problem by inspection from 1,024 ($2^{10}$) to 8 + 2 + 8 + 4 = 22 alternatives being evaluated.

The opportunities of a given project should be organized in much the same fashion as the entire set of the firm's opportunities was organized into projects. The implication of the approach is that each project should be divided into as many conditionally independent subprojects as possible. *A subproject is a set of opportunities whose returns are independent of other opportunities within the total project, but conditional on the undertaking of the project itself.* A subproject is not accepted or rejected in itself; rather, it is a device for organizing the analysis in an efficient manner by minimizing the number of alternatives that need to be evaluated. Some of the examples presented below of projects and their analyses will help clarify these points.

It should also be noted that the concept of independence means total independence for all time. Future opportunities that depend on current decisions must be included within the appropriate project in order to ensure the optimality of the current budget. Specification of the alternatives is a formidable task, one that calls for careful judgment by management to keep the problem within a controllable size by suitable approximation. This issue is discussed in more detail later in the chapter.

## Efficient Investment Analysis

To summarize the development to this point, the efficient approach to investment analysis involves the following steps:

1. Define the total set of opportunities available to the firm.
2. Divide the opportunities into the *maximum* number of projects achievable. Any two opportunities that are dependent must be included in the same project.
3. For each project:
   (*a*) Define every possible combination of opportunities within that project. Each combination is referred to as an "alternative." One of the alternatives is to accept none of the opportunities in the project (to reject the project). The other alternatives will contain one or more opportunities.
   (*b*) From the alternatives identified under (3*a*) above, determine and adopt that alternative which is "best," i.e., the one with the highest net present value (present value of all inflows less outflows).

For each project step (3) is performed.[7] Thus, once steps (1) and (2) have been completed, each project is analyzed separately. Each *alternative* (combination of project *opportunities*) within a project is *mutually exclusive* of each other alternative, and the best alternative is the one that should be adopted.

[7] In some cases, it is possible to avoid analyzing every combination of opportunities within a project, i.e., "subprojects" can be defined which reduce the number of steps in the analysis.

A problem arises in defining alternatives as required in step (3*a*) when the future options available to the firm are affected by its current choices. One common situation of this type occurs when an asset under one alternative differs in usable economic life from an asset under another alternative, where each alternative is in the same project. For example, building a concrete warehouse with a life of 50 years may be an alternative to building a wooden warehouse with a life of 25 years. The options available to the firm 25 years from now differ appreciably under these two alternatives. The correct method to deal with such problems is as follows:

(i) For each possible current alternative (e.g., concrete and wooden warehouses) determine the set of future possible options that is available for all future periods.
(ii) For each current alternative, select that series of future options which is best according to the criterion in use (e.g., present value).
(iii) In comparing current alternatives, the best set of future options associated with each alternative must be evaluated as part of the alternative in question. As before, the best current alternative (and its associated best future options) is the one that should be adopted. Keep in mind that the best alternative may be to reject the project (choose none of the opportunities).

These additions are simply an amplification of the basic approach outlined earlier. Actions taken by the firm today must be evaluated in light of the anticipated effect on possible future actions. Statement (i) indicates that this must be done. For example, if the wooden warehouse option is to be evaluated properly, we must consider what will be done at the end of 25 years. Will the building be torn down and the site used for something else? Will it be rebuilt in a style comparable to the present structure? Will new materials (such as plastic) be available that will make it cheaper to build? Will the site be sold and another location used? Future alternatives associated with the concrete warehouse must also be examined.

Steps (ii) and (iii) state that only the best future options should be used in evaluating current alternatives. The choices made today should not be based on inferior actions in the future. For example, suppose that the best action 10 years from now would be to tear down whichever warehouse has been built in order to build a new plant on the site. Clearly, assuming that we shall replace the wooden one with another 25 years from now is not the appropriate option to use in the analysis. Instead, the costs of tearing down each warehouse 10 years from now should be evaluated.

Three qualifications to these comments should be made here. First, although in theory one should examine all future actions for each current alternative, extending the analysis to eternity is impractical. It is also unnecessary in a theoretical sense since the present value of a quantity far into the future will (for any magnitudes a firm will deal with) be extremely small. The present value of any finite amount will approach zero as its time of occurrence approaches eternity. A casual examination of present-value tables will assure the reader that amounts beyond 50 or 60 years can generally be ignored entirely.

Second, strictly speaking, all possible future alternative actions for any given current actions must be considered for any given time span (e.g., if analysis of only 50 years is conducted, *all* possible actions over the 50 years must be considered). But, as with evaluating the firm's alternatives in any case, most possibilities can be disposed of out-of-hand since they are clearly unprofitable. The task of examining all combinations of actions over time seems overwhelming in the abstract; however, in practice the firm can usually limit the set to a sufficiently small number of reasonable series of actions so that analysis can proceed.[8] In effect, the firm's management is conducting the analytical procedure outlined here. In doing so, however, many alternatives are discarded very quickly because it is clear that they are inferior.

Third, under conditions of uncertainty when the distant future may be totally obscure, only a general recommendation is appropriate. Management must consider the long-run consequences of its current choices. Applied to the warehouse example, this means that some consideration must be paid to what future actions may be desirable. However, such consideration might involve only a restricted number of the more significant possibilities—to tear down the warehouse at some future time or to keep it for an indefinite period, replacing it with a comparable structure as needed. If one alternative is better under all conditions then there is no problem. If one is better under one possibility (wood is better if the warehouse is to be torn down in the next 10 years) and the other is better under another possibility (concrete is better if it will be kept for an indefinite period), then some evaluation of the likelihood of the possibilities will be needed for a decision. In any case the problem under uncertainty is more difficult, and in the final analysis managerial judgment will be needed.

In the preceding discussion, present value in step (3) was used as the criterion of choice since present value is a valid standard under the assumptions of this chapter and those of Chap. 2. In this case, the optimal budget is comprised of all projects with a positive present value. It should be carefully noted here that *even if present value were* not *the criterion being used, steps* (1), (2), *and* (3) *would still be the efficient method of analysis,* except that "best" would no longer be determined on a present-value basis. Step (3*b*) would no longer make reference to present value but to the alternative criterion appropriate under the circumstances. The best alternative under that criterion would be identified and adopted under step (3*b*).

## Projects—Some Examples

Suppose a real estate development firm is considering the purchase of a parcel of raw land. Assume that the profitability of any other investments made by the

[8] A "decision tree" may be helpful here. See J. F. Magee, Decision Trees in Decision Making, *Harvard Business Review,* vol. 42, July–August 1964.

firm is not affected by the choices of development of the property. The purchase and development of the land can therefore be considered a project. In order to decide whether or not to purchase the property (accept or reject the project), the firm must determine the best development plan, including the possibility that the land will be held undeveloped for future sale. Since there is only one plan that will be used if the land is purchased, the firm must find the best plan among a set of mutually exclusive alternatives. Each potential plan involves additional decisions that, at least theoretically, must be evaluated before the choice of plan is made.[9] Each of these decisions will normally be interdependent, and thus all alternatives must be considered; that is, we are unlikely to find subprojects here.

Suppose, however, that the seller of the land is offering as a package two parcels that are distant from one another. We have a project—accept or reject the entire deal. However, if the deal is accepted the firm may then have two subprojects within the overall project. That is, if the development of one of the parcels does not affect the cost or return from any use of the other parcel, the development decisions can be made independently at a considerable saving in analysis. For example, suppose there are three alternative plans for each parcel. If the parcels are independent we need only pick one plan from three alternatives for each parcel; i.e., we must evaluate six plans. If, on the other hand, the development plans are interdependent—what we do with one plot of land affects the other—a total of nine plans must be considered in combinations as shown below.

| *Parcel A plans* | *Parcel B plans* | *Possible development plans for both* | | |
|---|---|---|---|---|
| $A_1$ | $B_1$ | $A_1B_1$ | $A_1B_2$ | $A_1B_3$ |
| $A_2$ | $B_2$ | $A_2B_1$ | $A_2B_2$ | $A_2B_3$ |
| $A_3$ | $B_3$ | $A_3B_1$ | $A_3B_2$ | $A_3B_3$ |

In general, if there are $n_1$ plans for one parcel and $n_2$ plans for the other, we need only evaluate $n_1 + n_2$ alternatives if the parcels are independent. If they are dependent, we must evaluate $n_1 \times n_2$ alternatives. This illustrates the savings in analysis through identification of independent subprojects.[10]

Another example of a project might be the production of a new product by a firm. If the product, its production, and its sales are independent of the other opportunities of the firm, it can be considered a project. A number of interrelated decisions must be made before the profitability of introducing the product

[9] Actually, to make the accept decision it is only necessary to find one plan that would result in a positive present value if purchased and developed. That is, once you know there exists at least one profitable use of the land you can make the decision to purchase. You can then proceed to determine the *most* profitable one.

[10] Independence is generally only approximate (see discussion on p. 53).

can be determined—the size and location of the production facility, the type of manufacturing process, the inventory needed, and so forth. Some decisions may be approximately independent even though they are conditional on others. For example, the optimal level of inventories to be held will depend on production volume, manufacturing process, and location of the plant. The decision whether or not to air-condition the plant will also depend on the location and design of the plant; however, the inventory decision can often be made independently of the air-conditioning decision—*given* the other decisions. The decision to air-condition the plant will not be affected by whether we carry 1,000 units of finished goods or 2,000 units.[11] Therefore, we shall not have to consider combinations of the two decisions.

As a final example of a project, consider the problem of whether to make a subcomponent currently being purchased by the firm. If this decision is independent of other investment opportunities, it is a project. In general there will be a variety of processes for manufacturing the subcomponent, each of which must be evaluated. Presumably the advantage to be gained from manufacture is a lower cost of production. The manufacturing process with the least cost is the best, and if the cost savings from manufacture using the best processes provide a positive present value, then the project—manufacture—should be accepted. We shall present some other methods of evaluating projects involving choice among alternative cost streams.

In summarizing this section three points should be emphasized. First, no two investment opportunities undertaken by a single firm are entirely independent of each other. Approximate independence is probably the best that can be expected to hold; however, in many cases the approximation can be fairly close. In making business decisions such approximation must be exploited to minimize the costs of evaluation. Second, the question of whether or not the approximation is reasonable involves a judgment on the part of management. Independence will be assumed as long as the anticipated savings in analysis are viewed as sufficient to offset anticipated losses due to imprecision. Under uncertainty, all estimates are subject to error, and the importance of judgment and the potential for approximation are much greater than here. Third, implicit in the discussion so far is the concept that there are only two types of investment decisions faced by the firm: accept-reject and choices among alternatives. Earlier we noted that mutual exclusivity is a special kind of dependence among opportunities. It should be emphasized that any form of dependence requires an analysis of mutually exclusive alternatives. An example should clarify this point.

Suppose a firm is evaluating alternative heating-ventilation systems in a plant. Forced-air heating could be one alternative. However, if the ducts used

[11] Not necessarily, however. Suppose the spoilage rate of inventory depends on whether the facility is air-conditioned or not. The spoilage rate will be a factor in determining the optimal level of inventory, and all combinations of the two decisions must be evaluated.

for forced-air heating could also be used for air-conditioning, the two possibilities are dependent. The forced-air heating and air-conditioning opportunities would therefore represent part or all of a project. If these opportunities are independent of all other firm opportunities, they comprise a single "environment" project. The firm could use forced-air heating alone, air-conditioning alone, or both together. Each of the three alternatives must be evaluated in evaluating the environment project; it would be improper *not* to consider "both together" as a distinct alternative since the decisions on heating and air-conditioning are not independent. In other words, when dependencies exist among decisions, each package must be evaluated as a mutually exclusive alternative. Of course, if two *opportunities* are mutually exclusive (e.g., an office building and a hotel on the same plot of ground) the two together cannot occur in any alternative evaluated.

## Project Evaluation—A Numerical Illustration

Assume a firm with two restaurants $A$ and $B$ in different parts of the same city. The only decisions to be made by management regard the menus at $A$ and $B$. At both $A$ and $B$ the problem is to select that combination of chicken, hamburger, and shrimp which will maximize firm value. Assume that the market rate of interest is 10% per year, and that returns after an initial outlay (cash outflow at time 0) are level over time beginning one year from now. Designate the decision to serve chicken, hamburger, and shrimp by the letters $C$, $H$, and $S$, respectively; thus, for example, serving chicken and hamburger but not shrimp at $A$ is denoted by $CH_A$, or serving all three at $B$ is denoted by $CHS_B$, and so forth.

If any action regarding the menu problem taken at $A$ does not affect the profitability of any action taken at $B$ and vice versa, then the two menus can be planned separately. The two sets of opportunities—those associated with $A$ and those associated with $B$—are separate projects. Assume that at each restaurant the initial outlay in serving either chicken, hamburger, or shrimp is \$5,000; to serve any two requires an outlay of \$8,000; to serve all three requires an outlay of \$10,000. The cash flow each year from time 1 on for the alternatives at restaurant $A$ are shown in Table 3-1. These annual cash flows are level perpetuities. The last column is computed by taking the present value of the perpetual income and subtracting the relevant initial outlay; e.g., for $CH_A$ $(\$1{,}000/.1) - \$8{,}000 = \$2{,}000$. The investment opportunities at A are interdependent in two ways. First, the initial outlay required to serve two or three items is less than the sum of the outlays required to serve the items individually. For example, it costs only \$8,000 to serve both chicken and shrimp ($CS_A$), but the cost to serve each one separately is \$5,000 each. If the chicken and shrimp opportunities were independent, the outlay required to do both would be the sum of the separate outlays, or \$10,000. Second, there are substitutions or complementary relationships between the items as reflected in the cash

**table 3-1**

| *Alternative* | *Income per period, \$* | *Present value of income, \$* | *Initial Outlay, \$* | *Present value of income less initial outlay, \$* |
|---|---|---|---|---|
| $C_A$ | 400 | 4,000 | 5,000 | −1,000 |
| $H_A$ | 700 | 7,000 | 5,000 | 2,000 |
| $S_A$ | 800 | 8,000 | 5,000 | 3,000 |
| $CH_A$ | 1,000 | 10,000 | 8,000 | 2,000 |
| $CS_A$ | 1,300 | 13,000 | 8,000 | 5,000 |
| $HS_A$ | 1,300 | 13,000 | 8,000 | 5,000 |
| $CHS_A$ | 1,700 | 17,000 | 10,000 | 7,000 |

flows. For example, $C_A$ produces \$400 and $H_A$ produces \$700 but $CH_A$ produces only \$1,000; that is, by serving both chicken and hamburger, the cash flow of the two together differs from the sum of the individual cash flows. This might be due to an interrelationship of greater costs of producing hamburgers and chicken together; or because people buy fewer hamburgers when chicken is sold or vice versa (or both). In any case, since the sum of the individual cash flows for $C_A$ and $H_A$ is not equal to the cash flow of $CH_A$, there are interdependencies. This means that one cannot consider serving chicken and serving hamburgers as separate projects with each possibility analyzed independently of the other; alternative $CH_A$ must therefore be considered.

Notice that there is a complementary relationship between chicken and shrimp, since the cash flow generated by $CS_A$ (\$1,300) is greater than the sum (\$1,200) of the cash flow from serving chicken alone (\$400) plus cash flow from serving shrimp alone (\$800).

The best choice for restaurant $A$ is $CHS_A$. Since the present value of this alternative is positive, it is adopted. A similar analysis could be performed for restaurant $B$. Notice that for restaurant $A$ there are eight alternatives to consider; for restaurants $A$ and $B$ together, there are 16 alternatives.

Now assume that the wholesale prices of the chicken, hamburger, and shrimp at which the restaurant firm purchases these products are subject to quantity discounts. In this case, costs for restaurants $A$ and $B$ would be interdependent. The result would be that every combination of menus at the two restaurants would have to be considered; for example, $C_A$ and none of the three items at $B$, $C_A$ and $C_B$, $C_A$ and $CH_B$, and so forth. There are 64 alternatives that would have to be considered.[12] That with the highest present value would be identified and adopted.

[12] That is, $2^6$ combinations of the six opportunities of $C$, $H$, and $S$ at restaurants $A$ and $B$ including the alternatives of serving none of the three items at one or both of the two restaurants.

## Methods of Evaluation

The present-value rule used for both project selection and the evaluation of alternatives is always an appropriate method of analysis under our assumptions. The actual application of the rule requires some practice in setting up problems, but this is not an issue here. (See the Suggested Readings at the end of the chapter.) However, there are other methods in use that were developed because of computational convenience, ease of interpretation, or historical precedent. It is of some practical importance as well as theoretical interest to determine the circumstances under which these alternative methods are also appropriate. We examine two major alternatives to present value: rate of return and uniform annual series.[13]

Slightly different notation will be used in this discussion to keep the formulas simple and to center attention on the cash flows associated with the particular investment decision being considered. Define $B_t$ as the cash benefits (increase in the firm's cash inflow) that accrue to the firm at time $t$ because of a particular decision. $C_t$ is the cash cost (increase in the firm's cash outflow) at time $t$ because of the decision. $Z_t$ is the net cash flow from the decision (i.e., the resulting change in the firm's total cash flow) and

$$Z_t = B_t - C_t \tag{3-2}$$

The rate of interest or discount rate per period is $i$ as before. We assume that all options or projects being considered require a net initial outlay, that is, $Z_0 < 0$, although the rules stated below do not require this assumption.[14]

**Present value.** In terms of our notation we have the following definition of present value and its associated rules when used as a method of analysis:

$$\text{Present value} \equiv V \equiv \sum_{t=0}^{n} \frac{Z_t}{(1+i)^t} = \sum_{t=1}^{n} \frac{Z_t}{(1+i)^t} + Z_0 \tag{3-3}$$

Our basic objective is to maximize the present value of the firm's net cash flows. The rules for project analysis presented above can be stated as follows:

1. *Project-selection rule*: Undertake all projects for which $V > 0$.
2. *Alternative selection rule*: Choose that alternative for which $V$ is maximum. This rule follows directly from the objective of the firm. When we are dealing with alternatives that involve the same level of benefits but different costs a special version of rule (2) can be used:

2′. *Cost alternative rule*: Choose that alternative with the minimum present value of costs $V_c$. The present value of costs is

[13] For an extensive discussion of the use of these methods, see Grant and Ireson, *op. cit.* Another method that is most often used in the evaluation of public investments, the benefit-cost ratio, is also discussed by them.

[14] In later chapters, $-Z_0$ will be signified as $I_{Z0}$, the initial net outlay for the project.

$$V_c = \sum_{t=0}^{n} \frac{C_t}{(1+i)^t} \tag{3-4}$$

**Uniform annual series.** The uniform annual series (UAS) method is closely related to present value. It finds most common application in the comparison of alternative methods of achieving the same level of benefits. In such situations it is known as "annual cost." Essentially, the UAS method converts a cash-flow stream into an equivalent series of equal annual cash flows. This is in contrast to the present-value method, which converts a cash-flow stream into an equivalent cash amount to be received at time 0. Hence the annual series is related to the present value of a stream by the relationship

$$V = \text{UAS} \sum_{t=1}^{n} \frac{1}{(1+i)^t} \tag{3-5}$$

or

$$\text{UAS} = V \left\{ \frac{1}{\sum_{t=1}^{n} [1/(1+i)^t]} \right\} \tag{3-6}$$

The quantity in the braces is called the "capital recovery factor," and tables of its values for different $i$ and $n$ are usually included in books dealing with problems of engineering economy. The quantity $\Sigma_{t=1}^{n}[1/(1+i)^t]$ is more frequently tabulated and is the present value of \$1/year for $n$ years discounted at $i$.

The capital recovery factor is always greater than zero; therefore, we know that any project whose present value is greater than zero will have a UAS > 0 and vice versa. Hence adoption of those projects for which UAS > 0 is entirely consistent with the present-value rule (1) above.

As a measure of the merits of a particular project, UAS has a convenient economic interpretation. It is the average annual economic profit derived from undertaking the project.[15] The rule could be stated as "Undertake those projects that are profitable," and UAS measures the level of profits.

An example might be useful to illustrate the concepts involved here. Suppose a project has the following net cash flows associated with it:

| $t =$ | 0 | 1 | 2 | |
|---|---|---|---|---|
| $Z_t =$ | −100 | 60 | 60 | 0 thereafter |

and $i = .06$.

[15] The concept of economic profit differs of course from the accountant's concept of profit, since economic profit measures profits after a deduction for all costs (capital costs *including interest* as well as other costs). Accounting profit is economic profit plus the required return (interest) on shareholders' investments.

$$V = -100 + \frac{60}{1.06} + \frac{60}{(1.06)^2}$$

$$= -100 + 60 \sum_{t=1}^{2} \frac{1}{1.06^t}$$

$$= -100 + 60(1.833) = \$9.98$$

$$\text{UAS} = \frac{\$9.98}{1.833} = \$5.46/\text{year}$$

However, since our net cash receipts ($60) are already "uniform annual amounts" we could compute

$$\text{UAS} = \$60 - \$100/1.833 = \$60 - \$54.54$$
$$= \$5.46/\text{year}$$

The $5.46 is the annual profit from the project. We derive this profit by deducting the annual cost of invested funds, $54.54, from our annual cash receipts of $60.

In essence a similar procedure is being followed in situations where the cash receipts (as well as the costs) are not uniform from period to period. The method can be thought of as expressing all flows in the form of equivalent annual cash flow; the remainder after deducting costs from benefits is the average profit per period. From this point on we shall use the terms "annual profit" and "annual cost" to refer to the values derived from the UAS method.

Using the UAS method as a means of choosing among alternatives is less straightforward than using it as a means of project selection. If one picks the alternative with the largest annual profit or (in a cost-minimization problem) picks the one with the smallest annual cost, one is making an implicit assumption that the cash flows from all alternatives have the same *longevity*. This assumption is often incorrect. The problem is illustrated by the following example.

Suppose an oil company has two alternative methods available for pumping the oil from a particular well. Method $A$ requires a larger initial investment than method $B$, but removes the oil faster from the well. Since there is a limited amount of oil in the well, the total cash flow produced by sale of the oil is the same under both alternatives. The cash flows are assumed to be:

| | *Time* | | | | |
|---|---|---|---|---|---|
| *Method* | 0 | 1 | 2 | 3 | 4 *and thereafter* |
| $A$ | (12,000) | 15,000 | 15,000 | 0 | 0 |
| $B$ | (10,000) | 10,000 | 10,000 | 10,000 | 0 |

At $i = 8\%$ the annual profit for method $A$ is $8,268/year [$15,000 less (.561)($12,000), where .561 is the capital recovery factor at 8% for 2 years]. The annual profit for method $B$ is $6,120 per year [$10,000 less (.388)($10,000), where .388 is the capital recovery factor at 8% for 3 years]. If a choice were made on the basis of annual profit, $A$ would be chosen. However, the present value of the cash flows associated with $A$ is $14,740, and the present value for $B$ is $15,770, indicating that $B$ is the better choice.

The UAS method can be used to evaluate alternatives with assurance of reaching the correct conclusions only if the computations are made on an *incremental* basis. That is, the differences in the cash flows between two alternatives must be evaluated to determine which is the superior one. Using the example above, suppose we compare the cash flows of the two methods. If we choose $A$ over $B$ we pay an additional $2,000 initially in order to get cash sooner. The incremental stream is

| | *Time* | | | | |
|---|---|---|---|---|---|
| | 0 | 1 | 2 | 3 | 4 *and thereafter* |
| $A - B$ | (2,000) | 5,000 | 5,000 | (10,000) | 0 |

At $i = 8\%$ the annual profit from the incremental investment is −$255; that is, an "annual loss." On an incremental basis, choosing $A$ over $B$ is not desirable. Since $B$ is profitable, we should develop the oil well by method $B$. This decision is the same as the one reached above by computing the present value of the cash flows associated with each method. Since the present-value approach achieves this result directly, there would appear to be no particular reason to use the annual profit method to evaluate alternatives. However, if it is used properly as indicated, the method is valid.

A comparison of cost alternatives using annual cost does not present the same problem of longevity that annual profit does. The cash flows for all alternatives must have the same longevity since it is the *longevity of the benefits* that is relevant, and a minimum cost criterion (present value or annual cost) is not appropriate for alternatives whose benefit streams differ. In other words, if two alternatives have different benefit streams associated with them, it is improper to compare only the costs. Both the costs and the benefits from the two alternatives must be evaluated. There does arise a problem in application: namely, the complete specification of all the alternatives. Since this problem is common to all methods it will be discussed later in the chapter. From a theoretical point of view, the use of the annual cost method is completely consistent with the overall objective of the firm provided that the method is used properly. Its problems are comparable to those of all methods used to evaluate alternatives, and arise in the practical applications of the method rather than in the theory.

**Rate of return.** The rate-of-return method for evaluating investments requires the user to find that discount rate for which the present value of the cash flows is zero. That is, one must solve the following equation for $r$, the rate of return:

$$\sum_{t=0}^{n} \frac{Z_t}{(1 + r)^t} = 0 \tag{3-7}$$

Although there are some situations for which there is more than one solution, or only imaginary solutions, for $r$ (see Appendix 3A for proofs and discussions), a single real value for $r$ will be obtained if the initial (time 0) cash flow is negative ( an outlay) and all subsequent cash flows are nonnegative and some are positive (inflows). The method cannot be applied directly to alternative benefit streams or cost streams, i.e., if all flows (from time 0 on) are positive or all are negative.

The rate of return is interpreted as the "yield" of an investment and is commonly applied to securities. Its use in project selection follows directly from this interpretation. If a project has a greater yield than the market rate,[16] it is worthwhile. If it has not, the project is not worthwhile. Intuitively, this is reasonable. If a project's yield is greater than the market rate, the amount earned per period on the project exceeds the amount that could be earned per period in the market through lending the same sum; if the project's yield is less than the market rate, more could be earned by lending in the market than by investing in the project. The project-selection rule is therefore:

3. Select those projects for which $r > i$.

This rule will be fully consistent with the objective of the firm so long as there is a unique, real, internal rate of return associated with the project.

The rate-of-return method can be used in comparing a set of mutually exclusive alternatives provided that it is applied to the *incremental* cash flows of those alternatives.[17] The procedure is as follows. First, the alternatives are ranked by the size of their initial investment from the alternative with the smallest initial cost to the one with the largest. Then one must ask whether the additional investment in the second alternative compared to the first (and smallest) is justified based on its net incremental benefits. (The benefits can be lower costs.) In order to determine the answer, the rate of return of the incremental

[16] There is an obvious problem if the $i_j$ are not equal for all periods $j = 1 \ldots n$. Then one must decide *which* $i_j$ should be compared with $r$. See app. 3A for a discussion.

[17] If this procedure is not used, then a variety of errors is possible, as the rate of return is sensitive to the scale (size) of the initial investment and has problems of interpretation when the longevity of the cash flows differs among alternatives. An example of the improper use of the rate-of-return method is given in app. 3A. Further, notice that there must be a unique real internal rate of return for each incremental stream if the method is applicable. As noted in the text, such a unique rate will exist if the incremental stream involves a negative incremental flow (outlay) at time 0 and positive incremental flows (inflows) for some periods (and negative for no periods) thereafter.

cash flows can be computed and compared with the market rate $i$. The market rate is the firm's "hurdle rate" since it is the alternative rate the firm can earn in the market by lending and is the rate the firm must pay if it borrows funds in the market for investment. As long as an incremental investment yields more than the market rate, the firm can invest its own funds (and earn more than by lending in the market) or can borrow funds at the market rate and make the incremental investment. The net gain in terms of a rate of return is the difference between the incremental investment's yield and the market rate of interest (the "opportunity cost" of capital). We can think of the first alternative as the "defender" and the second as the "challenger." If the additional investment in the challenger does provide a profitable rate of return (greater than $i$), then *it* becomes the defender for comparison with the third alternative. Otherwise the first alternative is retained as the defender (the challenger is defeated) for comparison with the new challenger, the third alternative. The analysis proceeds in this fashion until all alternatives have been compared.[18] The "victor" of the analysis becomes a project to be considered for selection. By rule (3) the project is selected if its internal rate of return exceeds $i$.

As an example of this procedure, assume mutually exclusive investment alternatives $A$, $B$, and $C$ with the cash flows indicated in Table 3-2. For periods after period 3 all cash flows from the projects are assumed to be zero. Suppose that the market rate $i$ is 10%. In the bottom row is the internal rate of return for each column of cash flows. Comparing $B$ with $A$, $r_{B-A} = 3\% < i = 10\%$. Therefore, $B$ is rejected. Comparing $C$ with $A$, $r_{C-A} = 20\% > 10\%$. Therefore, $C$ is the "victor" over $A$. The last step is to compare $r_c$ with $i$. Since $r_c = 22.5\% > 10\%$, project $C$ is accepted.

Two comments are appropriate here. First, note that $A$, $B$, and $C$ considered individually all have rates of return greater than 10%. Any alternative with

[18] The method of analysis described here and in Grant and Ireson, *op. cit.*, involves ranking alternatives in ascending order of size. It has been pointed out by William Collins that this is not necessary. All that is needed is to compare any pair of alternatives, each time accepting the one with the larger outlay only if its incremental rate of return exceeds the market rate. This comparison and elimination proceeds until a single alternative remains and it will be the same as that determined using the method presented in the text above.

**table 3-2**

| | $A$ | $B$ | $C$ | $B-A$ | $C-A$ |
|---|---|---|---|---|---|
| $Z_0$ | −100 | −300 | −400 | −200 | −300 |
| $Z_1$ | 30 | 36 | 90 | 6 | 60 |
| $Z_2$ | 30 | 36 | 90 | 6 | 60 |
| $Z_3$ | 130 | 336 | 490 | 206 | 360 |
| $Z_4$–$Z_\infty$ | 0 | 0 | 0 | 0 | 0 |
| | 30% | 12% | 22.5% | 03% | 20% |

a return less than $i$ can be rejected without further consideration. The suggested procedure does not require computation of an alternative's own rate of return ($r_A$, $r_B$, or $r_C$) except in the last step when a decision must be made to accept or reject the project. Unprofitable alternatives will be defeated when compared to profitable ones. An efficient analysis would therefore require only the computation of $r_{B-A}$, $r_{C-A}$, and $r_C$ in the preceding example. Second, note that although $r_C < r_A$, alternative $C$ is preferred. The rate of return on the incremental investment for $C$ over $A$ is 20%, which is well above the required rate of 10%. The procedure presented here is correct and consistent with value maximization. Choosing the alternative with the highest rate of return is not correct in general and should not be done. (See Appendix 3A for further discussion.)

The procedure described above is time-consuming and would appear to offer no convincing benefits compared with other methods. The concept of a rate of return is useful in project selection as it has the intuitively appealing interpretation of the yield on the project's investment. It also has some advantages under conditions of uncertainty, as we shall see later. However, there are practical as well as theoretical grounds for preferring present value as a method of comparing alternatives.

## COST MINIMIZATION AND ECONOMIC LIFE

The three methods we have discussed will provide the same choice among alternative cost streams if used properly.[19] However, that which constitutes "proper use" is not obvious when the assets to be acquired have different economic lives. This problem was discussed earlier (see pages 50–51) in the context of our general rules for investment analysis. There we observed that when current choices affected the future options available to the firm, some care must be taken in analysis. This discussion deals with a particular type of problem that is common to most firms—the evaluation of alternative ways to accomplish a task (achieve a given level of benefits over time) when the economic lives of the assets acquired under the alternatives differ.

A simple example of this type of problem, which highlights the issues involved, is as follows. Suppose a firm is investigating which one of three types of pump to acquire to pump oil from an oil well. Each pump has the same capacity; therefore, the benefits to be derived are the same for each one, and it is appropriate to consider the problem as one of minimizing the costs of pumping oil. Pump $A$ has an economic life of 2 years, pump $B$ has a life of 3 years, and pump $C$ has a life of 6 years. The costs of operating each pump are assumed to

[19] When the alternative assets have different economic lives, the differences in cash flows between two alternatives frequently contain alternating inflows and outflows over time. The rate-of-return method applied to these cash flows may result in more than one solution and is therefore difficult to use for this type of problem. See app. 3A.

**table 3-3**

| *Pump* | *Life* | *Initial cost, \$* | *PVC, \$* | *AC, \$* |
|---|---|---|---|---|
| *A* | 2 | 5,000 | 5,000 | 2,800 |
| *B* | 3 | 6,000 | 6,000 | 2,330 |
| *C* | 6 | 10,000 | 10,000 | 2,160 |

be zero for simplicity. The cost of acquiring each pump, its life, the present value of the costs (PVC), and the annual cost (AC) are shown in Table 3-3.

The appropriate discount rate is assumed to be 8%. The PVC and AC shown are based on the "blind" procedure of simply applying the appropriate formulas [Eqs. (3-4) and (3-6)] to the cash flow, which is the initial cost in this example. The values shown for PVC are simply the initial outlays, and the values for AC are those outlays distributed over the lives of the pumps. Note that the two measures shown give radically different results. The minimum cost alternative by PVC is *A*; the minimum cost alternative by AC is *C*. Which one is correct? The answer to this question cannot be determined from the data above. We must know several additional items. First we need to know how long the oil in the well will last; that is, we need to know the longevity of the benefits of the task to be performed. Let us examine two possibilities: that the oil will last 2 years and that the oil will last 6 years.

If the oil will last only 2 years, the advantage of longer lives for pumps *B* and *C* over *A* may not amount to much. We must know what will be done with the pumps when the oil is exhausted. Suppose that pumps *B* and *C* have no recoverable value at the end of 2 years. The present values of costs shown in Table 3-3 are not affected; neither is the annual cost shown for pump *A*. Now, however, the annual costs of pumps *B* and *C* must be based on a life of 2 years for each one rather than 3 and 6 years, respectively, as used before. The annual cost of pump *B* becomes \$3,366 and the annual cost of *C* becomes \$5,610. Now both PVC and AC yield the same conclusion: that pump *A* is best.

Now suppose that the oil will last for 6 years. In this case we need to know what we shall do about the fact that pumps *A* and *B* will not last for 6 years. Either they must be replaced or we must stop pumping oil. However, if the latter alternative involves a different benefit stream, cost minimization is not appropriate. Assuming that it will be profitable to get all the oil out, we need to investigate the possibilities for replacing pumps *A* and *B*. Assume that we shall replace pump *A* with the same type of pump at the end of 2 years and again at the end of 4 years and replace *B* with another of the same type at the end of 3 years. The cash flows from the expanded alternatives and the cost measures are shown in Table 3-4.

Under these assumptions pump *C* is best. Also note that the annual costs in Table 3-4 are the same as in Table 3-3. Recall that the present values of costs when the oil was to be exhausted in 2 years were the same as those shown in Table 3-3. What has been demonstrated are the implicit assumptions made in a

**table 3-4 Cash Flows (Costs), in $**

| *Pump* | 0 | 1 | 2 | 3 | 4 | 5 | 6 | *PVC* | *AC* |
|---|---|---|---|---|---|---|---|---|---|
| *A* | 5,000 | 0 | 5,000 | 0 | 5,000 | 0 | 0 | 12,950 | 2,800 |
| *B* | 6,000 | 0 | 0 | 6,000 | 0 | 0 | 0 | 10,800 | 2,330 |
| *C* | 10,000 | 0 | 0 | 0 | 0 | 0 | 0 | 10,000 | 2,160 |

blind computation of PVC and AC when the assets have different lives. If we choose on the basis of PVC in Table 3-3, we are assuming implicitly that the task will end after 2 years (the life of the shortest-lived alternative) and that no assets will have recoverable values (or costs) after then. A choice made on the basis of AC in Table 3-3 implicitly assumes that the task will last as long as the longest-lived asset and that those assets with shorter lives will be replaced with similar assets at the same cost as the original.[20]

The point here is not to determine the conditions under which "blind" analysis is appropriate but to restate a more basic and important concept. The true "life" of alternative ways to accomplish a task is not the lives of the particular assets but the longevity or life of the task itself. A correct specification of alternatives requires the determination of a *sequence* of actions over the life of the task. This may require the examination of the prospects for technological improvements in the ways to accomplish the task. For example, suppose that a new pump, which would cost $4,000 and have a life of 4 years, was expected to be available at the end of 2 years. Since it is clearly better to replace pump *A* with the new pump at the end of 2 years, a revised alternative *A'* should be used in the analysis instead of the *A* in Table 3-4.

All the methods we have presented require the complete specification of the cash flows resulting from a given choice. Failure to do this (or implicitly assuming different cash flows with different methods) will result in unreliable methods for choosing among alternatives. The methods are consistent when applied to the same set of cash flows.[21]

## SUMMARY

Under conditions of perfect capital markets and certainty, the optimal investment budget for the firm is the one that includes all projects with positive present values and excludes any with negative present values. There are, however, methods other than present value that can be used to select projects—

[20] To be correct, the assumption is that the task will continue up to the smallest common multiple of the lives of the alternatives. For example, the smallest common multiple of two assets with lives of 3 years and 4 years is 12 years.

[21] It is impossible to perform a "blind" computation of the rate of return for cost streams since it is undefined for such streams. An incremental analysis is usually valid, but introduces the multiple-rate problem when applied to the streams of Table 3-4.

uniform annual series and rate of return. When used correctly, the methods are consistent; they will agree on the projects to be included in the investment budget.

The evaluation of projects involves specification of alternative combinations of opportunities in the project and adoption of the best alternative. Considerable care must be used in applying any of the methods, but the rate-of-return method requires special caution when comparing alternatives.

APPENDIX

# THREE A

# PROBLEMS IN USING THE RATE-OF-RETURN METHOD

In this appendix we discuss two problems in using the rate-of-return method: the possibility of multiple values for $r$ and the use of $r$ when the interest rate $i$ is not constant for future periods. An example of the improper use of the rate of return to evaluate alternatives is given.

## MULTIPLE AND IMAGINARY SOLUTIONS

The rate of return $r$ is a solution to an equation:

$$\sum_{t=0}^{n} \frac{Z_t}{(1+r)^t} = 0 \qquad \text{(3A-1)}$$

Equations may have more than one solution or imaginary solutions (involving $\sqrt{-1}$), and therein lies a potential problem in using $r$. If more than one solution results, which one is appropriate for comparison with $i$? And how does one interpret an imaginary solution? Let us examine the problem further.

Equation (3A-1) is a sum of $n + 1$ terms

$$\frac{Z_0}{(1+r)^0} + \frac{Z_1}{(1+r)^1} + \frac{Z_2}{(1+r)^2} + \frac{Z_3}{(1+r)^3} + \cdots + \frac{Z_n}{(1+r)^n} = 0 \qquad \text{(3A-2)}$$

Since $(1 + r)^0 = 1.0$, we can write (3A-2) as

$$Z_0 + \frac{Z_1}{(1+r)^1} + \frac{Z_2}{(1+r)^2} + \cdots + \frac{Z_n}{(1+r)^n} = 0 \qquad \text{(3A-3)}$$

Suppose we multiply through (3A-3) by $(1 + r)^n$ and replace $(1 + r)$ by $q$. We have

$$Z_0q^n + Z_1q^{n-1} + Z_2q^{n-2} + \cdots + Z_n = 0 \qquad (3A\text{-}4)$$

Equation (3A-4) is a polynomial equation of degree $n$. The question is this: How many roots exist and of what form are the roots? Descartes' rule of signs states that there are either as many positive real roots as there are changes of algebraic sign of the coefficients or less than that by an even number. Suppose that $Z_0 < 0, Z_1 > 0$, and $Z_t \geq 0$ for all $t \geq 2$; then there is only one change in sign (from $Z_0 < 0$ to $Z_1 > 0$) and there is one positive real root, that is, $q \geq 0$ and $r \geq -1$. However, if there are two changes in sign, e.g., if $Z_0 < 0$, $Z_1 > 0$, $Z_2 < 0$, and $Z_t = 0$ for $t > 2$, then there are two positive real roots or none. If there are two positive real roots, which should be used? If there is none, the two roots may be imaginary; and imaginary roots are not applicable for project selection. Thus, if $Z_0 = -10, Z_1 = 150, Z_2 = -140$, and $Z_t = 0$ for $t > 2$, then $q = [1,5.4]$. That is, there are two positive real solutions for $q$ and the corresponding values for $r$ are 0% and 440%, respectively. If $Z_0 = -100, Z_1 = +20$, $Z_2 = -10$, and $Z_t = 0$ for $t > 2$, then $q = .1 \pm .3\sqrt{-1}$ and the roots are imaginary. With multiple positive roots or all imaginary roots, the internal rate-of-return method is not easily applied.[22] We note in conclusion that some other method should be used when the cash flows have more than one sign change over the life of the investment.

The problem of multiple roots is most apt to arise in replacement problems of the sort discussed at the end of the body of Chap. 3. For example, consider the cash flows of the alternatives that were shown in Table 3-4 (reproduced in Table 3A-1 below).

To apply the rate-of-return method to choosing among these alternatives, an incremental analysis is necessary. Suppose the consequences of choosing $B$ instead of $A$ are examined. The incremental cash flows from this choice are shown in Table 3A-1 as $B - A$. Substituting these values for the cash flows in Eq. (3A-4) and simplifying, we get

[22] This problem has been carefully analyzed by D. Teichroew, Alexander A. Robichek, and M. Montalbano in Mathematical Analysis of Returns under Certainty, *Management Science*, pp. 395–403, January 1965, and in An Analysis of Criteria for Investment and Financing Decisions under Certainty, *Management Science*, November 1965, by the same authors.

**table 3A-1 Cash Flows, $**

| *Pump* | 0 | 1 | 2 | 3 | 4 | 5 | 6 |
|---|---|---|---|---|---|---|---|
| *A* | (5,000) | 0 | (5,000) | 0 | (5,000) | 0 | 0 |
| *B* | (6,000) | 0 | 0 | (6,000) | 0 | 0 | 0 |
| *C* | (10,000) | 0 | 0 | 0 | 0 | 0 | 0 |
| *B* − *A* | (1,000) | 0 | 5,000 | (6,000) | 5,000 | 0 | 0 |

$$-1000q^6 + 0q^5 + 5000q^4 - 6000q^3 + 5000q^2 + 0 + 0 = 0$$
$$-1000q^6 + 5000q^4 - 6000q^3 + 5000q^2 = 0$$
$$-q^4 + 5q^2 - 6q + 5 = 0 \qquad (3A\text{-}5)$$

The solutions to Eq. (3A-5) will provide the rates of return we are concerned with, where $q = 1 + r$.

There are three sign changes in (3A-5); so there are either three positive roots or only one. In this example there is only one positive real root at $q = 1.8$ or $r = 80\%$ that can be determined by trial and error or graphical methods. However, in general, when several replacement sequences are being compared, it is not unlikely that some of the incremental cash flows will have more than one positive real rate of return.[23]

## VARIABLE INTEREST RATES

The variable interest rate problem can be stated as follows: Given a single value for $r$ and interest rates that vary over time $i_1, i_2, i_3, \ldots, i_n$, which interest rate should be used to compare with $r$?

This is an issue of primarily theoretical interest, since in most practical applications the rate of interest is assumed to be a single value over time as a means of simplifying the analysis. Also, under uncertainty, the appropriate rate becomes an even more troublesome issue. In any case the problem arises because the rate of return is an *average* concept. It takes a series of $n$ numbers and converts them into an average value. An obvious possibility is to convert the $i_t$ into an average value for purposes of comparison with $r$. *Under perfect markets and certainty* such an average does exist; however, it must be determined for each set of cash flows being evaluated.[24] This is a time-consuming procedure and one not likely to commend itself to managers.

## IMPROPER USE OF THE RATE OF RETURN

In comparing alternatives with different benefit streams, a blind use of the rate-of-return method is incorrect under our assumptions. The rate-of-return

[23] Methods exist for determining whether or not there is a multiple rate problem for cash flows with multiple changes in sign. See Clovis de Faro, A Sufficient Condition for a Unique Non-Negative Internal Rate of Return, *Journal of Financial and Quantitative Analysis,* vol. 12, pp 577–584, September 1978.

[24] The problem is related to the expectations hypothesis concerning the term structure of interest rates when securities have a coupon payment. If $Z_1 = Z_2 = \cdots = Z_n$, the problem is identical; if not, the problem is much more complicated algebraically but still susceptible to solution. See J. W. Conard, "An Introduction to the Theory of Interest Rates," University of California Press, Berkeley, 1959, for a development of the constant-coupon case.

method can be used to compare two alternatives on an incremental basis as indicated in the body of Chap. 3; however, computation of the rate of return associated with each alternative and using those numbers to select the best alternative may result in nonoptimal choices. This problem is illustrated in the following examples.

1. Same life but different initial investments:

| | *Cash flows* | | | | |
|---|---|---|---|---|---|
| *Alternative* | 0 | 1 | 2 | 3 | $r$ |
| $A$ | (1,000) | 300 | 300 | 1,300 | 30% |
| $B$ | (2,000) | 500 | 500 | 2,500 | 25% |
| $B - A$ | (1,000) | 200 | 200 | 1,200 | 20% |

The rate of return associated with $A$ is 30%; that for $B$ is 25%. If one chose $A$ over $B$ on the basis of the magnitudes of the rates of return, one would be passing up the opportunity to invest an additional \$1,000 in $B$ that would earn 20%. If the firm can raise funds at any rate under 20%, ($i < 20\%$), $B$ is clearly the preferred alternative.

2. Same initial investments but different lives:

| | *Cash flows* | | | | |
|---|---|---|---|---|---|
| *Alternative* | 0 | 1 | 2 | 3 | $r$ |
| $C$ | (1,000) | 200 | 1,200 | 0 | 20% |
| $D$ | (1,000) | 200 | 200 | 1,200 | 20% |
| $D - C$ | 0 | 0 | (1,000) | 1,200 | 20% |

A blind analysis suggests that $C$ and $D$ are equivalent, since their rates of return are the same. However, failure to choose $D$ implies that the firm is passing up the opportunity to invest (in an opportunity cost sense) \$1,000 at time 2 to return \$1,200 at time 3. If the discount rate is less than 20%, $D$ is the proper choice.

3. Same initial investments and same lives:

| | *Cash flows at time* | | | | |
|---|---|---|---|---|---|
| *Alternative* | *0* | *1* | *2* | *3* | $r$ |
| $E$ | (1,000) | 1,300 | 100 | 100 | 42% |
| $F$ | (1,000) | 300 | 300 | 1,300 | 30% |
| $F$-$E$ | 0 | (1,000) | 200 | 1,200 | 20% |

The rates of return on $E$ and $F$ are 42% and 30%, respectively. Choosing $E$ over $F$ on the basis of these rates of return means passing up the opportunity to receive $1,000 less at time 1 in return for $200 more at time 2 and $1,200 more at time 3 (incremental investment $F–E$). If the discount rate is less than 20%, $F$ is the proper choice.

Blind ranking of alternatives using the rate-of-return method favors smaller initial investment and fast payoff alternatives. This in a sense is a "conservative" approach that some may feel is reasonable, particularly under conditions of uncertainty. However, even if management wishes to be "conservative," there does not appear to be any reason to be implicitly so through use of blind analysis. It would be far better to examine directly the implications of choosing one alternative over another as indicated by the incremental flows $B - A$, $D - C$, and $F - E$ and their associated rates of return.

## SUGGESTED READINGS

Bierman, Harold, Jr., and Seymour Smidt: "The Capital Budgeting Decision," 4th ed., pp. 1–127, The Macmillan Company, New York, 1975.

Grant, Eugene L. and W. Grant Ireson: "Principles of Engineering Economy," 6th ed., chaps. 1–9, 12, 15, 17, The Ronald Press Company, New York, 1976.

CHAPTER

# FOUR

# PROBABILITY AND RANDOM VARIABLES

The world of certainty assumed in Chaps. 2 and 3 is clearly a fiction, and the implications of such a world are more useful as an introduction to problems and concepts than as a practical guide to financial decisions. The world we live in is fundamentally subject to uncertainty and, therefore, so are our financial decisions. The purpose of this chapter is to provide a logical foundation for dealing with decisions made under uncertainty. We shall first discuss the question of whether the concepts of probability theory provide an appropriate basis for analyzing problems. Having concluded that this is at least a reasonable approach, we then develop some general mathematical relationships that will be useful in later chapters. A summary of the most important relationships is at the end of the chapter.

## PROBABILITY[1]

The mathematical structure of probability can be developed completely from three basic axioms; if those axioms are reasonable in the context of financial decisions, then the logical extensions of the axioms (probability theory) should be applicable to those decisions. As discussed in Chap. 2, the theory of finance is concerned with the rational choices of individuals and firms.

The axioms are developed in the context of a situation in which there exists a given set of "events." An event is a possible outcome or result that may arise

[1] A comprehensive treatment of decision making under uncertainty and the use of judgmental probabilities can be found in Schlaifer, "Analysis of Decisions under Uncertainty" (listed in the Suggested Readings at the end of this chapter).

from some action, or it can be a characteristic of the world. For example, rolling a pair of dice is an action, and the events in this situation may be defined as the possible values of the sum of the spots on the upper faces of the dice. Another action is the shooting of an arrow into the air; the events can be specified in terms of the location of the arrow on its return to earth. A characteristic of the world might be the condition of the United States economy in 1990. One might characterize the economy as having only two events, boom or bust. Alternatively, the economy could be characterized by the level of gross national product (GNP) in that year, the possible values constituting a large number of different events. An example we shall use throughout this chapter is the price per share of a company's common stock 1 year from now, the events being the possible values for that price.

Axiom (1) states that to every possible event a number equal to or greater than zero can be assigned which measures the relative likelihood of occurrence of the event. For example, this axiom requires that a number be associated with every possible price of a given stock at some moment in time and that those numbers in one way or another reflect how likely those prices are to occur. As noted in axiom (3) below, the numbers assigned to events must be scaled in a particular way if they are to be interpreted as "probabilities."

Axiom (2) states that the likelihood of either of two mutually exclusive events occurring is the sum of the likelihoods of each of the two events. "Mutually exclusive" means that if one event occurs, the other cannot occur. Prices of a given good at a given moment and location are mutually exclusive in that if the price is \$50 it cannot also be \$40. The axiom says that if the likelihood of a price of \$50 is .2 and the likelihood of a price of \$20 is .1, then the likelihood of the price being either \$50 or \$20 is .3.

Axiom (3) states that the sum of the likelihoods of *all possible mutually exclusive* events equals 1.0. The third axiom requires that the likelihoods be measured in a consistent fashion irrespective of the situation. This axiom coupled with axiom (1) means that all likelihoods must be measured so that each is a number between 0 and 1. When all three axioms are satisfied, we can refer to the numbers we have developed as "probabilities." The question now is whether the axioms are reasonable in the context of financial decisions made under uncertainty.

Let us look at the axioms in reverse order. Axiom (3) is of no fundamental difficulty since its primary purpose is to ensure a uniform scaling. The scale used is consistent with the concept of probabilities as relative frequencies. (For example, the probability of heads from the toss of a coin can be thought of as the number of times heads would appear in a large number of tosses divided by the number of tosses.) If we did not use axiom (3) there would be no special reason not to measure likelihoods on arbitrary scales, such as 0 to 10 or 1 to 100. However, as we shall see later, scaling likelihoods between 0 and 1.0 is very convenient and permits us to apply the mathematics of probability theory if axioms (1) and (2) also hold.

Axiom (2) should also present no special problem. The axiom imposes an addition relationship on likelihoods that seems very reasonable. For example, if the weatherman tells us that the chance of rain is 60% and the chance of snow is 20%, it seems quite proper and logical to say that the chance of rain or snow is 80%. Alternatively, if the likelihood of heads from the toss of a coin is considered to be .5 and the likelihood of tails to be .5, then is it not appropriate to say that the likelihood of either heads or tails is 1.0?

Axiom (1) requires the assessment of likelihoods and is therefore the most important axiom. In most financial problems likelihoods are at best a calibration of the degree of confidence an individual has about the outcome of a future event. As such, they seem to be very subjective. Yet in any given situation one's opinion about future events can be discussed with others. You can imagine a committee trying to come up with the best set of likelihoods they can. You might seek additional objective information about the situation, ask experts their opinions on various aspects of the problem, and so forth. One of the advantages of scaling likelihoods is to provide a uniform measurement system that aids in communication.

All of us make decisions based on our judgments of the likelihoods of future events. Axioms (1) to (3) simply suggest that it may sometimes be useful to measure these judgments in a careful and consistent manner. Of course you can continue to make such decisions as whether or not to carry an umbrella without going through all the trouble of calibrating and scaling your judgment of the chances of rain. When the problem is whether or not to build a $10 million plant, the extra effort may be worthwhile. Also, when we seek to describe the average behavior of large numbers of individual investors, it is helpful to analyze the situation in terms of probabilities even though we know that the individuals are making their decisions in a much less formal fashion. All we really require is that the decisions be made on the basis of the individual's judgments about the likelihood of future events.

It is important to understand that the preceding axioms apply to any given situation where each event [e.g., the price of General Motors (GM) stock equal to $100 or between $90 and $100] has a unique probability. That is, if each event is assigned a given probability, the resulting set of probabilities for all events must satisfy the three axioms. This does not mean that everyone agrees on the probability of any or all events. Indeed, disagreement clearly characterizes the world. People may make their own judgments about the likelihood of events. However, if an individual's assessment of likelihoods is to be consistent with probability theory, it must fulfill the axioms.

In the discussion below, the probability assignments are assumed to be given. That is, we assume some given judgments regarding the probability that a variable (e.g., the price of GM stock) will take on a particular value or range of values. This means we are viewing the situation through the eyes of one decision maker or through the eyes of many decision makers who all agree on the probabilities of the events in the situations.

## PROBABILITY DISTRIBUTIONS AND RANDOM VARIABLES

A *random variable* is any variable whose value is uncertain. We shall use the tilde over a symbol to indicate that the variable represented by the symbol is a random variable. The values taken on by a random variable $\tilde{X}$ are assumed to be described by a *probability distribution* $p(\tilde{X})$. A probability distribution is a function that assigns probabilities to the values of $\tilde{X}$ according to the axioms discussed above. For example, if $\tilde{X}$ is the stock price of a company 1 year from now, $p(\tilde{X})$ might be shown as

| $\tilde{X}$ *(price in \$)* | $p(\tilde{X})$ |
|---|---|
| 60 | .1 |
| 50 | .2 |
| 40 | .4 |
| 30 | .2 |
| 20 | .1 |

Note that the sum of the probabilities equals 1.0, which indicates that we have considered all possible values of $\tilde{X}$.

Note also that we appear to be assuming that the price of this stock cannot take on a value of, say, \$45. As we discuss below, it is often convenient to simplify variables so that "\$50" in the table may really mean "between \$45 and \$55." When a random variable takes on only a few particular values such as \$40 and \$50 above, it is called a *discrete* variable and $p(\tilde{X})$ would be called a *discrete probability distribution*. The other type of variable is a *continuous* variable. Such variables can take on all possible numerical values over the range (between the highest and lowest values) of their distributions. For example, if the price were a continuous variable, it could have the values \$50, \$49.86, or \$50.0001. Most financial variables are continuous in nature; however, it is hard to imagine anyone trying to estimate the probabilities for all possible values of a continuous variable. Such a procedure would be extremely impractical.

There are three solutions to this problem, each of which may be suitable depending on the situation. The first solution is to *approximate* a continuous variable with a discrete distribution.[2] Instead of thinking of the probability of a particular price, we evaluate the probability of the price's falling within a particular *range* of prices. Using this method we would determine the probability of obtaining a price between \$45 and \$55. Suppose that probability is .2. Since \$50 is the midpoint of that range, we could associate a probability of .2 with \$50 as shown above; but this is just "shorthand" for the range of \$45 to

[2] Whether a variable should be considered essentially continuous depends in part on the situation. Prices of stock are given only to the nearest eighths of a dollar. If you are concerned with the price tomorrow, as traders are, you may wish to consider the price to be a discrete variable. If you are interested in the price 10 years from now, it may be considered essentially continuous.

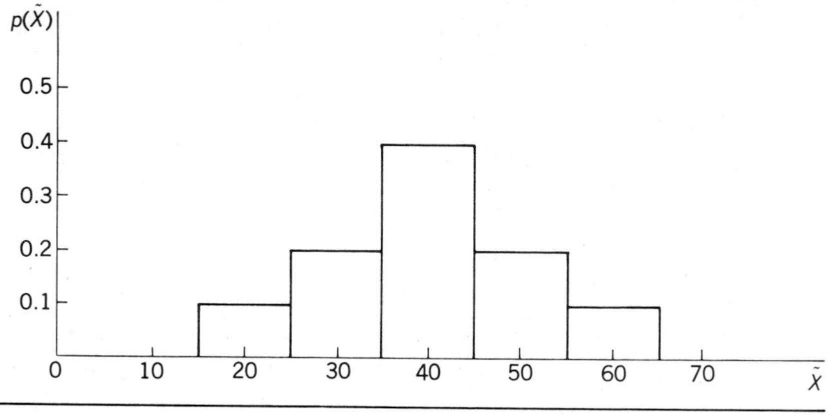


**figure 4-1**

\$55. This type of distribution can be most easily displayed by means of a graph such as Fig. 4-1, in which the distribution of the example above is shown assuming that the values were really midpoints of a range.

The second solution is to define $p(\tilde{X})$ as a continuous mathematical function. The typical procedure in this case is to choose a function (preferably one of the several commonly used ones) that seems to provide a "good fit" to the distribution. The alternative is to define one's own function, but this requires some skill in mathematics. A continuous distribution that has been widely used in the sciences is the *normal* distribution, the "bell-shaped curve." This distribution has been found to describe many types of frequency data very well and has some convenient mathematical properties.[3] A graph of the normal distribution is shown in Fig. 4-2.

[3] See Robert Schlaifer, "Probability and Statistics for Business Decisions," pp. 274–305, McGraw-Hill Book Company, New York, 1959.

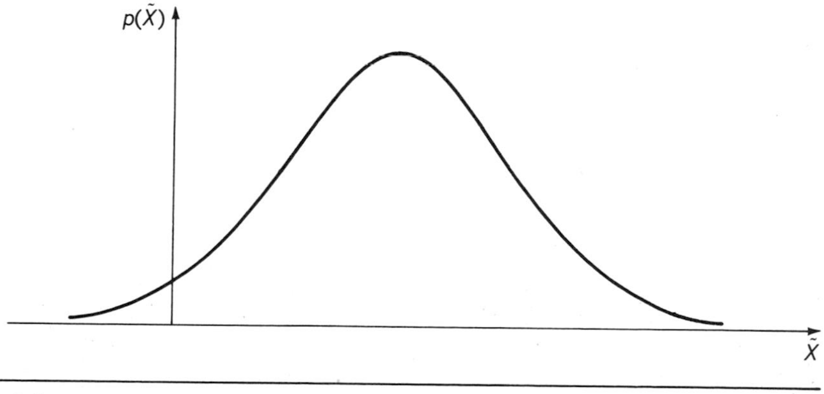


**figure 4-2**

The third solution is not so much a solution as a way of avoiding the problem. Instead of concerning ourselves with the precise form of the distribution, we assume that each random variable of interest has a distribution of some form and then concentrate on a few summary measures (e.g., mean and variance) that describe various characteristics of distributions in general. The next section is devoted to developing such measures. It is fortunate, as we shall see later, that for many purposes this solution is sufficient.

The examples and many of the formulas of the remainder of the chapter will use discrete probability distributions. All the results, however, apply equally well to continuous distributions. The only reason for using the discrete form is that continuous distributions require the use of calculus (or a computer) for computation.[4]

## EXPECTATIONS AND MOMENTS

The most commonly used and most important characteristic of the probability distribution of a random variable is the *mean* or *expected value*. The mean is a measure of the central tendency of a distribution and is related to the concept of an average value for the random variable. It is computed by multiplying each possible value by its probability and taking the sum of the results:

$$\bar{X} = E[\tilde{X}] = \Sigma X_i p(X_i) \qquad \text{for all } X_i \tag{4-1}$$

The mean $\bar{X}$ is the expected value of $\tilde{X}$, $E[\tilde{X}]$.

The concept of the mathematical expected value can be generalized to include functions of random variables [for example, $u(\tilde{X}) = a + b\tilde{X}$]. The expected value of $u(\tilde{X})$ can be written as $E[u(\tilde{X})]$ and computed as $\Sigma u(X_i)p(X_i) = \Sigma(a + bX_i)p(X_i)$. Since $a$ and $b$ are constants, $E[a + b\tilde{X}] = a + bE[\tilde{X}]$ or $a + b\bar{X}$. Three useful properties of the expected value idea are presented here:[5]

1. The expected value of a constant is that constant

$$E[a] = a$$

2. The expected value of a constant times a random variable is the constant times the expected value of the variable:

$$E[b\tilde{X}] = bE[\tilde{X}]$$

[4] The probability distribution of a continuous variable is called a *probability density function*. The probability of a continuous variable's assuming a particular value (for example, 40.00000) is zero; probabilities are greater than zero only for an interval of values for the variable. In other words, we speak only of the probability that $\tilde{X}$ will be between $A$ and $B$. This probability is determined by the integral of the density function from $A$ to $B$.

[5] These properties are based on the mathematical characteristics of expected value. Proofs are elementary; they require only the definition of expected value as discussed above and algebra.

3. The expected value of a sum equals the sum of the expected values:

$$E[a + b\tilde{X}] = E[a] + E[b\tilde{X}]$$

This third property is quite general and applies to sums of different random variables and to sums of functions of random variables. For example, $E[\tilde{Y} + \tilde{X}] = E[\tilde{Y}] + E[\tilde{X}]$, where $\tilde{Y}$ and $\tilde{X}$ are two different random variables; or $E[u_1(\tilde{X}) + u_2(\tilde{X})] + E[u_1(\tilde{X})] + E[u_2(\tilde{X})]$, where $u_1(\tilde{X})$ and $u_2(\tilde{X})$ are two different functions of $\tilde{X}$.

These properties may appear more complicated than they really are. Suppose you own one share of GM stock and one share of IBM. All property (3) says is that the expected value of your two shares 1 year from now is equal to the expected value of the GM share plus the expected value of the share of IBM. Property (2) says that if you own 100 shares of GM, the expected value of your 100 shares will be equal to 100 times the expected price per share. Property (1) says that if you have $10 in your hand, the expected value of the money in your hand is $10.

The concept of expected value is vital to an understanding of most of the rest of this book, since the theory of finance under uncertainty is based in good part on it. There are really two notions involved: one is the expected value of a particular variable; the other is the mathematical operation which produces that value. When we specify a quantity $\bar{X}$, we are thinking of a number—the mean of the distribution of $\tilde{X}$. The notation $E[\tilde{X}]$ calls attention to the fact that we are computing or taking the expected value of the random variable $\tilde{X}$.

## Moments

Consider the expected value of the $j$th power of a random variable $\tilde{X}$; $E[\tilde{X}^j]$. This expectation is called the $j$th *moment* of the distribution of $\tilde{X}$. When $j = 1$, we have the mean of $\tilde{X}$—its expected value, $E[\tilde{X}]$. The moments of a probability distribution are associated with some characteristics that we shall find highly useful in describing the distribution. To be more precise, the moments about the mean of a distribution (also called the *central moments*) will be found useful; that is, $E[(\tilde{X} - \bar{X})^j]$.

The first central moment, $j = 1$, is zero, as can be seen by applying property (3) above; $E[\tilde{X} - \bar{X}] = E[\tilde{X}] - E[\bar{X}] = \bar{X} - \bar{X} = 0$. Remember that given the probability distribution, the mean $\bar{X}$ is a particular number and not a random variable. Of more interest to us is the second central moment $E[(\tilde{X} - \bar{X})^2]$. This quantity is called the *variance* of the distribution of $\tilde{X}$, var$[\tilde{X}]$:

$$\text{var}[\tilde{X}] = E[(\tilde{X} - \bar{X})^2] \tag{4-2}$$

$$\begin{aligned}\text{var}[\tilde{X}] &= E[\tilde{X}^2 - 2\tilde{X}\bar{X} + \bar{X}^2] \\ &= E[\tilde{X}^2] - 2\bar{X}E[\tilde{X}] + \bar{X}^2 \\ &= E[\tilde{X}^2] - \bar{X}^2 \end{aligned} \tag{4-2a}$$

In other words, the variance is equal to the second moment minus the square of the mean. The square root of the variance is called the *standard deviation* and is commonly denoted as $\sigma$. Therefore, $\sigma^2$ can be used to refer to the variance. We frequently find the standard deviation more useful than the variance because it is in the same units of measurement as the random variable and the mean. The variance is measured in squared units. If $\tilde{X}$ is measured in dollars, $\sigma$ is also measured in dollars, but $\sigma^2$ is measured in squared dollars. These two numbers—$\sigma$ and $\sigma^2$—measure the amount of variation around the mean; that is, they measure the dispersion of the distribution. In Fig. 4-3 distribution $A$ is less dispersed than distribution $B$ and therefore has lower values for its variance and standard deviation. The means of the two distributions are the same. Note from the formulas above that these two measures are always greater than or equal to zero. They will be equal to zero only when $\tilde{X}$ has but one possible value, i.e., when that value is certain. Thus $\sigma$ and $\sigma^2$ are natural measures of the degree of uncertainty associated with the random variable $\tilde{X}$.

The mean, variance, and standard deviation can be readily computed given a discrete probability distribution such as those in the examples above. Using the definitions of Eqs. (4-1) and (4-2*a*),

$$\bar{X} = \Sigma X_i p(X_i)$$

and

$$\text{var}[\tilde{X}] = E[\tilde{X}^2] - \bar{X}^2 = \Sigma X_i^2 p(X_i) - \bar{X}^2$$

Suppose we apply these formulas to the distributions shown in Fig. 4-3.

| A | | | | | B | | | | |
|---|---|---|---|---|---|---|---|---|---|
| $X_i$ | $p(X_i)$ | $X_i^2$ | $X_i p(X_i)$ | $X_i^2 p(X_i)$ | $X_i$ | $p(X_i)$ | $X_i^2$ | $X_i p(X_i)$ | $X_i^2 p(X_i)$ |
| 15 | .1 | 225 | 1.5 | 22.5 | 10 | .2 | 100 | 2 | 20 |
| 20 | .2 | 400 | 4 | 80 | 20 | .3 | 400 | 6 | 120 |
| 25 | .4 | 625 | 10 | 250 | 30 | .3 | 900 | 9 | 270 |
| 30 | .2 | 900 | 6 | 180 | 40 | .2 | 1,600 | 8 | 320 |
| 35 | .1 | 1,225 | 3.5 | 122.5 | | | | $\Sigma$ = 25 | 730 |
| | | | $\Sigma$ = 25 | 655 | | | | | |

Therefore, both distributions have the same mean value $\bar{X}_A = \bar{X}_B = 25$. The variance of $A$ is $655 - (25)^2 = 30$; the variance of $B$ is $730 - (25)^2 = 105$. The standard deviation of $A(\sigma_A)$ is $= \sqrt{30} = 5.48$; the standard deviation of $B(\sigma_B)$ is $= \sqrt{105} = 10.25$. As we noted above, distribution $B$ is more dispersed than $A$, measured by either variance or standard deviation.

One of the most useful mathematical properties of variances and standard deviations is that

$$\text{var}[a\tilde{X}] = a^2 \, \text{var}[\tilde{X}] \tag{4-3}$$

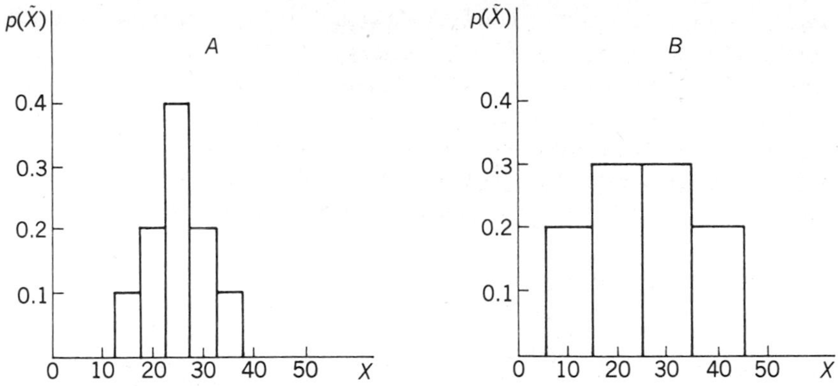


**figure 4-3**

where $a$ is a constant. Consequently, the standard deviation of a constant times a random variable is simply the constant times the standard deviation of the variable:

$$\sigma_{aX} = a\sigma_X \tag{4-3a}$$

These results follow algebraically from the definitions of the variance and standard deviation and properties (2) and (3) above. (Remember that the variance is simply the expected value of a function of the random variable.) The usefulness of the relationships can be seen from an example. In evaluating a particular stock, the variance of the value of 2 shares or 100 shares can easily be derived from the variance of the price per share by applying Eq. (4-3); that is, $\text{var}[n\tilde{P}] = n^2 \text{ var}[\tilde{P}]$, where $n$ is the number of shares and $\tilde{P}$ is the price per share.

The third central moment ($j = 3$) is a measure of the *skewness* of the distribution. We shall not define a special symbol for this moment, $E[(\tilde{X} - \bar{X})^3]$;

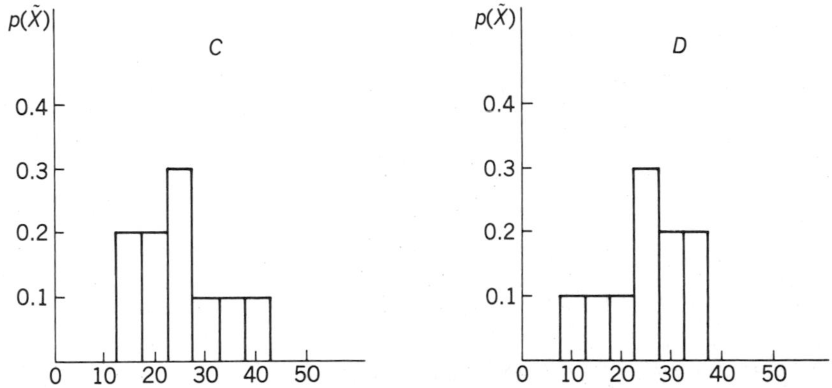


**figure 4-4**

knowledge of its properties is sufficient. It measures the degree of symmetry of the distribution and indicates the direction of the asymmetry if there is any. The distributions in Fig. 4-3 above are symmetric about their mean. The probability of $\tilde{X} = \bar{X} + \Delta$ is equal to the probability of $\tilde{X} = \bar{X} - \Delta$ for all values of $\Delta$. The third central moments of these distributions are equal to zero, as is true for all symmetric distributions. Compare them with the distributions in Fig. 4-4. All distributions have the same mean of 25. $C$ and $D$ have the same variance of 60. Distribution $C$ indicates a greater chance of getting a value for the random variable much larger than the mean than the chance of getting a much smaller value. This distribution can be described as having a "positive tail," a "tail" extending to higher values of the random variable. The skewness measure for this distribution is positive; therefore, $C$ is said to be "positively skewed." Distribution $D$ has a greater chance of values much smaller than the mean; therefore, its skewness measure would be negative. It has a "tail" extending to the lower values; it is negatively skewed.

Computation of the third central moment requires only the observation that $E[(\tilde{X} - \bar{X})^3] = \Sigma(X_i - \bar{X})^3 p(X_i)$. For the two distributions in Fig. 4-4, $\bar{X}_C = \bar{X}_D = 25$. Therefore, we have:

| | | *C* | |
|---|---|---|---|
| $X_i$ | $p(X_i)$ | $(X_i - 25)^3$ | $(X_i - 25)^3 p(X_i)$ |
| 15 | .2 | −1,000 | −200 |
| 20 | .2 | −125 | −25 |
| 25 | .3 | 0 | 0 |
| 30 | .1 | 125 | 12.5 |
| 35 | .1 | 1,000 | 100 |
| 40 | .1 | 3,375 | 337.5 |
| | | $\Sigma =$ | 225 |

| | | *D* | |
|---|---|---|---|
| $X_i$ | $p(X_i)$ | $(X_i - 25)^3$ | $(X_i - 25)^3 p(X_i)$ |
| 10 | .1 | −3,375 | −337.5 |
| 15 | .1 | −1,000 | −100 |
| 20 | .1 | −125 | −12.5 |
| 25 | .3 | 0 | 0 |
| 30 | .2 | 125 | 25 |
| 35 | .2 | 1,000 | 200 |
| | | $\Sigma =$ | −225 |

So we find that both distributions have the same amount of skewness (225), but one is positive and the other is negative.

The first three moments of a distribution capture its most interesting characteristics for financial decision making.[6] Given the general definition of a moment stated above, any desired moment can be determined. We shall stop at three.

## COMBINATIONS OF RANDOM VARIABLES

To this point the discussion has been concerned primarily with distributions of a single random variable. Many problems, however, involve combinations of different random variables. For example, consider the problem of simultaneously holding shares of two different firms. The returns from this portfolio depend on both share prices and must therefore be analyzed in terms of a "joint" probability distribution. An example of such a distribution is

| | $\tilde{X}$ (Price of Firm 1) 30 | 40 | 50 | 60 | |
|---|---|---|---|---|---|
| $\tilde{Y}$ (Price of Firm 2) 30 | .01 | .05 | .10 | .05 | .21 |
| 40 | .05 | .10 | .15 | .06 | .36 |
| 50 | .04 | .10 | .10 | .03 | .27 |
| 60 | .05 | .05 | .05 | .01 | .16 |
| | .15 | .30 | .40 | .15 | 1.0 |

The values in this table are the values of $p(\tilde{X},\tilde{Y})$, the joint probability distribution of the random variables $\tilde{X}$ and $\tilde{Y}$. Note that the sum of all the values in the table is 1.0. The numbers at the margins of the table are the sums of the row or column they are associated with. The sum of the probabilities in the column under $\tilde{X} = 30$ is .15. This is the probability of obtaining $\tilde{X} = 30$. Similarly, the probability of obtaining $\tilde{X} = 40$ is .30. The probability distribution of $\tilde{X}$ taken by itself is therefore

| $\tilde{X}$ | $P(\tilde{X})$ |
|---|---|
| 30 | .15 |
| 40 | .30 |
| 50 | .40 |
| 60 | .15 |

[6] Occasionally the fourth moment that measures the degree of "peakedness" of the distribution is discussed. This moment has found some use in evaluating the statistical properties of price changes in the stock market. See Eugene F. Fama, The Behavior of Stock-Market Prices, *Journal of Business*, January 1965, pp. 34–105.

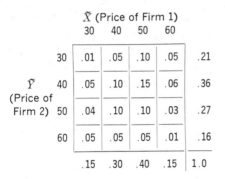

The distribution of $\tilde{Y}$ can be derived in a similar fashion. When we are discussing problems that involve more than one random variable, we must distinguish between the joint distribution of the variables and the "marginal" distributions of each variable considered separately. The joint distribution refers to the probability of obtaining a *pair* of values (in the case of two variables); for example, the probability of obtaining $\tilde{X} = 30$ *and* $\tilde{Y} = 30$ is .01. The marginal distributions provide the probability of obtaining a single value for the variable in question; for example, the probability of obtaining $\tilde{X} = 30$ is .15. We shall use these two types of distribution later in this chapter.

Specifying a joint distribution may be a difficult task; however, there are measures of the relationship between two variables that summarize some of the attributes of the distribution. One characteristic of the joint distribution is an expectation called the *covariance,* which measures the extent to which two variables vary together. The covariance is defined as

$$\text{cov}[\tilde{X},\tilde{Y}] = E[(\tilde{X} - \overline{X})(\tilde{Y} - \overline{Y})] \tag{4-4}$$

$$\begin{aligned}\text{cov}[\tilde{X},\tilde{Y}] &= E[\tilde{X}\tilde{Y} - \overline{X}\tilde{Y} - \tilde{X}\overline{Y} + \overline{X}\overline{Y}] \\ &= E[\tilde{X}\tilde{Y}] - \overline{X}\overline{Y}\end{aligned} \tag{4-4a}$$

An alternative measure of the relationship between two random variables is the *correlation coefficient*. This measure is computed from the covariance as

$$\rho_{XY} = \frac{\text{cov}[\tilde{X},\tilde{Y}]}{\sigma_X \sigma_Y} \tag{4-5}$$

where $\rho_{XY}$ is the correlation coefficient and $\sigma_X$ and $\sigma_Y$ are the standard deviations of $\tilde{X}$ and $\tilde{Y}$, respectively. The advantage of using the correlation between variables as a measure of their relationship is that it takes on values only within the range $\pm 1.0$. Since the maximum degree of positive relationship occurs when $\rho = 1.0$, we can speak of two variables as having *perfect positive correlation* when that condition holds. A positive relationship between two variables is one where high values of the first variable tend to occur with high values for the second variable. Also, low values of each variable tend to occur together. When there is no relationship between two variables, they are statistically independent—their correlation is zero. When two variables move in opposite directions from each other (high values of one occurring with low values of the other and vice versa), they are negatively correlated. At the extreme, when $\rho = -1.0$, they are said to be *perfectly negatively correlated.*

To gain some insight into the meaning and computation of the covariance and the correlation coefficient, consider the following simple distributions of $\tilde{X}$ and $\tilde{Y}$. The two variables have identical marginal distributions (looking at them separately):

| $\tilde{X}$ | $p(\tilde{X})$ | $\tilde{Y}$ | $p(\tilde{Y})$ |
|---|---|---|---|
| 10 | .5 | 10 | .5 |
| 20 | .5 | 20 | .5 |

$$\bar{X} = \bar{Y} = 15$$
$$\sigma_X = \sigma_Y = 5$$

There is an infinite number of joint distributions that are consistent with these two marginal distributions; three special joint distributions are shown below:

***A***

| $\tilde{Y}$ \ $\tilde{X}$ | 10 | 20 |
|---|---|---|
| 10 | .5 | 0 |
| 20 | 0 | .5 |

***B***

| $\tilde{Y}$ \ $\tilde{X}$ | 10 | 20 |
|---|---|---|
| 10 | 0 | .5 |
| 20 | .5 | 0 |

***C***

| $\tilde{Y}$ \ $\tilde{X}$ | 10 | 20 |
|---|---|---|
| 10 | .25 | .25 |
| 20 | .25 | .25 |

Distribution *A* has a covariance of 25 and a correlation of 1.0; the variables are perfectly correlated. Distribution *B* has a covariance of −25 and a correlation of −1.0; the variables are perfectly negatively correlated. Distribution *C* has a covariance of zero and a correlation of zero because the variables are independent. For another example using the same marginal distributions, look at distribution *D*. Are $\tilde{X}$ and $\tilde{Y}$ positively or negatively correlated?

***D***

| $\tilde{Y}$ \ $\tilde{X}$ | 10 | 20 |
|---|---|---|
| 10 | .4 | .1 |
| 20 | .1 | .4 |

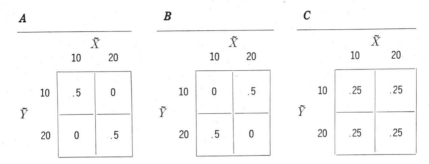

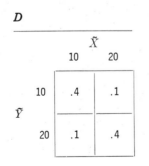

There are some properties of covariances and correlations that will be useful later on. Suppose that each of the values of $\tilde{X}$ and $\tilde{Y}$ in the examples above is multiplied by 10, as in the case of the variables being share prices with a purchase of 10 shares of each firm's stock. The covariances for each joint distribution increase by a factor of 10 times 10, or 100. For example, using distribution $A$, $\mathrm{cov}[10\tilde{X},10\tilde{Y}] = 2{,}500$. The standard deviation for each variable would increase by a factor of 10 to 50 as from Eq. (4-3*a*). The correlation coefficient would not change at all, $\rho = 2{,}500/[(50)(50)] = 1.0$. The fact that the correlation between two variables is unaffected by the absolute magnitude of the numbers, as compared to the covariance that is affected, makes $\rho$ useful as a "pure" measure of the degree of relationship.

The covariance, however, has some very helpful mathematical properties. One of these was illustrated above: that we can account for changes in the scale of the variables fairly easily. In general terms, if we multiply a variable $\tilde{X}$ by a constant $a$ and multiply a variable $\tilde{Y}$ by another constant $b$,

$$\mathrm{cov}[a\tilde{X},b\tilde{Y}] = ab\ \mathrm{cov}[\tilde{X},\tilde{Y}] \tag{4-6}$$

In the example above, $a$ and $b$ were both equal to 10.

A second characteristic of covariances that can be used to generate some important theoretical results is the fact that covariances are *additive;* given random variables $\tilde{X}$, $\tilde{Y}$, and $\tilde{Z}$,

$$\mathrm{cov}[(\tilde{X} + \tilde{Y}), \tilde{Z}] = \mathrm{cov}[\tilde{X},\tilde{Z}] + \mathrm{cov}[\tilde{Y},\tilde{Z}] \tag{4-7}$$

This characteristic follows from a property of the mathematical expectation—that the expected value of the sum of any functions of random variables is equal to the sum of the expected values of the functions. [Refer to property (3) of expected values discussed earlier.]

Let us return to the problem that introduced this section. Consider the purchase of stock in two different companies, where $\tilde{X}$ and $\tilde{Y}$ are the share prices of the two, respectively. The results from purchasing one share in each company can be expressed as a new random variable $\tilde{Z} = \tilde{X} + \tilde{Y}$. Of interest are the characteristics of the distribution of $\tilde{Z}$, given the joint distribution of $\tilde{X}$ and $\tilde{Y}$. Except for very simple distributions as in our examples, the general problem of determining the distribution of $\tilde{Z}$ is difficult and beyond the scope of this discussion. Fortunately, it is quite easy to determine the mean and variance of the distribution. The mean of $\tilde{Z}$ is equal to the sum of the means of $\tilde{X}$ and $\tilde{Y}$, as we know from the properties of expected values:

$$E[\tilde{Z}] = E[\tilde{X} + \tilde{Y}] = E[\tilde{X}] + E[\tilde{Y}] \qquad \text{or} \qquad \bar{Z} = \bar{X} + \bar{Y} \tag{4-8}$$

The variance of $\tilde{Z}$ can be derived readily from the definitions and the properties of expected values. The development goes as follows:

$$\begin{aligned}\mathrm{var}[\tilde{Z}] &= E[(\tilde{Z} - \bar{Z})^2] = E\{[(\tilde{X} + \tilde{Y}) - (\bar{X} + \bar{Y})]^2\} \\ &= E\{[(\tilde{X} - \bar{X}) + (\tilde{Y} - \bar{Y})]^2\} \\ &= E[(\tilde{X} - \bar{X})^2 + 2(\tilde{X} - \bar{X})(\tilde{Y} - \bar{Y}) + (\tilde{Y} - \bar{Y})^2] \\ &= E[(\tilde{X} - \bar{X})^2] + 2E[(\tilde{X} - \bar{X})(\tilde{Y} - \bar{Y})] + E[(\tilde{Y} - \bar{Y})^2] \\ &= \mathrm{var}[\tilde{X}] + 2\ \mathrm{cov}[\tilde{X},\tilde{Y}] + \mathrm{var}[\tilde{Y}]\end{aligned} \tag{4-9}$$

With a knowledge of the means, variances, and covariance of $\tilde{X}$ and $\tilde{Y}$, the mean and variance of the sum $\tilde{Z}$ of the two variables are easily determined.

This is so regardless of the exact form of the joint distribution of $\tilde{X}$ and $\tilde{Y}$. Moreover, Eqs. (4-8) and (4-9) generalize to the case of many variables each multiplied by a different constant, as in the problem of determining the results from purchasing different numbers of shares in several different companies. Given $\tilde{Z}$ equal to a linear combination of $n$ random variables $\tilde{X}_i$($\tilde{X}_1$ being one variable, $\tilde{X}_2$ another, etc.) and $b_i$ is a constant, that is,

$$\tilde{Z} = b_1\tilde{X}_1 + b_2\tilde{X}_2 + b_3\tilde{X}_3 + \cdots + b_n\tilde{X}_n$$

then

$$\bar{Z} = b_1\bar{X}_1 + b_2\bar{X}_2 + b_3\bar{X}_3 + \cdots + b_n\bar{X}_n \tag{4-10}$$

or, more compactly,

$$\bar{Z} = \sum_{i=1}^{n} b_i\bar{X}_i \tag{4-10a}$$

Expressing the variance of $\tilde{Z}$ in a reasonably compact form is more difficult than expressing the mean, since the variance includes terms that involve the covariances of all possible pairs of variables; for example, cov$[\tilde{X}_1\tilde{X}_2]$, cov$[\tilde{X}_1\tilde{X}_3]$, cov$[\tilde{X}_1\tilde{X}_n]$, cov$[\tilde{X}_2\tilde{X}_3]$, and so forth. However, recall that cov$[\tilde{X},\tilde{Y}] = E[(\tilde{X} - \bar{X})(\tilde{Y} - \bar{Y})]$. Now suppose we take the covariance of $\tilde{X}$ with itself: cov$[\tilde{X},\tilde{X}]$ will be equal to $E[(\tilde{X} - \bar{X})^2]$ = var$[\tilde{X}]$. In other words, we can express var$[\tilde{X}]$ as cov$[\tilde{X},\tilde{X}]$. Consequently, we can write the variance of $\tilde{Z}$ as

$$\text{var}[\tilde{Z}] = \sum_{i=1}^{n}\sum_{j=1}^{n} b_ib_j \,\text{cov}[\tilde{X}_i\tilde{X}_j] \tag{4-11}$$

where the double summation means that we sum first over $j$ for $i = 1$, then over $j$ again for $i = 2$, and so on until $i = n$. This procedure accounts for all possible pairs of variables and the variances of the $\tilde{X}_i$.

Equations (4-10) and (4-11) are the bases for the theory of portfolios of securities and for a major theory of capital market equilibrium under uncertainty. They also provide insight into some of the financial decisions of the firm. The next three chapters develop these ideas.

## SUMMARY

This chapter has been an introduction to the concepts and mathematics of probability theory and random variables. We discussed the meaning and measurement of probability and the concept of expected value. Summary characteristics of probability distributions—mean, variance or standard deviation, and skewness—were presented. These characteristics were suggested to be the most important attributes of the distribution of a single random variable. We next discussed problems involving two random variables and presented the concept of their joint distribution. Two measures of the relationship expressed by the joint distribution were the covariance and the correlation coefficient. Equations for determining the mean and variance of a linear function of random variables were developed from the mathematical properties of expected values. A summary of the definitions and the relationships that will be used in later chapters is presented below.

## Definitions

1. The expected value of a random variable or a function of a random variable for the discrete case is the sum of the values of the variable or function multiplied by the probability of obtaining these values:

$$E[\tilde{X}] = \sum_{i} X_i p(X_i) \tag{4-1}$$

2. The mean of the probability distribution of a random variable measures the central tendency or average size of the variable and equals the expected value of the variable. The mean value of $\tilde{X}$ is written as $\bar{X}$.
3. The variance of a probability distribution measures the amount of variation around the mean value. The square root of the variance, the standard deviation, measures the same thing. The variance is the expected value of the squared deviations around the mean:

$$\mathrm{var}[\tilde{X}] = E[(\tilde{X} - \bar{X})^2] \tag{4-2}$$

4. The skewness of a distribution refers to its degree of symmetry. Distributions may have positive, negative, or zero skewness. A measure of skewness is the third central moment of the distribution.
5. The covariance is a measure of the degree of relationship between two random variables. It is the expected value of the product of the deviations around the mean for each variable:

$$\mathrm{cov}[\tilde{X}, \tilde{Y}] = E[(\tilde{X} - \bar{X})(\tilde{Y} - \bar{Y})] \tag{4-4}$$

6. An alternative measure of the relationship between two variables is the correlation coefficient that takes on values between $\pm 1.0$ and is therefore not affected by the scale of measurement of the variables:

$$\rho_{XY} = \frac{\mathrm{cov}[\tilde{X}, \tilde{Y}]}{\sigma_X \sigma_Y} \tag{4-5}$$

## Relationships

Given a set of random variables $\tilde{X}_i$ and constants $b_i$, the following relationships hold:

1. The expected value of a constant is that constant.
2. The expected value of a constant times a random variable or a function of a

random variable is that constant times the expected value of the variable or function.

3. The expected value of a sum equals the sum of the expected values. This relationship holds, no matter what is being summed—different random variables, functions of a single variable, or functions of many variables.
4. The standard deviation of a constant times a variable is that constant times the standard deviation of the variable.
5. $\text{cov}[b_1\tilde{X}_1, b_2\tilde{X}_2] = b_1 b_2 \,\text{cov}[\tilde{X}_1, \tilde{X}_2]$ (4-6)
6. $\text{cov}[(\tilde{X}_1 + \tilde{X}_2), \tilde{X}_3] = \text{cov}[\tilde{X}_1, \tilde{X}_3] + \text{cov}[\tilde{X}_2, \tilde{X}_3]$ (4-7)
7. Let $\tilde{Z} = b_1\tilde{X}_1 + b_2\tilde{X}_2$
   (*a*) $\bar{Z} = b_1\bar{X}_1 + b_2\bar{X}_2$
   (*b*) $\text{var}[\tilde{Z}] = b_1^2 \,\text{var}[\tilde{X}_1] + b_2^2 \,\text{var}[\tilde{X}_2] + 2\, b_1 b_2 \,\text{cov}[\tilde{X}_1, \tilde{X}_2]$
8. Let $\tilde{Z} = b_1\tilde{X}_1 + b_2\tilde{X}_2 + b_3\tilde{X}_3 + \cdots + b_n\tilde{X}_n$
   then

$$(a)\ \bar{Z} = \sum_{i=1}^{n} b_i \bar{X}_i \qquad (4\text{-}10a)$$

$$(b)\ \text{var}[\tilde{Z}] = \sum_{i=1}^{n} \sum_{j=1}^{n} b_i b_j \,\text{cov}[\tilde{X}_i, \tilde{X}_j] \qquad (4\text{-}11)$$

9. Alternative ways of expressing Eq. (4-11) are

$$(a)\ \sigma_{\tilde{Z}}^2 = \sum_{i=1}^{n} \sum_{j=1}^{n} b_i b_j \sigma_{ij} \qquad (4\text{-}12)$$

which is based on our alternative notation for covariances and variances, and

$$(b)\ \sigma_{\tilde{Z}}^2 = \sum_{i=1}^{n} \sum_{j=1}^{n} b_i b_j \rho_{ij} \sigma_i \sigma_j \qquad (4\text{-}13)$$

where $\sigma_i$ = standard deviation of $X_i$
$\rho_{ij}$ = correlation between $X_i$ and $X_j$

The correlation of a variable with itself $\rho_{ii}$ is 1.0. See the definition of $\rho$, Eq. (4-5).

## SUGGESTED READINGS

Hogg, Robert V. and Allen T. Craig: "Introduction to Mathematical Statistics," chaps. 1 and 2, The Macmillan Company, New York, 1959.

Raiffa, Howard: "Decision Analysis," chaps. 0–5, Addison-Wesley Publishing Company, Inc., Reading, Mass., 1968. (This reading also applies to chap. 5 of this text.)

Schlaifer, Robert: "Analysis of Decisions under Uncertainty," pts. 1 and 2, McGraw-Hill Book Company, New York, 1969. (This reading also applies to chap. 5 of this text.)

CHAPTER

# FIVE

# INDIVIDUAL DECISIONS UNDER UNCERTAINTY: THE EXPECTED UTILITY MODEL

In the preceding chapter we suggested that probability theory is useful in describing and measuring the degree of uncertainty in a decision-making situation. In this chapter we shall consider the impact of individual preferences on decisions when the outcomes are uncertain. Taken together, Chaps. 4 and 5 lay the foundations for the development of the theory of investment in risky assets (called "portfolio theory") presented in Chap. 6. Portfolio theory in turn provides the basis for a theory of equilibrium in the capital markets under uncertainty which is presented in Chap. 7. We use the equilibrium conditions developed in Chap. 7 to determine optimal financial policies for firms in Chap. 8. The analysis in this part of the book is limited to single-period or "now-later" problems. Chapters 9 and on are devoted to decisions involving multiple periods. As we shall see, the multiperiod problem is considerably more difficult.

The particular model of decision making by individuals under uncertainty that will be presented in this chapter is called the *expected utility model.*[1] Al-

[1] More extensive discussion and development of this model can be found in the Suggested Readings at the end of this chapter. For an alternative introductory exposition see Robert L. Winkler, "An Introduction to Bayesian Inference and Decision," pp. 219–295, Holt, Rinehart and Winston, Inc., New York, 1972.

though most of the theory of financial decisions by individuals and firms which is developed in later chapters does not strictly require that this model be valid, the theory is nevertheless consistent with the model. The expected utility model is widely used in economic theory to provide formal treatments of individual attitudes toward risk. It has also been suggested as an appropriate guide to individual decision making under uncertainty. The model may therefore aid us in understanding the behavior of individuals who are making risky decisions.

## THE GENERAL PROBLEM FOR THE INDIVIDUAL

At any point in time an individual has two basic decisions to make: how much to consume in the current period (therefore, for a given amount of wealth, how much to invest) and which financial assets to hold. As discussed in Chap. 2, under conditions of certainty and perfect markets the latter problem is trivial since all financial assets provide the same yield (the risk-free rate of interest $i$). Under uncertainty, however, asset selection becomes much more difficult since the returns from holding most assets are uncertain. Moreover, the individual's consumption problem is more difficult because future income is, in general, uncertain. For the purposes of this chapter it will be assumed that the individual has decided upon the amount to consume in the current period and therefore how much is available for investment in financial assets. The consumption problem and its relationship to the investment problem is discussed in more detail in Appendix 5A.

Suppose that an individual has \$1,000 available for investment. We wish to determine the criterion the individual might use in achieving the most benefit from this investment of \$1,000. In a world of uncertainty we need to know how an individual may choose among risky alternatives. There are two issues here. We might be interested in providing a reasonable guide for individual choices and suggest that the model to be presented is such a guide. This is the normative issue that is developed by Raiffa and Schlaifer (see the Suggested Readings for this chapter and Chap. 4). However, our primary concern in this book is the financial decisions of the firm. Since the objective of the firm is assumed to be that of maximizing the welfare of its shareholders, we need a model that permits us to evaluate the consequences of the firm's decisions on its shareholders. In order to make this evaluation we require a model of individual preferences in risky situations, which we hope is a reasonable approximation to the actual behavior of individuals.

The expected utility model presented below may therefore be looked at in two ways: as a reasonable *guide* to individual decisions and as a reasonable *description* of individual decisions. In the next few pages our primary purpose is to describe the model itself. Support for the two points of view is provided in the Suggested Readings for this chapter, although some discussion of the reasonableness of the model in both its normative and its positive aspects is included below.

## ASSUMPTIONS OF RATIONAL CHOICE

The expected utility model is based on a theorem derived from axioms concerning individual behavior.[2] If the axioms are assumed to hold, the theorem follows. We can consider these axioms to be conditions imposed on the analysis or simply assumptions of how people behave; in any case they form the basis for the expected utility model. In essence they amount to a general assumption that people are rational and consistent in choosing among risky alternatives.

1. Individuals have preferences among alternatives and can express them. Given any two alternative choices $Q_1$ and $Q_2$, the individual either prefers $Q_1$ to $Q_2$, prefers $Q_2$ to $Q_1$, or is indifferent between them. The ability of an individual to rank alternative choices is a basic component of rational behavior. Economic theory generally assumes this condition to be true.
2. Individuals are *transitive* in their preferences. If $Q_1$ is preferred to $Q_2$ and $Q_2$ is preferred to $Q_3$, then $Q_1$ must be preferred to $Q_3$. Similarly, if an individual is indifferent between $Q_1$ and $Q_2$ and between $Q_2$ and $Q_3$, then he or she must be indifferent between $Q_1$ and $Q_3$. Although this requirement also would seem characteristic of rational behavior, it can present problems in some situations involving risky choices. People do not always conform to the transitivity principle.[3]
3. If an individual is indifferent between $Q_1$ and $Q_2$ and if $Q_3$ is any other alternative, then he or she will be indifferent between two gambles $A$ and $B$, where
   $A$ offers a probability $p$ of receiving $Q_1$ and a probability $(1-p)$ of receiving $Q_3$, and
   $B$ offers a probability $p$ of receiving $Q_2$ and a probability $(1-p)$ of receiving $Q_3$.
   Axiom (3) is called the *substitution principle*. It says essentially that preferences with respect to the outcomes of risky situations are not affected by the risky situation itself. For example, suppose you are flipping coins with a friend. You happen to be indifferent to chocolate or vanilla ice cream. You will also be indifferent to two choices—heads he gives you a vanilla ice cream cone, tails you pay him \$1; and heads he gives you a chocolate ice cream cone, tails you pay him \$1. This does not mean you are indifferent to either of the two gambles and the choice of not playing at all, only that the uncertainty of the outcome does not affect your relative evaluation of chocolate and vanilla. The principle becomes more complicated when the outcomes

[2] The following development is drawn from Harry M. Markowitz, "Portfolio Selection," chap. 10, John Wiley & Sons, Inc., New York, 1959. A more formal and detailed discussion of the assumptions is in R. D. Luce and Howard Raiffa, "Games and Decisions," John Wiley & Sons, Inc., New York, 1957.

[3] For a discussion and argument in favor of this axiom see Howard Raiffa, "Decision Analysis," pp. 75–80, Addison-Wesley Publishing Company, Inc., Reading, Mass., 1968.

are themselves risky (for example, if $Q_1$ were a ticket in the Irish Sweepstakes); however, the principle is assumed to apply in these cases as well.[4]

4. There exists a certainty equivalent to any gamble. If $Q_1$ is preferred to $Q_2$ and $Q_2$ is preferred to $Q_3$, then there exists some probability $p$ that the individual will be completely indifferent to getting $Q_2$ for certain or getting $Q_1$ with probability $p$ and $Q_3$ with probability $(1 - p)$. The problems with this assumption arise when $Q_3$ is a very bad outcome—bankruptcy, death, and so forth. People are apt to say they are completely unwilling to subject themselves to any chance of such an adverse outcome if they can avoid it. The counterargument is that the probability of getting $Q_3$ can be made very, very small, like .0000000001, which is one chance in 10 billion. People subject themselves to worse chances than that by crossing the street.[5]

There have been experiments to determine how well people actually conform to the axioms. The results indicate that people are not always rational and consistent in the sense of these axioms. However, it has also been found that if their inconsistencies are pointed out to them, people will generally change their behavior to conform to the axioms.[6] The applicability of the model is therefore still an issue that is not completely settled. However, let us go on to examine the consequences of assuming that these conditions have been met.

## UTILITY FUNCTIONS

If an individual conforms to axioms (1) to (4) above, an index that expresses the individual's preferences for both the certain outcomes and the choices in a risky situation can be derived.[7] In other words, this index can be used to represent the individual's preferences toward the ultimate results from a decision and to provide a measure of the merit of each possible decision. For example, suppose the decision to be made is which of two stocks to buy. You plan to sell 1 year from now. If you conform to the axioms, it will be possible to develop an index of your preferences with respect to the final outcomes (the value of your investment 1 year from now). Moreover, so long as you conform to the axioms, your index can be used to indicate which stock you should buy.

[4] Thorough discussion of the issues here can be found in Markowitz, *op. cit.*, pp. 230–233.

[5] An interesting discussion of the problems in determining acceptable levels of probabilities for disasters is in Pierre Masse, "Optimal Investment Decisions," chap. 8, sec. III, Prentice-Hall, Inc., Englewood Cliffs, N.J., 1962.

[6] Raiffa, *op. cit.*, pp. 80–86. See also Donald Davidson and Jacob Marschak, "Experimental Tests of a Stochastic Decision Theory," in C. West Churchman and Philburn Ratoosh (eds.), "Measurement: Definitions and Theories," pp. 233–269, John Wiley & Sons, Inc., New York, 1959.

[7] There are some additional axioms of a more technical nature. See Luce and Raiffa, *op. cit.*

To be specific, you should choose that stock which has the maximum expected value of the index of the outcomes.

The index is called a utility index or utility function.[8] The expected utility model consists of the axioms, the characteristics of the utility functions admissible under the axioms, and the theorem that behavior consistent with the axioms requires the maximization of expected utility. As noted above, we can think of the model in two ways: as a way to make decisions and as a hypothesis about the way people make decisions. Let us now look at a procedure for determining such an index that should help clarify the concept.

Suppose that Ms. H has $1,000 available for investment. She is considering investing this money in risky securities. Assume further that the worst possible outcome from investment is the loss of the entire amount, and that the best outcome she can hope for is a gain of $1,000. The magnitude or scale of the utility function is arbitrary. We can fix the scale of the index by specifying that its value for a loss of $1,000 is zero and that its value for a gain of $1,000 is 1.0. Symbolically we define $U(-1{,}000) = 0.0$ and $U(1{,}000) = 1.0$, where $U(Y)$ is the utility index of the gain or loss from the investment.

So far we have merely set up the problem. Nothing has yet been said about this person's preferences. Note, however, that we *have* specified her opportunities. The utility index is being based on a specific situation, not an abstract one. The index that will be developed is therefore unique both to the individual involved and to the particular circumstances or decision situation being analyzed.[9]

Two arbitrary points of this individual's utility index have been established. The problem now is to determine the complete index. This may be done by using axiom (4) above and the expected utility theorem. The expected utility theorem implies that for an individual to be indifferent between two risky choices, the expected value of the utility from the choices must be equal. When one of two equivalent choices provides an amount to be received for certain, that amount is called the "certainty equivalent" of the other, risky choice. Axiom (4) states that there exists a certainty equivalent for every risky choice. Ms. H would be asked to determine her certainty equivalent for simple gambles that will pay off the best possible amount ($1,000) with probability $p$ and the

[8] This index is often referred to as a "Von Neumann-Morgenstern utility function" after the people who derived it as a theorem from postulates about individual behavior. J. Von Neumann and O. Morgenstern, "Theory of Games and Economic Behavior," 2d ed., Princeton University Press, Princeton, N.J., 1947. A utility index $U$ will indicate a higher number for an object of choice the more it is preferred [for example, $U(R_2) > U(R_1)$ if $R_2$ is preferred to $R_1$]. The Von Neumann-Morgenstern utility function is "cardinal," which means that the rate of change in the level of $U$ is also significant [for example, $U(R_3) - U(R_2)$ relative to $U(R_2) - U(R_1)$]. A cardinal utility function provides the basis for a consistent ordering of preferences under uncertainty. See S. S. Stevens, "Measurement, Psychophysics, and Utility," in Churchman and Ratoosh (eds.), *op. cit.*, pp. 18–63.

[9] In economic theory it is generally agreed that interpersonal comparisons of utility are not appropriate. We observe here that intertemporal comparisons of utility for a single individual may also be inappropriate.

worst possible (−\$1,000) with probability $(1 - p)$. Let $Y$ be the certainty equivalent. By the expected utility theorem, the utility $U(Y)$ of $Y$ received for certain must equal the expected utility of the gamble. $U(Y) = pU(1{,}000) + (1 - p)U(-1{,}000)$. However, since we set $U(1{,}000) = 1.0$ and $U(-1{,}000) = .0$, $U(Y) = p(1.0) + (1 - p)(.0) = p$. Our choice of scale for $U(Y)$ turns out to be a very convenient one.[10]

As an example of the use of this technique let us look at the gamble when $p = .5$. In this case the *expected monetary value*[11] of the gamble is $(1{,}000)(.5) + (-1{,}000)(.5) = \$0$. Suppose Ms. H responds that she would just as soon take a \$250 loss for certain than gamble at those odds on losing \$1,000. We now have a third point on her index, $U(-250) = .5$. Looking at another gamble when $p = .8$, the expected monetary value of the gamble is $(1{,}000)(.8) + (-1{,}000)(.2) = \$600$. The decision maker might respond that \$400 would be her certainty equivalent for this gamble. This would provide an index value $U(400) = .8$. If we continued in this fashion, exploring the range of values for $p$ between 0 and 1.0, we would define a utility index for this person. An index $[U_1(Y)]$ consistent with the preceding data is shown in Fig. 5-1.

[10] Other scales may be used; however, they require an additional computational step. For example, we could let $U(-1{,}000) = 10$ and $U(1{,}000) = 100$. To find the value of $U(-250)$ resulting from the reference gamble of $p = .5$, the expected utility theorem is used:

$$\begin{aligned} U(-250) &= .5U(1{,}000) + .5U(-1{,}000) \\ &= .5(100) + .5(10) \\ &= 55 \end{aligned}$$

[11] The payoff need not necessarily be monetary. Utility functions can be developed for any set of outcomes, since a given function is based on a particular set of outcomes. Expected *monetary* value (EMV) is frequently used in decision theory to contrast with the value of expected *utility*. In succeeding discussions the term "expected value" will always refer to the expected value of the monetary outcomes as compared to the "expected utility" of those outcomes.

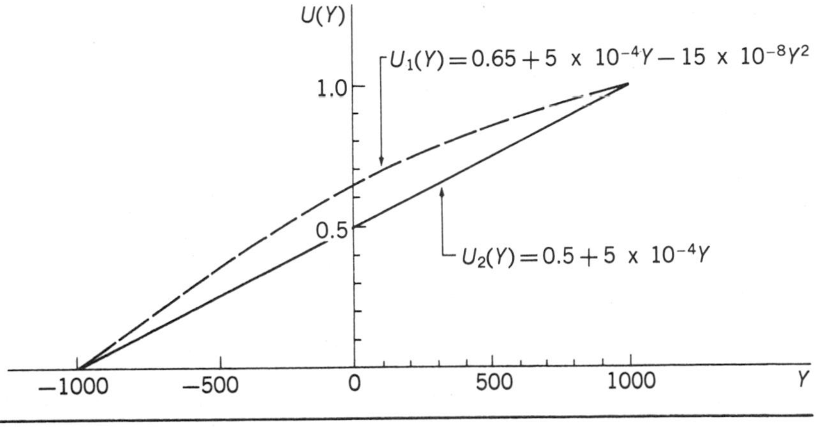


**figure 5-1**

The individual whose preferences are described by $U_1(Y)$ shown in Fig. 5-1 is said to be averse to risk because she would be willing to exchange a given gamble for a certain amount less than the expected value of the gamble. $U_2(Y)$ is a utility index for someone who is indifferent between having a gamble or its expected value to be received for certain. The certainty equivalent for this person is equal to the expected value of the gamble. A person indifferent to risk has a linear utility function. For such people $E[U(\tilde{Y})] = U(E[\tilde{Y}])$. As an example, consider the gamble when $p = .5$. The expected value of this gamble from the preceding is $0. The certainty equivalent for this person is also $0 since he or she is indifferent to risk. Therefore, $U(0) = .5 = U(E[\tilde{Y}])$. But $E[U(\tilde{Y})] = p[U(1{,}000)] + (1 - p)[U(-1{,}000)] = .5(1.0) + .5(0) = .5$. For Ms. H, whose preferences are described by $U_1(Y)$, $E[U(\tilde{Y})] < U(E[\tilde{Y}])$. In this example $E[U(\tilde{Y})] = .5$ as before, but $U(0) = .65$ from $U_1(Y)$ on the graph. In other words, for a person averse to risk the expected utility from a gamble $E[U(\tilde{Y})]$ is less than the utility of the expected value of the gamble $U(E[\tilde{Y}])$.

## APPLICATION OF THE MODEL

In the paragraphs above we showed how an index of individual preferences in risky situations might be derived. We assume that individuals in their investment decisions do, by and large, make rational choices in the sense of the conditions of the model we have described. We therefore assume that people make choices among investment alternatives by choosing that alternative which provides the maximum expected value for their personal utility functions. The individual will select that alternative which provides a cash return $\tilde{Y}$ with the maximum expected utility, i.e., with the maximum $E[U(\tilde{Y})]$ where, for discrete variables,

$$E[U(\tilde{Y})] = \sum_{i=1}^{n} p(Y_i)U(Y_i)$$

For example, suppose the individual whose utility function is shown by $U_1(Y)$ in Fig. 5-1 is choosing between the following alternatives, both of which require an investment of $1,000 and for which the outcomes are specified in terms of the profit or loss from the investment:

| *A* | | *B* | |
|---|---|---|---|
| $p(\tilde{Y})$ | $\tilde{Y}$ | $p(\tilde{Y})$ | $\tilde{Y}$ |
| 1.0 | $50 | .20 | −$200 |
| | | .60 | $ 50 |
| | | .20 | $300 |

Both alternatives have an expected value of their outcomes of \$50. The expected utility value for $A$ is simply $U(\$50)$, since the \$50 is received for certain. Using the function shown in Fig. 5-1 we get, approximately, $U(\$50) = .67$. In order to determine the expected utility value for alternative $B$, we find $U(-\$200) = .54$, and $U(\$300) = .79$. The expected value of $U(\tilde{Y})$ for alternative $B$ is therefore

$$E[U(\tilde{Y})] = .2(.54) + .6(.67) + .2(.79)$$
$$= .668$$

Since the expected utility of $A$ is greater than that of $B$, we would expect the individual to choose $A$ over $B$.

Clearly, people in practice do not go through such elaborate procedures in making their decisions. The concept of a utility function is useful, however, in thinking about attitudes toward risky situations. For example, we can now say more precisely what is meant by the term "risk aversion" and we can find ways to measure risk.

## RISK AVERSION AND MEASUREMENT

An individual who is averse to risk would generally prefer alternative $A$ to alternative $B$ in the example above. Both alternatives have expected returns of \$50, but the \$50 return from $A$ is certain and the \$50 from $B$ is not. Suppose that we had another alternative, $C$, which offered an uncertain set of returns also having an expected value of \$50. If someone were offered the choice between the two risky alternatives $B$ and $C$, how could you tell whether this person was averse to risk or not from the decision? You could not tell. Suppose you knew the certainty equivalents of the alternatives. If the certainty equivalent of any risky alternative is less than the expected value of the alternative, we can say that the individual is averse to risk. For example, the person might be indifferent between getting \$40 for certain and getting an expected value of \$50 from a risky alternative. If that person were offered \$41 for certain, this certain amount would be preferred to the risky alternative with an expected monetary value of \$50. In general we assume that individuals are averse to risk in their financial decisions.[12]

Given the assumption of general risk aversion, we would like to find some way to measure the "risk" of an alternative without specific knowledge of the utility functions of individuals. In one sense this is impossible since the risk of an alternative to an individual depends on personal preferences. However, the alternatives are described by probability distributions. We would like to be able to measure risk in terms of some general characteristics of those probability distributions if possible since this would greatly simplify the problem. Risk aversion and utility functions are examined in more depth in Appendix 5C.

[12] Risk aversion is not necessarily a general characteristic of individuals in all situations. See M. Friedman and L. Savage, The Utility Analysis of Choice Involving Risk, *Journal of Political Economy*, vol. 56, pp. 279–304, August 1948.

Let us begin with the utility function $U_1(Y)$ shown in Fig. 5-1. It has the general form

$$U(Y) = A + BY + CY^2 \tag{5-1}$$

We can think of this general form as being characteristic of different people, each having different values for $A$, $B$, and $C$.[13] If we think of the investment alternatives as securities that can be purchased in any desired amount, it is reasonable to convert the dollar returns into rates of return by dividing the outcomes by the amount of the investment for each person. For example, take the individual whose utility function was shown in Fig. 5-1. She has \$1,000 to invest; so a loss of \$1,000 is a return of $-100\%$. If we let the rate of return $r = Y/1{,}000$, then $Y = 1{,}000r$, and we can express her utility function as

$$U(r) = .65 + .5r - .15r^2 \tag{5-2}$$

simply by substituting for $Y$. For any given return, the value for the utility index is the same whether rates of return or dollar returns are used. We can now think of a new class of utility functions that could be common to many people (as an approximation):

$$U(r) = a + br + cr^2 \tag{5-3}$$

The coefficients in the function depend on how much money a particular individual has to invest, feelings toward risk, and anything else in that person's current situation that is relevant to the individual. Given this general form, what can we say about the appropriate measure of risk?

Suppose we take the expected value of the utility function of Eq. (5-3), given that $\tilde{r}$ is a random variable associated with an alternative:

$$E[U(\tilde{r})] = a + bE[\tilde{r}] + cE[\tilde{r}^2] \tag{5-4}$$

The expected value of the rate of return $E[\tilde{r}]$ for any given distribution is simply the mean of the distribution, $\bar{r}$. The expected value of a random variable squared is the second moment of the distribution of the variable and is equal [by Eq. (4-2$a$)] to the variance of the distribution plus the mean squared; that is,

$$E[\tilde{r}^2] = \sigma_{\tilde{r}}^2 + \bar{r}^2 \tag{5-5}$$

Substituting Eq. (5-5) into Eq. (5-4) we arrive at an expression for the expected utility containing two characteristics of probability distributions: the mean and the variance:

$$E[U(\tilde{r})] = a + b\bar{r} + c(\sigma_{\tilde{r}}^2 + \bar{r}^2) \tag{5-6}$$

[13] For a given quadratic function ($A$, $B$, and $C$ given) the implied upper limit to the range of outcomes over which the function would be considered a reasonable approximation of the individual's utility function is $B/2C$. For outcomes beyond $B/2C$, the function decreases as the outcome increases; i.e., it is implied that utility falls as returns increase. See app. 5B for proof and discussion.

We can think of the variance of a distribution as measuring the risk for individuals who have quadratic utility functions. This can be seen most easily by thinking of two alternatives, both of which have the same expected value ($\bar{r}$), but one of which is certain and the other risky. The variance of the certain return is zero; the variance of the other is greater than zero. If $c < 0$ in (5-6), then the expected utility of the certain alternative will be greater than the expected utility of the risky one. The condition that $c$ be negative is equivalent to an assumption that individuals are averse to risk. Given this condition, the higher the variance, the lower the expected utility at a given expected return. If $c$ were zero, then the individual would be indifferent to risk, since this person would make decisions solely on the expected returns. If $c$ were positive, the individual would prefer risk, since the higher the variance, the higher the expected utility.

Of course we have no particular reason to believe that people in general act as if their utility functions were quadratic. Other characteristics of probability distributions (such as skewness) may be important. However, we shall assume for now that the mean and variance (or standard deviation) are the most important characteristics; and we may be justified in making this assumption because it may be a reasonable approximation in many cases. Some problems with this assumption are discussed in Appendix 5B.

## †Mean-Variance Analysis as an Approximation

There are essentially two conditions, either of which can hold, that justify the use of the mean and the variance as the only characteristics of interest of the probability distributions of rates of return. The first condition is that the distributions under consideration can be completely specified by two or fewer parameters.[14] If this condition is met, then the mean and the variance can serve as the two parameters to be used to evaluate alternatives with different probability distributions. The second condition that would permit use of mean and variance as the sole choice criteria is if the individual's utility function is quadratic.

Even if a utility function is not quadratic, it may be that it can be approximated by a quadratic function. In this case, mean and variance may be reasonably good guides to selection of distributions. To see how such an approximation works and also to provide insight into the problem, let us take a Taylor series expansion of $U(Y)$ at an arbitrary point $h$ within the range of possible dollar outcomes:

[14] Strictly speaking, this condition is sufficient only for concave utility functions (for individuals who are risk averse over the entire range of outcomes) and for two-parameter distributions for which the mean and variance are independent. See M. S. Feldstein, Mean-Variance Analysis in the Theory of Liquidity Preference and Portfolio Selection, *Review of Economic Studies*, January 1969; and G. Hanoch and H. Levy, The Efficiency Analysis of Choices Involving Risk, *Review of Economic Studies*, July 1969.

$$U(Y) = U(h) + U'(h)(Y - h) + \frac{U''(h)}{2!}(Y - h)^2 + \frac{U'''(h)}{3!}(Y - h)^3 + \cdots \quad (5\text{-}7)$$

From basic calculus we know that the Taylor series expansion of a function is a way of approximating that function to any desired degree of accuracy, depending on the number of terms of the series and the choice of $h$. $U(h)$ is simply the value of the function at $h$. $U'(h)$ is the first derivative of $U(Y)$, $dU/dY$, evaluated at point $h$; therefore, it is a number characteristic of the function. Similarly, $U''(h)$ is the second derivative evaluated at $h$; $U'''(h)$ is the third derivative; and the terms can be continued in like fashion using higher-order derivatives. Since the derivatives evaluated at point $h$ are all numbers, we can replace them with symbols representing the constants. That is, we can express Eq. (5-7) as

$$U(Y) + a_0 + a_1(Y - h) + a_2(Y - h)^2 + a_3(Y - h)^3 + \cdots \quad (5\text{-}8)$$

Two items of interest arise here. First, suppose $h$ is set at zero *and* the original function was a quadratic. What does (5-8) look like in terms of the original quadratic? Answer: it is identical (proof is left to the reader). Second, at least conceptually, we can imagine finding that value of $h$ which minimizes the contribution to (5-8) of terms involving third and higher powers of $Y$. Consequently, we can consider a quadratic utility function to be an approximation of any utility function. How good that approximation is depends on how similar the function is to a quadratic; but so long as the real function looks something like the one shown in Fig. 5-1, we can have reasonable confidence in the ability of the approximation to make general discriminations among alternatives.

If a quadratic approximation is not assumed, Eq. (5-8) can be used to gain insight into the characteristics of probability distributions relevant to individuals. Recalling that Eq. (5-8) holds for any $h$, suppose $h$ is set equal to zero and we take the expected value of $U(\tilde{Y})$:

$$E[U(\tilde{Y})] = a_0 + a_1E[\tilde{Y}] + a_2E[\tilde{Y}^2] + a_3E[\tilde{Y}^3] + \cdots \quad (5\text{-}9)$$

where $a_0 = U(0)$
$a_1 = U'(0)$
$a_2 = [U''(0)]/2!$
$a_3 = [U'''(0)]/3!$, etc.

The expected utility of any alternative can be expressed, therefore, as a function of the moments of the probability distribution of returns. The number of moments that must be considered depends on the utility function (the $a$ terms), how good an approximation is desired, and the characteristics of the probability distribution. As for the latter point, suppose, for example, that a good approximation would require consideration of the first six moments of a distribution because of the complexity of the utility function. However, if the probability distributions of returns for all alternatives being considered are normal, the third through sixth moments can all be expressed in terms of the first two moments and thus we need only evaluate those two.[15]

Thus, in general, one must look at more characteristics of probability distributions than their means and variances. This raises an interesting philosophical point. Is it appropriate to think about financial decisions as making "tradeoffs between risk and return." More properly, it would seem that in general the decisions involve a comparison of alternatives along many dimensions and that the final choice should be based on a complex weighing of pros and cons.

## SUMMARY

The expected utility model introduced in this chapter provides a way to view the choices of individuals in risky situations. According to the model, if individuals are rational and consistent in their decisions or wish to be so in the sense of some general conditions, they will or should choose the alternative that has a maximum expected value for their utility index. An example of such an index was developed; it implied that the only characteristics of risky investments of concern to individuals who had utility indices of this type (quadratic) would be the expected value and standard deviation of the rate of return on the investments. Moreover, it was suggested that such an index may serve as an approximation to the utility indices of many individuals.

[15] The number of moments that must be considered depends on the information required to completely specify the distribution. The normal distribution can be completely specified by the first two moments. However, in order to be able to *choose* among normal distributions on the basis of mean and variance without knowing the coefficients in the utility function, the function must meet some regularity conditions. See the preceding footnote.

APPENDIX

# FIVE A

## THE INDIVIDUAL'S CONSUMPTION-INVESTMENT DECISION

Individuals seek to maximize the benefits from their lifetime consumption, i.e., to maximize their happiness over time. In the single-period case (with times 0 and 1 being one period apart), their decision is that of allocating their existing wealth between current consumption and consumption one period hence. Consumption one period hence is equal to the part of wealth that is invested at time 0 plus the amount earned on that investment.[16] Defining $C_0$ and $\tilde{C}_1$ as consumption at times 0 and 1, respectively, the investor maximizes expected utility $E[U(C_0,\tilde{C}_1)]$ [signified as $\epsilon(\tilde{C})$], where

$$E[U(C_0,\tilde{C}_1)] \equiv \epsilon(\tilde{C}) = E\{U[C_0, (W_0 - C_0)(1 + \tilde{r})]\} = E[U(C_0, \tilde{W}_1)]$$

$W_0$ and $\tilde{W}_1$ are wealth at times 0 and 1, and $\tilde{r}$ is the rate of return earned on the investment of $W_0 - C_0$, that rate of return being a random variable. $W_0$ is the market value at time 0 of the individual's present and future income from both human (labor) and nonhuman assets.[17] All $\tilde{W}_1$ is consumed at time 1 in this single-period model.

[16] If $(C_0, \tilde{C}_1)$ is to include all the individual's consumption, $W_0$ must include the time 0 market value of the individual's entire income stream at times 0 and 1 including that from labor. This is necessary because consumption at time 1 is $(W_0 - C_0)(1 + \tilde{r})$, that is, includes only that which can be purchased from invested wealth at time 0. If the individual can borrow on human capital, then it is included in $W_0$ and the part of it not borrowed against to enhance $C_0$ produces income for consumption at time 1.

[17] That is, $W_0$ is the total cash proceeds individuals would receive if they combined their time 0 income with the proceeds they could obtain by selling all their other nonhuman assets and sold their time 1 human income (i.e., offered to pay someone their entire time 1 labor income in exchange for a given amount at time 0). Not selling one's time 1 labor income can be viewed as an investment in one's own human capital. This income, like the income from nonhuman capital, can be uncertain; that is, the returns from human capital can be stochastic.

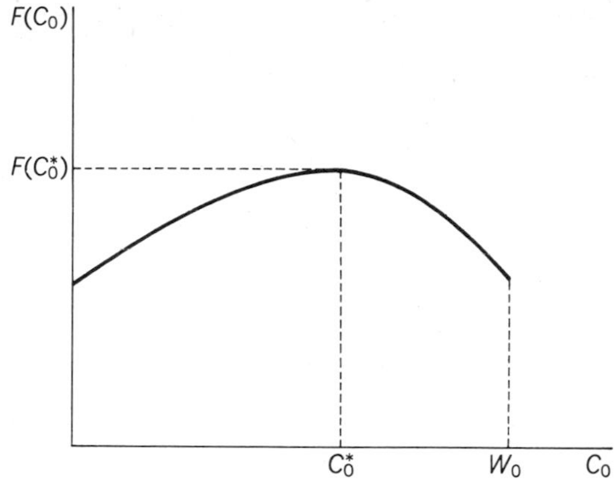


figure 5A-1

For each level of $C_0$, there is a particular maximum level of $\epsilon(\tilde{C})$ that can be achieved by appropriately selecting from the available set of investments. That is, for any given level of $C_0$, there is some portfolio of investments that maximizes $\epsilon(\tilde{C})$, that is, provides the most desirable distribution of $\tilde{W}_1$ for that given level of $C_0$ and given level of $W_0$. Define this maximum value of $\epsilon(\tilde{C})$ as $F(C_0)$. $F(C_0)$ states the maximum level of expected utility $\epsilon(\tilde{C})$ achievable for each level of $C_0$. $F(C_0)$ is shown in Fig. 5A-1. Assuming that $F(C_0)$ is a strictly concave function of $C_0$, that is, has a unique maximum as in the figure, the $C_0$ that provides the individual with the highest expected utility is $C_0^*$ in Fig. 5A-1. At $C_0^*$, the individual is able to attain the highest expected utility of consumption over time given the investment opportunities and initial wealth available at time 0. Therefore, $F(C_0^*) = \max \epsilon(\tilde{C})$. It follows that individuals set $C_0$ equal to $C_0^*$ in order to maximize their expected utility.

To determine $F(C_0)$, the individual must determine the maximum expected utility achievable for each level of $C_0$. $F(C_0)$ therefore depends on the distributions of $\tilde{W}_1$ that are possible from the investment opportunities available. For any given $W_0$ and $C_0$, there is a unique relationship between the rate of return on investment $\tilde{r}$ and $W_1$, since $W_1 = (W_0 - C_0)(1 + \tilde{r})$. Therefore, expected utility as a function of the distribution of $W_1$ for any $C_0$ can be expressed as a function of the distribution of $\tilde{r}$ for that $C_0$ as we showed in Chap. 5. Define the expected utility for $\tilde{r}$, for a given $W_0$ and $C_0$, as $\epsilon(\tilde{r})$. The objective for any *given* $C_0$ is to maximize $\epsilon(\tilde{r})$—to choose the investment and strategy that provide the distribution of $\tilde{r}$ which maximizes expected utility.

APPENDIX

# FIVE B

## QUADRATIC UTILITY FUNCTIONS

In the body of Chap. 5 quadratic utility functions that have the form

$$U(Y) = A + BY + CY^2 \tag{5B-1}$$

were suggested to be a reasonable approximation for individuals who have concave utility functions. The argument for the reasonableness of the approximation was based on the condition that individual utility functions are applicable only in the context of a particular decision situation. By "particular decision situation" we mean that the probability distributions of the outcomes of alternative courses of action (e.g., investments) are given, as are the circumstances of individuals—their wealth, health, tastes, etc. In other words, a given utility function is appropriate in general only at the time at which it is determined. In addition we limit the analysis to problems in which the relevant outcomes occur one period from the time of the decision. Although these are fairly restrictive conditions, they are sufficient for the development of the theory in the next three chapters.

Quadratic utility functions do have properties, however, that are not especially appealing from an economic point of view. One of these properties makes it necessary to impose a joint restriction on the coefficients in the utility function and on the maximum value obtainable from investment.

We begin by noting that higher monetary values or rates of return should probably be associated with larger values of "utility." Individuals are generally assumed to prefer more wealth to less. However, quadratic functions have the mathematical property of obtaining a maximum (or minimum) at some point.

Suppose that the utility function for a risk-averse individual is expressed as a quadratic function in *rates of return* as discussed in the text.[18]

$$U(r) = a + br - cr^2 \tag{5B-2}$$

where $a$, $b$, and $c$ are constants greater than zero. This function takes on a maximum value. The value of $r$ at the maximum value of $U(r)$ can be found by setting the derivative of the function to zero; that is,

$$\frac{d\,U(r)}{dr} = b - 2cr = 0$$

Now solve for $r^*$, the value of $r$ at which $U(r)$ is maximized:

$$b - 2cr^* = 0$$

$$r^* = \frac{b}{2c} \tag{5B-3}$$

In order for the utility function to be always increasing with $r$, no outcome can have a rate of return greater than $b/2c$. This means that the maximum rate of return available, $r_m$, must be less than or equal to $b/2c$:

$$r_m \leq \frac{b}{2c} \tag{5B-4}$$

The condition stated by (5B-4) is a joint condition on the utility function and the outcomes from investment. Given $r_m$, a value for the ratio $b/2c$ less than $r_m$ would imply decreasing utility for rates of return between $r^*$ and $r_m$. Alternatively, given the ratio $b/2c$, a rate of return greater than $r^*$ would have a lower value for $u(r)$ than the value at $r^*$. This means that if the maximum rate of return is very large, so must be the ratio $b/2c$. For the sample utility function in the body of Chap. 5, $r^* = .50/.30 = 1.67$ or 167%.

There are some interesting aspects to the problem as developed so far. First, we might note that $b$ indicates in a general sense the "preference for rates of return" and that $c$ is related to the "degree of risk aversion." This is an intuitive description of the effect of these two parameters and is not completely accurate, since the two parameters jointly describe the preferences of the individual.[19] However, with this description in mind we might then ask under what conditions will a quadratic utility function be appropriate if outcomes conform to common continuous probability distributions such as the normal distribution. The normal distribution ranges from $\pm\infty$; that is, the maximum rate of

[18] See eq. (5-3). The formulation here differs from that of the body of the chapter in that $c$ is assumed to be a positive constant. Given risk aversion on the part of the individual, the coefficient associated with the term $r^2$ is negative; that is, $-c$.

[19] For risk-indifferent individuals ($c = 0$) the value chosen for $b$ is arbitrary and does not affect the choices implied for the individual. Such individuals would always choose the alternative that has the highest expected return. A measure of risk aversion more correct than $c$ is $2c/(b - 2cr)$. See Appendix 5C.

return goes to infinity. Consequently, if condition (5B-4) is to hold, either $b$ must be infinitely large or $c$ must be zero. An infinite value for $b$ does not make sense, and if $c$ equals zero, the individual is not averse to risk. Therefore, quadratic utility functions are likely to be poor approximations for the utility functions of risk-averse individuals when the outcomes can take on extremely large values.

A second difficulty with quadratic utility is its inherently limited flexibility in describing the preferences of individuals. The value of $r^* = b/2c$ for an individual is sufficient information to permit us to tell which of any two alternatives will be preferred, given the expected returns and variances of the alternatives. In other words, only a single number, $r^*$, is needed to completely specify the choices that will be made by an individual. This fact can be shown as follows.

The choice between alternatives is assumed to be based on the criterion of maximizing the expected value of $U(\tilde{r})$. Therefore, given two alternatives I and II, I will be preferred to II if and only if

$$E[U(\tilde{r}_{\text{I}})] > E[U(\tilde{r}_{\text{II}})] \tag{5B-5}$$

The expected value of $U(\tilde{r})$ can be expressed for any distribution of $\tilde{r}$ as

$$E[U(\tilde{r})] = a + b\bar{r} - c(\sigma^2 + \bar{r}^2) \tag{5B-6}$$

Define $m^2$ as

$$m^2 \equiv \sigma^2 + \bar{r}^2 \tag{5B-7}$$

Then Eq. (5B-6) can be written

$$E[U(\tilde{r})] = a + b\bar{r} - cm^2 \tag{5B-8}$$

We can then state (5B-5) as

$$a + b\bar{r}_{\text{I}} - cm_{\text{I}}^2 > a + b\bar{r}_{\text{II}} - cm_{\text{II}}^2 \tag{5B-9}$$

Subtracting $a$ from both sides of (5B-9),

$$b\bar{r} - cm_{\text{I}}^2 > b\bar{r}_{\text{II}} - cm_{\text{II}}^2 \tag{5B-10}$$

Dividing both sides by $c$, we get

$$\frac{b}{c}\,\bar{r}_{\text{I}} - m_{\text{I}}^2 > \frac{b}{c}\,r_{\text{II}} - m_{\text{II}}^2 \tag{5B-11}$$

Rearranging terms, we arrive at

$$\frac{b}{c} > \frac{m_{\text{I}}^2 - m_{\text{II}}^2}{\bar{r}_{\text{I}} - \bar{r}_{\text{II}}} \tag{5B-12}$$

If expression (5B-12) holds, alternative I will be preferred. Therefore, in order to know whether this is true, we need only know the ratio of $b/c$ (which can be determined easily from $b/2c$) and the expected values and variances of the distributions of $\tilde{r}_{\text{I}}$ and $\tilde{r}_{\text{II}}$.

Since we would generally think that individual preferences are too complex to be adequately described by a single number ($b/c$ or $b/2c$), this result makes quadratic utility less appealing as a general characteristic of individuals. The approximation may be fairly rough. However, as noted earlier in the chapter, the use of expected values and variances does not rely solely on assumptions of quadratic utility. These two parameters may be sufficient to characterize the outcomes from financial decisions and thus the quadratic utility assumption may not be necessary.

APPENDIX

# FIVE C

# PROPERTIES OF UTILITY FUNCTIONS[20]

An individual's utility function reflects that person's preferences; the shape of the function is likely to vary from person to person. However, it is possible to limit the possible shapes that utility functions may have based on assumptions regarding what is reasonable economic behavior for people. In this appendix we examine some general mathematical attributes of utility functions and discuss their economic interpretation.

## BASIC PROPERTIES

Let $u(x)$ represent the utility function of a hypothetical person. The variable $x$ is measured in dollars and may be either wealth or income (change in wealth) at this point of the discussion. We assume that the function $u(x)$ is such that the first and higher-order derivatives exist. The first derivative is denoted as $u'(x)$, the second derivative as $u''(x)$, and so forth.

Consider the algebraic sign of the first derivative; what is its significance? If $u'(x)$ is greater than zero (its sign is positive), then the function $u(x)$ must be increasing as $x$ increases. Since larger values of utility represent greater satisfaction to the individual, positive values for $u'(x)$ mean that the person prefers more dollars to fewer. Conversely, negative values for $u'(x)$ imply decreasing utility as the dollars of wealth or income increase. The usual economic assumption regarding individuals is that more is preferred to less and therefore

$$u'(x) > 0 \qquad \text{for all } x \tag{5C-1}$$

[20] See Kenneth Arrow, "Essays in the Theory of Risk-Bearing," chap. 4, Markham Publishing Co., Chicago, 1971, for an alternative development.

The economic assumption that more money is preferred to less requires that the first derivative of the utility function always be positive.

Consider now the algebraic sign of the second derivative $u''(x)$. The second derivative has to do with the curvature of the utility function and, as we shall see, the individual's attitude toward risk. As we remarked on page 94, a linear utility function would imply that the person is indifferent to risk. The equivalent mathematical implication is that the second derivative equals zero. In general we can say that

| | |
|---|---|
| $u''(x) > 0$ | implies risk preference |
| $u''(x) = 0$ | implies risk indifference |
| $u''(x) < 0$ | implies risk aversion |

Figure 5C-1 illustrates the general shapes of utility functions corresponding to each of the three alternative assumptions regarding individual attitudes toward risk. Each function shown has a positive first derivative. For illustrative purposes the functions are scaled to have the same value at the point where they intersect the vertical axis. This point need not be where $x = 0$. We discuss the significance of the second derivative to risk aversion in more detail in the next section. For now we note only that the customary economic assumption is that people are generally risk averse. This assumption therefore requires that

$$u''(x) < 0 \qquad \text{for all } x \tag{5C-2}$$

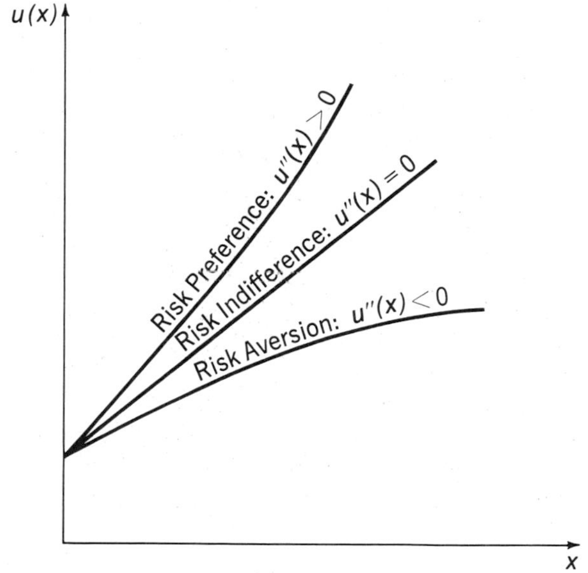


**figure 5C-1**

As an exercise, it would be useful to the reader to examine the general quadratic utility function of Appendix 5B, Eq. (5B-1), and work through the implications of conditions (5C-1) and (5C-2) for the coefficients in the function.

The third derivative, $u'''(x)$, indicates the individual's attitudes toward skewness. A positive value of $u'''(x)$ indicates a preference for positive skewness and vice versa. See Eq. (5-9) to verify this point. The third derivative is usually assumed to be positive; however, a complete economic interpretation is somewhat complex and is discussed as part of the next section. The higher-order derivatives (fourth and beyond) are virtually unexplored territory.

## MEASURING THE DEGREE OF RISK AVERSION[21]

Given that individuals are assumed to be risk averse [condition (5C-2) holds], the next interesting question is how to measure the degree or strength of risk aversion. To do this we need first consider the "risk premium," denoted as RP, of a gamble. We define the risk premium as the difference between the expected value of a gamble and its certainty equivalent. Recall that the certainty equivalent of a gamble is the amount a person would have to receive with certainty so as to be indifferent between having either that amount or the gamble. The certainty equivalent of a risky gamble is always less than the expected value of the gamble for a risk-averse person. (See page 95.) Therefore, risk premiums are always positive for risk-averse people. In the examples on pages 92 and 93, the certainty equivalent for the gamble with a \$0 expected value was $-\$250$; therefore, the risk premium for this gamble would be

$$\text{RP} = \text{expected value} - \text{certainty equivalent} \tag{5C-3}$$

$$\text{RP} = \$0 - (-\$250) = \$250$$

The certainty equivalent for the gamble having an expected value of \$600 was \$400; therefore, the risk premium for this gamble is \$200.

For a given gamble, the more risk-averse an individual is, the larger will be the risk premium. Thus, if we can derive a measure of the risk premium in terms of the general mathematical characteristics of the utility function, we obtain a measure of the degree of risk aversion.

First note that from the definition of a certainty equivalent, the utility of the certainty equivalent must equal the expected utility of the gamble. That is, both utility values must be equal for a person to be indifferent between the certainty equivalent and the gamble. But by the definition of the risk premium, Eq. (5C-3), the certainty equivalent of a gamble equals the expected value of the gamble minus the risk premium. Define a gamble with monetary outcomes $\tilde{G}$ and expected value $\bar{G}$; then

[21] This section is based on John Pratt, Risk Aversion in the Small and in the Large, *Econometrica*, vol. 32, pp. 122–136, January–April 1964.

Utility of certainty equivalent = expected utility of $\tilde{G}$

$$u(\overline{G} - \text{RP}) = E[u(\tilde{G})] \tag{5C-4}$$

Now take the Taylor series expansions of $u(x)$ around $\overline{G}$, the expected value of $\tilde{G}$, for each side of Eq. (5C-4). (See pages 97 and 98. We are setting $h = \overline{G}$, which is permissible since $\overline{G}$ is a number given the gamble $\tilde{G}$.)

$$u(\overline{G} - \text{RP}) = u(\overline{G}) - \text{RP}u'(\overline{G}) + \text{RP}^2 \frac{u''(\overline{G})}{2} + \cdots \tag{5C-5}$$

Also,

$$u(\tilde{G}) = u(\overline{G}) + (\tilde{G} - \overline{G})\, u'(\overline{G}) + (\tilde{G} - \overline{G})^2 \frac{u''(\overline{G})}{2} + \cdots \tag{5C-6}$$

The expected value of $u(\tilde{G})$, using Eq. (5C-6) and taking the expected value of both sides of the equation, is

$$E[u(\tilde{G})] = u(\overline{G}) + \text{var}\,[\tilde{G}]\frac{u''(\overline{G})}{2} + \cdots \tag{5C-7}$$

since $E[(\tilde{G} - \overline{G})] = \overline{G} - \overline{G} = 0$ and $E[(\tilde{G} - \overline{G})^2] = \text{var}\ [\tilde{G}]$. Using Eqs. (5C-5) and (5C-7) to substitute for the terms in (5C-4) and rearranging, we obtain

$$\text{RP} = \left[\frac{-u''(\overline{G})}{u'(\overline{G})}\right]\frac{\text{var}\,[\tilde{G}]}{2} + \text{other terms} \tag{5C-8}$$

For "small" gambles (the central moments of $\tilde{G}$ are small relative to the mean), the "other terms" are small; therefore, the risk premium is approximately equal to minus the ratio of the first two derivatives of the utility function times half the variance of the gamble. Observe that our conditions (5C-1) and (5C-2) above imply a positive value for the quantity $[-u''(\overline{G})/u'(\overline{G})]$, and hence a positive risk premium for any risky venture. Note that the magnitude of the risk premium required for a gamble with a given variance depends on the *ratio* of the derivatives, not just the size of the second derivative.

The above analysis provides us with a measure of the degree of risk aversion, "absolute risk aversion," $R_a$ where, in general[22]

$$\text{Absolute risk aversion} = R_a = \frac{-u''(x)}{u'(x)} \tag{5C-9}$$

This measure permits us to compare, at least in concept, the degree of risk aversion of two different people or the same person at two different points in time. That is, if individual $A$ has a larger value of absolute risk aversion than individual $B$, individual $A$ is more averse to risk in the sense that $A$ will require a

[22] The derivatives in Eq. (5C-8) are being evaluated at the point $\overline{G}$. Equation (5C-9) provides the general expression for the absolute-risk-aversion measure evaluated at any point $x$.

greater premium for a given gamble than $B$. Thus the ability to measure the degree of risk aversion possessed by different people provides the potential for empirical investigations of utility functions.[23]

A second and related measure of risk aversion is called "relative" or "proportional" risk aversion. This measure evaluates the degree of risk aversion for risks measured as a proportion of wealth or of the size of the gamble. We develop relative risk aversion from the measure of absolute risk aversion in the following way.

Consider the relative or proportional risk premium, RRP, for gambles with $\overline{G} > 0$, where

$$\text{RRP} = \frac{\text{RP}}{\overline{G}} \tag{5C-10}$$

Thus we are expressing the dollar risk premium RP as a proportion of the expected value of the gamble $\overline{G}$. Using (5C-8) to substitute into (5C-10),

$$\text{RRP} = \frac{-u''(\overline{G})}{u'(\overline{G})} \frac{\text{var}\,(\tilde{G})}{2\overline{G}} + \frac{\text{other terms}}{\overline{G}} \tag{5C-11}$$

Here again the "other terms" will be ignored. Express the outcomes of the gamble in relative terms:

$$\tilde{g} = \frac{\tilde{G}}{\overline{G}} \tag{5C-12}$$

then $\text{var}\,[\tilde{g}] = \text{var}\,[\tilde{G}]/\overline{G}^2$, or

$$\text{var}\,[\tilde{G}] = \text{var}\,[\tilde{g}]\overline{G}^2 \tag{5C-13}$$

From (5C-11) and (5C-13), we can express the relative risk premium as (assuming "other terms" are small)

$$\text{RRP} = (R_a\overline{G})\ \text{var}\,[\tilde{g}] \tag{5C-14}$$

For a "relative" gamble, $\tilde{g}$, we have a measure of relative risk aversion, $R_r$, where, from (5C-14)

$$R_r = R_a\overline{G} \tag{5C-15}$$

or, in general, using the form of Eq. (5C-9)

$$\begin{aligned} R_r &= xR_a \\ &= -xu''(x)/u'(x) \end{aligned} \tag{5C-16}$$

This relative measure of risk aversion is more widely used in theoretical and empirical work than the absolute measure $R_a$. In any case both measures are important.

[23] An excellent review of the literature and empirical study is Irwin Friend and Marshall Blume, The Demand for Risky Assets, *American Economic Review*, vol. 65, pp. 900–922, December 1975. The primary measure of risk aversion discussed in this paper is relative risk aversion, which is presented next.

## RISK AVERSION AND WEALTH

Most of the theoretical and empirical literature on the subject of utility functions and risk aversion is based on a somewhat different model for individual utility than the one presented in Chap. 5. The development so far in this Appendix applies to both models; however, it is useful at this point to examine the problem more deeply. Assume that an individual possesses a utility function $u(W)$ defined in terms of wealth ($W$) rather than income ($Y$) as presented earlier in Chap. 5. The results developed so far in this appendix all apply provided that we interpret the outcomes of the gamble $\tilde{G}$ as being alternative levels of wealth and that the expected value of $\tilde{G}$, $\overline{G}$, equals current wealth. Given these assumptions, we can make some further observations and analysis.

## INVESTMENT IN RISKY ASSETS

First let us consider the following problem.[24] An individual with current wealth (assets) $A$ is considering how to divide these assets between investments which offer a riskless rate of return of $i$ and risky investments (stock) which provide an uncertain rate of return $\tilde{r}$. Let $S$ be the amount invested in risky assets. Then the wealth of the individual one period hence is a random variable $\tilde{W}$, where

$$\begin{aligned}\tilde{W} &= (A - S)(1 + i) + S(1 + \tilde{r}) \\ &= A(1 + i) + S(\tilde{r} - i) \qquad \text{(5C-17)}\end{aligned}$$

Assume that the utility function is defined in terms of wealth one period from now. The individual will, by the expected utility hypothesis, invest an amount $S^*$ which maximizes the expected value of the utility function $u(\tilde{W})$. Therefore, the individual's problem is to find that amount $S^*$ which maximizes $E[u(\tilde{W})]$, given $i$ and the probability distribution of $\tilde{r}$. From (5C-17)

$$E[u(\tilde{W})] = E[u(A(1 + i) + S(\tilde{r} - i))] \qquad \text{(5C-18)}$$

Define $Q(S) = E[u(\tilde{W})]$; then a maximum for expected utility will be obtained at

$$Q'(S) = \frac{dQ}{dS} = 0 \qquad \text{provided that} \qquad Q''(S) = \frac{d^2Q}{dS^2} < 0$$

But

$$Q'(S) = \frac{d(E[u(\tilde{W})])}{dS} = E\left[\frac{du}{dS}\right]$$

from the properties of mathematical expectations, and using the chain rule for derivatives

$$Q'(S) = E\left[\frac{du}{d\tilde{W}}\frac{d\tilde{W}}{dS}\right]$$

[24] The development corresponds approximately to that of Arrow, *op. cit.*, pp. 98–101.

Since

$$\frac{du}{d\tilde{W}} = u'(\tilde{W}) \qquad \text{and} \qquad \frac{d\tilde{W}}{dS} = \tilde{r} - i$$

we obtain

$$Q'(S) = E[u'(\tilde{W})(\tilde{r} - i)] \tag{5C-19}$$

Taking the derivative of (5C-19) in the same fashion, we obtain

$$Q''(S) = E[u''(\tilde{W})(\tilde{r} - i)^2] \tag{5C-20}$$

Examining (5C-20), we note that $(\tilde{r} - i)^2$ is always a number greater than or equal to zero. Furthermore, for risk-averse individuals, $u''(\tilde{W}) < 0$ for all $\tilde{W}$ as per condition (5C-2). Therefore, $Q''(S)$ must be less than zero (for $\tilde{r}$ not identically equal to $i$) and $Q'(S)$ is a decreasing function of $S$. This satisfies the requirement that a maximum for $Q(S)$ will be obtained for some value of $S$ denoted as $S^*$. There are two possibilities (provided that the amount invested in risky assets cannot be less than zero)—that no risky assets are held ($S^* = 0$) or that some risky assets are held ($S^* > 0$). Let us examine the first possibility, that $S^* = 0$.

If $S^* = 0$, then $Q'(0) \leq 0$ because we know that $Q'(S)$ is always decreasing and the maximum value for $Q$ is obtained at $Q'(S) = 0$ if $S$ cannot be less than zero. But at $S = 0$, $\tilde{W} = A(1 + i)$ and $u'(\tilde{W}) = u'(A(1 + i))$, which is a known amount greater than zero by (5C-1).

$$\begin{aligned} Q'(0) &= E[u'(A(1 + i))(\tilde{r} - i)] \\ &= u'(A(1 + i))(\bar{r} - i) \end{aligned} \tag{5C-21}$$

where $\bar{r}$ is the expected value of $\tilde{r}$. For $S^* = 0$, $Q'(0) \leq 0$; so

$$u'(A(1 + i))(\bar{r} - i) \leq 0$$

Since $u'(A(1 + i)) > 0$, then

$$(\bar{r} - i) \leq 0 \qquad \text{or} \qquad \bar{r} \leq i \tag{5C-22}$$

If it is optimal for an individual to own no risky assets ($S^* = 0$), the expected rate of return on the risky assets must be less than or equal to the rate that could be earned on riskless assets. An interesting aspect of this result is its converse, namely, that *regardless of how risk averse a person is, if the expected rate of return on risky assets* ($\bar{r}$) *is greater than the riskless rate* ($i$), *individuals will invest some part of their wealth in risky assets.* The optimal amount to be invested $S^*$ must satisfy the following equation:

$$Q'(S) = E[u'(\tilde{W})(\tilde{r} - i)] = 0 \tag{5C-23}$$

We cannot say much more at this point without making additional assumptions regarding the utility function.

We could have formulated the individual's problem in a slightly different way. Instead of asking what the *dollar* amount of investment in risky assets ($S$)

would be, we could ask what *fraction* or proportion ($f_S$) of wealth would be invested. That is,

$$f_S = \frac{S}{A} \tag{5C-24}$$

and Eq. (5C-17) can be written as

$$\tilde{W} = A(1 + i) + Af_S(\tilde{r} - i) \tag{5C-25}$$

The individual's problem is to find the value of $f_S$ that maximizes expected utility. The analysis proceeds as above except that the derivative of $Q$ is taken with respect to $f_S$ instead of $S$ and the resulting first-order condition for the optimal value of $f_S$ is

$$Q'(f_S) = E[u'(\tilde{W})A(\tilde{r} - i)] = 0 \tag{5C-26}$$

instead of (5C-23). We use this alternative model below. As an exercise, the reader may find it useful to develop Eq. (5C-26) from (5C-25).

## WEALTH-INVARIANT UTILITY FUNCTIONS

One assumption commonly made in the literature is that the utility function $u(W)$ is invariant with the current wealth ($A$) of the individual. That is, regardless of how much wealth the person possesses, the utility function describing the person's preferences is the same. Thus the outcomes of a given gamble measured as the resulting levels of wealth ($\tilde{G} = \tilde{W}$) will provide the same values $u(\tilde{G})$ for all $A$ and we can evaluate the behavior of the utility function as wealth, $W = A$, changes. This assumption is in addition to those made above, so that models based on wealth invariance are more restrictive regarding individual preferences and the results are less general than those presented earlier. Let us examine some of the implications of this assumption.

First, consider the measure of absolute risk aversion, Eq. (5C-9), rewritten in terms of the utility of wealth $u(\tilde{W})$.

$$R_a = -\frac{u''(\tilde{W})}{u'(\tilde{W})} \tag{5C-27}$$

We can ask how an individual's absolute risk aversion varies with the amount of wealth. Recall that the risk premium demanded for a given-sized gamble is proportional to $R_a$. As wealth increases, most economists would argue that the risk premium should either be constant or, even more likely, decrease. Thus the general view is that absolute risk aversion decreases with increased wealth.

If $R_a$ decreases with wealth, then the derivative of $R_a$ with respect to $\tilde{W}$ must be negative,

$$\frac{dR_a}{d\tilde{W}} = \frac{(-u'''(\tilde{W})u'(W) + u''(\tilde{W})^2)}{u'(\tilde{W})^2} < 0 \tag{5C-28}$$

Since by (5C-1) we have $u'(\tilde{W}) > 0$, it follows that the third derivative of the utility function $u'''(\tilde{W})$ must be positive for absolute risk aversion to decrease with wealth. In other words, decreasing absolute risk aversion implies a positive third derivative for the utility function. We should note, however, that having a positive third derivative is not sufficient to guarantee decreasing absolute risk aversion. If $u''(\tilde{W})^2$ is greater than $u'''(\tilde{W})u'(\tilde{W})$, then absolute risk aversion will increase regardless of $u'''(\tilde{W})$.

The hypothesis of decreasing absolute risk aversion places restrictions on the form of permissible wealth-invariant utility functions. For example, the quadratic is ruled out since quadratic utility functions in wealth exhibit increasing absolute risk aversion. This can be seen most easily by examining (5C-28) given that the third derivative of a quadratic function is zero. Therefore, $dR_a/d\tilde{W}$ must be greater than zero and $R_a$ increases with $\tilde{W}$. However, as we show below, quadratic utility cannot be ruled out by this hypothesis under the more general assumption that the utility function is dependent on the initial level of wealth.

The most important economic implication of decreasing absolute risk aversion is that individuals will increase their dollar investment in risky assets as their wealth increases. Indeed it is this implication that provides the strongest backing for the hypothesis of decreasing $R_a$. To prove this is so, we can use the model developed earlier, which is summarized by Eq. (5C-23):

$$Q'(S) = E[u'(\tilde{W})(\tilde{r} - i)] = 0 \qquad \text{(5C-23)}$$

Recall that this equation must be solved to determine the optimal value of $S$, the amount invested in risky assets. We now consider $Q'(S)$ as a joint function of $S$ and current wealth $A$. We would like to know how the optimal value of $S(S^*)$, as determined from (5C-23), behaves as $A$ varies. Thus we want to find the derivative of $S^*$ with respect to $A$ where $S^*$ is the solution to (5C-23). To do this, we differentiate (5C-23) as follows:

$$\frac{\partial Q'}{\partial S^*} dS^* + \frac{\partial Q'}{\partial A} dA = 0$$

$$\frac{dS^*}{dA} = -\frac{\partial Q'/\partial A}{\partial Q'/\partial S^*}$$

$$\frac{\partial Q'}{\partial S^*} = Q''(S) = E[u''(\tilde{W})(\tilde{r} - i)^2] \qquad \text{from (5C-20)}$$

$$\frac{\partial Q'}{\partial A} = E\left[\frac{\partial(u'(\tilde{W})(\tilde{r} - i))}{\partial \tilde{W}} \frac{\partial \tilde{W}}{\partial A}\right]$$

But

$$\frac{\partial(u'(\tilde{W})(\tilde{r} - i))}{\partial \tilde{W}} = u''(\tilde{W})(\tilde{r} - i)$$

and

$$\frac{\partial \tilde{W}}{\partial A} = (1 + i) \qquad \text{from (5C-17)}$$

so
$$\frac{\partial Q'}{\partial A} = E[u''(\tilde{W})(\tilde{r} - i)(1 + i)]$$

Therefore
$$\frac{dS^*}{dA} = -\frac{E[u''(\tilde{W})(\tilde{r} - i)(1 + i)]}{E[u''(\tilde{W})(\tilde{r} - i)^2]} \tag{5C-29}$$

We know that the denominator of the fraction in Eq. (5C-26) is always negative, as discussed in conjunction with Eq. (5C-20). Therefore, the algebraic sign of Eq. (5C-29) depends only on the sign of the numerator. If the numerator is positive, $dS^*/dA$ will be positive, and the amount invested in risky assets increases with wealth.

The sign of the numerator depends on whether absolute risk aversion increases or decreases with wealth. We shall show that if $R_a$ decreases with wealth, the numerator is positive. The proofs for constant and for increasing absolute risk aversion can be done as an exercise by the reader.

We begin by examining all outcomes involving $\tilde{r} > i$; that is, $\tilde{r} - i > 0$. In this case the resulting wealth levels $\tilde{W}$ of the individual will be greater than $A(1+i)$. Assume decreasing absolute risk aversion. Then (using brackets to indicate where $R_a$ is evaluated),

$$R_a[\tilde{W}] < R_a[A(1 + i)]$$

Using the definition of $R_a$,

$$-\frac{u''(\tilde{W})}{u'(\tilde{W})} < R_a[A(1 + i)]$$

$$u''(\tilde{W}) > -R_a[A(1 + i)]u'(\tilde{W})$$

Multiply both sides by $(\tilde{r} - i)(1 + i)$, a positive number which preserves the inequality; then

$$u''(\tilde{W})(\tilde{r} - i)(1 + i) > -R_a[A(1 + i)]u'(\tilde{W})(\tilde{r} - i)(1 + i) \tag{5C-30}$$

Now examine all outcomes involving $(\tilde{r} - i) \leq 0$. In this case the resulting wealth levels are less than or equal to $A(1 + i)$. Using a parallel procedure to the above

$$R_a[\tilde{W}] > R_a[A(1 + i)] \qquad \text{since } \tilde{W} < A(1 + i)$$

Thus

$$u''(\tilde{W}) < -R_a[A(1 + i)]u'(\tilde{W})$$

Multiplying both sides by $(\tilde{r} - i)(1 + i)$ now reverses the inequality since $(\tilde{r} - i)(1 + i) < 0$ by assumption. We arrive at

$$u''(\tilde{W})(\tilde{r} - i)(1 + i) \geq -R_a[A(1 + i)]u'(\tilde{W})(\tilde{r} - i)(1 + i) \tag{5C-31}$$

This result (5C-31) holds as (5C-30) with the strong inequality when $\tilde{r} > i$. Therefore, we can take the expected value of both sides of (5C-31) over the entire probability distribution of $\tilde{r}$.

$$E[u''(\tilde{W})(\tilde{r} - i)(1 + i)] > -R_a[A(1 + i)](1 + i)E[u'(\tilde{W})(\tilde{r} - i)]$$

But $E[u'(\tilde{W})(\tilde{r} - i)] = 0$ from the optimality condition Eq. (5C-23); therefore,

$$E[u''(\tilde{W})(\tilde{r} - i)(1 + i)] > 0$$

if absolute risk aversion is decreasing. Consequently, $dS^*/dA$ is positive and the amount invested in risky assets $S^*$ increases with wealth $A$.

So far we have not said very much about the other measure: relative risk aversion. The importance of this measure is that it concerns proportions rather than absolute amounts. Recall the alternative investment problem for an individual where the amount invested in risky assets was treated as a proportion or fraction of wealth. The optimal fraction is determined as a solution to (5C-26), as explained earlier.

$$Q'(f_S) = E[u'(\tilde{W})A(\tilde{r} - i)] = 0 \qquad \text{(5C-26)}$$

We shall now show, in a manner similar to the proofs for absolute risk aversion, that if *relative* risk aversion $R_r$ decreases with wealth ($A$), the *proportion* of wealth invested in risky assets ($f_S$) increases. The analysis for constant $R_r$ and increasing $R_r$ will be left as an exercise.

We proceed as before to differentiate (5C-28) in order to obtain $df_S^*/dA$.

$$\frac{\partial Q'}{\partial f_S^*}\, df_S^* + \frac{\partial Q'}{\partial A}\, dA = 0$$

$$\frac{df_S^*}{dA} = -\frac{\partial Q'/\partial A}{\partial Q'/\partial f_S^*} \qquad \text{(5C-32)}$$

and

$$\frac{\partial Q'}{\partial f_S^*} = Q''(f_S) \qquad \text{(5C-33)}$$

We know from earlier arguments that (5C-33) is always negative in sign. Therefore, here again, it is the sign of the numerator of (5C-32) which determines the sign of $df_S^*/dA$.

$$\frac{\partial Q'}{\partial A} = E\left[\frac{\partial(u'(\tilde{W})A(\tilde{r} - i))}{\partial \tilde{W}}\frac{\partial \tilde{W}}{\partial A}\right]$$

$$= E\left[u''(\tilde{W})A(\tilde{r} - i)\frac{d\tilde{W}}{dA}\right]$$

$$\frac{d\tilde{W}}{dA} = \frac{d[A(1 + i) + f_S A(\tilde{r} - i)]}{dA} \qquad \text{from (5C-25)}$$

$$= (1 + i) + f_S(\tilde{r} - i)$$

Therefore,

$$\frac{\partial Q'}{\partial A} = E[u''(\tilde{W})A(\tilde{r} - i)((1 + i) + f_S(\tilde{r} - i))] \qquad \text{(5C-34)}$$

To evaluate the sign of $\partial Q'/\partial A$, we begin by examining outcomes for which $\tilde{r} - i > 0$. Give that relative risk aversion $R_r$ is a decreasing function of wealth, we know that

$$R_r[\tilde{W}] < R_r[A(1 + i)] \qquad \text{since } \tilde{W} > A(1 + i) \text{ for } \tilde{r} - i > 0$$

From the definition of relative risk aversion we have

$$-\tilde{W}\frac{u''(\tilde{W})}{u'(\tilde{W})} < R_r[A(1 + i)]$$

Substituting for $\tilde{W}$ using (5C-25) and rearranging the inequality, we have

$$u''(\tilde{W})(A(1 + i) + Af_S(\tilde{r} - i)) > -R_r[A(1 + i)]u'(\tilde{W})$$

Multiply both sides by $(\tilde{r} - i)$, always positive at this point, and we obtain

$$u''(\tilde{W})A(\tilde{r} - i)\{(1 + i) + f_S(\tilde{r} - i)\} > -R_rA(1 + i)u'(\tilde{W})(\tilde{r} - i) \quad (5C\text{-}35)$$

We can repeat the argument for all outcomes $\tilde{r} - i \leq 0$ as we did earlier in examining the absolute investment in risky assets. If this is done, we also arrive at the inequality (5C-35). This is left as an exercise for the reader. Since (5C-35) applies for the entire probability distribution of $\tilde{r}$, we now take expected values of both sides and obtain

$$E[u''(\tilde{W})A(\tilde{r} - i)((1 + i) + f_S(\tilde{r} - i))] > -R_r[A(1 + i)]E[u'(\tilde{W})(\tilde{r} - i)] \quad (5C\text{-}36)$$

The left-hand side is $\partial Q'/\partial A$, as shown by Eq. (5C-34); the right-hand side is zero by the optimality condition of (5C-26) since

$$E[u'(\tilde{W})A(\tilde{r} - i)] = AE[u'(\tilde{W})(\tilde{r} - i)]$$

given $A > 0$, $E[u'(\tilde{W})(\tilde{r} - i)]$ must be zero to satisfy Eq. (5C-32). Since $\partial Q'/\partial A$ is positive, $df_S^*/dA$ is also positive and the optimal proportion of wealth devoted to risky assets increases with wealth.

Although there is general agreement that absolute risk aversion decreases with wealth, the behavior of relative risk aversion is an issue of some controversy. Note that constant or increasing absolute risk aversion implies increasing relative risk aversion and constant or decreasing relative risk aversion implies decreasing absolute risk aversion. However, it is also possible to have increasing relative risk aversion with decreasing absolute risk aversion. The controversy will require empirical studies to settle the issue, and we believe that there will be considerable attention to this topic for some time.

## QUADRATIC UTILITY AND RISK AVERSION

Earlier we indicated that a quadratic utility function which was invariant to the current wealth ($A$) of the individual exhibited increasing absolute (and relative) risk aversion. In the view of most economists this property alone of the quadratic makes it unacceptable as a general representation of people's behavior.[25]

[25] Of course, there are other problems, as explained in Appendix 5B.

This has important implications for the applicability of mean-variance analysis of risk. If the quadratic is not a reasonable approximation of individual preferences and if the probability distributions of the returns from investments are not approximately normal, then use of the mean and variance (or standard deviation) to evaluate the investments is not valid. However, the quadratic may be partially rescued from oblivion by recognizing that this criticism is based on the assumption of wealth invariance, which itself is restrictive of individual behavior.

First let us examine the version of the quadratic presented in Chap. 5. Recall that we defined outcomes of gambles not in terms of wealth, but rather as changes in wealth. If this function is invariant to current wealth, the present level of wealth does not affect the individual's evaluation of any given gamble. This means that the risk premium of a given gamble is the same regardless of the individual's wealth and, hence, that absolute risk aversion is constant for a wealth-invariant quadratic function of income. For example, an investment of \$1,000 to return \$900 with probability of 0.5 or \$1,200 with probability of 0.5 involves a change in wealth of either −\$100 with 0.5 probability or \$200 with 0.5 probability. In this utility function it does not matter whether the individual had \$10,000 to start with or \$100,000. The changes in wealth are the same in both cases, and those changes are the only results of consequence.

If, instead, the utility function is defined in terms of wealth, then the initial wealth position of the individual must be considered in defining the outcomes of the gamble. For a current wealth of \$10,000 and the above gamble, the individual faces a final wealth of \$9,900 or \$10,200 depending on the outcome. For a current wealth of \$100,000, the possible outcomes are \$99,900 and \$100,200. The hypothesis of decreasing absolute risk aversion implies that the gamble would be considered more favorably if the individual had \$100,000 instead of \$10,000 to start with. As we know, a wealth-invariant quadratic exhibits increasing absolute risk aversion so that the gamble would be viewed more favorably at the lower level of wealth.

However, individual preferences can be represented as quadratic in final wealth (or income) *and* exhibit decreasing absolute risk aversion with increasing current wealth. This can be done by simply assuming that one or more of the *coefficients* in the function are dependent on current wealth. That is, suppose we have a utility function in terms of final wealth of the general form

$$u(W) = f(A) + g(A)W + h(A)W^2 \qquad \text{(5C-37)}$$

For simplicity, assume $f(A) = 0$ and $g(A) = b$, a constant. The coefficient $h(A)$ varies with current wealth $A$. Suppose we assume $h(A) = -c/A$, where $c$ is a constant. Then we can express the utility function of (5C-37) as

$$u(W) = bW - \frac{c}{A}W^2 \qquad \text{(5C-38)}$$

Absolute risk aversion for this function is

$$R_a = -\frac{u''(W)}{u'(W)}$$
$$= \frac{2c/A}{b - (2c/A)W} \tag{5C-39}$$

At the point $W = A$, which is the only point along the utility function that matters here,

$$R_a = \frac{2c/A}{b - 2c} \tag{5C-40}$$

Clearly as current wealth $A$ increases, absolute risk aversion decreases. Relative risk aversion at point $A$ is a constant for all $A$.

$$R_r = A\left[\frac{2c/A}{b - 2c}\right]$$
$$= \frac{2c}{b - 2c} \tag{5C-41}$$

An individual with a utility function described by (5C-38) will be concerned only with the mean and variance of the outcomes of investments. If the individual's wealth increases, an increasing amount will be invested in risky assets as a constant proportion of wealth $A$ provided that the probability distribution of the rates of return on risky assets do not change.

Depending on the characteristics of $f(A)$, $g(A)$, and $h(A)$ in the utility function of Eq. (5C-37), the function may exhibit increasing or decreasing relative risk aversion and still maintain decreasing absolute risk aversion. Therefore, the relationship between utility and wealth can be described in many ways even with a simple quadratic.

There is a distinction between the issue of what utility function best describes the preferences of individuals toward alternative risky investments (given their current situation including their assets) and the question of how preferences change as wealth changes. We have shown that hypotheses about risk aversion and wealth are not sufficient grounds for adopting or excluding any model of preferences (including the quadratic) for a given current wealth. This entire area remains open for further research.

## SUGGESTED READINGS

Bernoulli, Daniel: Exposition of a New Theory on the Measurement of Risk, *Econometrica*, vol. 22, pp. 23–26, January 1954, reprinted in Archer, Stephen H. and Charles A. D'Ambrosio, "The Theory of Business Finance," 2d ed., The Macmillan Company, New York, 1976.

Ellsburg, D.: Classic and Current Notions of "Measurable Utility," *Economic Journal*, vol. 44, pp. 528–556, September 1954.

Friedman, Milton and Leonard J. Savage: The Utility Analysis of Choices Involving Risk, *Journal of Political Economy*, vol. 56, pp. 279–304, August 1948, reprinted in Archer, and D'Ambrosio, *op cit*.

Pratt, John W.: Risk Aversion in the Small and in the Large, *Econometrica*, vol. 32, pp. 122–136, January–April 1964, reprinted in Archer and D'Ambrosio, *op. cit*.

See also the Suggested Readings for chap. 4.

CHAPTER

# SIX

# INDIVIDUAL INVESTMENT DECISIONS: PORTFOLIO THEORY

In the preceding chapter we argued that the consequences of individual investment decisions could be evaluated using the expected return and standard deviation (or variance) as an approximation. In this chapter we shall explore the nature of investment decisions when that conclusion is appropriate. It should be noted at the outset, however, that the discussion in this chapter is based on the assumption that individuals like expected returns and dislike variance or standard deviation of returns and that these are the only characteristics of streams of concern to the individual. Other than rationality, we do not require any other particular assumptions about individuals.

## SECURITIES

The first issue of concern is how an individual selects the specific securities to be held during the current period. Assume that our only knowledge of the individual's attitudes toward risky investments is that for a given expected return the alternative with the minimum standard deviation will be preferred, and for a given standard deviation the alternative with the maximum expected return will be preferred. The standard deviation as a measure of risk will be used here rather than variance, for reasons that will become obvious later.

Consider the following situation. There are five different securities that have the following characteristics to be evaluated:

**table 6-1**

| *Security* | *Expected return* ($\bar{r}$) | *Standard deviation* ($\sigma$) |
|---|---|---|
| *A* | .05 | 0 |
| *B* | .10 | .08 |
| *C* | .22 | .20 |
| *D* | .10 | .18 |
| *E* | .15 | .20 |

If you were to choose only one of these securities, which would you pick? As an aid in answering that question suppose we plot the securities as in Fig. 6-1. By the assumption of attitudes made above, securities *D* and *E* are ruled out as choices because *B* offers less risk for the same return than *D* and security *C* offers more return than *E* and has the same risk. We are left with the choice among *A*, *B*, and *C*. If there are no other alternatives, nothing else could be said without knowing the utility function of the individual faced with these choices. However, people have the option of investing in more than one security and may also be able to borrow to finance additional investment. If so, then there are many more alternatives available even in this simple situation.

## DIVERSIFICATION AND PORTFOLIOS

A combination of securities is called a *portfolio*. Roughly speaking, *diversification* means investing in more than one risky asset. In later chapters we shall be

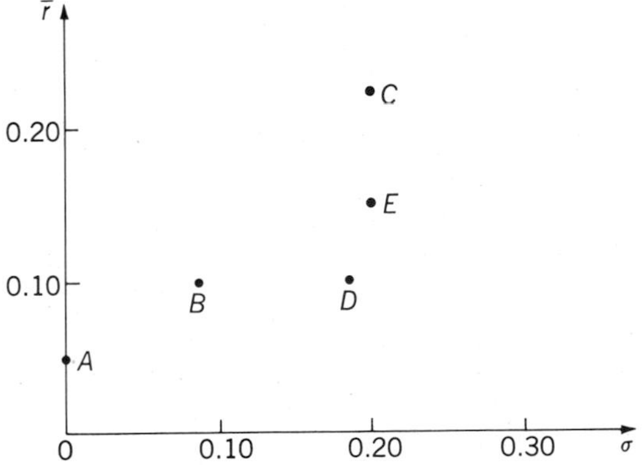


**figure 6-1**

interested in firm diversification decisions that involve changing the number of risky projects and activities engaged in by the firm; but here we are concerned with diversification by individuals in their acquisition of risky securities.

Let us examine the effects of holding a portfolio of securities $B$ and $C$. Let $x$ be the proportion of the total amount in the portfolio that is invested in $B$; $(1 - x)$ is the proportion invested in $C$. The rate of return realized on the portfolio ($\tilde{r}_P$) is a random variable and is a linear combination of the rates earned on $B$ and $C$, $\tilde{r}_B$ and $\tilde{r}_C$, respectively.

$$\tilde{r}_P = x\tilde{r}_B + (1 - x)\tilde{r}_C \tag{6-1}$$

The expected return on the portfolio is therefore

$$\bar{r}_P = x\bar{r}_B + (1 - x)\bar{r}_C \tag{6-2}$$

Since from Table 6-1 $\bar{r}_B = .10$ and $\bar{r}_C = .22$, $\bar{r}_P = .22 - .12x$. As we increase the proportion $x$ invested in $B$, we lower the expected return on the portfolio from that provided by $C$ (22%) at $x = 0$ to that provided by $B$ (10%) at $x = 1.0$.

In Chap. 4 we discussed the problem of finding the variance of a linear combination of random variables. The variance of a combination of two random variables depends on the variances of the two variables and their covariance or correlation [see Eq. (4-9)]. Equation (6-1) is a linear combination of the returns from securities $B$ and $C$. Applying the relationship developed in Chap. 4, the variance of the return on the portfolio can be expressed as

$$\sigma_P^2 = x^2\sigma_B^2 + (1 - x)^2\sigma_C^2 + 2x(1 - x)\,\text{cov}[\tilde{r}_B,\tilde{r}_C] \tag{6-3}$$

or

$$\sigma_P^2 = x^2\sigma_B^2 + (1 - x)^2\sigma_C^2 + 2x(1 - x)\rho_{BC}\sigma_B\sigma_C \tag{6-4}$$

where $\rho_{BC}$ is the correlation coefficient between $\tilde{r}_B$ and $\tilde{r}_C$. Let us now investigate the consequences of alternative assumptions as to the value of $\rho_{BC}$.

The correlation between two random variables can be any number between $-1.0$ and $1.0$. When $\rho_{BC}$ is 1.0, the returns on the two securities are perfectly correlated and Eq. (6-4) becomes

$$\begin{aligned}\sigma_P^2 &= x^2\sigma_B^2 + (1 - x)^2\sigma_C^2 + 2x(1 - x)\sigma_B\sigma_C \\ &= [x\sigma_B + (1 - x)\sigma_C]^2\end{aligned}$$

and

$$\sigma_P = x\sigma_B + (1 - x)\sigma_C \tag{6-5}$$

We can substitute the values for $\sigma_B = .08$ and $\sigma_C = .20$; so $\sigma_P = .2 - .12x$. As we increase our investment in $B$, $x$ increases and the risk of the portfolio is reduced. However, we pay for that reduction in risk with a proportional reduction in return. Figure 6-2$a$ shows the possible combinations of $\bar{r}_P$ and $\sigma_P$ when $\rho_{BC} = 1.0$ as we vary $x$. When the returns on the securities in the portfolio are perfectly correlated, there is a linear relationship between the expected return on the portfolio and its standard deviation.

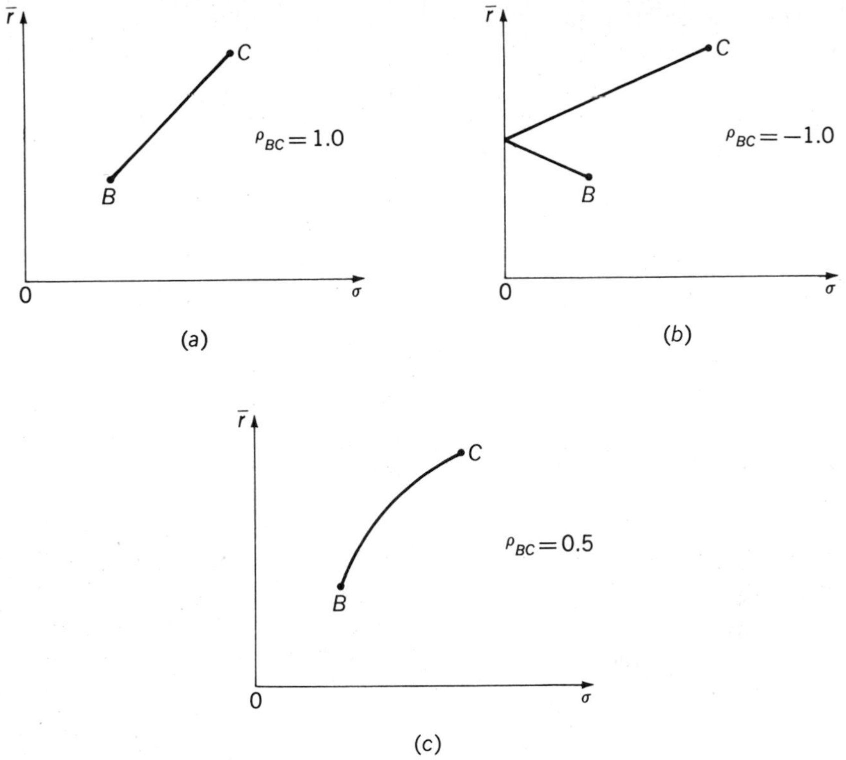


**figure 6-2**

Taking the other extreme value for $\rho_{BC} = -1.0$, the maximum benefit from diversification is possible. Substituting $\rho_{BC} = -1.0$ in Eq. (6-4), we get

$$\sigma_P^2 = x^2\sigma_B^2 + (1-x)^2\sigma_C^2 - 2x(1-x)\sigma_B\sigma_C$$
$$= [x\sigma_B - (1-x)\sigma_C]^2$$

and

$$\sigma_P = x\sigma_B - (1-x)\sigma_C \qquad (6\text{-}6)$$

Substituting the values of $\sigma_B$ and $\sigma_C$ into Eq. (6-6) and collecting terms, we arrive at $\sigma_P = .28x - .2$. It would appear that we can have "negative risk" when $x = 0$; however, this is not so, since the variance and standard deviation can never be less than zero. The standard deviation reaches zero as $x$ is reduced to $.2/.28 = .715$. The variance and standard deviation are zero at this point.[1] As

[1] The value for $x$ at the point where the variance of a portfolio of two perfectly negatively correlated securities reaches zero is $x_0 = \sigma_C/(\sigma_B + \sigma_C)$, where $\sigma_C > \sigma_B$.

$x$ is reduced further, the variance begins to increase and the *positive* square root of the variance, the standard deviation, is given by $(1 - x)\sigma_C - x\sigma_B = .2 - .28x$ and also increases. The important fact here is that the standard deviation is zero when $x = .715$; this is the point of maximum benefit from diversification. The relationship between $\bar{r}_P$ and $\sigma_P$ for this case of perfect negative correlation is displayed in Fig. 6-2*b*. It would be very nice if we could find in the market securities that have perfect negative correlation; however, as we shall see in Chap. 7, such securities would provide very low rates of return in equilibrium markets.

Compared to the cases above, most securities are not perfectly correlated, either negatively or positively, but have correlations between $-1.0$ and 1.0. In fact it is difficult to find securities whose returns, based on past history, have correlations with one another that are less than zero; most securities are positively correlated. Suppose the two securities have a correlation of .5. Even in this case there will be some benefits from diversification. If the values of the standard deviation and correlation coefficient of $B$ and $C$ are substituted into Eq. (6-4), we have $\sigma_P^2 = .0304x^2 - .064x + .04$ or $\sigma_P = (.0304x^2 - .064x + .04)^{1/2}$. If $\bar{r}_P$ and $\sigma_P$ are then plotted for different values of $x$, the results are as shown in Fig. 6-2*c*. The effect of diversification in this case is that as $x$ is increased (i.e., hold more $B$) risk is reduced proportionally more than is return, at least initially.

In general we can say that diversification is the more beneficial the lower the correlation between the returns of the securities in the portfolio. We generally expect correlation between securities to be less than 1.0 but greater than 0; therefore, the expected return and standard deviation of alternative two-security portfolios should plot on a curve that looks like Fig. 6-2*c*.

The analysis for two securities can be easily extended to many securities using the results developed in Chap. 4. Instead of having a linear combination of two random variables, we have a linear combination of $n$ random variables. If $\bar{r}_i$ is the expected rate of return on security i, and $x_i$ is the proportion of the total portfolio invested in that security, then the expected rate of return on the portfolio from Eq. (4-10) is

$$\bar{r}_P = \sum_{i=1}^{n} x_i \bar{r}_i \tag{6-7}$$

If $\sigma_i$ is the standard deviation of the returns from security i, and $\rho_{ij}$ is the correlation coefficient between the returns on securities, i and $j$, then from Eq. (4-13) the variance of the portfolio is

$$\sigma_P^2 = \sum_{i=1}^{n} \sum_{j=1}^{n} x_i x_j \rho_{ij} \sigma_i \sigma_j \tag{6-8}$$

Once the variance is known the standard deviation is simple to obtain.

## THE EFFICIENT FRONTIER

The fact that the expected return and standard deviation of a given portfolio of $n$ securities can be computed from the equations above does not answer the question of which securities should be held and in what proportions. There is an infinite number of possible portfolios that can be formed so long as there are at least two securities. This is because the total investment can be allocated among the securities in any of an infinity of ways. However, the set of possibilities can be thought of in general terms, assuming many securities. Suppose that the expected returns and standard deviations of all possible portfolios were plotted as in Fig. 6-3. We know that only those portfolios on the left boundary of the region are of interest to risk-averse investors. Any portfolio lying to the right of the boundary (curve $GH$) is inferior to portfolios lying on $GH$, since some portfolio on the boundary will provide higher expected returns for the same risk (standard deviation) or lower risk at the same expected return than a portfolio to the right of $GH$.

The portfolios lying on $GH$ are termed "efficient" because they are superior to any others. The boundary curve $GH$ is therefore called the "efficient frontier." The set of efficient portfolios constitutes a curve of the sort shown in Fig. 6-3 because even if two portfolios along the curve were perfectly correlated, the combinations of the two would lie between them on a straight line. (We can form new portfolios by combining two portfolios.) If the returns of securities or portfolios are not perfectly correlated, the efficient frontier will "bulge out" in the manner shown. Compare Fig. 6-3 with the examples of Fig. 6-2. There are computer codes that enable one to quickly determine the efficient

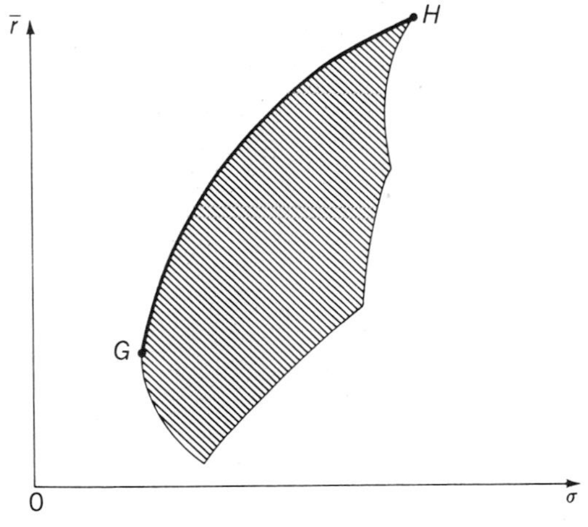


**figure 6-3**

frontier; however, the determination of it is beyond the scope of this book.[2] Our focus here is on the existence of the efficient frontier and its properties.

At this stage in the analysis we have found that an individual investor who likes expected returns and dislikes standard deviation of returns is very likely to want to own one of the portfolios along the efficient frontier, if he or she plans to own any risky assets. However, to complete our analysis of the individual's problem, we should consider two additional options that may be available to him or her: investing in a riskless asset (lending) and borrowing to finance investment.

## LENDING

In Chap. 2 individuals were able to invest at the riskless rate of interest, that is, *lend* part of their initial wealth. Since security $A$ of Table 6-1 is riskless, we can speak of investing in $A$ as lending. Suppose only part of the funds available for investment is used to purchase $A$ and the remainder is used to purchase security $B$. Let $f$ be the fraction of our initial capital invested in the risky security. For example, if we have \$1,000 to invest and we put \$250 into $B$, $f$ would equal .25 or 25%. The remaining funds are lent (i.e., invested in $A$) and the proportion of our investment in $A$ is $(1 - f)$. The rate of return on our investment is a random variable,

$$\tilde{r}_I = (1 - f)r_A + f\tilde{r}_B \tag{6-9}$$

the weighted average of the returns from the two securities. We are interested in the expected return on our investment and the standard deviation of the return. The expected return on the combination will be

$$\bar{r}_I = (1 - f)r_A + f\bar{r}_B \tag{6-10}$$

The standard deviation of $\tilde{r}_I$ can be derived from the equation we used previously to get the variance from investing in securities $B$ and $C$, Eq. (6-3). However, $\sigma_A = \rho_{AB} = \text{cov}[r_A, \tilde{r}_B] = 0$, since $A$ is riskless and the rate of return from investing in $A$, $r_A$, is a constant. Consequently,

$$\sigma_I^2 = f^2\sigma_B^2$$

and

$$\sigma_I = f\sigma_B \tag{6-11}$$

The possibility of combining lending with investment in a risky security provides us with a large number of alternatives, each determined by the value chosen for $f$. If the values of $\bar{r}_I$ and $\sigma_I$ are determined for various values of $f$ and

[2] A formal argument for the assumed shape of *GH* is in app. 6A. For a discussion of the computational problems involved in determining the efficient frontier see William F. Sharpe, "Portfolio Theory and Capital Markets," apps. A to C, McGraw-Hill Book Company, New York, 1970.

are plotted on a graph, we get a straight line between $A$ and $B$ as shown in Fig. 6-4$a$. Each point along the line represents a particular value for $f$; that is, a particular combination of $A$ and $B$. Similarly, the result of combining $C$ and $A$ is shown by the line between them. Now suppose the set of possible portfolios of the two risky securities $B$ and $C$ is as shown by curve $BC$ in Fig. 6-4$b$. The curve is drawn for a value $\rho_{BC} = .2$.

Consider the consequences of putting a portion of our initial funds into a portfolio of $B$ and $C$ and the rest in $A$. For example, suppose $I = \$500$ and we put \$100 into a portfolio of $B$ and $C$ and purchase \$400 of $A$. Given that \$100 has been allocated for $B$ and $C$, the amount to be invested in each must be determined. The proportion of the \$100 invested in $B$ corresponds to the value of $x$ earlier in the chapter. Think of the portfolio resulting from a given value of $x$ as a security with expected return $\bar{r}_P$ and standard deviation $\sigma_P$ from Eqs. (6-2) and (6-4). A given value of $x$ identifies a single point along curve $BC$ in Fig. 6-4$b$. Let $x = .75$; \$75 is invested in security $B$ and \$25 in security $C$. Point $P$ along the curve $BC$ indicates the values of $\bar{r}_P$ and $\sigma_P$ for $x = .75$ as determined from Eqs. (6-2) and (6-4) respectively.

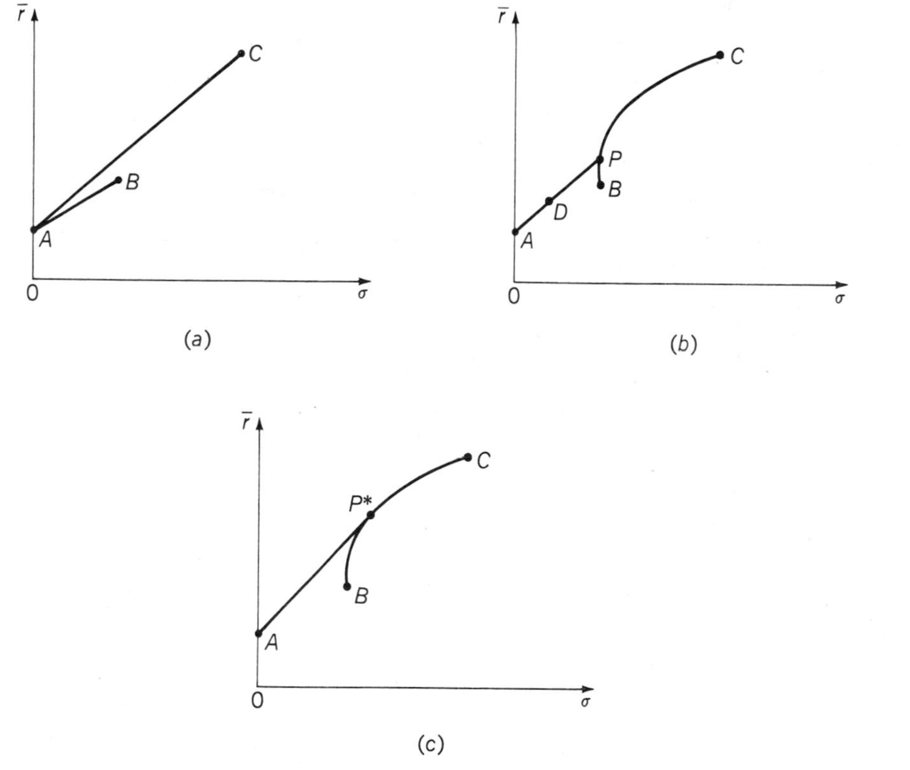


figure 6-4

If we invest part (proportion $f$) of our funds in portfolio $P$ (made up of $B$ and $C$) and the rest of our funds in $A$ [proportion $(1 - f)$], the expected return and standard deviation on total investment will lie along $AP$. The value of $f$ determines the point on $AP$, which describes the combination chosen. If, as was indicated above, \$100 is invested in $P$, $f = .2$. The expected rate of return and the standard deviation of the rate of return for an investment with 80% of initial funds in $A$ and 20% of those funds in a portfolio of 75% $B$ and 25% $C$ is shown by point $D$ on the line $AP$. The expected return on the combination represented by $D$ is 6.6% and the standard deviation is 1.7% from Eqs. (6-10) and (6-11), respectively.

We can carry the analysis one step further. It should be clear that there exists some portfolio $P^*$ which would be the best one to hold in combination with lending. This is illustrated in Fig. 6-4*c*. Without knowing any more about an individual than the individual's preference for return and dislike of standard deviation, we can say that the only investment combinations of interest to that investor would be those along $AP^*C$. The possibilities along that curve dominate all others. Compare the risk and return from lending in combination with portfolio $P^*$ against those available from lending in combination with $P$. Clearly, $P^*$ is a better portfolio to invest in than $P$, given the possibility of lending. In Fig. 6-4*c*, the line $AP^*$ is tangent to curve $BC$ at point $P^*$. That is, $P^*$ is that portfolio along $BC$ which is at the tangent point of $BC$ with a straight line emanating from point $A$.

The determination of the exact proportions of $B$ and $C$ included in $P^*$ is most easily accomplished by using calculus as given in Appendix 6B. An approximate value for $x$ can be estimated from Fig. 6-4*c*, by noting that $\bar{r}_{P^*}$ is approximately .15. Since we know from Eq. (6-2) that $\bar{r}_{P^*} = .22 - .12x$, we

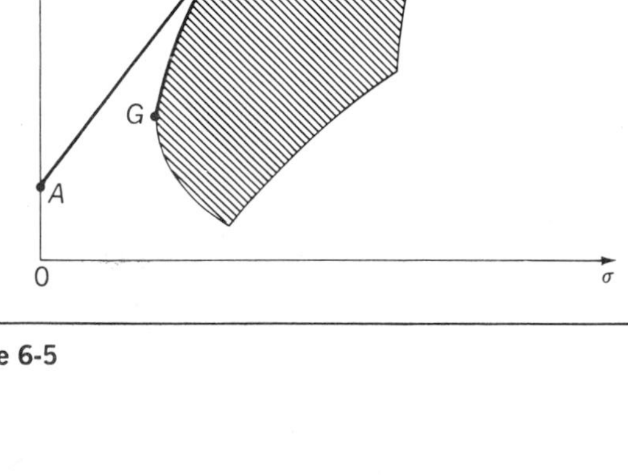

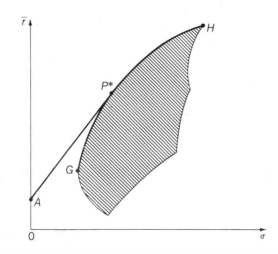

**figure 6-5**

can solve for $x^*$ the proportion of $B$ in $P^*$. $x^* = (.15 - .22)/(-.12) = .58$. The exact value from Appendix 6B is $x^* = .611$.

In reality, of course, there are many more than two risky securities available and thus the efficient frontier of risky portfolios is much more difficult to derive. However, the same general principle applies. There will be only one portfolio that will be a desirable combination with lending. The more general situation is illustrated in Fig. 6-5. The efficient frontier is $GH$; however, the only investments that would be considered lie along $AP^*H$, where $AP^*$ is tangent to $GH$ at point $P^*$. It should be clear that the particular choice of the investment combination will depend on the investor's preferences. One who is highly averse to risk may invest only in $A$, the riskless asset. One who is not very concerned about risk may invest in $H$, the most risky portfolio available. The investor may also invest in any combination or portfolio between $A$ and $H$, the choice of portfolio depending on his or her feelings about risk and return (i.e., depending on his or her utility function).

## BORROWING

Suppose that individuals can borrow to finance investment in risky assets. Assume that they can borrow at 6% and that payment of interest and principal is certain. Let us look at borrowing to invest in a single risky security. The amount invested in the risky security equals our initial capital plus the amount borrowed. Consequently $f$, the fraction of initial capital put into the risky security, is greater than 1.0 and $(1 - f)$ is a negative number. By defining $f$ as we have, the equations for the expected return on our capital and the standard deviation are the same as in the lending situation, except that we must replace the lending rate $r_A$ with the rate of interest on borrowed funds $r_F$. An example should make the point clear. Assume that we borrow to invest in security $C$.

Initial capital = \$1,000
Borrowed funds = \$500
Investment in the risky security = \$1,500, $f = 1.5$, $(1 - f) = -.5$
Expected rate of return on $C$ = 22%
Standard deviation of the return on $C$ = 20%
Expected dollar return from investing \$1,500 in $C$ = (.22)(\$1,500) = \$330
Interest on borrowed funds at 6% = (.06)(\$500) = \$30
Expected dollar return on capital = \$330 − \$30 = \$300
Expected rate of return on capital = $\bar{r}_I$ = \$300/\$1,000 = .30

Alternatively, we can simply compute

$$\begin{aligned}\bar{r}_I &= f\bar{r}_C + (1 - f)r_F \\ &= 1.5(.22) - (.5)(.06) \\ &= .33 - .03 \\ &= .30\end{aligned}$$

The standard deviation of the rate of return in this example would be $\sigma_I = f\sigma_C$. Since the standard deviation of security $C$ is .2, $\sigma_I = 1.5(.2) = .3$. Borrowing increases both the risk and the return. Just as in the case for lending, combinations of borrowing with a given risky security must lie along a straight line. Combinations involving borrowing lie on the extension of the line drawn from the borrowing rate through the values of $\bar{r}$ and $\sigma$ for the security. They provide expected returns and standard deviations higher than those provided by investment in the risky security by itself. Unless some limit is placed on the amount borrowed, the line extends indefinitely. In Fig. 6-6 the combinations of borrowing at 6% plus investment in either security $B$ or security $C$ are shown.

If we look at portfolios rather than individual securities, the effect of borrowing is no different, as was true in the lending case. Suppose we incorporate lending at 5%, borrowing at 6%, and the possibility of investing funds in both $B$ and $C$ into the same diagram. The result is Fig. 6-7. In this situation, the combinations along the segments $AP_1P_2$ and on out along the borrowing line dominate all other possibilities. The particular risk-return preferences of an individual in this situation would determine which of these possible combinations is most desirable.

One final point is important. Suppose that an individual can borrow and lend at the same rate of interest. In this case the lending combinations and the borrowing combinations lie along the same line as in Fig. 6-8. Note that there is only one portfolio of $B$ and $C$ ($P^*$) which would be held if any risky securities were held. Since we assumed that the borrowing rate $r_F = r_A$ (the lending rate), $P^*$ is the same portfolio as denoted by $P_1$ in Fig. 6-7 and $P_1$ is the same as portfolio $P^*$ in Fig. 6-4*c*. Note that the proportions of $B$ and $C$ in $P^*$ do not depend on the utility function or the preferences of an individual faced with the choices shown. Given the characteristics of the securities and the borrowing-

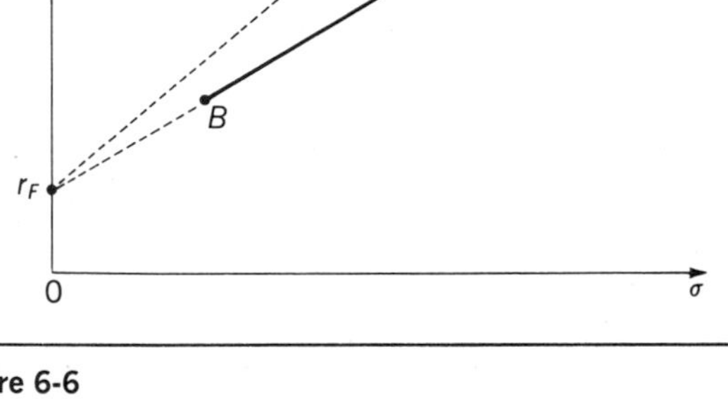

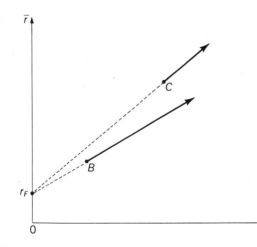

**figure 6-6**

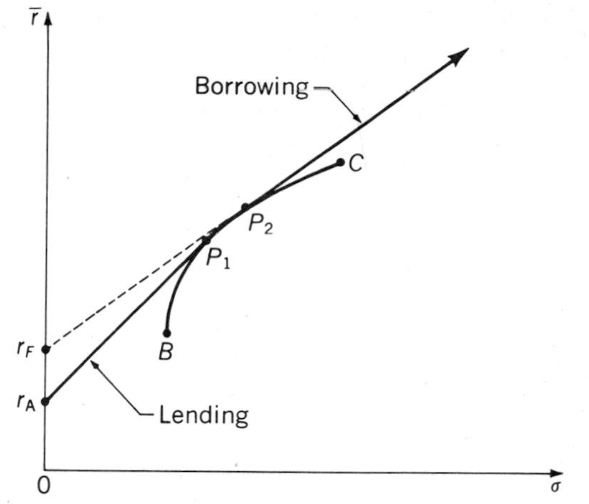


**figure 6-7**

lending rate, $P^*$ can be determined without reference to the risk-return preferences of individuals. We suggested earlier that the proportions of the securities in $P^*$ could be found by mathematical and graphical methods without assuming anything about the preferences of the decision maker. The conclusion here is that $P^*$ will be the only portfolio of $B$ and $C$ which will be of interest to the investor. Portfolio $P^*$ is that portfolio on line $BC$ which exists at the tangency point ($P^*$) of a straight line from point $r_A$ to curve $BC$. As explained in the next section, this result generalizes readily to the situation where we have a large number of risky securities available.

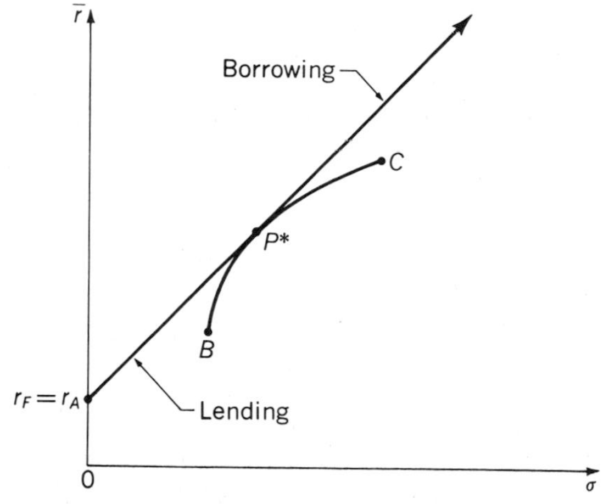


**figure 6-8**

## THE SEPARATION THEOREM[3]

Assuming that the individual investor can borrow and lend at the same rate of interest and given that he or she has determined the efficient boundary of risky securities, we can state a very important result:

> The individual's choice of a portfolio of risky securities to hold is independent (separate) of the individual's attitude toward risk.

In other words, provided that expected return and standard deviation are the only characteristics of interest to the individual, the optimal portfolio of *risky* securities for that individual is not related to the individual's feelings about risk. This statement is called the "separation theorem" and its proof is based on the point we made above. Figure 6-9 illustrates the situation for a large number of securities. The efficient frontier of portfolios consisting only of risky securities is curve $GH$. If the investor is going to invest in any risky assets, the investment will be in portfolio $P^*$.[4] Of course, the investor may choose to put all of his or her funds into the riskless asset and earn the riskless rate $r_A$. But if there is any investment in a risky combination, the investor will either hold $P^*$ plus some of the riskless asset (be at a point along $AP^*$), hold $P^*$ with no borrowing or lending, or borrow to invest in $P^*$.[5] In any case the investor's attitude toward risk does not affect the determination of $P^*$. The securities and the proportions of those securities in $P^*$ do not depend on the individual's risk preference—only on the individual's estimates of the probability distributions of the rates of return on the securities and the value of $r_A$.

The separation theorem turns out to be very useful in determining equilibrium conditions in the capital markets as developed in the next chapter. However, it should be noted before proceeding that the assumption that the individual can borrow and lend at the same rate of interest is critical to the theorem. If this point is not clear, refer to Fig. 6-8. There is more than one portfolio that might be considered when the two rates are not equal.

It is important to realize that the efficient frontier $GH$ and the value of $r_A$ are based on the perceptions and opportunities facing a given investor. In particular, we have not assumed that all investors have the same perceptions and opportunities. Nor have we assumed very much about the market in which the securities are traded. We have simply looked at the problem faced by an individual as that individual seeks to determine an optimal investment strategy

[3] The original development of the theorem is due to J. Tobin, Liquidity Preference as Behavior toward Risk, *Review of Economic Studies,* vol. 26, pp. 65–86, February 1958. In his analysis, "cash" is the riskless asset with an expected return of zero, no borrowing is permitted, and there exists only a single risky asset (or portfolio).

[4] If there are some perfectly correlated portfolios near $P^*$, then there may be more than one portfolio that lies on the line. Any one of these could be chosen by the individual.

[5] It is assumed that the investor can borrow at the rate $r_A$ at least up to a point at which the expected return of the portfolio equals that obtaining for portfolio $H$.

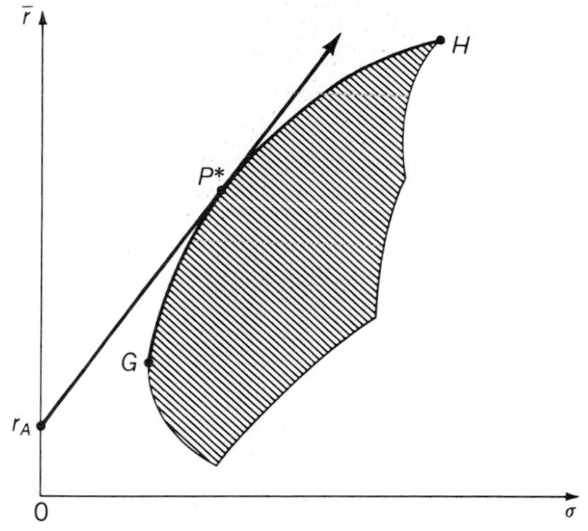


figure 6-9

under uncertainty. The separation theorem suggests that an individual can divide the investment problem into two parts if the individual can borrow and lend at the same rate of interest. The first part involves making an evaluation of available investment opportunities. This part of the problem involves the determination of the portfolio $P^*$ and hence the set of preferred (dominant) combinations of lending or borrowing in conjunction with investment in $P^*$. This is equivalent to determining the tangent line from $r_A$ through $P^*$ in Fig. 6-9. The second part of the investor's investment problem is to determine the point on that line that the investor prefers given the investor's attitude toward risk and return.

It should be noted that if two individuals have the same perceptions or expectations regarding the probability distributions of risky securities and if they can both borrow and lend at the same rate ($r_A$ for investor 1 equals $r_A$ for investor 2), they will both agree on the same portfolio $P^*$. In other words, the first part of the problem will be the same for each investor. Then each investor must determine the best combination to hold. The second part of the problem can and probably will result in a different combination for each. One may wish to invest 50% of his or her funds in $P^*$ and lend 50%; the other may wish to borrow 20% of his or her initial funds and invest 120% of the initial funds in $P^*$. The fact that different people may agree on $P^*$ and yet still be able to invest differently to suit their preferences is crucial to the analysis of the next chapter.

## SUMMARY

To some extent this chapter can be viewed as the development of the separation theorem. This theorem provides the basis for the theory of market equilibrium, which is the subject of the next chapter. The importance of the separation theorem is that it permits the development of a theory of valuation under uncertainty which does not depend directly upon knowledge of the degree of risk aversion of investors. However, the background to the theorem is as important as the result. We have introduced some of the essential concepts of portfolio theory, which is a substantial area in its own right with important theoretical and practical implications. The past three chapters form a foundation for the analysis to come.

APPENDIX

# SIX A

## DERIVATION OF THE EFFICIENT SET

As explained in the text, rates of return on assets can be defined in the mean-standard deviation space as in Fig. 6A-1. The figure depicts the expectations of investors with respect to the mean and standard deviation of every asset in the market. The shaded area $\Omega$ includes all risky assets that are traded.

The efficient set of portfolios (a portfolio can contain one or many assets) includes those portfolios for which:

1. There exists no other portfolio with a higher expected return and the same standard deviation of return.
2. There exists no other portfolio with a lower standard deviation of return and the same expected return.

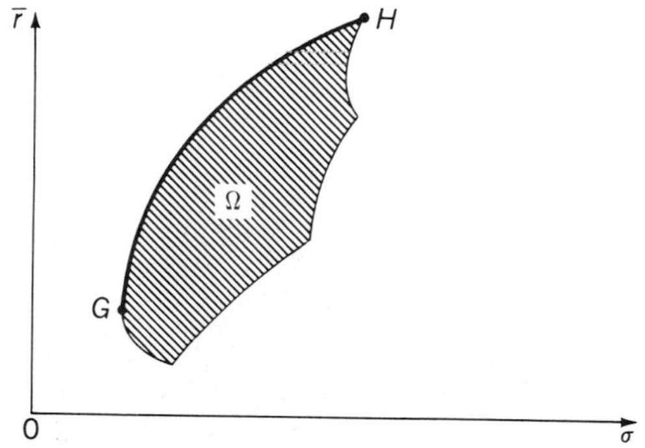


figure 6A-1

In Fig. 6A-1 the efficient set is segment *GH* along the rim of $\Omega$. To see why the efficient set has the concave shape of *GH*, assume any two portfolios *J* and *K* in Fig. 6A-2. It will be shown that any portfolios which comprise a weighted combination of *J* and *K* will have the concave shape of *GH*. It will then be shown that this implies the concavity of *GH*.

If all the investor's funds were in asset *J*, the expected rate of return and standard deviation of the rate of return on his or her holdings would be $\bar{r}_J$, $\sigma_J$ at point *J* in Fig. 6A-2. Similarly, if all the funds were in asset *K*, the expected return and standard deviation would be $\bar{r}_K$, $\sigma_K$ at point *K*. But what of $\bar{r}$ and $\sigma$ if a combination of *J* and *K* were purchased? Assume that the investor places fraction $\alpha$ of his or her investment in *J* and $(1 - \alpha)$ in *K*, where $0 \leq \alpha \leq 1$. The resulting portfolio *E* has rate of return $\tilde{r}_E$, where the $\bar{r}$ and $\sigma$ of this portfolio equal

$$\bar{r}_E = \alpha\bar{r}_J + (1 - \alpha)\bar{r}_K \tag{6A-1}$$

$$\begin{aligned}\sigma_E &= [\alpha^2\sigma_J^2 + (1 - \alpha)^2\sigma_K^2 + 2\alpha(1 - \alpha)\text{cov}(\tilde{r}_J,\tilde{r}_K)]^{1/2} \\ &= [\alpha^2\sigma_J^2 + (1 - \alpha)^2\sigma_K^2 + 2\alpha(1 - \alpha)\rho_{JK}\sigma_J\sigma_K]^{1/2}\end{aligned} \tag{6A-2}$$

where $\rho_{JK}$ is the correlation coefficient of $\tilde{r}_J$ and $\tilde{r}_K$. Equations (6A-1) and (6A-2) correspond to Eqs. (6-2) and (6-4) in the text, where the analysis was based on securities rather than portfolios. Of interest here is how all combinations of *J* and *K* can be represented. Terms $\sigma_J$ and $\sigma_K$ are numbers defined at points *J* and *K*. Furthermore, since the first two variance terms in Eq. (6A-2) must be positive, the maximum possible value of $\sigma_E$ for any given value of $\alpha$ is obtained when the returns from the two portfolios are perfectly positively correlated, that is, $\rho_{JK} = 1.0$. If $\rho_{JK} = 1.0$,

$$\sigma_E = \sigma_K + \alpha(\sigma_J - \sigma_K) \tag{6A-3}$$

which corresponds to Eq. (6-5) in the text. Equations (6A-1) and (6A-3) can be used to determine the manner in which the expected rate of return on portfolio

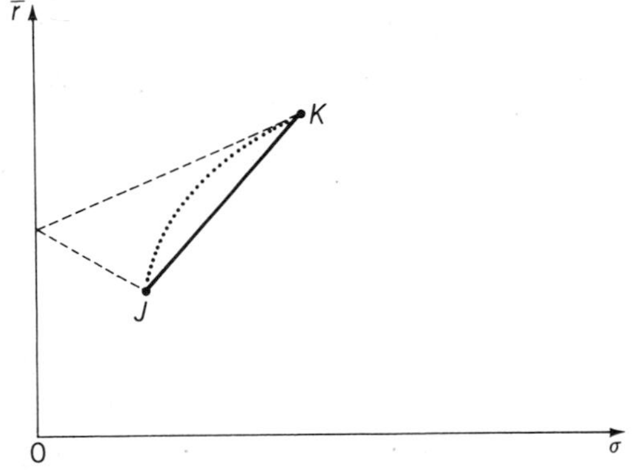


**figure 6A-2**

$E$ varies with respect to the standard deviation of the portfolio. From the "chain rule" of calculus

$$\frac{d\bar{r}_E}{d\sigma_E} = \frac{d\bar{r}_E/d\alpha}{d\sigma_E/d\alpha} \tag{6A-4}$$

From Eq. (6A-1)

$$\frac{d\bar{r}_E}{d\alpha} - \bar{r}_J - \bar{r}_K \tag{6A-5}$$

and from Eq. (6A-3)

$$\frac{d\sigma_E}{d\alpha} = \sigma_J - \sigma_K \tag{6A-6}$$

Substituting the derivatives with respect to $\alpha$ into Eq. (6A-4),

$$\frac{d\bar{r}_E}{d\sigma_E} = \frac{\bar{r}_J - \bar{r}_K}{\sigma_J - \sigma_K} \tag{6A-7}$$

The expected rates of return and standard deviations for portfolios $J$ and $K$ are values determined by the probability distributions, which are independent of $\alpha$. Therefore, given those values, the derivative of $\bar{r}_E$ with respect to $\sigma_E$ is a constant when $\rho_{JK} = 1.0$. As a consequence of this result, $\bar{r}_E$ and $\sigma_E$ for the combinations determined by various values of $\alpha$ must lie along a straight line between the points $J$ and $K$ in Fig. 6A-2. But $\rho_{JK} = 1$ provides the maximum $\sigma_E$ for any given level of $\alpha$ and thus for any given level of $\bar{r}_E$ in Eq. (6A-1). This implies that if $\rho_{JK} < 1$, then $\sigma_E$ must lie left of the straight line between $J$ and $K$. It follows that if $\rho_{JK} < 1$, the set of all $(\bar{r}_E, \sigma_E)$ points must lie left of straight line $JK$. It is easily shown that such a line will be of the concave form of the efficient frontier $GH$.[6] This is illustrated by the dotted line between $J$ and $K$ in Fig. 6A-2. The exception is if $\rho_{JK} = -1$, in which case $JK$ is of the dashed form in the figure. This case will be disregarded hereafter.

Assume now a third portfolio $D$ in Fig. 6A-3. Combinations of $J$ and $K$, $K$ and $D$, and $J$ and $D$ are represented by the solid lines. However, any weighted combination of $J$ and $K$ (portfolio $S$) can be combined with a combination of $K$ and $D$ (portfolio $T$), forming the set of possible portfolios along the dotted curve. But combinations of $T$ and $S$ can be combined with a different portfolio made up of $J$ and $K$ or of $K$ and $D$ to form another set of portfolio opportunities in the figure, and so on. It follows that the set of portfolio opportunities provided by $J$, $K$, and $D$ is a concave function of the form of the efficient set $GH$ in Fig. 6A-1. It also follows that any two or more portfolios satisfying the efficient set conditions (1) and (2) stated above provide a set of portfolio combination

[6] The concavity follows from the fact that

$$d(dr_E/d\sigma_E)/d\alpha < 0 \qquad \text{if } \rho_{JK} < 1.0$$

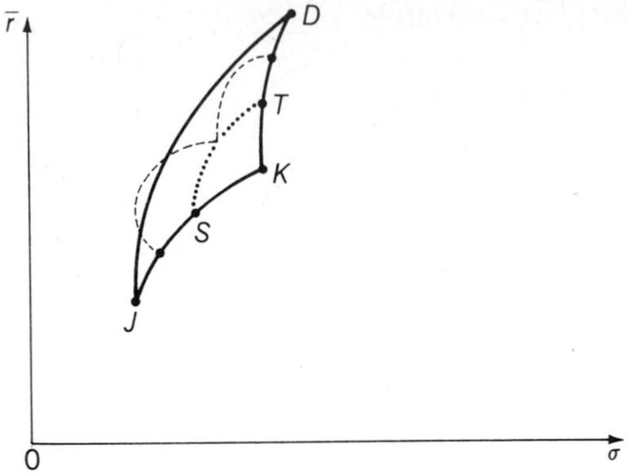


figure 6A-3

opportunities of a concave form. *GH* therefore has the concave form illustrated in Fig. 6A-1.

One final point concludes the analysis. If the individual can borrow and lend at the same rate $r_A$, it was shown in the text that in general there would be some particular portfolio $P^*$ which would produce the best (most efficient) set of alternatives for that investor. This was illustrated by Fig. 6-9. From Eqs. (6-10) and (6-11) the expected return $\bar{r}_I$ and standard deviation $\sigma_I$ of combinations of borrowing or lending at $r_A$ with $P^*$ are given by

$$\bar{r}_I = \alpha \bar{r}_{P*} + (1 - \alpha) r_A \tag{6A-8}$$

$$\sigma_I = \alpha \sigma_{P^*} \tag{6A-9}$$

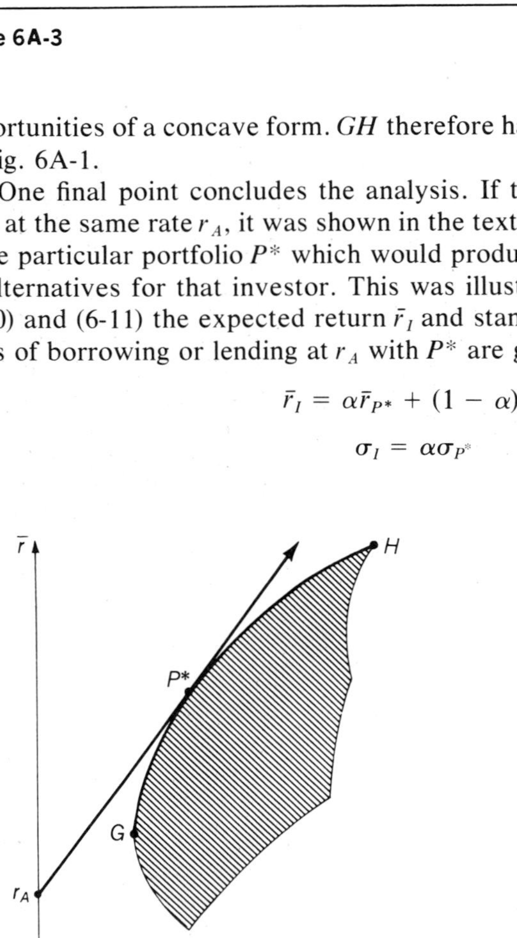


figure 6A-4

where $\alpha$ is the proportion of the initial funds of the individual that is invested in $P^*$.

The relationship between the expected return $\bar{r}_I$ and standard deviation $\sigma_I$ can be shown using the derivatives as was done above:

$$\frac{d\bar{r}_I}{d\sigma_I} = \frac{d\bar{r}_I/d\alpha}{d\sigma_I/d\alpha} = \frac{r_{P^*} - r_A}{\sigma_{P^*}} \tag{6A-10}$$

The values of $\bar{r}_{P^*}$, $r_A$, and $\sigma_{P^*}$ do not depend on $\alpha$. Therefore, the derivative is a constant and $\bar{r}_I$ and $\sigma_I$ for various values of $\alpha$ lie along a straight line passing through $A$ and $P^*$. This is the same result reached in the text and shown in Fig. 6A-4. The efficient set of investment combinations lies along this line, which dominates $GH$ using criteria (1) and (2) above.

Note that Eq. (6A-10) is the slope of the line through $A$ and $P^*$. It should be apparent that the line is tangent to curve $GH$. Therefore, the slope of curve $GH$ at $P^*$ is also given by Eq. (6A-10). This result is used in Appendix 6B and in Chap. 7.

APPENDIX

# SIX B

# DETERMINATION OF THE OPTIMAL PROPORTIONS OF A TWO-SECURITY PORTFOLIO

The problem to be analyzed in this appendix is the determination of the optimal proportions of two securities in a portfolio $P^*$ when the individual can borrow and lend at rate $r_A$. The setting of the problem is discussed in the text and is illustrated by Fig. 6B-1, which is identical to Fig. 6-6*c*.

At the end of Appendix 6A, it was noted that the line passing through $P^*$

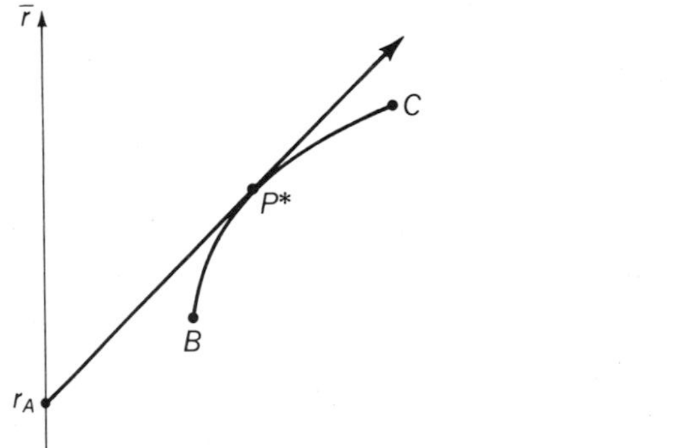


**figure 6B-1**

was tangent to the efficient frontier at $P^*$. The slope of the line must therefore equal the slope of the curve $BC$ at $P^*$ in Fig. 6B-1. That is,

$$\left.\frac{d\bar{r}_I}{d\sigma_I}\right|_{P^*} = \left.\frac{d\bar{r}_P}{d\sigma_P}\right|_{P^*} \tag{6B-1}$$

where the subscript $I$ refers to borrowing or lending combinations along the line through $A$ and $P^*$ and the subscript $P$ refers to portfolios along curve $BC$. From Eq. (6A-10)

$$\frac{d\bar{r}_I}{d\sigma_I} = \frac{\bar{r}_{P^*} - r_A}{\sigma_{P^*}} \tag{6B-2}$$

An expression for $d\bar{r}_P/d\sigma_P$ is now needed.

From Eqs. (6-2) and (6-4) in the text

$$\bar{r}_P = x\bar{r}_B + (1 - x)\bar{r}_C \tag{6B-3}$$

$$\sigma_P = [x^2\sigma_B^2 + (1 - x)^2\sigma_C^2 + 2x(1 - x)\rho_{BC}\sigma_B\sigma_C]^{1/2} \tag{6B-4}$$

Applying the "chain rule" as in Appendix 6A,

$$\frac{d\bar{r}_P}{d\sigma_P} = \frac{d\bar{r}_P/dx}{d\sigma_P/dx} \tag{6B-5}$$

The derivatives of Eqs. (6B-3) and (6B-4) with respect to $x$ are, respectively,

$$\frac{d\bar{r}_P}{dx} = \bar{r}_B - \bar{r}_C \tag{6B-6}$$

$$\frac{d\sigma_P}{dx} = \frac{2x\sigma_B^2 - 2(1 - x)\sigma_C^2 + (2 - 4x)\rho_{BC}\sigma_B\sigma_C}{2\sigma_P} \tag{6B-7}$$

Substituting Eqs. (6B-6) and (6B-7) into Eq. (6B-5),

$$\frac{d\bar{r}_P}{d\sigma_P} = \frac{\sigma_P(\bar{r}_B - \bar{r}_C)}{x\sigma_B^2 - (1 - x)\sigma_C^2 + (1 - 2x)\rho_{BC}\sigma_B\sigma_C} \tag{6B-8}$$

Equation (6B-8) expresses the derivative along the curve $BC$. At point $P^*$, this derivative is

$$\left.\frac{d\bar{r}_P}{d\sigma_P}\right|_{P^*} = \frac{\sigma_{P^*}(\bar{r}_B - \bar{r}_C)}{x^*\sigma_B^2 - (1 - x^*)\sigma_C^2 + (1 - 2x^*)\rho_{BC}\sigma_B\sigma_C} \tag{6B-9}$$

where $x^*$ is the proportion of security $B$ in portfolio $P^*$ and $(1 - x^*)$ is the proportion of $C$.

Now set the two derivatives from Eqs. (6B-9) and (6B-2) equal to each other as indicated by Eq. (6B-1). The objective is to determine the value of $x^*$.

$$\frac{\bar{r}_{P^*} - r_A}{\sigma_{P^*}} = \frac{\sigma_{P^*}(\bar{r}_B - \bar{r}_C)}{x^*\sigma_B^2 - (1 - x^*)\sigma_C^2 + (1 - 2x^*)\rho_{BC}\sigma_B\sigma_C} \tag{6B-10}$$

**table 6B-1**

| | |
|---|---|
| $r_A = .05$ | $\sigma_B = .08$ |
| $\bar{r}_B = .10$ | $\sigma_C = .20$ |
| $\bar{r}_C = .22$ | $\rho_{BC} = .20$ |

We can use the equations for the expected return on the portfolio (6B-3) and the standard deviation of the portfolio (6B-4) to substitute for $\bar{r}_{P*}$ and $\sigma_{P*}$ in Eq. (6B-10). Doing this and solving for the optimal proportion of security $B$, $x^*$, we obtain the general solution:

$$x^* = \frac{(\bar{r}_B - r_A)\,\sigma_C^2 - (\bar{r}_C - r_A)\,\rho_{BC}\,\sigma_B\sigma_C}{(\bar{r}_B - r_A)\,\sigma_C^2 + (\bar{r}_C - r_A)\,\sigma_B^2 - (\bar{r}_C + \bar{r}_B - 2r_A)\,\rho_{BC}\,\sigma_B\sigma_C} \qquad \text{(6B-11)}$$

Equation (6B-11) holds for any two-security problem where the securities are arbitrarily designated by $B$ and $C$ and where $r_A$ is the borrowing and lending rate. The particular values assumed in Chapter 6 and used to develop Figures 6-4C and 6B-1 are given in Table 6B-1. Using the values from the table in Eq. (6B-11) we find the value of $x^*$ in this particular case to be 0.611 which was noted on page 129.

## SUGGESTED READINGS

Brealey, Richard A.: "An Introduction to Risk and Return from Common Stocks," Chaps. 10 and 11, The M.I.T. Press, Cambridge, Mass., 1969.

Markowitz, Harry: Portfolio Selection, *Journal of Finance*, vol. 7, pp. 77–91, March 1952, reprinted in Archer, Stephen H. and Charles A. D'Ambrosio, "The Theory of Business Finance," 2d ed., The Macmillan Company, New York, 1976.

Sharpe, William F.: "Portfolio Theory and Capital Markets," pp. 18–58, McGraw-Hill Book Company, New York, 1970.

CHAPTER

# SEVEN

# CAPITAL MARKET EQUILIBRIUM

Chapter 6 presented a method, called portfolio theory, of dealing with the investment problem faced by a single individual. In the current chapter we shall consider the implications of assuming that investors act the way portfolio theory says they should. The primary concern of the analysis is to specify the value of risky securities as determined by the equilibrium conditions in the capital markets. Of particular interest is the determination of the price of a firm's common stock. Once we know how the value of the ownership interest in a firm is determined, we shall be in a position to examine the major financial decisions of the firm; we shall do this in Chap. 8.

Capital market theory is positive, since we are attempting to describe reality. However, we are forced to make a number of fairly restrictive assumptions in developing the theory. The assumptions may not appear realistic; but if the implications of the theory are reasonable approximations to the facts we observe, the theory will be worthwhile. The particular theory of capital markets developed in this chapter is based on a single time period. In later chapters we shall be able to describe some general characteristics of the capital markets in a multiperiod setting. However, we shall not be able to specify equilibrium conditions with anything like the precision that we can here. The theory presented in this chapter and the next can be considered special cases of more general approaches.

## ASSUMPTIONS

Theories of financial markets under uncertainty are based on assumptions about individual attitudes and behavior and about the market for financial assets.[1] The assumptions about individuals made here are developed from the discussion in Chap. 6. These assumptions are more restrictive than is strictly necessary to yield the results presented. However, the ones used are helpful for expository purposes since the arguments become more difficult with more general assumptions. The assumptions made here are:

1. Individuals seek to maximize the expected utility from their portfolios of securities. The only characteristics of portfolios of concern to an individual are the expected returns and standard deviations (or variances). Individuals prefer greater expected return; for any given variance of return, the portfolio with the highest expected return will be preferred. Individuals are averse to risk; for any given expected return, the portfolio with the lowest standard deviation will be preferred.
2. Investors are indifferent between equal dollar amounts of dividend and capital gains income (since they can always sell their shares or bonds).
3. All individuals have a single-period planning horizon, and forecast the probability distributions of the rates of return on securities and portfolios of securities for the coming period. The horizon period is the same for all investors.
4. Everyone in the market has the same forecast; that is, everyone agrees on the probability distributions of the rates of return (homogeneous expectations).
5. Everyone in the market has the same opportunities to invest, although the *amounts* to be invested may differ from person to person.
6. The market is perfect in the sense that there are no taxes and no transaction costs, securities are completely divisible, and the market is perfectly competitive.[2]
7. Individuals can borrow and lend freely at the riskless rate of interest $i$.[3]
8. The stock of risky securities in the market is given; all securities that were to be issued for the coming period have been issued, and all firm financial decisions have been made.

Assumptions 1 to 8 establish a world in which individuals differ in their attitudes toward risk and the amounts they will be investing, but they agree on the characteristics of securities available, are all averse to risk, and agree on what constitutes risk. They can freely invest in any combination of securities

[1] The theory developed here applies to all types of assets, not just financial assets. However, for simplicity we have assumed throughout this book that individuals invest only in financial assets and that all productive investment in real assets is undertaken by firms. For an alternative development see William F. Sharpe, "Portfolio Theory and Capital Markets," chap. 5, McGraw-Hill Book Company, New York, 1970.

[2] The costless availability of information is usually also included in the definition of perfect markets; however, assumptions (4) and (5) are sufficient.

[3] The debt issued by firms may be risky or riskless depending on the circumstances of the firm and the amount of debt issued.

desired and can borrow and lend at the same rate of interest. At best this world is an idealization of the actual case, but it may serve as a useful approximation of reality and will permit us to focus later on the implications of departures from the ideal case.

The rate of return on any security or portfolio of securities is given by

$$\tilde{r}_i = \frac{\tilde{Y}_i}{V_i} - 1 \tag{7-1}$$

where $\tilde{Y}_i$ is the dollar return one period from now and includes any cash distributions (assumed to be made at the end of the period) plus the market value at the end of the period. Variable $\tilde{Y}_i$ is a random variable and, therefore, so is $\tilde{r}_i$. Value $V_i$ is the *current* market value of the asset and is therefore known with certainty. As before, $\bar{r}_i$ and $\sigma_i$ denote the expected value and standard deviation of $\tilde{r}_i$. The relationships developed and discussed in Chap. 6 with respect to securities and portfolios can now be used to determine equilibrium conditions in the market.

## THE CAPITAL MARKET LINE

By assumption the only characteristics of securities and portfolios that matter to the individual are the expected returns and standard deviations. Suppose we display all available assets in terms of these two characteristics as in Fig. 7-1. Under these conditions in Chap. 6, $P^*$ was the only risky asset of interest to investors, since they could borrow or lend to achieve their preferred combination of risk and return. The same conditions hold true now. Relatively risk-averse investors will hold combinations of the riskless asset and $P^*$. The values for the expected return and standard deviations on their investments lie along the portion of the line between $i$ and $P^*$. Investors who are willing to incur

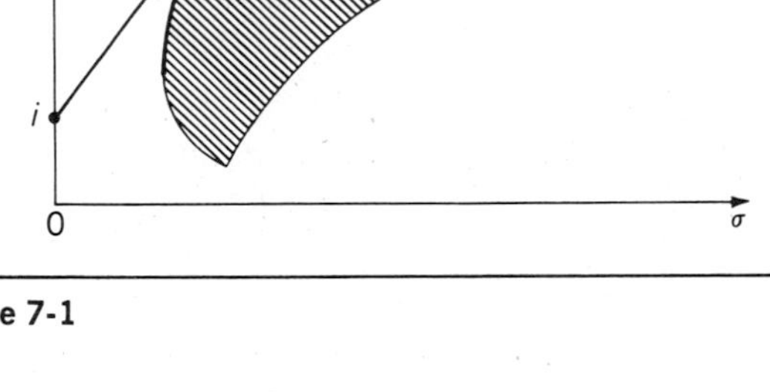

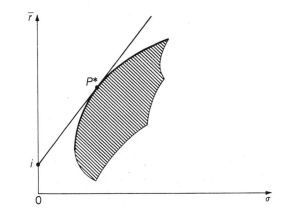

**figure 7-1**

higher risks for higher returns will borrow to finance investment in $P^*$. If they can borrow at a rate of interest of $i$, the resulting values of expected return and standard deviation lie along the line extending from $P^*$ with higher risks and returns than $P^*$. The result that the optimal portfolio of risky securities does not depend on individual preferences is the "separation theorem" presented in Chap. 6.

Given now that investors in the market have the same expectations regarding the risk and return from portfolios and that they can freely borrow and lend at $i$, the portfolio $P^*$ is the same for all investors. *Everyone* will wish to hold $P^*$ in some combination since everyone agrees that $P^*$ is best—except those highly risk-averse individuals who will invest only in the riskless asset.

If everyone wishes to hold the same portfolio ($P^*$), in order for the market to be in equilibrium that portfolio must contain all the securities in the market. This is so because all securities must be held by someone. If some securities were not in $P^*$, their prices would fall, thereby increasing their expected rate of return, until they became desirable and were included in $P^*$. Since all securities in the market are in $P^*$, the proportion (in terms of market value) of each security in $P^*$ must be the proportion its value is of the whole market. For example, suppose that there are only two securities in the market, $A$ and $B$. The total amount held by investors must be the market value of $A$ plus the market value of $B$ denoted by $V_A$ and $V_B$. Moreover, suppose that there are only two investors in the market, one with \$100 and the other with \$1,000. Both investors agree on the optimal proportions of $A$ and $B$ to be held in their portfolios. Suppose the proportions are 20% $A$ and 80% $B$. The first investor will try to buy \$20 worth of $A$ and \$80 worth of $B$, and the second will try to buy \$200 worth of $A$ and \$800 worth of $B$. If the value of $A$ is \$220 and the value of $B$ is \$880, both investors can and will achieve the proper proportions; otherwise the values of $A$ and $B$ will change and the optimal proportions of $A$ and $B$ will change until equilibrium is reached. Note that the optimal proportions of the securities do depend on the current values (prices). If those values change, then so will the proportions. The *process* by which the market is presumed to reach equilibrium is difficult to specify precisely. However, we can say something about the ultimate results of the process.

If the market is to be in equilibrium so that no one wishes to change his or her holdings of any security, $P^*$ must be the *market portfolio* $M$. In other words, in equilibrium the only risky asset held by individuals is a portfolio $M$ which contains all the risky securities in the market, and the proportion of the value of $M$ assumed by each security is equal to the value of that security divided by the value of all securities in the market.[4]

[4] If there exist some portfolios whose returns are perfectly correlated with the return on the market portfolio, these portfolios may also be held and would lie along the CML. This situation was the one used by Sharpe in his original development of the theory. See Sharpe, Capital Asset Prices: A Theory of Market Equilibrium under Conditions of Risk (listed in the Suggested Readings at the end of this chapter).

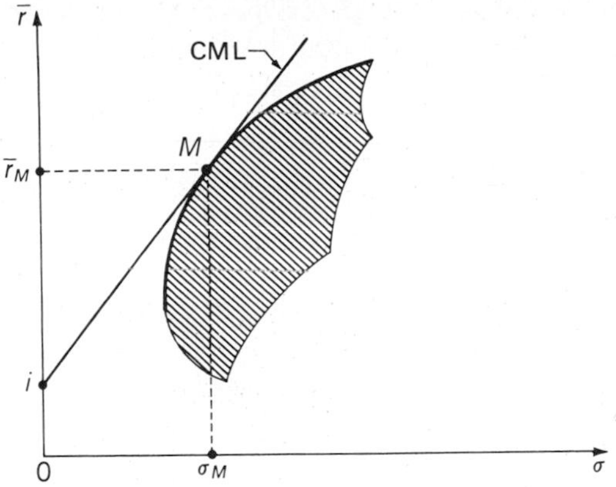


**figure 7-2**

All individuals will hold combinations that lie along the line passing through $i$ and $M$ shown in Fig. 7-2. This line is called the capital market line (CML) and can be expressed as

$$\bar{r}_j = i + \lambda'\sigma_j \tag{7-2}$$

where $\bar{r}_j$ is the expected return on *any* combination actually held by individuals and $\sigma_j$ is the standard deviation of the rate of return on the combination. $\lambda'$ is the slope of the CML and can be considered the "price of risk" in the market.[5] Since the CML passes through the point $(\bar{r}_M,\sigma_M)$, $\lambda' = (\bar{r}_M - i)/\sigma_M$ in equilibrium.

The CML expresses the *current* "trading terms" for risk and return for *efficient combinations*, the combinations investors will actually hold. It reflects current *expectations* regarding the distributions of future outcomes from investments. Realized rates of return will generally differ from the expected values. Also, there is no reason to believe that the trading terms for risk and return will remain constant over time. Both the interest rate $i$ and the price of risk $\lambda'$ reflect individual preferences and opportunities and as these change so should $i$ and $\lambda'$. Equilibrium conditions are therefore given only at the present point in time and reflect expectations of outcomes one period from now.

Over time, the equilibrium changes as new assets enter the market and old assets disappear. Indeed, if such asset changes occur with sufficient rapidity, an equilibrium may never be achieved since adjustments are not necessarily in-

[5] As part of the equilibrium process $i$ is also determined. The conditions for equilibrium include the fact that total borrowing at $i$ must equal total lending. The dynamics of the equilibrium process are quite complicated since both the consumption preferences of individuals and the activities of firms are involved. Equation (7-2) represents the "final" outcome of this complex process.

stantaneous. The theory presented in this chapter is meant to describe the equilibrium that the system at least approaches if not attains. The theory developed thus far will now be extended to derive an expression for the equilibrium rate of return on an asset.

## THE SECURITY MARKET LINE

The CML provides the equilibrium relationship for efficient combinations, but does not directly say anything about the expected returns on *inefficient* assets—either portfolios or individual securities. The equilibrium conditions for securities and inefficient portfolios can be determined from the mathematical relationships between the market portfolio $M$ which lies on the CML and the securities that comprise the portfolio. A formal derivation is presented in the next section; here we shall present the reasoning behind the results.

Very briefly, we know that each security is held as part of a portfolio $M$. The characteristics of any given security of concern to an investor are the effects of including that security in the portfolio. The expected return of a portfolio changes in proportion to the expected return on a security added to it. The risk (standard deviation) of a portfolio depends primarily on the *covariances* of the securities in it. Consequently, the risk of an individual security that matters to investors holding a highly diversified portfolio is the covariance of the security's return with the returns of all other securities in the portfolio; that is, the covariance of the security's return with the return on the market. In equilibrium the relationship depicted in Fig. 7-3 must hold. The equilibrium expected return on a security (or any portfolio) can be expressed as

$$\bar{r}_i = i + \frac{\lambda'}{\sigma_M} \operatorname{cov}[\tilde{r}_i, \tilde{r}_M] \qquad (7\text{-}3)$$

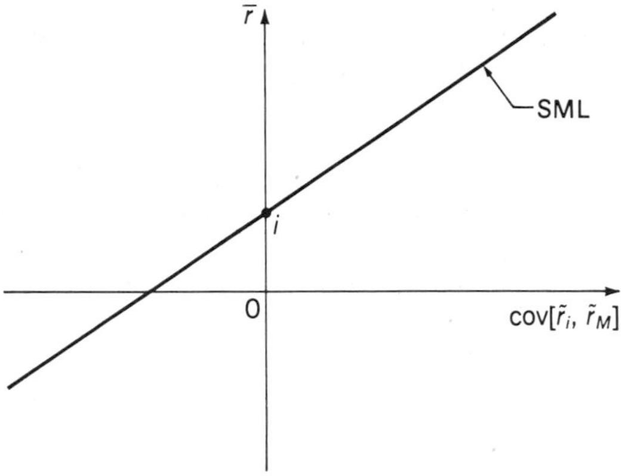


figure 7-3

or.[6]

$$\bar{r}_i = i + \lambda' \rho_{iM} \sigma_i \tag{7-3a}$$

where $\tilde{r}_i$ = return on an individual security
$\tilde{r}_M$ = return on the market
$\rho_{iM}$ = correlation between return on security i and return on the market
$\sigma_M$ = standard deviation of return on the market

The relationship shown in Fig. 7-3 and expressed as Eq. (7-3) is called the *security market line* (SML). The SML shows that in equilibrium the required expected rate of return on risky assets is a function of the risk-free rate of interest plus a premium for risk where the risk is measured by the covariance of the asset's return with the return on all assets.[7] One of the interesting properties of this relationship is that a security whose returns are uncorrelated with the market ($\rho_{iM} = 0$) will in equilibrium have an expected return equal to the risk-free rate. Such a security is riskless when included in a very large portfolio even though it would be risky to hold it alone. Adding an uncorrelated security to a large portfolio has a negligible effect on the variance of the portfolio. This result is caused by the effectiveness of diversification. Moreover, any security whose returns are negatively correlated with the market would have an expected return less than $i$ because such securities serve to *reduce* the risk of the total portfolio. These points are subsidiary to the principal result—that the risk of a security is not its total risk as measured by standard deviation but only that portion of the total risk which cannot be diversified away as measured by $\text{cov}[\tilde{r}_i, \tilde{r}_M]$ or by $\rho_{iM}\sigma_i$.[8] This portion of total risk which cannot be diversified away is called the security's *systematic risk*.

## †Derivation of the SML

The security market line, Eq. (7-3), is essentially a logical extension of the general equilibrium relationship in the market for risky assets that we called the capital market line (CML). The CML was expressed as Eq. (7-2):

$$\bar{r}_j = i + \lambda' \sigma_j$$

[6] Equation (7-3*a*) is obtained from (7-3) by substitution of $\rho_{iM}\sigma_i\sigma_M$ for $\text{cov}[\tilde{r}_i, \tilde{r}_M]$; see chap. 4.

[7] *All* assets and combinations plot along the SML in equilibrium. Efficient combinations are perfectly correlated with the market; hence $\rho_{iM} = 1.0$ and (7-3*a*) reduces to the CML for such combinations. Inefficient assets, both securities and portfolios, plot only along the SML, not on the CML.

[8] An alternative expression frequently used in portfolio theory is

$$\bar{r}_i = i + (\lambda' \sigma_M) b_i$$

where $b_i = \rho_{iM}\sigma_i/\sigma_M.b_i$ is called *volatility* and can be thought of as the slope of a regression line from the equation $r_i = a + b_i r_M$. See Sharpe (1970), *op. cit.*, p. 93.

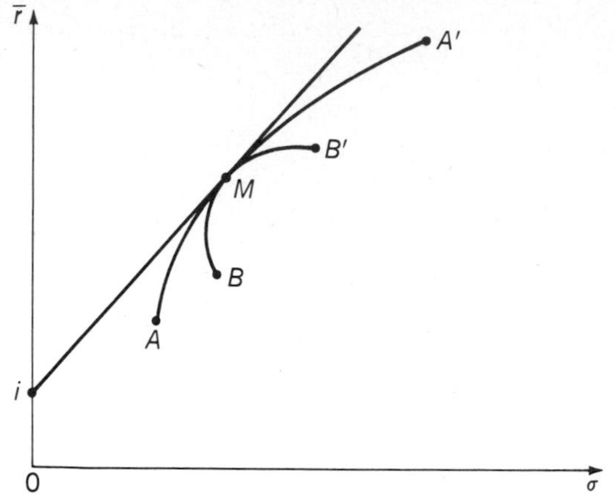


**figure 7-4**

This line is tangent to the equilibrium frontier ($AMA'$) of risky portfolios at point $M$, the market portfolio, as is shown in Fig. 7-4.

Let us take any asset i with $\bar{r}_i$ and $\sigma_i$ at point $B$ in Fig. 7-4. Consider the combinations that result from putting a fraction $x_i$ of funds into asset i and the rest $(1 - x_i)$ into the market portfolio $M$. At point $B$, $x_i = 1.0$ and all funds are invested in asset i. At $M$ the market portfolio is held ($x_i = 0$), which implies that some of asset i is held since the market portfolio includes asset i. At $B'$, *none* of asset i is held ($x_i = -v_i$, where $v_i$ is the proportion of $M$ that is represented by asset i), which implies that a sufficient amount of asset i must be sold short to cause the net holding of asset i to be zero.

The expected return ($\bar{r}_p$) and variance of return ($\sigma_p^2$) of the portfolios along $BMB'$ can be expressed as

$$\bar{r}_p = x_i\bar{r}_i + (1 - x_i)\bar{r}_M \tag{7-4}$$

$$\sigma_p^2 = x_i^2\sigma_i^2 + (1 - x_i)^2\sigma_M^2 + 2x_i(1 - x_i)\sigma_{iM} \tag{7-5}$$

where $\sigma_{iM} \equiv \text{cov}[\tilde{r}_i, \tilde{r}_M]$.

Note that $BMB'$ is drawn so that it is *tangent* to the efficient frontier $AMA'$ at point $M$. This is no accident. The two curves must touch at $M$ because point $M$ is common to both. However, $BMB'$ cannot pass through $AMA'$ because if this happened it would mean that $AMA'$ is not efficient. A point in $BMB'$ would dominate some point on $AMA'$, but by construction there is *no* combination of risky assets that is strictly superior to a point along the efficient frontier $AMA'$. Since $BMB'$ must touch but not pass through $AMA'$, $BMB'$ must be tangent at $M$. This fact enables us to derive the equilibrium rate of return on asset i.

The general argument can be presented simply; the mathematics follow. Both the capital market line and $BMB'$ are tangent to $AMA'$ at $M$. Therefore, the slope of the capital market line must equal the slope of $BMB'$ at $M$. We know the slope of the capital market line is $\lambda'$. All we need do is determine the slope of $BMB'$ at $M$ and set the two equal to find the equilibrium rate of return of asset i.

The slope of $BMB'$ is the derivative of $\bar{r}_p$ with respect to $\sigma_p$, $d\bar{r}_p/d\sigma_p$. By the chain rule of differentiation

$$\frac{d\bar{r}_p}{d\sigma_p} = \frac{d\bar{r}_p/dx_i}{d\sigma_p/dx_i} \tag{7-6}$$

From Eq. (7-4)

$$\frac{d\bar{r}_p}{dx_i} = \bar{r}_i - \bar{r}_M \tag{7-7}$$

From Eq. (7-5)

$$\sigma_p = [x_i^2\sigma_i^2 + (1 - x_i)^2\sigma_M^2 + 2x_i(1 - x_i)\sigma_{iM}]^{1/2} \tag{7-8}$$

$$\frac{d\sigma_p}{dx_i} = \frac{x_i(\sigma_i^2 + \sigma_M^2 - 2\sigma_{iM}) + \sigma_{iM} - \sigma_M^2}{\sigma_p} \tag{7-9}$$

We wish to know the slope at $M$. At $M$, $\sigma_p = \sigma_M$ and $x_i = 0$; therefore,

$$\left(\frac{d\sigma_p}{dx_i}\right)_{x_i=0} = \frac{\sigma_{iM} - \sigma_M^2}{\sigma_M} \tag{7-10}$$

We can substitute Eqs. (7-7) and (7-10) into Eq. (7-6) to arrive at the slope of $BMB'$ at $M$:

$$\left(\frac{d\bar{r}_p}{d\sigma_p}\right)_M = \frac{(\bar{r}_i - \bar{r}_M)\sigma_M}{\sigma_{iM} - \sigma_M^2} \tag{7-11}$$

Now we include the condition that the slope of the CML, $\lambda'$, must be equal to the slope of $BMB'$ at $M$; that is,

$$\frac{(\bar{r}_i - \bar{r}_M)\sigma_M}{\sigma_{iM} - \sigma_M^2} = \lambda' \tag{7-12}$$

solving Eq. (7-12) for $\bar{r}_i$, $\bar{r}_i - \bar{r}_M - \lambda'\sigma_M + \dfrac{\lambda'}{\sigma_M}\sigma_{iM}$ (7-13)

We further note that, setting $M = j$ in the CML equation, Eq. (7-2),

$$\bar{r}_M - \lambda'\sigma_M = i \tag{7-14}$$

and, therefore,

$$\bar{r}_i = i + \frac{\lambda'}{\sigma_M}\sigma_{iM} \tag{7-15}$$

and we have the security market line

$$\bar{r}_i = i + \frac{\lambda'}{\sigma_M}\operatorname{cov}[\tilde{r}_i,\tilde{r}_M] \tag{7-3}$$

as presented earlier in the chapter.

## THE VALUATION OF ASSETS

Equation (7-3) provides the equilibrium relationship between the expected return on an asset and its risk. Of more interest to the management of a firm is the relationship between the dollar returns provided and the current value (price) of the firm's shares. This relationship is provided by the substitution of Eq. (7-1) (which defined the return $\tilde{r}_i$) into Eq. (7-3):

$$\tilde{r}_i = \frac{\tilde{Y}_i}{V_i} - 1 \tag{7-1}$$

and, therefore,

$$\bar{r}_i = \frac{\bar{Y}_i}{V_i} - 1 \tag{7-1a}$$

but in equilibrium, as we have seen,

$$\bar{r}_i = i + \frac{\lambda'}{\sigma_M} \operatorname{cov}[\tilde{r}_i, \tilde{r}_M] \tag{7-3}$$

Substituting for $\tilde{r}_i$ and $\bar{r}_i$ into Eq. (7-3),

$$\frac{\bar{Y}_i}{V_i} - 1 = i + \frac{\lambda'}{\sigma_M} \operatorname{cov}\left[\left(\frac{\tilde{Y}_i}{V_i} - 1\right), \tilde{r}_M\right] \tag{7-16}$$

$V_i$ and 1 are constants; so from Chap. 4

$$\operatorname{cov}\left[\left(\frac{\tilde{Y}_i}{V_i} - 1\right), \tilde{r}_M\right] = \frac{\operatorname{cov}[\tilde{Y}_i, \tilde{r}_M]}{V_i} \tag{7-17}$$

Substituting Eq. (7-17) into Eq. (7-16) and solving for $V_i$,

$$V_i = \frac{\bar{Y}_i - (\lambda'/\sigma_M) \operatorname{cov}[\tilde{Y}_i, \tilde{r}_M]}{1 + i} \tag{7-18}$$

The standard deviation of the market $\sigma_M$ is a constant in equilibrium. We can therefore define a new "price of risk" $\lambda = \lambda'/\sigma_M$, which simplifies (7-18) to

$$V_i = \frac{\bar{Y}_i - \lambda \operatorname{cov}[\tilde{Y}_i, \tilde{r}_M]}{1 + i} \tag{7-19}$$

Equation (7-19) is a general expression for the value of an asset in equilibrium.[9] Given the joint probability distribution of the dollar returns $\tilde{Y}_i$ and the market rate of return, the riskless rate of interest, and the price of risk, the value of the asset may be determined from Eq. (7-19).

[9] This expression is essentially the same as that derived by John Lintner, The Valuation of Risk Assets and the Selection of Risky Investments in Stock Portfolios and Capital Budgets, *Review of Economics and Statistics*, vol. 47, pp. 13–37, February 1965. See sec. IV and eq. (29′) in this paper.

The expression in the numerator of the fraction $\bar{Y}_i - \lambda \text{ cov }[\tilde{Y}_i, \tilde{r}_M]$ has a simple interpretation—it is the cash or certainty equivalent of the random cash payment $\tilde{Y}_i$. Note that for riskless assets, $\text{cov}[\tilde{Y}_i, \tilde{r}_M] = 0$ and Eq. (7-19) becomes

$$V_i = \frac{\bar{Y}_i}{1 + i} \tag{7-20}$$

which is comparable to the valuation equation of Chap. 2 for perfect markets and certainly for a single period. Following this logic it should also be apparent that the value of a risky asset can be viewed as the value it would have if it were riskless less a "discount" for risk. This can be seen by writing Eq. (7-19) as

$$V_i = \frac{\bar{Y}_i}{1 + i} - \frac{\lambda \text{ cov}[\tilde{Y}_i, \tilde{r}_M]}{1 + i} \tag{7-21}$$

As an example of the application of the valuation equation and to illustrate some of its properties, consider the following two assets. The dollar return from asset $A$, $\tilde{Y}_A$, is twice as large as the dollar return from asset $B$, $\tilde{Y}_B$; $\tilde{Y}_A = 2\tilde{Y}_B$. Suppose that the joint distribution of $\tilde{Y}_B$ and the market rate of return $\tilde{r}_M$ are as shown below:

| | | $\tilde{Y}_B$ 10 | 20 | 30 |
|---|---|---|---|---|
| | .00 | .20 | .10 | 0 |
| $\tilde{r}_M$ | .10 | .10 | .20 | .10 |
| | .20 | 0 | .10 | .20 |

$\bar{Y}_B = 20$, $\text{cov}[\tilde{Y}_B, \tilde{r}_M] = .40$, $\bar{r}_M = .10$, $\sigma_M^2 = .006$

Assume that $i$ is 4%. From this information we can determine $\lambda$ because we know $\bar{r}_M$, $\sigma_M^2$, and $i$. We noted above that $\lambda' = (\bar{r}_M - i)/\sigma_M$, and by definition $\lambda = \lambda'/\sigma_M$. Therefore,

$$\begin{aligned} \lambda &= \frac{\bar{r}_M - i}{\sigma_M^2} \\ &= \frac{.10 - .04}{.006} \\ &= 10 \end{aligned} \tag{7-22}$$

We can now determine the value of asset $B$ from Eq. (7-19):

$$\begin{aligned} V_B &= \frac{\bar{Y}_B - \lambda \text{ cov}[\tilde{Y}_B, \tilde{r}_M]}{1 + i} \\ &= \frac{20 - (10)(.4)}{1.04} \\ &= \$15.38 \end{aligned} \tag{7-23}$$

We now ask what the value of asset $A$ is. If the dollar returns from asset $A$ are exactly and always twice those of asset $B$, one's intuition would suggest that the value of $A$ should be twice that of $B$. For example, if $B$ were one share of stock and $A$ were two shares, then this result seems obvious. In fact, the valuation relationship does precisely that. We know from prior work that $\bar{Y}_A = E[\tilde{Y}_A] = E[2\tilde{Y}_B] = 2E[\tilde{Y}_B] = 2\bar{Y}_B$; therefore, $\bar{Y}_A = 2(20) = 40$. Also, we know that $\text{cov}[\tilde{Y}_A, \tilde{r}_M] = \text{cov}[2\tilde{Y}_B, \tilde{r}_M] = 2 \ \text{cov}[\tilde{Y}_B, \tilde{r}_M]$; therefore, $\text{cov}[\tilde{Y}_A, \tilde{r}_M] = 2(.4) = .8$. The value of $A$ is therefore

$$V_A = \frac{\bar{Y}_A - \lambda \ \text{cov}[\tilde{Y}_A, \tilde{r}_M]}{1 + i} = \frac{40 - (10)(.8)}{1.04} = \$30.76 \qquad (7\text{-}24)$$

So far, all we have done is to show that Eq. (7-19) implies that asset values have some reasonable properties under uncertainty. Indeed, we might be concerned if the relationship did not imply these properties. In Chap. 8 the implications of the valuation equation for firm financial decisions will be developed. There we shall find that it has some not so obvious properties which are of considerable importance in developing a theory of firm financial decisions under uncertainty.

## CURRENT MARKET VALUE AND THE OBJECTIVE OF THE FIRM

Although this issue will be discussed in detail in Chap. 17, a comment is appropriate here regarding the suitability of maximization of the market value of the firm's stock as an objective for the firm's management. It may not be true that maximization of the current market value of the firm's shares is consistent with shareholder utility maximization. Therefore, a management seeking to act in the best interests of the firm's shareholders may not seek to maximize the current market value of the company's shares.

The problem can be posed in the following manner. Suppose that management is considering two alternative courses of action (e.g., mutually exclusive investments). One (alternative $A$) will result in a higher market value of the firm than the other (alternative $B$). Will all the shareholders prefer the firm to choose $A$? The answer depends on the market opportunities of the shareholders. If they can sell shares and undertake market transactions that will place them in a better position (achieve a preferred income stream) by the firm's choosing $A$ than they could achieve by having the firm choose $B$, then $A$ will be preferred. This is true even if any or all the shareholders view $B$ as the better of the two alternatives when evaluated by themselves. For example, if $B$ is a less risky investment than $A$, some or all shareholders might prefer $B$, other things being equal. However, if as a consequence of the firm's choosing $A$ those shareholders can sell a portion of their shares and use the proceeds to obtain a portfolio with a better risk-return than they could if *B* were chosen, then they will prefer the firm to choose *A*.

For example, let the firm having chosen *A* be designated firm *A*. If there exists another firm (firm *B*) that is identical to what the original firm would be had it adopted *B*, the shareholders of firm *A* could sell their shares and purchase shares of firm *B*. This transaction would leave them with shares equivalent to what they would have had if the original firm had adopted *B* and would also give them extra money to invest. Of course, if they cannot achieve a better position through their market transactions, they would be happier if the firm chose *B* despite the smaller resulting value of the firm. The consequence of this discussion is that whether market value maximization is an appropriate goal in general depends on the market opportunities of the shareholders.

Given such opportunities as exist in perfect and nearly perfect markets, management is acting in the best interests of its current shareholders by maximizing current share value, even if some of the shareholders are being forced to sell out (at a higher price) in order to reach their preferred positions.

The general result is, however, that maximization of the *current* market value of his or her assets is not necessarily an investor's objective. Consequently, in making financial decisions the goal of management should not *necessarily* be that of maximizing current share values. Some or all the firm's owners may prefer a decision inconsistent with that objective. However, throughout most of this book it will be assumed that the market opportunity conditions noted above which do imply preference for current asset-value maximization are applicable to all investors. Under these conditions the objective of the firm's financial decisions is current share-value maximization assuming that management is acting in the best interests of the firm's shareholders.

## SUGGESTED READINGS

Fama, Eugene F.: Risk, Return, and Equilibrium: Some Clarifying Comments, *Journal of Finance*, vol. 23, pp. 29–40, March 1968. (This paper should be read in conjunction with the paper by Sharpe and Lintner below.)

Lintner, John: Security Prices, Risk, and Maximal Gains from Diversification, *Journal of Finance*, vol. 20, pp. 587–615, December 1965.

Mossin, Jan: Equilibrium in a Capital Asset Market, *Econometrica*, vol. 34, pp. 768–783, October 1966, reprinted in Archer, Stephen H. and Charles A. D'Ambrosio, "The Theory of Business Finance," 2d ed., The Macmillan Company, New York, 1976.

Sharpe, William F.: Capital Asset Prices: A Theory of Market Equilibrium under Conditions of Risk, *Journal of Finance*, vol. 19, pp. 425–442, September 1964, reprinted in Archer and D'Ambrosio, *ibid*.

CHAPTER

# EIGHT

# FIRM FINANCIAL DECISIONS: THE SINGLE-PERIOD MODEL

In this chapter we shall apply the single-period valuation model of Chap. 7 to a firm that is expected to be liquidated one period from the present time. Despite the lack of realism in assuming such a firm, it is worthwhile examining because it provides a fairly simple and rigorous way to deal with firm financial decisions under uncertainty. Our treatment here should be helpful in developing and illustrating the issues faced in the more general discussion of later chapters, and it provides precise criteria for firm financial decisions that the more general models do not. Assuming a single-period firm permits us to examine some of the problems posed by uncertainty without the complications of the multiperiod analysis discussed later.

## BASIC ASSUMPTIONS

We assume that the firm will pay a liquidating dividend $\tilde{D}_1$ at time 1 to the owners of the shares outstanding just before time 0; the amount is uncertain although the probability distribution is known. After $\tilde{D}_1$ is paid, the value of the firm will be zero for certain. Let $S^o$ be the value of the firm's "old" shares at time 0 *just after current dividends are paid.* The old shares are those that are outstanding at time 0 and for at least one period before time 0. It is the wealth of investors owning the time 0 old shares that decisions at time 0 are meant to maximize. From Eq. (7-19) the value of $\tilde{D}_1$ will be

$$S^o = \frac{\bar{D}_1 - \lambda \operatorname{cov}[\tilde{D}_1, \tilde{r}_M]}{1 + i} \tag{8-1}$$

The wealth of the firm's shareholders provided by their ownership of the firm at time 0 is $W_S = S^o + D_0$. All of $D_0$ is paid to the time 0 old shares; any new shares issued at time 0 do not receive dividends until time 1. We assume that shareholders are indifferent between dividends and capital gains in the sense that they would be indifferent between obtaining an incremental dividend $\Delta D_0$ or an increment in the ex-dividend value of their shares $\Delta S^o$ of the same dollar amount.

Management should attempt to maximize $W_S$ if it is to act in the best interests of its current (or "old") shareholders. By current shareholders we mean those who own shares at the time management is making its decisions. These shareholders are the ones who will receive $D_0$. Management is also assumed to take market equilibrium conditions as given. (They are "price takers" in the language of economics.) Obviously the decisions made by management will have some effect on general equilibrium, but a very small one that can be safely ignored. The two decision areas of concern are financing policy and investment policy.

## FINANCING POLICY

The firm is assumed to have a certain cash income at time 0 of $X_0$ and an uncertain cash income produced at time 1 of $\tilde{X}_1$, where $\tilde{X}_1$ includes the funds realized from selling its assets. The capital budget of the firm at time 0 is $I_0$, which is also certain (once the investment decision is made) at time 0. The firm's cash income at time 1 includes the random returns from the firm's investment at time 0. These assumptions are very similar to the ones made in the single-period case discussed in Chap. 2; the only difference is that the dividends and income of the firm at time 1 are now assumed to be random variables rather than being known for certain at time 0.

The firm has two general sources of funds available to finance its current investments: internal (through retained earnings by reducing dividends) and external (bonds or stock). In Chap. 2 we noted that the issue of "dividend policy" was in essence a problem of financing policy; therefore, the discussion here includes "dividend policy." As in Chap. 2, paying a dividend of $D_0$ reduces the funds available to the firm, and external sources may be needed of amount $F_0$. At time 0 the cash-flow equation of the firm is

$$\underset{\text{(Inflow)}}{X_0 + F_0} = \underset{\text{(Outflow)}}{D_0 + I_0} \tag{8-2}$$

which is identical to Eq. (2-7). Similarly, we can use Eq. (8-2) to express the total dividends of the firm at time 0:

$$D_0 = X_0 - I_0 + F_0 \tag{8-3}$$

We now must determine the payments to current shareholders at time 1. Raising $F_0$ in the market will commit the firm to make some payment at time 1 to the suppliers of $F_0$. In general this payment is some uncertain amount $\tilde{Y}^F$, where everyone agrees on the distribution of $\tilde{Y}^F$. Since $I_1 = 0$ because the firm liquidates at time 1, the cash-flow equation at time 1 is

$$\tilde{X}_1 = \tilde{D}_1 + \tilde{Y}^F \tag{8-4}$$

all quantities being in general random variables. From Eq. (8-4), $\tilde{D}_1$ must therefore be

$$\tilde{D}_1 = \tilde{X}_1 - \tilde{Y}^F \tag{8-5}$$

We can now substitute for $\tilde{D}_1$ in our valuation Eq. (8-1) and perform some algebraic manipulations based on the additive property of covariances [Eq. (4-7)].

$$S^O = \frac{\bar{D}_1 - \lambda \operatorname{cov}[\tilde{D}_1]}{1+i}$$
$$= \frac{(\bar{X}_1 - \bar{Y}^F) - \lambda \operatorname{cov}[(\tilde{X}_1 - \tilde{Y}^F),\tilde{r}_M]}{1+i}$$

but $\operatorname{cov}[(\tilde{X}_1 - \tilde{Y}^F),\tilde{r}_M] = \operatorname{cov}[\tilde{X}_1,\tilde{r}_M] - \operatorname{cov}[\tilde{Y}^F,\tilde{r}_M]$ and therefore

$$S^O = \frac{\bar{X}_1 - \lambda \operatorname{cov}[\tilde{X}_1,\tilde{r}_M]}{1+i} - \frac{\bar{Y}^F - \lambda \operatorname{cov}[\tilde{Y}^F,\tilde{r}_M]}{1+i} \tag{8-6}$$

$F_0$ was raised in equilibrium capital markets by assumption. Therefore, the market value of the uncertain dollar return $\tilde{Y}^F$ must be $F_0$; that is,

$$F_0 = \frac{\bar{Y}^F - \lambda \operatorname{cov}[\tilde{Y}^F,\tilde{r}_M]}{1+i} \tag{8-7}$$

As a consequence, substituting Eq. (8-7) into Eq. (8-6),

$$S^O = \frac{\bar{X}_1 - \lambda \operatorname{cov}[\tilde{X}_1,\tilde{r}_M]}{1+i} - F_0 \tag{8-8}$$

The wealth provided by the firm to its current shareholders is $W_S = S^O + D_0$. If we substitute for $S^O$ and $D_0$ using Eqs. (8-8) and (8-3), respectively, we arrive at

$$W_S = X_0 - I_0 + \frac{\bar{X}_1 - \lambda \operatorname{cov}[\tilde{X}_1,\tilde{r}_M]}{1+i} \tag{8-9}$$

The conclusion expressed by Eq. (8-9) is that the wealth provided by the firm is independent of financing policy since neither $X_0$, $\tilde{X}_1$, nor $I_0$ is affected by financing policy. The wealth is solely a function of the basic cash flows of the firm and investment policy. An important and attractive feature of this expression is that it reduces directly to the equivalent relationship derived under certainty [Eq. (2-12)] when the cash flows of the firm are riskless.[1] Uncertainty in itself does not change the conclusions reached in Chap. 2 with respect to financing policy—it is irrelevant.

Note that no assumptions were made as to the *type* of external financing that is used, whether new shares, riskless debt, or risky debt. So long as the income provided to the suppliers of the financing is valued according to Eq. (8-7) (as it must be under the assumptions here) the type of financing used makes no difference. Since this conclusion is an important one, let us examine the two most interesting cases: new shares and risky debt.

## Stock Issues

If the firm issues new shares of common stock to finance investment in the current period, the new stockholders will acquire the right to share proportionally in the future returns of the firm. Suppose sufficient shares are issued that the new shares constitute 10% of the total outstanding. Of the total payment of the firm at time 1, $\tilde{X}_1$ (whatever it happens to be), 10% will be paid to the new shares and 90% to the original shares. The value of the new shares issued must be

$$S^N = \frac{.10\bar{X}_1 - \lambda \operatorname{cov}[.10\tilde{X}_1, \tilde{r}_M]}{1 + i} \tag{8-10}$$

assuming that the new shares are issued ex-dividend at time 0. The value of the old shares ex-dividend must also be

$$S^O = \frac{.90\bar{X}_1 - \lambda \operatorname{cov}[.90\tilde{X}_1, \tilde{r}_M]}{1 + i} \tag{8-11}$$

The wealth provided to the owners of the old shares is $W_S = S^O + D_0$, and $D_0 = X_0 - I_0 + S^N$ from the cash-flow accounting. Therefore,

$$W_S = X_0 - I_0 + S^N + S^O \tag{8-12}$$

but $(S^N + S^O)$ is just the total value of the firm after issuing the new shares. It should not make any difference to the total value as to how the income is split up between old and new shares. It does not.

[1] In chap. 2 the value of the firm was expressed at the instant in time before the current dividend $D_0$ was paid. Here the wealth of the shareholders provided by the firm is determined at the time the dividend is received by them. Both treatments are fully equivalent in perfect markets. In imperfect markets the wealth approach is more appropriate, although the specific relationship $W_S = D_0 + S^O$ does not necessarily apply. See also the discussion of the share-value maximization rule at the end of chap. 7.

$$S^N + S^O = \frac{.10\bar{X}_1 - \lambda \operatorname{cov}[.10\tilde{X}_1,\tilde{r}_M]}{1+i} + \frac{.90\bar{X}_1 - \lambda \operatorname{cov}[.90\tilde{X}_1,\tilde{r}_M]}{1+i}$$

$$= \frac{\bar{X}_1 - \lambda \operatorname{cov}[\tilde{X}_1,\tilde{r}_M]}{1+i} \tag{8-13}$$

Substituting Eq. (8-13) into Eq. (8-12), we end up with our earlier expression Eq. (8-9), in which the wealth of the original shareholders does not depend on whether new shares are issued or not.

## Risky Debt

Rather than present a variation of the basic proof applied to financing with risky debt,[2] an example will be used to illustrate the issues.

Assume the following simple joint probability distributions of the firm's income at time 1 and the market rate of return:

| $\tilde{r}_M$ \ $\tilde{X}_1$ | 2,000 | 4,000 | 6,000 |
|---|---|---|---|
| −.05 | .10 | 0 | 0 |
| .00 | .10 | .10 | .05 |
| .10 | .05 | .30 | .10 |
| .30 | 0 | .10 | .10 |

$\bar{X}_1 = \$4{,}000$, $\bar{r}_M = .10$, $\operatorname{cov}[\tilde{X}_1,\tilde{r}_M] = \$80$, $\sigma_M^2 = .01275$

Also let the riskless rate of interest be 5%. $\lambda$ can be determined from the relationship $\lambda = (\bar{r}_M - i)/\sigma_M^2$ and in this example is equal to 3.9. The ex-dividend value of the firm's shares if no external financing is used is [from Eq. (8-1)] $S^O = [\$4{,}000 - 3.9(\$80)]/1.05 = \$3{,}512$. The expected rate of return on the stock is 14% $[(\bar{D}_1 - S^O)/S^O = \$4{,}000/\$3{,}512 - 1 = .14]$.

Suppose that the firm attempts to issue \$2,000 in bonds at par value with a coupon rate of 6%. This bond issue commits the firm to pay \$2,120 in principal and interest at time 1. But according to the income possibilities above, under some conditions the most that the firm will be able to pay is \$2,000. (The bondholders, of course, have priority over the shareholders.) There is in fact a .25 probability that the bondholders will receive only the par value of \$2,000

[2] We have assumed in chap. 7 that individual investors can borrow and lend at the riskless rate $i$. One might well ask why it makes sense to worry about business firms issuing risky debt when individuals are assumed to be able to borrow at the riskless rate. There are two answers: (1) individual incomes produced from their human wealth were assumed certain and in perfect markets can therefore be borrowed against risklessly, and (2) the situation is interesting because it illustrates some basic issues in financing policy irrespective of the realism of the particular assumptions.

and a .75 probability that they will receive the payment promised them of \$2,120. The expected value of the payments is therefore only \$2,090, and the expected return to the bondholders if the bonds were issued at par would be only 4.5%, compared to the available riskless return of 5%. The bonds are unlikely to sell at par under these conditions. The market value of the bonds will be determined by the equilibrium conditions that apply to all securities and is based on the characteristics of the joint probability distribution of the payments to bondholders $\tilde{Y}^B$ and the market rate of return. This distribution can be derived from the distribution of the firm's total income:

| | | $\tilde{Y}^B$ | |
|---|---|---|---|
| | | 2,000 | 2,120 |
| $\tilde{r}_M$ | −.05 | .10 | 0 |
| | .00 | .10 | .15 |
| | .10 | .05 | .40 |
| | .30 | 0 | .20 |

$\bar{Y}^B = \$2{,}090$, $\mathrm{cov}[\tilde{Y}^B, \tilde{r}_M] = \$3.0$

The market value of the bonds is computed from Eq. (8-7) and is [\$2,090 − 3.9(\$3.0)]/1.05 = \$1,979. In other words, the firm will receive only \$1,979 from the sale of these bonds, which will be used to increase current dividends by \$1,979, over what they would have been if the bonds were not issued. The bondholders require an expected rate of return of 5.61% [(\$2,090/\$1,979) − 1] to compensate for the degree of risk assumed.[3]

The issuance of the bonds also changes the income provided to the shareholders, who will receive what is left after paying the bondholders. The distribution of the residual income ($\tilde{D}_1 = \tilde{X}_1 - \tilde{Y}^B$) is

| | | $\tilde{X}_1 - \tilde{Y}^B$ | | |
|---|---|---|---|---|
| | | 0 | 1,880 | 3,880 |
| $\tilde{r}_M$ | −.05 | .10 | 0 | 0 |
| | .00 | .10 | .10 | .05 |
| | .10 | .05 | .30 | .10 |
| | .30 | 0 | .10 | .10 |

$\bar{X}_1 - \bar{Y}^B = \$1{,}910$, $\mathrm{cov}[(\tilde{X}_1 - \tilde{Y}^B), \tilde{r}_M] = \$77$

[3] We must assume quadratic utilities for individuals in order to justify application of the valuation model to risky bonds, since in general the distribution of $\tilde{Y}_B$ is not a normal distribution or even one that can be described by two parameters. Refer to the discussion in chap. 5, p. 97.

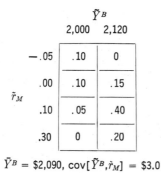

The value of the shares after issuing the bonds will be

$$
\begin{aligned}
S^O &= \frac{(\bar{X}_1 - \bar{Y}^B) - \lambda \operatorname{cov}[(\tilde{X}_1 - \tilde{Y}^B), \tilde{r}_M]}{1+i} \\
&= \frac{\$1{,}910 - 3.9(\$77)}{1.05} \\
&= \$1{,}533
\end{aligned}
$$

The expected return on the new value is now 24.6% [(\$1,910/\$1,533) − 1], as the risk to the shareholders has risen because of the bond financing.[4] The ex-dividend value of the shares has dropped from \$3,512 to \$1,533, reflecting both the reduction in income and increased risk. The change in value of the shares (\$3,512 − \$1,533) is \$1,979, which equals the receipts from the bond issue. Therefore, the only effect of the bond issue was to provide \$1,979 in higher current dividends at the expense of a reduction in the ex-dividend value of the firm. Since shareholders could sell their shares if they needed current income and could reinvest the dividends if they did not, no advantage or disadvantage results from financing with risky bonds.

The preceding example raises two issues of importance to future development of the theory and its applications. First, it should be clear from the example that the *coupon* rate of interest on a bond (6% in the example) has only an indirect relationship with the equilibrium required return of 5.61%. There are actually three interest rates in the example, the two just mentioned above and the yield to maturity. The yield to maturity is defined as the rate of interest computed *as if* the payments on the bonds were certain. In the preceding example the yield to maturity is computed by taking the *promised* payment of \$2,120 and determining the rate of return on the current market value of the bonds; that is, the yield to maturity equals 7.1% (\$2,120/\$1,979 − 1). The yield to maturity (henceforth, simply "yield") is therefore the *maximum* rate of return that will be earned on the bond and the maximum rate paid by the firm. In the example the bondholders either will earn 7.1% with probability .75 or will earn 1.1% (\$2,000/\$1,979 − 1) with probability .25. The expected rate of return can therefore be computed from these figures as 5.6%. The yield on a bond is the figure often found in the daily newspaper; but, as we have seen, the more relevant interest rate is the expected return. The yield is in fact derived from the other factors in the situation.

Given the expectations for the firm's cash flows, and the promised payments of the bond issue (coupon interest plus principal), the market determines the value of the bond issue and the required rate of return based on the risk of that issue. The yield is then computed from the market value of the bonds and the promised payments. It should be noted that if the firm in the example issued

[4] The "gross dollar risk" has actually fallen from \$80 to \$77; but the risk per dollar of expected income (a measure we shall see more of later) has gone from \$80/\$4,000 = .02 to \$77/\$1,910 = .04. The risk as measured by $\operatorname{cov}[\tilde{r}_i, \tilde{r}_M]$ has increased from \$80/\$3,512 = .023 to \$77/\$1,533 = .05.

only \$1,000 of par value bonds with a coupon rate of 7.5%, the bonds would sell for \$1,075/1.05 = \$1,025 because the promised payment of \$1,075 would be made for certain, given the probability distribution of $\tilde{X}_1$ assumed above. In this case the yield on the bonds will equal the required rate of return in the market, the riskless rate of 5%. In general, the yield to maturity will equal the market rate only when the bond payments are riskless. The coupon rate will equal the yield if the bonds are sold at par. For risky, one-period bonds the yield to maturity is always greater than the expected rate of return since the yield is the highest rate of return that can be earned on the bond.[5]

The second point to be made follows from the first one. In future discussions a distinction must be made between such rates as the yield on a bond and the expected rate of return on the bond as determined by the market in equilibrium. It will be convenient to distinguish between rates of return in general ($r$) and equilibrium values of the expected rate of return on securities ($k$). Notice that it is assumed here that there is a particular equilibrium expected rate of return in the market on a given stream since all investors agree on the probability distributions. Thus, a new variable is defined, $k$, which will always be used for the equilibrium market rate that applies to a security of a given risk. The market rate of return on a bond will be denoted as $k_B$ and the comparable rate for common stock will be $k_S$. Rates of return in general will continue to be denoted as $r$. The riskless rate of interest will also continue to be represented as $i$ since this rate has a special significance under uncertainty even though it, too, is an equilibrium rate.

## INVESTMENT POLICY

In the preceding section we found that the financing and dividend decisions of the firm do not affect its value to current stockholders, as was also true of the certainty case. In this section we shall examine criteria for investment decisions. Two aspects of the problem of investment for the firm are important here: the criterion for the optimal capital budget at time 0, and criteria for project selection and evaluation. As was done in Chap. 2 for the single-period case, $\tilde{X}'_1$ is the cash receipts the firm would have at time 1 if no investment were undertaken at time 0 ($I_0 = 0$); however, the receipts are now uncertain. Let the random variable $\Delta\tilde{X}$ be the increment to the cash receipts of the firm at time 1 from undertaking any particular capital budget $I_0$. The total cash income of the firm at time 1 is therefore $\tilde{X}_1 = \tilde{X}'_1 + \Delta\tilde{X}$. Substituting for $\tilde{X}_1$ in Eq. (8-9), we have the wealth of the original shareholders of the firm as a function of the investment undertaken at time 0 and its results:

[5] With bonds maturing more than one period hence, the bondholders could earn more than the current yield to maturity if bond prices increase because of a fall in market interest rates. In a multiperiod analysis the "holding period yield," the rate of return over the period held, is as important for bonds as it is for stocks.

$$W_S = X_0 - I_0 + \frac{(\bar{X}_1' + \Delta\bar{X}) - \lambda \operatorname{cov}[(\tilde{X}_1' + \Delta\tilde{X}), \tilde{r}_M]}{1 + i}$$

but $\operatorname{cov}[(\tilde{X}_1' + \Delta\tilde{X}), \tilde{r}_M] = \operatorname{cov}[\tilde{X}_1', \tilde{r}_M] + \operatorname{cov}[\Delta\tilde{X}, \tilde{r}_M]$ by the additivity rule we used earlier in the chapter. Therefore,

$$W_S = X_0 - I_0 + \frac{\bar{X}_1' - \lambda \operatorname{cov}[\tilde{X}_1', \tilde{r}_M]}{1 + i} + \frac{\Delta\bar{X} - \lambda \operatorname{cov}[\Delta\tilde{X}, \tilde{r}_M]}{1 + i} \tag{8-14}$$

Not all the terms in Eq. (8-14) are affected by the firm's investment decisions. Only $I_0$ and the term containing measures on the probability distribution of $\Delta\tilde{X}$ need be considered. The basic objective is to maximize $W_S$. Investment decisions should therefore be made so as to maximize the contribution of investment to $W_S$; that is,

$$\max \left\{ \frac{\Delta\bar{X} - \lambda \operatorname{cov}[\Delta\tilde{X}, \tilde{r}_M]}{1 + i} - I_0 \right\} \tag{8-15}$$

Expression (8-15) provides the objective of investment policy and is the increment to the wealth of the shareholders from undertaking $I_0$. As was true in the certainty case, the firm should evaluate its alternative capital budgets and choose the budget with the highest incremental value to the firm's shareholders.

In Chap. 3 we looked at the problem of organizing the firm's investment opportunities in a way that minimized the computational effort required. An efficient method was to separate opportunities into economically (as opposed to statistically) independent projects. Each project could then be accepted or rejected using any one of three methods: present value, uniform annual series, or rate of return. We also discussed in that chapter the use of these methods in comparing the alternatives which in general constitute a project. The organizational procedure is also appropriate under uncertainty; however, the use of the methods is somewhat more difficult. We shall examine the problem of project selection first.

## Project Selection

We wish to know whether a particular project should be included in the capital budget. The initial cost of the project is $I_{Z0}$ and it is expected to return an uncertain amount $\tilde{Z}$ at time 1.[6] From the condition of economic independence we know that the total investment budget of the firm if the project is undertaken will be $I_0 + I_{Z0}$ and that the returns at time 1 from the total budget will be $\Delta\tilde{X}$ +

[6] We assume that the project-evaluation approach to Chap. 3 (pages 47 to 51) has been used to identify the best alternative involving some investment outlay $I_{Z0}$. The task here is to determine whether that alternative is better than the alternative of doing nothing. Precisely how this investment alternative may be determined is discussed later. If this is bothersome, think of the project as involving only one opportunity.

$\tilde{Z}$, where $I_0$ and $\Delta\tilde{X}$ are the cost of the firm's other investments and returns from such investments, respectively. Using our criterion for the optimal budget [expression (8-15)], the project should be undertaken only if there is an increase in value over what it would be if the project were not undertaken; that is,

$$\frac{(\Delta\bar{X} + \bar{Z}) - \lambda \operatorname{cov}[(\Delta\tilde{X} + \tilde{Z}), \tilde{r}_M]}{1 + i} - (I_0 + I_{Z0}) > \frac{\Delta\bar{X} - \lambda \operatorname{cov}[\Delta\tilde{X}, \tilde{r}_M]}{1 + i} - I_0 \qquad (8\text{-}16)$$

but $\operatorname{cov}[(\Delta\tilde{X} + \tilde{Z}), \tilde{r}_M] = \operatorname{cov}[\Delta\tilde{X}, \tilde{r}_M] + \operatorname{cov}[\tilde{Z}, \tilde{r}_M]$; therefore, expression (8-16) reduces to

$$\frac{\bar{Z} - \lambda \operatorname{cov}[\tilde{Z}, \tilde{r}_M]}{1 + i} - I_{Z0} > 0 \qquad (8\text{-}17)$$

The ratio term in relation (8-17) is the value of stream $\tilde{Z}$, the cash flow generated by the project; i.e., relation (8-17) can also be stated as $V_Z - I_{Z0} > 0$. As might be expected, the rule for project selection is a direct reflection of the criterion for the optimal capital budget. If the project has a positive incremental value, it should be accepted. This rule is economically equivalent to the present-value rule under certainty and reduces to that case when the cash flows of the project are riskless. A riskless project is one for which $\operatorname{cov}[\tilde{Z}, \tilde{r}_M] = 0$; therefore, the project-selection rule becomes for a *riskless* project

$$\frac{\bar{Z}}{1 + i} - I_{Z0} > 0 \qquad (8\text{-}18)$$

The distinction between economic independence and statistical independence is of critical importance to understanding the significance of the project-selection rule developed above. In Chap. 3 a project was defined as an investment option whose acceptance would not alter the profitability or possibility of acceptance of any other project available to the firm. Under uncertainty the definition requires that the *probability distributions* of the cash flows of all opportunities not included in the project be unaffected by the acceptance of one or more of the opportunities included in the project. That is, the probability of any outcome from other investments of the firm not included in the project must be unaffected by the adoption of the project. The potential benefits and costs of all other opportunities must not be changed as the result of undertaking the project. This condition is what is meant by "economic independence." However, it does *not* mean that the cash flows from a project are *uncorrelated* with the cash flows from other projects. The projects' cash flows do not have to be statistically independent.

The project-selection rule (8-17) holds, no matter how the cash flows from the projects under consideration are correlated. Economically independent opportunities (projects) can still be evaluated independently; the firm *does not* have a portfolio problem as does the individual. In other words, the fact that the firm's shareholders hold highly diversified portfolios means that the firm does not have to concern itself with diversification. The firm does take into account [via the covariance term in (8-17)] the impact of its decisions on the risk of the portfolio held by its shareholders but does not have to consider the effects of taking on alternative combinations of projects or the combination of any given capital budget and the existing assets of the firm.[7]

The result is that the approach outlined on pages 47 to 51 of Chap. 3 is appropriate here. Opportunities are divided into the maximum number of projects attainable. For *each* project the best alternative (combination of opportunities) is selected and adopted. One of the alternatives is to do nothing, i.e., to reject the project. The best alternative in a project is the alternative that has the highest difference as expressed in relation (8-17) (the highest net present value $V_Z - I_{Z0}$) where "doing nothing" has a zero net present value.

An example may help clarify these points. Suppose that a firm is considering purchase of two separate parcels of land in the same city and has determined that the optimal development plan for each would be to build apartments on them. The two parcels are several miles apart, and the purchase and development of one will not affect the cost or cash returns from the purchase and development of the other. They are economically independent and can therefore be considered projects. The returns from the two projects are likely to be correlated because of their common dependence on local economic conditions; they are statistically dependent. This statistical dependence is irrelevant to the selection of either project. Their covariances with the total market are the only relevant characteristics in determining the risk of the projects. They may be accepted or rejected independently using the project-selection rule. Moreover, it does not matter what other activities the firm is pursuing or might undertake. The returns from the projects might even be negatively correlated with the results of some of the other activities, but that has no bearing on the decisions with respect to the two projects.

## Value Additivity

The project-selection rule (8-17) says that any project for which the value of the returns exceeds the cost should be undertaken and that the value can be assessed without taking into account the other projects under consideration. The derivations of both the criterion for the optimal budget (8-15) and the project-selection rule imply that the following is true:

$$V_{X_1} = V_{X_1'} + V_{\Delta X_1} \tag{8-19}$$

[7] This conclusion is counter to that reached by Lintner, the Valuation of Risk Assets and the Selection of Risky Investments in Stock Portfolios and Capital Budgets (listed in the Suggested Readings at the end of this chapter). The reason for the divergence in views is the assumption that the investment decisions of the firm do not affect market equilibrium conditions. See Charles W. Haley, Comment on the Valuation of Risk Assets . . . , *Review of Economics and Statistics*, May 1969.

and

$$V_{\Delta X} = \sum_{i=1}^{n} V_{Z_i} \tag{8-20}$$

where $V_{X_1}$ = current value of total cash flow of firm at time 1
$V_{X_1'}$ = value of cash flow that results if no investment is made
$V_{\Delta X}$ = value of incremental cash flow from total budget
$V_{Z_i}$ = value of cash return from project i

These variables are defined from (8-15) and (8-17) as

$$V_{X_1} = \frac{\bar{X}_1 - \lambda \operatorname{cov}[\tilde{X}_1, \tilde{r}_M]}{1 + i} \tag{8-21}$$

$$V_{X_1'} = \frac{\bar{X}_1' - \lambda \operatorname{cov}[\tilde{X}_1', \tilde{r}_M]}{1 + i} \tag{8-22}$$

$$V_{\Delta X} = \frac{\Delta\bar{X} - \lambda \operatorname{cov}[\Delta\tilde{X}, \tilde{r}_M]}{1 + i} \tag{8-23}$$

$$V_{Z_i} = \frac{\bar{Z}_i - \lambda \operatorname{cov}[\tilde{Z}_i, \tilde{r}_M]}{1 + i} \tag{8-24}$$

They are the market values of the respective cash returns and follow from the general valuation relationship (7-19); in particular, $V_{Z_i}$ can be thought of as the amount the firm (and its shareholders) would receive if the rights to $\tilde{Z}_i$ were sold in the market after the firm had paid the initial cost $I_{Z_i0}$.[8]

Equations (8-19) and (8-20) are examples of a valuation principle that holds in general under perfect markets; this will be referred to as the *value additivity principle*.[9] When this principle applies, as it does here, the value of a set of income streams (for example, $\Delta\tilde{X}$) is equal to the sum of the values of the individual streams (for example, the $\tilde{Z}_i$). Value additivity is a property of the capital markets of this chapter and is useful in dealing with the problem of project selection and evaluation.

One implication of value additivity is that there is no advantage to mergers between firms or firm diversification per se. If the combined income stream of two merged firms is simply the sum of the incomes of the firms without merger, the market value of the combination will simply equal the sum of the premerger values of the two firms. Only if there is some income benefit to a merger will there be an increase in value as a result of the combination.

[8] If the firm has not paid $I_{Z_i0}$ then the project would sell for $V_{Z_i0} - I_{Z_i0}$.

[9] This principle will be the subject of considerable discussion in later chapters. When it holds, diversification by the firm is irrelevant. Although it was not discussed at that point, the principle was operative in the proofs of the irrelevance of financing policy earlier in the chapter. In the context of financing policy the rule applies in reverse; i.e., no matter how you split up a given income stream the sum of the values of the component streams equals the value of the original stream.

## Risk-Adjusted Discount Rates

The project-selection rule (8-17) is directly comparable to the present-value rule under certainty. Of some interest is whether alternative rules can also be used. In particular, we would like to know whether there exists a "risk-adjusted discount rate" that could be used under uncertainty in the same fashion the riskless rate was used under certainty but applied to the *expected values* of the cash flows. That is, we would like to find a single rate $k_Z$ such that

$$\frac{\bar{Z}}{1 + k_Z} = V_Z \tag{8-25}$$

Equation (8-25) can be solved for $k_Z$ by substituting for $V_Z$ from its definition (8-24):

$$\frac{\bar{Z}}{1 + k_Z} = \frac{\bar{Z} - \lambda \operatorname{cov}[\tilde{Z},\tilde{r}_M]}{1 + i}$$

$$1 + k_Z = \frac{(1 + i)\bar{Z}}{\bar{Z} - \lambda \operatorname{cov}[\tilde{Z},\tilde{r}_M]}$$

$$1 + k_Z = \frac{1 + i}{1 - \lambda \operatorname{cov}[\tilde{Z},\tilde{r}_M]/\bar{Z}}$$

$$k_Z = \frac{1 + i}{1 - \lambda \operatorname{cov}[\tilde{Z}/\bar{Z},\tilde{r}_M]} - 1 \tag{8-26}$$

The quantity $(1 - \lambda \operatorname{cov}[\tilde{Z}/\bar{Z},\tilde{r}_M])$ can be thought of as a "risk-adjustment factor," $\alpha$, which converts the expected return $Z$ into its certainty (cash) equivalent, so that

$$V_Z = \frac{\alpha\bar{Z}}{1 + i}$$

This concept is discussed more thoroughly in Chap. 9.

Equation (8-26) is of interest because it introduces an alternative measure of the risk of an income stream, $\operatorname{cov}[\tilde{Z}/\bar{Z}, \tilde{r}_M]$. The ratio $\tilde{Z}/\bar{Z}$ adjusts the random variable $\tilde{Z}$ for scale—the magnitude of $\tilde{Z}$. This adjustment implies that the following two cash flows are equally risky in that the same risk-adjusted rate would apply to each even though they are not equally risky in an absolute sense:

$$A\colon \bar{Z}_A = 100 \qquad \operatorname{cov}[\tilde{Z}_A,\tilde{r}_M] = 5$$

$$B\colon \bar{Z}_B = 1{,}000 \qquad \operatorname{cov}[\tilde{Z}_B,\tilde{r}_M] = 50$$

From Eq. (8-26), $k_Z$ is a nonlinear function of the risk of the income. Figure 8-1 graphs $k_Z$ for $i$ equal to 5% and $\lambda$ equal to 3.9. Over the range of "normal" risks, $k_Z$ is in fact approximately linear.[10] Note that in the example used earlier the

[10] If managers are to estimate values of $k_Z$ for projects of different risks, it would be helpful for the relationship between the risk of a project and its required return to be approximately linear. That $k_Z$ is approximately linear in $\operatorname{cov}[\tilde{Z}/\bar{Z},\tilde{r}_M]$ is shown by the following: Let $z = \lambda \operatorname{cov}[\tilde{Z}/Z,\tilde{r}_M]$. Equation (8-26) can be expressed as

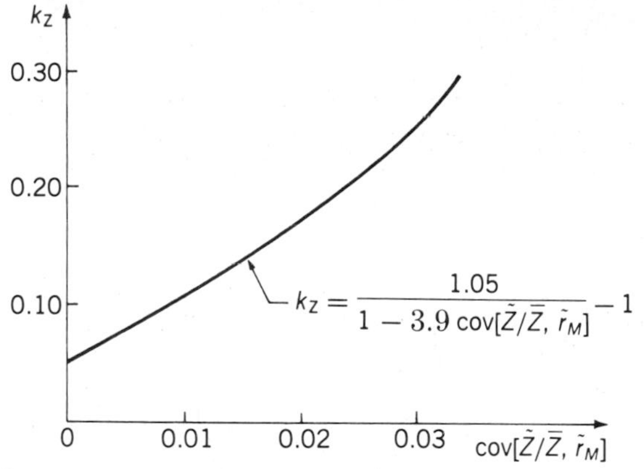


**figure 8-1**

total expected cash flow of the firm was \$4,000 and $\operatorname{cov}[\tilde{X}, \tilde{r}_M]$ was \$70. $\operatorname{Cov}[\tilde{X}/\bar{X}, \tilde{r}_M]$ is therefore \$70/\$4,000 = .0175 and $k$ for this amount is and was 16%. As implied from our use of $k$ for this rate and the comparison with the equilibrium rate for the firm, Eq. (8-26) is an alternative form of the security market line as developed in Chap. 7.[11]

---

$$k_Z = \frac{1+i}{1-z} - 1 \tag{a}$$

The Taylor series expansion of ($a$) around zero is

$$k_Z = i + (1+i)z + (1+i)z^2 + (1+i)z^3 + \cdots \tag{b}$$

Using the first two terms of ($b$) as a linear approximation,

$$k_Z' = i + (1+i)z \tag{c}$$

when $i = .05$, $\lambda = 3.9$, and $\operatorname{cov}[\tilde{Z}/\bar{Z}, \tilde{r}_M] = .01$, $k_Z$ from ($a$) is $1.05/.961 - 1 = .093$ or 9.3%. Computing $k_Z'$ from ($c$)

$$k_Z' = .05 + (1.05)(.039) = .091 \text{ or } 9.1\%$$

For practical purposes the difference between 9.3% and 9.1% is negligible. At higher risks, of course, the difference becomes larger, but still not excessive; e.g., for $\operatorname{cov}[Z/\bar{Z}, \tilde{r}_M] = .025$, $k_Z = 16.3\%$ and $k_Z' = 15.2\%$.

[11] $k_Z$ can be derived from the SML [eq. (7-3)] by using the relationship $\tilde{r} = \tilde{Y}/V - 1$ and the valuation relationship, eq. (7-19); however, the algebra is tedious. Alternatively, we note that the equilibrium expected return ($\bar{r}_Y$) on an asset is

$$\bar{r}_Y = \frac{\bar{Y}}{V_Y} - 1$$

or

$$V_Y = \frac{\bar{Y}}{1 + \bar{r}_Y}$$

We derived $k_Z$ from the requirement that $V_Z = \bar{Z}/(1 + k_Z)$. If $V_Z$ is the equilibrium value of $\tilde{Z}$, then $k_Z$ must be the equilibrium expected return on $V_Z$ and $\bar{r}_Y = k_Z$ for *any* stream $\tilde{Z}$ or $\tilde{Y}$. See also app. 8A.

The usefulness of Eq. (8-26) lies not so much in the fact that a required rate of return on projects can be computed from it, but in the fact that such a rate exists and that it is solely a function of the market equilibrium parameters $i$ and $\lambda$ and of the cash flow from the project in question. It is therefore theoretically sound under the assumptions of this chapter to speak of the required rate of return for an opportunity that is a function of the risk of the opportunity. The project-selection rules derived in Chap. 3 can therefore be applied under uncertainty except that the criterion rate in general differs from opportunity to opportunity depending on the risks. That is, instead of using $i$ as the criterion rate for all projects, $k_Z$ must be determined for each opportunity.

## Evaluation of Alternatives

In choosing the best alternative, the obvious extension of the rule for choosing the optimal capital budget applies. The alternative that has the maximum increment to the value of the firm should be chosen. The incremental value can be determined as

$$\Delta V = \frac{\overline{Z}}{1 + k_Z} - I_{Z0} \tag{8-27}$$

where $k_Z$ depends on the risk of the alternative under consideration, using Eq. (8-26).

The uniform annual series method can also be used, since it is closely related to present value. However, the rate-of-return method is difficult to apply here unless the risks of the alternatives are the same, so that the same rate would apply to each alternative.[12] If the equal-risk condition is met (risk being defined as $\text{cov}[\tilde{Z}/\overline{Z}, \tilde{r}_M]$), then the "challenger-defender" procedure of Chap. 3 can be used under uncertainty. Nevertheless, in general it is easier to use the present-value rules presented above for evaluating alternatives.

## The Firm's "Cost of Capital" and Investment Decisions

It is common in discussing investment decisions to assume that the "cost of capital" for the firm (also often called the firm's discount rate or capitalization rate) is an appropriate criterion provided that the investments are of the "same risk as the firm." We are now in a position to specify both the appropriate "cost of capital" and how risks must be measured to ensure they are the "same."

[12] If this condition is not met, then each alternative has a different criterion rate. The rate-of-return method requires a comparison between two alternatives; if the rates differ, then a new rate based on the differential risks between the two cash flows must be determined. Each comparison will require a different rate leading to an appreciable increase in computation. If the rates are basically judgments of management, it seems a bit much to require management to assess such differential risks as $\text{cov}\{[\tilde{Z}_A - \tilde{Z}_B]/[\overline{Z}_A - \overline{Z}_B], \tilde{r}_M\}$, where $A$ and $B$ are the two alternatives.

From the earlier discussion it should be apparent that the firm's cost of capital is another name for the expected rate of return on the value of the entire firm in equilibrium, and is therefore taken from the security market line. We also know that this rate of return is solely a function of the market parameters ($i$ and $\lambda$) and the risk of the firm's income stream. We can express the equilibrium rate of return for the firm $k_f$ as a function of the income $\tilde{X}'_1$ the firm would have if no investment took place

$$k_f = \frac{1 + i}{1 - \lambda \operatorname{cov}[\tilde{X}'_1/\overline{X}'_1, \tilde{r}_M]} - 1 \tag{8-28}$$

If $k_f$ is to be an appropriate criterion, then for any project income $\tilde{Z}$, the required rate of return for that project $k_Z$ must equal $k_f$ or

$$k_f = k_Z = \frac{1 + i}{1 - \lambda \operatorname{cov}[\tilde{X}'_1/\overline{X}'_1, \tilde{r}_M]} - 1 = \frac{1 + i}{1 - \lambda \operatorname{cov}[\tilde{Z}/\overline{Z}, \tilde{r}_M]} - 1 \tag{8-29}$$

Therefore, $\operatorname{cov}[\tilde{Z}/\overline{Z}, \tilde{r}_M]$ must equal $\operatorname{cov}[\tilde{X}'_1/\overline{X}'_1, \tilde{r}_M]$. One obvious situation in which the covariances are equal is for $\tilde{Z} = a\tilde{X}'$, $a$ being a constant; that is, when the project is simply an increase in the scale of the firm with no change in any other characteristics. There are other types of projects that will satisfy the condition; however, a complete analysis is beyond the scope of this discussion.[13] The main point here is that there do exist situations in which it is theoretically sound to use the firm's market rate of return or cost of capital before investment as a criterion for investment decisions.

## FIRM DECISIONS AND CORPORATE INCOME TAXES

In this section we depart from the idealized assumptions of the previous section to consider the impact of corporate income taxes on firm financial decisions. The existence of corporate taxation has a significant impact on both the financing and the investment decisions of the firm. We shall consider briefly why this is so; the discussion in later chapters will present a more extensive analysis. The assumption that investors are indifferent between dividend and capital gains income is retained.

[13] One fairly simple case is the following:

$$\tilde{Z} = a\tilde{X}'_1 + \tilde{\epsilon}$$

where $\bar{\epsilon} = 0$, $\operatorname{cov}[\tilde{\epsilon}, \tilde{r}_M] = 0$

In this situation the project's returns differ from the firm's returns not only proportionally but also by random amount uncorrelated with the market with an expected value of zero. Projects involving replacement of existing production equipment with some that embodies new and hence uncertain technology might fit into this case.

## Valuation of the Firm

The existence of corporate income taxes does not change the basic equilibrium relationships of the CML and the SML. The market parameters themselves may take on different values in a world with corporate taxes; but Eq. (7-19) remains valid because it is based on the opportunities and preferences of individual investors and the supply of securities in the market.[14] We can also continue to express the value of the firm's shares in terms of the cash payments to shareholders as in Eq. (8-1), even though the magnitude and risk characteristics of the payments may be different because of taxes. Whatever difference exists will affect the value of the firm but not the relationship between the cash payments and the values. The numbers may change; but the equation still holds. The ex-dividend value of the firm's original shares can be expressed as before:

$$S^o = \frac{\bar{D}_1 - \lambda \operatorname{cov}[\tilde{D}_1, \tilde{r}_M]}{1 + i} \tag{8-30}$$

and the wealth provided by the firm to its current shareholders is

$$W_S = D_0 + S^o \tag{8-31}$$

or

$$W_S = D_0 + \frac{\bar{D}_1 - \lambda \operatorname{cov}[\tilde{D}_1, \tilde{r}_M]}{1 + i} \tag{8-32}$$

The tax laws as they exist are complicated; so we simplify them in order to capture the major points. We assume that at time 1 all the firm's cash flow net of deductions for depreciation and debt payments will be subject to tax.[15] We shall also assume that no such deductions exist at time 0; that is, the firm is assumed to have no debt outstanding nor any depreciation deductions at time 0. At time 1 a depreciation deduction of $I_0$ (the firm's capital outlay at time 0) is permitted the firm. Also, at time 1 payments on any debt issued by the firm are deductible. If the firm's cash income $\tilde{X}_1$ is insufficient to cover its depreciation and debt payments, then an unlimited tax carry-back is assumed (the government re-

[14] These preferences and opportunities may differ from those in a no-tax situation: but *given* the existence of taxes, the market will come to equilibrium in the manner discussed earlier and the same equilibrium relationships apply.

[15] Since the firm is liquidating at time 1, part of the cash flow is a return of capital and would not be taxable. Assuming that all of $\tilde{X}_1$ is potentially taxable in the absence of debt payments and depreciation substantially reduces the algebra of the argument without affecting the general result. Without the assumption, we would have to separate the cash returns at time 1 into two components: for example, $\tilde{X}_1 = \tilde{L}_1 + \tilde{E}_1$, where $\tilde{L}_1$ is nontaxable and $\tilde{E}_1$ is taxable. The algebraic arguments become massive without contributing anything to the results. For similar reasons we assume that the total payment to bondholders is tax-deductible rather than merely the portion designated as "interest."

funds the taxes paid in prior periods).[16] Finally, the tax rate $\tau$ is assumed to be a constant proportion of taxable income. With these assumptions in mind, we can now look at financing policy.

## Financing Policy

Since a portion of the payments to some types of external financing (debt) are tax-deductible and the payments on other types (new shares) are not, we must distinguish more carefully between them than was necessary in the no-tax case. We shall therefore revert to the more standard categorization of financing policy into the two major areas: dividend policy (the choice between the sources of new equity—new shares and retained earnings) and capital structure policy (the choice between debt and equity).

**Dividend policy.** We assume as before that the pretax income of the firm is $X_0$ at time 0 (known for certain) and $\tilde{X}_1$ at time 1 (a random variable). The cash-flow equation at time 0 is

$$\underset{\text{(Inflow)}}{X_0 + S^N} = \underset{\text{(Outflow)}}{D_0 + I_0 + \tau X_0} \tag{8-33}$$

$\tau X_0$ is the taxes on $X_0$, which are paid at time 0. Suppose we define a new variable $X^\tau = (1 - \tau)X$. The reasoning behind this definition will be more obvious later. Using the definition of $X^\tau$, Eq. (8-33) can be restated as

$$X_0^\tau + S^N = D_0 + I_0 \tag{8-34}$$

or

$$D_0 = X_0^\tau + S^N - I_0 \tag{8-35}$$

The only difference now between this case and our previous expression for $D_0$, Eq. (8-3), is the use of $X_0^\tau$ rather than income in the absence of taxes. As before, $S^N$ is the value of any new shares issued at time 0, and $I_0$ is the firm's capital budget.

In a similar fashion the cash-flow equation at time 1 is

$$\tilde{X}_1 = \tilde{D}_1 + \tilde{D}^N + \tau(\tilde{X}_1 - I_0) \tag{8-36}$$

or

$$\tilde{D}_1 = \tilde{X}_1^\tau + \tau I_0 - \tilde{D}^N \tag{8-37}$$

where $\tilde{D}_1$ is the dividend payment to current shareholders and $\tilde{D}^N$ is the payment on the new shares that were issued. We assume that a depreciation deduc-

[16] An alternative assumption is that the firm can sell its tax losses in a perfect market so that the proceeds from sale of the loss would amount to the cash value of carry-back, assuming that other firms have the same tax rate.

tion of amount $I_0$ is permitted at time 1 so that taxable income at time 1 is $\tilde{X}_1 - I_0$. Note that the tax benefit from depreciation is certain because of our assumption of a tax-loss carry-back. If we now substitute for $D_0$ and $\tilde{D}_1$ from Eqs. (8-35) and (8-37) into Eq. (8-32), we find that

$$W_S = X_0^\tau + S^N - I_0 + \frac{(\bar{X}_1^\tau + \tau I_0 - \bar{D}^N) - \lambda \operatorname{cov}[(\tilde{X}_1^\tau + \tau I_0 - \tilde{D}^N),\tilde{r}_M]}{1+i}$$

$$= X_0^\tau - I_0 + \frac{\bar{X}_1^\tau + \tau I_0 - \lambda \operatorname{cov}[\tilde{X}_1^\tau,\tilde{r}_M]}{1+i} + S^N - \frac{\bar{D}^N - \lambda \operatorname{cov}[\tilde{D}^N,\tilde{r}_M]}{1+i}$$

But $S^N$ must equal $\{\bar{D}^N - \lambda \operatorname{cov}[\tilde{D}^N,\tilde{r}_M]\}/(1+i)$ by Eq. (8-30). Therefore,

$$W_S = X_0^\tau - I_0 + \frac{\bar{X}_1^\tau - \lambda \operatorname{cov}[\tilde{X}_1^\tau,\tilde{r}_M]}{1+i} + \frac{\tau I_0}{1+i} \tag{8-38}$$

The wealth relationship derived here [Eq. (8-38)] differs in only two respects from the one derived in the no-tax case [Eq. (8-9)]—the use of $X^\tau$ and the present value of depreciation deduction $\tau I_0/(1+i)$. Since the wealth of the shareholders is not a function of the dividend-financing decision, we conclude that dividend policy is irrelevant.

**Capital structure policy.** Having just shown that the choice between retained earnings and new shares as a means of financing is irrelevant, we can use either equity alternative to compare with the use of debt. Let us compare retained earnings and debt. The assumptions and definitions of the preceding discussion are retained; we need only specify the impact of the debt issue. The cash-flow equation at time 0 is

$$X_0 + B_0 = D_0 + I_0 + \tau X_0 \tag{8-39}$$

and

$$D_0 = X_0^\tau + B_0 - I_0 \tag{8-40}$$

where $B_0$ is the value of the new debt (bonds) issued. Since by the assumptions of this section there are no old bonds outstanding at time 0, bonds are signified here simply as $B_0$ rather than as $B_0^N$ to signify new bonds; the $N$ superscript is used in later chapters. The cash-flow equation at time 1 is

$$\tilde{X}_1 = \tilde{D}_1 + \tilde{Y}^B + \tau(\tilde{X}_1 - I_0 - \tilde{Y}^B) \tag{8-41}$$

and

$$\tilde{D}_1 = \tilde{X}_1^\tau + \tau I_0 - (1-\tau)\tilde{Y}^B \tag{8-42}$$

$\tilde{Y}^B$ is the uncertain payment to the bondholders; contrary to existing laws we are treating the entire payment as tax-deductible, as indicated earlier. Proceeding as we have in the past, the dividend payments as determined from Eq. (8-40) and (8-42) are substituted into Eq. (8-32):

$$W_S = X_0^\tau + B_0 - I_0 + \frac{[\bar{X}_1^\tau + \tau I_0 - (1-\tau)\bar{Y}^B] - \lambda \operatorname{cov}[[\tilde{X}_1^\tau + \tau I_0 - (1-\tau)\tilde{Y}^B],\tilde{r}_M]}{1+i}$$

$$= X_0^\tau - I_0 + \frac{\bar{X}_1^\tau - \lambda \operatorname{cov}[\tilde{X}_1^\tau, \tilde{r}_M]}{1+i} + \frac{\tau I_0}{1+i}$$
$$+ B_0 - (1-\tau)\left[\frac{\bar{Y}^B - \lambda \operatorname{cov}[\tilde{Y}^B, \tilde{r}_M]}{1+i}\right]$$

But the value of the bonds from Eq. (8-7) must be

$$B_0 = \frac{\bar{Y}^B - \lambda \operatorname{cov}[\tilde{Y}^B, \tilde{r}_M]}{1+i} \tag{8-43}$$

and therefore

$$W_S = X_0^\tau - I_0 + \frac{\bar{X}_1^\tau - \lambda \operatorname{cov}[\tilde{X}_1, \tilde{r}_M]}{1+i} + \frac{\tau I_0}{1+i} + \tau B_0 \tag{8-44}$$

Equation (8-44) differs from Eq. (8-38) in one crucial respect; the last term, which is the product of the tax rate and the value of the bonds that are issued. Equation (8-44) implies that the wealth of the current shareholders increases as the amount of bonds issued increases—the more debt financing the better. Moreover, this proof is based on the issue of *risky* bonds. It holds equally well for riskless bonds; but more important, it does not permit one to argue that the increase in value will not continue as more bonds are issued because of the increased risk. The results here imply that the firm should issue debt so long as it can still receive a tax deduction, paying out the proceeds of the debt issue to the shareholders.[17] This conclusion is due to our assumption of perfect capital markets and will be discussed under more general conditions in later chapters. For the moment it is sufficient to note that the tax-deductibility of debt payments is the *only* benefit we have been able to find for debt financing.

## Investment Policy

The problem of investment policy is appreciably more complicated when the firm must pay corporate income taxes under present tax laws,[18] so much so that the topic will not be developed in depth, but a few remarks are appropriate.

The complications arise from two sources: depreciation policy and the

[17] In fact, when debt levels get very high—85 to 90% of total firm value—the IRS will challenge the appropriateness of the deduction since usually at such levels of debt the bondholders are also closely related to the equity interest in the firm. In the markets we are assuming, everyone holds both the shares and the risky bonds of *all* firms. In the absence of restrictions by the IRS the limit to the process depends on the amount of tax rebates available to the firm and $\tilde{X}_1$. No more bonds can be sold when $\tilde{Y}^B = \tilde{X}_1$. If the firm exhausts its tax rebates before debt has reached that point, there will be no advantage to issuing any more debt.

[18] Two changes in tax laws would eliminate most of the problems: (1) allowing the firm to deduct the cost of depreciable assets when the assets are acquired rather than forcing the firm to make noncash deductions (depreciation) over the "life" of the asset, and (2) treating interest as a nondeductible payment to capital rather than as a business expense. See Charles W. Haley, Taxes, the Cost of Capital, and the Firm's Investment Decision, *Journal of Finance*, September 1971, for a discussion.

tax-deductibility of payments on the firm's debt. In Eq. (8-44) derived above, one term accounted for the tax effects of depreciation $[\tau I_0/(1 + i)]$. However, investment opportunities generally differ in the proportion of the initial cost that can be treated as an expense for tax purposes and also in the allowable timing of the expense. Some costs (such as advertising, research and development, and installation of equipment) can be deducted for tax purposes when spent. Other costs (purchase of "depreciable assets," such as machinery or buildings) must be deducted over the "life" (as determined by the IRS) of the asset. We assumed in the preceding development that the entire investment budget was used to acquire assets with single-period lives. Finally, some costs (land) cannot be deducted at all. Analyzing the tax effects of depreciation in project evaluation is no more difficult than determining the basic cash flows themselves. The tax laws simply make the problem more time-consuming. The basic arguments developed in the no-tax case still hold, except that tax payments must now be counted as part of the costs associated with a project. Such problems are dealt with in detail elsewhere and need not concern us here.[19]

Of more importance to the theory is the result that the financing decisions of the firm affect its value through the tax-deductibility of debt payments. As a consequence, investment decisions are likely to depend in part on financing decisions. The standard solution to this issue is to determine a solution to the problem of the optimal mix of financing sources and then to derive criteria for investment decisions, which depend on that financing policy. This solution is appropriate when the investments made by the firm do not affect financing policy.[20] Let us use this approach by assuming that the investment budget is financed in part with retained earnings and in part with debt. Since we know that dividend policy is irrelevant, the critical component is the use of debt financing.

The following definitions will be used:

$D'_0$ = dividend payment at time 0 if no investment is undertaken.
$B_0$ = debt issued to finance investment.
$d_0$ = *proportion* of $I_0$ that can be deducted as depreciation expense for tax purposes at time 0. Reduction in taxes that results from undertaking $I_0$ is therefore $\tau d_0 I_0$.
$D_0$ = dividend payments at time 0:

$$D_0 = D'_0 + B_0 - I_0 + \tau d_0 I_0 \tag{8-45}$$

[19] See, for example, Eugene L. Grant and W. Grant Ireson, "Principles of Engineering Economy," 6th ed., chaps. 10 and 16, The Ronald Press Company, New York, 1976.

[20] The astute reader might note that if the amount and composition of optimal financing are independent of investment policy, then investment decisions should be made without regard to financing policy. However, if the firm has reached some limit to the amount of debt that it can issue (see p. 175), then additional investment which increased the income of the firm would also increase the amount of debt that could be issued. Hence the investment decision would depend on the financing decision as presented below.

$\tilde{D}_1' =$ dividend payments at time 1 if $I_0 = 0$.
$\tilde{Y}^B =$ cash payments to $B_0$ at time 1.
$\Delta\tilde{X} =$ pretax incremental flow to firm at time 1 because of undertaking $I_0$.
$d_1 =$ proportion of $I_0$ that is deductible for tax purposes at time 1.
$\tilde{D}_1 =$ dividend payments at time 1:

$$\tilde{D}_1 = \tilde{D}_1' - \tilde{Y}^B + \Delta\tilde{X} - \tau(\Delta\tilde{X} - \tilde{Y}^B - d_1 I_0) \tag{8-46}$$

If $D_0$ and $\tilde{D}_1$ from Eqs. (8-45) and (8-46), respectively, are substituted into Eq. (8-32), we have (after some rearrangement):

$$W_S = D_0' + \frac{\bar{D}_1' - \lambda\,\text{cov}[\tilde{D}_1',\tilde{r}_M]}{1+i} + B_0 - (1-\tau)\left\{\frac{\bar{Y}^B - \lambda\,\text{cov}[\tilde{Y}^B,\tilde{r}_M]}{1+i}\right\} - I_0^\tau + \frac{\Delta\bar{X}^\tau - \lambda\,\text{cov}[\Delta\tilde{X}^\tau,\tilde{r}_M]}{1+i} + \frac{\tau d_1 I_0}{1+i} \tag{8-47}$$

where $I_0^\tau \equiv (1 - \tau d_0)I_0$ and $\Delta\tilde{X}^\tau \equiv (1-\tau)\,\Delta\tilde{X}$.

$I_0^\tau$ is the after-tax cost of the current capital budget, and $\Delta\tilde{X}^\tau$ is the increment to $X_1^\tau$ resulting from investment. Using the relationship for $B_0$ [Eq. (8-43)] we can express Eq. (8-47) as

$$W_S = D_0' + \frac{\bar{D}_1' - \lambda\,\text{cov}[\tilde{D}_1',\tilde{r}_M]}{1+i} + \tau B_0 - I_0^\tau + \frac{\Delta\bar{X}^\tau - \lambda\,\text{cov}[\Delta\tilde{X}^\tau,\tilde{r}_M]}{1+i} + \frac{\tau d_1 I_0}{1+i} \tag{8-48}$$

Let us assume that a decision has been made with respect to the proportion of $I_0^\tau$ to be financed with debt; that is, $\gamma$ is given where

$$\gamma = \frac{B_0}{I_0^\tau} \tag{8-49}$$

Furthermore, the terms involving $D_0'$ and $\tilde{D}_1'$ are not dependent on investment or financing by assumption. We can therefore express the criterion of investment policy as

$$\max\left[-(1-\tau\gamma)I_0^\tau + \frac{\Delta\bar{X}^\tau - \lambda\,\text{cov}[\Delta\tilde{X}^\tau,\tilde{r}_M]}{1+i} + \frac{\tau d_1 I_0}{1+i}\right] \tag{8-50}$$

Expression (8-50) contains three terms:

1. $(1 - \tau\gamma)I_0^\tau$ is the net current cost to the stockholders of the capital budget $I_0$, given current depreciation and financing policy.
2. $\{\Delta\bar{X}^\tau - \lambda\,\text{cov}[\Delta\tilde{X}^\tau,\tilde{r}_M]\}/(1 + \text{i})$ is the market value of the cash flow $\Delta\tilde{X}^\tau$ by itself.
3. $\tau d_1 I_0/(1 + i)$ is the present value of the tax reduction resulting from the depreciation deduction $d_1 I_0$. The deduction is riskless as discussed earlier.

Together these three terms account for the change in wealth of the firm's shareholders that will result from undertaking an investment of $I_0$ to be financed in part with debt and in part with equity. We have already shown that the source of the equity, new shares or retained earnings, does not matter.

Note that the investment criterion in the tax case [expression (8-50)] reduces directly to the criterion of the no-tax case [expression (8-15)] when the tax rate $\tau = 0$. Therefore, given financing policy and depreciation schedules, the existence of firm taxes complicates the investment problem; it has not been changed in any fundamental manner. The criteria for project selection and the evaluation of alternatives follow naturally from (8-50) with the indicated change in notation, and will not be restated. Projects are still evaluated independently. The value additivity principle still holds; diversification projects or mergers are not beneficial unless they result in income benefits. There are some increased difficulties in expressing a discount rate to be used in valuing expected income streams, but this topic will be reserved for more extensive development in later chapters.

## SUMMARY

We found that in an idealized version of the world the presence of uncertainty does not change the basic conclusions we reached in Chaps. 2 and 3 with respect to the financial decisions of the firm. Financing-dividend policy is still irrelevant in the absence of taxes, and investment policy is still important. The methods developed to deal with the problems of project analysis apply even when projects and alternatives differ in risk, although the computational requirements have increased. The only significant difference between the certainty case and this single-period idealization of uncertainty is that a different criterion discount rate must be determined for each project or alternative which has a different degree of risk. However, all alternatives with the same risk as the firm can be evaluated using the firm's market rate in the criteria in much the same fashion as the rate of interest was used under certainty.

When corporate income taxes are introduced into the analysis, some of the preceding conclusions must be modified. The tax-deductibility of interest on the firm's debt creates an incentive to use debt financing although dividend policy remains irrelevant. The rules regarding depreciation introduce additional complexity into the computation of the cash flows, but for a given financing policy the criteria for investment decisions remain essentially unchanged. The major difference from the no-tax case is that cash flows from investments must be determined on an after-tax basis.

APPENDIX

# EIGHT A

## AN ALTERNATIVE APPROACH TO PROJECT SELECTION

In Chap. 8 we developed present-value rules for project selection (8-17) and for evaluating alternatives (8-27). We also noted that a rate-of-return rule could be used for project selection where the criterion rate is $k_Z$ as defined by (8-26). There is an alternative approach to project selection based on a different criterion rate which we will denote as $\hat{k}$. This rate may be used in either a present-value rule or a rate-of-return rule for project selection; however, it is not valid for the evaluation of mutually exclusive opportunities.[21] The purpose of this appendix is to develop the expression for $\hat{k}$, to show how it can be used as a criterion for project selection, and to show why it should not be used for the evaluation of mutually exclusive opportunities.

### PROJECT SELECTION

The basic rule for project selection is that the net present value of the project cash flows should be greater than zero for a project to be acceptable,

$$V_Z - I_Z > 0 \tag{8A-1}$$

where $V_Z$ is the value at time 0 of the project's cash flows $\tilde{Z}$ and $I_Z$ is the time 0 investment required to undertake the project.

In the absence of taxes we have shown that [see (8-17) and discussion]

[21] This approach has been suggested by M. Rubinstein, A Mean-Variance Synthesis of Corporate Financial Theory, *Journal of Finance*, vol. 28, pp. 167–181, March 1973, and others. Rubinstein also does not recommend $\hat{k}$ for use in evaluating mutually exclusive investments.

$$V_Z = \frac{\bar{Z} - \lambda \operatorname{cov}[\tilde{Z},\tilde{r}_m]}{1 + i} \tag{8A-2}$$

therefore, we can write (8A-1) using (8A-2) as

$$\frac{\bar{Z} - \lambda \operatorname{cov}[\tilde{Z},\tilde{r}_m]}{1 + i} - I_Z > 0 \tag{8A-3}$$

which is our basic rule for project selection, (8-17).

Now divide (8A-3) through by $I_Z$ and rearrange terms. We obtain

$$\frac{\bar{Z}}{I_Z} - \lambda \operatorname{cov}\left[\frac{\tilde{Z}}{I_Z}, \tilde{r}_m\right] > 1 + i \tag{8A-4}$$

Define the rate of return earned on the project, $\tilde{r}_Z$,

$$\tilde{r}_Z = \frac{\tilde{Z}}{I_Z} - 1 \tag{8A-5}$$

and the expected value of $\tilde{r}_Z(\bar{r}_Z)$ is

$$\bar{r}_Z = \frac{\bar{Z}}{I_Z} - 1 \tag{8A-6}$$

Substituting our definitions for $\tilde{r}_Z$ and $\bar{r}_Z$ into (8A-4):

$$1 + \bar{r}_Z - \lambda \operatorname{cov}[\tilde{r}_Z,\tilde{r}_M] > 1 + i$$

$$\bar{r}_Z > i + \lambda \operatorname{cov}[\tilde{r}_Z,\tilde{r}_M] \tag{8A-7}$$

The rule shown by (8A-7) says that the expected rate of return on the project must exceed $(i + \lambda \operatorname{cov}[\tilde{r}_Z,\tilde{r}_M])$ for the project to be acceptable. Define $\hat{k}_Z$ as

$$\hat{k}_Z \equiv i + \lambda \operatorname{cov}[\tilde{r}_Z,\tilde{r}_M] \tag{8A-8}$$

Thus, our rule of (8A-7) is simply to accept every project with an expected rate of return greater than $\hat{k}_Z$ as defined in (8A-8), where $\hat{k}_Z$ may differ among projects. Equation (8A-8) provides a natural interpretation of $\hat{k}_Z$. The measure of risk for a project is the covariance of its rate of return with the market. Given the project's risk and the security market line ($i$ and $\lambda$), we determine the required rate of return appropriate for project selection.

We now show that $\hat{k}_Z$ can be used to calculate a value for project cash flow $\tilde{Z}$ which is appropriate for use in a present-value rule for project selection. We choose a somewhat roundabout approach, as the results are useful later.

We wish to know whether the rule

$$\hat{V}_Z - I_Z > 0 \tag{8A-9}$$

is appropriate for project selection given that

$$\hat{V}_Z \equiv \frac{\bar{Z}}{1 + \hat{k}_Z} \tag{8A-10}$$

That is, we want to know whether we can obtain a "present value," $\hat{V}_Z$, using $\hat{k}_Z$ as defined by (8A-8) to discount the expected future cash flow from the project $\bar{Z}$ and have $\hat{V}_Z$ be valid for use in the project-selection rule (8A-9). To do this, let us express $(\hat{V}_Z - I_Z)$ in terms of $(V_Z - I_Z)$. From the definition of $\hat{V}_Z$ and $\hat{k}_Z$, we have

$$\begin{aligned}\hat{V}_Z - I_Z &= \frac{\bar{Z}}{1 + \hat{k}_Z} - I_Z \\ &= \frac{\bar{Z} - I_Z(1 + \hat{k}_Z)}{1 + \hat{k}_Z} \\ &= \frac{\bar{Z} - I_Z(1 + i + \lambda \operatorname{cov}[\tilde{r}_Z, \tilde{r}_m])}{1 + \hat{k}_Z} \\ &= \frac{\bar{Z} - \lambda \operatorname{cov}[\tilde{Z}, \tilde{r}_m] - I_Z(1 + i)}{1 + \hat{k}_Z}\end{aligned} \tag{8A-11}$$

But from our definition of $V_Z$, (8A-2)

$$\bar{Z} - \lambda \operatorname{cov}[\tilde{Z}, \tilde{r}_m] = V_Z(1 + i) \tag{8A-12}$$

Therefore, we can substitute in (8A-11) using (8A-12) to obtain

$$\begin{aligned}\hat{V}_Z - I_Z &= \frac{V_Z(1 + i) - I_Z(1 + i)}{1 + \hat{k}_Z} \\ &= \frac{(V_Z - I_Z)(1 + i)}{1 + \hat{k}_Z}\end{aligned} \tag{8A-13}$$

From (8A-13) we can see that $\hat{V}_Z - I_Z$ will be greater than zero only if $V_Z - I_Z$ is greater than zero. But $V_Z - I_Z$, by our general arguments, will be greater than zero only if the project is desirable. Thus the present value rule of (8A-9) using $\hat{k}_Z$ as a discount rate is consistent with the general rule (8-17) for project selection.

Two other properties of (8A-13) are of interest. First, for risky investments ($\operatorname{cov}[\tilde{Z}, \tilde{r}_M] > 0$), $\hat{k}$ is greater than $i$ and therefore $\hat{V}_Z - I_Z$ is always less than $V_Z - I_Z$. In other words the rule based on $\hat{k}$ provides a downward-biased estimate of the true incremental value of risky projects. Second, when $V_Z = I_Z$, $\hat{V}_Z - I_Z = 0$, and therefore $\hat{V}_Z = I_Z = V_Z$. In other words, for marginal projects, the two present values $\hat{V}_Z$ and $V_Z$ are equal. But if this is true, then it must also be true that $\hat{k}_Z$ and $k_Z$ are equal for marginal projects.

So far we have shown that $\hat{k}_Z$ can be used as a discount rate for expected cash flow $\bar{Z}$ to obtain a present value which is suitable for project selection. This rate $\hat{k}_Z$ also is suitable as a criterion rate in a rate-of-return rule. Now let us consider the evaluation of alternatives. Here we shall consider only the present-value approach since, as noted in Chap. 8, rate-of-return rules are difficult to apply to alternatives differing in risk.

## EVALUATING ALTERNATIVES

We show in this section that $\hat{V}_Z$, which is based on $\hat{k}_Z$, should *not* be used in evaluating alternatives. We begin by restating (8A-13):

$$\hat{V}_Z - I_Z = \frac{(V_Z - I_Z)(1 + i)}{1 + \hat{k}_Z} \tag{8A-13}$$

**table 8A-1 Comparing $V_Z - I_Z$ and $\hat{V}_Z - I_Z$ as Measures of Investment Values**

*Assume $\lambda = 4.0$ and $i = 6\%$.*

| | Alternative Investments | | |
|---|---|---|---|
| | *A* | *B* | *C* |
| *Given variables* | | | |
| $\bar{Z}$ | \$1,200 | \$1,370 | \$1,120 |
| cov $[\tilde{Z},\tilde{r}_m]$ | \$ 10 | \$ 50 | \$ 40 |
| $I_Z$ | \$1,000 | \$1,000 | \$ 800 |
| *Calculated values* | | | |
| (1) $\bar{r}_Z$ | 20% | 37% | 40% |
| (2) cov $\left[\frac{\tilde{Z}}{\bar{Z}}, \tilde{r}_m\right]$ | 0.83% | 3.65% | 3.57% |
| (3) cov $\left[\frac{\tilde{Z}}{I_Z}, \tilde{r}_m\right]$ | 1% | 5% | 5% |
| (4) $V_Z$ | \$1,094 | \$1,104 | \$ 906 |
| (5) $\hat{k}_Z$ | 10% | 26% | 26% |
| (6) $\hat{V}_Z$ | \$1,091 | \$1,087 | \$ 889 |
| (7) $V_Z - I_Z$ | \$ 94 | \$ 104 | \$ 106 |
| (8) $\hat{V}_Z - I_Z$ | \$ 91 | \$ 87 | \$ 89 |

Alternative *C* is best, but $\hat{V}_Z - I_Z$ indicates *A* is best.

*Definitions and Comments*

(1) $\bar{r}_Z = \dfrac{\bar{Z}}{I_Z} - 1.0$

(2) $\text{cov}\left[\dfrac{\tilde{Z}}{\bar{Z}},\tilde{r}_m\right] = \text{cov}[\tilde{Z},\tilde{r}_m]/\bar{Z}$

(3) $\text{cov}\left[\dfrac{\tilde{Z}}{I_Z},\tilde{r}_m\right] = \text{cov}[\tilde{Z},\tilde{r}_m]/I_Z$

(4) $V_Z = \dfrac{\bar{Z} - \lambda\,\text{cov}[\tilde{Z},\tilde{r}_m]}{1+i}$

(5) $\hat{k}_Z = i + \lambda\,\text{cov}\left[\dfrac{\tilde{Z}}{I_Z},\tilde{r}_m\right]$

(6) $\hat{V}_Z = \dfrac{\bar{Z}}{1+\hat{k}_Z}$

(7) Ranking from highest to lowest *C*, *B*, *A*.

(8) Ranking from highest to lowest *A*, *C*, *B*.

The normal method of determining the best alternative is to choose that alternative which provides the maximum value, net of cost, to the shareholders. We know from Chap. 8 that choosing the alternative which has the greatest net present value (NPV)

$$\text{NPV} = V_Z - I_Z \tag{8A-14}$$

is a valid approach for maximizing shareholder wealth. It is clear from inspection of (8A-13) that, for any set of alternatives under consideration, if $\hat{k}_Z$ is the same for each alternative, then $(\hat{V}_Z - I_Z)$ will rank the alternatives in precisely the same order as $(V_Z - I_Z)$. Any problems with the use of $\hat{V}_Z$ will therefore arise only when $\hat{k}_Z$ differs from one alternative to another.

In Table 8A-1 we show that $\hat{V}_Z - I_Z$ does not rank alternatives correctly; that is, a ranking based on $\hat{V}_Z - I_Z$ is not consistent with the objective of maximizing shareholder wealth as measured by NPV. Therefore, $\hat{k}_Z$ is *not* an appropriate discount rate for general use in investment decisions.

## SUGGESTED READINGS

Hamada, R. S.: Portfolio Analysis, Market Equilibrium and Corporation Finance, *Journal of Finance,* vol. 24, pp. 13–31, March 1969, reprinted in Archer, Stephen H. and Charles A. D'Ambrosio, "The Theory of Business Finance," 2d ed., The Macmillan Company, New York, 1976.

Levy, Haim and Marshall Sarnat: Diversification, Portfolio Analysis, and the Uneasy Case for Conglomerate Mergers, *Journal of Finance,* vol. 25, pp. 795–802, September 1970.

Lintner, John: The Valuation of Risk Assets and the Selection of Risky Investments in Stock Portfolios and Capital Budgets, *Review of Economics and Statistics* vol. 47, pp. 13–37, February 1965, reprinted in Archer and D'Ambrosio, *op. cit.*

Rubenstein, Mark: A Mean-Variance Synthesis of Corporate Financial Theory, *Journal of Finance,* vol. 28, pp. 167–181, March 1973.

Stapleton, R. C.: Portfolio Analysis, Stock Valuation and Capital Budgeting Decision Rules for Risky Projects, *Journal of Finance,* vol. 26, pp. 95–117, March 1971.

Tuttle, D. L. and R. H. Litzenberger: Leverage, Diversification and Capital Market Effects on a Risk Adjusted Capital Budgeting Framework, *Journal of Finance,* vol. 23, pp. 427–443, June 1968, reprinted in Archer and D'Ambrosio, *op. cit.*

CHAPTER

# NINE

# MULTIPERIOD VALUATION

This chapter begins the development of the state of the art in financial theory. The primary issue of Chaps. 9 and 10 is the valuation of multiperiod income streams by individuals and the financial markets. Chapter 9 focuses on the discrete time case and Chap. 10 concerns valuation in continuous time. In subsequent chapters, the major strategic decisions of the firm—dividend policy, financial structure policy, and investment policy—will be examined in depth. The highly idealized assumptions of the preceding chapters will be modified in an attempt to develop criteria that can be applied in general to the real situation facing business firms in developed economies.[1]

The problem of valuation is central of the theory of firm financial decisions. Given the objective for management of maximizing the welfare of the owners of the firm, the value of the firm to its owners is an obvious gauge for measuring the contribution of the firm to its owners. The *market* value of the ownership interest is a measure of the firm's value to owners, and is therefore an index of firm performance for corporations with widely held shares.

The market value of a firm's shares is determined by many factors, including the attitudes of buyers and sellers in the market, their expectations regarding the performance of the firm, their current situation and the characteristics of the market itself (transaction costs, cost and availability of information, opportunities available in the market, etc.). Perhaps the most critical aspect of the problem and the most difficult to deal with is the question of how individuals

[1] The probable existence of substantial imperfections in the financial markets of underdeveloped countries would tend to make the analysis less applicable to them.

appraise the consequences of owning claims against uncertain future income streams. The emphasis in this chapter is on this individual appraisal. The implications of the analysis will be used in later chapters when we deal with the effects of firm financial decisions on the market value of the firm's shares.

## Introduction to the Multiperiod Problem

In Chaps. 6 to 8 we assumed that individuals and firms operated in a world where events occurred at only two points in time: "now" and "one period from now." However, from our discussion in Chap. 1 we know that only in special circumstances can the decisions of individuals and firms be assumed to be based on a single-period evaluation.[2] Financial decisions are intrinsically multiperiod problems.

A security or portfolio of securities provides the owner with a series of cash returns during the time the asset is held and some amount when it is sold. The basic issue is how the value of the returns from ownership, including the receipts from selling, can be determined. We assume that any prospective owner of such an asset forms some expectation of the future possibilities for the returns; for analytic convenience we can consider the returns at any future point in time to be a random variable. Therefore, we can say that the value of an asset depends on the characteristics of a multiperiod set of random cash receipts. The number of such receipts (or, equivalently, the number of periods) relevant to the individual depends on how long the asset will be held and hence may be uncertain. However, the planning horizon will be assumed given for an individual, although it can vary from person to person. With only this basic organization of the problem let us now examine some alternative approaches to the valuation of uncertain multiperiod cash flows. We shall begin with the most general models and proceed to more restrictive ones.

## A Comment on Vector Notation

Before proceeding, the use of vector notation in this and forthcoming chapters should be briefly explained. A boldface vector variable will be used to represent a stream over time. For example, stream $\tilde{\mathbf{Y}}_i = (\tilde{Y}_{i1}, \tilde{Y}_{i2}, \ldots, \tilde{Y}_{i\infty})$, where $\tilde{\mathbf{Y}}_i$ signifies the entire stream and $\tilde{Y}_{it}$, $t = 1, \ldots, \infty$, represents the amount associated with that stream at time $t$. For example, $\tilde{\mathbf{Y}}_i$ might be the dividend stream from a share of General Motors stock, where $\tilde{Y}_{it}$ is the dividend received in year $t$. Of course, some of the $\tilde{Y}_{it}$ in the vector can be zero or negative as well as positive. Use of the vector notation is therefore merely a compact way to

[2] Both J. H. Wood, Expectations and the Demand for Bonds, *American Economic Review*, September 1969, pp. 522–530, and Fama, Multiperiod Consumption-Investment Decisions (the Fama work is listed in the Suggested Readings at the end of this chapter) have suggested that the general multiperiod problem for the individual can be formulated as a single-period problem in some cases.

denote a stream over time where the values of that stream in each period can differ from period to period.

Just as with single-element variables, vectors can be added. Thus, for $\tilde{\mathbf{Y}}_i = (\tilde{Y}_{i1}, \tilde{Y}_{i2}, \ldots, \tilde{Y}_{i\infty})$ and $\tilde{\mathbf{Y}}_j = (\tilde{Y}_{j1}, \tilde{Y}_{j2}, \ldots, \tilde{Y}_{j\infty})$, $\tilde{\mathbf{Y}}_i + \tilde{\mathbf{Y}}_j = (\tilde{Y}_{i1} + \tilde{Y}_{j1}, \tilde{Y}_{i2} + \tilde{Y}_{j2}, \ldots, \tilde{Y}_{i\infty} + \tilde{Y}_{j\infty})$. That is, by adding the vectors all that is being done is adding the flows from the two streams at each point in time. For example, if $\tilde{\mathbf{Y}}_i$ and $\tilde{\mathbf{Y}}_j$ are the dividend streams from one share of General Motors and one share of DuPont stock, respectively, then $\tilde{\mathbf{Y}}_k = (\tilde{\mathbf{Y}}_i + \tilde{\mathbf{Y}}_j)$ would represent the dividend stream from a portfolio made up of one share of General Motors stock and one share of DuPont stock.

A given vector can be multiplied or divided by a constant. That is, $\alpha\tilde{\mathbf{Y}}_i = (\alpha\tilde{Y}_{i1}, \alpha\tilde{Y}_{i2}, \ldots, \alpha\tilde{Y}_{i\infty})$. Thus, if $\tilde{\mathbf{Y}}_i$ is the income from an apartment building and $\alpha = \frac{1}{2}$, then $\frac{1}{2}\tilde{\mathbf{Y}}_i$ is a stream providing one-half the income from the building in each period.

## TIME-STATE PREFERENCE (TSP)[3]

The special insight of the time-state preference (TSP) approach is the possibility that the value (utility) of a dollar received at a future point in time is not only a function of the length of time between now and then but also of the circumstances of the individual when the dollar is received. In other words, 10 years from now the value of a dollar to you will depend on whether you are rich or poor, whether you have one child or eight, etc. The value of a dollar depends not only on the time but also on the "state," from which comes the name time-state preference.

We develop the properties of this model in Appendix 9A. Here we present only the basic organization of the model.

### States

The critical construct of the TSP approach is the concept of "states" or "states of nature." The other characteristics of the model—return from assets, utility functions of individuals, and probabilities—are all based on the definition of states. The individual is assumed to have in mind a set of possible states of nature in which each state is a particular *sequence of events* occurring from the present to a future point in time where the state is defined. In other words, if state $s$ is said to occur at time $t$, the definition of state $s$ *includes a description of relevant events* which have happened up to that point. The precise definition of a

[3] The development here is based on Myers, A Time-State Preference Model of Security Valuation (listed in the Suggested Readings at the end of this chapter).

"sequence of events" depends on the characteristics of the world that are relevant in terms of the decision being made. The description of a state may be as detailed as desired.[4] For example, the states two periods from now could contain specifications of aggregate economic activity for the two periods, the government contracts won or lost by the firm where the person works; whether the person has been fired, obtained a raise, or been transferred; whether children have been born or not, etc. The idea is that if state 22 occurs at time 2, all events up to time 2, which are important in the context of the decision being made, are specified completely. Moreover, all possible states are identified, and only one state can occur at a given point in time (states are exhaustive and mutually exclusive). A necessary requirement for the valuation of income streams is that all possible combinations of returns from all assets are accounted for. If state $s$ occurs at time $t$, then the returns from each asset are given up to time $t$ and the states at time $t$ are sufficiently detailed that all possible different combinations of returns from the present until time $t$ are specified.

Associated with each state is a probability of its occurring. Since one and only one state will occur at a given time, the probabilities of all states at that time sum to 1.0. Therefore, there is a probability distribution across states for each period and there may be as many different probability distributions as there are time periods.

## Returns from Assets

The returns from any asset are described as a set of possible payments for each state and time. Given a particular state and time, the cash payment to the owner of the asset is known for certain. The only uncertainty in the system is what state will occur. The returns from an asset are said to be contingent on the occurrence of a state. For example, asset 420 pays \$16 if state 37 occurs in period 6. The \$16 is contingent on having state 37 occur in period 6. When the TSP model is used as a framework for determining market equilibrium, the additional assumption is often made that assets are held either to maturity or (for nonmaturing securities) to some distant future point in time. *From the viewpoint of individual valuation,* there is no need to restrict the model in this fashion, if we permit the state definitions to include personal emergencies or similar events that might create a need to dispose of the security. The receipts from sale of the security would then be the return contingent on the occurrence of a state in which the security must be sold.

[4] As the description of a state becomes more detailed, the number of possible states increases. The model becomes unwieldy for practical purposes very rapidly with the increase in states, although for theoretical purposes this is irrelevant. To use the approach as an equilibrium model, people must be assumed to agree on the states; hence the state definitions must be presumed to exclude the circumstances of the individual. When dealing with individual utility functions, this latter assumption presents some conceptual problems.

## Utilities

The utility functions of individuals in TSP models are somewhat different from the ones that were discussed previously. In Chap. 5 we assumed that given a particular decision situation the individual could be viewed as maximizing the expected value of an index reflecting that person's attitudes toward risky choices with cash outcomes. This index was referred to as a utility function $U(Y)$, where $Y$ is the outcome measured in dollars. In TSP models this concept is generalized. $U(Y)$ is thought of as reflecting an individual's preferences for money (or income or consumption) in general rather than in the context of a particular decision. These preferences are hypothesized to depend on both *when* (time) the money is received and the *conditions* (state) under which it is received. The individual is therefore assumed to have at the present time a set of utility functions, $U_{S,t}(Y)$, which reflect preferences toward money received in different states and time.[5] The decision rule is generally assumed to be to maximize the expected value of total utility defined as the sum of the expected values of the utility functions in each period.[6] This formulation of individual preferences clearly provides for a wide variety of possible preferences that can be encompassed in the model.

## Summary

We can summarize the TSP approach as follows. Assets provide returns in each period, which depend on the state that occurs. Individuals evaluate the consequences of acquiring an asset by determining the expected value of the utility of the returns provided by the asset in each period. For example, suppose there are 50 possible states that can occur in period 4. There are 50 possible dollar returns for any asset in this period, although for a given asset the amount of the returns in two or more states may be the same. The expected utility from owning an asset in period 4 is the expected value of the utilities of the returns in each state. The utility of a return of \$10 in state 16 may differ from the utility of a return of \$10 in state 22. The expected value is determined from the probability distribution of the states in period 4. The total utility from owning an asset is the sum of the expected utilities in each period for all periods of concern to the individual. The total utility is in some sense the "present sum" of the expected utility from holding the asset, since it incorporates the individual's present preferences for cash returns in the future.

The individual is assumed to maximize total utility; i.e., to select the asset (security or portfolio) that provides the most desirable level and pattern of

[5] Note that in this formulation "income" is synonymous with "consumption." The utility functions incorporate both attitudes toward risky situations and time preferences for consumption. A related approach was developed in app. 5A for the single-period model.

[6] This quantity, total utility, can be most easily interpreted as an index for choice. It cannot be directly converted into a cash equivalent value as could the expected utility of chap. 5.

returns over states and time. In the absence of specific assumptions about the markets for assets, there is no simple way to express the dollar value of a particular asset in this model. Associated with each asset is a total utility value, but this value cannot be transformed directly into a cash equivalent as was possible for the utility functions of Chap. 5. This is so because the value depends on time preferences for consumption. In the certainty case of Chap. 2 we used the assumption of perfect markets to develop a measure of the current dollar value of an asset (income stream) to an individual. Without such an assumption, we would have the same problem in the certainty case that we have here. With the introduction of perfect-market assumptions and some additional restrictions,[7] it is possible to determine equilibrium dollar values for assets as a function of their returns, the probability of occurrence of states, and the characteristics of individual utility functions.

The TSP approach is a powerful theoretical tool, but presents problems as a guide to decision making. The generality of the approach inhibits the formulation of criteria that can be readily applied. This is unfortunately a problem common to all financial models. Those models that provide simple criteria for decisions tend to be based on highly restrictive assumptions; those models that are more general in their assumptions are more difficult to apply. With this thought in mind, let us look at a simple model with more restrictive assumptions.

## CERTAINTY EQUIVALENTS (CE)[8]

Consider the problem of an individual, Mr. H, evaluating an asset that provides a multiperiod set of random cash returns. Mr. H assesses the probability distribution of returns in each period using a utility function of the sort discussed in Chap. 5. He imagines himself to be at the time the returns are to be received and determines the expected utility of the returns at that time using a utility function he currently feels is appropriate for that point in time. Expressed in mathematical symbols, he determines the expected utility of $\tilde{Y}_t$, $E[U_t(\tilde{Y}_t)]$. He then converts this value to its cash equivalent value or certainty equivalent using the same utility function. That is, he can be thought of as determining the certain amount $CE_t$ received at time $t$ satisfying the following equation:

$$U_t(CE_t) = E[U_t(\tilde{Y}_t)] \tag{9-1}$$

where $U_t(CE_t)$ equals $E[U_t(CE_t)]$, since $CE_t$ is a certain amount. The certainty equivalent is that amount of cash to be received for certain at time $t$ for which

[7] Including homogeneous expectations and unrestricted short sales.

[8] Certainty equivalent models have been the "traditional" method of dealing with problems of uncertainty in the economics literature. The development here is based on Alexander A. Robichek and Stewart C. Myers, "Optimal Financing Decisions," chap. 5, Prentice-Hall, Inc., Englewood Cliffs, N.J., 1965.

Mr. H would be indifferent between having that cash or receiving the uncertain payment $\tilde{Y}_t$. He is indifferent between $CE_t$ and $\tilde{Y}_t$ because they yield the same expected utility.[9]

The major difference between the CE approach and TSP models should be clear at this point. The utility functions now do not depend on the state but only on time. The cash receipts from owning assets are random variables in both models and can even be thought of as arising from different states of nature in CE models as well as TSP models.[10] The only differences so far are somewhat less generality in the assumptions about utility functions and the fact that the utility functions in the CE approach do not measure present preferences for future consumption.

Assume now that individuals can borrow and lend freely at $i$, the riskless rate of interest, and that $i$ is constant for all future periods.[11] The present value of a certain stream is therefore simply the discounted sum of the future payments. Since we can transform the risky stream $\tilde{Y}_t$ into an equivalent certain stream $CE_t$, the value to the individual must be the discounted sum of the certainty equivalents:

$$V = \sum_{t=0}^{n} \frac{CE_t}{(1+i)^t} \tag{9-2}$$

In other words, we can think of the value of a stream of risky cash payments as being the present value of the certainty equivalents of the individual payments discounted at the risk-free rate. The certainty equivalents depend on the characteristics of the probability distributions of the individual payments and on the individual's attitude toward risk.

To carry the model one step further we can define a new variable, the risk-adjustment factor ($\alpha_t$), in terms of the certainty equivalent of the random cash payment $\tilde{Y}_t$ and the expected value $\overline{Y}_t$ of the distribution of the payment:

$$\alpha_t \equiv \frac{CE_t}{\overline{Y}_t} \tag{9-3}$$

$CE_t$ is therefore equal to $\alpha_t \overline{Y}_t$ and the valuation equation (9-2) can be restated as

[9] It is assumed here that the expected utility approach is valid, i.e., that objects of choice are evaluated in terms of the expected utility they yield. If this were not the case, (9-1) would not be applicable. However, $CE_t$ would still be that certain amount deemed equivalent to $\tilde{Y}_t$ using whatever standard of choice the individual considers appropriate.

[10] At first glance the TSP approach may appear more restrictive than the CE approach in its assumptions about the sources of uncertainty. This is not so, since TSP models can be defined in terms of an infinite number of states and can encompass any possible distribution of returns. CE models of the form presented here require an assumption of independence of probability distributions from period to period for each asset. Moreover, the utility functions defined for each period must be independent of the cash receipts in prior periods.

[11] It is not necessary to assume that the rate of interest is constant over time.

$$V = \sum_{t=0}^{n} \frac{\alpha_t \overline{Y}_t}{(1 + i)^t} \tag{9-4}$$

The advantage of Eq. (9-4) is that we can interpret the $\alpha_t$ as adjustments for the riskiness of $\tilde{Y}_t$ and the discounting process as adjustments for their timing. The model is useful aside from the insight it provides into the nature of the problem of multiperiod valuation. It enables us to evaluate simpler models, in particular the one that follows.

## RISK-ADJUSTED DISCOUNT RATES

Perhaps the most widely used model in both theory and practice for valuing risky, multiperiod streams is the risk-adjusted discount rate (RADR). The concept follows rather simply from the use of the riskless rate under certainty. We express the present value of a risky stream $\tilde{\mathbf{Y}}$ as

$$V = \sum_{t=1}^{n} \frac{\hat{Y}_t}{(1 + r_y)^t} \tag{9-5}$$

where $\hat{Y}_t$ is a measure of the magnitude of the risky flow $\tilde{Y}_t$, and $r_y$ is a discount rate used by the individual, which takes into account in some fashion both the general riskiness of $\tilde{Y}_t, t = 1, \ldots, n$, and the rate of time preference (presumably the risk-free rate $i$).[12] $\hat{Y}_t$ is typically identified as the expected value of $\tilde{Y}_t$, $\overline{Y}_t$.[13]

As a model of individual evaluation of risky, multiperiod flows, this approach offers simplicity as its primary advantage. It requires the individual to form estimates of the future flows and apply a subjectively determined discount rate to them. The model is also fairly general in the sense that no special assumption as to what constitutes the "risk" of the stream is required. Furthermore, let us suppose that the estimates are expected values. Then there is an appealing result that follows from the use of the model.

Let $P$ be the purchase cost of the asset. The expected rate of return on the purchase cost ($\bar{r}$) can be determined from

$$P = \sum_{t=1}^{n} \frac{\overline{Y}_t}{(1 + \bar{r})^t} \tag{9-6}$$

If $\bar{r}$ is greater than the subjective rate $r_y$ determined for this stream, then the asset is a desirable purchase and the converse also holds. Given $P$ and a set of

[12] Note that here the stream is assumed to begin at time 1. The flow (if any) at time 0 is assumed to be certain and the value of the stream is assessed net of that initial flow.

[13] The assumption that $\hat{Y}_t = \overline{Y}_t$ is normally made for analytic convenience and to provide some consistency with models based on expected values. In practice, $\hat{Y}_t$ can be considered simply the estimated value of $\tilde{Y}_t$; whether that estimate corresponds to $\overline{Y}_t$ is debatable.

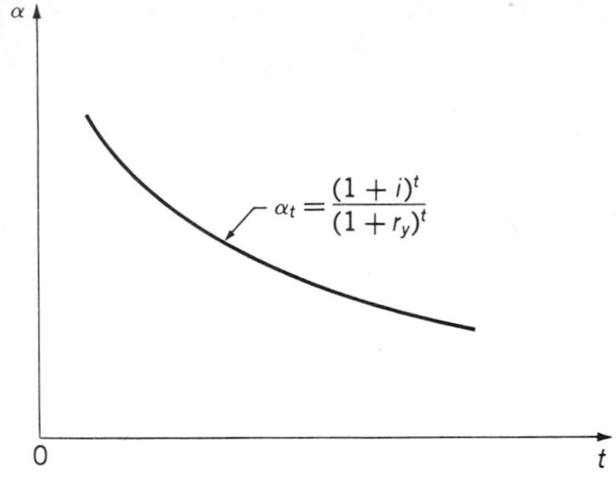


**figure 9-1**

expectations $\bar{Y}_t, t = 1, \ldots, n$, then $\bar{r}$ exists so long as $\bar{Y}_t \geq 0$ for all $t$ (refer to Appendix 3A). From a practical point of view the problem for the decision maker is greatly simplified by the RADR approach. For theoretical purposes the model is less appealing because it is difficult to determine $r_y$. At this point it must be considered a derived quantity resulting from some unspecified process.[14]

Perhaps the most serious deficiency in the RADR approach (with a constant rate) is that its use implies a specific pattern to the risk of future cash flows. This can be shown most readily by comparing valuation using a risk-adjusted rate with valuation using the certainty equivalent approach.

Let us examine the present value $V_{Y_t}$ of an expected payment $\bar{Y}_t$ in period $t$ using the two methods:[15]

$$\text{CE: } V_{Y_t} = \frac{\alpha_t \bar{Y}_t}{(1+i)^t} \tag{9-7}$$

$$\text{RADR: } V_{Y_t} = \frac{\bar{Y}_t}{(1+r_y)^t} \tag{9-8}$$

Since we presume that either method should yield the same result,

$$\frac{\alpha_t \bar{Y}_t}{(1+i)^t} = \frac{\bar{Y}_t}{(1+r_y)^t} \tag{9-9}$$

[14] In chap. 8 a rate of this sort was in fact derived for the single-period case. It was based on the particular equilibrium model of that chapter. In general such rates depend on individual preferences and the opportunities in the market. However, it must be emphasized that equilibrium prices plus a set of expectations yield a set of expected *equilibrium* rates of return derived from these expectations and prices. The theoretical issue is how equilibrium prices (or rates of return) are determined. An equilibrium model is presented in the next section.

[15] This is taken from Alexander A. Robichek and Stewart C. Myers, Conceptual Problems in the Use of Risk-Adjusted Discount Rates, *Journal of Finance*, December 1966, pp. 727–730.

**table 9-1**

| $t =$ | 1 | 2 | 3 | 4 | 5 | 10 | 15 | 20 |
|---|---|---|---|---|---|---|---|---|
| $\alpha_t =$ † | .96 | .93 | .90 | .86 | .83 | .69 | .58 | .48 |
| $CE_t =$ † | 96 | 93 | 90 | 86 | 83 | 69 | 58 | 48 |

† $\alpha_t = (1.06/1.10)^t = (.964)^t$; $CE_t = 100\alpha_t$.

or

$$\alpha_t = \frac{(1 + i)^t}{(1 + r_y)^t} \tag{9-10}$$

For risky cash flows $r_y$ generally exceeds $i$. Thus, the ratio $(1 + i)^t/(1 + r_y)^t$ is a decreasing function of $t$. If the two valuation approaches are to be consistent, $\alpha_t$ must decline with $t$ as illustrated in Fig. 9-1. Since $\alpha_t$ is a measure of the risk of the uncertain cash flow $\tilde{Y}_t$ as perceived by the individual, where the smaller the value of $\alpha_t$ the greater the perceived risk, the risk of the cash flows must be increasing over time. This result can be most easily demonstrated in an example when the expected values of the future cash flows are equal; $\bar{Y}_t = 100$ for all $t$. Let $r_y = .10$ and $i = .06$. The values of $\alpha_t$ and the certainty equivalent $CE_t$ as a function of time implied by Eq. (9-10) are shown in Table 9-1. Since the certainty value of the expected payment of $100 declines as $t$ increases, the payment must be considered more risky.[16]

## OTHER MODELS

A variety of other models have been developed to evaluate risky, multiperiod cash flows. Most have been proposed as methods for analyzing firm investment opportunities; however, in principle they should be equally applicable to the individual's problem.[17] An important class of models is based on the conversion of the multiperiod flows into a single probability distribution of a summary

[16] This argument is based on the concept that there are only two characteristics of the distribution of $\tilde{Y}_t$ which affect its value of the individual in period $t$: "return" as measured by the expected value, and "risk," which includes all other characteristics of concern to the individual. A more general statement would be that for a fixed expected value, the cash payments become less desirable as measured by the certainty equivalents.

[17] In fact, given our basic argument that optimal decision criteria for the firm must be derived from an analysis of shareholder preferences, we would say that only if the model is appropriate for the shareholder would it be appropriate for use by the firm. This is not to say that it is necessary that the approach used by shareholders be used by the firm, since in many cases (for example, chaps. 2 and 6) management does not have to concern itself with shareholder preferences. That is, the firm's problem may be simpler than the shareholder's problem. For example, in chap. 2, management did not have to concern itself with the consumption preferences of shareholders, but could concentrate instead on maximizing present value.

measure of the flows. The distribution of the rate of return on the purchase price, and distributions of the present value of the flows, have been suggested.[18] Presumably individuals could be viewed as assessing the risk implied from such distributions and determining the value of the income stream according to their judgment. A difficulty with such models is that they "collapse" a multiperiod set of risky payments into a single probability distribution. Hence a great deal of information is necessarily lost by the procedure and in general we cannot know how valuable that lost information is to the individual. In short we do not know the underlying assumptions that are needed to validate such models and hence whether such assumptions are reasonable.[19]

## MARKET VALUATION

The discussion so far in this chapter has been directed toward alternative ways individuals might value risky income streams. Implicit in the discussion was the idea that the value of any given stream to the individual depends on a variety of factors, including the individual's preferences and available alternatives. Moreover, it is clear that in a world of uncertainty individuals may have differing expectations about the stream provided by any particular asset. If management is to act in the best interests of its shareholders and its shareholders have differing views on what constitutes the best action, management faces a difficult problem. We remarked earlier that it is appropriate for management to maximize the market value of the firm's shares provided that the shareholders can transact in the market to achieve their preferred position. In fact, so long as shareholders can sell their shares, any alternative objective might well create a conflict of interest. That is, actions preferred by one group of shareholders may be objectionable to another. By maximizing market value, management is at least providing any unhappy shareholder with the highest current cash receipts if the shareholder wishes to sell out.

Thus we need to know how the capital market values risky streams. This is no easy problem. We approach the problem of market valuation here in two ways.[20] First, in this section we develop a market-valuation equation that is an

[18] Approaches of this form have been suggested in a number of papers including: F. S. Hillier, The Derivation of Probabilistic Information for the Evaluation of Risky Investments, *Management Science*, April 1963; D. B. Hertz, Risk Analysis in Capital Investment, *Harvard Business Review*, January–February 1964; and W. Beranek, "Analysis for Financial Decisions," chap. 6, Richard D. Irwin, Inc., Homewood, Ill., 1963.

[19] See the discussion by Robichek and Myers, Valuation of the Firm: Effects of Uncertainty in a Market Context (listed in the Suggested Readings at the end of this chapter). In particular, their argument that the manner in which uncertainty is expected to be resolved over time will affect value suggests that summary distributions are abstracted from important characteristics of multiperiod streams.

[20] In Chap. 10 an alternative approach to the entire "multiperiod" valuation problem is presented which examines the problem in continuous time.

extension of the single-period, mean-variance model of Chaps. 7 and 8. Although the assumptions required to produce the valuation equation are fairly restrictive, the model and its development provides insights into the general problem and illustrates some of the difficulties inherent in multiperiod valuation. Second, in the next section we present a general property of perfect markets called the "value-additivity principle," a property that was established for the single-period model in Chap. 8. The value-additivity principle is sufficient to deal with general questions about the impact of firm financial decisions on the value of the firm's shares. However, specification of the method of valuation becomes necessary to determine the specific numerical magnitude of the impact of a particular decision (for example, the net present value of an investment opportunity).

## Multiperiod Securities Pricing: Single Cash Flow

Suppose that the single-period valuation model of Chap. 7 holds in each future period $t$. Thus we can express the value of a security at time $t$-1 using Eq. (7-19) as

$$V_{t-1} = \frac{\bar{Y}_t - \lambda_t \operatorname{cov}[\tilde{Y}_t, \tilde{r}_{Mt}]}{1 + i_t} \tag{9-11}$$

Here $\tilde{Y}_t$ is the proceeds from sale of the security at time $t$ plus any income (dividends) received at time $t$. $\tilde{Y}_t$ would be the cash flow received for period $t$ by a person who sells the security at time $t$. Since part of this cash flow is the market value of the security at time $t$, the problem is pushed forward one period; that is, we would need to know how the security will be valued at time $t$. Ultimately we want to find the market value at time 0 of the entire income stream from $t = 1$ to $t = n$ for a security.

To simplify the analysis we assume that the market parameters $i$ and $\lambda$ are known and constant for all $t$; that is, the riskless interest rate is $i$ per period and the "price of risk" is $\lambda$ in each period. Also, for now, we look at a security that will pay an uncertain amount $\tilde{Y}_T$ in only one future period $T$. These assumptions will be discussed and a more general case presented after the basic result is established. The problem then is to find the market value at time 0 of the uncertain cash payment $\tilde{Y}_T$.

First, consider the market value of $\tilde{Y}_T$ at time $T$-1; that is, imagine we are at time $T$-1. From Eq. (9-11):

$$V_{T-1} = \frac{\bar{Y}_T - \lambda \operatorname{cov}[\tilde{Y}_T, \tilde{r}_{MT}]}{1 + i} \tag{9-12}$$

However, to be more precise, the value of the security at time $T$-1 will be based on expectations regarding $\tilde{Y}_T$ formed at time $T$-1. Therefore, we need to use a notation that will keep track of *when* the expectations are being formed:

$$\text{Expected value of } \tilde{Y}_T \text{ at time } T - j \equiv E_{T-j}[\tilde{Y}_T]$$

Covariance between $\tilde{Y}_T$ and $\tilde{r}_{MT}$ at time $T - j \equiv \text{cov}_{T-j}\,[\tilde{Y}_T,\tilde{r}_{MT}]$

Therefore,

Expected value of $\tilde{Y}_T$ at time $T - 1 = E_{T-1}\,[\tilde{Y}_T]$

Covariance between $\tilde{Y}_T$ and $\tilde{r}_{MT}$ at time $T - 1 = \text{cov}_{T-1}\,[\tilde{Y}_T,\tilde{r}_{MT}]$

Using this notation, Eq. (9-12) can be expressed as

$$V_{T-1} = \frac{E_{T-1}[\tilde{Y}_T] - \lambda\, \text{cov}_{T-1}[\tilde{Y}_T,\tilde{r}_{MT}]}{1 + i} \tag{9-13}$$

Having complicated the notation by these considerations, we now simplify somewhat to a form that turns out to be convenient later. Define the "relative covariance" (used in Chap. 8) as the Greek letter chi, $\chi$.

$$\chi_T^{T-1} = \frac{\text{cov}_{T-1}[\tilde{Y}_T,\tilde{r}_{MT}]}{E_{T-1}[\tilde{Y}_T]} \tag{9-14}$$

The superscript on $\chi$ indicates the timing of the expectations $(T - 1)$ and the subscript indicates the timing of the cash flow $(T)$. Then, using Eq. (9-14) in Eq. (9-13), we have

$$V_{T-1} = E_{T-1}[\tilde{Y}_T]\left(\frac{1 - \lambda\chi_T^{T-1}}{1 + i}\right) \tag{9-15}$$

At time $T - 1$, $V_{T-1}$ is given by Eq. (9-15) and its alternative version Eq. (9-13). Now consider the market value of the security at time $T - 2$. Applying the single-period model:

$$V_{T-2} = \frac{\overline{V}_{T-1} - \lambda\, \text{cov}[\tilde{V}_{T-1},\tilde{r}_{MT-1}]}{1 + i} \tag{9-16}$$

From the perspective of investors at time $T - 2$, the value of the security at time $T - 1$ is uncertain. Why?

Given $i$ and $\lambda$, the only reason $\tilde{V}_{T-1}$ is uncertain at time $T - 2$ is due to uncertainty as to what the probability distribution of $\tilde{Y}_T$ will be at time $T - 1$. That is, in Eq. (9-15), the only possible sources of uncertainty in $V_{T-1}$ are uncertainty as to $E_{T-1}[\tilde{Y}_T]$ and $\chi_T^{T-1}$. *We now assume that $\chi_T^{T-1}$ is known and the superscript can be dropped*; $\chi_T$ is assumed to be a given quantity from the perspective of investors from time 0 to time $T - 1$. This assumption turns out to be similar to the assumption that $i$ and $\lambda$ are known in future periods and is discussed later.[21] Given $\chi_T$, uncertainty in $\tilde{V}_{T-1}$ at time $T - 2$ is due solely to uncertainty as to the expected value of $\tilde{Y}_T$, $\tilde{E}_{T-1}\,[\tilde{Y}_T]$, and from the perspective of time $T - 2$, Eq. (9-15) becomes

[21] The significance and necessity for this assumption is discussed by E. F. Fama, Risk-Adjusted Discount Rates and Capital Budgeting under Uncertainty, *Journal of Financial Economics*, vol. 5, pp. 3–24, August 1977. This paper is the basic reference for the model presented here.

$$\tilde{V}_{T-1} = \tilde{E}_{T-1}[\tilde{Y}_T] \left(\frac{1 - \lambda\chi_T}{1 + i}\right) \tag{9-17}$$

At time $T - 2$, investors will have a probability distribution for $\tilde{Y}_T$ with expected value $E_{T-2}[\tilde{Y}_T]$. We can define a random variable $\tilde{e}_{T-1}$ which accounts for possible revisions in expectations during the period from time $T - 2$ to $T - 1$:

$$\tilde{e}_{T-1} = \frac{\tilde{E}_{T-1}[\tilde{Y}_T] - E_{T-2}[\tilde{Y}_T]}{E_{T-2}[\tilde{Y}_T]} \tag{9-18}$$

The variable $\tilde{e}_{T-1}$ is the proportional change in the expected value of $\tilde{Y}_T$ during period $T - 1$. And from Eq. (9-18):

$$\tilde{E}_{T-1}[\tilde{Y}_T] = (1 + \tilde{e}_{T-1})E_{T-2}[\tilde{Y}_T] \tag{9-19}$$

Under the assumptions of the model, all information about $\tilde{Y}_T$ at time $T - 2$ is contained in the time $T - 2$ probability distribution for $\tilde{Y}_T$. The expected value of $\tilde{e}_{T-1}$ must therefore be zero since any anticipated systematic changes would already be reflected in $E_{T-2}[\tilde{Y}_T]$. Substituting Eq. (9-19) for $\tilde{E}_{T-1}[\tilde{Y}_T]$ in Eq. (9-17), we obtain

$$\tilde{V}_{T-1} = (1 + \tilde{e}_{T-1})E_{T-2}[\tilde{Y}_T] \left(\frac{1 - \lambda\chi_T}{1 + i}\right) \tag{9-20}$$

and

$$\bar{V}_{T-1} = E_{T-2}[\tilde{Y}_T] \left(\frac{1 - \lambda\chi_T}{1 + i}\right) \tag{9-21}$$

and, using (9-20) and (9-21),

$$\text{cov}[\tilde{V}_{T-1},\tilde{r}_{MT-1}] = \bar{V}_{T-1} \text{ cov}[\tilde{e}_{T-1},\tilde{r}_{MT-1}] \tag{9-22}$$

The value of the security at time $T - 2$ is obtained by using Eqs. (9-21) and (9-22) to substitute into Eq. (9-16).

$$V_{T-2} = \frac{\bar{V}_{T-1}(1 - \lambda \text{ cov}[\tilde{e}_{T-1},\tilde{r}_{MT-1}])}{1 + i} \tag{9-23a}$$

$$= \frac{E_{T-2}[\tilde{Y}_T](1 - \lambda\chi_T)(1 - \lambda \text{ cov}[\tilde{e}_{T-1},\tilde{r}_{MT-1}])}{(1 + i)^2} \tag{9-23b}$$

For convenience, define the covariance of the change in expectations as Greek letter epsilon, $\epsilon$.

$$\epsilon_{T-1} = \text{cov}[\tilde{e}_{T-1},\tilde{r}_{MT-1}] \tag{9-24}$$

Then (9-23$b$) becomes

$$V_{T-2} = \frac{E_{T-2}[\tilde{Y}_T](1 - \lambda\chi_T)(1 - \lambda\epsilon_{T-1})}{(1 + i)^2} \tag{9-25}$$

We assume that the covariance $\epsilon_{T-1}$ is known at all preceding points in time as we did for $\chi_T$, $i$, and $\lambda$. We then can apply a similar procedure to find $V_{T-3}$, $V_{T-4}$, and so on to $V_0$.

$$V_{T-3} = \frac{E_{T-3}[\tilde{Y}_T](1 - \lambda\chi_T)(1 - \lambda\epsilon_{T-1})(1 - \lambda\epsilon_{T-2})}{(1 + i)^3}$$

$$V_{T-4} = \frac{E_{T-4}[\tilde{Y}_T](1 - \lambda\chi_T)(1 - \lambda\epsilon_{T-1})(1 - \lambda\epsilon_{T-2})(1 - \lambda\epsilon_{T-3})}{(1 + i)^4}$$

$$V_0 = \frac{E_0[\tilde{Y}_T](1 - \lambda\chi_T)(1 - \lambda\epsilon_{T-1}) \ldots (1 - \lambda\epsilon_t) \ldots (1 - \lambda\epsilon_1)}{(1 + i)^T} \quad \text{(9-26)}$$

where

$$\epsilon_t = \text{cov}[\tilde{e}_t, \tilde{Y}_{Mt}]$$

$$\tilde{e}_t = \frac{\tilde{E}_t[\tilde{Y}_T] - E_{t-1}[\tilde{Y}_T]}{E_{t-1}[\tilde{Y}_T]}$$

The market value at time 0 of a single cash flow in period $T$ is therefore the expected value of the cash flow as viewed from time 0, $E_0[\tilde{Y}_T]$, times the product of a series of risk-adjustment factors, all discounted at the riskless interest rate. Note that the risk is of two types. First, there is the "basic" risk of the cash flow in period $T$ as measured by its relative covariance $\chi_T$; and, second, there is the risk due to potential revisions of expectations regarding the expected value of the distribution as measured by the $\epsilon_t$, $t = 1 \ldots T - 1$. We would expect that the $\epsilon_t$ will be positive for most assets. For example, if the rate of return on the market is high in a given period $t$ because the outlook for the economy improves, the outlook for most future cash returns must improve; expectations in general are being revised upward. Conversely, a low rate of return on the market due to a worsening outlook for the economy would imply that expected returns on most assets are being revised downward.

Another way to see the significance of the $\epsilon_t$ terms is to assume that no such revisions in expectations will occur. Then, $\epsilon_t = 0$ for all $t$ and

$$E_t[\tilde{Y}_T] = E_0[\tilde{Y}_T] \qquad \text{for all } t$$

But if this is true, then there is no uncertainty associated with any $V_t$, $t = 1, \ldots, T - 1$. The market price of the asset is known with certainty for each future period and the only risk is in the final cash flow as measured by $\chi_T$. Since this result is not realistic, we conclude that the $\epsilon_t$ are not zero.

**Implications for CE and RADR models.** We can see from inspection of Eq. (9-26) and the definition of the "market" certainty equivalent factor $\alpha$, Eq. (9-4), the factor applicable to the cash flow $\tilde{Y}_T$ must be

$$\alpha_T = (1 - \lambda\chi_T)(1 - \lambda\epsilon_{T-1}) \ldots (1 - \lambda\epsilon_1) \quad \text{(9-27)}$$

Thus, a market-determined certainty equivalent factor contains information regarding both the basic risk $\chi_T$ and the potential for revised expectations, the

$\epsilon_t$. Notice that as $T$ increases, the number of multiplicative terms $(1 - \lambda\epsilon_t)$ in (9-27) also increases. Since these terms are typically less than 1.0, $\alpha_T$ tends to decline with $T$. We return to this point later.

Consider now the market expected rate of return at time $T - 1$ on the security for period $T$, $k_T$:

$$k_T = \frac{E_{T-1}[\tilde{Y}_T]}{V_{T-1}} - 1$$

From Eq. (9-15) and since $\chi_T$ is given by assumption so that the superscript $T - 1$ may be deleted,

$$k_T = \frac{(1 + i)}{(1 - \lambda\chi_T)} - 1 \tag{9-28}$$

Equation (9-28) is, in our present notation, the same as Eq. (8-26), where we derived the market discount rate in the single-period model. Remember that $k_T$ is an equilibrium value determined in the market. Note that by our assumption of known $i$, $\lambda$, and $\chi_T$, $k_T$ is also known for any prior time. We can express Eq. (9-28) as

$$\frac{1}{1 + k_T} = \frac{1 - \lambda\chi_T}{1 + i} \tag{9-29}$$

Now look at the market rate of return on the security expected for period $T-1$. Using Eq. (9-23$a$) and the definition of $\epsilon_{T-1}$ in (9-24)

$$\begin{aligned} k_{T-1} &= \frac{\overline{V}_{T-1}}{V_{T-2}} - 1 \\ &= \frac{1 + i}{1 - \lambda\epsilon_{T-1}} - 1 \end{aligned} \tag{9-30}$$

or

$$\frac{1}{1 + k_{T-1}} = \frac{1 - \lambda\epsilon_{T-1}}{1 + i} \tag{9-31}$$

In general, then, for any $t = 1 \ldots T - 1$

$$\frac{1}{1 + k_t} = \frac{1 - \lambda\epsilon_t}{1 + i} \tag{9-32}$$

Since the $\epsilon_t$ are known by assumption, $k_t$ is also known for any future period $t$. We can now use Eqs. (9-29) and (9-32) to express the value $V_0$ of Eq. (9-26) in terms of the discount rates $k_t$

$$V_0 = \frac{E_0[\tilde{Y}_T]}{\prod_{t=1}^{T} (1 + k_t)} \tag{9-33}$$

Eq. (9-33) is simply the general present value equation for the cash flow in a single period when the discount rate may differ from period to period.

There are several interesting things that are revealed by Eq. (9-33) and its development. First, note that (9-33) would apply, as is, for the more general case where $\lambda$ and $i$ vary from period to period. That is, Eq. (9-32) could be written as

$$\frac{1}{1 + k_t} = \frac{1 - \lambda_t \epsilon_t}{1 + i_t} \tag{9-34}$$

With $i_t$ and $\lambda_t$ used, all previous proofs follow except that $i_T$, $\lambda_T$, $i_{T-1}$, $\lambda_{T-1}$, etc., must be used in the appropriate places. Remember, however, all these values must be known with certainty. Next, given constant $i$ and $\lambda$, $k_t$ will not be constant for all $t$ except under unusual circumstances. It might be reasonable to assume, at least as an approximation, that $\epsilon_t$ are the same for all $t = 1 \ldots T - 1$. Remember that $\epsilon_t$ measures the risk of changes in expectations in period $t$ for the cash flow $\tilde{Y}_T$. We see no circumstances that would make the $\epsilon_t$ vary in any particular way over time. Thus we might well assume $k_t = k$ for $t = 1 \ldots T - 1$. However, $k_T$ results from somewhat different considerations. The risk in period $T$ is measured by $\chi_T$, the relative covariance of actual cash receipts with the economy in that period. Although $\chi_T$ and $\epsilon_t$ are related, they are not measuring the same thing and therefore are unlikely to be equal. Finally, we should note that the $k_t$ derived here apply only to the cash flow in period $T$.

## Valuation of Multiperiod Streams

The value of a stream of cash flows occurring in periods $t = 1, \ldots, n$ can be developed by summing the market values of its components. At this point we revert to our standard notation using $\bar{Y}_t$ as the expected income in period $t$ where the expectation is always as of the present time ($t = 0$), and we use this as standard in this book for all expectations. That is,

$$\bar{Y}_t = E_0[\tilde{Y}_t]$$

Then we can write the value at time 0, $V_0^t$ of a cash flow occurring at any time $t$, $\tilde{Y}_t$, as

$$V_0^t = \frac{\bar{Y}_t(1 - \lambda\chi_t)(1 - \lambda\epsilon_{t-1}^t)(1 - \lambda\epsilon_{t-2}^t) \ldots (1 - \lambda\epsilon_1^t)}{(1 + i)^t} \tag{9-35}$$

We use the superscript here to keep track of which flow is being valued, the superscript $t$ refers to $\tilde{Y}_t$. Under our assumptions, we can then express the value of a stream of $\tilde{Y}_t$, $t = 1, \ldots, n$ as

$$V_0 = V_0^1 + V_0^2 + \ldots + V_0^t + \ldots + V_0^n$$

$$V_0 = \frac{\bar{Y}_1(1 - \lambda\chi_1)}{1 + i} = \frac{\bar{Y}_2(1 - \lambda\chi_2)(1 - \lambda\epsilon_1^2)}{(1 + i)^2} + \frac{\bar{Y}_3(1 - \lambda\chi_3)(1 - \lambda\epsilon_2^3)(1 - \lambda\epsilon_1^3)}{(1 + i)^3} + \ldots + \frac{\bar{Y}_n(1 - \lambda\chi_n)(1 - \lambda\epsilon_{n-1}^n)(1 - \lambda\epsilon_{n-2}^n) \ldots (1 - \lambda\epsilon_1^n)}{(1 + i)^n} \tag{9-36}$$

The valuation equation (9-36) is complicated by the possible variations in the $\epsilon_t^T$ for cash flows occurring at times 2 through $n$. Note, for example, in period 1, changes in expectations regarding period 2, 3, . . . , $n$ cash flows may occur. In general, the proportional revisions in the expected value of $\tilde{Y}_n$ might be rather different from the proportional revision of the expected value of $\tilde{Y}_2$. One would suppose that the covariance for period 2 cash flows ($\epsilon_1^2$) would be greater than the covariance for period $n$ cash flows ($\epsilon_1^n$). This has important implications for the discount-rate model. In discount-rate form, Eq. (9-36) becomes

$$V_0 = \frac{\overline{Y}_1}{(1 + k_1^1)} + \frac{\overline{Y}_2}{(1 + k_1^2)(1 + k_2^2)} + \frac{\overline{Y}_3}{(1 + k_1^3)(1 + k_2^3)(1 + k_3^3)} + \cdots + \frac{\overline{Y}_n}{\prod_{t=1}^{n} (1 + k_t^n)} \tag{9-37}$$

where $k_t^T$ is the discount rate applicable in period $t$ to the cash flow occurring at time $T$. To obtain a single discount rate applicable to all flows for a given period $t$, the following equalities must hold:[22]

$$\chi_t = \epsilon_t^{t+1} = \epsilon_t^{t+2} = \cdots = \epsilon_t^n \qquad \text{for all } t \tag{9-38}$$

For condition (9-38) to hold, the covariance of revision in expectations for each cash flow subsequent to $t$ must be equal and equal to the relative covariance of the cash flow in period $t$. If (9-38) holds, then there is a single $k_t$ for each $t$ and the valuation equation (9-37) becomes

$$V_0 = \sum_{T=1}^{n} \frac{\overline{Y}_T}{\prod_{t=1}^{T} (1 + k_t)} \tag{9-39}$$

Equation (9-39) is the certainty model of Chap. 2 with variable interest rates applied under uncertainty. As noted above, (9-39) would apply also to the case for nonconstant market parameters $i_t$ and $\lambda_t$.

To obtain a single discount rate as used in the basic RADR model, given constant $i$ and $\lambda$, and given (9-38), the risk of each flow must be the same.

$$\chi_t = \chi \qquad \text{all } t \tag{9-40}$$

[22] As an alternative simplification, one might consider the conditions required for a single discount rate to apply to each flow; that is, $k_t^j = k^j$ for all $t \leq j$ and

$$V_0 = \frac{\overline{Y}_1}{(1 + k^1)} + \frac{\overline{Y}_2}{(1 + k^2)^2} + \frac{\overline{Y}_3}{(1 + k^3)^3} + \cdots + \frac{\overline{Y}_n}{(1 + k^n)^n} \tag{i}$$

The conditions are

($a$) Constant $i$ and $\lambda$, all $t$

($b$) $\epsilon_t^j = \chi_j$ for each cash flow $\overline{Y}_j$, all $t \leq j$.

Condition ($b$) says that the covariances of revisions of expectations about a given cash flow are all equal to the relative covariance of the cash flow.

Then $k_t = k$, all $t$, and

$$V_0 = \sum_{t=1}^{n} \frac{\bar{Y}_t}{(1+k)^t} \tag{9-41}$$

Note that embedded in the single-discount-rate model are changing expectations. The $\epsilon_t^T$ are not zero, but are constant and equal to $\chi$. The relative covariance is therefore the sole measure of risk in the single-discount-rate approach.[23]

## Discussion

We have shown how the single-period model of capital market equilibrium developed in Chap. 7 can be extended to a multiperiod analysis. However, the development of the general valuation equation (9-36) required assumptions that future riskless interest rates, the market price of risk, and the covariances $\chi_t$ and $\epsilon_t^T$ are all known, i.e., are not random variables. Fama, in his development of the model, argues that all these assumptions are implicit in the application of the model.[24] If any of the four types of variables listed above are stochastic in period $t$, the expected rate of return in period $t$ is a random variable and the value of the firm at $t - 1$ will be affected by this. Uncertainty in the expected rate of return produces a different and more complex equilibrium model. At this point there are two possible paths to follow. We can delve more deeply into the theory of multiperiod equilibrium. This is done to some degree in Appendix 9A, where we explore the time-state preference approach in more depth, and we examine valuation in continuous time in Chap. 10. However, most of our subsequent development is based on general properties of capital market valuation. As we shall see, considerable insight into firm financial decisions can be gained without assuming any particular valuation approach.

# THE VALUE-ADDITIVITY PRINCIPLE[25]

To this point in the chapter we have described several models for valuing a multiperiod income stream. The present section will discuss a valuation rela-

[23] Under the assumptions used to develop a single discount rate, the certainty equivalent factor for any cash flow $\tilde{Y}_t$ follows from Eq. (9-27):

$$\alpha_t = (1 - \lambda\chi)^t$$

Given that for a risky stream $0 < (1 - \lambda\chi) < 1.0$, the certainty equivalent factors follow precisely the pattern shown in Fig. 9-1.

[24] *Op. cit.*, p. 11.

[25] This discussion and Appendix 9B are based on Schall's Asset Valuation, Firm Investment, and Firm Diversification (listed in the Suggested Readings at the end of this chapter). The development here and the one in the Schall article differ somewhat because of a difference in the definitions

tionship, the value-additivity principle (VAP), which has a number of important implications for firm financial decisions. The VAP does not assume any particular valuation model by investors and all the models we discussed earlier (TSP, certainty equivalent, and RADR) are consistent with the VAP. It will be assumed initially that capital markets are transaction costless (no transaction costs or government constraints associated with transactions, and transaction costless infinite divisibility of assets) and competitive (no firm or individual can alter the structure of discount rates in the market), there is no personal tax bias in that all cash payments received by investors in the market are taxed at the personal level at the same effective tax rate for any given investor (but tax rates may vary among investors), and expectations are homogeneous. In Appendix 9B it is shown that the VAP holds with heterogeneous expectations, noncompetitive capital markets, and in a special form, even with personal tax biases. Note that no assumption concerning investor risk preferences is required. The value-additivity principle, or VAP, states that:

> At equilibrium, the total market value of any set of income streams (cash payments by firms to investors) received by investors in the market is the same regardless of how that set of streams is combined or divided into the debt or equity streams of one or more firms.

Put algebraically, for a set of $n$ debt and/or equity streams of one or more firms, $\tilde{\mathbf{Y}}_1, \ldots, \tilde{\mathbf{Y}}_n$, the VAP states that

$$V_T = \sum_{i=1}^{n} V_i \qquad \text{if} \qquad \tilde{Y}_T = \sum_{i=1}^{n} \tilde{Y}_i \tag{9-42}$$

where $V_j$ is the equilibrium market value of stream $\tilde{\mathbf{Y}}_j, j = T, i, i = 1, \ldots, n.$[26] $V_j$ is the value that $\tilde{\mathbf{Y}}_j$ would have if $\tilde{\mathbf{Y}}_j$ were available in the market *as an individual income stream*. The above relationship means that the sum of the values of *any* streams $\tilde{\mathbf{Y}}_1, \ldots, \tilde{\mathbf{Y}}_n$, which in total equal stream $\tilde{\mathbf{Y}}_T$, will be the same as the value of $\tilde{\mathbf{Y}}_T$ in the market. Thus any arbitrary division of $\tilde{\mathbf{Y}}_T$ into separate streams will not alter total market value. For example, if $\tilde{\mathbf{Y}}_1$ and $\tilde{\mathbf{Y}}_2$ were the cash flows and $V_1$ and $V_2$ the values of firms 1 and 2, the VAP states

---

of the streams involved. The original proof was divided into Proposition I for the no-tax case and Proposition II for the tax case. The propositions were defined in terms of precorporate tax rather than postcorporate tax streams as is done here. Defining all streams as postcorporate tax cash flows to investors, as is done here, allows all results (no-tax and tax) to be stated in a single proposition. This proposition, the value-additivity principle, applies with or without firm taxes, with risky as well as riskless debt, and with or without firm bankruptcy costs. The cash flow $\tilde{Y}$ is the net flow (net of firm taxes, bankruptcy costs, etc.) paid by the firm to investors in the market.

[26] Note that $\tilde{\mathbf{Y}}$ in (9-42) is defined as a cash payment by the firm to investors in the market and does not include capital gains, which are changes in the value of the cash flow. See app. 9B for a discussion of this issue.

that merging the two firms into one would produce a merged value $V_T$ such that $V_T = V_1 + V_2$ if $\tilde{Y}_T = \tilde{Y}_1 + \tilde{Y}_2$ (no synergy). The sum of the values of the premerger firms 1 and 2 equals the value of the firm resulting from the merger if there are no economies or diseconomies, that is, if $\tilde{Y}_T = \tilde{Y}_1 + \tilde{Y}_2$. Further, a division of $\tilde{Y}_T$ into *any* other streams $\tilde{Y}_1 \ldots \tilde{Y}_n$ results in a total value of those streams equal to $V_T$, that is, $V_T = \Sigma_{i=1}^n V_i$.

Thus, *no matter how the firms divide or combine the cash-flow streams in making them available to the market as debt or equity streams of one or more firms, the total value will be the same by the VAP.* The reason for this is that arbitragers (market participants) will always pay for any stream (or set of streams) that amount which they can receive by reselling that stream to investors in the form most desired by investors. We can use a simple example to explain the arbitraging process that causes the VAP to hold (a formal proof is provided in Appendix 9B). Assume that there are no corporate taxes and firm H offers its returns to investors in the market as a dividend stream $\tilde{Y}_T$ (i.e., the firm has no debt and therefore pays its stockholders all returns that are not reinvested by the firm). The value of the firm is $V_T$, the value of stream $\tilde{Y}_T$. But assume that investors in the market would prefer that $\tilde{Y}_T$ be paid out as a debt stream $\tilde{Y}_1$ (interest) and as a dividend stream $\tilde{Y}_2$, where $\tilde{Y}_1 + \tilde{Y}_2 = \tilde{Y}_T$ (i.e., some investors would like stream $\tilde{Y}_1$ and others would like $\tilde{Y}_2$). The prices investors will pay for streams $\tilde{Y}_1$ and $\tilde{Y}_2$ are $V_1$ and $V_2$, respectively, where, $V_1 + V_2 > V_T$ (since investors will pay more for the firm when its income stream is divided up as they prefer). But, even if firm H decides to offer its income in the form of a single dividend stream $\tilde{Y}_T$, arbitragers can purchase $\tilde{Y}_T$ for price $V_T$ and divide dividend stream $\tilde{Y}_T$ into interest stream $\tilde{Y}_1$ and dividend stream $\tilde{Y}_2$, sell $\tilde{Y}_1$ and $\tilde{Y}_2$ to investors in the market for $V_1$ and $V_2$, and make a profit of $(V_1 + V_2) - V_T$. Thus, if a firm offers its income stream in a form investors don't prefer most (and consequently the firm is worth less than if the firm offered its income as investors prefer), arbitragers can buy up the firm's securities and reissue new claims (securities) against the firm's securities where the new claims pay out the firm's returns as investors prefer. At equilibrium, arbitraging profit will be zero because competing arbitragers will pay for the firm's income stream (pay for $\tilde{Y}_T$) what can be received for that stream $(V_1 + V_2)$ after they most profitably convert it. That is, at equilibrium, arbitragers will drive up the price of $\tilde{Y}_T$, $V_T$ until it equals $V_1 + V_2$. Similarly, if firm H initially offered its income as debt stream $\tilde{Y}_1$ and dividend stream $\tilde{Y}_2$, and if investors preferred a single stream $\tilde{Y}_T$, where $\tilde{Y}_T = \tilde{Y}_1 + \tilde{Y}_2$, arbitragers (or investors themselves) could buy up $\tilde{Y}_1$ and $\tilde{Y}_2$ for $(V_1 + V_2)$, combine $\tilde{Y}_1$ and $\tilde{Y}_2$ and offer them as single stream $\tilde{Y}_T$, receiving $V_T$ for stream $\tilde{Y}_T$. Since investors prefer $\tilde{Y}_T$ to $\tilde{Y}_1$ and $\tilde{Y}_2$, they will pay more for $\tilde{Y}_T$ than for $\tilde{Y}_1$ and $\tilde{Y}_2$; therefore, arbitragers will make a profit by buying $\tilde{Y}_1$ and $\tilde{Y}_2$, combining the streams into $\tilde{Y}_T$, and selling $\tilde{Y}_T$ to investors. At equilibrium, with arbitragers competing for the $\tilde{Y}_1$ and $\tilde{Y}_2$, the arbitraging profit will be zero and $V_T = V_1 + V_2$.

The above arguments imply that, regardless of how the firm initially offers its income to the market, it will ultimately have the same value. If it is initially offered in a form that is not most desired by investors, arbitragers will compete for the firm's streams and pay the value of the most desired set of streams into which the firm's income can be converted. If the firm does initially provide its income to the market in the most desired form, the same total equilibrium value will of course obtain, but without the necessity of arbitrage.

In Appendix 9B it is shown that investors themselves can also perform arbitrage and that the VAP will result from such "investor arbitrage" just as from the "pure arbitrage" discussed above. It should be noted here that the arbitrage just described (or investor arbitrage) can be performed by individuals or by such institutions as banks, insurance companies, mutual funds, or other financial institutions. In perfect markets, individuals and financial institutions can freely purchase and sell claims on income streams. They can issue fixed promises to pay (debt) or can issue equity claims. Although the perfect-market assumption permits us to assume the ability of individuals to issue equity claims, in actuality such a practice is more readily performed by financial institutions, including mutual funds, commercial banks, insurance companies, and savings and loan firms, all of which purchase one form of income stream in the market and issue claims promising streams with different risk-return properties. This process of transformation is referred to here as "arbitrage."

Given the ability to perform the arbitrage transactions described above, arbitragers can combine a group of individual streams and issue debt or equity claims against the combination; they can also purchase a given stream and split it up into component parts. If there are profits to be made in performing such operations, participants will engage in them. The outcome is that regardless of how a firm initially offers its income stream $\tilde{\mathbf{Y}}_T$ to the market (as $\tilde{\mathbf{Y}}_T$ or any set $\tilde{\mathbf{Y}}_1 \ldots \tilde{\mathbf{Y}}_k$ that can be generated from $\tilde{\mathbf{Y}}_T$), arbitragers will convert the stream(s) into the most desired set and it will be the total value of that most desired set which is the ultimate equilibrium value of the initial stream(s) offered by the firm.[27]

Clearly the concept is an idealization of conditions in actual markets. Yet we do observe financial institutions in particular engaging in the kinds of activities required. The fact that such actions are not costless means only that value additivity is an approximation and not an exact relationship. The degree of approximation is essentially an empirical question.[28]

Observe that nothing has been said regarding the existence of firm taxes. The preceding results hold with or without firm taxes. The cash-flow streams referred to in the discussion are streams *received by investors after corporate*

[27] The assumption of zero transaction costs is particularly important here. The ability of market participants in reality to aggregate and disaggregate income streams to eliminate arbitraging profits depends on how easily financial assets can be created and sold, which in turn depends on the magnitudes of transaction costs.

[28] There is some evidence that actual capital-market asset pricing is consistent with the value-additivity principle, although there may be price adjustment time lags. See Malcom Burns, "The Time Series Behavior of the Value Additivity Principle," unpublished manuscript, University of Kansas, 1977.

*taxes have been paid* if such taxes exist. That is, all streams were *after-tax* streams; the VAP states that a set of streams received by investors (which means after firm taxes are paid) has the same total value regardless of how such a set of after-tax streams is divided into equity or debt streams. As will be shown in Chap. 11, this does not imply that a firm is indifferent to how it divides its *pretax* cash flow into debt and equity streams; with taxes, the division of the pretax stream affects the *after-tax* stream valued by investors and to which the VAP applies. The VAP holds that it makes no difference how the *after-tax* stream is divided into debt and equity streams.[29] This is explored in detail in Chap. 11.

As a closing point, note that the VAP only requires a degree of perfection of *capital markets*; the VAP will hold even with imperfect product markets (e.g., if the firm is a monopolist or if product markets involve transaction costs), with firm bankruptcy costs, with agency costs (see Chaps. 14 and 15), with an inability to sell tax losses, and with other tax imperfections. The VAP applies to the net returns to investors after all these costs have been netted out. The capital market requirement that must be met for the VAP to hold is simply costless capital markets (zero transaction costs; no government restrictions that create transaction costs or prevent transactions; transaction costless, infinite divisibility of financial assets); capital markets do not even have to be competitive in the sense that the firm's stream of returns has substitutes in the market. Even if the firm provides the only stream in the market with particular risk-return properties, the arbitraging mechanism described above will ensure that the firm's returns will be converted in the market into the form that investors prefer. The assumption of competitive capital markets was made above only to simplify the discussion (see Appendix 9B for details). The VAP holds with heterogeneous expectations as well as with homogeneous expectations as long as information about present and past events is costlessly available to investors in the market. A version of the VAP also holds with personal tax biases (e.g., in favor of capital gain income) as long as the income streams are properly defined. Heterogeneous expectations and tax biases are discussed in Appendix 9B.

[29] To see the distinction between dividing the *after-tax* stream and dividing the *pretax* stream into debt and equity streams, first note that it is the streams received by investors to which the value-additivity principle relates. It is these streams that are arbitraged in the market. Thus, assume two firms 1 and 2 with different debt-equity ratios and different *pretax* cash flows; but assume that the total payments to stockholders and bondholders *combined* are identical for the two firms (for all periods). That is, the distribution of the stockholder plus bondholder stream of firm 1 is identical to (same distribution and correlation of 1.0) the distribution of the stockholder plus bondholder stream of firm 2, both payment streams over time being net of firm taxes. The division between stockholders and bondholders of the total stream differs between the two firms. The value-additivity principle holds that the values of the two firms would be identical (even though the bond values would differ, as would the stock values in the opposite direction). The two firms would have the same values since the VAP states that the value of a total stream *received by investors* is independent of how it is divided into debt and equity streams.

**table 9-2**

| *Firm A* | *Firm B* | *Firm C* |
|---|---|---|
| $E[\tilde{Y}_A] = 120$ | $E[\tilde{Y}_B] = 55$ | $E[\tilde{Y}_C] = 57.50$ |
| $\text{var}[\tilde{Y}_A] = 36$ | $\text{var}[\tilde{Y}_B] = 16$ | $\text{var}[\tilde{Y}_C] = 25$ |
| $k_A = .20$ | $k_B = .10$ | $k_C = .15$ |
| $V_A = \dfrac{E[\tilde{Y}_A]}{1 + k_A} = 100$ | $V_B = \dfrac{E[\tilde{Y}_B]}{1 + k_B} = 50$ | $V_C = \dfrac{E[\tilde{Y}_C]}{1 + k_C} = 50$ |
| | $\text{cov}[\tilde{Y}_A, \tilde{Y}_B] = 20$ | $\text{cov}[\tilde{Y}_A, \tilde{Y}_C] = -30$ |

**An illustration of the VAP with mergers.** A simple example may help to clarify the meaning and significance of the value-additivity principle. For simplicity, assume that investors discount expected streams to determine value. Assume three all-equity firms *A*, *B*, and *C*, which will dissolve at time 1 after paying liquidating dividends at time 1 of $\tilde{Y}_A$, $\tilde{Y}_B$, and $\tilde{Y}_C$, respectively. Assume the data regarding firms *A*, *B*, and *C* shown in Table 9-2.

Values $V_A$, $V_B$, and $V_C$ are the values of firms *A*, *B*, and *C*, respectively, where $k_A$, $k_B$, and $k_C$ represent the discount rates applicable to the firm dividend streams. Firm *A* is considering a merger with either firm *B* or firm *C*. Firm *A* must issue its own stock in the merger and must determine which merger will be more beneficial. Define $\tilde{Y}_{A+B}$ and $\tilde{Y}_{A+C}$ as the time 1 dividend streams from a firm resulting from a merger of firm *A* and firm *B* and from a merger of firm *A* and firm *C*, respectively. Assume that the merger produces no real economies or diseconomies in production; i.e., the cash flow of the new firm created by the merger equals the sum of the cash flows of the two firms had they not merged. Therefore, $\tilde{Y}_{A+B} = \tilde{Y}_A + \tilde{Y}_B$ and $\tilde{Y}_{A+C} = \tilde{Y}_A + \tilde{Y}_C$. Assuming the merger of firm *A* with firm *B*, and firm *A* with firm *C*, the postmerger cash flows would have the following distributions:

Merger of firm *A* and firm *B*:

$$E[\tilde{Y}_{A+B}] = E[\tilde{Y}_A + \tilde{Y}_B] = E[\tilde{Y}_A] + E[\tilde{Y}_B] \qquad = 175$$
$$\text{var}[\tilde{Y}_{A+B}] = \text{var}[\tilde{Y}_A + \tilde{Y}_B]$$
$$= \text{var}[\tilde{Y}_A] + \text{var}[\tilde{Y}_B] + 2\,\text{cov}[\tilde{Y}_A, \tilde{Y}_B] = 92$$

Merger of firm *A* and firm *C*:

$$E[\tilde{Y}_{A+C}] = E[\tilde{Y}_A + \tilde{Y}_C] = E[\tilde{Y}_A] + E[\tilde{Y}_C] \qquad = 177.50$$
$$\text{var}[\tilde{Y}_{A+C}] = \text{var}[\tilde{Y}_A + \tilde{Y}_C]$$
$$= \text{var}[\tilde{Y}_A] + \text{var}[\tilde{Y}_C] + 2\,\text{cov}[\tilde{Y}_A, \tilde{Y}_C] = 1$$

The dividend stream resulting from a merger of firm *A* and firm *C* has a higher expected level and a lower variance than does the dividend stream resulting from a merger of firm *A* and firm *B*. One might expect that the value of the new firm ($A + B$) would be different from that of the new firm ($A + C$); the higher expected dividend and lower dividend variance of firm ($A + C$) than of firm ($A + B$) might suggest a higher value for firm ($A + C$) since the dividends are larger and less "risky." However, even though the two dividend streams differ, the value-additivity principle implies that firm $(A + B)$ has the same value as firm $(A + C)$. This is so since

$$\tilde{Y}_{A+B} = \tilde{Y}_A + \tilde{Y}_B$$

and, therefore, by the VAP,

$$V_{A+B} = V_A + V_B = 100 + 50 = 150$$

Also, $$\tilde{Y}_{A+C} = \tilde{Y}_A + \tilde{Y}_C$$

and, therefore, by the VAP,

$$V_{A+C} = V_A + V_C = 100 + 50 = 150$$

The stochastic relationship between $\tilde{Y}_A$ and the stream of the firm with which $A$ is merged is irrelevant. The value of the sum of a set of streams provided to investors equals the sum of the values of the individual streams: so by the VAP.

The issue of mergers in perfect markets is considered again in Chap. 16, where it is shown that even with real economies (synergy) or diseconomies in a merger, the VAP applies and stochastic relationships are irrelevant. The VAP is also used in Chaps. 11 and 12 in considering financing and investment policy in perfect markets.

## FIRM CASH FLOW

The purpose of this section is to provide precise definitions of terms that will be used throughout the remainder of the book. The reader is encouraged to review Chap. 1 before proceeding further, since that background discussion should help clarify the concepts presented here.

A basic assumption we have used in prior chapters and shall continue to use is that the value of any asset is determined by the cash receipts associated with the ownership of the asset. We assume that this is true regardless of the nature of the market in which the asset may be bought or sold, whether perfect or imperfect. The discussion in this section is devoted to an examination of the cash flows associated with ownership of the firm's securities and the relationships among the flows as affected by the financing and investment decisions of the firm. We are concerned with definitions and accounting relationships that apply in both perfect and imperfect capital markets and make no assumptions as to the valuation of cash streams other than the assumption that such streams determine value. The value of the firm is the current market value of all outstanding claims on the firm's present and future cash flow; the value of any given claim (security) is based on the stream of (uncertain) receipts associated with its ownership.

To simplify the discussion we shall consider the firm to have only two classes of securities outstanding: debt (bonds) and equity (stock). This is sufficient for our purposes, and expansion of the arguments to more than two classes is straightforward.[30] The value of the bonds is determined by investors' expectations about the future cash returns to the owners of the bonds. These returns are designated as interest (usually paid semiannually by the firm) and repayment of principal. Principal payments occur through retirement of debt, either at maturity or when the bonds are called, or through purchases by the firm in the market (treasury bonds). All such payments by the firm are cash outflows from the firm. Similarly, the value of the currently outstanding shares is determined by expectations about the cash payments (dividends and capital distributions through treasury stock purchases) to the owners of those shares. However, note that current shareholders and bondholders together own all outstanding claims against the future cash flow of the firm. Therefore, the current stockholders *own* the entire future cash flow of the firm less that which is owned by current bondholders. As shown below, this cash-flow stream may not equal the cash-payments stream paid to currently outstanding shares. Now how about the relationship between the two streams and the current value of the firm's shares? The next few chapters deal with this question; the concern here is with the nature of the two streams and why they differ, but first some definitions and relationships must be presented.

The following definitions will be used throughout the remainder of the book. Initially we shall assume that no taxes are levied on firm income. All variables below are defined for period $t$, which is equivalent to a flow occurring at time $t$ under our timing conventions (see Chap. 1).

$X_t$ = the cash income of the firm, which is equal to cash revenues from sale of goods and services less the current costs of producing them.

$I_t$ = the net cash outlay for investment made by the firm, which is equal to expenditures for new assets less receipts from sale of old assets. *Note that the cash balances held by the firm are part of firm assets and that an increase in the cash balance to be maintained for the coming period is considered an investment.* By this definition $I_t$ may be positive (net investment), zero, or negative (net disinvestment).[31]

[30] The basic division of claims worth examining is the division between the claims held by the owners of the firm and stockholders, and all other claims. This division is necessary because of the assumption that the objective of the firm is maximization of the current owners' wealth. Some of the various types of nonequity securities other than bonds are discussed in chap. 14.

[31] This definition of investment would seem to imply that using the proceeds from sale of an asset (or using cash by reducing firm average cash balances) to acquire some other assets does not constitute "investment" since *net* investment $I_t$ would be zero. This is not so. In this case there are two *investment decisions* involved that have resulted in a net investment outlay, $I_t$, of zero. One decision was a "negative" investment decision in which the firm received cash in exchange for a loss in future benefits from the assets sold; the other was a "positive" investment decision resulting in the acquisition of assets with associated future benefits in exchange for cash. The merits of both decisions must be evaluated. For ease of exposition in subsequent chapters we shall assume that all investment decisions are "positive," i.e., involve current cash outlays to achieve future benefits and therefore $I_t \geq 0$.

$Y_t^B$ = the net cash payments to bondholders of the firm, including the owners of the bonds issued at time $t$. This equals the cash payments on the old bonds outstanding before the issuance of new bonds at time $t$ less the inflow of cash from sale of new bonds (if any).

$Y_t^S$ = the net payments to the stockholders of the firm, including the owners of any new shares issued at time $t$. This equals the cash paid to the owners of the old shares outstanding before the issuance of any new shares at time $t$ less the inflow of cash from the sale of new shares.

$Y_t$ = the net cash flow of the firm, which is equal to the total cash payment to the security holders of the firm. That is,

$$Y_t \equiv Y_t^S + Y_t^B \tag{9-43}$$

Several comments regarding these definitions need to be made. First, the reader must take the usefulness of these definitions on faith for the present; their worth will be demonstrated in a few pages. Second, all variables defined above may take on positive, negative, or zero values; but the meaning of the algebraic sign differs for $X_t$ compared to the others. The cash income of the firm is a cash inflow (to the firm) when it carries a positive sign; the other variables are cash outflows (from the firm) when they are positive. It should also be clear that, except for firm taxes, the variables above account for all cash flows in and out of the firm in period $t$.[32] A summary of the cash flows included in the definition of each variable is provided in Table 9-3.

Variable $X_t$ is an inflow less outflow (revenue less expense). Variables $I_t$, $Y_t^B$, and $Y_t^S$ are outflows from the firm less inflows to the firm. Therefore, $I_t$ is asset purchases less asset sales, plus the net change in firm cash; $Y_t^B$ is interest and principal (and treasury bond purchases) less new bond sale proceeds; and $Y_t^S$ is dividends and treasury stock payments less new stock sale proceeds.

[32] Ignored here are miscellaneous transaction costs associated with purchase and sale of securities. These will be discussed in chap. 14.

**table 9-3**

| | | *Inflows and outflows associated with variable* | |
|---|---|---|---|
| *Cash-flow variable* | *Nature of transaction* | *Inflows to firm* | *Outflows from firm* |
| $X_t$ | Operations | Revenues | Expenses |
| $I_t$ | Asset transactions (investment) | Sale of assets | Purchase of assets |
| $Y_t^B$ | Bond transactions | Sale of bonds (new bonds) | Interest, principal repayments, and purchases of treasury bonds |
| $Y_t^S$ | Stock transactions | Sale of stock (new shares) | Dividends (including liquidating dividends and capital distributions) and stock purchases |

Since it must be true that cash inflows to the firm equal cash outflows (given our inclusion of changes in cash balances in $I_t$), the following will be true by our definitions of the variables:

$$X_t = I_t + Y_t^B + Y_t^S \tag{9-44}$$

and

$$X_t - I_t = Y_t^B + Y_t^S$$

Therefore,

$$\begin{aligned} Y_t &\equiv Y_t^B + Y_t^S \\ &= X_t - I_t \end{aligned} \tag{9-45}$$

From Eq. (9-44) the net cash flow paid to the security holders of the firm in any period $t$ depends on the cash generated from operations of the firm in that period less net investment undertaken. This flow in no way depends on financing except to the extent that past and current investment decisions depend on financing. However, the market *value* at any time $t$ of all subsequent cash flows may depend on the manner in which the firm is financed. This topic will be developed in Chaps. 11, 14, and 15.

To illustrate the preceding definitions, assume that in period $t$ the following occurs for the firm:

1. Cash revenues from product sales less current expenses equal \$200; therefore, $X_t = \$200$
2. The firm:
   (*a*) Purchases new machinery for \$300
   (*b*) Increases inventory by \$110
   (*c*) Increases its cash balances by \$50
   (*d*) Sells old machinery for \$100
   Net investment is therefore

   $$I_t = 300 + 110 + 50 - 100 = 360$$

3. The firm sells new bonds for \$300 and retires \$200 of old (outstanding just before time $t$) bonds; the firm also pays interest of \$10 on old bonds. Therefore, total net cash flow to all bondholders (outflows less inflows) equals

   $$Y_t^B = -300 + 200 + 10 = -90$$

   There is therefore a net inflow of \$90 to the firm from bond transactions.
4. The firm sells new shares for \$100 and pays \$30 in dividends on old shares (those existing just before time $t$). Therefore,

   $$Y_t^S = -100 + 30 = -70$$

   That is, the net cash flow (outflows less inflows) to stockholders in period $t$ is a negative \$70; equivalently, the net cash inflow to the firm from shareholders is \$70.

Assuming that all cash transactions are accounted for in **1** through **4**, it follows that

$$Y_t = X_t - I_t = 200 - 360 = -160$$

or

$$Y_t = Y_t^S + Y_t^B = -70 - 90 = -160$$

Thus, the equality $Y_t = X_t - I_t = Y_t^S + Y_t^B$ is satisfied.

Let us now return to an earlier topic; specifically, what it is that *current* stockholders own. Time 0 will be used as the point in time referred to as "current." It was pointed out at the beginning of this section that current stockholders own a claim on everything the firm will ever generate for current and future investors less that which is owed to *current* bondholders. A very important distinction should be made here between cash that will be paid by the firm on *current* (time 0) shares and bonds and the *total* cash paid by the firm at time $t$ to all *time t* shares and bonds. If new stocks or bonds are issued between time 0 and time $t$, $Y_t^S$ is the net cash flow to those new shares as well as to those shares that were outstanding at time 0 and are still outstanding at time $t$ (note that some of the time 0 shares may have been purchased by the firm, as treasury shares, between time 0 and time $t$). The value of the firm at time 0 equals the value of shares plus bonds outstanding at time 0. We shall refer to these stocks and bonds as the "current" or "old" shares and bonds. More precisely, the "current" shares and bonds are those outstanding at time 0 that were outstanding before time 0; therefore, any new shares or bonds issued at time 0 are not "current" shares or bonds at time 0.[33]

At time 0, the market value of the stock $S$ is the market value of the *ownership* or claim to all future cash flow of the firm less that owed to current bonds; $B$ is the market value of the cash flow to be received by the currently outstanding bonds. Firm value at time 0 is $V = S + B$. Notice that $S$ is defined as the value of *ownership* of *all* future cash flow of the firm not owned by $B$. This is not inconsistent with our statement in the last paragraph that not all the cash flow at some future time $t$ will go to current shares and bonds if new shares and bonds are issued after time 0; the new shares and bonds receive a part of the firm's cash flow after their issuance. What has happened is that current (time 0) stockholders have *sold* part of their claim on the firm's future cash flow when new bonds or stock are issued. That is, *the issuance of new stock or bonds by the firm at time t is effectively a sale by existing stockholders of part of their claim on the future (after time t) cash flow of the firm.* Thus, at time 0 the current stockholders own all firm cash flow less that claimed by current (time 0) bondhold-

[33] This definition of "old" or "current" stock and bonds is useful when considering financing-investment decisions at a point in time, e.g., at time 0. The objective is to maximize the wealth of shareholders in the firm at the time the decisions are made. If new shares are issued at time 0, it is in order to benefit holders at time 0 of shares other than the new shares, i.e., to benefit the "old" shareholders at time 0. This will become clearer in the discussion of chaps. 11 and 12.

ers. The current stockholders may at time 0 or at some future date "sell" part of that claim on firm cash flow through the firm's issuing new stock or bonds, but this does not alter the fact that, at time 0, current shareholders do own the entire cash-flow stream of the firm less the part owned by time 0 bondholders.

These arguments imply that $Y_t^S$ will not equal the period $t$ cash flow to time 0 shares if new shares are issued or if old shares are purchased by the firm between time 0 and time $t$; similarly, $Y_t^B$ will not be the cash flow to time 0 current bondholders in period $t$ if new bonds are issued or old bonds are retired between time 0 and time $t$. Using the definition that $Y_t^{Bo}$ is the cash payment at time $t$ to the time 0 *old* bonds (i.e., to bonds that were outstanding at time 0), it follows that $Y_t - Y_t^{Bo}$ is the cash flow at time $t$ owned at time 0 by current stockholders at time 0; this equals the entire cash flow of the firm $Y_t$ less that which is owned by current (time 0) bondholders, $Y_t^{Bo}$.

From the preceding discussion it follows that $(Y_t - Y_t^{Bo})$ does not necessarily equal $Y_t^S$, the net cash flow to shares outstanding at *time t*; this is so since $Y_t^S = (Y_t - Y_t^B)$ and $Y_t^B \neq Y_t^{Bo}$ if new bonds have been issued or old bonds retired between time 0 and time $t$. Moreover, $(Y_t - Y_t^{Bo})$ does not necessarily equal the cash paid at time $t$ to the shares that were outstanding at time 0. This is so since $(Y_t - Y_t^{Bo})$ is all cash flow at time $t$ not paid to the owners of the time 0 bonds and therefore equals the cash flow to all other security holders of the firm at time $t$, including the owners of the time 0 shares and the owners of all securities (bonds and stocks) outstanding at time $t$ that were issued between time 0 and time $t$.

A simple example may help to clarify these points. Assume that we are at time 7 and are reviewing the history of the firm from time 0. Assume that there are no taxes and that the following has happened:

1. There were bonds outstanding at time 0 that paid interest of $10/period to time 6 and were then retired at time 6; the par value of the bonds was $200, which was paid, in addition to interest of $10, to holders of the bonds upon retirement at time 6.
2. There were 100 shares of common stock outstanding at time 0.
3. At time 2, 25 new shares of common stock were sold for $300.
4. At time 4, new bonds were sold for $100 that pay interest of $4/period beginning at time 5 and continuing forever (perpetual bonds).
5. No transactions occur at time 7.

Define a new variable:

$Y_t^{So}$ = the cash paid in period $t$ to time 0 old shares. This equals the total cash payments to all stockholders at time $t$ less that paid on shares sold to investors by the firm between time 0 and time $t$.

Table 9-4 indicates the level of each of the major variables for periods 0 through 7. Several points are illustrated in the example of Table 9-4. First, the

**table 9-4**

| *Time* | $Y_t$ | $Y_t^{BO}$ | $Y_t^B$ | $Y_t^{SO}$ | $Y_t^S$ | $Y_t - Y_t^{BO}$ |
|---|---|---|---|---|---|---|
| 0 | $(X_0 - I_0)$ | 10 | 10 | $(X_0 - I_0 - 10)$ | $(X_0 - I_0 - 10)$ | $(X_0 - I_0 - 10)$ |
| 1 | $(X_1 - I_1)$ | 10 | 10 | $(X_1 - I_1 - 10)$ | $(X_1 - I_1 - 10)$ | $(X_1 - I_1 - 10)$ |
| 2 | $(X_2 - I_2)$ | 10 | 10 | $(X_2 - I_2 + 290)$ | $(X_2 - I_2 - 10)$ | $(X_2 - I_2 - 10)$ |
| 3 | $(X_3 - I_3)$ | 10 | 10 | $.8(X_3 - I_3 - 10)$ | $(X_3 - I_3 - 10)$ | $(X_3 - I_3 - 10)$ |
| 4 | $(X_4 - I_4)$ | 10 | −90 | $.8(X_4 - I_4 + 90)$ | $(X_4 - I_4 + 90)$ | $(X_4 - I_4 - 10)$ |
| 5 | $(X_5 - I_5)$ | 10 | 14 | $.8(X_5 - I_5 - 14)$ | $(X_5 - I_5 - 14)$ | $(X_5 - I_5 - 10)$ |
| 6 | $(X_6 - I_6)$ | 210 | 214 | $.8(X_6 - I_6 - 214)$ | $(X_6 - I_6 - 214)$ | $(X_6 - I_6 - 210)$ |
| 7 | $(X_7 - I_7)$ | 0 | 4 | $.8(X_7 - I_7 - 4)$ | $(X_7 - I_7 - 4)$ | $(X_7 - I_7)$ |

total cash flow to bondholders after time 0 includes that to the new bonds sold as well as to the old bonds. The cash flow to bondholders $Y_t^B$ reflects the sale of the new bonds at time 4 and thereafter. Indeed, since the old bonds are retired at time 6, no cash flow is associated with the old bonds after time 6. The sale of the new bonds at time 4 is a sale by stockholders of part of their claim to the cash flow of the firm after time 4. That is, the shareholders at time 4 promise a future interest stream of \$4/period to new bondholders in return for \$100 (sale price of new bonds). Second, notice that at time 2 the cash flow to *old* stockholders is $Y_t^{SO} = (X_2 - I_2 + 290)$ but to old and new stockholders combined it is $Y_t^S = (X_2 - I_2 - 10)$; the difference is the cash inflow to the firm of \$300 paid by the new stockholders. This \$300 is paid into the firm as a payment to old stockholders for selling 20% of their claim to the cash flow of the firm after time 2.[34] As a consequence of the stock sale, the old stockholders receive a dividend in period 4 of \$300 more than they would have received if there had been no sale of stock but if the same $X_4$ and $I_4$ had occurred.[35]

The example also illustrates which stream is relevant in determining the value of the stock at time 0. Two candidates are available: $\mathbf{Y}^{SO}$ and $(\mathbf{Y} - \mathbf{Y}^{BO})$.

[34] There were 100 shares originally; 25 new shares were sold at time 2; therefore, there are 125 shares outstanding after the sale. The old shareholders consequently own 80% of the stock after the sale, whereas they owned 100% before.

[35] The cash flow in a period $t$, $Y_t = (X_t - I_t)$, will be negative (see example on p. 211) if investment $I_t$ exceeds cash income $X_t$. In this case, $(Y_t - Y_t^{BO}) = (X_t - I_t - Y_t^{BO})$ will be negative so long as $Y_t^{BO} \geq 0$. It is pointed out in the text that $(\mathbf{Y} - \mathbf{Y}^{BO})$ is the stream *owned* by the time 0 "old" shareholders. The question arises as to what it means to "own" a stream $(\mathbf{Y} - \mathbf{Y}^{BO})$ if $(Y_t - Y_t^{BO})$ is negative for some $t$. It means that the stream not only provides a positive cash inflow in those periods for which $(Y_t - Y_t^{BO}) > 0$ but also requires the inflow into the firm of the amount $|(Y_t - Y_t^{BO})|$ from investors when $(Y_t - Y_t^{BO}) < 0$, that is, involves the obligation to contribute to the firm in order to sustain investment at level $I_t$ and pay out $Y_t^{BO}$ to time 0 old bondholders. Of course, this difference can be contributed by old stockholders (by selling themselves more shares); or, old stockholders can sell new shares or bonds to outsiders to make up the difference. Therefore, the ownership of $(\mathbf{Y} - \mathbf{Y}^{BO})$ by time 0 old stockholders is not only ownership of a positive cash flow (when $Y_t = (X_t - I_t) > Y_t^{BO}$) but can also entail ownership of an obligation to provide additional funds to the firm (if $Y_t < Y_t^{BO}$) in order to undertake investment $I_t$. Note that $Y_t$ may also be negative if the firm experiences cash losses $X_t < 0$ in period $t$. Similar considerations apply as above.

Stream $\mathbf{Y}^{SO}$ in column 5 of the table is the cash flow to the shares outstanding at time 0. This stream is affected by the bond transactions at times 4 and 6 and by the stock transaction at time 2 of the firm as well as by the revenues, expenses, and investments ($X$ and $I$) of the firm. Clearly, $\mathbf{Y}^{SO}$ is a valid measure of the returns to the old shares, and current share values will reflect future expectations regarding this stream. However, in examining firm investment policy, the use of $(\mathbf{Y} - \mathbf{Y}^{BO})$ as a measure of what is generated for current shareholders by firm assets may also be valid. Current owners of the firm have a claim to the entire future cash flow of the firm less that committed to current bonds; this stream is $(\mathbf{Y} - \mathbf{Y}^{BO})$. The shareholders in future periods may find it desirable (or necessary to undertake profitable investment) to "sell" part of their claim to $(\mathbf{Y} - \mathbf{Y}^{BO})$ by issuing new shares or new bonds. This, however, does not alter the fact that it is stream $(\mathbf{Y} - \mathbf{Y}^{BO})$ that is currently owned. If a portion of the stream is sold by issuing new securities, the price received will be the market value of the claim against $(\mathbf{Y} - \mathbf{Y}^{BO})$ that was issued; that value will depend upon $(\mathbf{Y} - \mathbf{Y}^{BO})$ and the characteristics of the claim (debt or equity).[36]

## The Effects of Firm Taxes

In order to determine the effects of taxes on the cash flows of the firm, some additional variables need to be defined.

$R_t$ = interest payments in period $t$ on the outstanding bonds in period $t$. We can divide $Y_t^B$ into two parts: interest payments $R_t$ and all other cash flows $K_t$; therefore, $K_t \equiv Y_t^B - R_t$. "Interest" is, for our purposes, merely the portion of $Y_t^B$ that may be deducted from firm income before computation of firm income taxes and is therefore based on the tax laws. Stream $K_t$ accounts for the net effect of all other bond transactions in period $t$.

$DP_t$ = the depreciation deduction permitted the firm in period $t$ for tax purposes. This variable is *not* a cash flow but an amount allowed under the tax laws as a tax-deductible "expense" to reflect declines in the productivity of physical assets owned by the firm.

$\text{Tax}_t$ = the taxes paid by the firm. It is assumed that taxes are a net outlay by the firm and equal

$$\text{Tax}_t = \tau(X_t - DP_t - R_t) \tag{9-46}$$

[36] Note that $\mathbf{Y}^{SO}$ reflects firm financing policy after time 0 (stock and bonds issued or retired after time 0) since it is the net payments to current (time 0) shares after netting out *all* cash inflows and outflows to the firm. $(\mathbf{Y} - \mathbf{Y}^{BO})$, on the other hand, does not reflect financing policy after time 0. In perfect capital markets and no taxes, financing policy is irrelevant and therefore a given $(\mathbf{Y} - \mathbf{Y}^{BO})$ implies a unique value of the firm's current shares. However, with firm taxes or with market imperfections, financing policy is also relevant and therefore it is more appropriate to use $\mathbf{Y}^{SO}$ rather than $(\mathbf{Y} - \mathbf{Y}^{BO})$ to value the firm's equity. It should also be added that with personal tax biases (e.g., favoring capital gain income relative to dividend income), we would have to break $\mathbf{Y}^{SO}$ into the portion paid out to retire stock (treasury stock purchases) and the portion paid out as dividends, since the two kinds of cash payments are taxed differently.

> The tax rate $\tau$ is assumed constant over time. Quantity $(X_t - DP_t - R_t)$ is the taxable income of the firm. By this definition taxes may be positive, negative, or zero depending on the value for taxable income. "Negative taxes" may be cash payments by the government to the firm that reflect refunds of past taxes paid or may result from sale of the firm's tax losses if no such refunds are available.[37]

The inclusion of firm taxes forces the following modifications of the relationships presented above. Since taxes are cash outflows, the inflow-outflow equation (9-44) becomes

$$X_t = I_t + Y_t^B + Y_t^S + \text{Tax}_t \tag{9-47}$$

Therefore,

$$Y_t \equiv Y_t^B + Y_t^S = X_t - I_t - \text{Tax}_t \tag{9-48}$$

Since $\text{Tax}_t$ depends on the interest payments on the firm's debt, the total cash flow of the firm $Y_t$ must also depend on the level of interest payments. Substituting the definition for $\text{Tax}_t$ [Eq. (9-46)] into (9-48),

$$\begin{aligned} Y_t &= X_t - I_t - \tau(X_t - DP_t - R_t) \\ &= (1 - \tau)X_t - I_t + \tau DP_t + \tau R_t \end{aligned} \tag{9-49}$$

An increase in the level of interest payments on the firm's debt results in an increase in the total cash flows of the firm $(\Delta Y_t = \tau \Delta R_t)$. Of course, the cash flow to stockholders $Y_t^S$ *alone* will fall with a rise in $R_t$, since

$$\begin{aligned} Y_t^S = Y_t - Y_t^B &= [(1 - \tau)X_t - I_t + \tau DP_t + \tau R_t] - (R_t + K_t) \\ &= (1 - \tau)X_t - I_t + \tau DP_t - K_t - (1 - \tau)R_t \end{aligned} \tag{9-50}$$

where $Y_t^B = (R_t + K_t)$ as defined earlier.

Term $K_t$ (the repayment of principal on debt less the inflow of new cash from sale of bonds) will be zero for a firm with a level amount of debt over time. Therefore, a greater average but level amount of debt will not affect $K_t$ but will raise interest expense $R_t$ and therefore lower $Y_t^S$. Thus, for a given firm investment policy (i.e., if $I_t$ and $X_t$ are unaffected), increased debt raises firm total after-tax cash flow $Y_t$, raises debt flow $Y_t^B$, and lowers stock cash flow $Y_t^S$. In estimating the future cash flow accruing to current shares, future financing policy must be specified regardless of whether $\mathbf{Y}^{SO}$ or $(\mathbf{Y} - \mathbf{Y}^{BO})$ is used. With taxes, both streams are affected by bond transactions.

The reader may have noticed that in this discussion of cash flow no tildes appeared above any of the variables to signify uncertain quantities. The tildes were omitted merely to simplify the notation, since it was the flow relationships that were of central interest. These results hold completely under certainty or

[37] If neither tax refunds nor sale of tax losses are available in the amount implied by eq. (9-46), the tax consequences of losses must be evaluated separately.

uncertainty. With uncertainty, the future flows are unknown and tildes are appropriate; all the definitions and relationships described above apply but are in terms of uncertain variables.

## SUMMARY

Three approaches to the problem of valuing multiperiod income streams were presented: (1) time-state preference, (2) certainty equivalents, and (3) risk-adjusted discounting. The time-state preference approach is the most general of the three, as it incorporates a wide variety of possible preferences for individuals. Risk-adjusted discounting was suggested to be the simplest method to apply in practice.

Under assumptions of costless financial markets, the value-additivity principle holds. This principle does not require any particular assumption about individual preferences or expectations and applies to the perfect-market case in general. In later chapters, this principle will be shown to simplify greatly the analysis of firm financial decisions in perfect markets.

In the last section, the cash-flow variables of the firm were defined and related to one another. The relationships developed here will be important in analyzing firm financing and investment decisions.

APPENDIX

# NINE A

# THE TIME-STATE PREFERENCE MODEL AND MARKET VALUATION

The basic framework of the time-state preference model was sketched in the body of Chap. 9. This appendix provides additional details of the model. We shall begin by defining certain terms and then identifying the assumptions that are made in the time-state analysis.

## DEFINITIONS

In this appendix, we shall use various terms and expressions. The expression "pays off in $(s,t)$" means "provides a payment at time $t$ if state $s$ occurs at time $t$." Thus, security $h$ pays off \$3 in $(s,t) = (4,10)$ if $h$ provides the security owner with a \$3 cash flow (from the issuer of the security) at time 10 if state 4 occurs at time 10. The following variables will be used:

$p_{st}$ = the *probability* that state $s$ will occur at time $t$.

$e(s,t)$ = an *elementary security* or *Arrow-Debreu security*, which is one which pays off one unit (one dollar) in one $(s,t)$, e.g., in (5,7), and zero in all other states in $t$ and zero in all states at all other points in time; thus, $e(1,1)$ is any elementary security that pays off 1 dollar in state 1 at time 1 and zero in all other states at time 1 and zero in all states for all $t \neq 1$.

$v_{st}$ = the price at time 0 (now) of a claim to a return (payoff) of \$1 if state $s$ occurs at time $t$ [the price of an $(s,t)$ "elementary security" $e(s,t)$].

$V[\ ]$ = the value at time 0 of the term in brackets, e.g., $V[\tilde{Y}]$ = the value of stream $\tilde{Y}$, where $\tilde{Y}$ may be a state-dependent income stream.

$Y^{i}_{st}$ = the payoff of security i in state $s$ at time $t$.

As elsewhere in this text, $i$ is the riskless rate of interest, $k$ is a risk-adjusted discount rate, and $B$ and $S$ are bond and stock values.

A security represents a claim to a payoff in one or more $s$ and $t$; such a security can be represented by a vector as follows:

$$\tilde{\mathbf{Y}}^{\mathrm{i}} = (Y_0; Y^{\mathrm{i}}_{11}, Y^{\mathrm{i}}_{21}, \ldots, Y^{\mathrm{i}}_{n(1)1}; Y^{\mathrm{i}}_{12}, Y^{\mathrm{i}}_{22}, \ldots, Y^{\mathrm{i}}_{n(2)2}; \ldots; Y^{\mathrm{i}}_{1T}, Y^{\mathrm{i}}_{2T}, \ldots, Y^{\mathrm{i}}_{n(T)T}) \quad \text{(9A-1)}$$

where it is assumed that the asset begins to pay off at time 0 (but the time 0 payment of $Y_0$ is certain) and continues to pay off to time $T$, and there are $n(t)$ states at time $t$. In the (9A-1) vector, we use a semicolon to separate points in time. Also, since the time 0 state is known with certainty and therefore $Y_0$ is known with certainty, there is only one Y entry for time 0. Thus, for example, $\tilde{\mathbf{Y}}^{\mathrm{i}} = (5; 3,1)$ signifies a security that will pay \$5 at time 0 (for certain) and, at time 1, will pay \$3 if state 1 occurs at time 1 and \$1 if state 2 occurs at time 1.

Note that to maximize clarity in this appendix we shall use notation here that differs from that used elsewhere in the book in the following respect: whereas in this appendix, $\tilde{\mathbf{Y}}^{\mathrm{i}}$ signifies stream i [Eq. (9A-1)] and $\tilde{\mathrm{Y}}^{\mathrm{i}}_t$ signifies the time $t$ set of stream i state-contingent payoffs [$\tilde{\mathrm{Y}}^{\mathrm{i}}_t = (Y_{1t}, \ldots, Y_{n(t),t})$], elsewhere in this book we use $\tilde{\mathbf{Y}}_i$ and $\tilde{\mathrm{Y}}_{it}$, respectively, to represent these same variables; $\tilde{\mathbf{Y}}_i$ and $\tilde{\mathrm{Y}}_{it}$ are defined on page 185. The reason for the difference in notation is that in this appendix we also have a state subscript, and therefore we have made the stream reference i a superscript here.

## ASSUMPTIONS

The time-state approach assumes that everyone agrees that at any time $t$, one and only one of $n(t)$ possible states will occur, where $n(t)$ can depend on $t$. Each individual assigns a subjective probability $p_{st}$ to each state in $t$; thus, for any $t$,

$$p_{1t} + p_{2t} + \ldots + p_{n(t)t} = 1 \quad \text{(9A-2)}$$

For each individual, Eq. (9A-2) must hold for each $t$ with homogeneous expectations or with heterogeneous expectations. However, whereas with homogeneous expectations everyone places the same numerical magnitude on each $p_{st}$, with heterogeneous expectations individuals may disagree on the $p_{st}$ magnitudes. That is, the state-preference model allows the assumption of homogeneous or heterogeneous expectations, with the differences in expectations embodied in the subjective probabilities of the different states. With homogeneous or heterogeneous expectations, however, all investors agree on the states that can obtain and agree on the dollar payoffs of each and every asset (or security) in each state; differences of opinion relate, at most, to the probabilities of the states.

At first blush, the assumption that all investors agree on the payoff of each security in every state might appear very restrictive. However, it is not restric-

**table 9A-1 Expectations of Investors $A$ and $B$ Concerning the Payoffs of Assets i and j**

| | State | |
|---|---|---|
| | *Boom* | *Recession* |
| *A's view* | | |
| Asset i | $2 | $1 |
| Asset j | $3 | $1 |
| Probability of state | 0.6 | 0.4 |
| *B's view* | | |
| Asset i | $4 | $2 |
| Asset j | $2 | $1 |
| Probability of state | 0.5 | 0.5 |

tive, since we can assume any number of states, a separate state for each set of payoffs over all individuals. For example, suppose there are only two individuals, $A$ and $B$, and two assets i and j. The assets pay off only at time 1, one period hence. Individual $A$ feels that in a boom i pays $2 and j pays $3 and that in a recession, i pays $1 and j pays $1. $B$ feels that in a boom i pays $4 and j pays $2 and that in a recession, i pays $2 and j pays $1. This is shown in Table 9A-1. To make this situation conform to the state-preference model assumption that all agree on the payoffs in each state, we define some additional states as shown in Table 9A-2. Instead of state Boom, we have Boom 1 and Boom 2; and instead of state Recession, we have states Recession 1 and Recession 2. By properly assigning a zero probability to the appropriate states for each investor, we now have a set of states, securities, and payoffs with disagreement only about the probabilities of the states. There is agreement about the definitions of the states and the payoffs for each state.

**table 9A-2 Restatement of Table 9A-1**

| | State | | | |
|---|---|---|---|---|
| | *Boom 1* | *Boom 2* | *Recession 1* | *Recession 2* |
| *A's view* | | | | |
| Asset i | $2 | $4 | $1 | $2 |
| Asset j | $3 | $2 | $1 | $1 |
| Probability of state | 0.6 | 0 | 0.4 | 0 |
| *B's view* | | | | |
| Asset i | $2 | $4 | $1 | $2 |
| Asset j | $3 | $2 | $1 | $1 |
| Probability of state | 0 | 0.5 | 0 | 0.5 |

It should be noted here that prices $v_{st}$ will, in general, for any given $t$, vary among the states $s$. Thus, investors might currently be willing to pay \$ .50 for a dollar payoff in state $a$ (say depression) in one year but only \$ .30 for a dollar payoff in state $b$ (say boom), i.e., $v_{a1} = \$ .50$ and $v_{b1} = \$ .30$; the reason might be that a dollar in a depression is worth more (generates more happiness) than a dollar in a boom (since income is more scarce in a depression). We shall discuss the determinants of the $v_{st}$ in greater detail later.

## MARKET PERFECTION AND MARKET COMPLETENESS

We begin by defining two distinct but related market concepts: perfection and completeness.

**A. Perfect markets.** Markets with zero transaction and information costs, zero costs of financial intermediation (e.g., no costs of performing arbitrage), no government constraints on transactions, infinite divisibility of financial assets, and competitive capital markets (no firm or individual significant enough to alter state prices).[38]

**B. Semiperfect markets.** These are markets that are perfect except that it is "prohibitively" costly for a financial intermediary or investor to disaggregate a payoff vector (security) into its parts. Thus, with $t = 0$, 1, and states 1 and 2 at time 1, if $\tilde{\mathbf{Y}}^i = (6;2,8)$ exists in the market, we can with perfect or semiperfect markets, *transaction* costlessly (i.e., with no brokerage fees, etc.) acquire or sell short, for example, one-half of $\tilde{\mathbf{Y}}^i$ (acquire $(\tilde{\mathbf{Y}}^i/2) = (3;1,4)$). But, whereas with *perfect* markets, arbitragers and investors can disaggregate (6;2,8) into say (6;0,0), (0;2,0), and (0;0,8), such disaggregation *cannot* be performed at acceptable cost in *semiperfect* markets. Of course, even in semiperfect markets *a firm* can disaggregate its payoff vectors; e.g., a firm with (6;2,8) could issue security I which pays 6 at time 0, and security II which pays 2 in $(s,t) = (1,1)$ and 8 in $(s,t) = (2,1)$. The point is, though, that only the firm, not investors or arbitragers in the market, can do the disaggregation in semiperfect markets. As we shall see, this means that if firms issue securities that do not represent a complete market, in a semiperfect market investors and arbitragers cannot make the market complete, whereas in perfect markets, investors and arbitragers can make the market complete.

[38] Divisibility here means that if security i has payoff vector $\tilde{\mathbf{Y}}^i$, then $\tilde{\mathbf{Y}}^i$ could be divided into parts $(\tilde{\mathbf{Y}}^i/\gamma)$, any $\gamma > 1$, where $(\tilde{\mathbf{Y}}^i/\gamma) = (Y_0^i/\gamma;\ Y_{11}^i/\gamma,\ Y_{21}^i/\gamma,\ \ldots,\ Y_{st}^i/\gamma\ \ldots\ Y_{n(T)T}^i/\gamma)$, where there are $T$ periods and $n(t)$ states in each period. For example, if $\tilde{\mathbf{Y}}^i = (10;8,4)$, we could divide $\tilde{\mathbf{Y}}^i$ into two vectors $(\tilde{\mathbf{Y}}^i/2)$, where $\tilde{\mathbf{Y}}^i/\gamma = (\tilde{\mathbf{Y}}^i/2) = (5;4,2)$. Note that divisibility does *not* mean that we can disaggregate $\tilde{\mathbf{Y}}^i = (10;8,4)$ into $\tilde{\mathbf{Y}}^{i1} = (10;0,0)$, $\tilde{\mathbf{Y}}^{i2} = (0;8,0)$, and $\tilde{\mathbf{Y}}^{i3} = (0;0,4)$; the division under the infinite-divisibility assumption means only that all payoffs in all states are divided by $\gamma$. As explained below, whereas divisibility exists with perfect and semiperfect markets, the disaggregation capability is limited to perfect markets.

**C. Complete markets.** Markets in which there exist as many linearly independent securities (i.e., securities with payoff vectors that are linearly independent) as there are time periods and states of the world.[39] Complete markets are discussed in detail below.

Before discussing the implications of the perfection and completeness of markets, we shall clarify the complete market concept. To do this we begin by defining linear independence:

*Linear independence.* Any vectors $\mathbf{Y}_1, \mathbf{Y}_2, \ldots, \mathbf{Y}_Q$ are linearly independent if it is *not* possible to find numbers $c_1, c_2, \ldots, c_Q$, where one or more of the $c$'s are nonzero, such that

$$c_1\mathbf{Y}_1 + c_2\mathbf{Y}_2 + \cdots + c_Q\mathbf{Y}_Q = \sum_{j=1}^{Q} c_j\mathbf{Y}_j = 0 \qquad \text{(9A-3)}$$

Equivalently, $\mathbf{Y}_1, \ldots, \mathbf{Y}_Q$ are linearly independent if there are no numbers $d_j$, $j = 1, \ldots, Q$, $j \neq i$, such that for any $i = 1, \ldots, Q$,

$$\mathbf{Y}_i = \sum_{j=i} d_j\mathbf{Y}_j \qquad \text{(9A-4)}$$

Thus, if there were two points in time, time 0 (now) and time 1, and two states at time 1, then markets would be complete if there were securities i, j, and k with payoff vectors $\tilde{\mathbf{Y}}^i = (4;1,0)$, $\tilde{\mathbf{Y}}^j = (1;2,0)$, and $\tilde{\mathbf{Y}}^k = (0;0,1)$. Markets would also be complete if $\tilde{\mathbf{Y}}^i = (4;0,0)$, $\tilde{\mathbf{Y}}^j = (0;6,0)$, and $\tilde{\mathbf{Y}}^k = (0;0,2)$. But markets would be incomplete if the only three securities were $\tilde{\mathbf{Y}}^i = (1;0,0)$, $\tilde{\mathbf{Y}}^j = (2;0,0)$, and $\tilde{\mathbf{Y}}^k = (0;4,4)$; markets are incomplete because $2\tilde{\mathbf{Y}}^i + (-1)\tilde{\mathbf{Y}}^j + 0\tilde{\mathbf{Y}}^k = 0$ ($c_i = 2$, $c_j = -1$, and $c_k = 0$ in (9A-3)).

If markets are complete, then there are as many linearly independent payoff vectors (securities) as there are points in time and states.[40] Thus, if there are points in time $0, 1, \ldots, T$, and $n(t)$ states at time $t$, then markets are complete for $0, 1, \ldots, T$ if there are $[n(0) + n(1) + \ldots + n(T)]$ linearly independent payoff vectors (with payoffs for times $0, \ldots, T$) in the market. In this case we would say that the securities "span" the time-state space over all states and all dates $t = 0, \ldots, T$. Mathematically, this is equivalent to $k$ linearly independent $k$-element vectors spanning a $k$-dimensional vector space. If $k$ linearly independent vectors span the $k$-dimensional space, then we can create any vector $(a_1, a_2, \ldots, a_k)$, where $a_1, \ldots, a_k$ are elements of the vector, by taking the proper linear combination of the $k$ vectors (i.e., by combining the proper proportions of each of the vectors).

[39] If there are times $0, 1, \ldots, T$, and $n(t)$ states in period $t$, $t = 0, 1, \ldots, T$, then there must be $\sum_{t=0}^{T} n(t)$ linearly independent security payoff vectors for complete markets.

[40] If there is a state in which there is no payoff in the economy at all (e.g., nuclear war), then we would say that the markets are complete for each of those states in which there is a positive payoff somewhere in the economy if, for those states, there are as many linearly independent payoff vectors as states and time periods.

A consequence of having complete perfect (*A* and *C*) or complete semiperfect (*B* and *C*) markets is therefore that any payoff vector can be obtained by taking a linear combination of the linearly independent payoff vectors (i.e., by taking the proper proportions of each vector). To illustrate, assume that there are two points in time, time 0 and time 1, with two states 1 and 2 at time 1. Assume that there exist three securities $\tilde{\mathbf{Y}}^i = (4;1,0)$, $\tilde{\mathbf{Y}}^j = (1;2,0)$, and $\tilde{\mathbf{Y}}^k = (0;0,1)$. Since $\tilde{\mathbf{Y}}^i$, $\tilde{\mathbf{Y}}^j$, and $\tilde{\mathbf{Y}}^k$ are linearly independent and span the time-state space, we can create any payoff vector we choose simply by creating linear combination $[a_i\,\tilde{\mathbf{Y}}^i + a_j\,\tilde{\mathbf{Y}}^j + a_k\,\tilde{\mathbf{Y}}^k]$ out of $\tilde{\mathbf{Y}}^i$, $\tilde{\mathbf{Y}}^j$, and $\tilde{\mathbf{Y}}^k$. Assume we want elementary security (1;0,0); then we set $a_i = \frac{2}{7}$ (buy two-sevenths of $\tilde{\mathbf{Y}}^i$), $a_j = -\frac{1}{7}$ (issue or sell short one-seventh of $\tilde{\mathbf{Y}}^j$), and $a_k = 0$ (do not transact in $\tilde{\mathbf{Y}}^k$).[41] This makes

$$(1;0,0) = (\tfrac{2}{7})\,(4;1,0) - (\tfrac{1}{7})\,(1;2,0) + 0(0;0,1)$$

With complete perfect or complete semiperfect markets (*A* or *B*, and *C* above), by assumption investors *can* acquire two-sevenths of $\tilde{\mathbf{Y}}^i$ and sell short one-seventh of $\tilde{\mathbf{Y}}^j$. Thus we have the following conclusion:

> In complete perfect or complete semiperfect capital markets, any security payoff, including any elementary security, is obtainable by investors as a linear combination of existing securities.

In complete perfect or in complete semiperfect markets, any payoff can be created by investors.[42] But note that for the markets to be complete, the issuers of securities (firms, government agencies, etc.) must provide the complete markets, i.e., must in the aggregate offer the set of linearly independent securities that span the time-state space. Furthermore, *in addition to* the completeness, markets must be perfect or semiperfect or all possible payoff vectors cannot be obtained. Thus *completeness alone is insufficient to allow investors to acquire any payoff vector*.

Now observe that if markets are perfect (*A* above), then even if the securities offered by the market by productive (nonintermediary) firms do not provide a complete market, any payoff vector is still obtainable by investors in the market because, unlike semiperfect markets (*B* above), in perfect markets investors or arbitragers can *without transaction costs* "break up" any payoff

[41] Selling short one-seventh of $\tilde{\mathbf{Y}}^j$ means borrowing one-seventh unit of $\tilde{\mathbf{Y}}^j$ and selling that one-seventh unit at time 0; at time 1, if state 1 obtains, the short seller must acquire (to cover the short position) one-seventh of $\tilde{\mathbf{Y}}^j$ for $\frac{2}{7}$ (the payoff of one-seventh of $\tilde{\mathbf{Y}}^j$ in state 1 is $\frac{2}{7}$, and is therefore what one-seventh of $\tilde{\mathbf{Y}}^j$ will be worth at time 1 if state 1 obtains at time 1); and, if state 2 obtains, the short seller will acquire one-seventh of $\tilde{\mathbf{Y}}^j$ for 0 (zero payoff by $\tilde{\mathbf{Y}}^j$ in state 2). On the other hand, issuing one-seventh of $\tilde{\mathbf{Y}}^j$ at time 0 means promising stream $(\frac{1}{7};\frac{2}{7},0) = (\frac{1}{7})\,\tilde{\mathbf{Y}}^j$ in return for which the promiser receives the time 0 market price of one-seventh of $\tilde{\mathbf{Y}}^j$.

[42] That is, any *proportions* of payoffs in all states and time periods can be achieved. The magnitudes of the payoffs that can be obtained by any investor will depend on the investor's wealth (budget constraint).

vector into parts. For example, (6;3,5) could be broken up (e.g., through arbitrage) into (6;0,0), (0;3,0), and (0;0,5). This means that even if firms issue a set of securities that do not span the time-state space, arbitragers or investors can disaggregate the existing securities and create a spanning set of linearly independent payoff vectors.[43] For example, if there are times 0 and 1, with two states at time 1, and if the only security types in the market are $\tilde{\mathbf{Y}}^{\mathrm{i}} = (1;3,5)$ and $\tilde{\mathbf{Y}}^{\mathrm{j}} = (2;4,8)$, arbitragers could transform $\tilde{\mathbf{Y}}^{\mathrm{i}}$ into (1;0,0), (0;3,0), and (0;0,5), which alone span the time-state space. The implication is that any market equilibrium conditions that hold with complete, semiperfect markets ($B$ and $C$) also hold with perfect markets ($A$), and this is so *whether or not* the perfect markets are complete.[44] One of these conditions, value additivity, is discussed in the next section.

## MARKET EQUILIBRIUM

With perfect markets ($A$ above), all securities can be combined (added together) or divided into parts and short selling and arbitrage are possible; this is so whether or not markets are complete. This implies that the market value of any security is equal to the sum of the values of its time-state components; that is, for any stream $\tilde{\mathbf{Y}}^{\mathrm{i}}$, the value-additivity principle holds, which means that with $n(t)$ states at time $t$

$$\begin{aligned} V[\tilde{\mathbf{Y}}^{\mathrm{i}}] &= V[Y_0^{\mathrm{i}}] + V[Y_{11}^{\mathrm{i}}] + V[Y_{21}^{\mathrm{i}}] + \cdots + V[Y_{n(1)1}^{\mathrm{i}}] + V[Y_{12}^{\mathrm{i}}] \\ &\qquad + V[Y_{22}^{\mathrm{i}}] + \cdots + V[Y_{n(2)2}^{\mathrm{i}}] + \cdots + V[Y_{n(T)T}^{\mathrm{i}}] \\ &= \sum_s \sum_t V[Y_{st}^{\mathrm{i}}] \\ &= \sum_s \sum_t v_{st} Y_{st}^{\mathrm{i}} \end{aligned} \tag{9A-5}$$

As noted earlier, $v_{st}$ is the time 0 price per dollar of payoff in state $s$ of period $t$. Relation (9A-5) states that the value of any security (payoff vector) is equal to the sum of the values of the elementary securities of which it is comprised. Thus, for example, the value of $\tilde{\mathbf{Y}}^{\mathrm{i}} = (Y_0^{\mathrm{i}}; Y_{11}^{\mathrm{i}}, Y_{21}^{\mathrm{i}}) = (6;3,1)$ is equal to six times the value of (1;0,0), plus three times the value of (0;1,0), plus the value of (0;0,1).

Interestingly, it can be shown that value additivity [relation (9A-5)] holds not only in perfect markets (whether or not complete) but also in complete,

[43] It is assumed that there is a payoff by some firms in every state (more than one firm if we are to assume competitive markets). If this is not so, then we cannot have complete markets or payoffs over *all* states, but only over all states for which there is a positive payoff in the economy. But for all states in which there are payoffs in the economy, with perfect markets, arbitrage will ensure that any payoff vector pattern is possible. See footnote 3, p. 222.

[44] If markets are perfect, they will become complete through the action of arbitragers or investors if investors demand streams that require the existence of complete markets.

semiperfect markets.[45] In complete or incomplete perfect markets and in complete semiperfect markets, no payoff vector can sell for more or for less than the sum of the market values of the elementary securities of which it is composed. The proof of the VAP on pages 230 to 234 applies with complete semiperfect markets or with perfect markets (whether complete or incomplete). Whether or not a state-preference model or a different notation (such as that used in the proof) is used, the existence of the VAP [relation (9A-5)] rests on the ability of investors or arbitragers to combine or divide streams (securities) so as to provide investors with the income streams (time-state claims) that they prefer. In complete markets investors or arbitragers need only combine, divide, and sell short securities; in incomplete markets, investors or arbitragers are also likely to have to disaggregate securities (which they can do in perfect markets) in order to provide the set of income streams most desired by investors.

To illustrate (9A-5), for $\tilde{\mathbf{Y}}^{i}$ in the one-period example above, using (9A-5),

$$V[\tilde{\mathbf{Y}}^{i}] = v_0 Y_0^i + v_{11} Y_{11}^i + v_{21} Y_{21}^i \tag{9A-6}$$

As we observed earlier, $v_{11}$ will differ from $v_{21}$ if a dollar of income in state 1 has a different value to investors than does a dollar of income in state 2. Value $v_{st}$ depends on the demand and supply of state-contingent consumption claims and will generally differ for different magnitudes of $s$ or $t$. Generally, the more money is valued in state $s$ relative to other states (e.g., the more impoverished is the state, such as the states of depression or plague) and the closer $t$ is to the present (the smaller $t$ is), the higher $v_{st}$ will be [the more investors will pay for a dollar of payoff in $(s,t)$]. Observe that since we assume that investors agree on the division of contingencies into states and on the state payoffs of each security, $v_{st}$ is an observable datum in a complete market that is perfect or semiperfect—it is the current price in the market for an asset (or the net price of

[45] To show that (9A-5) holds with complete semiperfect markets, note first that it must be that

$$V[\tilde{\mathbf{Y}}^{i}] \le \sum_{s,t} v_{st} Y_{st}^i \tag{$a$}$$

If ($a$) did not hold [i.e., if in ($a$), we had $>$ instead of $\le$] no one would purchase $\tilde{\mathbf{Y}}^{i}$ directly for $V[\tilde{Y}^{i}]$ since $\tilde{\mathbf{Y}}^{i}$ could be obtained more cheaply by acquiring, for each $s$ and $t$, $\tilde{\mathbf{Y}}_{st}^{i}$ elementary securities $e(s,t)$ [and we know in complete, semiperfect markets the $e(s,t)$ are obtainable]; thus at equilibrium we know that ($a$) must apply. But also observe that it must be that

$$V[\tilde{\mathbf{Y}}^{i}] \ge \sum_{s,t} v_{st} Y_{st}^i \tag{$b$}$$

If ($b$) did not hold [i.e., if in ($b$) we had $<$ instead of $\ge$], then investors could purchase $\tilde{\mathbf{Y}}^{i}$ and appropriate proportions of other securities to create elementary securities (since this can be done with complete semiperfect markets) with greater value; this will continue to occur as long as ($b$) fails to hold. But, since *both* ($a$) and ($b$) must hold at equilibrium, it must be that (9A-5) holds [the equalities in ($a$) and ($b$) must both be satisfied] at equilibrium.

a linear combination of securities) that will pay \$1 under particular circumstances (in a particular state) at time $t$.[46] We can use this fact to determine the risk-adjusted discount rates applicable to different streams.

First let us determine the riskless rate $i$. A riskless stream of \$1 at time 1 is a stream that pays exactly \$1 at time 1 regardless of which of the $n(1)$ states obtains at time 1. To acquire such a stream, we can buy $n(1)$ elementary securities, each of which pays \$1 in a different state at time 1. The price of each elementary security is, by definition, $v_{s1}$, $s = 1, \ldots, n(1)$. The price of the riskless time 1 stream is defined here as $V[Y_1 = \$1]$, where

$$V[Y_1 = \$1] = v_{11} + v_{21} + \cdots + v_{n(1)1} = \frac{1}{1 + i_1} \tag{9A-7}$$

or

$$(1 + i_1) = \frac{1}{\sum_{s=1}^{n(1)} v_{s1}} \tag{9A-8}$$

Similarly, letting $i_2$ equal the riskless rate *from time 1 to time 2,*

$$V[Y_2 = \$1] = v_{12} + v_{22} + \cdots + v_{n(2)2} = \frac{1}{(1 + i_1)(1 + i_2)} \tag{9A-9}$$

and

$$(1 + i_1)(1 + i_2) = \frac{1}{\sum_{s=1}^{n(2)} v_{s2}} \tag{9A-10}$$

In general,

$$\prod_{q=1}^{t} (1 + i_q) = \frac{1}{\sum_{s=1}^{n(t)} v_{st}} \tag{9A-11}$$

where $i_q$ is the current riskless rate for time $q - 1$ to time $q$ and

$$\prod_{q=1}^{t} (1 + i_q) = (1 + i_1)(1 + i_2) \ldots (1 + i_t).^{47}$$

[46] Value $v_{st}$ is observable in complete semiperfect or complete perfect markets either because elementary security $e(s,t)$ exists and has price $v_{st}$ or because a particular linear combination of certain existing payoff vectors (each with a market price) will produce $e(s,t)$ where that linear combination has a net price of $v_{st}$.

[47] We can also define a single riskless rate $i(t)$ applicable to the time $t$ expected payoff where

$$i(t) = \left[\prod_{q=1}^{t} (1 + i_q)\right]^{1/t} - 1$$

To show how to determine the risk-adjusted discount rate applicable to the income stream from a particular asset i, assume a single-period situation where asset i pays off at time 1 in states $a$ and $b$; there is no payoff at time 0. The single-period risk-adjusted discount rate for $\tilde{\mathbf{Y}}^{i}$ is $\mathbf{k_i(t)}$. Consider first the perspective of a single investor with particular probability beliefs; we shall consider "market" risk-adjusted rates in a moment. We can express $V[\tilde{\mathbf{Y}}^{i}]$ as the present value of the expected time 1 cash flow; thus, using Eq. (9A-5),

$$\begin{aligned} V[\tilde{\mathbf{Y}}^{i}] &= \frac{p_{a1}Y^{i}_{a1} + p_{b1}Y^{i}_{b1}}{1 + k_{i}(t)} \\ &= v_{a1}Y^{i}_{a1} + v_{b1}Y^{i}_{b1} \end{aligned} \tag{9A-12}$$

and, rearranging (9A-12), we have

$$1 + k_{i}(t) = \frac{p_{a1}Y^{i}_{a1} + p_{b1}Y^{i}_{b1}}{v_{a1}Y^{i}_{a1} + v_{b1}Y^{i}_{b1}} \tag{9A-13}$$

Observe that $k_i(t)$ in (9A-13) is defined in terms of investor i's probability beliefs, $p_{a1}$ and $p_{b1}$. If investors differ concerning thc probabilities (that is, they differ in their views about the expected cash flow from asset i), then there is no "market" discount rate since there is no single "expected cash flow" (this is true in general, whether or not we use the state-preference model). If we assume homogeneous expectations, however, $k_i(t)$ in (9A-13) is the same of all investors and is the "market" rate on an asset with a time-state payoff distribution such as that of asset i.

Observe that any asset j with payoffs in states $a$ and $b$ which are proportionate to asset i payoffs in $a$ and $b$ will have the same risk-adjusted discount rate $k_i(t)$ in (9A-13); that is, any asset j for which

$$\frac{Y^{j}_{a1}}{Y^{j}_{b1}} = \frac{Y^{i}_{a1}}{Y^{i}_{b1}} \tag{9A-14}$$

will have the same rate $k_i(t)$ [the reader can substitute into (9A-13) to see that this is so]. This means that a "risk class" is defined by the relative distribution of payoffs over states. Two streams in the same risk class differ at most by a scale factor.

In general, we know that for a stream $\tilde{\mathbf{Y}}^{i}$ paying off at times $t = 1, \ldots, T$,

$$\begin{aligned} V[\tilde{\mathbf{Y}}^{i}] &= \sum_{t=1}^{T} \frac{\sum_{s=1}^{n(t)} p_{st}Y^{i}_{st}}{(1 + k_{i}(t))^{t}} \\ &= \sum_{t=1}^{T} \sum_{s=1}^{n(t)} v_{st}Y^{i}_{st} \end{aligned} \tag{9A-15}$$

where $k_i(t)$ is the risk-adjusted discount rate for i's risk class for the expected payoff at time $t$. Using (9A-15), it follows that

$$(1 + k_i(t))^t = \frac{\sum_{s=1}^{n(t)} p_{st} Y^i_{st}}{\sum_{s=1}^{n(t)} v_{st} Y^i_{st}} \tag{9A-16}$$

As in the single-period case described above, the series of rates $k_i(t)$, $t = 1, \ldots, T$, are applicable to any stream with payoffs over states $s = 1, \ldots, n(t)$, $t = 1, \ldots, T$, which are proportional to those of stream i.

## THE USEFULNESS OF THE TIME-STATE PREFERENCE MODEL

The time-state preference (TSP) model is a very useful way of conceptualizing the array of possible outcomes (payoffs) in the future. Its major function in finance is to provide a framework for stating and analyzing the valuation of the consumption or dollar payoffs of securities, where the payoff at a particular time $t$ is dependent on the state that obtains at time $t$. The advantage of the model over, for example, the risk-adjusted discount rate (RADR) model is that it allows a very precise statement of the problem being analyzed. However, there is total consistency between the TSP approach and other valid approaches including the RADR approach. Indeed, as explained above, the TSP and RADR models have a close and definable relationship to one another. It must be emphasized, though, that the TSP model does not in and of itself contain or imply any significant theories of finance. The model is simply a way of describing the existence and valuation of state-contingent consumption claims; that is, it notes that future payoffs (consumption returns) depend on states of the world and have current prices in the market. Theoretical results are derived by using this time-state format to analyze the system under various assumptions about the degree of perfection and completeness of markets. Equivalent results are generally derivable (although often with less clarity of exposition) using the RADR model or other models as long as the same assumptions are made about the degrees of perfection and completeness of markets. It is the assumptions about these market conditions, and not the TSP model or any other model, that imply the important principles of finance.

Just as the interesting theoretical ideas of finance do not require the TSP model for their proofs or validity, any limitations on the usefulness or realism of the TSP valuation analysis are properly attributed not to the TSP model but, rather, to the assumptions made in the analysis. The assumptions of complete or perfect or semiperfect markets may not hold in actuality even as a good approximation.[48] In this case, the propositions derived under such assumptions

[48] The assumption of complete markets has its nonstate preference equivalent in the assumption that securities are obtainable in the market which provide any pattern of payments over time that can possibly be achieved given the production of goods and services possibilities of the economy; the TSP framework provides an extremely clear and precise way of expressing such an assumption.

are of limited importance. The appropriate next step in such a case is to make new assumptions that better describe reality. The TSP framework can be used under these more realistic assumptions.

A problem with the application of the TSP model is that in actuality an enormous (perhaps infinite) number of states exists at any future point in time. This means that a complete specification of conditions is not a practical alternative. However, this does not imply that the model is useless. States can be combined into several "aggregate states" such as boom, semiboom, normal, . . . , etc., with middle estimates used for each of the aggregate states. Of course, in actual business situations, it may be more feasible to use probability distributions and risk-adjusted discount rates, but this is to a major extent due to custom, not because the TSP approach is intrinsically less functional. Eventually, it may be that the TSP approach will become a common tool of financial analysis. In Chap. 10 we show a possible application.

## SUMMARY

The time-state preference (TSP) model conceptualizes income streams as time-state consumption (dollar) payoffs. An elementary or Arrow-Debreu security is one which pays off one dollar in one state in one time period. The model assumes that everyone agrees on the number of states in each period and on the payoff of each security in each state; investors may disagree on the probabilities of states. The model can be made very general, however, by simply defining a sufficient number of states, some with zero probability in the view of some investors. Thus any analysis that can be performed using the risk-adjusted discount rate (RADR) model can also be performed using the TSP model.

The TSP model can be applied under any assumptions concerning capital markets. However, certain assumptions have been used in the literature. These include perfect markets, semiperfect markets, and complete (and incomplete) markets. Perfect markets are transaction costless, competitive, and allow for complete disaggregation of securities by investors or arbitragers into elementary securities. Semiperfect markets are perfect except that disaggregation of securities into elementary securities cannot be achieved economically by investors or arbitragers. If markets are complete, there are as many linearly independent payoff vectors (securities) as there are points in time and states.

As long as markets are perfect, the operations of investors and arbitragers will ensure that markets are also complete if completeness is necessary in order to provide investors with the income streams they most prefer; this is so even if firms offer securities that initially only provide an incomplete market. The value-additivity principle holds with perfect markets (whether or not complete) and with complete semiperfect markets. The TSP model and the risk-adjusted discount-rate model are fully consistent with one another. Both riskless rates and risk-adjusted discount rates can be expressed in terms of time-state payoffs, their probabilities, and the market prices of claims to future payoffs.

APPENDIX
# NINE B
## THE VALUE-ADDITIVITY PRINCIPLE

It will be assumed initially that capital markets are transaction costless (no transaction costs or government constraints associated with transactions, and transaction costless, infinite divisibility of assets) and competitive (no firm or individual can alter the structure of discount rates in the market), there are no personal tax biases (e.g., capital gains are not favored), and expectations are homogeneous. These assumptions will be relaxed later. Note that all streams referred to below are cash-flow streams paid by the firm to its shareholders and bondholders; if there are any corporate taxes, these streams are therefore after-corporate-tax streams.[49]

Define $V_i$ as the market value of stream $\tilde{\mathbf{Y}}_i$, where $\tilde{\mathbf{Y}}_i$ may be a vector of returns over time.[50] The value-additivity principle (VAP) can be expressed algebraically as

[49] The analysis here is multiperiod in the sense that income can extend over any number of periods into the future and can vary over time. The results here apply with or without risky debt even in the presence of firm taxes. For clarity, there is a slight difference in the presentation of the proof and that in Schall's Asset Valuation, Firm Investment and Firm Diversification, *op. cit.* To replicate the proof here, simply use Schall's proof of Proposition I and define Schall's **X** as an after-corporate-tax stream received by investors, i.e., Proposition I applies to any **X** *received by investors in the market,* whether **X** is in a no-corporate-tax world or is the after-corporate-tax returns to investors in a world with corporate taxes. Note that we need not assume that tax losses are salable in the market and we need not assume zero bankruptcy costs (**X** is simply defined as net of any firm taxes, whatever they are, and net of bankruptcy costs).

[50] Thus stream i is designated $\tilde{\mathbf{Y}}_i$, where $\tilde{\mathbf{Y}}_i = (\tilde{Y}_{i1}, \tilde{Y}_{i2}, \ldots, \tilde{Y}_{i\infty})$, where $\tilde{Y}_{it}$ is the cash flow at time $t$. Investors obtaining stream i at time 0 therefore receive a claim to a cash flow commencing at time 1.

$$V_T = \sum_{i=1}^{n} V_i \qquad \text{at equilibrium if } \tilde{\mathbf{Y}}_T = \sum_{i=1}^{n} \tilde{\mathbf{Y}}_i \tag{9B-1}$$

The VAP states that the total value of a set of cash-flow streams received by investors is unaltered regardless of how that set of streams is combined or divided into the debt and equity streams of one or more firms.

With $\tilde{\mathbf{Y}}_T = \sum_{i=1}^{n} \tilde{\mathbf{Y}}_i$ under homogeneous expectations, not only do all investors believe that $\tilde{\mathbf{Y}}_T$ necessarily equals the sum of the $\tilde{\mathbf{Y}}_i$ but all investors agree on the distribution of each of the $\tilde{\mathbf{Y}}_i$ and therefore on the distribution of $\tilde{\mathbf{Y}}_T$. Homogeneous expectations are initially assumed and then this assumption is relaxed. Two types of arbitrage will be considered, either of which will ensure the VAP. The first is referred to as "pure arbitrage" and involves the transformation of streams by arbitragers who seek arbitraging profits rather than ownership of the streams being arbitraged. The second type of arbitrage is performed by the investor.

With either type of arbitrage the arbitrager may be a financial institution (e.g., mutual fund, insurance company, or bank) or an individual. In both cases it is assumed that the arbitrager who owns a part of stream $\tilde{\mathbf{Y}}_T$, say $\alpha\tilde{\mathbf{Y}}_T$, can issue debt or equity claims against $\alpha\tilde{\mathbf{Y}}_T$, promising a part or all of the set of streams $(\alpha\tilde{\mathbf{Y}}_1 \ldots \alpha\tilde{\mathbf{Y}}_n)$, where the latter set of streams is any arbitrary division of $\alpha\tilde{\mathbf{Y}}_T$ into smaller streams. In the case of pure arbitrage, the arbitrager buys $\alpha\tilde{\mathbf{Y}}_T$ and sells claims against all of the streams $(\alpha\tilde{\mathbf{Y}}_1 \ldots \alpha\tilde{\mathbf{Y}}_n)$, retaining no net ownership in the streams. In the case of investor arbitrage, the investor sells only part of the set of streams $(\alpha\tilde{\mathbf{Y}}_1 \ldots \alpha\tilde{\mathbf{Y}}_n)$, retaining some net ownership. This sale of part or all of the set $(\alpha\tilde{\mathbf{Y}}_1 \ldots \alpha\tilde{\mathbf{Y}}_n)$ by the investor will be referred to as "liquidation." The result of the liquidation is that investors can retain a net claim on any part of $\alpha\tilde{\mathbf{Y}}_T$ they desire and can thereby always duplicate the situation in which each $\tilde{\mathbf{Y}}_i$ is available separately instead of combined, as it might be, as $\tilde{\mathbf{Y}}_T$.

Pure arbitrage will be considered first. The VAP states that the market structure of asset prices at equilibrium must be such that an added unit of any stream $\tilde{\mathbf{Y}}_T$ has the same total value whether available as $\tilde{\mathbf{Y}}_T$ or as any set of separate equity and debt streams $(\tilde{\mathbf{Y}}_1 \ldots \tilde{\mathbf{Y}}_n)$, where $\tilde{\mathbf{Y}}_T = \sum_{i=1}^{n} \tilde{\mathbf{Y}}_i$. Arbitragers can always purchase or sell $\tilde{\mathbf{Y}}_T$ for $V_T$ and purchase or sell $(\tilde{\mathbf{Y}}_1 \ldots \tilde{\mathbf{Y}}_n)$ for $\sum_{i=1}^{n} V_i$.[51] The arbitraging profit is $\left|V_T - \sum_{i=1}^{n} V_i\right|$ from transforming $\tilde{\mathbf{Y}}_T$ to the set of individual streams $(\tilde{\mathbf{Y}}_1 \ldots \tilde{\mathbf{Y}}_n)$ if $V_T < \sum_{i=1}^{n} V_i$ and from transforming $(\tilde{\mathbf{Y}}_1 \ldots$

[51] The most that arbitragers will pay for $\tilde{\mathbf{Y}}_T$ or any set of streams $(\tilde{\mathbf{Y}}_1 \ldots \tilde{\mathbf{Y}}_n)$ generated from $\tilde{\mathbf{Y}}_T$ equals the total value of that set of streams which can be produced from $\tilde{\mathbf{Y}}_T$ that is most desired by investors. Notice that it has been assumed here for simplicity that the purchase and sale price of $\alpha\tilde{Y}_T$ is $\alpha V_T$ and $(\alpha\tilde{\mathbf{Y}}_1 \ldots \alpha\tilde{\mathbf{Y}}_n)$ is $\sum_{i=1}^{n} \alpha V_i$ for any $0 < \alpha \leq 1$, where $V$ for any stream $\tilde{\mathbf{Y}}$ is the market price per claim times the number of claims on $\tilde{\mathbf{Y}}$ (for example, price per share times the number of shares if $\tilde{\mathbf{Y}}$ is a firm's equity income). This assumption of an infinite demand elasticity for claims on the firm's income stream follows from the assumption of competitive capital markets made here for simplicity. As is explained at the end of this section, this assumption is not required for the VAP to hold.

$\tilde{\mathbf{Y}}_n$) to $\tilde{\mathbf{Y}}_T$ if $V_T > \sum_{i=1}^n V_i$.[52] The transformation of $\tilde{\mathbf{Y}}_T$ into ($\tilde{\mathbf{Y}}_1 \ldots \tilde{\mathbf{Y}}_n$) involves dividing the claim on stream $\tilde{\mathbf{Y}}_T$ into the set of $n$ separate claims, each promising the streams $\tilde{Y}_i$, $i = 1, \ldots, n$. Transforming individual streams ($\tilde{\mathbf{Y}}_1 \ldots \tilde{\mathbf{Y}}_n$) into $\tilde{\mathbf{Y}}_T$ merely requires combining the claims on the former into a single claim promising the stream $\tilde{\mathbf{Y}}_T$, $\tilde{\mathbf{Y}}_T = \sum_{i=1}^n \tilde{\mathbf{Y}}_i$. Competing arbitragers will pay the same for $\tilde{\mathbf{Y}}_T$ and the set of streams ($\tilde{\mathbf{Y}}_1 \ldots \tilde{\mathbf{Y}}_n$) since they are equivalent; i.e., either can be transformed into the other or into any other set of streams that can be generated from $\tilde{\mathbf{Y}}_T$. At equilibrium, arbitraging profits are zero and the value of $\tilde{\mathbf{Y}}_T$ and any set ($\tilde{\mathbf{Y}}_1 \ldots \tilde{\mathbf{Y}}_n$) generated from $\tilde{\mathbf{Y}}_T$ will have the same market value; i.e., the value-additivity principle holds.

The second type of arbitrage, investor arbitrage, is based upon the same principle: that streams can be transformed into the form most desired by investors. To see that equilibrium must involve $V_T = \sum_{i=1}^n V_i$, first note that equilibrium market rates cannot imply that $V_T > \sum_{i=1}^n V_i$ since this implies that investors demanding fractions of $\tilde{\mathbf{Y}}_T$ are not willing to pay as much for equal fractions of each stream of the set of stream ($\tilde{\mathbf{Y}}_1 \ldots \tilde{\mathbf{Y}}_n$) comprising $\tilde{\mathbf{Y}}_T$. That is, this implies investor $g$ will pay $\alpha_g V_T$ for $\alpha_g \tilde{\mathbf{Y}}_T$ but will not pay as much for $\sum_{i=1}^n \alpha_g \tilde{\mathbf{Y}}_i$. Market rates cannot imply this, since $\alpha_g \tilde{\mathbf{Y}}_T = \sum_{i=1}^n \alpha_g \tilde{\mathbf{Y}}_i$ for $\tilde{\mathbf{Y}}_T = \sum_{i=1}^n \tilde{\mathbf{Y}}_i$; that is, $\alpha_g \tilde{\mathbf{Y}}_T$ and the set ($\alpha_g \tilde{\mathbf{Y}}_1, \alpha_g \tilde{\mathbf{Y}}_2, \ldots, \alpha_g \tilde{\mathbf{Y}}_n$) are equivalent, and investor $g$ will pay as much for the latter as for the former. This must be true for all investors $g$ demanding a fraction of stream $\tilde{\mathbf{Y}}_T$ and it follows that if $\tilde{\mathbf{Y}}_T$ has equilibrium value $V_T$, the set of streams ($\tilde{\mathbf{Y}}_1 \ldots \tilde{\mathbf{Y}}_n$) must have a total equilibrium value no less than $V_T$. Therefore,

$$V_T \leq \sum_{i=1}^{n} V_i \tag{9B-2}$$

By definition, $V_j$ is the equilibrium price of individual stream $\tilde{\mathbf{Y}}_j$ and at such an equilibrium investor $k$ pays $\alpha_k V_j$ for $\alpha_k \tilde{\mathbf{Y}}_j$. Now observe that if $\tilde{\mathbf{Y}}_T$, $\tilde{\mathbf{Y}}_T = \sum_{i=1}^n \tilde{\mathbf{Y}}_i$, is available in the market, investor $k$ can obtain a net claim on stream $\alpha_k \tilde{\mathbf{Y}}_j$ from the set ($\tilde{\mathbf{Y}}_1 \ldots \tilde{\mathbf{Y}}_n$) comprising $\tilde{\mathbf{Y}}_T$ by purchasing $\alpha_k \tilde{\mathbf{Y}}_T$ and selling individual claims against each of the $\alpha_k \tilde{\mathbf{Y}}_i$ streams making up $\alpha_k \tilde{\mathbf{Y}}_T$, $i = 1 \ldots n$, $i \neq j$. The proceeds from the sale of the latter $\alpha_k \tilde{\mathbf{Y}}_i$ streams are $\sum_{i \neq j} \alpha_k V_i$. By buying $\alpha_k \tilde{\mathbf{Y}}_T$, investor $k$ can therefore always obtain $\alpha_k \tilde{\mathbf{Y}}_j$, for which he is willing to pay $\alpha_k V_j$, and also receive proceeds $\sum_{i \neq j} \alpha_k V_i$ from selling that $\alpha_k \tilde{\mathbf{Y}}_i$ streams. He is therefore willing to pay a price $\alpha_k V_T$ for $\alpha_k \tilde{\mathbf{Y}}_T$ that at least equals $(\alpha_k V_j + \sum_{i \neq j} \alpha_k V_i) = \alpha_k \sum_{i=1}^n V_i$. This is true for all investors $k$ demanding some of stream $\tilde{\mathbf{Y}}_j$ and it follows that if $\tilde{\mathbf{Y}}_j$ has equilibrium value $V_j$, equilibrium market rates must imply a market value $V_T$ of stream $\tilde{\mathbf{Y}}_T$ that is no less than $\sum_{i=1}^n V_i$. That is,

$$V_T \geq \sum_{i=1}^{n} V_i \tag{9B-3}$$

Combining (9B-2) and (9B-3) it follows that

[52] As noted in the text below, $V_T > \sum V_i$ will not occur, even without arbitrage.

$$V_T = \sum_{i=1}^{n} V_i \tag{9B-4}$$

which is the value-additivity principle.

In the above proof it was assumed for simplicity that capital markets were competitive, that is, that neither the firm nor investors could alter the market structure of interest rates in the market. However, this assumption is *not* necessary for the VAP (the VAP holds even if $\tilde{Y}_T$ is unique in the market). Since market arbitrage can transform an income stream into any form (any division of debt or equity streams) in which the firm can provide that stream, the ultimate form will be independent of how the stream is provided by the firm to investors in the market. All streams will ultimately take the form preferred by investors because any other equilibrium will imply potential arbitraging profits. That is, if an income stream $\tilde{Y}_T$ is not divided in a manner most preferred by investors, an arbitrager i can acquire proportion $\alpha_i$ of $\tilde{Y}_T$ (by buying proportion $\alpha_i$ of each $\tilde{Y}_j$, $j = 1, \ldots, k$, where $\tilde{Y}_T$ is currently divided into $\tilde{Y}_j$, $j = 1, \ldots, k$) and reselling $\alpha\tilde{Y}_T$ in the form investors prefer (i.e., are willing to pay the most for). The process will cease when no such arbitraging opportunities remain.

## HETEROGENEOUS EXPECTATIONS

The preceding derivation of the VAP also holds with heterogeneous expectations. The VAP states that $V_T = \sum_{i=1}^{n} V_i$ if $\tilde{Y}_T = \sum_{i=1}^{n} \tilde{Y}_i$. As with homogeneous expectations, *all* investors must still expect that $\tilde{Y}_T = \sum_{i=1}^{n} \tilde{Y}_i$. However, in contrast with the homogeneous expectations case, investors may differ with regard to the distributions of $\tilde{Y}_T$ and of the $\tilde{Y}_i$. Thus, if $\tilde{Y}'_T$ is the preinvestment cash flow of the firm, $\tilde{Y}_n$ is the cash flow from a new investment, and $\tilde{Y}_T = \tilde{Y}'_T + \tilde{Y}_n$, all investors still agree that $\tilde{Y}_T = \tilde{Y}'_T + \tilde{Y}_n$ but may disagree on the distribution of $\tilde{Y}'_T$, $\tilde{Y}_n$, and $\tilde{Y}_T$. This is a restricted case of heterogeneous expectations in that all investors do agree that $\tilde{Y}_T = \sum_{i=1}^{n} \tilde{Y}_i$.

A second difference between the homogeneous and heterogeneous expectations cases is that in the latter it is necessary to add the assumption that investors know the ex-post values of each $\tilde{Y}_i$ of the set $(\tilde{Y}_1 \ldots \tilde{Y}_n)$ even if the $\tilde{Y}_i$ are combined into the single stream $\tilde{Y}_T$. This condition will be met if information is costlessly available to investors in the market. This allows the arbitrager (professional arbitrager or investor) to promise stream $\tilde{Y}_i$ as a claim against $\tilde{Y}_T$ even though investors have varying expectations regarding $\tilde{Y}_i$; the arbitrager merely pays the amount that investors would have earned if $\tilde{Y}_i$ were an individual stream in the market.[53] For example, if a firm has two divisions with cash flows

[53] The assumption that information is costless and available to all investors implies that the realized values of the $\tilde{Y}_i$ are revealed by firm $T$. This may not be too restrictive an assumption since this information is used by arbitragers to divide $\tilde{Y}_T$ into the form that is most desired by investors, i.e., the form that maximizes firm value assuming perfectly competitive markets. Management might therefore desire to provide such information to investors in the company.

paid to investors of $\tilde{Y}_1$ and $\tilde{Y}_2$ but provides the market with stream $\tilde{Y}_T = \tilde{Y}_1 + \tilde{Y}_2$, the arbitrager can promise to pay investors $\tilde{Y}_1$ and $\tilde{Y}_2$ individually, thereby duplicating the situation in which the two divisions are separate firms. With heterogeneous expectations, the arbitrager can do this only if he knows (ex-post) the realized outcomes of $\tilde{Y}_1$ and $\tilde{Y}_2$. With homogeneous expectations, however, it is easily shown that some predetermined method of division of $\tilde{Y}_T$ for any outcome of $\tilde{Y}_T$ will provide investors with income of the distributions of the $Y_i$ for $\tilde{Y}_T = \sum_{i=1}^{n} \tilde{Y}_i$. In this case, only the realized value of $\tilde{Y}_T$ and not the realized values of the $\tilde{Y}_i$ need be known. This is so because all investors agree exactly on the distribution of all the $\tilde{Y}_i$ and of $\tilde{Y}_T$ and will therefore agree on the method of division of $\tilde{Y}_T$ into the set of streams $(\tilde{Y}_1 \ldots \tilde{Y}_n)$. No such predetermined division of $\tilde{Y}_T$ is likely to provide streams with distributions of the $\tilde{Y}_i$ under heterogeneous expectations, since the distributions of the $\tilde{Y}_i$ differ among investors.[54]

## THE DEFINITION OF $\tilde{Y}$: CASH PAYMENTS VS. CAPITAL GAINS

In the discussion of the VAP in the text, $\tilde{Y}$ was defined as a cash payment *by the firm* to security holders. The VAP holds for cash payments $\tilde{Y}$ as long as all *cash* payments are subject to the same personal tax treatment (i.e., there is no difference in the taxability at the personal level of dividends, interest, principal payments, treasury stock purchases, etc.). Stream $\tilde{Y}_j$, $j = i, T$, in the statement of the VAP in (9B-1) includes all *cash* payments from the firm associated with stream j over the life of the stream. It does not include capital gains. It is not correct to include capital gains in the $\tilde{Y}_j$ because a capital gain is a change from one period to the next in the *value* of the cash flow $\tilde{Y}$ that is being valued. To include capital gains in $\tilde{Y}$ would be confusing the thing being valued (the cash flow) with changes in the value of the thing being valued.

What if a firm invests in a project that provides an $n$ period after tax cash flow $\widetilde{CF} = (\widetilde{CF}_1, \widetilde{CF}_2, \ldots, \widetilde{CF}_n)$, which could be reinvested in other projects, thus producing a capital gain, or could be paid out as a dividend? If capital markets were perfect, including the condition that the effective tax rate on capital gains is the same as that on all cash payments by the firm (e.g., if gains were taxed as they accrue and at the same tax rate as dividends, interest, etc.), then dividend policy would be irrelevant and the value of the cash flow from the investment would be the same whether paid out or retained to produce a capital

[54] With homogeneous expectations, there is some unique distribution of $\tilde{Y}_T$ and of the $\tilde{Y}_i$ generated from any given division of $\tilde{Y}_T$. There is, therefore, a set of $n$ conditional distributions (for each possible $\tilde{Y}_T$), one for each $\tilde{Y}_i, i = 1 \ldots n$. Thus, for any $\tilde{Y}_T$ there is a distribution of possible *divisions* of $\tilde{Y}_T$ into the $\tilde{Y}_i$ conforming to these conditional distributions. This distribution of divisions of $\tilde{Y}_T$ can be simulated to divide that $\tilde{Y}_T$ into the $\tilde{Y}_i$. With heterogeneous expectations, however, this predetermined division technique for each $\tilde{Y}_T$ cannot, in general, be applied; the ex-post values of the $\tilde{Y}_i$ must be known in order to disaggregate $\tilde{Y}_T$.

gain. That is, the cash flows from firm projects can be valued in perfect markets (with no tax biases) using the VAP even if the cash flow is retained and reinvested in other projects. This is so because under such assumptions the incremental value to the firm of $\widetilde{\mathbf{CF}}$ is the same whether the cash flow is paid out or is not paid out (is reinvested).

## A COMMENT ON PERSONAL TAXES

The above proof of the VAP referred to the valuation of cash flows paid by the firm to investors in the market. It was assumed that personal taxes were neutral, i.e., that they do not discriminate in favor of one kind of personal income over another. The critical part of the assumption was that personal taxes do not discriminate in favor of any kind of cash payment by the firm (note that $\tilde{Y}$ is defined as a cash payment). Thus, purchasing $\tilde{\mathbf{Y}}_i$ or $\tilde{\mathbf{Y}}_j$, $\tilde{\mathbf{Y}}_i = \tilde{\mathbf{Y}}_j$, implied the same personal taxes regardless of how $\tilde{\mathbf{Y}}_i$ and $\tilde{\mathbf{Y}}_j$ differed in terms of financing type (debt or equity streams) or nature of payment (debt interest, debt principal, dividend, or treasury stock purchase payment). Now let us see how the VAP applies if cash flows can differ in terms of their personal taxability. Assume personal taxability categories $k = 1, \ldots, q$, e.g., debt interest, dividends, and debt principal repayments. Assume that each stream paid by the firm is in one of personal tax categories $k = 1, \ldots, q$, and that the category is independent of who receives the stream. Thus, if the firm pays a dividend, it is taxed by the IRS as a dividend regardless of who receives the dividend (although the tax rate on the dividend can depend on who receives it). Define $\tilde{\mathbf{Y}}_i^k$ as stream i which is in personal tax category $k$. The VAP (using a proof identical to the one presented earlier for the no personal tax bias case) holds that

$$V_T = \sum_{i=1}^{n} V_i \qquad \text{if} \qquad \tilde{\mathbf{Y}}_T^k = \sum_{i=1}^{n} \tilde{\mathbf{Y}}_i^k \tag{9B-5}$$

where $V_j$ is the market value of $\tilde{\mathbf{Y}}_T^k$, and $V_i$ is the market value of $\tilde{\mathbf{Y}}_i^k$; $\tilde{\mathbf{Y}}_i^k$, $i = 1, \ldots, n$, are streams of one or more firms, and each $\tilde{\mathbf{Y}}_j^k$, $j = T$, i, $i = 1, \ldots, n$, is in personal tax category $k$.[55] For example, tax category $k$ might be dividends and $\tilde{\mathbf{Y}}_1^k$ the dividend stream from the Class A stock of firm 1, $\tilde{\mathbf{Y}}_2^k$ the dividend stream from the Class B stock of firm 1, $\tilde{\mathbf{Y}}_3^k$ the dividend stream of firm 2, etc. The VAP states that combining or dividing those dividend streams into any other set of dividend streams does not affect total value. The reason is that arbitragers will always convert any stream paid out

[55] It is assumed here that an arbitrager *cannot* change the personal tax category of a stream, e.g., transform a debt interest stream into a dividend stream. If such conversion could take place, then the VAP as originally stated (without the $k$ superscript) would hold; i.e., (9B-1) rather than (9B-5) would hold. Also, streams $\tilde{\mathbf{Y}}_i$ and $\tilde{\mathbf{Y}}_j$ are in the same tax category $k$ only if the cash payments $\tilde{\mathbf{Y}}_i$ and $\tilde{\mathbf{Y}}_j$ are taxed in the same way when received by the investor *and* if changes in the values of those streams (capital gains and losses) are taxed in the same way.

by the firm into the form preferred by investors, regardless of how the stream has been combined or divided by the firms (although we do assume that arbitragers cannot change the personal tax category of streams).

The implication of personal taxes is that it becomes relevant how firms offer income streams to the market; i.e., it is relevant what personal tax class firm returns assume. Thus, the economic equilibrium will differ for different levels of total (for the economy) debt relative to equity that is issued by firms, since the total personal taxes paid by investors will differ. Before, with no personal tax bias, the level of firm debt payments relative to equity payments *in the economy* was irrelevant since, first, debt payments and equity payments were taxed at the same tax rate and, second, the arbitraging mechanism could restructure the income streams offered by firms into any other form that could have been provided by the firms; the form in which firms offered income streams was irrelevant. It is different for personal tax biases. The total value of a set of streams in a *given* personal tax class is independent of how the streams are combined or divided into individual streams [by (9B-5)]. The value of type $k$ streams will depend on the economy's supply of income streams in each tax class.

An important point must be made here. When we say that value will depend on personal tax class, we mean for the economy as a whole; i.e., the aggregate value of income streams in the economy will depend on how the firms' returns are allocated among streams of different personal tax classes. Thus, if the personal tax rates on stock and bond incomes were different, and if firms in the economy only issued stock, even with no corporate taxes the total value of all securities would be different than if firms issued some debt too (since the personal taxes collected by the government would be different).

The question arises as to how the VAP applies if personal tax biases exist (and therefore valuation depends on the economy's relative supply of debt and equity streams) but at equilibrium an *individual firm's* financial structure (debt-equity ratio) and dividend policy (proportion of earnings paid out as dividends) are irrelevant. This situation, which is discussed in Chap. 15, can exist with a sufficiently wide diversity among investors of personal tax rates on debt and equity income. Thus, for example, the corporate tax bias in favor of debt financing may be compensated for by a *personal* tax bias in favor of equity income (a lower effective tax rate if equity returns are reinvested so as to produce larger dividends in the future and capital gains on the stock in the interim). High-tax-bracket investors will be attracted to low-dividend-paying stocks and low-tax-bracket investors will be attracted to high-dividend-paying stocks and to bonds.[56] A different financial structure or dividend policy may

[56] When we refer to a high- or a low-tax-bracket taxpayer, we mean a taxpayer subject to a high or low marginal tax rate on the type of investment income being discussed. Thus an individual earning $250,000 per year may be a low-tax-bracket investor with regard to bond income if the individual has put the bonds in a tax-sheltered trust, for example, if the bonds are in a pension trust under a Keogh Plan (bond interest would not be taxed when received by the trust but when withdrawn from the trust upon the taxpayer's retirement).

mean no difference in firm value, but simply a different clientele buying the firm's securities. The value of *precorporate tax* returns from firm assets may consequently be the same regardless of financial structure or dividend policy. *If* we assume that conditions are such that the dividend and financial structure policies are irrelevant, then the VAP can be applied as follows:[57]

$$V_T = \sum_{i=1}^{n} V_i \quad \text{if} \quad \tilde{\mathbf{E}}_T = \sum_{i=1}^{n} \tilde{\mathbf{E}}_i \tag{9B-6}$$

where

$$\tilde{\mathbf{E}} = \tilde{\mathbf{X}} - \tilde{\mathbf{I}} - \tau(\tilde{\mathbf{X}} - \widetilde{\mathbf{DP}})$$

where $\tilde{\mathbf{X}}$ is cash revenues minus cash expenses, $\tilde{\mathbf{I}}$ is capital outlays, $\tau$ is the corporate tax rate, and $\widetilde{\mathbf{DP}}$ is depreciation. Term $\tilde{\mathbf{E}}$ in relation (9B-6) is that part of firm returns that is independent of the proportion of financing that is debt or equity; (9B-6) states that the financing-dividend decision is irrelevant since the value of $\tilde{\mathbf{E}}_T$ equals the sum of the individual values that the $\tilde{\mathbf{E}}_i$ would have (regardless of whether the $\tilde{\mathbf{E}}_i$ are in the form of debt or equity streams). Of course, $\tilde{\mathbf{E}}_i$ is *not* the stream received by investors in the market since, in computing $\tilde{\mathbf{E}}$, interest on any debt has not been deducted in computing corporate taxes. Relation (9B-6) holds by applying the VAP arbitraging mechanism (which means that combining or dividing streams into parts does not alter total value, since arbitraging can reconstitute the streams into the form preferred by investors).[58]

## SUGGESTED READINGS

Arrow, Kenneth J.: The Role of Securities in the Optimal Allocation of Risk Bearing, *Review of Economic Studies,* vol. 31, April 1974.

Borch, Karl: "The Economics of Uncertainty," Chap. 8, Princeton University Press, Princeton, N.J., 1968.

Debreu, Gerard: "Theory of Value," Chap. 7, John Wiley & Sons, Inc., New York, 1959.

Diamond, Peter: The Role of a Stock Market in a General Equilibrium Model with Technological Uncertainty, *American Economic Review,* vol. 57, pp. 759–786, September 1967.

[57] For financial structure and dividend policies to be irrelevant, in addition to a costless capital market and adequate array of tax rates, we must assume zero bankruptcy costs and the salability of tax losses. It must also be assumed that there are many existing substitutes in the market for each of those debt and equity streams [i.e., that $(\tilde{\mathbf{X}}_T - \tilde{\mathbf{I}}_T)$ is an insignificant part of the economy and of its risk class]. The reason for the last assumption is that $(\tilde{\mathbf{X}}_T - \tilde{\mathbf{I}}_T)$ must be sufficiently insignificant that any change in the proportion of $(\tilde{\mathbf{X}}_T - \tilde{\mathbf{I}}_T)$ that is debt or equity can be compensated for by an offsetting change by other firms in the market so as to reestablish the equilibrium quantities of debt and equity streams in the market.

[58] For a more detailed discussion of the VAP and the financial policy irrelevancy condition with personal taxes, see L. D. Schall, Valuation and Firm Financial Policies With Personal Tax Biases, *Journal of Business Research,* 1980.

Fama, Eugene F.: Multiperiod Consumption-Investment Decisions, *American Economic Review*, vol. 60, pp. 163–174, (March 1970).

———: Risk Adjusted Discount Rates and Capital Budgeting under Uncertainty, *Journal of Financial Economics*, vol. 5, pp. 3–24, August 1977.

Hirshleifer, Jack: Investment Decisions under Uncertainty: Choice-Theoretic Approaches, *Quarterly Journal of Economics*, vol. 79, pp. 509–536, November 1965, reprinted in Archer, Stephen H. and Charles A. D'Ambrosio, "The Theory of Business Finance," 2d ed., The Macmillan Company, New York, 1976.

———: Investment Decision under Uncertainty: Applications of the State-Preference Approach, *Quarterly Journal of Economics*, vol. 80, pp. 252–277, May 1966.

Myers, Stewart C.: A Time-State Preference Model of Security Valuation, *Journal of Financial and Quantitative Analysis*, vol. 3, pp. 1–34, March 1968.

———: Procedures for Capital Budgeting under Uncertainty, *Industrial Management Review*, vol. 9, pp. 1–15, Spring 1968.

Robichek, Alexander A. and Stewart C. Myers, Valuation of the Firm: Effects of Uncertainty in a Market Context, *Journal of Finance*, vol. 21, pp. 215–227, May 1966.

Schall, Lawrence D., Asset Valuation, Firm Investment, and Firm Diversification, *Journal of Business*, vol. 45, no. 1, pp. 11–28, January 1972.

CHAPTER

# TEN

# THE VALUATION OF OPTIONS IN CONTINUOUS TIME

This chapter was written for two purposes—to provide an introduction to continuous-time models under uncertainty and to present the option-pricing model developed by Black and Scholes. The importance of continuous-time models is their ability to produce well-specified valuation equations in a multiperiod framework. As we noted in Chap. 9, there is a general lack of such results; the continuous-time models are the exceptions. The option-pricing model is the premier example of a multiperiod valuation equation and, moreover, is one that seems to work well when applied to actual securities. It is also being used as a theoretical foundation for examining corporate financial decisions, as we discuss at the end of this chapter.

First we look at the concept of continuous time and the assumptions made in typical continuous-time models. Then we briefly describe the various types of options found in the capital market. In the third section we use the concepts of the first two sections to present the Black-Scholes model of option values and show how the model can be applied. Finally we discuss applications and extensions of the option-pricing model to corporate financial decisions. Appendix 10A provides some mathematical background and a formal development of the Black-Scholes model.

## VALUATION IN CONTINUOUS TIME

Until the early 1970s the methods used to analyze financial decisions under uncertainty fell into one of two general types—discrete-time analysis, used predominately in this book, and continuous-time analysis involving simple extensions of the certainty model of Appendix 2B. Led by Robert Merton, a new approach using continuous-time analysis has now become highly important in the theoretical literature and has provided at least one result of much practical interest, the option-pricing model presented later in the chapter. The traditional continuous-time approach simply assumed the existence of a risk-adjusted discount rate applicable to a given expected continuous stream of cash flows. Thus the value of any asset in traditional continuous-time models is determined as the present value of the cash flows discounted at the appropriate rate. The problem with this approach is that it provides no information on the determinants of the discount rate; that is, the underlying market processes that are presumed to result in a discount rate applicable to a given stream are not well specified and there is no way to tell what the appropriate discount rate should be. For many theoretical problems the traditional approach is convenient and serves as a useful simplification. But in practical and empirical problems it leaves the most difficult issue, the determination of the proper discount rate to use, purely to the judgment of the decision maker in the situation. The new approach focuses directly on the issue of risk measurement and derives valuation relationships from the stochastic properties of cash flows and assumptions regarding the structure of the capital markets and the individual's consumption-investment problem.[1] We hope this new approach will result in valuation models whose parameters can be more easily estimated from actual data.

In this section we discuss the basic assumptions used in continuous-time analysis and contrast them with the discrete-time approach. Our emphasis here is on the conceptual issues. The formal development of continuous-time models requires an understanding of the mathematical techniques of stochastic calculus. A brief introduction to stochastic calculus is provided in Appendix 10A; however, this is not necessary for the material presented here. We examine one of the simplest continuous-time models. More complex problems have been analyzed in the literature, but the essential differences between the continuous-time and discrete-time approaches show up even in this simplified case.

## Individual Financial Decisions

Assume here, as was done in Chap. 7, that the only sources of uncertainty facing an individual are the rates of return earned on any risky assets owned. The basic problems for the individual are to determine: (1) the amount of wealth to be devoted to present consumption (the consumption problem), and (2) the assets to be acquired with that portion of wealth which is not consumed (the investment or portfolio problem). We assume also that the individual is

[1] For a general discussion, see Merton, Theory of Finance from the Perspective of Continuous Time, as listed in the Suggested Readings at the end of the chapter.

averse to risk but need not make any additional assumptions regarding individual utility functions. Recall that to develop the valuation model of Chap. 7 and to apply it to risky debt in Chap. 8 we had to assume that individual utility functions were approximately quadratic or, at least, that the expected value and standard deviation of an asset's returns were the only characteristics of concern to the individual. Therefore, the assumption of simple risk aversion made here is much less restrictive regarding individual attitudes toward risk. One of the most important advantages of the continuous-time approach is that minimal assumptions regarding individual utility functions are required.[2]

However, as noted in Chap. 5, if rates of return on assets all have normal probability distributions, it does not matter what forms individual utility functions take so long as individuals are risk averse. As we discuss below, continuous-time models restrict the stochastic behavior of rates of return to achieve much the same result as the normality assumptions did in the single-period, discrete-time case.

## Capital Markets

In continuous-time models the capital markets are assumed to be always operating or "open," and therefore trading opportunities are continuous. This is a fundamental assumption of continuous-time models. It says that individual investors can revise their portfolios of assets instantly as the desire or need arises. This explicit assumption may be contrasted with the corresponding implicit assumptions made in discrete-time analysis.

There are in reality several relevant time intervals which deserve explicit recognition:[3]

1. There is the minimum interval of time required between market transactions. We could call this the *trading interval*. This is determined by the structure of the capital markets, not by the individual investor. The trading interval actually depends on the time of day, the day of the week, and the asset in question. For example, the markets are not open for most transactions during weekends. However, during business hours, one can buy and sell securities virtually minute by minute through the organized exchanges. Furthermore, the trading interval for real estate is longer than that for U.S. Treasury Bills.
2. Individual investors normally do not continuously revise their portfolios; instead they do so periodically. We can therefore think of investors as hav-

[2] Wealth invariance as discussed in Appendix 5C is normally assumed in continuous-time models. This assumption is implicit in the use of a time integral for the utility of consumption as is typical of continuous-time models. See also R. A. Pollack, Additive Von Neumann-Morgenstern Utility Functions, *Econometrica*, vol. 35, pp. 485–494, July–October 1967.

[3] Merton (*op. cit.*, p. 662) refers to these as "horizons." He also includes an "observation horizon" which applies to empirical research. This is the time between successive observations of the data.

ing a *decision interval* which is the time between successive portfolio decisions. This interval clearly will vary from investor to investor and from time to time. That is, some investors ("traders") may be actively buying and selling securities minute by minute; whereas others may consider revising their asset portfolios only once a month or once a year.

3. Individual investors also have a planning horizon. This is the furthest future time considered by an investor when determining the most desirable portfolio to hold. The *planning interval* would then be the time between the present and the planning horizon. For many individuals the planning interval can be considered their expected remaining lifetimes.
4. Assets provide cash flows which are paid only periodically, for example, quarterly dividends on stock or semiannual interest payments on bonds. The length of time between cash flows can be called the *cash-flow interval* and will depend on the asset in question.

Normally in discrete-time analysis we assume that trading intervals, decision intervals, and cash-flow intervals are all equal and constant over future time. (Recall the discussion on pages 8 and 9 in Chap. 1). For ease of exposition, we often take this constant interval as being one year. In continuous-time models these intervals are assumed to be zero; that is, all events are occurring continuously or at least have the potential to do so. Clearly neither assumption is "realistic" in the sense of accurately describing the world; moreover, it is not clear whether one assumption is more realistic than the other. In our view, discussions of the relative realism of unrealistic assumptions are rarely fruitful. The more important question is which mode of analysis produces the more useful results or is the more direct approach to a given result, and the answer is likely to depend on the problem being attacked. Presently many problems previously analyzed in discrete time are being reformulated into continuous time to see whether any new insights can be developed. Some of these explorations will surely prove fruitful; others will not. In any case continuous time offers a promising alternative to standard discrete-time approaches.

One aspect of real markets which inhibits continuous trading is transaction costs, such as brokerage fees. Consequently, continuous-time models almost always assume the absence of transactions costs and usually make the general assumption that capital markets are perfect. Of course, the assumption that capital markets are perfect is made frequently in discrete models, just as we do throughout most of this book.

## Asset Returns

Assets or securities in continuous-time models are typically assumed to provide cash returns in two ways. First, most assets are assumed to have only a single cash return obtained either through sale of the asset or through a given liquidating (maturity) payment at the end of some finite period of time. For example, non-dividend-paying common stock and U.S. Treasury bills fall into this category. Second, some assets are assumed to provide a continuous cash flow at a given rate per unit time in addition to the proceeds from their sale. Thus a dividend-paying stock would be assumed to pay a continuous stream of cash dividends. The total cash returns from the stock would be the dividends received while it was owned plus the selling price when sold.

Two general random (stochastic) processes are assumed to apply to these returns—diffusion processes, and "jump" processes. For a diffusion process, returns are assumed to change randomly but continuously so that in any small interval of time only a small change in the return on the asset can occur. Uncertainty in the returns increases with their distance into the future in a predictable fashion. That is, we know the probability distribution of the returns and we know that the variance of the returns, from now to any given future time $t$, increases with $t$. In jump processes, the returns in any interval may "jump"—increase or decrease by a discrete amount—but the probabilities of arrival and potential magnitudes of the jumps are known. Jump processes are used to model such things as the arrival of a major piece of new information about a security. Generally the probability of having a jump occur becomes close to 1.0 as the time into the future becomes long.

An analogy for the two processes might be helpful. Imagine you are floating on an inner tube in the middle of a large lake. There is a slight wind blowing, the lake is choppy, and you are gradually drifting with the wind. Your path will be continuous with some uncertainty as to where precisely you will end up. The forecast error in your ultimate location from a given initial point increases with time. This is a diffusion process. Alternatively, suppose the lake is absolutely still with no wind. You would remain in one spot except that several of your friends are swimming in the vicinity. At irregular intervals one of them passes by and gives you a shove. This is a jump process.[4]

The returns from any given asset can be modeled by a mixture of a diffusion process for part of the returns and a jump process for the rest. Therefore, even though these two processes appear quite special, the resulting models are fairly general. And, as we mentioned earlier, the analysis of these models in continuous time often produces analytical formulas which can be solved using actual data.

We now move from idealized concepts of continuous time to the practical aspects of options in the securities markets.

## INTRODUCTION TO OPTIONS

In its most basic form an option is the right to buy or sell an asset at a stated price during the period of the contract. There are many different types of

[4] For further discussion of diffusion processes, see Appendix 10A. For a more complete discussion of jump processes, see J. Cox and S. Ross, The Valuation of Options for Alternative Stochastic Processes, *Journal of Financial Economics*, vol. 3, pp. 145–166, January 1976, in particular the first six pages.

options depending on the asset (common stock, land, wheat, etc.), on the issuer (individual or corporation), and on various provisions in the option contract. In this section we consider only options on common stock; for information regarding options on other types of assets, specialized publications in the particular area should be consulted.

## Options on Common Stock

Common-stock options are negotiable contracts providing for the right to purchase or sell a given number of shares at a designated price per share. The price per share stated in the contract may be called the contract price, option price, exercise price, or striking price—all of which mean the same thing. Option contracts apply generally only for a specific period of time. The date at which the option expires is called the maturity date or expiration date. An American option may be exercised at any time prior to and including the expiration date; a European option can be exercised only on the expiration date.

Corporations sometimes issue options to purchase common stock of the firm. These options are called *warrants*.[5] Warrants are usually issued in conjunction with other financing activities of the corporation. Warrants ordinarily have long maturities; some have been issued which have no expiration date and are therefore perpetual. Warrants are publicly traded securities just like the stock of the corporation. Corporations may issue *rights* (stock subscription warrants) to existing stockholders as a method of selling new stock. The owners of the rights can purchase stock from the corporation at a fixed price, usually at a moderate discount from the present stock price. These rights are also traded securities, but they normally expire 20 to 30 days after issue. Thus a substantial number of new options are issued each year as part of the financing activities of corporations. Furthermore, corporations frequently issue debt or preferred stock which is convertible into common stock at the option of the investor. These convertible securities can be viewed as a combination of straight debt or preferred stock plus an option to purchase common stock. Therefore, an understanding of option values is important to corporate financial officers, not just to investors.

Individuals may also create options on common stock. A *call* is an option to purchase stock; a *put* is an option to sell stock. These option contracts are endorsed by a stockbroker so that the purchaser is assured that the contract will be fulfilled. Puts and calls usually have a 30-day to 1-year initial maturity. There is an active secondary market in options; for example, an option purchased with an original maturity of one year can be sold rather than exercised at any time prior to its expiration date. The option-pricing model was developed specifically for call options; so we shall examine them more closely than the other types.

[5] Corporations often provide stock options to executives, but these are restricted to use by the individual, whereas warrants are marketable securities. Here we are concerned only with marketable options.

## Call Options

An example of a call will illustrate the basic concepts. Consider a call option for 100 shares of a stock having a current price of $40 per share. Suppose the maturity is 180 days from the present and the exercise price is the same as the current stock price, i.e., $40. The price of this option contract might be about $400. Our concern later is a formula for determining the value of the option contract. Let us price the contract on a per share basis; that is, we say that the price of the option on one share is $4 (price of the contract, $400, divided by 100, the number of shares in the contract). Option prices are now normally stated on a per share basis. Suppose that you purchase the call for $400 or $4 per share. What do you have? You have obtained the right to acquire the stock at a price of $40 per share at any time in the next 180 days (for an American option). Suppose that the price of the stock rises to $45 one month later. You could exercise the option and obtain the stock for $40, then sell it for $45. This would result in a net profit of $1 per share ($5 on the stock transaction less the $4 paid for the option), or $100 for the 100-share contract. However, it is likely that the value of the option itself will be greater than $5 at this time. This is because the option still has 150 days left before expiration and there is a good chance that the price of the stock will rise above $45 in the next 150 days. If the option's price is above $5, you will certainly prefer to sell the option rather than exercise it yourself since the net profit obtained from sale will exceed the net profit from exercising the option and selling the stock. Even if the option price were only $5, you would prefer simply to sell the option rather than go through the extra trouble of exercising the option and then selling the stock. Furthermore, the brokerage commissions on sale of $4,500 worth of stock will be

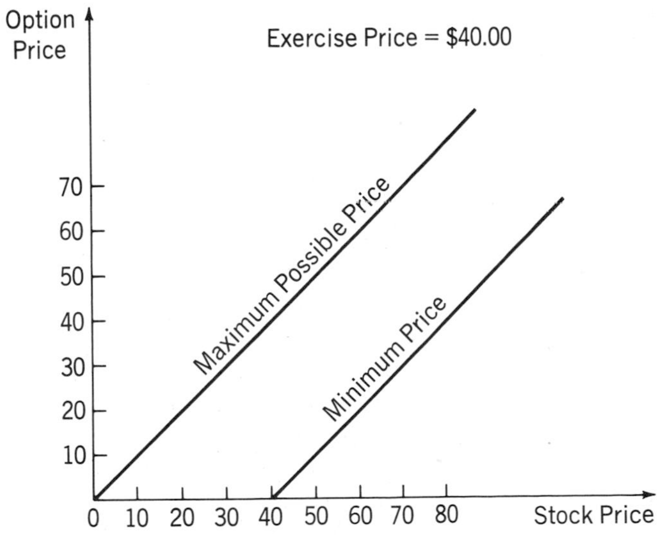


**figure 10-1**

greater than the commissions on $500 worth of options; so you would prefer to sell the option.

Figure 10-1 illustrates the general behavior of call option prices (per share of stock) as a function of the stock price and time to maturity. The maximum possible value for an option is the stock price because you must pay the exercise price to obtain the stock and you can always buy the stock directly. Theoretically, the value of a perpetual call on a stock that does not pay dividends is the stock price, since the option never needs to be exercised and the exercise price never needs to be paid. However, with a perpetual option, there is always some chance that dividends will be paid on the stock, making the option less valuable than the stock. For options with finite maturities, we would expect the option price to be well below the stock price because of the need to pay the exercise price at maturity.

The minimum value for an option is either zero (since no assessments can be made on the owner) or the difference between the stock price and the exercise price, if that difference is greater than zero. The option price cannot be less than this difference (ignoring transaction costs), because otherwise it would pay an investor to purchase the option, immediately exercise it, sell the stock, and thereby obtain an immediate riskless profit.

Accordingly, the value of the option will be somewhere between the two lines shown (and typically closer to the minimum line than to the maximum line). Generally, the difference between the actual option price and the minimum price (often called the "premium" on the option) will be greatest when the stock is selling close to the exercise price with an appreciable time to go before maturity of the option. As the option gets closer to maturity, its price will shift toward the minimum price line for a given stock price. On the expiration date, the price of the option will be the minimum price, either zero (if the exercise price is greater than the stock price) or the difference between the stock price and the exercise price (if the stock price exceeds the exercise price).

Some examples of options—the corporation, time to maturity, exercise price, current stock price (maximum possible option price), minimum price (stock price minus exercise price), and the current price of the option per share of stock—are shown in Table 10-1. Note that an option is identified by the corporation whose stock is being optioned, maturity, and exercise price.

Our analysis in the next section will focus on call options issued by individuals. Further we assume that the calls are European; that is, the option can be exercised only at its expiration date. As it turns out, the analysis for European call options is believed to apply directly to American call options provided the stock in question is not expected to pay a dividend prior to the expiration date of the option. We assume that the stock will not pay a dividend prior to the option's expiration. The payment of dividends complicates the analysis of any option, European or American, because the exercise price is reduced by any dividends paid on the stock during the period the option is in effect and the dividends are, in general, uncertain.[6]

[6] See Merton, Theory of Rational Option Pricing, *op. cit.*, for a discussion of the application of the European call model to American calls and for a model of dividends being paid on the stock.

**table 10-1 Examples of Options**

| *Corporation* | *Time to maturity* | *Exercise price* | *Stock price* | *Minimum price*[a] | *Option price per share* |
|---|---|---|---|---|---|
| Avon | 4 months | 45 | 45 | 0 | 2¼ |
| Burroughs | 4 months | 70 | 67⅛ | 0 | 2⅞ |
| 3-M | 4 months | 50 | 50 | 0 | 2½ |
| Xerox | 4 months | 50 | 52⅛ | 2⅛ | 4¼ |
| IBM | 1 month | 240 | 257⅝ | 17⅝ | 18⅜ |
| IBM | 4 months | 240 | 257⅝ | 17⅝ | 21¼ |
| IBM | 7 months | 240 | 257⅝ | 17⅝ | 24 |
| IBM | 7 months | 260 | 257⅝ | 0 | 12⅛ |
| Braniff[b] | 110 months | 23 | 9⅛ | 0 | 2¼ |

[a] Minimum price = stock price − exercise price, if positive
= 0, otherwise.
[b] Warrant traded on AMEX. All others are call options traded on the Chicago Board or, for Burroughs, AMEX.
*Source: Wall Street Journal*, September 23, 1977.

## CALL OPTION VALUATION

We discuss the valuation of call options in two stages. First, we examine the problem under certainty. This model provides insight into the Black-Scholes option-pricing model under uncertainty which is covered in the second stage of the discussion. We begin by developing our basic assumptions and notation.

1. The riskless interest rate, $i$, per year is known and constant, at least until the option expires.
2. Security markets are perfect (including option markets). There are no taxes or transaction costs and funds may be borrowed or lent in unlimited amounts at rate $i$ (continuously compounded).
3. There are no restrictions on short sales of options or stock.
4. Trading in the market is continuous.
5. The present time (now) is designated as time zero; a future point in time is designated as time $t$ measured in years ($t = .085$ would be 1 month from now, $t = 1.5$ would be 18 months from now, etc.).
6. The option is written against a non-dividend-paying stock and is of the European type.
7. $P_t$ is the price at time $t$ of the stock on which the option is written.
8. The option has an exercise (contract) price of $C$, expires at $t = t^*$, and has a value at time $t$ of $W_t$.

### Option Value under Certainty

Under certainty we know precisely what a call option will be worth at its expiration date, $t^*$. If the stock price will be less than the exercise price at time $t^*$, the option will have zero value at $t^*$. However, if it has zero value at $t^*$, the only time it can be exercised, then its value at any time prior to $t^*$ must also be zero. Therefore,

$$\text{If } P_{t^*} < C, \qquad W_t = 0 \qquad \text{for all } t \leq t^* \tag{10-1}$$

The more interesting situation is when the stock price will be greater than the exercise price at $t^*$. The value of the option at $t^*$ is simply the difference between the stock price and the exercise price.

$$W_{t^*} = P_{t^*} - C \tag{10-2}$$

Since we know the future value of the option with certainty, its value now (at $t = 0$) must be the discounted present value of the future amount. In a continuous-time world with an interest rate of $i$ per year, the present value of \$1 to be received $t$ periods from now is

$$\text{Present value of \$1} = e^{-it}$$

where $e$ is the base for natural logarithms, $e = 2.783. \ . \ . \ .$ (See Appendix 2B for discussion of continuous compounding and discounting.) Therefore, the present value of $W_{t^*}$ is

$$W_0 = W_{t^*}e^{-it^*} \tag{10-3}$$

since $W_{t^*} = P_{t^*} - C$ from (10-2)

$$W_0 = [P_{t^*} - C]e^{-it^*} \tag{10-4}$$

However, the future price of the stock is also known with certainty; therefore, it must be true that the stock's current price is the present value of the future price

$$P_0 = P_{t^*}e^{-it^*} \tag{10-5}$$

or, conversely, the future price must simply be the compounded value of the current price:

$$P_{t^*} = P_0e^{it^*} \tag{10-6}$$

Substituting for $P_{t^*}$ in (10-4) using (10-6), we obtain

$$W_0 = P_0 - Ce^{-it^*} \tag{10-7}$$

Equation (10-7) shows that the present value of an option under certainty in perfect markets is the present stock price minus the present value of the exercise price discounted back from the expiration date. Its primary usefulness is in interpreting solutions to more complicated models involving uncertainty and in checking to see whether such solutions can be applied to the certainty case. (They should be applicable.)

To see how the certainty formula works, consider the IBM option in Table 10-1 which had a maturity of 7 months ($t = \frac{7}{12} = 0.58$ year) and an exercise price of \$240. Interest rates on U.S. Treasury Bills at that time were about 6% per year ($i = .06$). The stock price was \$257.62. We would calculate the price of the option as

$$\begin{aligned} W_0 &= P_0 - Ce^{-it^*} \\ &= \$257.62 - \$240.00e^{-.06(0.58)} \\ &= \$257.62 - \$240.00\ (0.966) \\ &= \$257.62 - \$231.84 \\ &= \$25.78 \end{aligned}$$

Since the actual option price was \$24, the certainty model did not do so badly here. However, if we apply the same formula to the 7-month IBM option with a \$260 exercise price, we obtain a predicted value of \$6.46 as compared to the actual price of \$12.12. Thus the certainty model is clearly unsuited to be a general pricing formula. The failure of the certainty model should not be surprising, since the model assumes away the most interesting aspect of options—the uncertainty in future stock prices and, hence, the uncertainty in the future value of the option. A model addressing these uncertainties is needed.

## The Black-Scholes Model[7]

To assumptions 1 to 8 made earlier, we need add only the following:

9. The stock price is a random variable in continuous time. The instantaneous rate of return on the stock (change in price divided by price in a small interval) follows a diffusion process with a constant mean and a constant variance $s^2$. The resulting distribution of the stock price is a log-normal (the logarithm of the stock price has a normal probability distribution).

This assumption is examined in detail in Appendix 10A. The essential points are the diffusion process as discussed earlier and that the variance of the instantaneous rate of return on the stock ($s^2$) is a constant over the life of the option. The variance of the rate of return from time zero to time $t$ is $s^2t$; thus the degree of uncertainty increases with $t$.

Given perfect markets, Black and Scholes point out that it is possible to develop a "hedged" position in the stock and the option, that is, an investment which has no risk. The basic idea is that the value of an option is dependent primarily on the price of the stock and some known constants (exercise price, maturity, etc.). Suppose that we can estimate roughly over the next small period of time (a day, for example), what the change in option price will be for a given change in stock price. That is, suppose we know that if tomorrow the stock price increased by \$1, the option price would increase by \$0.25, and a

[7] The model was originally developed by F. Black and M. Scholes, The Pricing of Options and Corporate Liabilities, as listed in the Suggested Readings at the end of the chapter. See also the discussion in C. Smith, Option Pricing, listed there.

decrease in the stock price of \$1 would cause a decrease in the option price of \$0.25. The ratio of the change in option price to the change in stock price is sometimes called the "hedge" ratio, $h$.[8] In this example the hedge ratio is 0.25. The hedge ratio tells us how many shares of stock should be held long (owned) relative to options sold short (borrowed and sold) in order to achieve a riskless position.[9] A ratio of 0.25 says for every four options sold short, one share of stock should be held long. A ratio of 0.5 would indicate that to hedge four options sold short, two shares of stock must be held long.

What happens if we follow this rule? Suppose that the present option price is \$5, the present stock price is \$40, and the hedge ratio is 0.25.

We establish a position (net investment) per share of stock of

$$\begin{aligned} \text{Investment} &= P_0 - [1/h]W_0 \\ &= \$40 - (1/.25)\$5 \\ &= \$40 - (4)\$5 \\ &= \$20 \end{aligned} \tag{10-8}$$

Now suppose the stock price increases by \$2.00. The option price should also increase by approximately $0.25 \times \$2.00 = \$0.50$. Thus the new price for the stock would be \$42.00 and the new price for the option would be \$5.50. The value of our investment would remain unchanged.

$$\$42 - 4 \times \$5.50 = \$20$$

Suppose the price of the stock falls \$2.00 and the option price falls accordingly by \$0.50. Then the new prices for the stock and the option would be \$38.00 and \$4.50, respectively, and the value of our position would still be \$20. This simple example illustrates the risk elimination of the hedge. If we adjust our position as the hedge ratio changes, then the risk on the net investment remains very low (with precise and continuous adjustment it would be zero). However, in our example, there is also no apparent return on the investment. In a perfect market, any net investment should provide some returns to the investor. Since we know that risk can be eliminated by appropriate hedging, the rate of return on the position should be the riskless rate of interest $i$. To illustrate this, consider the certainty model of Eq. (10-7). In the certainty model the hedge ratio is a constant 1.0; therefore, the net investment per share of stock would be

$$\begin{aligned} \text{Investment} &= P_0 - W_0 \\ &= P_0 - [P_0 - Ce^{-it^*}] \\ &= Ce^{-it^*} \end{aligned}$$

[8] More precisely it is the partial derivative of the option price (with respect to the stock price $\partial W/\partial P$). See F. Black, Fact and Fantasy in the Use of Options, as listed in the Suggested Readings.

[9] Under the assumptions of the Black-Scholes model, the investor can either sell the options short or write a call against the stock to achieve the hedged position, and these two alternatives would be economically equivalent.

At maturity the value of the position will be

$$\begin{aligned}\text{Value at maturity} &= P_{t^*} - W_{t^*}\\ &= P_{t^*} - [P_{t^*} - C]\\ &= C\end{aligned}$$

Since $Ce^{-it^*}$ is the time zero present value of $C$ to be received at $t^*$ (remember the option is sold short or written), the rate of return earned must be $i$.

Black and Scholes use this economic argument plus some mathematics to arrive at the following valuation formula for a call option:[10]

$$W_0 = P_0N(d_1) - Ce^{-it^*}N(d_2) \tag{10-9}$$

where $N(d)$ is the cumulative normal probability function and

$$d_1 = \frac{\ln (P_0/C) + (i + s^2/2)t^*}{s\sqrt{t^*}}$$

$$d_2 = d_1 - s\sqrt{t^*}$$

This formula is simpler than it appears at first glance. The two terms $N(d_1)$ and $N(d_2)$ are probabilities which can be obtained, given values for $d_1$ and $d_2$, from standard tables as discussed below. The probabilities take on values between 0 and 1.0. Suppose, for whatever reason, these probabilities are very close to 1.0, as would be the case if the variance ($s^2$) of the stock is very small (the stock is almost riskless), or if $t^*$ is very small (the option is very close to its maturity). Then Eq. (10-9) reduces to our certainty model, which is quite reasonable given the assumptions of either riskless stock or very little time left on the option.

If $N(d_1) \approx N(d_2) \approx 1.0$,

$$W_0 \approx P_0 - Ce^{-it^*}$$

as in (10-7). Therefore, the Black-Scholes model is basically the certainty model adjusted by a couple of probabilities. These probabilities, $N(d_1)$ and $N(d_2)$, modify the certainty model to account for the uncertainty in the future stock price.

A precise interpretation of the probabilities is somewhat difficult. They are not the probabilities of any particular event's occurring; rather the formula results from the structure of the problem. We obtain the probabilities by calculating $d_1$ and $d_2$ given values for the following required variables: $t^*$, the time to maturity of the option; $s^2$, the variance of the stock's rate of return; $C$, the exercise price of the option; and $i$, the interest rate. Notice that of these numbers, only the variance $s^2$ poses any problems in application. Use of the formula requires us to estimate $s^2$, presumably from historical data on realized rates of return on the stock. In practice there will always be questions as to the accuracy of our estimate of $s^2$ for the particular stock and whether $s^2$ is a stable number over time.

[10] See app. 10A for the derivation.

Given values for $t^*$, $s^2$, $C$, and $i$, the calculated values for $d_1$ and $d_2$ are then used to find values for $N(d_1)$ and $N(d_2)$ in a table for the cumulative normal distribution which is available in a variety of statistical handbooks and in many computer systems. An abbreviated version in terms of $d$ is shown below:

| | | | | | | | | | |
|---|---|---|---|---|---|---|---|---|---|
| $d$: | $-\infty$ | −2.30 | −1.65 | −1.29 | −1.04 | −0.85 | −0.53 | −0.25 | 0.0 |
| $N(d)$: | 0.0 | 0.01 | 0.05 | 0.10 | 0.15 | 0.20 | 0.30 | 0.40 | 0.50 |
| $d$: | $\infty$ | 2.30 | 1.65 | 1.29 | 1.04 | 0.85 | 0.53 | 0.25 | 0.0 |
| $N(d)$: | 1.0 | 0.99 | 0.95 | 0.90 | 0.85 | 0.80 | 0.70 | 0.60 | 0.50 |

The values are shown here in such a way as to indicate the symmetry of the function. Actual tables usually indicate differences from the center point of $d = 0$, $N(0) = .5$, and appropriate additions or subtractions must be made to obtain the correct value.[11] For rough work, interpolation can be used in conjunction

[11] For example, only positive values for $d$ are shown in standard tables, so that for $d = -0.25$, look up 0.25 and you would obtain a table value of 0.10. Subtract this from 0.50 to obtain $N(-0.25) = 0.40$. Similarly if $d = 0.25$, you would have to add 0.10 to 0.50 to obtain $N(0.25) = 0.60$.

**table 10-2 Black-Scholes Option Values using Eq. (10-9) and Assumed Characteristics as Shown**

| | *Interest rate = 5% (i = 0.05)* | | | | | |
|---|---|---|---|---|---|---|
| | *3-month maturity (t* = 0.25)* | | | *9-month maturity (t* = 0.75)* | | |
| | *Stock price ($P_0$)* | | | *Stock price ($P_0$)* | | |
| *Standard deviation (s)* | *$36* | *$40* | *$44* | *$36* | *$40* | *$44* |
| 0.20 | $0.36 | 1.85 | 4.80 | $1.50 | 3.51 | 6.38 |
| 0.40 | 1.57 | 3.42 | 6.04 | 3.96 | 6.17 | 8.82 |
| 0.60 | 2.96 | 4.99 | 7.54 | 6.44 | 8.81 | 11.46 |
| | *Interest rate = 10% (i = 0.10)* | | | | | |
| | *3-month maturity t* = 0.25)* | | | *9-month maturity (t* = 0.75)* | | |
| | *Stock price ($P_0$)* | | | *Stock price ($P_0$)* | | |
| *Standard deviation (s)* | *$36* | *$40* | *$44* | *$36* | *$40* | *$44* |
| 0.20 | $0.45 | 2.12 | 5.22 | $2.01 | 4.35 | 7.49 |
| 0.40 | 1.72 | 3.67 | 6.38 | 4.49 | 6.87 | 9.67 |
| 0.60 | 3.12 | 5.22 | 7.83 | 6.95 | 9.43 | 12.19 |

All table values are in dollars per share of stock optioned. Exercise price ($C$) is $40. Stock prices are prices at $t = 0$.
*Source:* F. Black, *Financial Analysts Journal,* vol. 31, pp. 66–68, July–August 1975).

with the data above. Also Black has tabulated values of Eq. (10-9) for various combinations of the variables. We show some of these values in Table 10-2 for a call option with an exercise price of $40.

From the data in Table 10-2, we can see strong dependence of the option value on current stock price, standard deviation of the stock's rate of return, and maturity. The effect of interest rates is less important—doubling the rate from 5% to 10% increases the option price by at most 30% and usually by less than 10%. This might be compared to the impact of a 10% increase in stock price, which can increase the price of the option by 400% or more.

The use of the formula in evaluating option investments and its empirical validation is beyond the scope of this book. The interesting aspect from a theoretical point of view is that it can be derived at all. Except for the variance of the stock's rate of return, the other factors in the formula are essentially known at any point in time when the option is to be valued.[12] The actual variance over the period of the option is not known, but it may be fairly well approximated by historical estimates, although one might be concerned as to the reliability of such estimates for long-maturity options. Basically, then, we have an operational and fairly accurate way to value a complex security in a multiperiod setting under uncertainty. This is a major achievement. Furthermore, the option concept can be applied to other assets, in particular to the ownership interest in a business firm.

## APPLICATIONS OF THE OPM TO FIRM FINANCIAL DECISIONS

The option-pricing model has much more important applications than valuing call options. With suitable modifications, the model can be applied to a wide variety of financial instruments including convertible and subordinated debt, collateralized loans, underwriting contracts, insurance contracts, and others.[13] One of the more intriguing applications was pointed out by Black and Scholes—that the model might apply directly to the common stock of a corporation. The general concept of common stock as an option presents some interesting possibilities for theoretical analysis. Galai and Masulis, for example, combine the Black-Scholes model and a continuous-time version of the single-period, mean-variance model of Chap. 8 to obtain theoretical results regarding acquisitions and mergers, spin-offs, and corporate investment decisions.[14] Although the basic results achieved by these authors are implied by the value-additivity principle developed in Chap. 9, the alternative analysis is of some

[12] Interest rates may change, but use of the rate on U.S. Treasury issues of the same maturity as the option should produce reasonable results. Also, as we noted above, option prices are not very sensitive to interest rates.

[13] A review of these applications has been done by C. Smith, "Applications of Option Pricing Analysis," University of Rochester Working Paper 7804, March 1978.

[14] D. Galai and R. Masulis, The Option Pricing Model and the Risk Factor of Stock, *Journal of Financial Economics*, vol. 3, pp. 53–81, January 1976.

importance since it suggests avenues for future research. Along entirely different lines, the option-pricing model is being used to obtain estimates of "time-state" prices which may then be applied to firm investment decisions. Here we first discuss the concept of stock's being an option on the firm; then we examine the application to investment decisions.

## Common Stock as an Option on the Firm

Consider a business firm with only two outstanding securities issues—common stock and a debt issue payable in a lump sum at maturity. Assume further that the assets of the firm consist of undeveloped land and cash. The purpose of the corporation is to develop the land (using the cash presently on hand) and to sell the land when the debt is due. The debtholders are to be repaid from the proceeds of the sale and the remaining funds distributed to the stockholders. No financing or distributions of funds are to be made prior to sale of the land. In this situation *the common stock is an option* on the assets (proceeds from sale) of the firm. If the developed property can be sold for an amount in excess of the money due the debtholders, then the stockholders will exercise their option, pay off the debt, and keep the difference for themselves; otherwise the stockholders will let the debtholders acquire all the rights to the property, in which case the stockholders will receive nothing and pay nothing to the debtholders (due to the limited liability of stockholders). In terms of the option-pricing formula

$W_0$ = the current value of the stock.
$P_0$ = the current value of the firm's assets (entire firm).
$P_0 - W_0$ = the current value of the debt.
$C$ = the amount owed on the debt at maturity.
$s^2$ = the variance of the rate of return on the value of the firm as a whole.

The option-pricing formula might be directly applicable in special situations such as this, subject to the other assumptions (perfect markets for the securities and constant variance in particular). However, the concept appears generally valid.

Any time a debt issue matures, the stockholders (through their representatives, firm management) have the option of walking away from the firm leaving the assets to be divided among creditors. Otherwise they can choose to exercise their option and pay off the debt. In some cases (often termed equity bailouts) the stockholders may prefer to contribute additional funds to the firm in order to keep it going, i.e., to exercise their option to retain ownership. Since the option-pricing model (or derivatives of it) can apply to common stock valuation, the potential for investigation of the impact of financial decisions clearly exists. As indicated earlier, much research is proceeding in this area. Now let us consider a rather different application of the model, as a means to empirical estimates of time-state prices.

## State Prices and Capital Budgeting

One of the more vexing issues in finance remains the development of methods to estimate risk-adjusted discount rates for business investment decisions. In Chap. 12 we develop the basic rules for investment decisions in perfect markets; however, these rules assume that managers can estimate the values of risky, multiperiod cash flows. There we offer some guidelines for application of the risk-adjusted discount-rate approach to capital budgeting. As was discussed in Chap. 9, there are other approaches to valuation, the most important being the certainty-equivalent and time-state preference models. The time-state preference model, in particular, is an extremely powerful theoretical tool, but it has appeared to be too general for practical application owing to the difficulty of estimating the value of cash flows occurring in a given state of the world. Recent work indicates that the option-pricing model may offer a solution to the problem of estimating time-state values, thereby opening up this model to application in corporate capital budgeting. Here we explain the basis for the estimating procedure; actual estimates have been developed by Banz and Miller.[15] We begin with a simple illustration to motivate the subsequent discussion.

**An illustration.** Suppose that a toy manufacturer is considering the introduction of a new toy. Management expects that it will be a fad item and therefore it will be profitable to produce for only 3 years. The cash flow received in a given year is dependent on which one of three possible states of the economy will occur in that year. We assume that the uncertainty with respect to the state of the economy is the only aspect of risk that is relevant to shareholders; all other risk can be diversified away. Thus, for each future period and future state of the economy, management estimates the expected cash flow. A set of such estimates is shown in Exhibit 10-1.

To apply the time-state preference model to this problem, we must know the current value (price) of a dollar to be received in each future time and state. Let $v_{st}$ be a set of such prices for each state $s$ and time $t$. Then the present value of the cash flows $Z_{st}$ can be written in general as

[15] For the theoretical development, see D. Breeden and R. Litzenberger, Prices of State-Contingent Claims Implicit in Option Prices, *Journal of Business*, October 1978. Our discussion is drawn primarily from R. Banz and M. Miller, Prices for State-Contingent Claims: Some Estimates and Applications, *Journal of Business*, October 1978.

**Exhibit 10-1 Expected Cash Flows from Toy Project, $Z_{st}$**

| *State of economy* | *Year 1* | *Year 2* | *Year 3* | *Year 4 and beyond* |
|---|---|---|---|---|
| Boom | $1,000 | $500 | $300 | 0 |
| Normal | $ 800 | $400 | $200 | 0 |
| Recession | $ 500 | $200 | $100 | 0 |

**Exhibit 10-2 Time-State Prices, $v_{st}$**

| *State of economy* | *Year 1* | *Year 2* | *Year 3* |
|---|---|---|---|
| Boom | .1672 | .1693 | .1686 |
| Normal | .2912 | .2915 | .2903 |
| Recession | .5398 | .5333 | .5313 |

*Source:* Banz and Miller, *op. cit.*, Table 2. Their states 1, 2, and 3 are here referred to as recession, normal, and boom, respectively. To use their data it is necessary to specify the current state of the economy; here state 2 (normal) is assumed to be the current state.

$$PV = \sum_{s=1}^{n} \sum_{t=1}^{T} v_{st} Z_{st} \tag{10-10}$$

In our example the number of states, $n$, is 3 and the number of time periods, $T$, is 3. Therefore, to apply the model we must know the complete set of prices $v_{st}$ or $n \times T = 9$ prices. Where or how are these to be obtained? That is the problem Banz and Miller solved using the option-pricing model. A set of state prices based on their results is shown in Exhibit 10-2.

Substituting the prices from Exhibit 10-2 and the cash flows from Exhibit 10-1 into the valuation equation (10-10), we obtain

$$\begin{aligned} PV &= \$1{,}000\,(.1672) + \$800\,(.2912) + \$500\,(.5398) \\ &\quad + \$500\,(.1693) + \$400\,(.2915) + \$200\,(.5333) \\ &\quad + \$300\,(.1686) + \$200\,(.2903) + \$100\,(.5313) \\ &= \$670 + \$308 + \$162 \\ &= \$1{,}140 \end{aligned}$$

Therefore, if the initial outlay in the project is less than \$1,140, the investment has a positive net present value and should be undertaken.

**The single-period case.**[16] To see how the time-state prices $v_{st}$ may be determined from the option-pricing model, we begin by examining the single-period case. Suppose that we can identify "states of the world" with payoffs provided by the market portfolio. To obtain a finite set of discrete states, we define each state as a range of rates of return on the market. For example, in the three-state case used in Exhibit 10-2, "Recession" is defined as rates of return from −86.47% to 0.06%, "Normal" is defined as rates of return from 0.06% to 20.42%, and "Boom" is defined as rates of return from 20.42% to 171.83%.[17] The attractive features to this definition of "states" are:

(*a*) It is possible to determine the historical frequency of occurrence of any given state.

[16] An understanding of Appendix 9A on the time-state preference model is helpful but not necessary for this section.

[17] See Table 2 in Banz and Miller, *op. cit*. The ranges here are based on historical rates of return and have occurred historically with approximately equal frequency.

(*b*) The number of states considered may be as few or as many as desired.
(*c*) The state definitions are "objective" and therefore capable of being readily communicated.

Thus this definition is highly practical.[18]

Let the current value of the market portfolio be $M_0$ and consider an option which pays \$1 one period from now ($t = 1$) if the value of the market portfolio is equal to or greater than a specified level $M_j$ at that time and pays off zero otherwise. Breeden and Litzenberger show that the value of such an option $V_j$ can be derived from the Black-Scholes model Eq. (10-9) as the second partial derivative of Eq. (10-9) with respect to the exercise price evaluated at an exercise price of $M_j$. The resulting equation for $V_j$ is[19]

$$V_j = e^{-i}N[d_2(M_j)] \tag{10-11}$$

where

$$d_2 \equiv \frac{\ln (M_0/M_j) + (i - s_M^2/2)}{s_M}$$

and $s_M^2$ is the instantaneous variance of the rate of return on the market portfolio.

Compare (10-11) with (10-9), keeping in mind that we are considering a single period so $t^* = 1$. The differences between the pricing formula of (10-9) and that of (10-11) are due to the differences in the options considered. First, this option has no exercise price as such; that is, no payment is required to exercise the option. Second, the payoff when the value of the market portfolio equals or exceeds $M_j$ is limited to \$1. The call options valued by (10-9) pay the difference between the stock price and the exercise price at maturity ($t^* = 1$ here) and therefore the potential payoff is unlimited. Taking (10-11) as given, how can it be used? First, note that the ratio $(M_0/M_j)$ can be written as

$$\frac{M_0}{M_j} = \frac{1}{1 + r_{Mj}} \tag{10-12}$$

[18] There are some theoretical problems, however. See Breeden and Litzenberger, *op. cit.*, for a discussion of the limitations of this definition.

[19] The more general formula derived by Breeden and Litzenberger and presented by Banz and Miller is in terms of a "single period" of length $T$ (the exercise date $t^* = T$).

$$V_j = e^{-iT}N[d_2(M_j)]$$

$$d_2 \equiv \frac{\ln (M_0/M_j) + (i - s_M^2/2)T}{s_M \sqrt{T}}$$

Also note that Banz and Miller use an "exercise price" $E_j$ in their Eq. (1) with

$$E_j = \frac{M_j}{M_0}$$

so that

$$-\ln (E_j) = \ln \left(\frac{M_0}{M_j}\right)$$

where $r_{Mj}$ is the rate of return on the market portfolio for the period if the value of the market portfolio becomes $M_j$. Thus large negative values of $r_{Mj}$ result in large (positive) values of the ratio and its logarithm. As $r_{Mj}$ increases, $M_0/M_j$ and $\ln(M_0/M_j)$ decrease. The result is, for a given variance $s_M^2$ and riskless rate of interest $i$, the value of the option decreases as $r_{Mj}$ increases. As $r_{Mj}$ approaches $-100\%$, the option becomes certain of paying off \$1; therefore, its value becomes the present value of \$1 to be received with certainty one period from now, $e^{-i}$. As $r_{Mj}$ gets very large, the option becomes certain of not paying off, and its value becomes zero.

Now consider the value of a security that pays off \$1 when state $s_j$ occurs where state $s_j$ is defined as the range of rates of return in the market portfolio, $r_{Mj}$ to $r_{Mj+1}$, or corresponding values $M_j$ to $M_{j+1}$. Given the perfect market assumptions of this chapter, the value of this security must be the difference between the option values $V_j$ and $V_{j+1}$:

$$v_j = V_j - V_{j+1} \tag{10-13}$$

and, substituting for $V_j$ and $V_{j+1}$ from (10-11),

$$v_j = e^{-i}(N[d_2(M_j)] - N[d_2(M_{j+1})]) \tag{10-14a}$$

or, equivalently,

$$v_j = e^{-i}(N[d_2(r_{Mj})] - N[d_2(r_{Mj+1})]) \tag{10-14b}$$

Equation (10-13) follows from the value-additivity principle and is more clearly written as

$$V_j = v_j + V_{j+1} \tag{10-14}$$

$V_{j+1}$ is the value of a security (option) that pays \$1 if the value of the market portfolio is greater than or equal to $M_{j+1}$ or, equivalently, if the rate of return equals or exceeds $r_{Mj+1}$. If a security which pays \$1 when the market portfolio is greater than or equal to $M_j$ and less than $M_{j+1}$ is $v_j$, then a security paying \$1 for all values of the market portfolio greater than or equal to $M_j$ should be worth the sum of $v_j$ and $V_{j+1}$.

For example, suppose that $M_0 = 100$, $M_j = 110$ ($r_{Mj} = 10\%$), and $M_{j+1} = 120$ ($r_{Mj+1} = 20\%$). Assume that $V_j$ calculated from Eq. (10-11) is \$0.30 and that $V_{j+1}$ is calculated to be \$0.18. The value of a security paying \$1 when the market portfolio provides a rate of return within the range of 10% to 20% is \$0.30 − \$0.18 = \$0.12. Thus, provided that it is reasonable to define "states" as ranges of the market portfolio, we can estimate the price of any given state from Eqs. (10-11) to (10-14). The data required to do this for a single period are merely

1. The interest rate $i$.
2. The variance rate for the market portfolio, $s_M^2$.

**Multiperiod-state prices.** The single-period model described above can be applied to periods of any given length (one month, one year, etc.); however, for capital budgeting applications we require multiperiod-state prices since the cash flows from normal investments are multiperiod. Banz and Miller have developed a fairly simple way to calculate multiperiod-state prices from a set of single-period (one-year) estimates. We take as given that the appropriate definition of a "period" is one year, since this conforms to standard capital budgeting procedures.

The additional assumptions required are[20]

1. State definitions (ranges for the rate of return on the market portfolio) are constant for all future periods under consideration.
2. Transitions from one state to another follow a stationary Markov process.
3. Everyone agrees on the state definitions and believes that the transitions follow a stationary process.

These assumptions mean that the probability that the rate of return on the market portfolio will be in a given range (state) in period $t$ depends only on the range (state) it fell in for period $t - 1$. Further, the probabilities of going from one state at $t - 1$ to another state at $t$ do not vary with $t$. That is, the probabilities of transition from one state to another are stationary (constant over time). If these assumptions are valid historically and are perceived as valid for future periods by investors in the market, historical data on the actual rates of return on the market can be used to estimate future state prices. Since the probability of reaching any given state next period depends on which state we are currently in, the set of prices for states one period from now is a matrix.

Let **V** be an $n \times n$ matrix of single-period state prices where $n$ is the number of states. The rows in the matrix are identified by alternative "current states" and the columns are identified by alternative states in the next period. The values in the matrix are the $v_j$ from Eqs. (10-13) and (10-14). For example,

| | | *Next-period states* | | |
|---|---|---|---|---|
| | | *Boom* | *Normal* | *Recession* |
| Current-period states | Boom | \$.174 | \$.294 | \$.554 |
| | Normal | \$.167 | \$.291 | \$.540 |
| | Recession | \$.161 | \$.289 | \$.525 |

Each row is calculated using the single-period equations (10-11) to (10-14) based on the given current state and whatever dependencies are assumed between states. In the Banz-Miller analysis these dependencies are captured by estimating a different riskless interest rate for each current state. From assumptions 1 and 2 above, the matrix for any future period $T$ periods from the

[20] The stationarity assumption is not strictly necessary, but the problem is much more complicated without it, and it was used by Banz and Miller.

present is $\mathbf{V}^T$, the matrix $\mathbf{V}$ taken to the $T$th power.[21] The resulting matrix $\mathbf{V}^T$ is also $n \times n$ where the rows are the current period ($t = 0$) states, only one of which will apply in actuality, and the columns are the states in period $T$. Thus, given matrix $\mathbf{V}$, a complete set of time-state prices can be calculated.

To see what this procedure involves, let us examine the simplest case where only two states can occur, "high" and "low." High and low have equal probabilities of .5 each. We represent the one-period state prices as a $2 \times 2$ matrix $\mathbf{V}$ as follows:

| | | *Next-period states* | |
|---|---|---|---|
| | | *High* | *Low* |
| Current-period states | High | $H_H$ | $H_L$ |
| | Low | $L_H$ | $L_L$ |

$H$ signifies high and $L$ signifies low. The current prices of \$1 received next period if the *present* state is "high" are $H_H$ and $H_L$, where the subscripts of the $H$ indicate the state obtaining *next* period. Thus, for example, $H_L$ is the value at time 0 (now) of a dollar received at time 1 if the current state is high and the state at time 1 is low. $L_H$ and $L_L$ are the current prices of \$1 next period if the current state is low ($L$). Now consider the matrix of state prices two periods from the present, which will be $\mathbf{V}^2$. We calculate $\mathbf{V}^2$ according to the rules of matrix multiplication.

$$\begin{aligned}\mathbf{V}^2 &= \mathbf{V} \cdot \mathbf{V} \\ &= \begin{bmatrix} H_H & H_L \\ L_H & L_L \end{bmatrix} \cdot \begin{bmatrix} H_H & H_L \\ L_H & L_L \end{bmatrix} \\ &= \begin{bmatrix} (H_H H_H + H_L L_H) & (H_H H_L + H_L L_L) \\ (L_H H_H + L_L L_H) & (L_H H_L + L_L L_L) \end{bmatrix}\end{aligned}$$

The rows of $\mathbf{V}^2$ remain associated with the current ($t = 0$) states, but the columns now refer to states two periods from now.

Thus the value of \$1 to be received two periods from now (at time 2), if state "high" occurs at time 2 given that "high" is the current state, is $(H_H H_H + H_L L_H)$. The economic explanation of this result can be seen by first considering ourselves forward in time to time 1. At time 1, the value of \$1 to be received at time 2 if "high" occurs at time 2 depends on what state we are in at time 1. If we are in "high" at time 1, then the time 1 value will be $H_H$, and if we are in "low" at time 1, then the time 1 value will be $L_H$, since $H_H$ and $L_H$ are the one-period state prices that are constant by assumption. We have transformed

[21] More precisely, $\mathbf{V}^T$ is derived from the repeated matrix multiplications:

$$\mathbf{V}^M = \mathbf{V} \cdot \mathbf{V}^{M-1}$$

For example, $\mathbf{V}^2 = \mathbf{V} \cdot \mathbf{V}$, $\mathbf{V}^3 = \mathbf{V} \cdot \mathbf{V}^2$, $\mathbf{V}^4 = \mathbf{V} \cdot \mathbf{V}^3$, etc.

the \$1 payoff at time 2 under state $H$ at time 2 to a set of equivalent payoffs in period 1, $H_H$ and $L_H$. Think of this as an asset which will pay off $H_H$ in period 1 if state $H$ occurs at time 1 and $L_H$ if state $L$ occurs at time 1. Now consider the time 0 value of this asset. Remember, we are examining prices for a current state of $H$. The present value (at time 0) of any asset which pays amount $Z_H$ at time 1 if state $H$ occurs at time 1 and pays amount $Z_L$ at time 1 if state $L$ occurs at time 1 is simply $H_H Z_H + H_L Z_L$ by our basic valuation rule, Eq. (10-10). For our "asset" $Z_H = H_H$ and $Z_L = L_H$ and its present value is therefore $H_H H_H + H_L H_H$ as described in matrix $\mathbf{V}^2$. Thus the repeated multiplication of the single-period matrix to obtain future-period state prices follows from the basic logic of the time-state system and assumptions 1 to 3 above.

Banz and Miller provide such time-state price matrices in their paper based on the best data available at that time. Our interest here is not to show how to replicate their work, but rather to explain the theoretical basis for it. The basic theory may be summarized as follows:

1. Given perfect capital markets with continuous trading, the prices of state-contingent claims (elementary securities) are implicit in option prices and these option prices must conform to specific valuation equations.
2. If states can be defined as ranges of the rate of return on the market portfolio and if the transition from one state to another is a stationary Markov process, then the state prices for any period in the future can be calculated from a matrix of single-period prices.
3. Given the state prices for future periods, the state-time payoffs from an investment can be valued using Eq. (10-10).

From the point of view of financial theory, the weakest link in the analysis is step 2 above. In this stage the basic theory is made operational via the assumptions of a specific stochastic process for the market portfolio and through use of ranges of rates of return to define states. Problems, both theoretical and empirical, abound here, and we expect further developments in this area.

## SUMMARY

This chapter has covered a broad range of topics centered on the problem of option valuation in continuous time. Continuous-time analysis under uncertainty uses two types of stochastic process to model the cash flows of assets—diffusion processes in which random movements occur continuously over time and jump processes in which changes occur abruptly. In continuous-time analysis capital markets are assumed to be always open for trading so that investors can adjust their asset portfolios whenever they desire to do so.

Options are contracts enabling the owner either to buy or to sell an asset at a stated price during the period of the contract. The analysis focused on call options—the right to purchase common stock at a fixed exercise price. In general the value of an option is the present value of the expected difference between the price of the stock and the exercise price. Under certainty with perfect markets the value of a call option is simply the current price of the stock minus the present value of the exercise price. Under uncertainty with perfect markets and a simple continuous diffusion process assumed for the rate of return on the stock, the value of an option depends on five variables—the stock price, the exercise price of the option, maturity date of the option, the instantaneous variance of the stock's rate of return, and the riskless rate of interest.

The option-pricing model is being applied to many problems of asset valuation. Common stock can be viewed as an option on the total firm. The model has also been used to develop a method of estimating prices for future cash payoffs contingent on the rate of return realized on the market portfolio. These time-state prices can then be used in the analysis of firm investment opportunities by providing an estimate of the present value of the future cash returns from an investment.

APPENDIX

# TEN A

# STOCHASTIC CALCULUS AND DERIVATION OF THE OPTION-PRICING MODEL

Stochastic calculus is simply the mathematics of continuous-time random variables. Here we provide an elementary introduction to some of the basic concepts and procedures of stochastic calculus and use these concepts to derive the option-pricing model. Our interest is not to make the reader a competent user of the mathematics. Our purpose is to provide a general familiarity with the concepts so that research papers using them are not totally obscure. In addition we develop the option-pricing model so that its theoretical structure may be better understood. We begin with a brief review of ordinary calculus. Throughout we are assuming continuous time as per our discussion at the beginning of Chap. 10.

## DERIVATIVES AND DIFFERENTIAL EQUATIONS

### Functions of One Variable

In ordinary calculus we know how to determine the derivative of a continuous function. That is, given some function $f(x)$ we can differentiate the function with respect to $x$ to find its derivative expressed as $df/dx$. For example, if

$$f(x) = e^{ax}$$

$$\frac{df}{dx} = ae^{ax} \qquad (10A\text{-}1)$$

The derivative measures the rate of change in the function as $x$ changes. The first derivative has a geometric interpretation as the slope of the function at $x$. We can differentiate derivatives to generate higher-order derivatives. For example, the second derivative of $e^{ax}$ is

$$\frac{d^2f}{dx^2} = \frac{d(df/dx)}{dx} = a^2e^{ax}$$

We can also use derivatives to estimate the impact of small changes in the independent variable ($x$). If we wish to determine the change in $f(x)$, $\Delta f$, for a small change in $x$, $\Delta x$, $\Delta f$ will be approximately equal to the derivative times $\Delta x$.

$$\Delta f = \frac{df}{dx}\,\Delta x = (ae^{ax})\,\Delta x \qquad \text{(10A-2)}$$

This points out that $df/dx$ is a ratio of the two differentials $df$ and $dx$ where $\Delta f$ approaches $df$ as $\Delta x$ approaches $dx$ ($\Delta x \rightarrow 0$). Therefore, for small $\Delta$'s we could write (10A-1) as

$$df = ae^{ax}dx \qquad \text{(10A-3)}$$

## Functions of Two Variables

Now consider functions of two variables $x$ and $y$. Let $G(x,y)$ be such a function. There are two types of derivatives for such functions, partial derivatives and total derivatives. A partial derivative indicates how the function changes as *one* of the variables changes, assuming all other variables in the function do not change (are held constant). The partial derivatives of $G$ with respect to one of the variables are taken by using the normal rules of differentiation with the other variable being treated as a constant. For example, let

$$G(x,y) = e^{xy}$$

Then the partial derivatives are

$$\frac{\partial G}{\partial x} = ye^{xy}$$

$$\frac{\partial G}{\partial y} = xe^{xy}$$

For any given value of $y$, we could use the partial derivative $\partial G/\partial x$ to estimate $\Delta G$ for a $\Delta x$ as we did before. We can use $\partial G/\partial y$ in a similar fashion. Suppose that we wished to estimate the change in $G$, $\Delta G$, when both $x$ and $y$ are changing by $\Delta x$ and $\Delta y$. We can do this using the following relationship for the differential of $G$, $dG$:

$$dG = \frac{\partial G}{\partial x}\,dx + \frac{\partial G}{\partial y}\,dy \qquad \text{(10A-4)}$$

$$\Delta G = \frac{\partial G}{\partial x}\,\Delta x + \frac{\partial G}{\partial y}\,\Delta y \qquad \text{(10A-5)}$$

Equation (10A-4) is an exact expression; Eq. (10A-5) is an approximation which becomes exact [becomes (10A-4)] as $\Delta x$ and $\Delta y$ approach zero. Equation (10A-4) provides the basic relationship for derivatives of functions of more than one variable. Note that the *total* derivative of $G$ with respect to $x$, $dG/dx$, is simply

$$\frac{dG}{dx} = \frac{\partial G}{\partial x} + \frac{\partial G}{\partial y}\frac{dy}{dx}$$

In order to go further, we must specify how $y$ changes with $x$.

In some cases $x$ and $y$ are both related to a third variable such as time $t$. $G$ then varies with $t$ because of its dependence on $x$ and $y$. If we would like to know how $G$ changes with time, $dG/dt$, we could substitute for $x$ and $y$ to obtain $G$ as a function of $t$ or we can use (10A-4) to obtain

$$\frac{dG}{dt} = \frac{\partial G}{\partial x}\frac{dx}{dt} + \frac{\partial G}{\partial y}\frac{dy}{dt} \tag{10A-6}$$

## Differential Equations

Suppose that we know, hypothesize, or observe that the derivative (rate of change) of a function has some particular form. For example, suppose that we observe the savings account balance in our bank. Despite our not adding to it or withdrawing money from it, the account increases because the bank is paying interest at a rate of 5% per year "continuously compounded." We find that for a small interval $\Delta t$, the change in the account $\Delta A$ is

$$\Delta A = .05\, A\, \Delta t \tag{10A-7}$$

where $t$ is measured in years. We wish to know the value of the account at the end of $n$ years given that we began with $A_0$ in the account at $t = 0$. (The specification of $A = A_0$ at $t = 0$ is called the initial conditions.) We can express (10A-7) in differential form because the continuous compounding assumption is interpreted as compounding over very small intervals of time, that is, $t \rightarrow 0$. Therefore, (10A-7) can be rewritten as

$$dA = .05\, A\, dt \tag{10A-8a}$$

or

$$\frac{dA}{dt} = .05\, A \tag{10A-8b}$$

or, in a slightly different notation which is quite common, let $dA/dt \equiv A'$; then

$$A' = .05\, A \tag{10A-8c}$$

Equations (10A-8*a*), (10A-8*b*), and (10A-8*c*) are alternative forms of the same differential equation; that is, they involve the derivative of a function. The solution to a differential equation is the unknown function, in this case the value of a continuously compounded savings account with a constant interest rate. In other words, we would like to find the unknown function $f(n)$ such that $A = f(n)$ is a solution to (10A-8*a*), (10A-8*b*), and (10A-8*c*). Basically there are two general procedures for solving differential equations: (1) integration of the components of the equation or (2) systematic search, trial and error, and luck. There are a variety of mathematical techniques which aid in method (2), but these need not concern us here. The solution to a differential equation is a problem in mathematics (really more of an art than a science); establishing the equation is the financial part. Method (1) works well when it works but often cannot be used.

In our example, we can integrate the components as follows:

$$dA = .05\,A\,dt \qquad \text{(10A-8}a\text{)}$$

$$\left(\frac{1}{A}\right) dA = .05\,dt$$

$$\int_{A_0}^{A_n} \frac{1}{A}\,dA = \int_0^n .05\,dt$$

$$\ln A_n - \ln A_0 = .05\,n$$

$$\ln\left(\frac{A_n}{A_0}\right) = .05\,n$$

$$\frac{A_n}{A_0} = e^{.05\,n}$$

$$A_n = A_0\,e^{.05\,n} \qquad \text{(10A-9)}$$

Thus we develop an expression (function) for the value of the account after $n$ years which is the solution of our problem. If we let $i$ be the interest rate per period, we have a general expression for the value of an investment compounding continuously for $n$ periods

$$A_n = A_0 e^{in} \qquad \text{(10A-10)}$$

[See Appendix 2B for an alternative development of (10A-10).]

Differential equations have a vast number of applications in the physical and biological sciences and some in economics, but relatively few to date in finance. Our simple example is meant merely to illustrate the concept. Let us now go on to stochastic calculus. First we discuss the properties of random variables in continuous time.

## RANDOM VARIABLES IN CONTINUOUS TIME

Consider a random variable $\tilde{x}(t)$. At any point in time $t$, the value of $\tilde{x}(t)$ is uncertain; that is, $\tilde{x}(t)$ may take on different values $x_1(t)$, $x_2(t)$, etc. In general the probability distributions which describe the likelihood of occurrence of $x_i(t)$

must be defined at each point in time $t$. If the probability distribution does not change over time, the distribution is said to be *stationary*. The random variable $\tilde{x}(t)$ may be either a discrete or a continuous variable.

Variables such as $\tilde{x}(t)$ which are both uncertain and changing through time are called *stochastic processes*.[22] If the variable $\tilde{x}(t)$ can be observed only at periodic points in time, it is called a *discrete-time* stochastic process. An example would be the dividend payments of a corporation which occur only quarterly. If we can observe values of $\tilde{x}(t)$ at any point in time, $\tilde{x}(t)$ is called a *continuous-time* stochastic process or diffusion process. An example of a continuous-time stochastic process is the total cash assets of a multinational corporation which vary continuously because offices somewhere in the world are open for business all the time. Note that $\tilde{x}(t)$ itself may be either discrete or continuous regardless of the timing. Stochastic calculus deals with continuous-time stochastic processes, and here we shall consider only variables of the continuous type.[23] Our discussion from this point on, therefore, assumes the continuous-time, continuous-variable case.

## Wiener Processes

The starting point for an understanding of stochastic calculus and its finance applications is a simple stochastic process called the Wiener process. Intuitively, such processes are "purely random." More formally, let the stochastic process $\tilde{\epsilon}(t)$ have the following characteristics:

(1) $\tilde{\epsilon}(t)$ is normally distributed with expected value of zero and variance of 1.0, each $t$.
(2) For any two times, $t_i$ and $t_j$, $i \neq j$, the covariance (correlation) between $\tilde{\epsilon}(t_i)$ and $\tilde{\epsilon}(t_j)$ is zero.

Thus $\tilde{\epsilon}(t)$ has the same distribution for all $t$ (is stationary) and values for $\tilde{\epsilon}(t)$ at any two points in time or over any two nonoverlapping small intervals are statistically independent.

Now consider a process $\tilde{z}(t)$ and its value after some small interval $\Delta t$. Assume that

$$\tilde{z}(t + \Delta t) = z(t) + \tilde{\epsilon}(t) \sqrt{\Delta t}$$

or

$$\Delta \tilde{z}(t) = \tilde{\epsilon}(t) \sqrt{\Delta t} \qquad (10A\text{-}11)$$

[22] Our discussion and terminology are based largely on that used by Cox and Miller, listed in the references for this Appendix. Some authors restrict the term "stochastic process" to continuous variables and use "stochastic sequence" to describe discrete variables.

[23] Mathematics are available for dealing with discrete variables in continuous time. Discrete stochastic processes are often called "jump processes" (as we discussed in chap. 10) and are usually modeled with a Poisson distribution.

The expected value of $\Delta\tilde{z}(t)$, $E[\Delta\tilde{z}(t)]$, is zero since the expected value of $\tilde{\epsilon}(t)$ is zero for all $t$. The variance of $\Delta\tilde{z}(t)$ is

$$\begin{aligned}\text{var}\,[\Delta\tilde{z}(t)] &= E[\{\Delta\tilde{z}(t) - E[\Delta\tilde{z}(t)]\}^2] \\ &= E[\Delta\tilde{z}(t)^2] \\ &= E[(\tilde{\epsilon}(t)\sqrt{\Delta t})^2] \\ &= \Delta t\, E[\tilde{\epsilon}(t)^2] \\ &= \Delta t\ \text{var}\,[\tilde{\epsilon}(t)] \\ &= \Delta t \end{aligned} \tag{10A-12}$$

Thus we can interpret (10A-11) as an assumption that changes in $\tilde{z}(t)$ are proportional to their standard deviation, $\sqrt{\Delta t}$. As $\Delta t$ becomes very small, we can express (10A-11) in differential form (dropping the $t$ in parentheses to simplify our notation slightly)

$$d\tilde{z} = \tilde{\epsilon}\sqrt{dt} \tag{10A-13}$$

Equation (10A-13) is a stochastic differential equation and is the definitional equation for the basic Wiener process $\tilde{z}$. At any time $t$, $\tilde{z}$ has a normal distribution with expected value (mean) of zero and variance of $t$.[24] Thus, from a given initial point at $t = 0$, the uncertainty in the value of $\tilde{z}$ increases with time $t$. A fundamental attribute of this process is that $d\tilde{z}^2 = dt$ with probability of 1.0. This attribute is due to the assumed continuity of the process.[25]

Given the basic Wiener process $\tilde{z}$, we can develop more general Wiener processes which have expected values other than zero and variances other than $t$. The general Wiener process $\tilde{x}$ is described by the following stochastic differential equation which is often used as a model of the rate of return on stock.

$$d\tilde{x} = a\,dt + b\,d\tilde{z} \tag{10A-14}$$

[24] The normality of $\tilde{z}$ follows from the normality of $\tilde{\epsilon}$. Further we assume as a convention that $\tilde{z}$ at $t = 0$ is zero. Thus, from (10A-12),

$$\text{var}\,[z(t)] = \int_0^t dt = t$$

[25] This can be shown by examining the variance of $d\tilde{z}^2$. From (10A-13) we have

$$\begin{aligned} d\tilde{z}^2 &= (\tilde{\epsilon}\sqrt{dt})^2 \\ &= \tilde{\epsilon}^2 dt \end{aligned}$$

The expected value of $d\tilde{z}^2$ is

$$E[d\tilde{z}^2] = E[\tilde{\epsilon}^2 dt] = E[\tilde{\epsilon}^2]\,dt = dt$$

since $E[\tilde{\epsilon}^2]$ is simply var $[\tilde{\epsilon}]$, which is 1.0 by assumption. The variance of $d\tilde{z}^2$ is

$$\begin{aligned}\text{var}\,[d\tilde{z}^2] &= E[(d\tilde{z}^2 - E[d\tilde{z}^2])^2] \\ &= E[(\tilde{\epsilon}^2 dt - dt)^2] \\ &= E[\tilde{\epsilon}^4 dt^2 - 2\tilde{\epsilon}^2 dt^2 + dt^2] \\ &= dt^2\, E[\tilde{\epsilon}^4 - 2\tilde{\epsilon}^2 + 1] \end{aligned}$$

But $dt^2$ is effectively zero ($\Delta t^2$ vanishes before $\Delta t$ does as $\Delta t \to 0$). Therefore, the variance of $d\tilde{z}^2$ is zero. If the variance is zero, $d\tilde{z}^2 = E[d\tilde{z}^2] = dt$ with probability $= 1.0$.

where $d\tilde{z}$ is as defined by Eq. (10A-13) and $a$ and $b$ are constants. The process $\tilde{x}$ is a Wiener process with *drift* $a$ and variance $b^2$. The expected value of $d\tilde{x}$ is $a\,dt$. The drift, $a$, is often called the expected *instantaneous* rate of change of $\tilde{x}$ and is often denoted as $\mu$. Similarly, the instantaneous standard deviation of the change in $\tilde{x}$ is $b$ and is often denoted as $\nu$. From the condition that $d\tilde{z}^2 = dt$, we also have $d\tilde{x}^2 = b^2\,dt$ with probability of 1.0. From (10A-14) we see that Wiener processes are "smooth" in the sense that no abrupt changes in $\tilde{x}$ will occur within small intervals of time.

Given a value for $\tilde{x}$ of $x_0$ at $t = 0$, the expected value at time $t$ is

$$E[\tilde{x}_t] = x_0 + a\,t \tag{10A-15}$$

and the variance at time $t$ is

$$\text{var}\,[\tilde{x}_t] = b^2 t \tag{10A-16}$$

From an initial value of $x_0$, the process $\tilde{x}$ "drifts" through time around a possible trend line (10A-15), but the actual movement becomes difficult to predict (uncertain) as time into the future increases (10A-16). Both $a$ and $b$ are constants for Wiener processes. The basic Wiener process $\tilde{z}$ can be considered to be a special case of the general form with $a = 0$, $b = 1.0$.

Therefore, when someone assumes a particular variable (such as a stock's rate of return) to be described by a Wiener process (or Brownian motion) with given instantaneous mean (or drift) and variance, they are asserting that the variable has the form of (10A-14).[26]

## Itô Processes

Using our concept of Wiener processes, we can now examine more complex and general types of stochastic processes called Itô processes after the mathematician K. Itô who first examined their properties.[27] Consider the following stochastic differential equation

$$d\tilde{x} = m(x,t)dt + s(x,t)d\tilde{z} \tag{10A-17}$$

Again $\tilde{z}$ is the basic Wiener process. Compare (10A-17) with (10A-14). The differences are that instead of having a constant mean $a$, we now have a function of $x$ and $t$, $m(x,t)$, and instead of a constant standard deviation $b$, we have a function of $x$ and $t$, $s(x,t)$. However, these functions have the same interpreta-

[26] There is some confusion in the literature regarding the use of such terms as "Wiener processes," "Brownian motion," "diffusion processes," and "white noise." Some people use these terms interchangeably; others distinguish one from another. We consider Brownian motion and white noise to be processes found in nature that may be described by a Wiener process which is a formal (mathematical) model. Here we focus on the mathematical model. A diffusion process is a general term describing continuous stochastic variables in continuous time.

[27] K. Itô, On Stochastic Differential Equations, *Memoirs, American Mathematical Society*, no. 4, pp. 1–51, 1951.

tions as before, that of the instantaneous expected value [$a$ or $m(x,t)$] and standard deviation [$b$ or $s(x,t)$]. Now, however, the mean and standard deviations are no longer constants but may vary with $x$ and $t$. A variable $\tilde{x}$ which conforms to (10A-17) is said to follow an Itô process. When $m(x,t)$ and $s(x,t)$ are constants, $\tilde{x}$ is a Wiener process; thus Wiener processes are special cases of Itô processes.

We can also have Itô processes involving more than the two variables $x$ and $t$. For example, let $\tilde{x}$ and $\tilde{y}$ be Itô processes. Then, in general,

$$d\tilde{x} = m_x(x,y,t)dt + s_x(x,y,t)d\tilde{z}_x \tag{10A-18}$$

$$d\tilde{y} = m_y(x,y,t)dt + s_y(x,y,t)d\tilde{z}_y \tag{10A-19}$$

where the $x$ and $y$ subscripts indicate that the functions may differ for $x$ and $y$. The instantaneous expected rate of change in $\tilde{x}$ depends on $x$, $y$, and $t$ as described by $m_x(x,y,t)$, and so on. Note that we now distinguish $\tilde{z}_x$ from $\tilde{z}_y$. Therefore, there must be corresponding random variables $\tilde{\epsilon}_x$ and $\tilde{\epsilon}_y$, both normally distributed with expected values of zero and variances of 1.0. However, $\tilde{\epsilon}_x$ and $\tilde{\epsilon}_y$ may be correlated with each other; that is, cov $[\tilde{\epsilon}_x,\tilde{\epsilon}_y]$ need not be zero. Since the variances and standard deviations of $\tilde{\epsilon}_x$ and $\tilde{\epsilon}_y$ all equal 1.0, cov $[\tilde{\epsilon}_x,\tilde{\epsilon}_y]$ is equal to the correlation coefficient $\rho_{xy}$ for the variables $\tilde{\epsilon}_x$ and $\tilde{\epsilon}_y$, which is the correlation between $\tilde{x}$ and $\tilde{y}$.[28]

## An Example

Assume that the instantaneous rate of return $d\tilde{r}$ on a share of common stock is a Wiener process with mean value $k$ and variance $s^2$; then

$$d\tilde{r} = k\,dt + s\,d\tilde{z} \tag{10A-20}$$

Let $P_t$ be the price per share at time $t$; then for a non-dividend-paying stock

$$d\tilde{r} = \frac{d\tilde{P}}{P_t} \tag{10A-21}$$

Combining (10A-20) and (10A-21), we have

$$\frac{d\tilde{P}}{P_t} = k\,dt + s\,d\tilde{z} \tag{10A-22a}$$

or equivalently,

[28] Intuitively, since the only sources of uncertainty for $\tilde{x}$ and $\tilde{y}$ are due to $\tilde{\epsilon}_x$ and $\tilde{\epsilon}_y$, the only way they can be correlated is through the correlation between $\tilde{\epsilon}_x$ and $\tilde{\epsilon}_y$. Furthermore, the correlation $\rho_{xy}$ must be constant through time since $\tilde{\epsilon}_x$ and $\tilde{\epsilon}_y$ are individually time independent. It is fairly easy to show that

$$\text{cov}\,[d\tilde{x},d\tilde{y}] = s_x(x,y,t)s_y(x,y,t)\,\text{cov}\,[\tilde{\epsilon}_x,\tilde{\epsilon}_y]$$

Therefore,

$$\rho_{xy} = \text{cov}\,[\tilde{\epsilon}_x,\tilde{\epsilon}_y]$$

$$d\tilde{P} = kP_t\,dt + sP_t\,d\tilde{z} \tag{10A-22b}$$

Thus (10A-22*b*) indicates that the stock price is described by an Itô process of the form of (10A-17) with

$$m(P,t) = k\,P_t \qquad \text{and} \qquad s(P,t) = s\,P_t \tag{10A-23}$$

The stochastic process describing the stock price, given (10A-20) and (10A-21), is therefore a very simple Itô process since $k$ and $s$ are constants. This form for stock prices is often called "geometric Brownian motion" and is the continuous-time version of the "random-walk hypothesis" (which applies to discrete time).[29]

The model of stock prices expressed by (10A-22) is widely used for theoretical analysis and, as indicated by the references in the last footnote, has been empirically tested. We cannot solve stochastic differential equations as simply as we can the nonstochastic variety, but the solution to (10A-22) is known to be

$$\tilde{P}_t = P_0\,e^{[(k-s^2/2)t+sz_t]} \tag{10A-24}$$

or

$$\ln\left[\frac{\tilde{P}_t}{P_0}\right] = \left(k - \frac{s^2}{2}\right)t + s\tilde{z}_t \tag{10A-25}$$

We prove (10A-24) is the solution to (10A-22) later in the Appendix.

Since $\tilde{z}_t$ has a normal distribution with expected value of zero and variance of $t$, the natural logarithm of the stock price has a normal distribution with an expected value of $(k - s^2/2)t$ and a variance of $s^2t$. Thus if stock prices follow geometric Brownian motion, they have a log-normal probability distribution. This is a reasonable probability distribution for stock prices since it is consistent with limited liability on the part of stockholders. The worst that can happen is that the stock price reaches zero; negative stock prices are not possible. Notice also what happens if $s = 0$; i.e., the stock is riskless. Equation (10A-22b) reduces to

$$\frac{dP}{P_t} = k\,dt \tag{10A-26}$$

and (10A-24) reduces to

$$P_t = P_0 e^{kt} \tag{10A-27}$$

which is consistent with our earlier solution in the case of certainty [see (10A-8) and (10A-10)].

[29] The random-walk hypothesis is now more broadly termed the "efficient markets hypothesis." See, for example, J. C. Francis, "Investments," 2d ed., chap. 21, McGraw-Hill Book Company, New York, 1977, for a discussion of the hypothesis and citations to the empirical literature. The first modern continuous-time investigation was carried out by M. F. M. Osborne, Brownian Motion in the Stock Market, *Operations Research,* vol. 7, pp. 145–73, March–April 1959.

## THE FUNDAMENTAL THEOREM OF STOCHASTIC CALCULUS

Given that we know something about stochastic processes, we are in a position to examine Itô's lemma, often called the fundamental theorem of stochastic calculus. Itô's lemma provides the basic rule for finding differentials for functions of stochastic variables. The parallel rule was shown for ordinary calculus as Eq. (10A-4). For reference, consider the total differential, $dF$, of a function $F(x,t)$, where $x$ is known with certainty. Applying (10A-4), we have

$$dF = \frac{\partial F}{\partial x}\,dx + \frac{\partial F}{\partial t}\,dt \tag{10A-28}$$

Now let us state Itô's lemma as it applies to functions of a single stochastic variable $\tilde{x}$.

### Itô's Lemma

Given the random variable $\tilde{x}$ which follows an Itô process defined as

$$d\tilde{x} = m(x,t)\,dt + s(x,t)\,d\tilde{z} \tag{10A-29}$$

function $F(x,t)$, which is differentiable in $t$ and twice differentiable in $x$, is the solution to the following stochastic differential equation:

$$d\tilde{F} = \frac{\partial F}{\partial x}\,d\tilde{x} + \frac{\partial F}{\partial t}\,dt + \frac{1}{2}\frac{\partial^2 F}{\partial x^2}\,(d\tilde{x})^2 \tag{10A-30}$$

Equivalently, by substitution of (10A-29) into (10A-30) and ignoring products of differentials (except for $d\tilde{z}^2$, since $d\tilde{z}^2 = dt$ so that it cannot be neglected), we obtain

$$d\tilde{F} = \left[\frac{\partial F}{\partial t} + \frac{\partial F}{\partial x}\,m(x,t) + \frac{1}{2}\frac{\partial^2 F}{\partial x^2}\,s(x,t)^2\right]dt + \frac{\partial F}{\partial x}\,s(x,t)\,d\tilde{z} \tag{10A-31}$$

[It would be useful as an exercise to develop (10A-31) from (10A-29) and (10A-30).]

Comparing (10A-28), the certainty case, with (10A-30), we see that the only difference is in the addition of a term involving the second partial derivative of $F$ with respect to $x$. In ordinary calculus the higher-order derivatives do not appear because they would involve squared differentials and products of differentials which vanish at the limit. In stochastic calculus, terms involving $d\tilde{z}^2$ do not vanish because $d\tilde{z}^2 = dt$ by the nature of the stochastic processes involved.

There is a general form of the theorem which applies to functions of any number of Itô processes. We shall state it without further discussion for reference purposes. The single-variable form will be adequate for this appendix.

## General Form of Itô's Lemma

Let $\tilde{x}_i$ be a set of Itô processes, $i = 1, \ldots, n$, with

$$d\tilde{x}_i = m_i(x_1, \ldots, x_n, t)\, dt + s_i(x_1, \ldots, x_n, t)\, d\tilde{z}_i$$

Then function $F(x_1, \ldots, x_n, t)$ assumed twice differentiable in $x_i$ solves the stochastic differential equation

$$d\tilde{F} = \sum_{i=1}^{n} \frac{\partial F}{\partial x_i} d\tilde{x}_i + \frac{\partial F}{\partial t} dt + \frac{1}{2} \sum_{i=1}^{n} \sum_{j=1}^{n} \frac{\partial^2 F}{\partial x_i\, \partial x_j} d\tilde{x}_i\, d\tilde{x}_j$$

where $d\tilde{x}_i\, d\tilde{x}_j$ are determined by the rules

$$d\tilde{z}_i\, d\tilde{z}_j = \rho_{ij}\, dt$$

$$d\tilde{z}_i\, dt = 0$$

and $\rho_{ij}$ is the coefficient of correlation between $d\tilde{z}_i$ and $d\tilde{z}_j$ ($\tilde{\epsilon}_i$ and $\tilde{\epsilon}_j$).

## Discussion and Example

Itô's lemma can be used in several ways. It can be used to check the solutions to a stochastic differential equation. That is, given a function which is claimed to be the solution to a stochastic differential equation, we use Itô's lemma in trying to replicate the equation. It is also used to develop stochastic differential equations for functions of random variables which are described by Itô processes. We shall use it in this section to check our solution to the common stock price relationship of (10A-22*b*). In the next section we shall use it to develop the option-pricing model.

Equation (10A-24) was said to be the solution of the stochastic differential equation of (10A-22*b*)

$$d\tilde{P} = kP_t\, dt + sP_t\, d\tilde{z} \qquad \text{(10A-22}b\text{)}$$

$$\tilde{P}_t = P_0 e^{[(k - s^2/2)t + s\tilde{z}_t]} \qquad \text{(10A-24)}$$

Let us apply Itô's lemma (10A-30) to (10A-24) and see whether we come up with (10A-22*b*). Let $P = F(t,z)$; then by Itô's lemma, $d\tilde{P}$ must be

$$d\tilde{P} = \frac{\partial F}{\partial z} d\tilde{z} + \frac{\partial F}{\partial t} dt + \frac{1}{2} \frac{\partial^2 F}{\partial z^2} d\tilde{z}^2 \qquad \text{(10A-32)}$$

From (10A-24) the partial derivatives are

$$\frac{\partial F}{\partial z} = sP \qquad \frac{\partial^2 F}{\partial z^2} = s^2 P \qquad \frac{\partial F}{\partial t} = \left(k - \frac{s^2}{2}\right) P$$

Substituting the derivatives into (10A-32), we obtain

$$d\tilde{P} = sP\, d\tilde{z} + \left(k - \frac{s^2}{2}\right) P\, dt + \frac{1}{2} s^2 P\, d\tilde{z}^2$$

but $d\tilde{z}^2 = dt$; therefore, canceling terms, we obtain (10A-22*b*).

## THE OPTION-PRICING MODEL

The option-pricing model presented in Chap. 10 is a simple application of Itô's lemma to a nicely developed problem in finance. Financial theory combined with the formal mathematics produces a stochastic differential equation for the option-pricing function. In this section we develop the differential equation for the price of a call option which was obtained first by Black and Scholes. The basic assumptions and the solution were provided in Chap. 10.

Let $P$ be the price per share of stock, $W$ be the price of a call option (warrant), and $I$ be the value of the net investment in stock and options. Suppose that we form a portfolio consisting of $n_s$ shares of stock owned and $n_0$ call options sold against the stock. Then the net value of the position at any time $t$ is

$$I_t = n_{st}P_t - n_{0t}W_t \tag{10A-33}$$

Dividing (10A-33) through by $n_{st}$, the investment per share of stock held would be

$$\frac{I_t}{n_{st}} = P_t - \frac{n_{0t}}{n_{st}} W_t \tag{10A-34}$$

Let $\alpha$ be the ratio of options sold to shares of stock held at any time $t$; then (10A-34) becomes

$$\frac{I_t}{n_{st}} = P_t - \alpha_t W_t \tag{10A-35}$$

The change in the net position per share of common stock is

$$\Delta\left(\frac{I_t}{n_{st}}\right) = \Delta P_t - \alpha_t \Delta W_t - W_t \Delta\alpha_t \tag{10A-36}$$

$W_t \Delta\alpha_t$ measures the change in the net position due to changes in the number of shares held (or options written). In other words, $W_t \Delta\alpha_t$ is the amount of added investment or disinvestment in the position. The net return on the position is the total change in value of the position [as in (10A-36)] plus any funds withdrawn, or less any additional funds invested. With $\Delta\alpha > 0$, funds are being withdrawn since the number of options sold are increasing relative to the number of shares held long and vice versa. Therefore, the net return $\Delta R_t$ is

$$\begin{aligned} \Delta R_t &= \Delta\left[\frac{I_t}{n_{st}}\right] + W_t \Delta\alpha_t \\ &= \Delta P_t - \alpha_t \Delta W_t \end{aligned} \tag{10A-37a}$$

or, in differential form,

$$dR_t = dP_t - \alpha_t dW_t \tag{10A-37b}$$

We are interested only in the changes in the net position due to changes in the prices of the stock and the option. In a perfect market, additions and withdrawals from the portfolio ($W_t \Delta\alpha_t$) are not important, as funds can be freely borrowed or invested at the riskless interest rate.

We now would like to investigate the characteristics of $dR$ (for notational simplicity, we shall drop the $t$ subscript in this discussion). We begin by assuming that the instantaneous rate of return on the stock price is a Wiener process (geometric Brownian motion) as discussed above (no dividends are paid on the stock).

$$\frac{d\tilde{P}}{P} = k\,dt + s\,d\tilde{z} \tag{10A-38}$$

or

$$d\tilde{P} = k\,P\,dt + sP\,d\tilde{z} \tag{10A-39}$$

As we noted above, $\tilde{P}$ follows an Itô process. Furthermore we assume (assert) that the price of an option in the stock depends only on the price of the stock and time, all other factors being constants. Thus

$$\tilde{W} = W(\tilde{P},t)$$

Use Itô's lemma and (10A-39) to find $d\tilde{W}$,

$$\begin{aligned} d\tilde{W} &= \frac{\partial W}{\partial P}\,d\tilde{P} + \frac{\partial W}{\partial t}\,dt + \frac{1}{2}\frac{\partial^2 W}{\partial P^2}\,d\tilde{P}^2 \\ &= \frac{\partial W}{\partial P}(k\,P\,dt + sP\,d\tilde{z}) + \frac{\partial W}{\partial t}\,dt + \frac{1}{2}\frac{\partial^2 W}{\partial P^2}\,s^2P^2\,dt \end{aligned} \tag{10A-40}$$

Now substitute for $d\tilde{P}$ using (10A-39) and for $d\tilde{W}$ using (10A-40) into (10A-37*b*), to obtain

$$\begin{aligned} dR = \left(1 - \alpha\,\frac{\partial W}{\partial P}\right)k\,P\,dt + \left(1 - \alpha\,\frac{\partial W}{\partial P}\right)sP\,d\tilde{z} \\ - \alpha\left(\frac{\partial W}{\partial t} + \frac{1}{2}\frac{\partial^2 W}{\partial P^2}\,s^2P^2\right)dt \end{aligned} \tag{10A-41}$$

From (10A-41) we can see that if $\alpha = 1(\partial W/\partial P)$, the first two terms in (10A-41) become zero. Notice that the only term involving $d\tilde{z}$ is one of those two. Suppose that we do set $\alpha = 1/(\partial W/\partial P)$; we then obtain

$$dR = -\alpha\left(\frac{\partial W}{\partial t} + \frac{1}{2}\frac{\partial^2 W}{\partial P^2}\,s^2P^2\right)dt \tag{10A-42}$$

Question: Is $dR$ a random variable in (10A-42)? The answer is no, since the only potential source of uncertainty was $d\tilde{z}$ and $d\tilde{z}$ has been eliminated. Therefore, if the portfolio is continuously adjusted so that $\alpha = 1/(\partial W/\partial P)$, the investment is riskless, and the return on a riskless investment must equal the riskless rate of interest. Assume the instantaneous riskless rate $i$ is a constant over time. The amount invested (net position per share) at any time is $(P - \alpha W)$. The instantaneous return on the position, $dR$, must be

$$dR = i(P - \alpha W) \tag{10A-43}$$

Substituting for $dR$ on the left side of (10A-43) using (10A-42), and using $\alpha = 1/(\partial W/\partial P)$ on the right side of (10A-43), we have

$$-\frac{1}{\partial W/\partial P}\left(\frac{\partial W}{\partial t}+\frac{1}{2}\frac{\partial^2 W}{\partial P^2}s^2P^2\right)=i\left(P-\frac{W}{\partial W/\partial P}\right)$$

and solving for $\partial W/\partial t$ we obtain

$$\frac{\partial W}{\partial t}=iW-iP\frac{\partial W}{\partial P}-\frac{1}{2}s^2P^2\frac{\partial^2 W}{\partial P^2} \tag{10A-44}$$

Equation (10A-44) is a nonstochastic differential equation and is, with appropriate changes in notation, identical to Black and Scholes' Eq. 7.[30]

Black and Scholes then provide us with a solution for the differential equation of (10A-44) using the conditions that the value of the option at maturity must be either the stock price minus the call price when the difference is greater than zero or zero when it is not. Obtaining solutions to such equations, as we noted earlier, is often difficult to do; however, the problem at this point becomes an exercise in ordinary calculus.[31] The solution and its properties were discussed in Chap. 10. The interesting part of the development was finished when we reached (10A-44).

## REFERENCES FOR ADDITIONAL STUDY

The person who wishes to go further into stochastic calculus and its applications to finance will find several sources helpful. We should note first that Itô's lemma is only the starting point. The next concept of importance is the "maximum principle." This principle or theorem is used to determine optimal decision rules for a stochastic process. Further study leads into modifications of Itô's lemma as it applies to discrete variables and into a corresponding maximum principle.

As starting points the following articles provide example applications:

Fischer, S.: The Demand for Index Bonds, *Journal of Political Economy,* June 1975; see especially Appendix 1.

Merton, R.: Optimum Consumption and Portfolio Rules in a Continuous Time Model, *Journal of Economic Theory,* vol. 3, pp. 373–413, December 1971.

Merton, R.: An Intertemporal Capital Asset Pricing Model, *Econometrica,* vol. 41, pp. 867–887, September 1973.

[30] Black and Scholes, *op. cit.,* p. 643.

[31] There is another way to develop a solution which is described by Smith, *op. cit.,* pp. 22–23, as due to Cox and Ross. From inspection of (10A-44), we note that there are no variables related to the degree of risk aversion of investors (except indirectly through the stock price). Therefore, the solution must be the same regardless of any risk premiums in the market. The Cox and Ross method is to treat the problem as if investors are risk neutral and therefore the expected rates of return on the option and the stock are equal to the riskless rate. Given the probability distribution of the stock price (10A-24) with $k = i$, we find the expected future value of the option and discount that value back to the present ($t = 0$) at $i$. This produces the option-pricing formula (10-9). This general method can be applied to other problems in which a riskless (hedged) position can be established.

For mathematics, the following books are useful:

Arnold, L.: "Stochastic Differential Equations," John Wiley & Sons, Inc., New York, 1974.
Astrom, K.: "Introduction to Stochastic Control Theory," Academic Press, Inc., New York, 1970.
Cox, D. R. and H. D. Miller: "The Theory of Stochastic Processes," Chapman & Hall, Ltd., London, 1965.
Gihman, I. and A. Skorohod: "Stochastic Differential Equations," Springer-Verlag Inc., New York, New York, 1972.
Kushner, H.: "Introduction to Stochastic Control," New York: Holt, Rinehart and Winston, Inc., New York, 1972.

## SUGGESTED READINGS

Black, Fischer: Fact and Fantasy in the Use of Options, *Financial Analysts Journal,* vol. 31, pp. 36–72, July–August 1975.
Black, Fischer and Myron Scholes: The Valuation of Option Contracts and a Test of Market Efficiency, *Journal of Finance,* vol. 27, pp. 399–417, May 1972.
———: The Pricing of Options and Corporate Liabilities, *Journal of Political Economy,* vol. 81, pp. 637–654, May–June 1973.
Kruizenga, Richard: Introduction to the Option Contract, in P. Cootner (ed.), "The Random Character of Stock Prices," pp. 377–391, The M.I.T. Press, Boston, 1964.
Merton, Robert: Theory of Finance from the Perspective of Continuous Time, *Journal of Financial and Quantitative Analysis,* vol. 10, pp. 659–674, November 1975.
———: Theory of Rational Option Pricing, *Bell Journal of Economics and Management Science,* vol. 4, pp. 141–183, spring 1973.
Smith, Clifford: Option Pricing, *Journal of Financial Economics,* vol. 3, pp. 3–51, January 1976.

CHAPTER

# ELEVEN

# FINANCING DECISIONS IN PERFECT MARKETS

Given the firm's investment policy, management must determine the means of financing. The issue of how investment policy is affected by financing is developed in Chaps. 12 to 16. The question considered in this chapter is how financing decisions affect the value of the firm to its shareholders. We examine this problem here under assumptions of perfect markets, and we are concerned only with the general categories of retained earnings, common stock, and debt as the means of financing. In Chaps. 14 and 15 we consider the impact of various market imperfections on the financing decision. The use of such financial instruments as preferred stock, convertible bonds, and negotiated loans will also be discussed there. In Chap. 16 leasing as a method of financing is examined. The present chapter provides a basic structure that is helpful in understanding the more complicated situations discussed later.

## FINANCING DECISIONS IN GENERAL

The financing decisions of the firm can be viewed as two related problems: financing tactics and financing policy. *Financing tactics* will be used to refer to the choice of particular means of financing in the current period, i.e., the financing of the current capital budget. Under the simplified assumptions of our analysis all such financing takes place at time 0. The possibilities for the financing to be examined in this chapter are retained earnings, new shares, or debt, either individually or in combination. *Financing policy* refers to the question of what the long-run appropriate mix of financing should be. If the current financing decision is irrelevant (financing tactics do not affect the value of the firm), then presumably the long-run financing mix is irrelevant. On the other hand, when financing tactics affect value so will financing policy. Typical discussions of the effect of financing on the value of the firm are presented in terms of financing policy; however, so far we have focused in this text on financing tactics. The basic theoretical issues of financing decisions are common to both policy and tactics. To apply the theory to the practical problems facing management there is considerable advantage in distinguishing between the two. We shall discuss some tactical issues in Chap. 14. In the present chapter the proofs of propositions on the choice between debt and equity as the means of financing will be expressed in terms of financing policy. Dividend policy also will be viewed as part of the firm's financing policy, in particular as the choice between paying out dividends and selling new shares to finance investment or using internally generated funds to finance investment and thereby curtailing dividends. Before proceeding with the discussion of particular financing methods, let us examine the general question of financing in taxless, perfect markets.

## THE IRRELEVANCE OF THE FINANCING DECISION WITH NO TAXES

The basic proposition to be developed in this section is that the financing decisions of the firm do not affect the total market value of the firm's cash flows in perfect markets with no taxes, assuming a given investment policy. The perfect-market assumption means that both individuals and firms can transact freely in the financial markets with no costs and with no systematic differences in information available.[1] In addition there are no transaction costs associated with financial distress (i.e., no legal costs, delays, etc., associated with insolvency, reorganization, or liquidation).[2] The complete set of assumptions we use as constituting perfect markets is shown in Table 11-1. Under these conditions a given investment policy implies that the firm's net cash flows over time are given. This flow is

$$\tilde{\mathbf{Y}} = (\tilde{Y}_1, \tilde{Y}_2, \tilde{Y}_3, \ldots) = \tilde{X}_1 - \tilde{I}_1, \tilde{X}_2 - \tilde{I}_2, \tilde{X}_3 - \tilde{I}_3, \ldots)$$

[1] There are some important implications of the condition that individuals and firms can "transact freely with no cost," which may not be obvious to the reader. In particular, investors must be free to finance the purchase of stock in part with debt, and their liability to the lender can be limited to the value of the stock purchased. In other words, investors must be free to establish what amounts to "closed-end" investment companies. See David Durand, The Cost of Capital, Corporation Finance, and the Theory of Investment: Comment, *American Economic Review,* vol. 49, September 1959, and secs. I and II of the "Reply" by Modigliani and Miller in the same issue for a discussion of the significance of this condition.

[2] See Alexander A. Robicheck and Stewart C. Myers, Problems in the Theory of Optimal Capital Structure, *Journal of Financial and Quantitative Analysis,* vol. 1, pp. 16–19, June 1966, for a discussion of this point.

**table 11-1 Perfect-Market Assumptions**

A.1. Costless capital markets: No capital market transaction costs, no government restrictions which interfere with capital market transactions, and transaction costless infinite divisibility of financial assets.

A.2. Neutral personal taxes: There are no personal taxes or the effective tax rates on interest, dividends, and capital gains (realized or unrealized) are equal; sufficient for this is the same tax rate for a given investor (rates may differ among investors) on dividend, interest, and capital gain income, with capital gains taxed when the gains accrue and not when realized through sale of the asset.

A.3. Competitive markets: There are many perfect substitutes for all securities of a firm at any point in time and they can be acquired at the same market price regardless of a given firm's behavior or a given investor's behavior; this implies that a firm cannot create a new type of security (one that is different from any already available in the market and issued by another firm). In addition, the firm is a "price taker," i.e., the firm cannot affect the structure of interest rates in the market by its actions.

A.4. Equal access: Investors and firms can borrow, lend, and issue claims on the same terms.

A.5. Homogeneous expectations: Everyone has the same expectations.

A.6. No information costs: Firms and individuals have available the same information, and this information is acquirable at a zero cost.

A.7. No financial distress costs: Firms and individuals incur no costs of financial distress or bankruptcy (legal costs, accounting costs, disruption of operations, etc.), although financial distress, including bankruptcy, can occur.

A.8. Salability of tax losses: Firms and individuals can sell tax losses in the market. Thus a loss of $L$ can be sold for $\tau L$, where $\tau$ is the tax bracket of the seller of the loss.

$\tilde{Y}$ (in the no-tax case) is available to the security holders of the firm in aggregate; the assets of the firm (including cash and other liquid assets) are completely unaffected by financing policy.

It is helpful at this point to recapitulate briefly some of the points in the discussion of firm cash flow in Chap. 9 and to draw a parallel with the treatment in Appendix 2A. In the absence of taxes the total *net* cash flow to *all* security holders of the firm at time $t$, $\tilde{Y}_t$, equals $\tilde{X}_t - \tilde{I}_t$. Recall that in Eq. (2A-2) of Appendix 2A, $[D_t + (1 + i_t)F_{t-1}]$ was the total outflow to existing stockholders and lenders to the firm; $\tilde{Y}_t$ corresponds to this amount here. The same accounting relationship must also hold here; the net cash payment by the firm is

$$\tilde{Y}_t = (\tilde{X}_t - \tilde{I}_t + \tilde{F}_t) - \tilde{F}_t = \tilde{X}_t - \tilde{I}_t$$

Quantity $(\tilde{X}_t - \tilde{I}_t + \tilde{F}_t)$ is the cash payment (dividends, interest, treasury stock and bond purchases, retirement of matured debt) to the old security holders of the firm—the stock and bonds outstanding just before time $t$; and $\tilde{F}_t$ is the cash inflow from new security owners (the receipts from sale of new securities at time $t$). That is, $\tilde{X}_t + \tilde{F}_t$ is the inflow from firm assets $\tilde{X}_t$ and the sale of new securities $\tilde{F}_t$; $\tilde{I}_t$ is the outflow for new investment; the difference is the cash flow to owners not including those new investors paying in $\tilde{F}_t$. Thus, the net flow to all investors (new and old) is the flow to old owners, $\tilde{X}_t + \tilde{F}_t - \tilde{I}_t$, less the amount paid in by new investors, $\tilde{F}_t$, this difference equaling $(\tilde{X}_t - \tilde{I}_t)$. Consequently, the net flow from the firm is $(\tilde{X}_t - \tilde{I}_t)$, which may be positive or negative in any given period. Quantity $\tilde{F}_t$ is the price paid by new security holders for their claims on cash flows beyond period $t$, that is, $\tilde{Y}_{t+1}, \tilde{Y}_{t+2}, \ldots$. Thus, firm cash flow $\tilde{\mathbf{Y}} = (\tilde{X}_1 - \tilde{I}_1, \tilde{X}_2 - \tilde{I}_2, \ldots)$; given investment policy, $\tilde{I}_t$ and $\tilde{X}_t$ are given and, therefore, so is $\tilde{\mathbf{Y}}$.

Financing decisions by the firm are no more than the determination of who has rights to what part of the future cash flows of the firm. Note that *investment policy* is given, with changes in firm cash viewed here as a firm investment. Thus, if the firm pays a higher dividend, it must sell new bonds or shares or both to finance it, thereby reducing current shareholders' claims on future cash flows. If it finances through debt issues rather than stock issues, it changes the distribution of future payments to existing shareholders. However, no choice by the firm can change the *ultimate* distribution of ownership of the firm's cash flow so long as investors can freely transact in the market. Regardless of the firm's decisions, the highest bidders in the market will obtain ownership of the cash flows, and the value of the firm will be based on those cash flows rather than on the separations of the cash flows between old and new shareholders or between shareholders and bondholders as determined by the firm. That is, regardless of how the firm divides its cash flow between old or new investors (by varying dividend policy) or between stockholders and bondholders, the highest bidders in the market will ultimately obtain ownership of that cash flow. This will occur by means of transactions between investors in the market, and it follows that, in perfect, taxless markets, firm value is independent of dividend policy and financial structure policy. It should also be noted that this conclusion is an implication of the value-additivity principle discussed at the end of Chap. 9. The arguments there should be reviewed in the context of the comments above.

## FIRM VALUE AND SHARE VALUE

In both the discussion in this chapter with respect to capital structure policy and in the forthcoming discussion on investment policy it is convenient to deal with the total value of all the outstanding securities of the firm rather than just the value of the common stock. The question arises as to whether maximizing the value of the firm is in general equivalent to maximizing the value of the firm's shares. We examine this problem rigorously in Chap. 17; however, a few comments are appropriate here. Clearly, if the market value of the outstanding bonds (and other types of securities exclusive of common stock) does not change as the result of management decisions, the decisions that maximize the value of the firm must also maximize the value of the firm's shares. However, it is conceivable that some decisions might increase the value of the firm's bonds at the expense of the shareholders, leading to higher total value but lower share values. Moreover, other decisions might reduce the total value of the firm while increasing the value of the shares if lower bond values resulted.

This means that firm value maximization would not necessarily be achieved if share value maximization is the goal. However, this latter case of lower bond values can be ruled out by making either of the following two arguments.

First, existing bondholders may have restricted management's decisions by covenants in the bond contract in order to eliminate the possibility of a decision that would adversely affect them while benefiting the shareholders. For example, a requirement that all subsequent debt be subordinated to existing debt would prevent management from issuing new senior debt and thereby causing existing bondholders to suffer capital losses. Suppose the firm has $100 of certain income (all other income being risky) and has bonds outstanding valued at $2,000 with a coupon rate of 5% being paid on them; i.e., interest payments are $100/period. All interest is therefore riskless. If the firm were to issue new bonds with coupon interest of $100, the value of the new bonds would depend on whether they were subordinated to the old ones or not. Clearly, it is in the shareholder's interest to maximize the value of the new bonds sold. If the new bonds shared equally with the old bonds, $50 of the payment to the new bondholders would be riskless and $50 would be risky. However, the old bondholders would have their interest payments changed from $100 for certain to $50 for certain and $50 at risk. Therefore, the value of the old bonds would decline. If new bonds must be subordinated to existing bonds, then the entire payment to the new bondholders would be risky and hence new bonds would be sold at a lower price while the value of old bonds would remain unchanged. In the absence of such subordination it would appear that management could benefit their shareholders by selling new bonds and paying out the proceeds as dividends (or spending them on investments). Frequently, however, bonds are issued with the restriction that future bond issues will be subordinated, thereby preventing shareholders from gaining by imposing capital losses on old bondholders by means of new bond issues.

As a second argument, note that if management were able to (and frequently did) impose capital losses on existing bondholders, the market would anticipate such actions. The risk would be compensated for by lower prices for the future bond issues of the firm and no further benefits to shareholders would accrue. Shareholders may be hurt by such actions in the long run because of the increased uncertainty on the part of bondholders as to those actions. Consequently, the second argument is that attempting to benefit shareholders by imposing losses on bondholders may not achieve maximum share value even if subordination restrictions are not imposed. The market will evaluate not only the immediate effect of management decisions but also the consequences of those decisions on the long-run financing opportunities of the firm.

Now let us consider the other possibility, that maximizing total firm value might imply increasing the value of outstanding bonds while reducing the value of the shares. It will now be shown that if a decision by management results in a higher total value for the firm, it will be to the shareholders' benefit to make such a decision *even if share prices fall.*

Suppose the firm currently has a value of $V = S + B$, where $S$ and $B$ are the values of the shares and bonds outstanding. Management is considering a decision that will result in a firm value of $V^* = S^* + B^*$, where $V^* > V$ and new values for the firm's share of $S^* < S$ and for the bonds of $B^* > B$. The firm can sell new shares to shareholders of amount $B$, use the proceeds to retire existing bonds, and then distribute a new package of bonds worth $B^*$ to their shareholders *after taking the action that would result in a firm value of* $V^*$. The shareholders can then sell the bonds for $B^*$; their shares are now worth $S^*$.[3] Their current wealth position has been changed by these transactions as follows:

$$\begin{aligned}
\text{Change in value of shares} &= S^* - S \\
\text{Change in cash position} &= B^* - B \\
\text{Net change in wealth} &= (S^* - S) + (B^* - B) \\
&= S^* + B^* - (S + B) \\
&= V^* - V
\end{aligned}$$

Since $V^*$ is greater than $V$, the position of the shareholders has been bettered by the decision. The point is not that such a set of transactions is required; other strategies are also available. It is rather that even when the value of the firm's shares declines as a result of management decisions, shareholders can be made better off if $V^*$ is greater than $V$. That is, the action raising $V$ to $V^*$ should be adopted, since shareholders can be made to benefit by such an action.

In general we can say, with perfect capital markets, that maximizing total value is consistent with maximizing shareholder wealth.

## FIRM VALUE AND THE DEBT-EQUITY RATIO

There is general agreement that the equilibrium expected rates of return on debt and equity depend upon the proportion of debt financing used by the firm. As the proportion of debt increases, the probability of default may increase, bond prices may fall, and the expected rate of return on the bonds may rise. Similarly, as the debt increases, the riskiness of the equity stream also rises and so will the associated required rate of return.[4] Consequently, in a risk-averse market, the expected rates on both the debt and equity streams increase as the proportion of debt increases. The debate between the perfect market and traditional schools rests with how firm value varies with the debt-equity ratio. The traditionalists argue that, up to a point, increased debt increases firm value; the perfect-market hypothesis holds that firm value is independent of the debt-equity ratio (in the absence of taxes). Several models can be used to establish the perfect-market view; two will be described here.

[3] These transactions are cost-free by the perfect-markets assumption. Perfect markets also imply that outstanding bonds can be obtained at their market value $B$, for example, by an all-or-nothing tender offer from the firm.

[4] Refer to the discussion on debt financing in chap. 6 for a demonstration of this effect.

## The Modigliani-Miller (M-M) Proof

**The M-M proof without taxes.** Assume that there are no taxes or transaction costs, debt is riskless, and capital markets are competitive.[5] Also, assume the existence of two firms $u$ and $l$ with net cash flows $\tilde{Y}_u$ and $\tilde{Y}_l$ that are viewed as identical by the market; $\tilde{Y}_u = \tilde{Y}_l$ in the view of all investors.[6] Thus the streams have identical distributions and have a correlation coefficient of 1. Since the streams are identical, we can refer to both of them simply as $\tilde{Y}$. Although the proof to follow could be fully expressed in terms of cash-flow *vector* $\tilde{\mathbf{Y}}$, $\tilde{Y}$ is here assumed to be a single number representing each of the firms' cash flows. This is consistent with the development by Modigliani and Miller and simplifies the discussion.[7] The proof will demonstrate that $V_u = V_l$ must hold at equilibrium regardless of the differences in debt used between the two firms. This equality will hold because of investors' ability to arbitrage. No investor will hold shares of firm $l$ if $V_u < V_l$, and no investor will hold shares of firm $u$ if $V_u > V_l$. Investors will always sell out of the shares of the higher-valued firm (thus driving down its share price) and switch to the lower-valued firm (raising its share price) until $V_u = V_l$. Thus the M-M proposition for the no-tax case is:

> The equilibrium value of a firm is independent of its debt-equity ratio.

Assume that firm $u$ is unlevered (has no debt) and that firm $l$ is levered. Therefore, $V_u = S_u$ and $V_l = S_l + B_l$. For the levered firm, the return to stockholders equals $(\tilde{Y} - iB_l)$, where $iB_l$ is the total interest payment per period on the firm's debt (debt is riskless by assumption and yields rate $i$). Assume an investor with fraction $\alpha$ of the unlevered firm. The investor is entitled to income stream $\alpha\tilde{Y}$ for a total investment of $\alpha S_u = \alpha V_u$. However, an identical return

[5] The proofs presented in this chapter are based on Modigliani and Miller, Reply to Heins and Sprenkle (listed in the Suggested Readings at the end of this chapter). Their original arguments are in The Cost of Capital, Corporation Finance and the Theory of Investment, also listed in the Suggested Readings.

[6] The proof follows almost identically if $\tilde{Y}_u = \gamma\tilde{Y}_l$, $\gamma > 0$, that is, if $\tilde{Y}_u$ and $\tilde{Y}_l$ differ only by a scale factor, where $\gamma$ is viewed as the same by all investors. $\tilde{Y}_u = \tilde{Y}_l$ is assumed here only for simplicity.

[7] Miller and Modigliani do not distinguish between net cash flow $\tilde{Y}$ and firm income $\tilde{X} = \tilde{Y} + \tilde{I}$. It is assumed here that $\tilde{X} = \tilde{Y}$, that is, that all investment costs are considered as expenses in the period incurred (and can be deducted from $\tilde{X}$ for tax purposes). Also, the original M-M proof (1958) assumed that $Y$ is a single number reflecting the firm's income stream over time (see their footnote 8). However, as noted in the text above, the proof here does not require that $\tilde{X}$ or $\tilde{Y}$ be a single number even though Miller and Modigliani treat it as such. The value of the firm's bonds and the interest income on those bonds are also represented by single numbers $B_l$ and $iB_l$, respectively, instead of a vector. In general, however, $Y$ can be a vector of returns over time, $\tilde{\mathbf{Y}} = (\tilde{Y}_1, \tilde{Y}_2, \ldots, \tilde{Y}_\infty)$, in which case $i\mathbf{B}_l = (iB_{l1}, iB_{l2}, \ldots, iB_{l\infty})$, where $iB_{lt}$ is the interest payable on the debt of firm $l$ in period $t$. $B_{lt}$ can change over time. The use of single variables in the text proof has heuristic advantages. The proof of the perfect-market financing propositions in generalized perfect markets in the next section (using the value-additivity principle) will be in terms of vectors.

**exhibit 11-1**

| *Transaction* | *Amount of investment* | *Return provided* |
|---|---|---|
| 1. Purchase fraction $\alpha$ of the stock of levered firm $l$ | $\alpha S_l = \alpha(V_l - B_l)$ | $\alpha(\tilde{Y} - iB_l)$ |
| 2. Purchase fraction $\alpha$ of the bonds of levered firm $l$ | $\alpha B_l$ | $\alpha i B_l$ |
| Total investment | $\alpha V_l$ | |
| Total return | | $\alpha \tilde{Y}$ |

can be obtained by conducting the two transactions shown in Exhibit 11-1. It follows that if $V_u > V_l$ then the investor will be able to gain by selling shares in firm $u$ and conducting these two transactions. By switching, the investor obtains the same return and a profit of $\alpha(V_u - V_l)$. If $V_u > V_l$, all investors in firm $u$ will conduct the operation and drive down the price of the shares of firm $u$ (as they sell) and drive up the price of the shares of firm $l$ (as they buy) until $V_u = V_l$. At that point, no gain accrues from further shifting since $\alpha(V_u - V_l) = 0$ when $V_u = V_l$.

Now assume that $V_l > V_u$. The holder of fraction $\alpha$ of the shares of firm $l$ receives income stream $\alpha(\tilde{Y} - iB_l)$ with an investment of $\alpha S_l = \alpha(V_l - B_l)$. However, in perfect markets if firm $l$ can borrow at $i$, so can shareholders. Suppose this investor sells shares in $l$ for $\alpha S_l$ and conducts the two transactions shown in Exhibit 11-2.

Total return from these two transactions equals $\alpha\tilde{Y}$ from buying fraction $\alpha$ of firm $u$ less $\alpha i B_l$, the interest payable on the debt incurred on personal account. The investor has the same return as when owning $\alpha$ of the shares of firm $l$, $\alpha(\tilde{Y} - iB_l)$. However, if $V_l > V_u$, the new investment required by borrowing and investing in firm $u$ is less, that is, $\alpha(V_u - B_l) < \alpha S_l = \alpha(V_l - B_l)$, and the gain from selling the shares of firm $l$ and conducting the two transactions above equals $\alpha(V_l - B_l) - \alpha(V_u - B_l) = \alpha(V_l - V_u) > 0$ for $V_l > V_u$. Investors in firm $l$ will continue to switch from firm $l$ to firm $u$ so long as $V_l > V_u$. This switching will drive down the price of shares of firm $l$ and drive up the price of the shares of firm $u$ until $V_l = V_u$.

**exhibit 11-2**

| *Transaction* | *Amount of investment* | *Return provided* |
|---|---|---|
| 1. Purchase fraction $\alpha$ of the stock of unlevered firm $u$ | $\alpha S_u = \alpha V_u$ | $\alpha\tilde{Y}$ |
| 2. Borrow $\alpha B_l$ on personal account | $-\alpha B_l$ | $-\alpha i B_l$ |
| Total investment | $\alpha(V_u - B_l)$ | |
| Total return | | $\alpha(\tilde{Y} - iB_l)$ |

To illustrate this, assume two firms $u$ and $l$ with identical cash-flow streams equal to $\tilde{Y}$. Assume that Mr. $A$ invests in the shares of firm $u$ owning 10% of the firm's outstanding stock, that is, $\alpha = .10$. Also assume the following:

$$\begin{aligned} i &= .06 \\ S_u = V_u &= 1{,}000 \\ S_l &= 400 \\ B_l &= 500 \\ V_l &= 900 \end{aligned}$$

For the unlevered firm, total return to stockholders equals $\tilde{Y}$. Interest on the debt of the levered firm equals $iB_l = .06(500) = 30$. Returns to stockholders of the levered firm equal income less interest to bondholders, i.e., equals $\tilde{Y} - 30$. The cash return of Mr. $A$ from his shares of firm $u$ equals $\alpha\tilde{Y} = .1\tilde{Y}$; his investment in firm $u$ equals $\alpha S_u = .10(1{,}000) = 100$. Let $A$ now conduct the transactions indicated in Exhibit 11-1 and described in Exhibit 11-3 for the present example.

From Exhibit 11-3 it follows that $A$ can obtain a return of $.1\tilde{Y}$—the same return he had from his previous ownership of shares in the unlevered firm—for an investment of 90. Since he sold his 10% of firm $u$ for 100, he has 10 left over. This cash gain equals $\alpha(V_u - V_l) = .10(1{,}000 - 900) = 10$. Mr. $A$ is therefore better off. He initially had a stream of $.1\tilde{Y}$; after switching from the unlevered to the levered firm as described above, he has a stream of $.1\tilde{Y}$ *plus* a profit of 10.

By similar arguments, the transactions indicated in Exhibit 11-2 will provide the investor in the levered firm with a gain in switching to the unlevered firm if the latter firm has a lower market value. The investor in the higher-valued firm will always be able to gain by switching to the lower-valued firm. The switching will cause the share prices to adjust so that both firms have the same total value even though they have different debt-equity ratios. Thus, regardless of the debt-equity ratio established by a firm, that firm will have the same market value at equilibrium as all other firms in the same risk class (i.e., with the same distribution of cash flow).

**exhibit 11-3**

| *Transaction* | *Amount of investment* | *Return provided* |
|---|---|---|
| 1. Purchase fraction $\alpha$ (10%) of the stock of the levered firm $l$ | $\alpha S_l = .10(400)$<br>$= 40$ | $\alpha(Y - iB_l)$<br>$= .10(\tilde{Y} - 30)$<br>$= .1\tilde{Y} - 3$ |
| 2. Purchase fraction $\alpha$ (10%) of the bonds of levered firm $l$ | $\alpha B_l = 50$ | $\alpha i B_l$<br>$= .10(.06)500$<br>$= 3$ |
| Total investment | 90 | |
| Total return | | $.1\tilde{Y}$ |

**The M-M proof with firm taxes.** If corporate taxes exist, the preceding results do not hold. Given the presence of such taxes, Modigliani and Miller establish the following proposition:

> The equilibrium value of a levered firm equals:
>
> $$V_l = V_u + \tau B_l \tag{11-1}$$
>
> where $V_l$ is the equilibrium value of the levered firm, $V_u$ is the equilibrium value that the firm would have if it were unlevered, $\tau$ is the tax rate, and $B_l$ is the equilibrium value of the levered firm's bonds.

To establish (11-1), assume that there are taxes on the equity stream of the firm's income; interest is tax-deductible. Assume also that any investment of the firm is deductible from firm income as an expense in the year the investment is made, so that issues of depreciation policy can be avoided. If the pretax return of the levered firm is $\tilde{Y}$, then the return to stockholders equals $(1 - \tau)(\tilde{Y} - iB_l)$ and the total after-tax return of the firm equals $(1 - \tau)(\tilde{Y} - iB_l) + iB_l$, income to stockholders plus income to bondholders. For an unlevered firm, all income goes to stockholders where this income equals $(1 - \tau)\tilde{Y}$.[8] It will now be shown that at equilibrium (11-1) holds.

Assume any investor holding fraction $\alpha$ of the shares of the levered firm $l$. The investment in firm $l$ is $\alpha S_l$, which entitles the investor to stream $\alpha(1 - \tau)(\tilde{Y} - iB_l) = \alpha(1 - \tau)\tilde{Y} - \alpha(1 - \tau)iB_l$. If $V_l > V_u + \tau B_l$, then the investor can obtain the same return with a smaller investment in firm $u$. After selling $\alpha S_l$ shares in $l$, the investor conducts the two transactions shown in Exhibit 11-4.

[8] Note that the unlevered firm here is defined as a firm which is *forever* unlevered, since its cash flow over time is represented by $(1 - \tau)\tilde{\mathbf{Y}}$, where $\tilde{\mathbf{Y}}$ represents firm taxable income (see footnote 7, p. 284) assuming no firm debt. A levered firm is here defined as one for which bonds are currently outstanding and for which no new additional bonds will be issued in the future; $B_l$ is the value of currently outstanding bonds, the bonds yielding a perpetual stream. The bonds are perpetuities (given that only interest is tax-deductible) since Miller and Modigliani define the tax-deductible cash flow to bondholders as $iB_l$, which excludes principal repayment. Future repayment of principal is cash flow to bondholders and is valued in the market; its exclusion in Miller's and Modigliani's analysis implies perpetual bonds.

**exhibit 11-4**

| *Transaction* | *Amount of investment* | *Return provided* |
|---|---|---|
| 1. Purchase fraction $\alpha$ of the stock of unlevered firm $u$ | $\alpha S_u = \alpha V_u$ | $\alpha(1 - \tau)\tilde{Y}$ |
| 2. Borrow $\alpha(1 - \tau)B_l$ on personal account | $-\alpha(1 - \tau)B_l$ | $-\alpha(1 - \tau)iB_l$ |
| Total investment | $\alpha[V_u - (1 - \tau)B_l]$ | |
| Total return | | $\alpha(1 - \tau)(\tilde{Y} - iB_l)$ |

The same return as that provided by holding the shares of firm $l$ is received after the two transactions shown in Exhibit 11-4. If $S_l > V_u - (1 - \tau)B_l$, which implies that $S_l + B_l > V_u + \tau B_l$, then the investor gains on the transactions by selling $\alpha S_l$. The investor receives the same return as with $\alpha S_l$ and has a cash gain of $\alpha S_l - \alpha[V_u - (1 - \tau)B_l] = \alpha[V_l - (V_u + \tau B_l)]$. The gain equals the returns from selling $\alpha S_l$ less the net investment from the two transactions in Exhibit 11-4.

Finally, assume that $V_l < V_u + \tau B_l$. An investor holding fraction $\alpha$ of firm $u$ has stream $\alpha(1 - \tau)\tilde{Y}$ for investment $\alpha S_u = \alpha V_u$. Assume this investor sells shares in firm $u$ for $\alpha V_u$ and then performs the two transactions shown in Exhibit 11-5. If $V_l < V_u + \tau B_l$, then $\alpha V_l < (\alpha V_u + \alpha\tau B_l)$ and $\alpha[S_l + (1 - \tau)B_l] < \alpha V_u$ (recall that $V_l = S_l + B_l$). This means that the same return, $(1 - \tau)\tilde{Y}$, can be obtained by a smaller investment in the levered firm. The investor has sold the holdings in firm $u$ for $\alpha V_u$ and obtained the same return (through the transaction above) by investment $\alpha[S_l + (1 - \tau)B_l]$ in firm $l$. The cash gained from the switch is equal to $\alpha V_u - \alpha[S_l + (1 - \tau)B_l] = \alpha[V_u - S_l - (1 - \tau)B_l] = \alpha[V_u + \tau B_l - V_l]$. As shareholders of the unlevered firm switch to shares of the levered firm, firm $u$ shares fall in price and firm $l$ shares rise in price; this continues until Eq. (11-1) is satisfied.

To illustrate the preceding results, assume that Mr. $A$ owns 10% of the levered firm, that is, $\alpha = .10$.

Assume that

$$
\begin{aligned}
i &= .06 \\
\tau &= .50 \\
S_u = V_u &= 800 \\
S_l &= 600 \\
B_l &= 600 \\
V_l &= 1{,}200
\end{aligned}
$$

It is clear from these figures that $V_l > V_u + \tau B_l$. The return to stockholders of firm $u$ equals the entire after-tax cash flow of $(1 - \tau)\tilde{Y} = .5\tilde{Y}$. The interest to debtholders of firm $l$ equals $iB_l = .06(600) = 36$. The return to stockholders of firm $l$ is firm income less debt interest less taxes, i.e., equals $(1 - \tau)(\tilde{Y} - iB_l) =$

**exhibit 11-5**

| *Transaction* | *Amount of investment* | *Return provided* |
|---|---|---|
| 1. Purchase fraction $\alpha$ of the stock of levered firm $l$ | $\alpha S_l$ | $\alpha(1 - \tau)(\tilde{Y} - iB_l)$ |
| 2. Purchase fraction $\alpha(1 - \tau)$ of the bonds of levered firm $l$ | $\alpha(1 - \tau)B_l$ | $\alpha(1 - \tau)iB_l$ |
| Total investment | $\alpha[S_l + (1 - \tau)B_l]$ | |
| Total return | | $\alpha(1 - \tau)\tilde{Y}$ |

$.5(\tilde{Y} - 36) = .5\tilde{Y} - 18$. Mr. $A$ in the levered firm's stock receives 10% of the stock return, i.e., receives $.10(.5\tilde{Y} - 18) = .05\tilde{Y} - 1.8$. His investment is equal to 10% of the value of the firm's stock, i.e., is $.10S_l = 60$. However, $A$ can gain by shifting to the unlevered firm. The transactions of Exhibit 11-4 are shown for this example in Exhibit 11-6. As is apparent from Exhibit 11-6, $A$ earns a return of $.05\tilde{Y} - 1.8$, as was so by holding shares in the levered firm. However, by switching to the unlevered firm, he has also secured an additional sum of 10, equal to the liquidating value of his old stock less the net cost of his new investment in the unlevered firm. That is, his cash gain equals $\alpha[V_l - (V_u + \tau B_l)] = .10[1{,}200 - (800 + 300)] = 10$. Such gains are available to all holders of stock in the levered firm so long as $V_l > V_u + \tau B_l$. As investors in the shares of firm $l$ shift to shares of firm $u$ to obtain the gain, firm $l$ share prices will fall and firm $u$ share prices will rise until Eq. (11-1) is satisfied. At that point, no further gains are possible. Similar arguments hold in a situation where $V_l < V_u + \tau B_l$, in which case the transactions indicated in Exhibit 11-5 would be appropriate.

With the tax-deductibility of interest, bonds are clearly favored. Every dollar of income going to bond interest is untaxed, whereas that going to equity is taxed. Therefore, the higher value for a levered firm should not be surprising. Equation (11-1) would seem to imply that the firm should increase its debt to the point at which stock is an infinitesimal portion of the firm's capitalization, since $V$ necessarily increases as $B$ increases. Additional arguments must be introduced if this conclusion is not to hold. Clearly, in reality firms do not raise debt to its maximum level attainable. At this point it is useful to examine the assumptions underlying the M-M analysis.

**The M-M assumptions.** A shortcoming of the M-M proof lies in the assumption of perfect markets. Modigliani and Miller assume that there are no transaction costs and that firms and individuals can borrow and lend at the rate of interest. Neither assumption holds in reality. If all investors in the firm prefer that the stock be levered to a higher degree, it would be less expensive in terms of transaction costs for the firm to increase its debt than for all investors to borrow on their own accounts. In addition, margin requirements on personal borrowing against listed securities and the existence of limited liability of corporations (in

**exhibit 11-6**

| *Transaction* | *Amount of investment* | *Return provided* |
|---|---|---|
| 1. Purchase fraction $\alpha$ (10%) of the stock of unlevered firm $u$ | $\alpha S_u = 80$ | $\alpha(1 - \tau)\tilde{Y} = .05\tilde{Y}$ |
| 2. Borrow $\alpha(1 - \tau)B_l$ [$= .10(.5)600 = 30$] on personal account | $-\alpha(1 - \tau)B_l = -30$ | $-\alpha(1 - \tau)iB_l = -1.8$ |
| Total investment | 50 | |
| Total return | | $.05\tilde{Y} - 1.8$ |

contrast with unlimited liability for individuals) clearly place the individual and firm on a different footing in the money markets. Furthermore, transaction costs may render the individual's arbitrage transactions uneconomical.

Other factors may also imply that the firm is not indifferent to the level of debt it incurs. Bankruptcy transaction costs may discourage extremely high proportions of debt. Other capital market imperfections that might prevent the firm from obtaining additional capital even if required for an extremely profitable venture (or to prevent a major loss) might encourage firms to maintain a reserve of borrowing capacity. These same considerations may explain why firms do not increase debt to the upper limit possible even though interest is tax-deductible. The implications of market imperfections will be explored in more detail in Chaps. 14 and 15.

It should be noted that the existence of imperfections does not in itself negate the perfect markets results. To reject such results, it must be shown that the imperfections are significant and that they bias the system in a particular direction (that is, that their effects do not cancel each other out). Therefore, it is very possible that, although perfect market models ignore imperfections, they do provide close approximations of reality.

Even with perfect markets, the M-M assumption that firms can be placed into risk classes with returns that have identical distributions (except for a possible scale factor) and are perfectly correlated is of questionable validity. No such risk classes may exist, or, if they do exist, a risk class may include streams with differing distributions but equivalent risk. With differing distributions, however, streams within a risk class are not equivalent in the sense necessary for the M-M proof. The M-M proof requires that streams exist which are identical (except for a scale factor) and not merely equivalent in terms of some measure of "risk." An evaluation of the debt-equity choice under more general assumptions is needed. This is the subject of the next section.

## Value Additivity

**Value additivity and debt financing without taxes.** The value-additivity principle (VAP) developed in Chap. 9 was based only on the assumption of perfect markets, i.e., assuming zero transaction costs and competitive capital markets. In particular, no assumptions were made about the existence of identical firms and identical expectations on the part of investors. The VAP states that the value of the sum of a set of streams received by investors equals the sum of the values of the individual streams.

$$\text{If } \tilde{\mathbf{Y}}_T = \sum_{i=1}^{n} \tilde{\mathbf{Y}}_i \qquad V_T = \sum_{i=1}^{n} V_i \tag{11-2}$$

The equations in (11-2) are simply a repetition of (9-42); the $\tilde{\mathbf{Y}}_i$ are the individual streams and the $V_i$ are the market values of those streams. The value-additivity principle also implies that the division of a given stream into components does as follows. (For the relationship between firm cash flows and value see the discussion of firm cash flows in Chap. 9, directly related to the material below.)

Given the investment policy of the firm its total cash flow is given, $\tilde{\mathbf{Y}}$. The current value of this total cash flow provided to the market is $V$. Suppose the income stream is divided into two components: one owned by current bondholders, $\tilde{\mathbf{Y}}^{BO}$; the remainder $(\tilde{\mathbf{Y}} - \tilde{\mathbf{Y}}^{BO})$ owned by current shareholders, where,

$$\tilde{\mathbf{Y}}^{BO} + (\tilde{\mathbf{Y}} - \tilde{\mathbf{Y}}^{BO}) = \tilde{\mathbf{Y}} \tag{11-3}$$

As noted in the discussion of cash flow in Chap. 9, $(\tilde{\mathbf{Y}} - \tilde{\mathbf{Y}}^{BO})$ is the cash flow currently owned by shareholders and the value of which is $S$, the value of current shares outstanding. The value of $\tilde{\mathbf{Y}}^{BO}$ is $B$. (The superscript $O$ on $S$ and $B$ is not necessary here since $S$ and $B$ without the superscript always refer to currently outstanding shares and bonds.)

Given firm cash flow $\tilde{\mathbf{Y}}$, the more that is to be paid out to bondholders, the less that will be available for shareholders. Therefore, the value of outstanding shares $S$ will be lower and the value of outstanding bonds $B$ will be higher as $\tilde{\mathbf{Y}}^{BO}$ is increased.[9] However, the VAP states that the *total* value $V = S + B$ is the same irrespective of how the stream $\tilde{\mathbf{Y}}$ is divided between the two types of securities. That is, as $\tilde{\mathbf{Y}}^{BO}$ increases, $B$ rises and $S$ falls by the same amount. Therefore, the choice of financing does not affect the total value of the firm. This is the same result as stated in the M-M no-tax proposition.

**Value additivity and debt financing with taxes.** In Chap. 9, the period $t$ total after-tax cash flow to bondholders and stockholders combined, $\tilde{Y}_t$, was defined in Eq. (9-49); representing the related streams over time in vector notation, (9-49) becomes

$$\tilde{\mathbf{Y}} = (1 - \tau)\tilde{\mathbf{X}} + \tau\widetilde{\mathbf{DP}} - \mathbf{I} + \tau\tilde{\mathbf{R}} \tag{11-4}$$

where $\tau$ = firm tax rate
$\tilde{\mathbf{X}}$ = cash income before deductions for interest and depreciation
$\widetilde{\mathbf{DP}}$ = depreciation deduction for tax purposes
$\tilde{\mathbf{R}}$ = interest on firm debt
$\tilde{\mathbf{I}}$ = cash outlay by the firm on investment

[9] The concept of an "increase" (or decrease) in a vector representing a multiperiod random variable has a special meaning as used here. Given an initial vector $\tilde{\mathbf{Q}}'$ and a new vector $\tilde{\mathbf{Q}}$, time $t$ element $\tilde{Q}_t$ is "larger" than time $t$ element $\tilde{Q}'_t$ if

(*a*) prob $(\tilde{Q}_t \geq \hat{Q}_t) \geq$ prob $(\tilde{Q}'_t \geq \hat{Q}_t)$ for all $\hat{Q}_t$, where $\hat{Q}_t$ takes on all possible values attainable by $Q'_t$ and $Q_t$, and
(*b*) prob $(\tilde{Q}_t \geq \hat{Q}_t) >$ prob $(\tilde{Q}'_t \geq \hat{Q}_t)$ for some $\hat{Q}_t$.

For the vector $\tilde{\mathbf{Q}}$ to be greater than the vector $\tilde{\mathbf{Q}}'$, condition (*b*) must be satisfied for at least one $t$. These conditions imply that the expected values of the variables must be larger in at least one period and no smaller in any period for the vector to have increased.

At time zero, future levels of these variables are unknown and therefore the tilde appears over the vector terms. As discussed earlier, the terms in Eq. (11-4) are vectors representing streams over time. All the terms in (11-4) except for $\tilde{\mathbf{R}}$ are independent of financing policy. Tax rate $\tau$ depends upon the government's policy; $\widetilde{\mathbf{DP}}$ depends both upon the government's policy on depreciation and upon the firm's decision; $\tilde{\mathbf{X}}$ and $\tilde{\mathbf{I}}$ depend upon the firm's production and investment policies and upon economic conditions (demand for firm's products, supply conditions for inputs, etc.). The debt-equity ratio will affect only $\tilde{\mathbf{R}}$ in Eq. 11-4, and as $\tilde{\mathbf{R}}$ increases, $\tilde{\mathbf{Y}}$ increases. That is, as the firm increases the proportion of its returns from operations that is paid to debt (increases the debt-equity ratio), the total cash flow to stockholders and bondholders *combined,* $\tilde{\mathbf{Y}}$, increases. This is so because interest $\tilde{\mathbf{R}}$ is tax-deductible, whereas the returns to shareholders are not tax-deductible but are taxed at rate $\tau$.

With an increase in total firm cash flow $\tilde{\mathbf{Y}}$, it follows from the value-additivity principle that firm value must increase. Raising the debt interest that is paid adds incremental stream $\tau\ \Delta\tilde{\mathbf{R}}$ to the total cash flow of the firm and therefore increases the total value of the cash flow by the value of that incremental stream. Therefore, the value-additivity principle implies that firm value increases with debt, assuming the presence of firm taxes.

The results derived by Modigliani and Miller discussed above also follow using the value-additivity principle. However, in order for perfect markets to imply Eq. (11-1), certain restrictive assumptions must be made. In general, Eq. (11-1) would have to be replaced with a more complex relationship, although such a relationship would nevertheless indicate a similar bias in favor of debt financing. The assumptions made here to produce relation (11-1) are:

1. All debt yields a perpetual interest stream and investors expect the bonds to be outstanding forever.
2. Investors expect the firm never to issue new debt in the future above that currently outstanding, whether it is currently levered or unlevered.

Assumptions (1) and (2) imply that all future cash flow to bonds is in the form of interest on current bonds and is therefore all tax-deductible, that is, $\tilde{\mathbf{Y}}^B = \tilde{\mathbf{Y}}^{BO} = \tilde{R}^O$; thus, represent the bond stream simply as $\tilde{\mathbf{R}}^O$.[10]

Define $\tilde{Y}_t$ as the cash payments (cash flow) made by the firm to its security holders in period $t$. The total cash flow of the firm to stockholders and bondholders in any period $t$ is

$$\tilde{Y}_t = \tilde{X}_t - \tilde{I}_t - \widetilde{\text{Tax}}_t \tag{11-5}$$

where $\tilde{X}_t$ = pretax cash earnings (inflow) of firm
$\tilde{I}_t$ = investment outlay of firm
$\widetilde{\text{Tax}}_t$ = tax payment

[10] If it were assumed that *all* cash flow paid out to bondholders is tax-deductible, then assumption (1) would not be necessary. This was assumed in chap. 8.

All values are assumed uncertain. Recall from Chap. 1 that an increase in cash held by the firm in period $t$ is viewed as an investment (in the productive asset cash), i.e., as part of $\tilde{I}_t$. For ease of analysis we assume that the tax rate $\tau$ is constant and certain. As explained on page 215, the tax in any period is determined as[11]

$$\tilde{\text{Tax}}_t = \tau(\tilde{X}_t - \tilde{Y}_t^{BO} - \widetilde{DP}_t) \tag{11-6}$$

where $\tilde{Y}_t^{BO}$ is the tax-deductible interest payment to bondholders [since $\tilde{Y}_t^{BO} = \tilde{R}_t^O$ by assumption (1) above] and $\widetilde{DP}_t$ is the depreciation deduction. We can substitute (11-6) into (11-5) and get

$$\tilde{Y}_t = [(1 - \tau)\tilde{X}_t - \tilde{I}_t + \tau\widetilde{DP}_t] + \tau\tilde{R}_t^O \tag{11-7}$$

Using the vector concept, (11-7) becomes

$$\tilde{\mathbf{Y}} = [(1 - \tau)\tilde{\mathbf{X}} - \mathbf{I} + \tau\widetilde{\mathbf{DP}}] + \tau\tilde{\mathbf{R}}^O \tag{11-8}$$

where each variable in (11-8) is a vector with elements for $t = 1, \ldots, \infty$.[12]

First note that the total stream paid to stockholders and bondholders together, $\tilde{\mathbf{Y}}$ in (11-8), increases as the debt stream increases. Note also that the set of terms in brackets in (11-8) is the total cash flow owned by current stockholders if there were no current (and no future) debt, since in that case $\tilde{\mathbf{R}}^O = 0$ and the last term in (11-8) would drop out.[13] That is, if the firm were permanently unlevered, the cash flow would all go to stockholders and would equal the amount in brackets. Thus, the total cash flow to bondholders and stockholders together equals the cash flow that would be paid if the firm were unlevered (no debt) plus $\tau\tilde{\mathbf{R}}^O$ (the tax rate times the amount payable to the debt):

$$[\tilde{\mathbf{Y}} - \tilde{\mathbf{R}}^O] + \tilde{\mathbf{R}}^O = [(1 - \tau)\tilde{\mathbf{X}} - \tilde{\mathbf{I}} + \tau\widetilde{\mathbf{DP}}] + \tau\tilde{\mathbf{R}}^O \tag{11-9}$$

The VAP can be applied here. We know that the value of the firm's cash flow $\tilde{\mathbf{Y}}$ is equal to $V = S + B$; this is so by definition. The market value of $[\tilde{\mathbf{Y}} - \tilde{\mathbf{R}}^O]$ is $S$ and the value of $\tilde{\mathbf{R}}^O$ is $B$. But since the left-hand side of (11-9) necessarily equals the right-hand side of (11-9), by the VAP the market value of the stream on the left-hand side must equal the value that the streams on the right-hand side would have if they were available in the market. The value of the stream in brackets is the value the firm would have if it were an unlevered firm since, as just noted, the stream in the brackets is that which would be available in the market were the firm unlevered. Define this value of the firm if unlevered as $V_u$. The second stream on the right-hand side of (11-9), $\tau\tilde{\mathbf{R}}^O$, must have a value equal to $\tau B$ since the stream is just a fraction ($\tau$) of the debt stream to the firm's

[11] By assumption A.8, tax losses can be sold in the market for $\tau L$. Also, note that depreciation in any period $DP_t$ is *not* a cash outlay but is an "expense" in the sense that it is deductible from income $\tilde{X}_t$ to compute taxable income.

[12] Thus, in (11-8), $\tilde{\mathbf{Y}} = (\tilde{Y}_1, \tilde{Y}_2, \ldots, \tilde{Y}_\infty)$, $\tilde{\mathbf{X}} = (\tilde{X}_1, \tilde{X}_2, \ldots, \tilde{X}_\infty)$, $\tilde{\mathbf{I}} = (\tilde{I}_1, \tilde{I}_2, \ldots, \tilde{I}_\infty)$, etc. See the discussion in chap. 9 regarding firm cash flows.

[13] By assumption (2), p. 292, if there is no current debt there is no future debt; i.e., the firm is permanently unlevered.

current bonds. Thus, since the value of the left-hand side of (11-9) is $(S + B)$ and the value of the right-hand side is $V_u + \tau B$, it follows that

$$V = S + B = V_u + \tau B \tag{11-10}$$

Equation (11-10) states that the value of the firm, $V = S + B$, equals the value the firm would have if permanently unlevered plus the tax rate times the value of the firm's currently outstanding bonds. This is the same result as that derived by Modigliani and Miller. As before, it is clear that the value of the firm increases with debt; i.e., as $B$ rises, $V$ rises.

Equations (11-6) through (11-10) were based on assumptions (1) and (2) on page 292 which stated that interest $\tilde{\mathbf{R}}$ in equation (4) is comprised entirely of interest on debt outstanding at time 0 (no new debt in the future) and that the current debt is perpetual (therefore, the value of current bonds is simply the value of the tax deductible interest to be paid to current bondholders). However, if we drop these assumptions and assume the more general case in which there may be future debt issues and in which the payments to bondholders include principal repayments, then the present value of $\tilde{\mathbf{R}}$ in (11-4) is not equal to the value of currently outstanding debt. In this general case, the current market value of the firm, $V$, becomes (using the VAP)

$$\begin{aligned} V &= S + B \\ &= V[\tilde{\mathbf{Y}}] = V[(1 - \tau)\tilde{\mathbf{X}} + \tau\widetilde{\mathbf{DP}} - \tilde{\mathbf{I}}] - V[\tau\tilde{\mathbf{R}}] \\ &= V_u + \tau V[\tilde{\mathbf{R}}] \end{aligned} \tag{11-11}$$

where $V_u$ is, as before, the current market value of the firm if it had no debt and where $V[\tilde{\mathbf{R}}]$ is the current market value of the stream of interest payments on *all* debt (present and future debt) of the firm. Thus, $V[\tau\tilde{\mathbf{R}}] = \tau V[\tilde{\mathbf{R}}]$ is the current market value of the tax benefit to the firm from the interest deduction on all present and future debt. As with the simple case of equation (11-10), we see in the more general case of (11-11) that the value of the firm $V$ increases as debt increases (greater debt means greater $\tilde{\mathbf{R}}$ and therefore, from [11-11], greater firm value).

In perfect markets, therefore, there is an incentive for the firm to maximize its use of debt.[14] A perfect capital market with no costs of bankruptcy imposes no constraint on the use of debt; however, the government may do so and thereby determine the degree of debt financing to be used by the firm. The

[14] A number of other proofs have been developed for the perfect-market case. R. S. Hamada, in Portfolio Analysis, Market Equilibrium, and Corporation Finance, *Journal of Finance,* vol. 24, March 1969, derives proofs similar to those presented in chap. 8. Jan Mossin, Security Pricing and Investment Criteria in Competitive Markets, *American Economic Review,* vol. 59, pp. 749–756, December 1969, reaches the same results for the no-tax case under assumptions of single-period returns, no default risk, and homogeneous expectations regarding yields on securities. J. E. Stiglitz, A Re-examination of the Modigliani-Miller Theorem, *American Economic Review,* vol. 59, pp. 784–793, December 1969, shows that the debt-equity ratio is irrelevant in the no-tax case with default risk on bonds and without the assumption that firms can be placed in homogeneous risk classes.

perfect capital markets assumption does impose certain restrictions on the admissible values for capital market discount rates. This issue is examined in Appendix 11A.

## INTERNAL FINANCING AND DIVIDEND POLICY

A firm's decision to finance part or all of the current capital budget through retained earnings implies that the current dividend payment of the firm will be reduced by the amount retained. Since the value of the firm is determined by payments to security holders, we must ask whether such a decision is in the best interest of the shareholders. In previous discussions we argued that the decision should be a matter of indifference to shareholders. We shall now examine the impact of the retention of earnings (internal financing) on the value of the firm to current shareholders in generalized perfect markets. As before we shall take the investment decision as given.

### The M-M Dividend Policy Proof[15]

Assume that investors are indifferent between capital gains and dividend income; no taxes are levied on investor income. Furthermore, each investor imputes the same indifference to all other investors in the market.[16] Under these conditions the value of the firm to current shareholders will now be shown to be independent of the current dividend payment by the firm.

For simplicity we shall assume an all-equity firm. Investment policy is given. Since we have already shown that tax-deductibility creates a preference for debt over equity sources, it should be obvious that the firm will not finance internally so long as debt provides an advantage. In general, once the firm has attained the level of debt it seeks, the dividend policy decision is whether to keep dividends at a particular level or to increase dividends by selling (or to decrease by buying) the firm's shares in the market. Under the simplifying assumptions here, the firm has no debt. However, the irrelevancy of dividend policy with debt can be shown to follow in a similar fashion.

Let $\hat{S}_0$ be the current value of the firm's shares that is given in the market. Quantities $\tilde{D}_0$, $\dot{I}_0$, and $\tilde{S}_0^N$ are the uncertain values for current dividends, investment, and the value of new shares issued, respectively. Amount $\tilde{S}_0$ is the value of the *firm* immediately after $\tilde{D}_0$ is paid and investment and financing have taken place. The sequence of action being assumed is as follows. In a brief space of time the firm will pay a dividend, issue new shares if needed, and invest. The value of the firm just before this activity is $\hat{S}_0$ and just after, $\tilde{S}_0$.

[15] The proof here is based on that presented by Miller and Modigliani, Dividend Policy, Growth, and the Valuation of Shares (listed in the Suggested Readings at the end of this chapter).

[16] Miller and Modigliani refer to this assumption as "symmetric rationality."

The total shareholder return $\widetilde{SR}$ to the old shares will be

$$\widetilde{SR}_0 = \tilde{D}_0 + \tilde{S}_0 - \tilde{S}_0^N \qquad (11\text{-}12)$$

where $\tilde{S}_0$ is the postdividend value of the *firm* and $(\tilde{S}_0 - \tilde{S}_0^N)$ is postdividend value of the old shares (those outstanding before the new shares with value $\tilde{S}^N$ are issued). A shareholder who sold shares after the dividend was paid would receive a proportionate fraction of $\widetilde{SR}_0$ in cash. A shareholder who owned a fraction $\alpha$ of $\hat{S}_0$ would receive $\alpha\tilde{D}_0 + \alpha(\tilde{S}_0 - \tilde{S}_0^N)$. Shareholders retaining their shares would also receive cash dividends and own shares worth the appropriate proportion of $\tilde{S}_0 - \tilde{S}_0^N$; that is, would receive $\alpha\tilde{D}_0$ in dividends and own $\alpha(\tilde{S}_0 - \tilde{S}_0^N)$ in shares. Notice again that, by definition, the value of the current shares after the decisions of the firm have been executed must be $\tilde{S}_0 - \tilde{S}_0^N$, since $\tilde{S}_0$ is the total value of all shares outstanding after financing has occurred.

As we have established before, the cash inflows to the firm at time 0 must equal cash outflows:

$$\tilde{X}_0 + \tilde{S}_0^N = \tilde{I}_0 + \tilde{D}_0 \qquad (11\text{-}13)$$

where $\tilde{X}_0$ is the (uncertain) net cash income of the firm for the present period. The perfect-market assumption ensures that the receipts from the sale of new shares is equal to the market value of those shares. Hence, we can use (11-13) to find the amount of new shares required and substitute back in (11-12). From (11-13),

$$\tilde{S}_0^N = \tilde{I}_0 + \tilde{D}_0 - \tilde{X}_0$$

and

$$\widetilde{SR}_0 = \tilde{X}_0 - \tilde{I}_0 + \tilde{S}_0 \qquad (11\text{-}14)$$

Both $\tilde{X}_0$ and $\tilde{I}_0$ are unaffected by the dividend-financing decision. $\tilde{S}_0$ can depend only on the future prospects of the firm so long as investors are rational and assume that everyone else is. The current dividend decision therefore has no effect on the total returns to current shareholders except to change their source; i.e., dividends vs. change in share values. For any period, the dividend decision of that period is of no concern to owners. Furthermore, owners at time 0 know that they (and all other investors) will be indifferent in any future period $t$ to dividends in period $t$. Therefore, investors at time 0 are indifferent at time 0 to the dividend policy that they anticipate will be applicable to any future period $t$. This is true for all periods $t$. Firm value at time 0 is therefore independent of dividend policy and dividend policy is irrelevant given investment policy.

## SUMMARY

With perfect capital markets and no taxes, the financing decisions of the firm do not affect the total market value of its securities for a given investment policy. This is so because investors in the firm's securities are able to offset the effects of actions by the firm through market transactions. The existence of corporate income taxes causes debt financing to be the preferred method as the tax-deductibility of debt interest provides an advantage to debt over retained earnings and common stock issues. In the absence of constraints imposed on the firm by the government, only debt securities would be issued, since the total value of the firm will be maximized by committing all future cash flow to interest payments.

Dividend policy does not affect the value of the firm since, in the absence of taxes on dividends and capital gains, shareholders are indifferent between the two sources of return. For a given investment policy, an increase in dividend payments necessarily results in an exactly offsetting decline in the value of the firm's shares. That is, the increase in dividends is offset by an equal loss in share value, resulting in no change in shareholder wealth.

Thus, under the assumptions of this chapter, retained earnings and common stock issues are equivalent financing methods; but, with corporate taxes, debt will be preferred over equity.

APPENDIX

# ELEVEN A

## INTERRELATIONSHIPS AMONG CAPITAL MARKET RATES

The arbitrage possibilities inherent in perfect capital markets impose restrictions on admissible values of income streams. In terms of the risk-adjusted discount rate model of valuation, these restrictions imply some interrelationships among capital market discount rates. Here we shall develop these interrelationships and also provide some interesting and useful results for the case of level perpetuities.[17] Throughout we assume perfect capital markets.

The value of the firm's shares ($S$) at any point in time must equal the total value of the firm's outstanding debt and equity securities ($V$) less the value of currently outstanding bonds ($B$), that is, $S = V - B$. Given the limited liability of corporate stockholders, $S \geq 0$. Therefore, a fundamental restriction on the value of the firm's bonds in both perfect and imperfect markets, is

$$B \leq V \tag{11A-1}$$

Given perfect markets with corporate taxes (no taxes is simply a special case where $\tau = 0$), we found in Chap. 11, Eq. (11-11), that

$$V = V_u + V[\tau\tilde{\mathbf{R}}] \tag{11A-2}$$

Thus, combining (11A-1) with (11A-2) we have the basic restriction on valuation in perfect markets:

$$B \leq V_u + V[\tau\tilde{\mathbf{R}}] \tag{11A-3}$$

Condition (11A-3) says that the value of the bonds currently outstanding must be less than or equal to the sum of the value of the firm if unlevered and the

[17] A more complete analysis and an application to some imperfect market cases is in C. Haley, "Stream Effects and Capital Market Rates," University of Washington, 1978.

value of the tax benefit from debt interest where $\tilde{\mathbf{R}}$ includes both interest on the present debt and interest on future debt issues. The equality will hold in (11A-3) only if the firm is all debt. Condition (11A-3) does not *appear* to pose any significant restrictions on bond values; but, as we show now for the case of level perpetuities, there is more here than is obvious on first glance.

## Level Perpetuities

Assume a firm of the type examined for the classic Modigliani-Miller analysis which has pre-tax income $\tilde{\mathbf{X}}$, interest payments $\tilde{\mathbf{R}}$, and dividends $\tilde{\mathbf{D}}$—all streams being uncertain, level (constant mean) prepetuities. All firm income $\tilde{\mathbf{X}}$ is to be paid out as dividends, tax-deductible interest payments, and taxes. Therefore, with a constant, certain tax rate $\tau$,

$$\tilde{\mathbf{X}} = \tilde{\mathbf{D}} + \tilde{\mathbf{R}} + \tau(\tilde{\mathbf{X}} - \tilde{\mathbf{R}})$$

or

$$\tilde{\mathbf{D}} = (1 - \tau)(\tilde{\mathbf{X}} - \tilde{\mathbf{R}}) \tag{11A-4}$$

Define the following expected rates of return as determined by the valuation process of the capital markets:

$$\text{Stock rate} = k_S \equiv \frac{\overline{D}}{S} \tag{11A-5}$$

$$\text{Debt rate} = k_B \equiv \frac{\overline{R}}{B} \tag{11A-6}$$

where $\overline{D}$ and $\overline{R}$ are the expected dividend and interest per period, respectively. If the firm were debt-free (unlevered) the expected dividend payment would be $(1 - \tau)\overline{X}$. Define the expected rate of return on the stock (or total value) of the unlevered firm, $k_u$, as

$$\text{Unlevered Rate} = k_u \equiv \frac{(1 - \tau)\overline{X}}{S_u} = \frac{(1 - \tau)\overline{X}}{V_u} \tag{11A-7}$$

Consider the restriction expressed as (11A-3). Since the only debt to be outstanding is current debt, which by assumption is perpetual (no principal payments), and since the tax rate is a given constant, it follows that

$$V[\tau\tilde{\mathbf{R}}] = \tau V[\tilde{\mathbf{R}}] = \tau B \tag{11A-8}$$

Using (11A-8), condition (11A-3) becomes

$$B \le V_u + \tau B$$

$$(1 - \tau)B \le V_u$$

$$B \le \frac{V_u}{1 - \tau} \tag{11A-9}$$

Now substitute into (11A-9) $B$ from (11A-6) and $V_u$ from (11A-7):

$$\frac{\overline{R}}{k_B} \leq \frac{\dfrac{(1-\tau)\overline{X}}{k_u}}{1-\tau}$$

$$\frac{\overline{R}}{k_B} \leq \frac{\overline{X}}{k_u}$$

$$k_B \leq \frac{\overline{R}}{\overline{X}} k_u \qquad \text{(11A-10)}$$

It is convenient here to define a new variable, the ratio of expected interest payments to expected pre-tax income, denoted as the Greek letter omega ($\omega$):

$$\omega \equiv \frac{\overline{R}}{\overline{X}} \qquad \text{(11A-11)}$$

$\omega$ is the reciprocal of a ratio that is widely used in the evaluation of corporate bonds, the "interest coverage ratio." Omega can only take on values in the range $0 \leq \omega \leq 1.0$ and serves as a measure of the degree of leverage used by the firm. equals 1.0 only if the firm is all debt ($\tilde{R} = \tilde{X}$). Restating (11A-10) in terms of $\omega$, we have

$$k_B \geq \omega k_u \qquad \text{(11A-12)}$$

where the equality in (11A-12) holds only if $\omega = 1.0$ (firm is all debt).

Condition (11A-12) indicates that there is an interrelationship between $k_B$ and $k_u$ imposed by the perfect markets assumption. Note that seemingly reasonable rate combinations are ruled out by (11A-12). For example, with $\omega = 0.8$ and $k_u = 12\%$, $k_B$ cannot be 9%; it must be greater than 9.6% [with $\omega = 0.8 < 1.0$, $k_B > \omega k_u$ in (11A-12)].

There is also a relationship between the riskless rate of interest $i$ and $k_u$ which follows from (11A-11). To see this, suppose that a portion $X_r$ of periodic firm income $\tilde{X}$ is certain (riskless) and the firm issues debt such that $R \leq X_r \leq \tilde{X}$. The per period interest payment $R$ is certain and therefore $k_B = i$. Let $\omega_r = X_r/\overline{X}$; then it must be true by (11A-12) that

$$i \geq \omega_r k_u \qquad \text{(11A-13)}$$

or

$$k_u \leq \frac{i}{\omega_r} \qquad \text{(11A-14)}$$

Relation (11A-13) holds because for $R = X_r$, $\omega_r = X_r/\overline{X}$; using (11A-12) (which must hold for all levels of $R$ the firm can choose) relation (11A-13) follows.

The interest rate $i$ applies throughout the economy, whereas $k_u$ is firm specific. Thus, in (11A-14) we have rewritten (11A-13) in the form of a constraint on $k_u$ in terms of the riskless rate $i$. This condition also rules out some apparently reasonable rates. For example, suppose that $\omega_r = 0.5$ and $i = 6\%$.

No matter how uncertain the total income of the firm $\tilde{X}$ is, $k_u$ must be less than or equal to 12%.

Our final relationship is an equation for $k_S$ that follows from the basic valuation relationships and cash flow accounting. We defined $k_S$ as:

$$k_S = \frac{\bar{D}}{S} \tag{11A-5}$$

From above

$$\begin{aligned} S &= V - B \\ &= V_u + \tau B - B \\ &= V_u - (1 - \tau)B \\ &= \frac{(1 - \tau)\bar{X}}{k_u} - (1 - \tau)\frac{\bar{R}}{k_B} \\ &= \frac{(1 - \tau)\bar{X}k_B - (1 - \tau)\bar{R}k_u}{k_u k_B} \\ &= \frac{(1 - \tau)\bar{X}(k_B - \omega k_u)}{k_u k_B} \end{aligned} \tag{11A-15}$$

Also,

$$\begin{aligned} \bar{D} &= (1 - \tau)(\bar{X} - \bar{R}) \\ &= (1 - \tau)\bar{X}(1 - \omega) \end{aligned} \tag{11A-16}$$

Using (11A-15) and (11A-16) in (11A-5), we obtain

$$k_S = \frac{(1 - \omega)k_u k_B}{k_B - \omega k_u} \tag{11A-17}$$

Equation (11A-17) completes the set of interrelationships implied by the perfect market assumptions (assuming perpetuities). Conditions (11A-12) and (11A-14) plus equation (11A-17) define the admissible risk-adjusted discount rates applicable to level perpetuities in perfect markets. Note that under the assumptions used here (which conform to those used in the Modigliani and Miller analysis), the corporate tax rate $\tau$ is not a variable in these relationships. Therefore they apply with and without corporate taxes. Interestingly, alternative expressions for $k_S$, as explored in Chap. 13, normally involve the tax rate. The use of $\omega$ to measure the extent of debt financing used by the firm allows us to easily remove the tax term $\tau$ from the $k_S$ equation. Note, too, that $\omega$ is a determinant of how the market will regard the firm's debt burden and therefore how it will assess the risk and value of the firm's debt and equity (i.e., $\omega$ affects $k_B$, $B$, and $k_S$ and $S$). Thus $\omega$ is a more fundamental measure of the company's debt burden than is $B/S$ or $B/V$, since $\omega$ is a determinant of these latter ratios and not vice versa.

As a final point, relationships similar to (11A-12), and (11A-14) and (11A-17) hold in perfect market with variable (over time) and non-perpetual streams, although the relationships for this more general case will be more complex. To establish these relationships we would use relations (11A-1) and (11A-2) (for example, $k_S$ would be the solution to $S = \Sigma_{t=0}^{\infty} \overline{D}_t/(1 + k_S)^t$). Although the relationships would be far more complex than for the perpetuity case, the interesting point is that market rate interrelationships (between $k_S$, $k_B$, $k_u$ and $i$) would still be implied by (11A-1) and the perfect markets assumption (which implies (11A-2).

## SUGGESTED READINGS


Lintner, John: Dividends, Earnings, Leverage, Stock Prices, and the Supply of Capital to Corporations, *Review of Economics and Statistics,* vol. 44, pp. 243–269, August 1962.

Miller, Merton H. and Franco Modigliani: Dividend Policy, Growth and the Valuation of Shares, *Journal of Business,* vol. 34, pp. 411–432, October 1961, reprinted in Stephen H. Archer and Charles A. D'Ambrosio, "The Theory of Business Finance," 2d ed., The Macmillan Company, New York, 1976.

Modigliani, Franco and Merton H. Miller: The Cost of Capital, Corporation Finance, and the Theory of Investment, *American Economic Review,* vol. 48, pp. 261–297, June 1958, reprinted in Archer and D'Ambrosio, *ibid.*

——— and ———: Reply to Heins and Sprenkle, *American Economic Review,* vol. 59, pp. 592–595, September 1969, reprinted in Archer and D'Ambrosio, *ibid.*

Stiglitz, Joseph E.: A Reexamination of the Modigliani-Miller Theorem, *American Economic Review,* vol. 59, pp. 851–866, December 1969.

———: On the Irrelevance of Corporate Financial Policy, *American Economic Review,* vol. 64, pp. 851–866, December 1974.

CHAPTER

# TWELVE

## FIRM INVESTMENT DECISIONS IN PERFECT CAPITAL MARKETS

This chapter is concerned with the investment decisions of the firm under assumptions of perfect capital markets. The perfect-market assumptions are stated in Table 11-1 on page 280. The analysis here is based on the results of Chaps. 9 and 11. In Chaps. 14 and 15 we shall look at the impact of imperfections in the capital markets on firm investment decisions.

Under the assumption of perfect capital markets, the value-additivity principle discussed in Chaps. 9 and 11 holds. This principle will be used extensively in the present chapter. We shall begin by developing the investment criterion for perfect capital markets, which is applicable *both* without and with the presence of firm taxes. The no-tax case and the tax case will then be examined separately.[1] The following definitions will be used:

$V'$ = The value of the firm (stock plus bonds) if no current investment is made nor funds committed (if $I_0 = 0$); this is the "zero-investment" value of the firm.

$V$ = the value of the firm given the capital budget that is adopted: this is referred to as the "postinvestment" firm value.

$S^{o\prime}$ and $S^{o}$ = the zero-investment and postinvestment values, respectively, of the old shares, i.e., of the shares that are outstanding before the investment decision (excluding any new shares issued to finance the investment).

[1] For simplicity, it is assumed in this chapter that personal income taxes do not exist. It is easily shown that the results as presented here would apply with personal taxes given certain modifications of the cash flow definitions and given that taxes are such that individuals are indifferent between ordinary income (dividends, interest) and capital gains.

$B^{O\prime}$ and $B^{O}$ = the zero-investment and postinvestment values, respectively, of the old bonds, i.e., of the bonds outstanding before the investment decision (excluding any new bonds issued to finance the investment).

$S^N$ and $B^N$ = the values of new shares and new bonds issued, the proceeds being used to finance current investment.[2]

$\phi = \dfrac{S^N + B^N}{I_0}$ = the proportion of current investment financed by external means, i.e., by the issuance of new stocks $S^N$ and new bonds $B^N$.

$D_0'$ and $D_0$ = the zero-investment and postinvestment values, respectively, of the current (time 0) cash flow to old shareholders.[3]

It is important to understand that there is no *time* difference between the postinvestment and zero-investment values; *post* signifies "given the investment budget that is adopted." Postinvestment quantities equal zero-investment quantities when the investment budget includes no investment. As a second point, all zero-investment and postinvestment terms are at time 0; the 0 time subscript is left off the $V$, $S$, and $B$ terms to simplify notation.

As indicated in the preceding definitions, the stockholders and bondholders that hold the securities of the firm before any new shares and bonds are sold to finance current investment are referred to as the "current" or "old" stockholders and bondholders.[4] The objective of the current (time 0) investment and associated financing decision is to maximize the current value of that part of old shareholders' wealth associated with the firm, $W_S$. This amount equals the sum of dividends paid at time 0 plus the ex-dividend value of the shares at time 0. Therefore,

$$W_S = D_0 + S^O \tag{12-1}$$

The objective of investment policy is to select the ensemble of investments that increases $W_S$ by the greatest amount relative to the level of $W_S$ if current investment were zero. That is, the investment-financing policy that maximizes

[2] It is assumed here for simplicity that no new shares or bonds would currently be issued if investments were zero. This assumption merely simplifies the discussion and in no way alters the investment criteria that are derived. It is easily shown that the same results would hold even if new stocks and bonds were issued with no current investment.

[3] It should be clear from the discussion of firm cash flows, chap. 9, that cash flow paid to old stockholders includes both dividends and cash paid by the firm in purchasing its own shares in the market (treasury shares). However, it is assumed here for simplicity in discussing investment policy that current purchases of treasury shares are zero regardless of investment policy; therefore, any difference between cash currently paid to old shareholders because of a change in the level of investment is entirely reflected in a change in the amount of dividends currently paid out. This difference, as discussed below, is because some of the investment may be financed by reducing the current dividend payout. Introducing treasury shares would mean adding a term in eq. (12-1) representing cash paid for treasury shares; all conclusions regarding investment policy presented in the text would remain essentially unaltered.

[4] If an investment of zero during the current period is determined to be the share-value maximizing strategy, then, of course, $V = V'$, $S = S'$, $B = B'$, and $S^N = B^N = 0$.

$\Delta W_S$ relative to no investment is the best investment plan. The investment strategy is therefore to maximize $W_S$; using Eq. (12-1) this is equivalent to selecting the budget that will

$$\max\left[\Delta D_0 + \Delta S^o\right] \tag{12-2}$$

The criterion of (12-2) states that the best investment-financing strategy is the one which maximizes the increase in wealth of the shareholders resulting from adoption of the strategy.

As defined above, $S^N$ and $B^N$ are new stocks and bonds issued specifically to finance new investment. If new investment is zero ($I_0 = 0$), then $S^N = B^N = 0$. Investment $I_0$ can also be financed by reducing dividends to current stockholders below what they would be if investment were zero.[5] That is, instead of paying dividends the firm could use the same funds for investment. The proportion of $I_0$ that is financed with $S^N$ and $B^N$ is $\phi$. That is,

$$S^N + B^N = \phi I_0 \tag{12-3}$$

The remainder of new investment $(1 - \phi)I_0$ must be financed by reducing dividends relative to what they would be if investment were zero.[6] Recall that $D_0'$ and $D_0$ are the dividends paid to old shareholders given zero investment and given the capital budget that is adopted, respectively. Therefore, since $D_0 - D_0' = \Delta D_0$ (which is negative if dividends are reduced for investment), it follows that

$$D_0 - D_0' = \Delta D_0 = -(1 - \phi)I_0 = (\phi - 1)I_0 \tag{12-4}$$

We know from the definitions stated above that once the capital budget is adopted the value of the current stock and bonds will change to $S$ and $B$. In

[5] Investment at any time $t$, $t = 0, \ldots, \infty$, is defined to include all time $t$ firm cash outlays to enhance firm income $\tilde{X}$ in any or all periods after $t$. This includes the purchase of equity or debt claims issued by other firms or by government agencies. As noted in chap. 1, investment also includes increases in the firm's cash holdings, demand deposits, etc. See footnote 7, p. 10 regarding a slightly different definition that was used in chap. 2 in discussing dividend policy.

[6] Recall from chap. 1 that investment includes any increment to firm cash since firm cash is viewed as a productive asset. It follows that using firm cash to purchase another asset is not net investment (included in $I_0$) but merely the exchange of one productive asset (cash) for another (some noncash asset). Therefore, any net investment $I_0$ must be financed either by selling new securities or by reducing the cash paid out by the firm during the current period to old shareholders or to old bondholders. This cash flow to old security holders of the firm includes payments by the firm to stockholders as dividends or to acquire the firm's own shares (treasury stock); and payments to bondholders as interest, principal (at the time of debt retirement), or to purchase the firm's own bonds in the open market (treasury bonds). However, it will be assumed here that the financing of investment from a reduction in cash to old security holders is *only from a reduction in dividends*. That is, zero-investment and postinvestment cash flow to old bondholders (as interest, principal, or for treasury bonds) are assumed to be equal. And, as noted in footnote 3, p. 304, any effect of investment on cash paid to old stockholders is only through a change in dividends; zero-investment and postinvestment purchases of treasury stock are assumed to be zero. Therefore, the difference between $D_0$ and $D_0'$ (if there is any financing by reducing cash paid to old stockholders) is due entirely to a reduction in dividends currently paid.

addition, new securities ($S^N$ and $B^N$) may be sold to finance the capital budget. The value of the firm once the budget is adopted and financed will be $V = S^O + B^O + S^N + B^N$; that is, the sum of the values of the old securities once investment is made plus the values of any new securities issued. Since $V' = S^{O'} + B^{O'}$, the value of the firm's shares if investment is zero can be expressed as

$$S^{O'} = V' - B^{O'} \tag{12-5}$$

Similarly, the postinvestment value of old shares is

$$S^O = V - B^O - S^N - B^N \tag{12-6}$$

Since $\Delta S^O$ appears in the investment criterion of (12-2), it is the difference in $S^O$ and $S^{O'}$ that is of interest. Subtracting Eq. (12-5) from Eq. (12-6),

$$\Delta S^O = S^O - S^{O'} = \Delta V - \Delta B^O - S^N - B^N \tag{12-7}$$

where $\Delta V = V - V'$ and $\Delta B^O = B^O - B^{O'}$.

Although the term $\Delta B^O$ in Eq. (12-7) is generally assumed equal to zero in capital budgeting discussions, this assumption may not be valid. Quantity $\Delta B^O$ is the change in the value of the old bonds (not including new bonds $B^N$) due to the new investment. This change can occur from two sources:

1. If $B^N \neq 0$, that is, if new bonds are sold to finance the investment, and if the old bonds do not have priority over the new bonds, the existing bonds may become more risky.
2. Even if the old bonds have priority over the new bonds or if no new bonds are issued, the investment will alter the distribution of firm earnings. This can alter the distribution of returns to the existing bonds, either lowering or raising the riskiness of the bonds. A fall in risk could occur if the investments of the firm shifted the entire income stream of the firm upward, reducing the likelihood that interest payments on the old bonds could not be met. Or the firm's income stream could become more risky if investment were undertaken that promised a high possible return but also increased the probability of a very large loss. Therefore, the result of investment can be to produce $\Delta B^O > 0$ or $\Delta B^O < 0$ (or $\Delta B^O = 0$), depending upon the particular case.

Therefore, even if all new bonds $B^N$ are assumed to be subordinated to (have lower priority than) old bonds, the firm's investment decisions may affect the value of the old bonds. Acknowledging this fact, we shall assume from now on that investment and its associated financing do not change the distribution of returns or the value of existing debt. This assumption is ordinarily made in capital budgeting theory since it significantly simplifies the discussion. Furthermore, as explained in Chap. 17, with the perfect-markets assumptions (A.1 to A.8 on p. 280) made in this chapter, maximization of firm value and shareholder wealth are consistent with one another; therefore the investment criteria developed in this chapter fully apply even with 1 and 2 above a possibility. Simplifying, we assume that $\Delta B^O = 0$. Letting $\Delta B^O = 0$ in Eq. (12-7),

$$\Delta S^O = \Delta V - S^N - B^N \tag{12-8}$$

Substituting Eq. (12-3) into Eq. (12-8), it follows that

$$\Delta S^O = \Delta V - \phi I_0 \tag{12-9}$$

Substituting $\Delta D_0$ of Eq. (12-4) and $\Delta S^O$ of Eq. (12-9) into the investment criterion (12-2), that criterion becomes

$$\max \{[(\phi - 1)I_0] + [\Delta V - \phi I_0]\}$$

or, simplifying,

$$\max [\Delta V - I_0] \tag{12-10}$$

Thus, the investment criterion becomes (12-10). The ensemble of current investments that achieves a maximum difference between firm value change $\Delta V$ and the cost of the ensemble of investments $I_0$ is that which maximizes current shareholder wealth. *The criterion of* (12-10) *holds with or without firm taxes.* As will become clear in the discussion below, $\Delta V$ is independent of the method of financing the budget if there are no firm taxes but is dependent upon financing method if such taxes exist.

## PERFECT MARKETS AND THE INVESTMENT CRITERION WITH NO FIRM TAXES

The investment criterion (12-10) holds with or without firm taxes. In the present section, it will be assumed that no such taxes exist. In addition to the terms defined at the beginning of this chapter, the following terms will also be used:

$\tilde{\mathbf{Y}}' = (\tilde{Y}'_1, \tilde{Y}'_2, \ldots, \tilde{Y}'_\infty)$ = the total future cash-flow stream of the firm paid to stockholders and bondholders if no investment is currently made, that is, $I_0 = 0$; this is referred to as the zero-investment cash flow since it is the cash flow if no funds arc committed for investment. Term $\tilde{Y}'_t$, $t - 1, \ldots, \infty$, is cash flow for period $t$.

$\tilde{\mathbf{Y}} = (\tilde{Y}_1, \tilde{Y}_2, \ldots, \tilde{Y}_\infty)$ = the total future cash-flow stream of the firm given adoption of the capital budget; this is referred to as the postinvestment cash flow.

$\Delta\tilde{\mathbf{Y}} = \tilde{\mathbf{Y}} - \tilde{\mathbf{Y}}'$ = the change in the firm's future cash flow due to the investment budget.

$V_{\Delta Y}$ = the value of the incremental stream $\mathbf{\Delta Y}$ if it were available as a single stream in the market.

From earlier discussion, we know that $V'$ and $V$ are the zero-investment and postinvestment values of the firm; they are the firm values given cash flows paid to investors of $\tilde{\mathbf{Y}}'$ and $\tilde{\mathbf{Y}}$, respectively. Other terms will be defined as introduced.

In the previous section, nothing was indicated with regard to whether $\Delta V$ depends upon:

1. The stochastic (statistical) relationship of the earnings from the capital budget to the other earnings of the firm or of any statistical relationships of the earnings of the projects that comprise the capital budget.
2. The method of financing the capital budget.

**1** concerns the issue of firm diversification. That is, it deals with whether or not the effect of a new investment on firm value depends upon the stochastic relationship of a project's returns to the returns of the firm's other assets, including the returns from other current projects being undertaken. Of course, there is no question that *economic* relationships are important; it is the *statistical* (or *stochastic*) relationship that is being referred to here with regard to diversification. See Chap. 3 (on economic relationships) and Chap. 8 (pages 165–166) for a discussion of this distinction between economic and statistical relationships. Two opportunities are economically independent if adoption of one does not affect returns from the other; statistical independence means that the probability of any particular return from one is the same regardless of the return from the other, implying that returns from the two opportunities are uncorrelated.

**2** confronts the question of whether the effect of investment on total firm value may depend upon how it is financed, e.g., by the issuance of new bonds or new stock, or by the use of retained earnings. From the analysis of Chap. 11 we know that, in the absence of taxes, financing policy is irrelevant in perfect markets. Let us therefore consider the no-tax case first.

## The Optimal Capital Budget

In this section we shall look at the criterion that must be used to determine the optimal capital budget assuming perfect capital markets and no firm taxes. Under these assumptions we shall show that the optimal budget can be determined without considering the stochastic relationships between the earnings from undertaking any budget and the earnings from the existing assets of the firm. Furthermore, the method of financing the budget is irrelevant; that is, the same criterion arises for any combination of financing from new stock, new bonds, or internal financing.

It was shown in Chap. 9 that in perfect markets

$$\text{If } \tilde{\mathbf{Y}}_T = \sum_{i=1}^{n} \tilde{\mathbf{Y}}_i \qquad \text{then } V_T = \sum_{i=1}^{n} V_i$$

where $V_i$ is the market value of the stream $\tilde{\mathbf{Y}}_i$. This relationship was termed the value-additivity principle (VAP) and states that, at equilibrium, the total value of any set of streams received by investors is the same regardless of how those streams are divided into the debt and/or equity streams of one or more firms.

We shall use the VAP throughout this chapter, since it forms the basis for all our general proofs regarding investment policy in perfect markets. Indeed, it will be found that project evaluation is *not* valid in most cases unless the value-additivity principle holds. With respect to our present problem of an optimal budget, we shall make the general point first and then work through the formal proof.

Essentially our proposition is that, in perfect markets, the value of the firm (and the value of outstanding shares) is maximized if the difference between the value of the incremental cash flow of the firm provided by the budget $V_{\Delta Y}$ and the cost of the budget $I_0$ is maximized. Formally, we shall argue that the general criterion stated earlier in the chapter,

$$\max\,[\Delta V - I_0] \tag{12-10}$$

in perfect markets becomes

$$\max\,[V_{\Delta Y} - I_0] \tag{12-11}$$

Quantity $V_{\Delta Y}$ is the market value of the incremental stream $\mathbf{\Delta\tilde{Y}}$ that would obtain if $\mathbf{\Delta\tilde{Y}}$ were currently available in the market as an individual stream. For example, if the firm were to spin off its current investment as a separate firm providing $\mathbf{\Delta\tilde{Y}}$ to the market, that separate firm would be worth $V_{\Delta Y}$. Notice that $V_{\Delta Y}$ does *not* depend upon how $\mathbf{\Delta\tilde{Y}}$ might be divided into debt and equity streams since in perfect markets we know from Chap. 11 that the debt-equity division of a stream does not affect its value in the no-tax case. This will be alluded to again in the discussion below.

An understanding of the meaning of the variable $\mathbf{\Delta\tilde{Y}}$ is critical to an understanding of the general problem, the proof, and subsequent arguments. The variable $\mathbf{\Delta\tilde{Y}}$ represents the set of *future* incremental cash returns provided by the current investment of $I_0$. Symbolically, $\mathbf{\Delta\tilde{Y}} = [\Delta\tilde{Y}_1, \Delta\tilde{Y}_2, \Delta\tilde{Y}_3, \ldots, \Delta\tilde{Y}_n]$, where the subscripts refer to the points in time of the particular cash flows.[7] For any time $t$, $\Delta\tilde{Y}_t = \Delta(\tilde{X}_t - I_t) = \Delta\tilde{X}_t - \Delta\tilde{I}_t$; that is, the change in cash flow to security holders equals the change in cash income $\tilde{X}_t$ less the change in firm capital outlays $\tilde{I}_t$ that are occasioned by the current (time 0) investment com-

[7] See chap. 9 for a more detailed discussion of firm cash flow. As explained in chap. 9. $\tilde{\mathbf{Y}}$ is the net cash "pumped" into the capital markets by the firm via its current and new stockholders and bondholders; this equals the difference between what is paid out as dividends, interest, principal payments, and for purchase of the firm's own securities (treasury stock and bonds) and the amount received by the firm in selling new stock and bonds. As noted above, for simplicity it is assumed that bonds and stock are currently issued only if there is investment (footnote p. 304) and that the current investment budget does not affect firm policy regarding current treasury stock purchases (assumed zero; footnote 3, p. 304). Under these assumptions, it follows from the chap. 9 discussion of firm cash flows that the current (time 0) cash flow to stockholders (old and new) equals $Y_0^S = (D_0 - S^N)$ and to bondholders (old and new) equals $Y_0^B$ = [(interest on old debt) + (principal on retired debt) + (treasury bonds) $- B^N$]. With no taxes, $(Y_0^S + Y_0^B) = Y_0 = (X_0 - I_0)$; and, with firm taxes, $(Y_0^S + Y_0^B) = Y_0 = (X_0 - I_0 - \text{Tax}_0)$, where $Y_0^S$ is the after-tax equity cash flow, $Y_0^B$ is the untaxed debt stream (debt payments are not taxed), and $\text{Tax}_0$ is taxes currently paid by the firm.

mitment $I_0$. The particular values assumed in each period are of course uncertain, as is reflected by the tilde. That is, since $\Delta\tilde{\mathbf{Y}}$ is the change in future cash flow as anticipated by investors who value the firm at time 0, $\Delta\tilde{\mathbf{Y}}$ represents a multiperiod set of random variables, $\Delta\tilde{Y}_t$, $t = 1, \ldots, \infty$. The cash flows are incremental to the firm from undertaking the capital budget. The incremental flows represent the changes in firm cash flow at each point in time due to the investment $I_0$. Variable $\Delta\tilde{\mathbf{Y}}$ includes any increase (or decrease) in returns from other assets already owned by the firm due to the investment, as well as the direct returns of the new assets added by the expenditure of $I_0$.

To make (12-10) reduce to (12-11) we must show that the change in total value of the firm $\Delta V = V - V'$ is equal to $V_{\Delta Y}$, the market value of the incremental income provided by $I_0$. In other words, we must show that $V = V' + V_{\Delta Y}$. The market value of the firm is based upon the cash flow $\tilde{\mathbf{Y}}$ generated by the firm and received by investors in the market. Investment can change the distribution of that cash-flow stream and can therefore change firm value. The current investment budget changes $\tilde{\mathbf{Y}}$ from $\tilde{\mathbf{Y}}'$ to $\tilde{\mathbf{Y}}$, this change of $\Delta\tilde{\mathbf{Y}} = \tilde{\mathbf{Y}} - \tilde{\mathbf{Y}}'$ being the incremental cash flow from the investment budget. That is,

$$\tilde{\mathbf{Y}} = \tilde{\mathbf{Y}}' + \Delta\tilde{\mathbf{Y}} \tag{12-12}$$

Applying the VAP to (12-12) we get[8]

$$V = V' + V_{\Delta Y} \tag{12-13}$$

Since $\Delta V = V - V'$ (by definition), it follows from (12-13) that $\Delta V = V_{\Delta Y}$ and, substituting into (12-10), the criterion for the optimal capital budget becomes what we set out to prove it to be, namely,

$$\max\,[V_{\Delta Y} - I_0] \tag{12-11}$$

Expression (12-11) reveals two very important points. First, notice that this criterion is entirely in terms of the value of the marginal income stream $V_{\Delta Y}$ and of the current outlay $I_0$ associated with the capital budget. The *stochastic* relationship of $\Delta\tilde{\mathbf{Y}}$ to $\tilde{\mathbf{Y}}'$ is irrelevant since $\tilde{\mathbf{Y}}'$ or its value $V'$ does not enter (12-11). Second, nothing was indicated regarding the relative proportions of $I_0$ financed from $B^N$ and $S^N$. Quantities $V_{\Delta Y}$ and $I_0$ and therefore the criterion of (12-11) are independent of the method of financing the project. As noted above, $V_{\Delta Y}$—the value that an incremental stream of the distribution of $\Delta\tilde{\mathbf{Y}}$ would have if available as a separate stream in the market—is a given value independent of how $\Delta\tilde{\mathbf{Y}}$ is divided into debt and equity streams. That is, the incremental stream has a value $V_{\Delta Y}$ that is independent of debt-equity considerations since, in taxless

[8] The assumption of perfect markets means that the firm is sufficiently small that its investment $I_0$ will not affect the valuation which investors place on other streams in the market. These latter streams include $\tilde{\mathbf{Y}}'$, the zero-investment returns of the firm. That is, the market valuation of a stream of the form of $\tilde{\mathbf{Y}}'$ is assumed to be unaltered by the introduction to the market of new stream $\Delta\tilde{\mathbf{Y}}$.

perfect markets (assumed in this section), all streams have a value that is independent of how those streams are divided into flows to equity and debt claims. These two conclusions regarding the irrelevancy of stochastic relationships and of the method of financing also hold with partial or total internal financing ($\phi < 1$) since, as is clear from the derivation of (12-10) and therefore (12-11), (12-11) also holds in that case.

It is very important that the meaning of the argument that the stochastic relationship of $\mathbf{\Delta\tilde{Y}}$ to $\mathbf{\tilde{Y}'}$ is irrelevant be understood. This means that a given distribution for $\mathbf{\Delta\tilde{Y}}$, the added future cash flow due to the investment budget, implies a particular incremental value for the firm due to $\mathbf{\Delta\tilde{Y}}$; this is so regardless of the correlation between $\mathbf{\Delta\tilde{Y}}$ and $\mathbf{\tilde{Y}'}$. Amount $\mathbf{\Delta\tilde{Y}}$ incorporates all benefits to the firm from the investment budget; it is the change in firm cash flow from all types of gains due to the investment. Therefore, the synergistic production effects between the assets generating $\mathbf{\tilde{Y}'}$ and those additional assets that raise $\mathbf{\tilde{Y}'}$ to $\mathbf{\tilde{Y}}$ (where $\mathbf{\Delta\tilde{Y}} = \mathbf{\tilde{Y}} - \mathbf{\tilde{Y}'}$) are taken into account in determining the level of $\mathbf{\Delta\tilde{Y}}$. But, given whatever $\mathbf{\Delta\tilde{Y}}$ turns out to be, the correlation between $\mathbf{\Delta\tilde{Y}}$ and $\mathbf{\tilde{Y}'}$ is irrelevant. Thus, if two firms $G$ and $H$ with different zero-investment cash flows adopt investment budgets that happen to raise firm cash flow by identical amounts $\mathbf{\Delta\tilde{Y}}$, both firms will raise the values of their total firm cash flows (i.e., will raise total firm value) by $V_{\Delta Y}$. This is so even though the preinvestment cash flows of the two firms differ, i.e., even though $\mathbf{\tilde{Y}}'_G$ and $\mathbf{\tilde{Y}}'_H$ differ completely.[9]

## Project Returns and Firm Cash Flow: The Equivalence of $\mathbf{\tilde{Z}}$ and $\mathbf{\tilde{Y}}_Z$

In the preceding discussion, $\mathbf{\Delta\tilde{Y}}$ was defined as the increment to the future cash flow paid to investors in the market as a consequence of the current investment outlay. Since investors value the firm on the basis of the cash flow generated over time by the firm, it is clearly this effect on firm cash flow that is relevant in determining the impact of the investment budget on the value of the firm and on the value of the firm's shares. In the discussion below treating project evaluation, the effect on firm cash flow from a project $Z$ will be desig-

[9] To see how statistical dependencies could matter in *imperfect* markets, assume for simplicity a one-period world and assume that the mean and variance of the cash flows of firms $G$ and $H$ are $\bar{Y}'_G = 100$, $\sigma^2(\tilde{Y}'_G) = 36$, $\bar{Y}'_H = 100$, $\sigma^2(\tilde{Y}'_H) = 36$. Assume a project $Z$ yielding incremental stream $\tilde{Z}$ with mean and variance $\bar{Z} = 40$, $\sigma^2(\tilde{Z}) = 16$, where the incremental stream $\tilde{Z}$ is the same for firms $G$ and $H$, that is, $\tilde{Y}_G - \tilde{Y}'_G = \tilde{Z} = \tilde{Y}_H - \tilde{Y}'_H$. However, assume that correlation coefficient $\rho(\tilde{Y}'_G, \tilde{Z}) = \frac{1}{2}$ and $\rho(\tilde{Y}'_H, \tilde{Z}) = -\frac{1}{2}$. If firm $G$ adopts the project, $\bar{Y}_G = 140$, $\sigma^2(\tilde{Y}_G) = 76$; if firm $H$ adopts the project, $\bar{Y}_H = 140$, $\sigma^2(\tilde{Y}_H) = 28$. The project raises the variance of firm $G$'s cash flow and lowers the variance of firm $H$'s cash flow. Thus, it is clear that firm $G$ and firm $H$ might, in *imperfect* markets, value project $Z$ differently. This is so even in this simple case, in which $\bar{Y}'_G = \bar{Y}'_H$ and $\sigma^2(\tilde{Y}'_G) = \sigma^2(\tilde{Y}'_H)$. But with *perfect markets* and the VAP, project $Z$ is of the same value to firm $G$ and firm $H$ since $\tilde{Z}$ is the same for each firm; therefore, $V_Z$, the value of $\tilde{Z}$, is the same. The stochastic relationship between $\tilde{Y}'$ and $\tilde{Z}$ is irrelevant; only the distribution of $\tilde{Z}$ is relevant.

nated $\tilde{\mathbf{Z}}$, where

$$\tilde{\mathbf{Z}} = \tilde{\mathbf{X}}_Z - \tilde{\mathbf{I}}_Z = (\tilde{X}_{Z1} - \tilde{I}_{Z1}, \tilde{X}_{Z2} - \tilde{I}_{Z2}, \ldots, \tilde{X}_{Z\infty} - \tilde{I}_{Z\infty})$$

vectors $\tilde{\mathbf{X}}_Z$ and $\tilde{\mathbf{I}}_Z$ are the vectors of future cash income and future capital outlays, respectively, caused by project $Z$. That is, $\tilde{\mathbf{X}}_Z$ is the change in future cash income (revenues less noninvestment expenses) and $\tilde{\mathbf{I}}_Z$ is the change in future firm investment due to adopting project $Z$. Stream $\tilde{\mathbf{Z}}$ is the added net cash flow received by the firm from the project.

Of great importance is the point that $\tilde{\mathbf{Z}}$ is by definition equal to the change in future cash flow paid to investors in the market which arises as a consequence of adopting the project. This is so since $(\tilde{\mathbf{X}}_Z - \tilde{\mathbf{I}}_Z)$ is the incremental effect on firm $(\tilde{\mathbf{X}} - \tilde{\mathbf{I}})$, where $(\tilde{\mathbf{X}} - \tilde{\mathbf{I}})$ equals $\tilde{\mathbf{Y}}$. Recall from Chap. 1 that $\tilde{\mathbf{I}}$ includes any addition to firm cash, since firm-held cash is viewed here as a productive investment. Thus, in determining $\tilde{\mathbf{Z}}$ the firm examines the effect on future cash income and on future investment (including that in cash) to determine the relevant return from an investment; this relevant return is the increment to the cash flow paid to investors in the market resultant from the project.

The question arises as to why we have used the notation $\tilde{\mathbf{Z}}$ instead of, for example, $\tilde{\mathbf{Y}}_Z$, since $\tilde{\mathbf{Y}}$ is used throughout to signify cash flow. This could have been done, but it was felt that in treating project evaluation it would be helpful to highlight the fact that firm management is observing the cash flow at the stage at which the *firm* is receiving the flow from a given project. The firm can be viewed as a conduit through which the cash flow passes; that cash flow as it is received by the firm is referred to as $\tilde{\mathbf{Z}}$. It then pays out the entire cash flow $\tilde{\mathbf{Z}}$ to investors, who receive it as $\tilde{\mathbf{Y}}_Z$ in the market. The two quantities are necessarily identical in all cases since both $\tilde{\mathbf{Z}}$ and $\tilde{\mathbf{Y}}_Z$ are defined as $(\tilde{\mathbf{X}}_Z - \tilde{\mathbf{I}}_Z)$ [or as expressed in (12-31) in the tax case].

## Project Selection

**The general problem.** A "project" was defined in Chap. 3 as a group of investment opportunities, each of which is economically independent of all opportunities not included in that project. Two opportunities are economically independent if the adoption of one does not affect the profitability (net cash flow generated) or possibility of acceptance of the other. The same definition of project is applicable here.

The rule for project selection is developed as follows. Let $I_{Z0}$ be the initial (time 0) cost of project $Z$, which would yield to the firm the incremental cash flow of $\tilde{\mathbf{Z}}$. We know from (12-11) that the objective is to select the overall investment budget that maximizes the difference between the value of the incremental stream from the total budget and the investment outlay. Any new project is therefore justified only if its addition to the budget increases $[V_{\Delta Y} - I_0]$. From the definition of a project we know that the addition of project $Z$ to the capital budget would result in a new budget outlay of $I_0 + I_{Z0}$ and a new incremental stream $\mathbf{\Delta\tilde{Y}} + \mathbf{\tilde{Z}}$. By the VAP, the value of $(\mathbf{\Delta\tilde{Y}} + \mathbf{\tilde{Z}})$ equals $V_{\Delta Y} + V_Z$, where $V_Z$ is the value that stream $\mathbf{\tilde{Z}}$ would have if available in the market as an individual stream. Thus, project $Z$ raises the value of the stream from the investment budget by $V_Z$ and raises capital outlays at time 0 by $I_{Z0}$. Since it is the difference between the incremental value and the investment outlay that we wish to maximize [criterion (12-11)], it follows that project $Z$ should be undertaken (i.e., one or more of the project's opportunities should be adopted) if and only if

$$[(V_{\Delta Y} + V_Z) - (I_0 + I_{Z0})] > [V_{\Delta Y} - I_0]$$

or

$$V_Z - I_{Z0} > 0 \tag{12-14}$$

In short, we get the same general project-selection rule we had in Chaps. 3 and 8: namely, that the net present value $(V_Z - I_{Z0})$ be greater than zero.[10]

The significance of (12-14) lies in the fact that *each project available to the firm can be evaluated separately*. The comments in Chap. 8 with respect to *economic* and *statistical* (or *stochastic*) independence apply here as well since (8-18), the project-selection rule of Chap. 8, is simply a special case of (12-14). Firm diversification per se (i.e., consideration of *stochastic* dependencies between $\mathbf{\tilde{Z}}$ and any other cash flow of the firm) still has no role in the firm's investment strategy. The criterion is that the market value of $\mathbf{\tilde{Z}}$ if it were available individually in the market, $V_Z$, must exceed the time 0 cost of the investment, $I_{Z0}$.

It is important to appreciate the importance of being able to disregard stochastic relationships between projects. If the VAP did not hold, then the effect on firm value of every combination of opportunities available to the firm would have to be evaluated. This is so since not only *economic* dependencies but also *statistical* dependencies between opportunities would determine how a set of adopted opportunities affected the postinvestment firm cash flow and therefore firm value. The statistical dependencies between the cash flows of the various new opportunities available to the firm and the statistical dependencies between the cash flows of those opportunities and of the existing assets of the firm would all be relevant.[11] Thus, for example, if statistical dependencies could *not* be ignored, and if the firm had 20 *economically independent* opportunities (each, therefore, a "project"), the firm would have to analyze not 20 alternatives (adopt or reject each of the 20 projects), but $2^{20}$ alternatives. With the VAP, however, each of these 20 economically independent opportunities could be treated separately as projects since statistical dependencies between

[10] There is indifference regarding adoption of project $Z$ if $V_Z - I_{Z0} = 0$.

[11] See the footnote on p. 311 for an illustration of how the statistical correlation between project cash flow $\mathbf{\tilde{Z}}$ and zero-investment cash flow $\mathbf{\tilde{Y}}'$ affects the distribution of postinvestment cash flow $\mathbf{\tilde{Y}}$.

projects can be ignored; only 20 decisions must be made.[12] As with the certainty case described in Chap. 3, only *economic* dependencies and not *statistical* dependencies are relevant in dividing opportunities into independent packages (projects) if the VAP holds.

Notice that the investment project $Z$ discussed above can assume any of a variety of forms. Project $Z$ can be investment in an additional machine for a factory or it can be the purchase of any entire corporate entity. The former is the more usual form of investment; the latter is frequently termed "diversification." Both, however, are correctly regarded as investment. In either case, it has just been shown that regardless of the type of investment, the value of the cash-flow stream from the investment is the market value of that stream if it were individually available in the market.

The preceding discussion does *not* imply that stream $\tilde{\mathbf{Z}}$ from a given project is the same for all firms regardless of who adopts the project. A given investment opportunity may be more profitable to one firm than to another. For example, a hotel may be an unprofitable investment to a foodpacker just as a packing machine is useless to a hotel-management firm. Different skills and production advantages exist for different companies and, consequently, any given project is likely to have differing profitability between firms. The results established in the discussion above show that for any project $Z$ yielding $\tilde{\mathbf{Z}}$ (where $\tilde{\mathbf{Z}}$ may differ between firms), the value of that project to the adopting firm is $V_Z$. The statistical relationship between $\tilde{\mathbf{Z}}$ and $\tilde{\mathbf{Y}}'$, or between $\tilde{\mathbf{Z}}$ and cash flows from other projects currently adopted, is irrelevant. Of course, $\tilde{\mathbf{Z}}$ and therefore $V_Z$ may vary between firms for the given project $Z$, for example, as with a packing machine between a foodpacker and hotel firm. But for any firm adopting project $Z$, the resulting $\tilde{\mathbf{Z}}$ implies a resulting $V_Z$ from the project if adopted by that firm, and it is this $V_Z$ that equals the benefits of the project to that firm.

It is worth repeating that it makes no difference how any project is financed in taxless perfect markets. Value $V_Z$ is the market value of a cash stream of the form $\tilde{\mathbf{Z}}$ and, as established in Chap. 11, the value of a cash-flow stream in taxless perfect markets is independent of how it is divided into debt or equity streams. Thus $V_Z$ is a unique value that holds regardless of financing method.

[12] It is extremely important to note here that it is *every* combination of *opportunities* and not just of *projects* that must be evaluated if statistical dependencies are relevant. This is discussed in detail in chap. 14. Thus, assume that a firm has five investment opportunities, with two in project $A$ and three in project $B$. Assume that none of the opportunities is mutually exclusive. Using the project-evaluation procedure appropriate here with perfect capital markets (in which case statistical dependencies are *not* relevant), in project $A$ there are four *alternatives* (opportunity one alone, two alone, one and two together, and none), and in project $B$ there are eight alternatives. This is a total of 12 alternatives requiring evaluation. As explained below, the procedure of chap. 3 is still relevant here; the best alternative in each project is accepted. If statistical dependencies were *relevant* (as in the *imperfect* markets case considered in a later chapter), every combination of the total of five opportunities would have to be evaluated; this is 32 ($2^5$) combinations. Project evaluation is no longer applicable.

**Mutually exclusive alternatives.** The implications of (12-11) for the problem of choosing among mutually exclusive alternatives are fairly obvious. Given a project that consists of a set of mutually exclusive investment alternatives, let $\tilde{\mathbf{Z}}_i$ and $I_{Z_i0}$ represent the future cash flow and initial cost of alternative i which are incremental to the firm if alternative **i** is chosen.[13] $V_{Z_i}$ is then the value of the incremental cash flow $\tilde{\mathbf{Z}}_i$ if it were available in the market as an individual stream. From the VAP, we know that (12-11) implies that for each project we should choose the "best" alternative i that satisfies the following condition:

$$[V_{Z_i} - I_{Z_i0}] \quad \text{is maximum} \tag{12-15}$$

The best alternative must satisfy relation (12-16) below since one alternative is to not accept any opportunity in the project (which would have a zero $V_Z - I_{Z0}$):

$$V_{Z_i} - I_{Z_i0} \geq 0 \tag{12-16}$$

Expression (12-16) states the requirement that no project will be undertaken unless it yields an incremental cash flow with a market value exceeding its cost. In short, the general criteria developed in Chaps. 3 and 8 apply here as well.

**Summary of the procedure for investment analysis.** In summary, the procedure the firm should follow in analyzing its investment opportunities, assuming perfect markets, no taxes, and uncertainty is:

1. Define the total set of investment opportunities available to the firm.
2. Divide the opportunities into the *maximum* number of projects achievable. Any two opportunities that are *economically* dependent must be included in the same project; thus, an opportunity is *economically* independent of all opportunities not within the same project. All opportunities are within some project; it is possible for a project to be made up of only one opportunity.
3. For *each* project defined in (2) above:
   (*a*) Define every possible combination of opportunities within that project. Each combination is referred to as an "alternative." One of the alternatives is to accept none of the opportunities in the project (to reject the project). The other alternatives contain one or more opportunities.
   (*b*) From the alternatives identified under 3(*a*) above, determine and adopt the alternative i that has the maximum value less cost. That is, for project $Z$ select the alternative i that has the

$$\max\,[V_{Z_i} - I_{Z_i0}]$$

[13] See chap. 3 on the meaning of investment "alternatives" within a project and on the process of evaluating alternatives.

where $V_{Z_i}$ is the market value of the cash-flow stream $\tilde{\mathbf{Z}}_i$ that will be generated by alternative i and $I_{Z_i0}$ is the current outlay associated with alternative i. All alternatives other than the best alternative i are rejected. The alternative of accepting none of the opportunities has a $[V_Z - I_{Z0}]$ of zero; this will be the alternative that is adopted if every other alternative in the project has a negative $[V_Z - I_{Z0}]$.

The steps above are essentially the same as those outlined in Chap. 3 for the certainty case. Opportunities are divided into projects; each project contains a set of opportunities, each of which is *economically* independent of all opportunities not within the same project. Statistical dependencies are completely ignored (of course, there were no statistical dependence problems in Chap. 3 since all streams were certain). For each project $Z$, the alternative with the highest "net value" $(V_{Z_i} - I_{Z_i0})$ is determined; project $Z$ is accepted if and only if $(V_{Z_i} - I_{Z_i0}) > 0$. This is identical to the certainty case except that a market value of an uncertain stream $V_{Z_i}$ is used instead of the present value of a certain stream.

It should be clear that although the rules we have derived are very powerful and completely general in the case of taxless perfect markets, we have not said anything about how management is supposed to estimate $V_Z$. This is a difficult problem. However, at least our analysis here has reduced it to one of manageable size. Management can make optimal investment decisions on a project-by-project basis rather than considering all kinds of stochastic interaction effects among all present and potential opportunities. A particular valuation model is examined next, because it has practical application and because it illustrates some interesting aspects of the decision process.

## Applications of the Investment Criterion

The problem faced by management is to determine the market value of the incremental cash flows of proposed projects and alternatives. An implication of the analysis of Chap. 9 is that there is no way for management to know with certainty what $V_Z$ is. In other words, management must estimate $V_Z$. With homogeneous expectations, which are assumed in this chapter, management and investors will agree on the estimate of $V_Z$ and therefore this estimate is an appropriate basis for the firm's investment decision.

It is important to note that *the investment strategy described in the previous section is fully applicable regardless of how the cash-flow streams vary over time and regardless of how investors in the market value cash-flow streams.* Although a particularly useful model (the discount model) will be suggested in this section, the discussion of the previous sections would fully hold even if this model were not appropriate.

For an estimating procedure to be useful in the capital budgeting procedures of large, multidivisional corporations, it must have certain particular features:

1. The procedure must be such that many people within the corporation can understand it and be able to use it.
2. The procedure must not require managers at all levels to be intimately familiar with current conditions in the capital markets.
3. The procedure must provide reasonable estimates.

There does exist a valuation model that meets these criteria—the risk-adjusted discount-rate approach. We shall now develop this model formally.

**The discount-rate model.** Assume that income streams are discounted in the market by investors at rates which depend on the investors' risk preferences and on the perceived distributions of the streams. Assume also that management and investors agree on the expected values of the stream provided by any project $Z$ and that a single discount rate is used. For any given stream $\tilde{\mathbf{Z}}$ there is some equilibrium rate of discount $k_Z$. The market value of cash-flow stream $\tilde{\mathbf{Z}} = (\tilde{Z}_1, \tilde{Z}_2, \ldots, \tilde{Z}_\infty)$.

$$V_Z = \sum_{t=1}^{\infty} \frac{\bar{Z}_t}{(1 + k_Z)^t} \tag{12-17}$$

where $\bar{Z}_t$ is the expected value of the cash flow in time $t$ from project $Z$. Note that for some $t$, $\tilde{Z}_t = 0$ may hold. Thus, the stream may be of finite length in time, e.g., extending only to time $n$ if $\tilde{Z}_t = 0$ for all $t > n$. $V_Z$ is the value that cash-flow stream $\tilde{\mathbf{Z}}$ would have in the market. The resulting level of $V_Z$ can be used in the investment criteria stated earlier, given the assumptions that imply the discount model. Note that the model is a general version of the discount-rate model of Chap. 8. Under the much more restrictive assumptions of Chap. 8 we were there able to specify precisely how $k_Z$ should be determined.

In general we cannot be certain that the discount model is the basis for valuation in the capital markets. However, this is not strictly necessary as we saw in Chap. 9, where we noted that a unique discount rate will usually exist that will equate the discounted stream of expected values of the cash flows to the market value of the stream.[14] If the discount rates applicable to different streams are not dependent on the magnitudes of the streams (but only on the distribution per dollar of expected return), then it may well be easier to estimate the rates rather than to estimate the market values of the streams directly. In other words, if a unique rate is associated with the perceived risk of a stream, then the discount-rate model can be used. In Chap. 9 we were able to derive an expression for such rates from the equilibrium conditions in the market. The reader should refer back to the discussion on risk-adjusted discount rates in that chapter if this idea is not clear.

[14] This rate will approximate the expected rate of return from ownership of the stream if purchased in the market. The reason it may only be an approximation to the expected rate has to do with the mathematical-probabilistic relationships involved. See P. L. Cheng and M. K. Deets, Statistical Biases and Security Rates of Return, *Journal of Financial and Quantitative Analysis*, vol. 6, pp. 977–994 (especially pp. 978–980), June 1971.

If every investment opportunity available to the firm differs in its risk, there is no particular advantage to the discount model. A different discount rate would have to be estimated for each opportunity. Lacking any more specific guides to aid management in determining the appropriate rate, management might as well estimate $V_Z$ directly. The advantage to the model lies in the likelihood that opportunities may be classifiable into groups of comparable risk. In this case a single discount rate may be usable for all opportunities within a classification. If the number of rates to be estimated is less than the number of opportunities to be evaluated there is an obvious advantage to the model. In any case the model lends support to the following practices:

1. The use of different discount rates ("costs of capital") in different divisions of the same firm or for investments associated with different product lines.
2. The classification of investments by the degree of confidence management has in their estimates of future incremental returns. For example, cost-saving investments, increases in capacity to produce existing product lines, and additional facilities to produce new products may have different rates associated with them.
3. The use of the evaluation methods of Chap. 3 using $k_Z$ as the appropriate criterion rate. (Note that in evaluating alternatives it may be necessary to use the present-value rule with a different rate for each alternative.)

In short, the discount model with rates depending on the risk of the opportunity has some appealing features for investment decisions in perfect markets. In the imperfect markets of Chaps. 14 and 15 we shall argue that there are some additional advantages. True, there are significant theoretical problems with the method, but no alternative method available is superior on theoretical grounds comparable in ease of application to investment decisions.

**The cost of capital.** The term "cost of capital" is often used to refer to the "rate of return" an investment must earn in order for old shareholder wealth [$W_s$ in Eq. (12-1)] to not decline as a consequence of the investment. Using this terminology, the cost of capital for project $Z$ is $k_Z$ in (12-17). In Chap. 13, a more detailed discussion of the cost-of-capital concept is presented.

## Numerical Illustrations

As noted earlier, the investment strategy developed in this chapter and summarized on pages 315 to 316 is applicable regardless of how investors value income streams (i.e., whether the discount-rate model or some other model holds) and regardless of how the cash flows vary over time. In illustrating the criterion, however, it will be assumed that the discount-rate model is applicable and that streams are perpetual. If this simple case is well understood, applications to more complex situations should not be difficult.

Assume a firm with current investment opportunities relating to its restaurant division and to its gas station division. Decisions are to be made with regard to accepting each of the following investment opportunities:

| | |
|---|---|
| Restaurant chain: | To purchase new signs (*S*) |
| | To establish a delivery service (*D*) |
| | To add cigar-dispensing machines at the restaurant (*C*) |
| Gas station chain: | To add a car wash at each station (*W*) |
| | To provide a muffler service at each station (*M*) |

The letters after each investment opportunity (*S, D, C, W,* and *M*) refer to the particular decision. Assume that the returns from the restaurant chain are completely independent *economically* of the returns from the gas station chain. This means that the decisions relating to the two divisions can be treated separately, i.e., opportunities *S, D,* and *C* are in one project and opportunities *W* and *M* are in another. This is so regardless of the statistical relationship between the returns from the two projects, i.e., regardless of the correlation coefficient between returns from the two projects. Assume the further economic relationships:

| | |
|---|---|
| Restaurant chain: | The existence of signs will positively affect returns from at-restaurant business and will also positively affect returns from a delivery service if established. However, the added customers from the signs will be nonsmokers and will therefore have no effect on returns from a cigar-dispensing machine. |
| | The existence of the delivery service will have no effect on the restaurant chain's at-restaurant trade. |
| | The cigar-dispensing machine will not affect returns from adding signs or from adding a delivery service. |
| Gas station chain: | The existence of a car wash will add to sales and to the number of customers. This is also true for the muffler service, which will attract some customers who use the car wash. |

These economic dependency relationships imply that for the restaurants *S* and *D* are dependent but that *C* is independent of *S* and *D*. Opportunity *C* is therefore a project since it is economically independent of all the other opportunities of the firm. For the gas station chain, *W* and *M* are dependent. Therefore, the projects of the firm are:

| | |
|---|---|
| Project *R*: | includes opportunities *S* and *D* |
| Project *C*: | includes opportunity *C* |
| Project *G*: | includes opportunities *W* and *M* |

The *alternatives* (combinations of opportunities) possible for each project are:

| | |
|---|---|
| Project *R*: | adopt only *S*, designated by *S* |
| | adopt only *D*, designated by *D* |
| | adopt both *S* and *D*, designated by *SD* |
| | do not adopt *S* or *D* |

Project $C$: adopt $C$, designated by $C$
do not adopt $C$

Project $G$: adopt only $W$, designated by $W$
adopt only $M$, designated by $M$
adopt both $W$ and $M$, designated by $WM$
do not adopt $W$ or $M$

Each project is to be considered separately, and the best alternative i from each (that with the highest value of future cash flows, $V$, less initial cost of investment $I_0$) should be adopted.

For simplicity, we shall assume that each project is expected to produce a stream of returns beginning *one period hence* (at time 1) but that the distributions of returns (means, variances, etc.) may differ between alternatives. This means that the riskiness of the stream from any given alternative within a project may differ from the riskiness of the stream from any other alternative within that project. For each alternative, the initial cost of investment ($I_{Z0}$), the mean per period future cash income ($\bar{X}_{Zt}$), the mean per period future capital outlays ($\bar{I}_{Zt}$), and therefore the mean per period future net cash flow ($\bar{Z}_t = \bar{X}_{Zt} - \bar{I}_{Zt}$) are indicated in Table 12-1. It is assumed that $\bar{X}_{Zt}$, $\bar{I}_{Zt}$, and therefore $\bar{Z}_t$ are constant for all $t = 1, \ldots, \infty$; that is, they are all perpetuities with a constant mean over time. Therefore, drop the $t$ subscript and designate these annual amounts as $\bar{X}_Z$, $\bar{I}_Z$, and $\bar{Z}$, respectively.

Two points should be noted. First, the fact that all flows have constant means over time obviously does not imply that the streams are riskless. All that is implied is that the mean of the distribution of the flow remains the same from period to period; in any given period the flow may be above or below the mean. Second, recall that the future capital outlay per period $\bar{I}_Z$ is the amount the firm

**table 12-1**

| *Alternative* | *Initial outlay* ($I_{Z0}$) | *Mean annual cash income* ($\bar{X}_Z$) | *Mean annual capital outlay* ($\bar{I}_Z$) | *Mean annual cash flow* [$\bar{Z} = (\bar{X}_Z - \bar{I}_Z)$] |
|---|---|---|---|---|
| Project $R$: | | | | |
| $S$ | 100 | 20 | 8 | 12 |
| $D$ | 200 | 45 | 21 | 24 |
| $SD$ | 300 | 80 | 29 | 51 |
| Project $C$: | 50 | 6 | 2 | 4 |
| Project $G$: | | | | |
| $W$ | 250 | 60 | 8 | 52 |
| $M$ | 100 | 30 | 9 | 21 |
| $WM$ | 325 | 99 | 17 | 82 |

must expend to replace or add to capital goods which is occasioned by the project. Thus, for a restaurant $\bar{I}_Z$ per period beginning at time 1 would involve purchase of new utensils, replacement of a stove, etc., which must be incurred in future periods to sustain the project. Quantity $\bar{I}_Z$ also includes any other increases in firm capital outlays caused by project $Z$ but not directly related to the restaurant, e.g., increased central office accounting equipment due to the greater firm sales resulting from project $Z$. These expenditures are included in $\bar{I}_Z$ because they are capital outlays (costs to enhance revenues in periods after the cost is incurred, i.e., investments). Current outlays are subtracted from current revenues to determine $\bar{X}_Z$. The initial outlay $I_{Z0}$ for the restaurant would include all *initial* (time 0) investment in utensils, fixtures such as ovens and refrigerators, etc., which would produce revenues in future periods.

Unless it is specified how investors value income streams, the analysis cannot proceed any further, since a measure of $V_Z$ is needed. Therefore, assume that the discount model described in the previous section is applicable, i.e., that the value of a cash-flow stream received by investors equals the discounted expected cash flows in all future periods using a discount rate appropriate to the particular stream. Assume that the discount rate, value of the cash flow, and value of the cash flow less the initial outlay are as indicated in Table 12-2 for each investment alternative. Recall that a constant amount $\bar{Z}$ per period in perpetuity discounts to $(\bar{Z}/k_Z)$ as is indicated in the table.

The alternative i with the highest $(V_{Z_i} - I_{Z_i0})$ is $SD$ for project $R$, to not adopt opportunity $C$ for project $C$ and $WM$ for project $G$. Since the $(V_{Z_i} - I_{Z_i0})$ is positive for $SD$, zero for $C$, and positive for $WM$, it follows from the project-evaluation criterion stated earlier in the chapter [relation (12-14)] that $SD$ (and therefore project $R$) is accepted, $C$ (and therefore project $C$) is rejected, and $WM$ (and therefore project $G$) is accepted.

The preceding example was a very simple case meant only to illustrate the

**table 12-2**

| *Alternative* | *Market discount rate applicable to cash flow* $(k_Z)$ | *Discounted value of cash flow* $(V_Z = \bar{Z}/k_Z)$ | *Value less initial outlay* $(V_Z - I_{Z0})$ |
|---|---|---|---|
| Project $R$: | | | |
| $S$ | .10 | 120 | 20 |
| $D$ | .15 | 160 | −40 |
| $SD$ | .12 | 425 | 125 |
| Project $C$: | .10 | 40 | −10 |
| Project $G$: | | | |
| $W$ | .125 | 416 | 166 |
| $M$ | .15 | 140 | 40 |
| $WM$ | .133 | 615 | 290 |

approach to analyzing various projects and their associated alternatives. In general, cash flows may vary over time, noncomplementary and mutually exclusive relationships between opportunities within a project often exist, and the number of opportunities and projects will frequently be far greater. An added example of a project involving mutually exclusive and noncomplementary options might be helpful.

Assume a hotel that must make a decision as to whether it will establish a restaurant *R* or a bookstore *B* in a particular location on its main floor; these are mutually exclusive options. Assume also that if it installs the bookstore, it can sell paperback *P* or hard-cover *H* books. The *opportunities* available to the hotel are therefore *three* in number: to add the restaurant, to add the bookstore with paperbacks, and to add the bookstore with hard-cover books. These opportunities form a single project since *R* and *B* are mutually exclusive, and the action to sell hard-cover books or paperbacks depends upon whether the bookstore is built. But observe that there are *five alternatives* within the project since *both* paperback and hard-cover books may be sold in the bookstore (this is a combination of *B-P* and *B-H*). The five alternatives associated with the project are therefore:

Restaurant: designated by *R*
Bookstore with only paperbacks: designated by *B-P*
Bookstore with only hard-cover books: designated by *B-H*
Bookstore with both paperbacks and hard-cover books: designated by *B-PH*
Do not adopt *R, B-P, B-H,* or *B-PH*

The cash flows from the first four alternatives would be computed, the values determined using the appropriate discount rates (assuming the discount model is appropriate), and the net present value ($V_Z - I_{Z0}$) of each determined. From the five alternatives, the one with the highest net present value would be selected. (Note that the net present value of not adopting *R*, *B-P*, *B-H* or *B-PH* is zero.) The cash flows might be of amounts (assume again constant mean amounts over time and perpetual streams) shown in Table 12-3.

In this case, stocking both paperbacks and hard-cover books produces less cash flow than only paperbacks and also involves a higher initial outlay. The

**table 12-3**

| *Alternative* | *Initial outlay* ($I_{Z0}$) | *Mean annual cash flow* ($\bar{Z}$) | *Discount rate* ($k_Z$) | *Value less initial outlay* ($V_Z - I_{Z0}$) = $[(\bar{Z}/k_Z) - I_{Z0}]$ |
|---|---|---|---|---|
| *R* | 1,000 | 130 | .125 | 40 |
| *B-P* | 200 | 60 | .15 | 200 |
| *B-H* | 275 | 35 | .10 | 75 |
| *B-PH* | 350 | 50 | .133 | 25 |

cash-flow effect could arise because of limited space in the bookstore; thus, replacing the faster-moving paperbacks with hard-cover books might reduce cash flow. It might also be that the hard-cover books draw customers away from paperbacks and that the profit margin on paperbacks is higher; this could be so even if no space constraint in the store existed, i.e., even if the same selection of paperbacks were possible whether or not hard-cover books were also offered. From Table 12-3 it is apparent that the best choice is *B-P* since it is the alternative i with the highest $(V_{Z_i} - I_{Z_i 0})$.

## PERFECT MARKETS AND THE INVESTMENT CRITERION WITH FIRM TAXES

When firm taxes are assumed we know from our analysis of Chap. 11 that the value of the firm is not independent of financing decisions. The tax-deductibility of interest payments on the firm's debt creates an incentive for the firm to use debt in otherwise perfect markets. Moreover, as we saw in Chap. 11, the presence of depreciation deductions complicates the after-tax cash flow from investment. In the next few pages we shall show that despite the complications introduced by the existence of firm taxes, our basic conclusions about investment policy in perfect markets remain unaltered. In particular the firm can still evaluate opportunities on a project-by-project basis and can compare alternatives without regard to the stochastic relationships among the earnings streams of projects in the capital budget or between the earnings streams of the capital budget and the zero-investment stream offered by the firm.

### Cash Flow and Valuation

Some of the discussion here repeats the discussion of cash flow in Chap. 9. We begin by specifying the cash payments made by the firm to its stockholders and bondholders when taxes are included. This cash flow in period $t$ is defined as $\tilde{Y}_t$ and equals

$$\tilde{Y}_t = \tilde{X}_t - \tilde{I}_t - \tilde{\text{Tax}}_t \tag{12-18}$$

where $\tilde{X}_t$ = pretax cash earnings of firm
$\tilde{I}_t$ = capital budget of firm
$\tilde{\text{Tax}}_t$ = tax payment

All values are assumed uncertain. For ease of analysis we assume that the tax rate $\tau$ is constant over time and certain. The tax in any period is determined as

$$\tilde{\text{Tax}}_t = \tau(\tilde{X}_t - \widetilde{DP}_t - \tilde{R}_t) \tag{12-19}$$

where $\tilde{R}_t$ = tax-deductible interest to time $t$ bondholders
$\widetilde{DP}_t$ = depreciation deduction

Quantity $(\tilde{X}_t - DP_t - \tilde{R}_t)$ is the "taxable income" of the firm. We can substitute (12-19) into (12-18) and get

$$\tilde{Y}_t = (1 - \tau)\tilde{X}_t - \tilde{I}_t + \tau(\widetilde{DP}_t + \tilde{R}_t) \tag{12-20}$$

Using our concept of a vector of cash flow over time, (12-20) becomes a simpler and more general expression:

$$\tilde{\mathbf{Y}} = (1 - \tau)\tilde{\mathbf{X}} - \tilde{\mathbf{I}} + \tau(\widetilde{\mathbf{DP}} + \tilde{\mathbf{R}}) \tag{12-21}$$

where each variable is a vector with elements for $t = 1, \ldots, \infty$.[15]

We can take $\tilde{\mathbf{Y}}'$ to be the zero-investment, after-tax, cash-flow vector as before. That is, $\tilde{\mathbf{Y}}'$ is the cash flow of the firm if no projects under consideration in the current period are adopted. The adoption of the current capital budget $I_0$ (investment at time 0) may produce changes for all the cash flows of (12-21), *where any changes are assumed to begin at time 1.* Letting $\tilde{\mathbf{Y}}$ be the postinvestment, after-tax, cash-flow vector if the capital budget is adopted, we define the incremental cash flow from investment of $I_0$ as

$$\mathbf{\Delta}\tilde{\mathbf{Y}} = \tilde{\mathbf{Y}} - \tilde{\mathbf{Y}}' \tag{12-22}$$

To see more clearly what is being assumed, we can also express the incremental cash flow in any period $t \geq 1$ in the form of (12-20):

$$\Delta\tilde{Y}_t = (1 - \tau)\,\Delta\tilde{X}_t - \Delta\tilde{I}_t + \tau(\Delta\widetilde{DP}_t + \Delta\tilde{R}_t) \tag{12-23}$$

The Δ's all refer to the differences between zero-investment and postinvestment values of the variable. Finally, we can express $\mathbf{\Delta}\tilde{\mathbf{Y}}$ in the form of the change in the vectors of cash flows:

$$\mathbf{\Delta}\tilde{\mathbf{Y}} = (1 - \tau)\,\mathbf{\Delta}\tilde{\mathbf{X}} - \mathbf{\Delta}\tilde{\mathbf{I}} + \tau(\mathbf{\Delta}\widetilde{\mathbf{DP}} + \mathbf{\Delta}\tilde{\mathbf{R}}) \tag{12-24}$$

where $\mathbf{\Delta}\tilde{\mathbf{Y}} = (\Delta\tilde{Y}_1, \Delta\tilde{Y}_2, \ldots, \Delta\tilde{Y}_\infty)$.

All the manipulations so far have been definitional in nature. We have simply stated in a general form (12-24) the future consequences of adopting the current capital budget. We developed a general criterion (applicable with or without taxes) for the capital budget earlier in this chapter:

$$\max\,[\Delta V - I_0]$$

Our aim now is to determine what this general criterion becomes under the present perfect-market assumptions with taxes. As we shall see, the effects of financing with bonds as opposed to new shares are reflected in the incremental cash-flow equation (12-24) through the term $\mathbf{\Delta}\tilde{\mathbf{R}}$.

The incremental cash flow from the investment budget $\mathbf{\Delta}\tilde{\mathbf{Y}}$ equals the postinvestment *after-tax* cash flow less the zero-investment after-tax cash flow, that is, $\mathbf{\Delta}\tilde{\mathbf{Y}} = \tilde{\mathbf{Y}} - \tilde{\mathbf{Y}}'$; the firm values associated with $\tilde{\mathbf{Y}}$ and $\tilde{\mathbf{Y}}'$ are $V$ and $V'$,

[15] Therefore, $\tilde{\mathbf{Y}} = (\tilde{Y}_1, \tilde{Y}_2, \ldots, \tilde{Y}_\infty)$, $\tilde{\mathbf{X}} = (\tilde{X}_1, \tilde{X}_2, \ldots, \tilde{X}_\infty)$, $\tilde{\mathbf{I}} = (\tilde{I}_1, \tilde{I}_2, \ldots, \tilde{I}_\infty)$, and so forth.

respectively. Using the same reasoning as with the no-tax case, since $\tilde{\mathbf{Y}} = \tilde{\mathbf{Y}}' + \Delta\tilde{\mathbf{Y}}$ the value-additivity principle implies that

$$V = V' + V_{\Delta Y} \tag{12-25}$$

where in the present case $V_{\Delta Y}$ is the value that incremental *after-tax* stream $\Delta\tilde{\mathbf{Y}}$ would have in the market if available in the market as a separate stream. Since $\Delta V = V - V'$, it follows from (12-25) that $\Delta V = V_{\Delta Y}$. Substituting $V_{\Delta Y}$ for $\Delta V$ in (12-10), the investment criterion becomes

$$\max\,[V_{\Delta Y} - I_0] \tag{12-26}$$

Relations (12-25) and (12-26) are identical in form to relations (12-13) and (12-11), respectively, except that $\Delta\tilde{\mathbf{Y}}$ is an *after-tax* stream in (12-25) and (12-26). As before, the decision as to the optimal current budget is independent of any stochastic relationships between the earnings from investment and the existing earnings stream of the firm. This follows as before since the investment criterion is expressed only in terms of the value of the incremental stream and its cost $I_0$ and with no reference to the other income of the firm. This is the same conclusion we reached in the no-tax case. Moreover, as we know from Chap. 11, tax-deductibility of payments to debtholders does affect the value of the firm and hence its choice of investments. From (12-24) it is apparent that the greater the fraction of the investment financed with new debt (greater $\Delta\tilde{\mathbf{R}}$), the greater the $\Delta\tilde{\mathbf{Y}}$ and the greater the value to the firm of the investment. The larger the proportion of investment financed with debt, the greater the chance of acceptability of the investment by increasing the value of the stream generated by the investment. Theoretically, therefore, all investment in perfect capital markets will be financed with debt. This is discussed further in the sections below.

## Project-Selection Criterion with Taxes

The increase in after-tax cash flow to shareholders and bondholders due to project $Z$ is $\tilde{\mathbf{Z}}$. Using arguments essentially identical to those for Eq. (12-21), we know that $\tilde{\mathbf{Z}}$ can be expressed as

$$\tilde{\mathbf{Z}} - [(1 - \tau)\tilde{\mathbf{X}}_Z + \tau(\widetilde{\mathbf{DP}}_Z + \tilde{\mathbf{R}}_Z)] \tag{12-27}$$

Terms $\tilde{\mathbf{X}}_Z$, $\tilde{\mathbf{I}}_Z$, $\widetilde{\mathbf{DP}}_Z$, and $\tilde{\mathbf{R}}_Z$ are the increases in firm cash income, investment outlays, depreciation, and bond interest of the firm beginning at time 1. Since there is no change in the returns on old bonds (see previous discussion on page 306). $\tilde{\mathbf{R}}_Z$ is the cash flow to any new bonds $B_Z$ used to finance project $Z$ *and* to any future bonds that might be issued to sustain project $Z$.

By arguments identical to those for developing (12-16) for the no-tax case, it follows that a project is acceptable if and only if the value of $\tilde{\mathbf{Z}}$, $V_Z$, exceeds the initial investment cost of project $Z$, $I_{Z0}$, for the best alternative i associated with the project. That is, criterion (12-16) applies here just as before, except that $V_{Z_i}$ is now the value of the *after-tax* cash flow $\tilde{\mathbf{Z}}$ generated by the best alternative associated with project $Z$. Restating criterion (12-16), the best alternative must satisfy

$$V_{Z_i} - I_{Z_i0} \geq 0 \qquad (12\text{-}28)$$

where $V_{Z_i}$ and $I_{Z_i0}$ are the values and initial investment associated with the best alternative provided by project $Z$.

By the VAP we know that the value of stream $\tilde{\mathbf{Z}}$ defined in (12-27) is the same regardless of whether it is available in the market as a single stream or as two streams (stock and bond). Value $V_Z$ is the market value that $\tilde{\mathbf{Z}}$ would have if available as the single stream of (12-27). The value in (12-28) is that associated with the alternative i from project $Z$ with the maximum net present value. Criterion (12-28) is equivalent to criterion (12-16) for the no-tax case.

The discussion on pages 313 to 314 regarding the irrelevancy of diversification considerations and the fact that a given project may be more profitable to one firm than to another hold here as in the no-tax case. The bases of the arguments are the same here. The criterion expressed in Eq. (12-28) depends only upon the distribution of $\tilde{\mathbf{Z}}$ and not upon the returns generated from the other assets of the firm. And, of course, $\tilde{\mathbf{Z}}$ may vary between firms since the benefits from a given opportunity are as frequently dependent upon who adopts the opportunity as upon the opportunity itself. The reader is encouraged to review the earlier discussion since it is fully applicable here.

The method of project selection is identical to that described on pages 315 to 316 for the no-tax case. Opportunities are divided into the maximum number of projects and the alternative for each project with the highest net present value is determined. This best alternative will satisfy (12-28). The problem that must now be resolved is how the market value $V_Z$ of stream $\tilde{\mathbf{Z}}$ is determined. As with the no-tax case, the risk-adjusted discount-rate model provides a possible approach. This is discussed in the next section.

The question arises as to how much debt a firm will use in financing investment. Clearly, the criterion of Eq. (12-28) is completely correct in perfect markets regardless of what level of debt financing the firm chooses to employ. However, it is also clear from the preceding discussion and from Chap. 11 that theoretically the firm will be virtually all debt since the after-tax stream provided to the market (and therefore the value of that after-tax stream) necessarily increases as debt increases. This conclusion is reflected in the preceding discussion. The level of $\tilde{\mathbf{Z}}$ rises as $\tilde{\mathbf{R}}_Z$ rises, as is clear from Eq. (12-27) and, as a consequence, the total value of $\tilde{\mathbf{Z}}$ increases. If this is not clear, the reader should refer to the discussion of firm value and taxes in Chap. 11. It is also true, however, that in reality firms do use internal financing and the sale of new stock to finance capital expenditures. It follows that the perfect-market assumptions are empirically invalid in one or more respects. It is not clear to what extent imperfections in the market invalidate the conclusions we have reached. It may be that the investment criteria we have developed are good approximations and that the imperfections which do exist merely imply there is some upper limit on debt financing that is appropriate. This issue is examined in Chaps. 14 and 15.[16]

## The Discount Model With Taxes

**The general problem.** The basis of the discount model was discussed in Chap. 9 and its application to the no-tax, perfect-market investment case was presented earlier in this chapter. The value of a stream is the sum of the discounted expected flows in all future periods using a discount rate appropriate to the distribution ("riskiness") of the stream being discounted.

The discount model can be applied to the investment criterion expressed in (12-28). Define the after-tax stream from the best alternative i associated with project $Z$ as $\tilde{\mathbf{Z}}$ and its value as $V_Z$, where $V_Z$ would equal

$$V_Z = \sum_{t=1}^{\infty} \frac{\bar{Z}_t}{(1 + k_Z)^t} \tag{12-29}$$

Discount rate $k_Z$ is the rate the market would use in discounting a stream of the form of $\tilde{Z}$ if $\tilde{Z}$ were available as a single stream in the market. Term $\bar{Z}_t$ is the expected (mean) level of $\tilde{Z}_t$, where $\tilde{Z}_t$ is the time $t$ element in the $\tilde{Z}$ vector defined by (12-27). That is,

$$\bar{Z}_t = (1 - \tau)\bar{X}_{Zt} - \bar{I}_{Zt} + \tau(\overline{DP}_{Zt} + \bar{R}_{Zt}) \tag{12-30}$$

where the bars over the variables signify expected values. Thus, a project would be acceptable if and only if (12-28) were satisfied by alternative i in project $Z$, where the value of the stream from that alternative is defined by (12-29).

**An alternative expression for the project-selection criterion.** It was explained in Chap. 11 (pages 287 to 295) that under certain conditions the value of a levered stream can be expressed as the sum of the value it would have if unlevered, plus the tax rate times the value of current debt associated with the stream. This was expressed in Eq. (11-1). Conditions that allow the value of the stream from a project to be expressed in the form of Eq. (11-1) are:[17]

[16] We have not explored here how the firm's output, investment, and financing decisions are interrelated; for a discussion of this topic, see Gailen L. Hite, Leverage, Output Effects, and the M-M Theorems, *Journal of Financial Economics,* vol. 4, pp. 177–202, 1977.

[17] As noted in chap. 11, it would also be sufficient to ensure a valuation equation of the form of expression (11-1) if, instead of (1) and (2) below, the value of the debt were constant from period to period. That is, if any debt is retired, it is refunded with an identical amount of debt, and, further, the value of the debt does not vary from period to period.

1. All debt used to finance project $Z$ at time 0 yields a perpetual interest stream.
2. No new debt is expected to be issued after time 0 in order to sustain project $Z$.

In this case, $\tilde{\mathbf{R}}_Z$ in Eq. (12-27) is entirely associated with the debt issued at time 0 to finance the project. Notice that $\tilde{Z}$ can be represented as the sum of stream $\tilde{\mathbf{Z}}_u$ and stream $\tau\tilde{\mathbf{R}}_Z$, that is,

$$\tilde{\mathbf{Z}} = \tilde{\mathbf{Z}}_u + \tau\tilde{\mathbf{R}}_Z = [(1 - \tau)\tilde{\mathbf{X}}_Z - \tilde{\mathbf{I}}_Z + \tau\widetilde{\mathbf{DP}}_Z] + \tau\tilde{\mathbf{R}}_Z \tag{12-31}$$

This is of the form of Eq. (11-7). Stream $\tilde{\mathbf{Z}}_u$ is equal to the expression in brackets in Eq. (12-31) and is the after-tax stream that project $Z$ would yield if financed entirely without debt ($\tilde{\mathbf{R}}_Z = 0$). Define $V_{Z_u}$ as the value that $\tilde{\mathbf{Z}}_u$ would have as an individual stream in the market. Since it is assumed in (1) and (2) above that all current debt is perpetual and that no new debt will be issued, it follows that $\tilde{\mathbf{R}}_Z$ in Eq. (12-31) is the cash flow to bonds used to initially finance the project and is the only cash flow that such bonds will ever receive (the debt is never retired). Using the same reasoning that implied valuation equation (11-7), it follows that under these assumptions

$$V_Z = V_{Z_u} + \tau B_Z \tag{12-32}$$

where $B_Z$ is the value of the bonds used to finance project $Z$.

As before, we select the best alternative i in project $Z$, where, substituting (12-32) into (12-28), that best alternative will satisfy

$$V_{Z_u} + \tau B_Z - I_{Z0} \geq 0 \tag{12-33}$$

The i subscript is dropped in (12-33) to simplify the notation.

Criterion (12-33) clearly reveals the conclusion reached in the last section: that debt financing is favored. As the proportion of financing of investment that is from debt sources increases (as $B_Z$ increases), the value of the cash flow generated by the investment, $V_Z = (V_{Z_u} + \tau B_Z)$, also increases. This is so—as explained earlier—because of the tax-deductibility of interest.

The discounting model can be used in criterion (12-33) just as it was used with criterion (12-28). In this case,

$$B_Z = \sum_{t=1}^{\infty} \frac{\bar{R}_{Zt}}{(1 + k_{ZB})^t} \tag{12-34}$$

and

$$V_{Z_u} = \sum_{t=1}^{\infty} \frac{\bar{Z}_{ut}}{(1 + k_{Z_u})^t} \tag{12-35}$$

where, from Eq. (12-31),

$$\bar{Z}_{ut} = (1 - \tau)\bar{X}_{Zt} - \bar{I}_{Zt} + \tau\overline{DP}_{Zt} \tag{12-36}$$

where $k_{ZB}$ is the discount rate applicable to the bond stream $\tilde{\mathbf{R}}_Z$ and $k_{Zu}$ is the discount rate applicable to the unlevered stream $\tilde{\mathbf{Z}}_u$. The two values in (12-34) and (12-35) can then be substituted into criterion (12-33) to produce a more precise relationship.

Carrying the analysis a little further, assume that the proportion of debt financing used ($\gamma$) is independent of the particular projects which make up the capital budget but that some limit other than unity is imposed. In perfect markets, the object is to maximize $\gamma$ for *any* set of projects and this is so regardless of the nature of the projects themselves. Therefore, some imperfection is assumed here that favors a limit on $\gamma$, this imperfection not depending upon the projects themselves but upon some other factor making borrowing beyond some point undesirable. As discussed in Chap. 14, in *imperfect* markets in general different projects may warrant different levels of $\gamma$; to the extent that there exists an optimal proportion of debt to use, that optimal proportion may depend upon the characteristics of the projects undertaken. It should also be pointed out that the assumption of a $\gamma$ independent of the type of projects simplifies investment decisions considerably (and is widely used both for theoretical work and in practice for that reason).

The expression of the project-selection criterion we seek here follows directly by substituting into (12-33). Assume that for all projects the same proportion of debt financing is adopted, that is, $B_Z/I_{Z0} = \gamma_Z$ is the same for all $Z$. Designating $\gamma$ as this proportion, $B_Z/I_{Z0} = \gamma$ and therefore $B_Z = \gamma I_{Z0}$. Substituting $\gamma I_{Z0}$ for $B_Z$ in (12-33),

$$V_{Z_u} - (1 - \gamma\tau)I_{Z0} \geq 0 \tag{12-37}$$

Expression (12-37) is particularly useful if $\gamma$ is given, since those performing the project-selection task need only determine $V_{Z_u}$ and $I_{Z0}$ without being concerned about what part of $\tilde{\mathbf{Z}}$ must go to $\tilde{\mathbf{R}}$ to achieve a particular level of $\gamma_Z$; the latter task is assumed by the financial manager, who will treat all projects together as a single capital budget financed in proportion $\gamma$ by debt. That is, the division of the project cash flows to achieve a particular $\gamma$ need be performed only once for the overall investment budget. The practical advantages of this procedure are obvious.

## An Illustration

The analysis of investment opportunities proceeds with taxes just as in the no-tax case. The only difference is that the returns from investment are now measured on an after-tax basis. Referring back to the first illustration (page 319) for the no-tax case, with taxes the same procedure would still hold. The projects are divided just as before. To determine the after-tax cash flow, the degree of debt financing must first be ascertained, however, since debt interest is tax-deductible. As explained above, theoretically the entire capital budget would be financed with debt in perfect markets since $V_Z$ increases as debt increases with taxes. However, it will be assumed that the firm may select an investment-financing plan that includes some equity funds, either from the sale of new stock or from internal sources (firm cash). It will be assumed that the proportion of debt financing for any given project is independent of which *other* projects are also adopted as part of the capital budget for the period.[18] Whatever the basis for determining the level of debt associated with the adoption of a given investment alternative by the firm, each alternative identified with a given project is appraised and the alternative i with the highest net present value is adopted.

For simplicity, an example will be presented that is consistent with assumptions (1) and (2) on page 328 so that condition (12-33) as well as the more general (12-28) can be illustrated. Assume that the tax rate $\tau$ is 40% and that the firm is evaluating alternative $N$ of project $G$ of the no-tax example on page 319.

The $Z$ notation (rather than using $G$ and $W$ scripts) will be retained here for simplicity in referring to the cash flows from alternative $W$ of project $G$. Assume also that the firm has decided to finance $W$ (which requires an initial outlay of $250) with 60% debt, that is, $\gamma_Z = .60$. The first problem is: How much of the cash flow from $W$ must be paid to bondholders in order to obtain $150 in debt [$\gamma_Z I_Z = .60(\$250) = \$150$]? This depends upon the discount rate on the debt for each level of promised interest to bondholders. The higher the debt-equity financing ratio, the riskier the debt and the higher the discount rate on the debt. Assume that an expected payment to bondholders of $9/period in perpetuity implies a discount rate $k_{ZB}$ of 6% and therefore a $B_Z = \$150( = \$9/.06)$.[19] Assume that the discount rate $k_Z$ which would be applicable to the entire after-tax debt and equity stream combined [$\tilde{Z}$ of (12-27)] would be 10%; let the rate $k_{Z_u}$ that would be applicable to $\tilde{Z}_u$ be 10.83%. Assume that the expected depreciation deduction allowed by the government for tax purposes each period, $\overline{DP}_{Zt}$, is equal to $8 for all $t$. The data associated with alternative $W$ and its related financing are summarized in Table 12-4.

From the cash flows in Table 12-4 the expected cash flows $\overline{Z}_t$ and $\overline{Z}_{ut}$, for all $t$, $t = 1, \ldots, \infty$, can be determined and are stated below. Equations (12-30) and (12-36) identify the cash flows computed below.

From (12-30)

$$\begin{aligned} \overline{Z}_t &= (1 - \tau)\overline{X}_{Zt} - \bar{I}_{Zt} + \tau(\overline{DP}_{Zt} + \overline{R}_{Zt}) \\ &= .6(\$60) - \$8 + .4(\$17) = \$34.80 \end{aligned} \tag{12-38}$$

[18] Obviously, if this were not assumed, then projects could not be evaluated separately. That is, since the after-tax cash flow from a project depends upon the proportion that is financed with debt, a dependence of this proportion of debt financing on the other projects adopted implies that the project's cash flow depends on *which* other projects are adopted. The consequence would be a need to evaluate all investment options simultaneously to get a joint maximizing solution. The necessity of this approach in imperfect markets is discussed in chap. 14. Indeed, it is explained that such joint maximization implies that the concept of a project is no longer useful and that all combinations of investment *opportunities* must be considered. See also the footnote on p. 314.

[19] See chap. 8 on the difference between the *promised* payment to debt and the *expected* payment to debt. Recall that the expected payment is less than the promised payment if there is any chance of default.

**table 12-4**

| | |
|---|---|
| Tax rate $\tau$ = 40% | |
| Discount rates: | |
| $k_{ZB}$ = .06 | |
| $k_Z$ = .10 | |
| $k_{Zu}$ = .1083 | |
| Cash flows: | |
| Initial outlay ($I_{Z0}$) | \$250 |
| Expected cash income ($\bar{X}_{Zt}$) | \$ 60 |
| Expected future capital outlays ($\bar{I}_{Zt}$) | \$ 8 |
| Expected future depreciation deduction ($\overline{DP}_{Zt}$) | \$ 8 |
| Expected future bond interest ($\bar{R}_{Zt}$) | \$ 9 |

From (12-36)

$$\begin{aligned} \bar{Z}_{ut} &= (1 - \tau)\bar{X}_{Zt} - \bar{I}_{Zt} + \tau\overline{DP}_{Zt} \\ &= .6(\$60) - \$8 + .4(\$8) = \$31.20 \end{aligned} \qquad (12\text{-}39)$$

Since the expected amounts are the same for all periods, the $t$ subscript will be dropped, for example, $\bar{Z}_t \equiv \bar{Z} = \$34.80$, and so forth. Let us compute each of the values in conditions (12-28) and (12-33) using the discount equations (12-29), (12-34), and (12-35). Recalling that the value of a perpetual stream is the amount per period divided by the discount rate and that the streams considered here have level means over time, it follows that

$$V_Z = \frac{\bar{Z}}{k_Z} = \frac{\$34.80}{.10} = \$348$$

$$B_Z = \frac{\bar{R}_Z}{k_{ZB}} = \frac{\$9}{.06} = \$150$$

$$V_{Z_u} = \frac{\bar{Z}_u}{k_{Z_u}} = \frac{\$31.20}{.1083} = \$288$$

Substituting these values into (12-28) and (12-33), the total value of the after-tax cash flow from the project is \$348 and its initial cost is \$250; the net gain to the firm is therefore \$98.

In evaluating alternatives associated with a given project, the net present values are computed for each as was done for alternative $W$ of project $G$ above. The alternative i with the highest net present value is adopted. For project $G$, the computation performed for $W$ (which produced a net gain of \$98) would also be performed for alternatives $M$ and $WM$. From the alternatives $W$, $M$, $WM$, and none of these, we adopt the alternative with the highest net present value (since the net present value of $W$ is positive, we know that one of alternatives $W$, $M$ or $WM$ will be adopted).

The use of the investment criterion as expressed in (12-37) is straightforward. Assuming a given $\gamma$ for all alternatives being compared ($\gamma = .6$ in the example here), $[V_{Z_u} - (1 - \gamma\tau)I_{Z0}]$ would be computed for each alternative and that with the highest net present value would be adopted. For alternative $W$ this would equal

$$\frac{\bar{Z}_u}{k_{Z_u}} - (1 - \gamma\tau)I_{Z0} = \frac{\$31.2}{.1083} - (1 - .24)\$250 = \$98 \qquad (12\text{-}40)$$

The result in (12-40) is, of course, consistent with the net present value computed using the other methods.

## SUMMARY

There are three *potential* attributes of investments that affect the investment decision:

1. The characteristics of the incremental cash flows provided by investment (capital budget, project, or alternative).
2. The method of financing investments.
3. The stochastic relationships among cash flows (either between the flows resulting from the total budget and the firm's zero-investment flow or among projects within the budget).

In Chap. 11 and again in this chapter we argued that in the absence of taxes, financing, (2), does not affect investment decisions. The presence of firm taxes, however, does favor debt over equity financing and (2) becomes relevant. With or without taxes we have argued that (3) is irrelevant in perfect markets. The firm does not have a "portfolio" problem, and diversification considerations are irrelevant. Of course (1) is always important regardless of the assumptions. The problem in perfect markets is determining how incremental income streams are valued. We suggested that the discount model is a reasonable solution to the problem, at least in practice. For theoretical purposes other models, such as the time-state preference model, may be more appropriate. However, as we remarked in Chap. 9, the question of multiperiod valuation is still unsettled.

## SUGGESTED READINGS

Fama, Eugene F.: Risk Adjusted Discount Rates and Capital Budgeting under Uncertainty, *Journal of Financial Economics,* vol. 5, pp. 3–24, August 1977.

Jorgenson, Dale W.: Econometric Studies of Investment Behavior: A Survey, *Journal of Economic Literature,* vol. 9, pp. 1111–1147, December 1971.

Lintner, John: The Evaluation of Risk Assets and the Selection of Risky Investments in Stock Portfolios and Capital Budgets, *Review of Economics and Statistics,* vol. 47, pp. 13–37 (especially secs. V and VI), February 1965. Also, see Charles W. Haley, Comment and John Lintner, Reply, *Review of Economics and Statistics,* vol. 51, pp. 220–224, May 1969.

Mao, James C. T.: Survey of Capital Budgeting: Theory and Practice, *Journal of Finance,* vol. 25, pp. 349–360, May 1970.

Myers, Stewart C.: Procedures for Capital Budgeting under Uncertainty, *Industrial Management Review*, vol. 9, pp. 1–15, spring 1968.

Nelson, Charles R.: Inflation and Capital Budgeting, *Journal of Finance*, vol. 31, pp. 923–932, June 1976.

Sarnat, Marshall: A Note on the Implications of Quadratic Utility for Portfolio Theory, *Journal of Financial and Quantitative Analysis*, vol. 9, no. 4, pp. 687–690, September 1974.

——— and Haim Levy: The Relationship of Rules of Thumb to the Internal Rate of Return: A Restatement and Generalization, *Journal of Finance*, vol. 24, pp. 479–489, June 1969.

Schall, Lawrence D.: Asset Valuation, Firm Investment and Firm Diversification, *Journal of Business*, vol. 45, no. 1, pp. 11–28, January 1972.

———, Gary L. Sundem, and William R. Geijsbeek, Jr.: Survey and Analysis of Capital Budgeting Methods, *Journal of Finance*, pp. 281–287, March 1978.

Schlaifer, Robert: *Analysis of Decisions under Uncertainty*, McGraw-Hill Book Company, New York, 1969.

———: *Probability and Statistics for Business Decisions*, McGraw-Hill Book Company, New York, 1959.

Schwab, Bernhard and Peter Lusztig: A Comparative Analysis of the Net Present Value and the Benefit-Cost Ratios as Measures of the Economic Desirability of Investments, *Journal of Finance*, vol. 24, pp. 507–516, June 1969.

Stapleton, Richard C.: Portfolio Analysis, Stock Valuation and Capital Budgeting Decision Rules for Risky Projects, *Journal of Finance*, vol. 26, pp. 95–118, March 1971.

Sundem, Gary L.: Evaluating Capital Budgeting Models in Simulated Environments, *Journal of Finance*, vol. 30, pp. 977–992, September 1975.

See, too, the Suggested Readings for chap. 11, especially Miller and Modigliani, 1958 and 1963.

CHAPTER

# THIRTEEN

# THE COST OF CAPITAL

The discussion in this chapter is intended to accomplish two goals:

1. To review and bring together some of the major conclusions of the previous chapters in a form that is particularly suited to application to real-world problems, and
2. To make more explicit the relationship between our approach to the theory of finance and the approach followed in much of the literature—the "cost-of-capital" model

Throughout this book we have been concerned with two basic issues: the impact of financing decisions on the value of the firm, and the derivation of criteria for firm investment decisions. Under assumptions of perfect markets we have shown that these two issues can be treated separately. There exists a substantial body of literature that is devoted to a somewhat different issue—the impact of financing policy on the discount rate used in the criteria for investment decisions.[1] That discount rate is identified as the firm's "cost of capital." As we noted in Chaps. 8 and 12, the use of the cost of capital as a standard for different investments is appropriate with perfect markets provided that all investments are of the same risk as the firm and given that a discount-rate model is valid to begin with. The cost-of-capital approach is widely used in introduc-

[1] Prominent examples are the papers by Modigliani and Miller (1958) and (1963), listed in the Suggested Readings at the end of this chapter. A representative sample of the literature can be found in Archer, Stephen H. and Charles A. D'Ambrosio, "The Theory of Business Finance," 2d ed., selections 23 to 36 (which include the two Modigliani and Miller papers), The Macmillan Company, New York, 1976.

tory textbooks and in many advanced works dealing with business finance and capital budgeting.[2] The reason for the emphasis on the cost of capital appears to be the potential applicability of the model to the actual investment decisions of the firm, at least for those investments which are typical for the firm.

We develop the cost-of-capital model in this chapter following the lines of our basic approach. First, we consider a cost-of-capital formulation of the financing problem. Our principal goal is to express the results of Chap. 11 in a cost-of-capital format. Then the application of the model to investment decisions will be explored. Here we shall be concerned primarily with the use of the weighted average cost of capital as the discount rate for investments of the same risk as the firm. Perfect capital markets will be assumed throughout most of the chapter; imperfect markets are introduced in the discussion of the "traditional" case at the end of the chapter.

## FINANCING POLICY

### No Taxes

The cost-of-capital approach to financing policy usually separates the issue of dividend policy from that of capital structure policy. This separation is accomplished by using the static model presented in Chap. 11. The static approach takes the firm at a given point in time and asks whether or not the mix of debt and equity affects the value of the firm, i.e., whether the value of the firm would be different if a different mix of financing had been used. The source of equity, whether retained earnings or sale of new shares, is not an issue here. Of course, when new money is raised, the issue of dividend policy arises; however, under perfect markets and no personal taxes, we have already shown dividend policy to be irrelevant.[3]

Assume the existence of a firm that is expected to earn a cash income stream of $\tilde{X}$ in perpetuity.[4] The actual value of $\tilde{X}$ achieved in any future period is uncertain, but the probability distribution of $\tilde{X}$ is the same for each period. The expected value of $\tilde{X}$ in any future period is therefore $\overline{X}$, which is the same value for each future period. Assume that no investment is anticipated so that the cash flow $\tilde{Y}$ to investors is equal to $\tilde{X}$ and that no new shares or bonds are

[2] Most of the recent introductory textbooks contain a chapter entitled "The Cost of Capital" and virtually all discuss the concept. The same is true of most capital budgeting and engineering economy texts. There is also a book devoted almost exclusively to the model, Wilbur G. Lewellen, "The Cost of Capital," Wadsworth Publishing Company, Inc., Belmont, Calif., 1969.

[3] The assumptions constituting perfect capital markets are summarized in Table 11-1 at the beginning of chap. 11.

[4] The assumption that streams are level perpetuities is not realistic but will be used throughout this chapter for two reasons. The assumption substantially reduces the mathematical complexity and is commonly used in the literature in this area. More general approaches were provided in chaps. 11 and 12.

anticipated for the future as claims on $\tilde{Y}$. Ignoring all taxes for the moment, this stream will be paid out to current shareholders as dividends $\tilde{D}$ and to current bondholders as interest $\tilde{R}$. Effectively, the firm can be considered to have issued perpetual bonds. Of course, $\tilde{Y} = \tilde{D} + \tilde{R}$. In perfect markets with no taxes we showed in Chap. 11 that the value of the firm $V$ is independent of the division of the income stream $\tilde{Y}$ into payments to the two classes of securities. It is customary to state this conclusion in a slightly different fasion—namely, that the firm's "capitalization rate" or "cost of capital" is unaffected by the division. Define this cost of capital as[5]

$$k_V = \frac{\overline{Y}}{V} \tag{13-1}$$

where $k_V$ is the expected return on the total value of the firm ($V$) in equilibrium. In other words, $k_V$ is the rate of return expected to be earned by the owners of the firm's securities (debt and equity) in aggregate. Clearly, if $V$ is unaffected by the mix of debt and equity, $k_V$ is also unaffected given $\bar{Y}$. The value of the firm is the sum of the value of outstanding shares $S$ and the value of outstanding bonds $B$; that is, $V = S + B$. The expected return on shares is

$$k_S = \frac{\overline{D}}{S} \tag{13-2}$$

and the expected return on bonds is

$$k_B = \frac{\overline{R}}{B} \tag{13-3}$$

We can use these relationships to express $k_V$ in terms of the rates on the individual securities.

Equations (13-2) and (13-3) can be used to express the expected streams $\overline{D}$ and $\overline{R}$ as the products of the expected returns and the values of the respective securities; this is, $\overline{D} = k_S S$ and $\overline{R} = k_B B$. Since the expected cash flow to all security holders, $\overline{Y}$, is simply the sum of $\overline{D}$ and $\overline{R}$, $\overline{Y} = k_S S + k_B B$. But by definition $k_V = \overline{Y}/V$; therefore, we can substitute for $\overline{Y}$ in Eq. (13-1) and $k_V$ becomes

$$k_V = \frac{S}{V} k_S + \frac{B}{V} k_B \tag{13-4}$$

Equation (13-4) merely expresses $k_V$ as the weighted average of the rates of return on the shares and bonds of the firm. Given the distribution of the cash income of the firm $\tilde{X}$, we know that the value of the firm does not depend on the amount of debt $B$ under the assumptions of the analysis. Neither $V$ nor $k_V$

[5] As we shall see, there is more than one way to define the firm's "cost of capital." Equation (13-1) is the only one that is totally consistent with the concept that the capital markets "capitalize" the payments to the securities.

depends on $B$. However, the value of the firm's outstanding bonds is one of the variables in Eq. (13-4). If $k_V$ is invariant with respect to the value of $B$, then other variables in Eq. (13-4) must adjust to compensate unless $k_V = k_S = k_B$, in which case Eq. (13-4) reduces to an identity, $k_V = k_V$. We generally assume that the expected return on a given firm's bonds $k_B$ is less than the expected return on the shares of that firm $k_S$ because of the lower risk borne by bondholders, given that bondholders have first priority on the firm's income. Let us investigate the behavior of $S$ and $k_S$ for different values of $B$ and $k_B$.

First, we note that $S = V - B$. $V$ is constant with respect to $B$ since the value of the firm does not depend on the debt-equity ratio. If the firm had issued \$100 additional debt, the value of the shares must be lower by precisely \$100. Of more interest is the behavior of $k_S$. By definition, since $V = S + B$, it must be true that

$$\frac{S}{V} = 1 - \frac{B}{V} \quad \text{or} \quad \frac{S}{V} = 1 - \theta \tag{13-5}$$

where $\theta$ is the ratio of debt to total value $(B/V)$.[6] (An alternative expression for $k_S$, using $\bar{R}/\bar{X}$ rather than $\theta$ to measure leverage, is provided in Appendix 11A. The use of $\theta$ is conventional in cost of capital discussions.) We can use Eq. (13-5) and the definition of $\theta$ to substitute into Eq. (13-4) and solve for $k_S$.

$$k_V = (1 - \theta)k_S + \theta k_B \tag{13-6}$$

and

$$k_S = \frac{k_V - \theta k_B}{1 - \theta} \tag{13-7}$$

Since $k_V$ and $V$ are given, $k_S$ depends on the values of $k_B$ and $\theta$. Of course, $k_B$ will also depend on $\theta$ in some fashion. We assume that if the firm had issued only a small amount of bonds as compared to $V$ (small values of $\theta$), the expected yield on the bonds $k_B$ would be appreciably less than the overall cost of capital for the firm $k_V$. Also, we know that under our assumptions if the firm issues sufficient bonds to make the cash flow to bondholders equal to the cash flow of the firm, $\tilde{R} = \tilde{Y}$, then $S = 0$, $\theta = 1.0$, and $k_B = k_V$.

The general implications of these arguments regarding the behavior of $k_B$ are displayed in Fig. 13-1. The expected yield on the firm's bonds $k_B$ rises with the ratio of bonds to total value $\theta$, reaching $k_V$ when the firm is financed exclusively with bonds. The expected rate of return on the firm's shares $k_S$ must also increase as $\theta$ increases in order to maintain a constant value for $k_V$, as indicated by Eq. (13-7).

[6] Equation (13-7) is essentially the same relationship as Proposition II of Modigliani and Miller (1958), except that they assume riskless debt. Proposition II in our notation is $k_S = k_B + (k_V - k_B)B/S$. Since $B/S = \theta/(1 - \theta)$, eq. (13-7) can be derived from Proposition II.

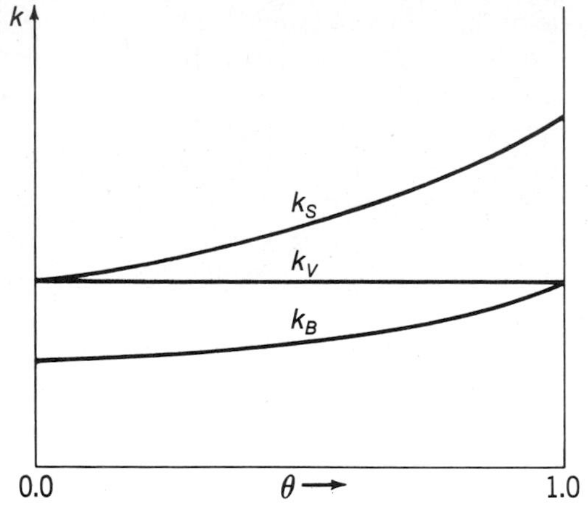


**figure 13-1**

The behavior of $k_S$ can be determined more precisely if a specific relationship between $\theta$ and $k_B$ is assumed. Suppose that $k_B$ depends on $\theta$ according to the following relationship:

$$k_B = i + (k_V - i)\theta^2 \tag{13-8}$$

where $i$ is the riskless rate of interest. We are assuming that small amounts of bonds can be issued at very little more than the riskless rate $i$, but as $B$ approaches $V$, $k_B$ approaches $k_V$. As the value of bonds issued approaches the total value of the firm (as $\tilde{R} \rightarrow \tilde{Y}$, $B \rightarrow V$, and $\theta \rightarrow 1.0$), the rate of return on shares[7] goes to a value of $(3k_V - 2i)$.

As an example, suppose that the total value of the firm is \$1 million, that the firm's cost of capital $k_V = 10\%$, and that $i = 6\%$. If the firm has \$500,000 in bonds outstanding, the expected return on the bonds from Eq. (13-8) is 7%. The expected return on shares from Eq. (13-7) is therefore 13%. If the firm has \$900,000 in bonds outstanding, $k_B = 9.24\%$ and $k_S = 16.84\%$. If $B = \$999{,}999$, then $k_S$ is approximately 18% and $k_B$ is approximately 10%. Naturally, different assumptions regarding the behavior of $k_B$ will alter these results but the general characteristics are not dependent on the precise form of Eq. (13-8).

## Firm Taxes

The existence of taxes on the firm's income complicates the analysis. As noted in Chap. 11, the firm is still valued on the basis of its cash flow to its security holders, $\tilde{Y}$, but that cash flow is net of firm taxes. Assuming that the properties of the firm's income are the same as before and that interest payments, which are the only cash payments to bondholders, are tax-deductible,

[7] See app. 13A.

$$\tilde{Y} = \tilde{X} - \tau(\tilde{X} - \tilde{R}) \\ = (1 - \tau)\tilde{X} + \tau\tilde{R} \tag{13-9}$$

We assume here that all tax losses either result in tax rebates from the government or may be sold at full value to other firms or individuals. The quantity $(1 - \tau)\tilde{X}$ is equal to $\tilde{Y}$ for the firm if no debt is outstanding ($\tilde{R} = 0$). The dividends paid to shareholders are $\tilde{D} = (\tilde{Y} - \tilde{R})$. Note that with taxes the cash flow to security holders of a levered firm $[\tilde{Y} = (1 - \tau)\tilde{X} + \tau\tilde{R}]$ is greater than $(1 - \tau)\tilde{X}$ which equals the cash flow to security holders of an unlevered firm. As was shown in Chap. 11, this difference in cash flows causes the value of the firm to increase with the amount of debt issued under the assumption of perfect markets. Let $V_u$ be the value of the unlevered firm [which is the value of $(1 - \tau)\tilde{X}$]. The total value of the firm can be expressed as

$$V = V_u + \tau B \tag{13-10}$$

which is the same as Eq. (11-1) and indicates the higher value for a levered firm than for an unlevered firm. So far we have simply repeated the conclusions of Chap. 11. Let us now examine the implications for the cost-of-capital model.

Equation (13-1) still defines the firm's capitalization rate as the expected rate of return on the firm's securities; that is,

$$k_V = \frac{\overline{Y}}{V}$$

Now, however, both $\overline{Y}$ and $V$ depend on the amount of debt the firm has outstanding. Let us express the value of the firm in terms of the ratio of debt to total value, $\theta = B/V$. Take Eq. (13-10), divide both sides by $V$, and rearrange terms:

$$V = V_u + \tau B$$

$$\frac{V}{V} = \frac{V_u}{V} - \tau\frac{B}{V}$$

$$1 = \frac{V_u}{V} + \tau\theta$$

$$V = \frac{V_u}{1 - \tau\theta} \tag{13-11}$$

where, as defined earlier, $\theta = B/V$.

Equation (13-11) will be used in the derivations below. Note, however, that when $\theta = 1.0$, the value of the firm is $V_m = V_u/(1 - \tau)$. We shall argue that this is the maximum value for the firm which occurs when the income of the firm is committed exclusively to the bondholders ($\tilde{R} = \tilde{X}$). The value of the shares at this point is zero.

Using Eqs. (13-9) and (13-1),

$$\bar{Y} = (1 - \tau)\bar{X} + \tau\bar{R}$$

$$k_V = \frac{\bar{Y}}{V} = \frac{(1 - \tau)\bar{X} + \tau\bar{R}}{V}$$

$$= \frac{(1 - \tau)\bar{X}}{V} + \tau\frac{\bar{R}}{V} \tag{13-12}$$

But $k_B = \bar{R}/B$ by definition from Eq. (13-3); therefore, $\bar{R} = k_B B$. Substituting $k_B B$ for $\bar{R}$ in Eq. (13-12) and noting that $\theta = B/V$, we can express Eq. (13-12) as

$$k_V = \frac{(1 - \tau)\bar{X}}{V} + \tau\frac{k_B B}{V}$$

$$= \frac{(1 - \tau)\bar{X}}{V} + \tau k_B \theta \tag{13-13}$$

Substituting for $V$ from Eq. (13-11) into Eq. (13-13), we have

$$k_V = \frac{(1 - \tau)\bar{X}}{V_u}(1 - \tau\theta) + \tau k_B \theta \tag{13-14}$$

The ratio $(1 - \tau)\bar{X}/V_u$ is simply the expected rate of return (cost of capital) on the firm if unlevered ($B = 0$), $k_u$, which does not depend on $B$ (or $\theta$) and can be considered a function of the risk of $(1 - \tau)\tilde{X}$. We therefore express $k_V$ from Eq. (13-14) as[8]

$$k_V = k_u(1 - \tau\theta) + \tau k_B \theta$$

$$= k_u - \tau(k_u - k_B)\theta \tag{13-15}$$

In Eq. (13-15), $k_u$ and $\tau$ do not depend on $\theta$; however, in general $k_B$ does vary with $\theta$. The manner in which the average cost of capital $k_V$ varies with $\theta$ therefore depends on the relationship between $k_B$ and $\theta$. To understand what might be reasonable, we must examine carefully the nature of the interest payments to bondholders $\tilde{R}$.

When $\tilde{R} < \tilde{X}$, the interest payments are less risky than is the firm's unlevered stream $(1 - \tau)\tilde{X}$. Therefore, $k_B$ should be less than $k_u$. We know that the maximum value of $\tilde{R}$ is $\tilde{X}$. At the point where $\tilde{R} = \tilde{X}$, no taxes are being paid whatsoever and $\tilde{Y} = \tilde{X} = \tilde{R}$. Beyond this point no more bonds can be issued since all the firm's pretax income has been committed to interest payments. Also, since the entire cash flow of the firm $\tilde{Y}$ is being paid to bondholders, the value of the firm's shares at this point is zero. Hence $B = V$ when $\tilde{R} = \tilde{X}$. We also argue that the risk borne by bondholders when $\tilde{R} = \tilde{X}$ is identical to the risk borne by the shareholders of the firm if no debt is used.[9] Consequently, $k_B = k_u$ at $\tilde{R} = \tilde{X}$ and $\theta = 1.0$. By these arguments we have suggested only that the

[8] The comparable relationship is Miller and Modigliani (1963), Equation 11.c.

[9] The risk per dollar of expected return of the stream $\tilde{X}$ is the same as that for $(1 - \tau)\tilde{X}$; that is, $\tilde{X}/\bar{X} = [(1 - \tau)\tilde{X}]/[(1 - \tau)\bar{X}] = \tilde{X}/\bar{X}$. The two streams differ only by a scale factor. See chap. 8, p. 171.

expected rate on bonds $k_B$ is less than $k_u$ if $\theta < 1$ and equals $k_u$ when $\theta = 1.0$. As a check on the internal consistency of this argument note that the value of the bonds when $\tilde{R} = \tilde{X}$ (desginated $B_m$) is

$$\begin{aligned} B_m &= \frac{\overline{X}}{k_B} \\ &= \frac{\overline{X}}{k_u} \end{aligned} \tag{13-16}$$

But $V_m = B_m$ when $\tilde{R} = \tilde{X}$ since firm value is maximized with all debt financing under the assumptions used here. Therefore, $V_m = \overline{X}/k_u$. By the definition of $k_u$,

$$V_u = \frac{(1 - \tau)\overline{X}}{k_u}$$

$$V_u = (1 - \tau)V_m$$

$$\frac{V_u}{1 - \tau} = V_m \tag{13-17}$$

But Eq. (13-17) is simply Eq. (13-11) for $\theta = 1.0$; therefore, the model is consistent.

The reason for stressing the internal consistency of this model is that the analysis implies a behavior for $k_V$ which is counterintuitive. The capitalization rate for the firm, $k_V$, under these conditions has a minimum value for $\theta < 1.0$, and $V$ reaches a maximum at $\theta = 1.0$. A minimum cost of capital is obtained at a point different from that at which the value of the firm is maximized. This can be seen simply by comparing Eq. (13-11) with Eq. (13-15):

$$V = \frac{V_u}{1 - \tau\theta} \tag{13-11}$$

$$k_V = k_u - \tau(k_u - k_B)\theta \tag{13-15}$$

The value of the firm as expressed by Eq. (13-11) increases with $\theta$ and reaches its maximum value at $\theta = 1.0$. The average cost of capital as expressed by Eq. (13-15) has a value of $k_u$ at $\theta = 0$. For values of $\theta < 1.0$, $k_u > k_B$; therefore, for values of $\theta < 1.0$, $k_V$ must be less than $k_u$. However, at $\theta = 1.0$ we have strongly argued that $k_B = k_u$ and therefore $k_V = k_u$. Since $k_V$ started off at $k_u$, is less than $k_u$ for $\theta < 1.0$, and comes back to $k_u$ at $\theta = 1.0$, there must be a minimum value for $k_V$ at some point between $\theta = 0$ and $\theta = 1.0$. Thus, although $V$ is maximized at $\theta = 1$, $k_V$ is minimized at some $\theta$ between 0 and 1. The behavior of $V$ and $k_V$ will be shown later for a specific functional relationship between $k_B$ and $\theta$. However, it should be clear that the existence of a minimum for $k_V$ at a point different from the maximum for $V$ does *not* depend on our choice of a particular functional relationship.

Before the results derived to this point are summarized graphically and an example is given, one final general relationship in the model is needed, an expression for the return on the firm's shares, $k_S$. Note first that the basic relationships of the no-tax case are all valid in the case of firm taxes; that is,

$$V = S + B$$

$$\overline{Y} = \overline{D} + \overline{R}$$

$$k_V = \frac{\overline{Y}}{V} \tag{13-1}$$

$$k_S = \frac{\overline{D}}{S} \tag{13-2}$$

$$k_B = \frac{\overline{R}}{B} \tag{13-3}$$

Therefore Eqs. (13-4) to (13-6), which were derived from the preceding relationships, are also valid. In particular,

$$k_S = \frac{k_V - \theta k_B}{1 - \theta} \tag{13-7}$$

In the no-tax case $k_V$ is constant; however, when firm income taxes are levied $k_V$ varies according to Eq. (13-15). Therefore, we substitute for $k_V$ from Eq. (13-15) into Eq. (13-6) to get

$$\begin{aligned} k_S &= \frac{k_u - \tau(k_u - k_B)\theta - k_B\theta}{1 - \theta} \\ &= \frac{(1 - \tau\theta)k_u - (1 - \tau)\theta k_B}{1 - \theta} \end{aligned} \tag{13-18}$$

Equation (13-18) provides the relationship between $k_S$, $k_B$, and $\theta$. In order to investigate this relationship, a more precise specification of how $k_B$ varies with $\theta$ is required.[10] We shall use the same general form as in the no-tax case, Eq. (13-8), modified to reflect the conclusion that $k_B = k_u$ at $\theta = 1.0$:

$$k_B = i + (k_u - i)\theta^2 \tag{13-19}$$

Equations (13-15), (13-18), and (13-19) provide the means to display the behavior of the rates of return on the firm's securities and the cost of capital. These functions are shown in Fig. 13-2*a*. The value of $\theta$ at which $k_V$ reaches a minimum is denoted by $\hat{\theta}$.

Figure 13-2*b* displays the behavior of the dollar values of the firm's securi-

[10] The firm's average capitalization rate $k_V$ can be considered as being determined by the rates on the individual securities, $k_S$ and $k_B$. The theory provides us with the total value of the firm, eq. (13-10), and we have some idea as to how $k_B$ varies with $\theta$. It is therefore convenient to express $k_V$ and $k_S$ as a function of $k_B$. This is not meant to imply that $k_V$ and $k_S$ are "determined" by $k_B$; only that the three rates must be consistent. Given a value for any two of them plus a value for $\theta$, the third rate can be solved for using the equations above. We develop the interrelationships between $k_u$, $k_S$, and $k_B$ in app. 11A using an alternative measure of leverage, $\overline{R}/\overline{X}$. A much simpler relationship for $k_S$ than (13-18) is derived there.

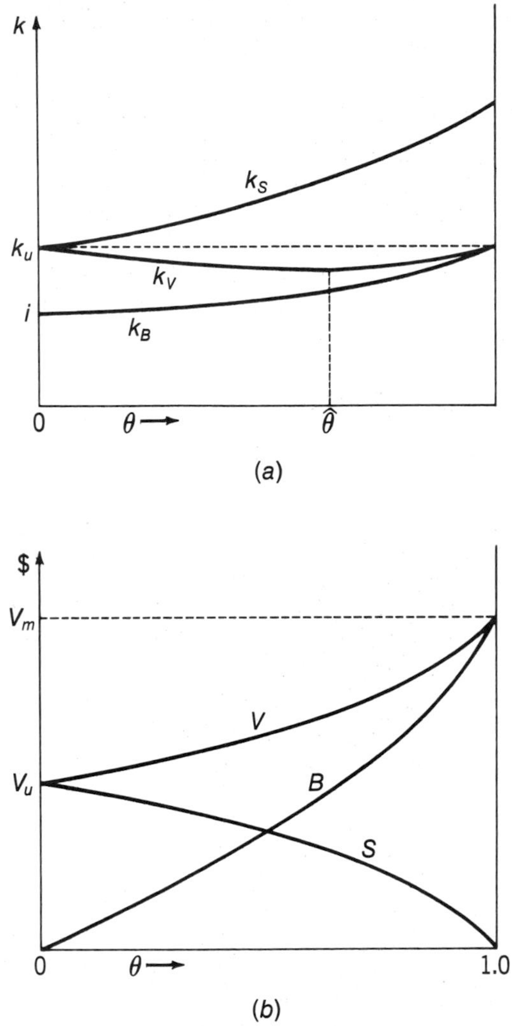


**figure 13-2**

ties as a function of $\theta$. As indicated by Eq. (13-11), $V$ increases smoothly to its maximum value of $V_u/(1 - \tau\theta)$ at the point where $B = V$ (that is, when $\theta = 1$). It should be emphasized again that the general behavior of the variables displayed in Fig. 13-2 follows from the general argument and does not require the specific assumption that $k_B$ follows the functional form of Eq. (13-19).

As an illustration of the model given Eq. (13-19), assume that $\overline{X} = \$200$, $k_u = 10\%$, $i = 6\%$, and $\tau = 50\%$. These data are all that is necessary to determine the values of the firm's securities and the rates of return on these securities as a function of $\theta$. Several such values are shown in Table 13-1.

**table 13-1**

| $\theta = B/V$ | $V(\$)$ | $B(\$)$ | $S(\$)$ | $k_V(\%)$ | $k_B(\%)$ | $k_S(\%)$ |
|---|---|---|---|---|---|---|
| 0.0 | 1,000 | 0 | 1,000 | 10.0 | [6.0] | 10.0 |
| 0.1 | 1,053 | 105 | 948 | 9.80 | 6.04 | 10.2 |
| 0.5 | 1,333 | 667 | 666 | 9.25 | 7.0 | 11.5 |
| 0.58 | 1,408 | 816 | 592 | 9.23 | 7.3 | 11.9 |
| 0.7 | 1,538 | 1,077 | 461 | 9.29 | 8.0 | 12.3 |
| 0.9 | 1,818 | 1,636 | 182 | 9.64 | 9.2 | 13.6 |
| 1.0 | 2,000 | 2,000 | 0 | 10.0 | 10.0 | [14.0]† |

† This is the value of $k_S$ at the limit, as determined in app. 13A. It can be thought of as the expected rate of return on shares when $S = \$1$.

The value for $\hat{\theta}$ for which $k_V$ is minimum is approximately .58.[11] As indicated by the data in Table 13-1, $k_V$ is less at $\theta = .58$ than it is for the neighboring values of $\theta$, and $V$ is not a maximum until $\theta = 1.0$.

Perhaps the most interesting result of the analysis is the finding that, even under perfect markets and a static firm with level cash income, the average capitalization rate, which is one definition of the cost of capital for the firm, reaches a minimum at a point where the value of the firm is not at its maximum. This result has both theoretical and practical implications. *It means that, with firm taxes, neither in theory nor in practice can the optimal capital structure of the firm be generally specified as the point of minimum cost of capital.* Instead, direct attention must be paid to the impact of debt financing on the value of the firm. The use of the cost-of-capital model for this purpose is not in general appropriate.

Despite the limitations of the model in evaluating alternative financing policies, it does have some advantages in application to the problem of investment policy. We shall now examine the cost of capital as used in investment decisions.

## INVESTMENT DECISIONS

### Investment Decisions and the Cost of Capital

In a general sense the "cost of capital" is any discount rate used to value cash streams. The discount-rate models presented in previous chapters can therefore be considered as "cost-of-capital" models of investment decisions. In the present discussion we shall focus on a narrower problem. Given that the cash income streams from the investment opportunities available to the firm have the same risk as the firm's income in the absence of investment, we wish to

[11] A solution for the minimum is provided in app. 13A.

develop criteria for investment decisions based on the discount rates used to value the cash flows provided by the firm. In other words, we wish to derive investment criteria from the model presented above.

In Chap. 12 we developed criteria for investment policy that apply in general. The basic purpose of the discussion here is to develop a discount rate that incorporates the effects of financing policy to be used in evaluating the cash income from investments. This discount rate is the one most often associated with the concept of the cost of capital; however, it is not the same as the definition we have been using in this chapter up to this point.

The cost of capital $k_V$ defined above was the expected rate of return on the total value of the firm's securities. This rate can also be described as the capitalization rate for the expected cash payments to the security holders of the firm. If one were to use this rate to evaluate investment opportunities, all incremental cash flows including the interest payments to bondholders would have to be considered. For example, the incremental interest payments to bondholders resulting from the financing associated with a particular project would have to be included in the cash flows of the project. Rather than evaluating this procedure, we show that an alternative definition of the cost of capital is possible, one that does not require direct consideration of the incremental interest payments. Moreover, it is this definition that is commonly suggested as the appropriate standard for the firm's investment decisions.[12]

There are two reasons for the attention paid to this problem. First, if a discount rate or cost of capital can be developed that includes the impact of financing policy, it can be used in the analytic apparatus discussed in Chap. 3. The discounting procedure of Chap. 3 is widely known and has significant practical advantages over the alternative procedures available, Second, if such a rate exists, it can be supplied to lower-level management as a standard for their evaluations of investment opportunities. This permits decentralization of investment decisions within the firm. Decentralized decision making is generally believed to offer savings in managerial time and effort. If criteria for optimal decentralized decisions are available, these savings may be realized.

The analysis for the case of no taxes on firm income is relatively straightforward and was developed in Chap. 12. The existence of firm taxes makes the problem more difficult; therefore, we shall consider this case in detail. The no-tax case will be presented as a special case when the tax rate is zero.

## Investment Criteria with Firm Taxes

Let us begin by stating precisely what we wish to accomplish. We wish to derive a cost of capital $k^\tau$ that can be used as a discount rate in the criteria for project selection and for the evaluation of alternative investment options. It will be necessary to assume that all projects and alternatives are such that the firm's

[12] For example, by Modigliani and Miller (1963), footnote 16.

cost of capital is the same with reinvestment as it would be if no investment were made by the firm.[13] It is also necessary to assume that the firm has chosen and will maintain a given ratio of debt to total value ($\theta^*$). This latter assumption will be discussed at the end of the chapter. For the present it is sufficient to note that nothing precludes $\theta^*$ from being any number between 0 and 1.0. All investments are assumed to provide level perpetual additions to the pretax cash income of the firm, which is also a level perpetual stream as before. By "level" we mean that the uncertain streams resulting from a given investment opportunity have the same probability distribution in each future period and hence have a constant expected value. The total investment budget is financed through a combination of debt and equity; the cash income of the firm less taxes is paid out as interest and dividends. In perfect capital markets it does not matter whether the equity portion is derived from retained earnings or from sale of shares. Finally, we assume that no additional profitable investment opportunities are anticipated in the future.[14] This assumption is implied by the previous assumption of level streams; we are simply making it explicit.

## The Criterion for the Optimal Capital Budget

From Chap. 12 the objective of investment policy in perfect capital markets was shown to be

$$\max\,[\Delta V - I_0] \tag{13-20}$$

where $\Delta V$ is the increase in value of the firm resulting from undertaking the investment budget $I_0$. [It might be useful to review the development of expression (12-10) in Chap. 12.] Our first goal will be to find an expression for a cost of capital $k^\tau$ such that the criterion above becomes

$$\max\left[\frac{(1-\tau)\,\Delta\bar{X}}{k^\tau} - I_0\right] \tag{13-21}$$

[13] The usual assumption made is that the investment be "of the same risk as the firm." This assumption is not sufficient unless diversification considerations are irrelevant, as in perfect capital markets. The assumption that the cost of capital for the firm is invariant with respect to the firm's investment decisions is less susceptible to imperfections and will be needed later in this chapter in the discussion of the "traditional" case.

[14] This assumption ensures that the expected values of the streams do not increase in the future. However, in order to maintain level perpetual streams as required by the models of this chapter, there may be future investment opportunities already included in the expected income stream of the firm with no current investment. Future opportunities may also be included in the incremental streams of currently available opportunities. For example, physical assets may deteriorate and require regular replacement. Such replacements are assumed to be accounted for in the expected income streams—the streams are net of such expenditures. To put the point more directly, the maintenance of *level* streams whether of the total firm or from current investment would most likely *require* periodic replacement of physical assets. We are assuming here that such expenditures are treated as "costs" which are tax-deductible when incurred.

where $\Delta\overline{X}$ is the expected value of the increment to the pretax cash income of the firm that results from the adoption of capital budget $I_0$. We shall then show that under our assumptions $k^\tau$ is the appropriate discount rate for project selection and the evaluation of alternative opportunities.

The two criteria presented above are consistent if and only if

$$\frac{(1 - \tau)\,\Delta\overline{X}}{k^\tau} = \Delta V \qquad (13\text{-}22)$$

We now need to examine the change in the value of the firm $\Delta V$. Let the value of the firm in the absence of investment be $V'$, where

$$V' = V'_u + \tau B' \qquad (13\text{-}23)$$

from Eq. (13-10). $V'_u$ is the value of the unlevered firm if no investment is undertaken and $B'$ is the value of the outstanding bonds of the firm with no investment. Similarly, the value of the firm with investment $V$ is

$$V = V_u + \tau B \qquad (13\text{-}24)$$

The change in value of the firm resulting from investment $\Delta V$ is the difference between $V$ and $V'$, or

$$\begin{aligned} \Delta V &= V - V' \\ &= (V_u + \tau B) - (V'_u + \tau B') \\ &= (V_u - V'_u) + \tau(B - B') \end{aligned} \qquad (13\text{-}25)$$

We assume that the only change in the value of the outstanding bonds of the firm is due to the issuance of new bonds $B^N$ to finance investment. That is, the value of the bonds outstanding before investment, $B'$, does not change because of the investment,[15] and the value of outstanding bonds after investment is $B = B' + B^N$. Therefore,

$$B - B' = B^N \qquad (13\text{-}26)$$

Substituting Eq. (13-26) into Eq. (13-25), we obtain

$$\Delta V = (V_u - V'_u) + \tau B^N \qquad (13\text{-}27)$$

The value of the firm if it were unlevered in the absence of investment, $V'_u$, can be expressed as the capitalized value of the income stream $(1 - \tau)\overline{X}'$ using the unlevered rate $k'_u$:

$$V'_u = \frac{(1 - \tau)\overline{X}'}{k'_u} \qquad (13\text{-}28)$$

Similarly, given the investment budget,

$$V_u = \frac{(1 - \tau)\overline{X}}{k_u} \qquad (13\text{-}29)$$

[15] See the discussion at the beginning of chap. 12 on this point.

The rate $k'_u$ is the capitalization rate on the unlevered firm with no investment, and $k_u$ is the rate after investment. By definition $\Delta\overline{X}$ is equal to the difference between the expected cash income of the firm with investment, $\overline{X}$, and the expected cash income of the firm without investment, $\overline{X}'$. Hence,

$$\overline{X} = \overline{X}' + \Delta\overline{X} \tag{13-30}$$

Furthermore, we assume that the discount rates for both streams are identical, that is, $k_u = k'_u$. In effect we are therefore assuming that the "risk" of $\tilde{X}$ is the same as that of $\tilde{X}'$. Equation (13-29) can now be expressed as

$$\begin{aligned} V_u &= \frac{(1-\tau)(\overline{X}' + \Delta\overline{X})}{k'_u} \\ &= \frac{(1-\tau)\overline{X}'}{k'_u} + \frac{(1-\tau)\,\Delta\overline{X}}{k'_u} \\ &= V'_u + \frac{(1-\tau)\,\Delta\overline{X}}{k'_u} \end{aligned} \tag{13-31}$$

Thus

$$V_u - V'_u = \frac{(1-\tau)\,\Delta\overline{X}}{k'_u} \tag{13-32}$$

Equation (13-32) shows that the difference between the unlevered value of the firm with investment and the unlevered value without investment is simply the capitalized value of the expected incremental cash income of the firm adjusted for taxes. The discount rate here is the rate that was applicable to the unlevered firm in the absence of investment $k'_u$. Thus we can now express the change in value of the firm. Substituting Eq. (13-32) into Eq. (13-27),

$$\Delta V = \frac{(1-\tau)\,\Delta\overline{X}}{k'_u} + \tau B^N \tag{13-33}$$

We will now assume that the firm maintains a constant ratio of debt to total value equal to $\theta^*$. Therefore, both the ratios of debt to value with and without investment must equal $\theta^*$:

$$\theta^* = \frac{B'}{V'}$$

or

$$B' = \theta^* V' \tag{13-34}$$

and

$$\theta^* = \frac{B}{V}$$

or

$$B = \theta^* V \tag{13-35}$$

From Eq. (13-26), the difference between $B$ and $B'$ is the value of new bonds issued, $B^N$. From Eqs. (13-34) and (13-35) this difference must be

$$\begin{aligned} B^N &= B - B' \\ &= \theta^* V - \theta^* V' \\ &= \theta^*(V - V') \\ &= \theta^* \Delta V \end{aligned} \tag{13-36}$$

Consequently, in financing investment the firm must issue new bonds equal to $\theta^*$ times the incremental value of the firm resulting from investment in order for the ratio of debt to firm value to remain constant. Substituting Eq. (13-36) into Eq. (13-33), we have

$$\Delta V = \frac{(1 - \tau)\, \Delta \overline{X}}{k'_u} + \tau\theta^* \Delta V \tag{13-37}$$

Solving Eq. (13-37) for $\Delta V$, we get

$$\Delta V = \frac{(1 - \tau)\, \Delta \overline{X}}{k'_u(1 - \tau\theta^*)} \tag{13-38}$$

If we now substitute for $\Delta V$ in Eq. (13-22), we arrive at[16]

$$k^\tau = k'_u(1 - \tau\theta^*) \tag{13-39}$$

Equation (13-39) expresses the discount rate for the stream $(1 - \tau)\, \Delta \overline{X}$ as a function of the rate on the unlevered firm in the absence of investment, the tax rate, and the debt ratio of the firm. This formulation is difficult to apply in practice, however, since the firm probably uses some debt, and $k'_u$ is the rate that would apply if no debt were used. The difficulty arises in estimating the value of $k'_u$. A more useful expression for $k^\tau$ would be one based on the current rates that are applicable to the outstanding securities of the firm $k'_S$ and $k'_B$. This expression is the weighted average cost of capital developed next.

**The weighted average cost of capital.** From our earlier analysis we know by Eq. (13-18) a relationship between $k'_S$, $k'_B$, and $k'_u$, that is,

$$k'_S = \frac{k'_u(1 - \tau\theta^*) - (1 - \tau)\theta^* k'_B}{(1 - \theta^*)} \tag{13-40}$$

Since all required rates of return on the securities of the firm are assumed to be unaffected by investment and given $\theta^*$, we can drop the "primes" without loss of generality. Let us solve Eq. (13-40) for $k_u$, and obtain

$$k_u = \frac{(1 - \theta^*)k_S + (1 - \tau)\theta^* k_B}{(1 - \tau\theta^*)} \tag{13-41}$$

[16] The difference between our $k^\tau$ and Modigliani and Miller's $\tilde{\rho}^*$ of footnote 16 in Modigliani and Miller (1963) is the use here of $\theta^*$, the ratio of bonds to value, as compared to their $L^*$, which is $B^N/I_0$ or the same as our $\gamma$ in eq. (12-37). Modigliani and Miller are assuming that the proportions of current investment to be financed with debt are given, whereas we have assumed above that the firm is seeking to maintain a constant ratio of debt to value. The significance of this difference is discussed later in this chapter.

Since $k_u = k'_u$, substitute $k_u$ in Eq. (13-41) for $k'_u$ in Eq. (13-39). We have

$$k^\tau = (1 - \theta^*)k_S + (1 - \tau)\theta^* k_B \qquad (13\text{-}42)$$

Equation (13-42) expresses $k^\tau$ as the weighted average of the rates on the individual securities adjusted for the tax-deductibility of interest on the firm's debt. It is the "weighted average cost of capital" found in most finance textbooks. The fact that $k^\tau$ is commonly presented as the "cost of capital" for investment decisions is a major reason for deriving it.

In our derivation three points should be kept in mind. First are the assumptions regarding risk: that the risk of the firm's securities is unaffected by investment in the sense that the applicable zero-investment and postinvestment discount rates are the same. Second, we have assumed that the firm maintains a constant ratio of debt to total value. Note by Eq. (13-36) that this assumption implies that the amount of bonds issued to finance investment cannot be determined before a determination of the increment in the value of the firm resulting from investment. In particular, $\theta^*$ is not generally equal to the proportion of the investment budget $I_0$ to be financed with bonds $B^N$; that is,

$$\theta^* \neq \frac{B^N}{I_0} \qquad \text{unless } I_0 = \Delta V$$

Since $I_0 = \Delta V$ only for those budgets that result in no benefit for shareholders ($\Delta V - I_0 = 0$), we would not expect to find $\theta^* = B^N/I_0$ very often.

The third point is our assumption of level perpetuities. Suppose that we wish to use $k^\tau$ as the discount rate applied to a general stream of the form $\Delta\overline{X}_1$, $\Delta\overline{X}_2$, $\Delta\overline{X}_3$, . . . , $\Delta\overline{X}_n$, where the expected values are not all equal and the stream has a finite life $n$. The cost of capital $k^\tau$ as defined by Eq. (13-42) can be used under these conditions provided that $k_S$, $k_B$, $\tau$, and $\theta$ are constant over $n$ and some additional conditions are met.[17]

## Criteria for Project Evaluation

Given that the criterion for the optimal capital budget is

$$\max \left[\frac{(1 - \tau)\,\Delta\overline{X}}{k^\tau} - I_0\right] \qquad (13\text{-}21)$$

where $k^\tau$ is determined from either Eq. (13-39) or Eq. (13-42), the criteria for project selection and the evaluation of alternatives follow directly.

Define $\overline{Z}$ as the increment to the cash income of the firm before taxes from undertaking project $Z$. Quantity $\overline{Z}_Z$ is a level perpetuity in the same sense as was used to describe $\Delta\overline{X}$. As was also true of $\Delta\overline{X}$, we assume that no future depreciation charges or future investment opportunities result

[17] See C. Haley and L. Schall, Problems with the Concept of the Cost of Capital, *Journal of Financial and Quantitative Analysis,* vol. 13, app. B, December 1978, for proofs and discussion.

from the adoption of project $Z$ (see page 346). The current investment required to undertake project $Z$ is $I_{Z0}$. Given that project $Z$ is economically independent of all other projects available to the firm, the incremental income $\Delta\overline{X}$, after the adoption of project $Z$ must be

$$\Delta\overline{X} = \Delta\overline{X}' + \overline{Z} \tag{13-43}$$

where $\Delta\overline{X}'$ is the incremental income if project $Z$ is not adopted. Similarly,

$$I_0 = I_0' + I_{Z0} \tag{13-44}$$

Under our assumptions that the debt ratio is constant and that the same discount rate $k^\tau$ applies to both $(1 - \tau)\,\Delta\overline{X}$ and $(1 - \tau)\,\Delta\overline{X}'$, the criterion for project selection follows from expression (13-21):

$$\frac{(1 - \tau)\overline{Z}}{k^\tau} - I_{Z0} \geq 0 \tag{13-45}$$

An equivalent alternative criterion can be derived from (13-45) based on the "internal rate of return" $\bar{r}_Z$:

$$\bar{r}_Z \equiv \frac{(1 - \tau)\overline{Z}}{I_{Z0}} \geq k^\tau \tag{13-46}$$

Expression (13-45) is a "present-value" form of the criterion and expression (13-46) is a "rate-of-return" form.

The criterion for choosing the best alternative from a set of mutually exclusive opportunities directly reflects the criterion for the optimal budget. Therefore, if $\overline{Z}_i$ and $I_{Z_i0}$ are the cash income and investment associated with alternative i of project $Z$, the criterion is to choose the alternative with

$$\max\left[\frac{(1 - \tau)\overline{Z}_i}{k^\tau} - I_{Z_i0}\right] \tag{13-47}$$

In general, then, given the assumptions with respect to risk and financing policy made in this chapter, the procedures of Chap. 3 can be applied using $k^\tau$ as the discount rate.

**The no-tax case.** The preceding analysis for the case of taxes on firm income also applies when no taxes are levied. The no-tax situation is simply a special case ($\tau = 0$) of the more general analysis. The results for this case can be expressed simply by setting $\tau = 0$ in all relevant expressions; that is,

1. $k^\tau = k_u(1 - \tau\theta^*)$ (13-39)

   becomes[18]

   $k^\tau = k_u = k_V$ (13-48)

[18] Recall that for the no-tax case the cost of capital for the firm does not vary with $\theta$ and therefore $k_V = k_u$ for all values of $\theta$.

2. $$\max\left[\frac{(1-\tau)\,\Delta\bar{X}}{k^{\tau}} - I_0\right] \tag{13-21}$$

becomes

$$\max\left[\frac{\Delta\bar{X}}{k_V} - I_0\right] \tag{13-49}$$

3. $$\frac{(1-\tau)\bar{Z}}{k^{\tau}} - I_{Z0} \geq 0 \tag{13-45}$$

becomes

$$\frac{\bar{Z}}{k_V} - I_{Z0} \geq 0 \tag{13-50}$$

4. $$\max\left[\frac{(1-\tau)\bar{Z}}{k^{\tau}} - I_{Z_i0}\right] \tag{13-47}$$

becomes

$$\max\left[\frac{\bar{Z}_i}{k_V} - I_{Z_i0}\right] \tag{13-51}$$

The tax case is clearly the more interesting and important of the two and the more difficult to analyze. The no-tax case summary is given for purposes of completeness; the general arguments of the tax case are also applicable here.

## A Comparison with the Results of Chap. 12

In Chap. 12 we developed criteria for firm investment decisions with taxes using the discount model. The analysis there was based on more general assumptions than the cost-of-capital model just presented. The differences in assumptions between the two models fall into three general classes:

1. The type of cash returns examined—level perpetuities with no future investment or depreciation in the cost-of-capital model as compared to general cash flows in Chap. 12.
2. The risk of the cash returns as indicated by the discount rate applied to those returns—in Chap. 12 each alternative could be evaluated with its own appropriate rate, which in general may not be the same for each alternative.
3. The impact of financing policy on the criteria.

In this section we shall be concerned with the assumptions regarding financing policy in the two models, since this has been an important issue in the literature. To highlight the differences between the two models, we shall first express the criteria of Chap. 12 as they apply to investment opportunities of the type assumed in the development of the cost-of-capital model. The discussion here is based on the "alternative expression for project selection" (12-37).

The project-selection criterion presented as (12-37) in Chap. 12 reduces to

$$\frac{(1-\tau)\bar{Z}}{k_u} - (1-\tau\gamma)I_{Z0} \geq 0 \tag{13-52}$$

when applied to the projects of this chapter. The rate $k_u$ is the discount rate that applies to the unlevered cash flow of the firm; we assume that the unlevered cash flow provided by project $Z$ is of the same "risk" as the cash flow of the firm. Term $\bar{Z}_{ut}$ as defined by Eq. (12-36) reduces to $(1-\tau)\bar{Z}$ in the absence of depreciation charges and future investment. Recall that $\gamma$ is the proportion of the current capital budget that will be financed with debt and is assumed to be independent of the projects selected.

Contrast expression (13-52) with the project-selection rule derived above:

$$\frac{(1-\tau)\bar{Z}}{k^\tau} - I_{Z0} \geq 0 \tag{13-45}$$

where $k^\tau = k_u(1-\tau\theta^*)$ from Eq. (13-39). Substituting for $k^\tau$ in (13-45), we have

$$\frac{(1-\tau)\bar{Z}}{k_u(1-\tau\theta^*)} - I_{Z0} \geq 0 \tag{13-53}$$

The only differences are the use of $\theta^*$ as compared to $\gamma$ and the fact that the term $(1-\tau\theta^*)$ appears associated with $k_u$ in (13-53), whereas $(1-\tau\gamma)$ is associated with $I_{Z0}$ in (13-52). It is also clear that (13-53) can be multiplied through by $(1-\tau\theta^*)$ to arrive at an equivalent project-selection criterion:

$$\frac{(1-\tau)\bar{Z}}{k_u} - (1-\tau\theta^*)I_{Z0} \geq 0 \tag{13-54}$$

The difference between the project-selection criterion of Chap. 12, expression (13-52), and the cost-of capital model [expression (13-54)] appear slight. Yet the two are not equivalent in general. The assumption used in deriving (13-52) is that adoption of a project $Z$ will result in additional bonds being issued of amount $B_Z^N = \gamma I_{Z0}$. The assumption underlying (13-54) is that the project will require additional bonds of amount $B_Z^N = \theta^* V_Z$, where $V_Z$ is the *value* of the incremental cash flow from project $Z$ as defined in Chap. 12. These assumptions are not consistent in general; thus criteria based on them are not necessarily consistent. To see why this is true, note

$$V_Z = \frac{(1-\tau)\bar{Z}}{k_u} + \tau B_Z^N \tag{13-55}$$

$$= V_{Zu} + \tau B_Z^N \tag{13-55a}$$

applying the arguments of Chap. 12 to the projects assumed here.

Also, $B_Z^N = \theta^* V_Z$ by assumption and therefore

$$V_Z = \frac{(1-\tau)\bar{Z}}{k_u} + \tau\theta^* V_Z$$

$$V_Z = \frac{(1-\tau)\bar{Z}}{k_u(1-\tau\theta^*)} \tag{13-56}$$

Equation (13-56), which applies to projects, compares directly with the expression for $\Delta V$, Eq. (13-38), which applies to the entire budget. The project-selection rule of this chapter, expression (13-53), is therefore simply

$$V_Z - I_{Z0} > 0 \tag{13-57}$$

which is the same as the general rule (12-28) of Chap. 12. In the derivation, we assumed that $B_Z^N = \theta^* V_Z$ and that neither $\theta^*$ nor $V_Z$ depends on $I_{Z0}$. Suppose that $V_Z = \$500$ and $\theta^* = .4$. In this case $B_Z^N = \$200$. Term $I_Z$ could be any value, but suppose it is \$400. This project is therefore desirable. Now consider another project to be included in the same capital budget. $V_Z = \$800$ and $\theta^*$ is still 40%; therefore, $B_Z^N$ for this project is \$320. Let $I_{Z0} = \$400$ so that this project too is worthwhile. In the case of the first project, the proportion of debt to initial investment is \$200/\$400 = 50%; in the case of the second project the proportion is \$320/\$400 = 80%. Therefore, a constant $\theta^*$ does not result in a constant value for $\gamma$.

When a criterion based on $\gamma$ is used, the firm should be planning to finance a fixed proportion of the *initial outlays* with debt. When a criterion based on $\theta^*$ is used, the firm should be planning to maintain a constant ratio of debt to *value*. The two are not the same thing.[19]

## IMPERFECT MARKETS AND INVESTMENT DECISIONS: THE "TRADITIONAL" CASE

A discussion of the cost-of-capital model would be incomplete without pointing out that there are other views regarding the influence of debt financing on the criteria for investment decisions.[20] The model to be presented here is roughly consistent with many of the arguments of other authors, although it is primarily a logical extension of our prior results for level perpetuities. The problem concerns the existence of an optimal capital structure and the criteria for investment decisions if such exist.

We have argued that corporate income taxes and the tax-deductibility of interest on the firm's debt result in an advantage to the use of debt in otherwise

[19] It should be noted in passing that the question of whether "book value" or "market value" weights should be used in determining the cost of capital is in part a question of which assumption is more appropriate. $\theta^*$ is a "market value weight" and $\gamma$ is a "book value weight." As used in the criteria above either may be correct. However, it is not in general correct to estimate a cost of capital of the form $(1 - \gamma)k'_S + (1 - \tau)\gamma k'_B$ when $B^N = \gamma I_0$. As should be obvious from the discussion, the rates on the firm's securities are unlikely to be invariant with respect to $\gamma$. Hence a weighted average cost of capital based on book value weights is apt to be invalid. We were able to derive a weighted average cost of capital with market weights, eq. (13-42), which is valid under the assumptions of the analysis.

[20] For example; see Eli Schwartz, Theory of the Capital Structure of the Firm, *Journal of Finance*, vol. 14, pp. 18–39, March 1959; and Solomon, Leverage and the Cost of Capital (listed in the Suggested Readings at the end of the chapter).

perfect capital markets. Under these assumptions the value of the firm is at a maximum when the entire income of the firm is paid out to bondholders. Therefore, the optimal capital structure is 100% debt ($\theta = 1.0$). Instead, suppose that the value of the (static) firm is at a maximum at some value of $\theta$ between 0 and 1.0. Presumably this condition results from some type of imperfection in the capital markets, although the precise nature of the imperfections is left unspecified. We assume that the pre-tax income of the firm, $\tilde{X}$, is *not* affected by firm leverage; thus those imperfections that affect $\tilde{X}$ (such as bankruptcy costs) are ruled out. Denote the value of $\theta$ at the point of maximum value for the firm as $\theta^*$ and that maximum value as $V^*$. Given the assumption that $0 < \theta^* < 1.0$, we wish to develop criteria for investment decisions that correspond to those for the perfect-market model with taxes. Here again all streams are assumed to be level perpetuities, the firm maintains debt ratio $\theta^*$, and all investments are such that the firm's zero investment and postinvestment costs of capital are the same.

Under these assumptions we argue that there exists a weighted average cost of capital $k^*$ which is the appropriate discount rate for use in investment decisions. We shall find that the weighted average formulation for $k^\tau$ above [Eq. (13-42)] also provides a value for $k^*$ and that $k^*$ is a minimum cost of capital for the firm.

Let us define a cost of capital for the firm that is equal to the expected after-tax income of the firm if it were unlevered, $(1 - \tau)\overline{X}$, divided by the total value of the firm at the point of maximum value:

$$k^* \equiv \frac{(1 - \tau)\overline{X}}{V^*} \tag{13-58}$$

Let $\overline{X}'$ be the expected income of the firm and $V'^*$ be the maximum value of the firm in the absence of investment. We assume that the investment decisions of the firm do *not* change $k^*$.

$$k^* = \frac{(1 - \tau)\overline{X}'}{V'^*} = \frac{(1 - \tau)\overline{X}}{V^*} \tag{13-59}$$

But $\overline{X} = \overline{X}' + \Delta\overline{X}$, where $\Delta\overline{X}$ is the expected increase in firm income as the result of undertaking capital budget $I_0$. Applying the relationships assumed in (13-59),

$$\begin{aligned} V^* &= \frac{(1 - \tau)\overline{X}}{k^*} = \frac{(1 - \tau)(\overline{X}' + \Delta\overline{X})}{k^*} \\ &= \frac{(1 - \tau)\overline{X}'}{k^*} + \frac{(1 - \tau)\,\Delta\overline{X}}{k^*} \\ &= V'^* + \frac{(1 - \tau)\,\Delta\overline{X}}{k^*} \end{aligned}$$

$$\Delta V^* = V^* - V'^* = \frac{(1 - \tau)\,\Delta\overline{X}}{k^*} \tag{13-60}$$

Equation (13-60) is very similar to Eq. (13-22) with $k^*$ substituted for $k^\tau$. However, the arguments leading up to the two equations differ. Equation (13-22) is essentially the definition of $k^\tau$; no assumptions were made regarding the impact of investment decisions on the "risk" of the firm or of the effects of financing policy. Equation (13-60) is based on a particular, value-maximizing financing policy and on the assumption that the ratio of income to total value is invariant to the firm's investment decisions. Our argument from this point will also differ from the one that follows Eq. (13-22).

From Eq. (13-60) we know that the criterion for the optimal capital budget

$$\max\,[\Delta V - I_0] \qquad \text{implies} \qquad \max\left[\frac{(1-\tau)\,\Delta\bar{X}}{k^*} - I_0\right] \tag{13-61}$$

It remains to express $k^*$ in another form. We observe that the following relationships hold for level perpetuities:

$$V^* = S^* + B^* \tag{13-62}$$

$$\bar{D} = (1-\tau)(\bar{X} - \bar{R}) \tag{13-63}$$

$$k_S^* = \frac{\bar{D}}{S^*} \tag{13-64}$$

$$k_B^* = \frac{\bar{R}}{B^*} \tag{13-65}$$

We can express Eq. (13-63) as

$$\bar{D} = (1-\tau)\bar{X} - (1-\tau)\bar{R} \tag{13-66}$$

and using the definitions of $k^*$, $k_S^*$, and $k_B^*$ [Eqs. (13-59), (13-64), and (13-65)] to substitute into (13-66),

$$k_S^* S^* = k^* V^* - (1-\tau) k_B^* B^*$$

$$k^* = k_S^*\left(\frac{S^*}{V^*}\right) + (1-\tau)k_B^*\left(\frac{B^*}{V^*}\right)$$

$$k^* = k_S^*(1-\theta^*) + (1-\tau)k_B^*\theta^* \tag{13-67}$$

Equation (13-67) expresses $k^*$ as the weighted average of the expected rates of return on the individual securities of the firm with the rate on bonds $k_B^*$ adjusted for tax-deductibility. We are assuming that the optimal debt-value ratio $\theta^*$ is not affected by the firm's investment decisions. It should be clear that $k_S^*$ and $k_B^*$ are also assumed to be unaffected by investment.

The cost of capital derived here can be used for project evaluation just as $k^\tau$ was used above. This use is subject to the same qualifications as for $k^\tau$ plus the requirement that the optimal capital structure is unaffected by the firm's investment decisions.

A final point is of interest. By the definition of $k^*$ [Eq. (13-58)], at the point where $V^*$ is maximum, $k^*$ must also be a minimum value. This is so because, by

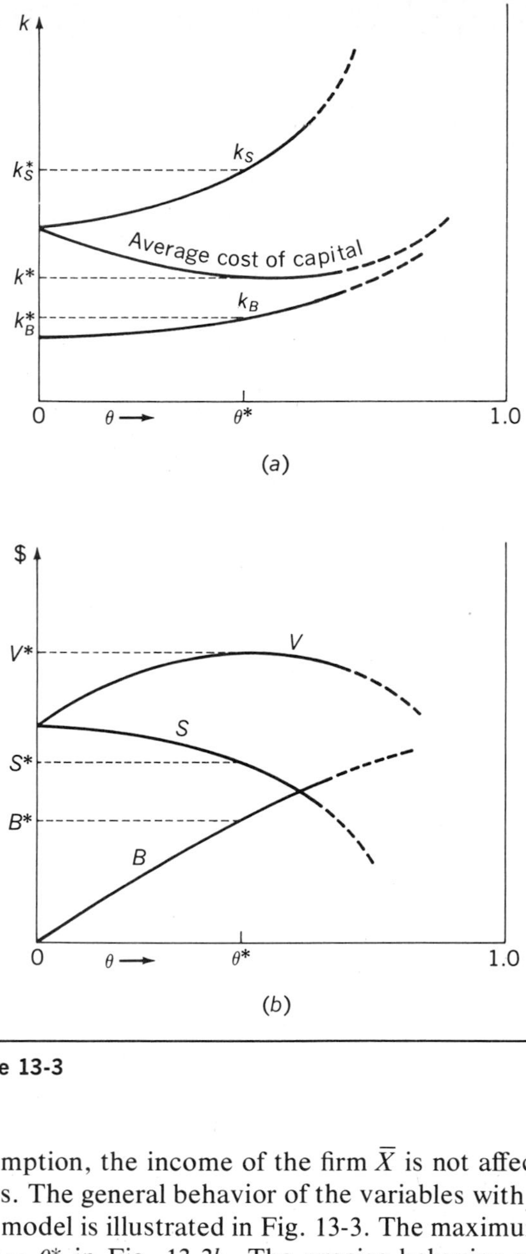


**figure 13-3**

assumption, the income of the firm $\bar{X}$ is not affected by capital structure decisions. The general behavior of the variables with respect to $\theta$ that is assumed in this model is illustrated in Fig. 13-3. The maximum value for the firm is reached at $\theta = \theta^*$ in Fig. 13-3*b*. The precise behavior of the values of the individual securities as a function of $\theta$ is hypothetical. Similarly, the rates on the securities and $k^*$ are shown in Fig. 13-3*a*. Here again we know very little about what might be reasonable behavior for these variables. Imperfect markets are difficult to analyze. We shall attempt to deal with the problem in more depth in the following chapters.

## SUMMARY

This chapter has presented variations on the cost-of-capital model, which has seen widespread use in theoretical articles, textbooks, and practical applications. A weighted average cost of capital was developed that can be used as a standard for investment decisions by the firm when some fairly restrictive conditions are met. These conditions are

1. Investments made by the firm do not affect the required yields on the firm's securities.
2. The firm maintains a constant debt ratio.

We noted that there are alternative approaches to investment decisions which do not require these assumptions in perfect markets. These approaches were developed in Chap. 12.

APPENDIX

# THIRTEEN A

## MATHEMATICAL PROOFS

In this appendix three problems will be considered:

1. The limit of $k_S$ for the no-tax case
2. The limit of $k_S$ for the tax case
3. The minimum value of $k_V$ for the tax case

### NO TAXES

From Eq. (13-6) we have

$$k_S = \frac{k_V - \theta k_B}{1 - \theta} \tag{13A-1}$$

We are interested in the value that $k_S$ approaches as $\theta$ approaches 1.0. We argued in the body of the chapter that at $\theta = 1.0$, $k_B = k_V$. Substitution of the limiting values in (13A-1) yields $k_S = 0/0$, which cannot be interpreted. The formal problem is

$$\lim_{\theta \to 1} [k_S] = \lim_{\theta \to 1} \left[ \frac{k_V - \theta k_B}{1 - \theta} \right] \tag{13A-2}$$

The solution to (13A-2) can be found by applying L'Hospital's rule as explained in any basic calculus text. We take the derivative of the numerator and the derivative of the denominator of the function and then examine the limit of the ratio of the derivatives. The derivative of the numerator is:

$$\frac{d(k_V - \theta k_B)}{d\theta} = -k_B - \theta \frac{dk_B}{d\theta} \tag{13A-3}$$

as $k_V$ is independent of $\theta$ in taxless, perfect markets. The derivative of the denominator is:

$$\frac{d(1-\theta)}{d\theta} = -1 \tag{13A-4}$$

Hence, by L'Hospital's rule

$$\lim_{\theta \to 1} [k_S] = \lim_{\theta \to 1} \left[k_B + \theta \frac{dk_B}{d\theta}\right] \tag{13A-5}$$

Note that $[k_B + \theta\, dk_B/d\theta]$ equals the marginal rate on debt $d(k_B B)/dB$, since $\theta = B/V$ and $V$ is a constant with respect to $\theta$. Therefore, we have the general proposition that the limit of $k_S$ is equal to the limit of the marginal rate on debt. If the marginal rate on debt has a finite limit, so will the average rate on the firm's shares $k_S$. Little more can be done without assuming a functional relationship between $k_B$ and $\theta$. Using the relationship assumed in the body of the chapter [Eq. (13-8)],

$$k_B = i + (k_V - i)\theta^2 \tag{13A-6}$$

and

$$\frac{dk_B}{d\theta} = 2(k_V - i)\theta \tag{13A-7}$$

Therefore, the marginal rate on debt is $k_B + 2(k_V - i)\theta^2$ and

$$\lim_{\theta \to 1} [k_B + 2(k_V - i)\theta^2] = 3k_V - 2i \tag{13A-8}$$

$$\therefore \lim_{\theta \to 1} [k_S] = 3k_V - 2i \tag{13A-9}$$

This limit is clearly positive and finite, since $k_V > i$.

## THE LIMIT OF $k_S$ WITH TAXES

In the tax case, problems similar to the above exist; the relationships between $k_S$, $k_B$, and $\theta$ are simply more complicated. From Eq. (13-18) we have

$$k_S = \frac{k_u(1-\tau\theta) - (1-\tau)\theta k_B}{1-\theta} \tag{13A-10}$$

The derivative of the numerator of (13A-10), $D_N$, is

$$D_N = -\tau k_u - (1-\tau)\left(k_B + \theta \frac{dk_B}{d\theta}\right) \tag{13A-11}$$

and the derivative of the denominator of (13A-10) is again $-1$. The ratio of the derivatives is $-D_N$, where

$$-D_N = \tau k_u + (1-\tau)\left(k_B + \theta \frac{dk_B}{d\theta}\right) \tag{13A-12}$$

Since $k_u$ and $\tau$ are constants, a finite limit of $k_S$ again depends on the existence of a finite limit for the marginal rate on debt. Using the relationship of the text [Eq. (13-19)],

$$k_B = i + (k_u - i)\theta^2 \tag{13A-13}$$

$$\frac{dk_B}{d\theta} = 2(k_u - i)\theta \tag{13A-14}$$

Substituting (13A-13) and (13A-14) into (13A-12) and taking the limit of (13A-12) as $\theta \rightarrow 1.0$, we have

$$\lim_{\theta \rightarrow 1.0} [k_S] = k_u + 2(1 - \tau)(k_u - i) \tag{13A-15}$$

Again, $k_S$ approaches a positive, finite value.

## THE MINIMUM VALUE OF $k_V$

Equation (13-15) in the body of the chapter provides a relationship between $k_V$, $k_u$, $\theta$, and $k_B$:

$$k_V = k_u - \tau(k_u - k_B)\theta \tag{13A-16}$$

The behavior of $k_V$ depends to a great extent on the relationship between $k_B$ and $\theta$. The derivative of $k_V$ with respect to $\theta$ is

$$\frac{dk_V}{d\theta} = -\tau(k_u - k_B) + \tau\theta \frac{dk_B}{d\theta} \tag{13A-17}$$

Setting (13A-17) to zero we find that a minimum value for $k_V$ is reached at the point where

$$k_B + \theta \frac{dk_B}{d\theta} = k_u \tag{13A-18}$$

i.e., the marginal rate on debt equals the rate on the unlevered firm. If the marginal rate on debt were never to reach $k_u$, then no minimum would exist. However, since we argued that the average rate on debt $k_B$ equals $k_u$ for an all-debt firm, the marginal rate must be greater than $k_u$ at some point $\theta < 1.0$. Using (13A-13) as an expression for $k_B$, and substituting (13A-13) and (13A-14) into (13A-18), we find that

$$i + (k_u - i)\theta^2 + 2(k_u - i)\theta^2 = k_u$$

$$3(k_u - i)\theta^2 = k_u - i$$

$$\theta^2 = \frac{1}{3}$$

$$\theta^* = \left(\frac{1}{3}\right)^{1/2} = .577 \tag{13A-19}$$

The interesting point about this result is that the value of $\theta$ where $k_V$ is minimum is independent of $k_u$, $i$, and $\tau$. This independence is characteristic of functions of $k_B$ of the form

$$k_B = k_0 + (k_u - k_0)\theta^n \tag{13A-20}$$

where $k_0$ equals the limit of $k_B$ as $\theta$ approaches zero. Note that

$$\frac{dk_B}{d\theta} = n(k_u - k_0)\theta^{n-1} \tag{13A-21}$$

Substituting (13A-20) and (13A-21) into (13A-18) we get

$$k_0 + (k_u - k_0)\theta^n + n(k_u - k_0)\theta^n = k_u$$

$$\theta^n = 1/(n + 1)$$

$$\theta^* = [1/(n + 1)]^{1/n} \tag{13A-22}$$

## SUGGESTED READINGS


Brennan, Michael: A New Look at the Weighted Average Cost of Capital *Journal of Business Finance,* vol. 5, pp. 24–30, January 1973.

Haley, Charles W. and Lawrence D. Schall: Problems with the Concept of the Cost of Capital, *Journal of Financial and Quantitative Analyses,* vol. 13, pp. 847–870, December 1978.

Lerner, Eugene M. and Willard T. Carleton: The Integration of Capital Budgeting and Stock Valuation, *American Economic Review,* vol. 54, pp. 683–702, September 1964, reprinted in Archer, Stephen H. and Charles A. D'Ambrosio, "The Theory of Business Finance," 2d ed., The Macmillan Company, New York, 1976.

Lewellen, Wilbur G.: "The Cost of Capital," Wadsworth Publishing Company, Inc., Belmont, Calif., 1969.

Modigliani, Franco and M. M. Miller: The Cost of Capital, Corporation Finance, and the Theory of Investment, *American Economic Review,* vol. 48, pp. 261–297, June 1958, reprinted in Archer and D'Ambrosio, *op. cit.*

Modigliani, Franco and M. M. Miller: Taxes and the Cost of Capital: A Correction, *American Economic Review,* vol. 53, pp. 433–443, June 1963, reprinted in Archer and D'Ambrosio, *op. cit.*

Nantell, T. J. and C. R. Carlson: The Cost of Capital as a Weighted Average, *Journal of Finance,* vol. 30, pp. 1343–1355, December 1975.

Robichek, Alexander A. and John G. MacDonald: The Cost of Capital Concept: Potential Use and Misuse, *Financial Executive,* vol. 33, pp. 2–8, June 1965.

Solomon, Ezra: Leverage and the Cost of Capital, *Journal of Finance,* vol. 17, pp. 273–279, May, 1963, reprinted in Archer and D'Ambrosio, *op. cit.*

Vickers, Douglas: The Cost of Capital and the Structure of the Firm, *Journal of Finance,* vol. 25, pp. 35–46, March 1970.

CHAPTER

# FOURTEEN

# INTRODUCTION TO FINANCIAL DECISIONS IN IMPERFECT MARKETS

With the exception of the simple model presented at the end of Chap. 13, our analysis so far in this book has been based on the general assumption of perfect capital markets. Using this assumption we have found that the value-additivity principle applies to risky, multiperiod cash flows; that financing decisions (in the absence of corporate taxes) did not affect the value of the firm; and that investment decisions could be made on a project-by-project basis, all projects with positive net present values being adopted. With corporate taxes and the tax-deductibility of interest payments on debt, we found that firms should finance exclusively with debt so long as the tax-deductibility of interest is permitted. Our investment decision rules must be modified somewhat to take into account the tax effects of debt financing, but these modifications are straightforward. Thus in perfect markets the primary concern of the financial manager of a firm is to find and evaluate investments. The major theoretical and practical problems under perfect markets concern the measurement and evaluation of investment risks or, equivalently, the estimation of the value of multiperiod risky cash flows.

We turn now to considerations of the impact of departures from the perfect-market assumptions on the financing and investment decisions of business firms. We examine in this chapter the general nature of imperfections in the capital markets and their significance for individuals and firms.[1] We then

[1] Although we use the terms ''imperfections'' and ''imperfect markets'' to refer to departures from the perfect-market assumptions, this usage is not technically accurate. Most of the ''imperfections'' we discuss are real economic costs imposed on various types of transactions as opposed to true capital market imperfections such as the existence of monopoly power in securities trading. See G. Stigler, Imperfections in the Capital Markets, *Journal of Political Economy*, vol. 74, pp. 287–292, June 1967.

**table 14-1 Some Observed Types of Imperfections**

(1) *Investor trading costs:* brokerage fees and commissions on securities purchases and sales by individuals.
(2) *Limitations on personal borrowing:* margin requirements, lenders fees, and other factors limiting personal borrowing or increasing its cost.
(3) *Personal tax structure biases:* favored treatment of capital gains over ordinary income, dividends over interest income, and any other biases built into the tax laws.
(4) *Information access and cost:* information is not costlessly available to everyone.
(5) *Issue or flotation costs:* commissions to investment bankers, legal fees, and other expenses paid by firms issuing securities.
(6) *Costs of financial distress:* accounting and legal expenses incurred in bankruptcy; loss of sales and increased costs due to disruption of operations during periods of financial distress including bankruptcy.
(7) *Agency costs:* costs imposed on the firm by creditors to ensure that the firm abides by its contractual obligations.*
(8) *Asset indivisibilities:* many financial assets are not perfectly divisible into small units.
(9) *Limited markets:* some financial assets such as the common stock of small companies and loans made by financial institutions are not freely traded in the capital market.

* Agency costs in general refer to costs which are involved in insuring that an agent fulfill his or her responsibilities and obligations to the principal. The agency costs of interest here and in subsequent chapters are those relating to the firm (stockholders) and its creditors.

provide an overview of the material discussed in Chaps. 15, 16, and 17. Thus this chapter serves as a general introduction to imperfect markets and the consequences of imperfections for financial decisions.

Table 14-1 summarizes the types of imperfections we examine in the chapter. Each one of these imperfections is discussed and its impact on financial decisions is evaluated. We begin with comments on the general impact of market imperfections before considering them in detail.

## THE SIGNIFICANCE OF MARKET IMPERFECTIONS

The perfect-market assumptions present an idealized version of the world. We know that none of the assumptions holds precisely. Nevertheless, they are useful so long as they hold approximately. To present the issue in another way, so long as departures from the assumptions are not *systematic* and *material,* a theory based on such assumptions can be presumed to hold in the absence of empirical evidence to the contrary.

Imperfections must be *systematic* in the sense that they imply a departure from the theory's results in only one direction. For example, corporate income taxes imply that debt financing is preferred; hence corporate income taxes are a systematic influence on the firm's financing policy. An example of an unsystematic imperfection is the trading costs assessed on the purchase and sale of securities. Such costs limit the degree to which arbitrage can operate. Only gross differences between the values of equivalent income streams will be eliminated, since the profits from arbitraging away small differences would be eliminated by the costs of the transactions. Hence the value-additivity principle would hold only as an approximation; the extent of the approximation is dependent on the type of transaction required and the magnitude of the resulting costs. Unsystematic departures from the perfect-market assumptions introduce some vagueness into what would otherwise be exact relationships.

Imperfections must also be *material* as they relate to firm decisions. Unfortunately, materiality is a difficult quality to assess since it involves comparisons between alternatives. An easy example that carries the discussion toward the next section involves the impact of issue costs on the use of debt by the firm. Firms incur costs in issuing bonds to the public. It can easily cost more than \$600,000 to issue \$50 million in bonds. That cost appears "material" by most standards. However, what if the proceeds from issuing the debt are used to retire some of the firm's stock? The theory developed to date (under simplifying assumptions) would predict an increase in the value of the firm of $\tau B$ or (with $\tau = .5$) \$25 million because of the tax effect. Hence \$600,000 is not "material" in this decision; i.e., it would not prevent the firm from issuing the debt. On the other hand, the \$600,000 may well be material in the decision as to the type of debt to issue; for example, whether to issue bonds or to obtain a long-term bank loan (thereby avoiding issue costs). Note also that materiality is definitely an empirical issue. We must assess the actual magnitudes of any imperfections; it is not sufficient merely to observe that they exist.

## INDIVIDUAL FINANCIAL DECISIONS

The general impact of imperfections on individuals is to make their investment-consumption decisions much more complex, dependent on past decisions regarding their asset portfolios, and more dependent on personal circumstances. To put it more succinctly, the individual's problems are messy and very difficult to treat analytically.

For example, imperfections (1), (3), and (9) in Table 14-1 mean that people cannot costlessly and easily restructure their asset portfolios. This means that the particular assets owned at a given point in time affect the desirability of alternative assets that might be owned. In other words, the desirability of investing in IBM stock today depends on whether or not you currently own the stock of General Motors (or any other company). Since purchase of IBM may imply selling some or all of your General Motors, you cannot make the decision to purchase IBM independently. You must consider the costs involved in rearranging your portfolio, that it would require the sale of several shares of GM stock to equal the purchase cost of one share of IBM stock, the personal tax implications, etc. Imperfections (1), (2), (3), (4), (8), and (9) all affect individual financial decisions. The existence of such imperfections and that the problems posed by them are difficult is attested to by the large numbers of firms and individuals selling personal financial services including estate planning, investment counseling, and tax planning. In this text, we shall not explore the impact of imperfections on individuals beyond that needed for the analysis of the effects of company policies on the firm's stockholders.

## FIRM FINANCIAL DECISIONS

We can relate the financial problems of the firm to the following questions:

1. What is the proper financing policy for any given portfolio of firm assets?
2. In evaluating investments (new assets), how should the following factors be included in the analysis?
   (*a*) The probability distribution of $\Delta\tilde{\mathbf{Y}}$ (the added cash flow from investment).
   (*b*) The means of financing.
   (*c*) The stochastic relationship between the incremental cash flow $\Delta\tilde{\mathbf{Y}}$ and the cash flow from the other assets of the firm $\tilde{\mathbf{Y}}'$.

In Chaps. 11 and 12 we have shown that in perfect markets *with no corporate taxes,* only 2(*a*) is a relevant problem for the firm. Financing policy does not affect the firm's value nor is it necessary to consider financing in evaluating investments. Moreover, it is not necessary to consider the stochastic relationship between a project's cash flow and the cash flow produced by the other assets of the firm. *With corporate taxes,* the use of debt becomes advantageous both in financing existing assets and in financing new assets. Thus, regarding considerations 1 and 2(*b*), all firm assets should be financed with debt so long as the debt interest is tax-deductible, and this is true regardless of the risk or nature of the assets. Consideration 2(*c*) remains irrelevant even with corporate taxes.

Imperfections cause all the above issues—1 through 2(*c*)—to be important in management's decisions. Debt policy becomes more complex. Not only may an optimal capital structure including both debt and equity exist, but other aspects of financing strategy must be considered. Issues such as debt maturity, the source of debt (banks vs. insurance companies vs. the public market), the analysis of provisions in the debt contract, and the use of various types of debt (senior vs. subordinated vs. convertible) all become relevant. Equity financing is more complicated and dividend policy is important. As a consequence, the means of financing any given project affects the value of the project and we must consider interactions between financing and investment decisions. Finally, single-project evaluation is ordinarily no longer appropriate, and alternative project packages and their associated financing must be evaluated relative to the existing cash flows of the firm.

If optimal decisions require a simultaneous solution of both the investment and the financing problems, it is no longer possible for management to decentralize investment decisions within the firm. In other words, all investment and financing decisions must be made "at the top." As a practical matter this would be an intolerable situation in large firms. Even though there exist both the theory and the solution procedures to deal formally with the joint problem, the costs incurred by firms in solving it may be large.[2] The capital budgeting procedures used by large firms can be explained in part by these observations. The provision of discretionary budgets to divisional managers plus the establishment of limits on the size of investments undertaken and the use of formal planning procedures all can be looked at as ways to provide top management with some controls on investment decisions without requiring full consideration by them. The budgeting-planning process includes as inputs information from financial management regarding the financing prospects for the firm. At present such procedures are largely arrived at by experience and judgment. It may be that as we understand more fully the theoretical issues involved, the budgeting-planning process can be improved.

We have said nothing about the problem of "diversification" [factor 2(*c*)] so far in this discussion. The paragraph above was based on the assumption that this problem did not exist for the firm. It is possible for the firm to have financing problems and a joint investment-financing problem without having to worry about the stochastic relationships among income streams. A formal discussion of this proposition is presented in the next chapter. Suppose that diversification is important; what does this mean in terms of firm decisions? The answer currently is that we do not really know except in a very general way; nor does it appear that corporate management has many ideas on the subject. Let us sketch out what happens to the investment decisions of the firm when diversification is a relevant consideration. We shall ignore any joint investment-financing effects in the following discussion. The reader should appreciate that introduction of joint effects compounds the problem greatly.

If the stochastic relationship between the incremental income from the current capital budget ($\mathbf{\Delta\tilde{Y}}$) and the stream that would exist in the absence of any current investment ($\mathbf{\tilde{Y}}'$) affects the value of $\mathbf{\Delta\tilde{Y}}$, then the following is also true in general:

1. The value of the incremental income stream associated with any given investment depends on the stochastic relationship between that stream and all other streams included in the optimal budget. The firm has a "portfolio" problem. Stochastic as well as economic relationships are now important to the total value of a set of streams. Therefore, in general, the efficient organization of opportunities into projects proposed in Chaps. 3 and 12 is no longer optimal. The firm must consider all feasible "packages" of opportunities confronting the firm.

[2] A theoretically correct solution may require enumeration of all alternatives, which is impractical. Practical solution methods available require formulation of the problem as a mathematical program involving specific assumptions about the objective function, which may have little theoretical or empirical support.

2. The value of each feasible package of opportunities depends on the stochastic relationship between the stream provided by the particular package under consideration and the streams provided by both the existing assets of the firm and *future* assets the firm may acquire. Therefore, the firm must consider not only *economic* relationships between present investment opportunities and future ones, but also the *stochastic* relationships involved.

No general analytic solution to the full-blown financing and investment problem of the firm is currently available. The only recommendation that can be made at present is that management must evaluate all options and do the best it can. Financial theory is of only partial help in coping with the general problem. However, we can explore various aspects of the problem and consider the effects of particular imperfections on firm decisions. In examining the problem, it is useful to separate imperfections into two groups—those that invalidate value additivity (rate effects) and those that do not (stream effects). We now consider the implications of this categorization of imperfections assuming that a discount model is appropriate.[3]

## RATE EFFECTS AND STREAM EFFECTS

At a conceptual level we can think of departures from the perfect-market assumptions as affecting the relationship between financing decisions and the value of the firm in two ways—via changes in the magnitudes of the cash streams and via changes in the discount rates applicable to those streams. A change in the total cash flow the firm provides to investors that is due to an imperfection is termed a "stream effect." A stream effect alone does not invalidate the value-additivity principle, since the total value of a given total stream will still be invariant with respect to how that stream is divided among different types of securities. This can occur if investors' transaction costs are zero, but the firm itself incurs costs such as those due to financial distress or securities issues. Therefore, the streams provided by the firm are affected but identical streams will have equal values. The second type of imperfection affects the discount rates applicable to streams and invalidates the value-additivity principle. This type of imperfection is called a "rate effect."

The distinction between rate effects and stream effects is important for the following reason. The value-additivity principle by its very nature indicates that if the total cash flow received by investors is affected by firm decisions, the value of the firm will be affected. If firm decisions reduce the total cash flow

[3] Similar arguments apply to certainty-equivalent models. A stream effect corresponds to a modification of the stream for which the certainty equivalent is determined and a rate effect modifies the certainty-equivalence process itself; that is, two identical streams may not have the same certainty equivalent.

represented by a set of streams, the value of the firm will be lowered. Similarly, if the total cash flow is increased, the value of the firm will increase. Therefore, even if the VAP holds, stream effects must be considered. An obvious example that we have already discussed is the impact of corporate income taxes and the tax deductibility of interest. The value of the firm with taxes is dependent on the amount of debt issued even though value additivity holds. Rate effects result from a breakdown of the VAP itself. If the total value of a set of streams provided by the firm to investors in the market is affected by the division of the total cash flow into those streams, even though the total cash flow is unaffected by the division (no stream effects), then a rate effect is presumed to exist. Rate effects may make the value of the firm dependent on the debt-equity choice in the absence of corporate taxes and may mean that the diversification implications of firm investment decisions are important. (Stream effects can also make diversification relevant.)

It is important to distinguish a "true" rate effect where the VAP does not hold from a discount rate adjustment for stream effects. In Chap. 13 we showed how the tax effects of debt financing could be incorporated into a "cost of capital" for use in evaluating investments. This was a convenience for analysis, not a rate effect. However, at the end of Chap. 13 we presented a model which assumed rate effects were present and that an optimal capital structure might exist even without tax deductibility of debt interest.

In general, rate effects result from restrictions or costs that inhibit arbitrage in the capital markets. Imperfections such as (1), (2), (4), (8), and (9) in Table 14-1 may result in a failure of the VAP, and therefore these imperfections would be classified as rate effects.[4] Despite the obvious existence of such imperfections, it is not clear that they are material enough to invalidate the VAP. There exists a large body of empirical evidence on the efficiency of capital markets and the adjustment of market prices to new information.[5] This evidence strongly suggests that such imperfections as (1), (2), (4), (8), and (9) do not prevent prices from "fully reflecting" all available information. Furthermore, there is some evidence that the value-additivity principle may hold in the capital markets.[6] These results are reassuring but do not conclusively answer the question of whether the VAP actually holds in general. Given the empirical results to date, and because rate effects are more difficult to deal with analytically, we concentrate our attention on the impact of stream effects on firm decisions in Chaps. 15 and 16; however, rate effects will not be ignored.

[4] The VAP holds even with imperfection (3), but in an altered form, with income streams defined in terms of their net of personal tax magnitudes. See app. 9B for a discussion.

[5] See E. F. Fama, Efficient Capital Markets: A Review of Theory and Empirical Work, *Journal of Finance,* vol. 35, pp. 383–417, May 1970; and M. Jensen, Capital Markets: Theory and Evidence, *Bell Journal of Economics and Management Science,* vol. 3, pp. 357–398, autumn 1972.

[6] See Malcolm Burns, "The Time Series Behavior of the Value Additivity Principle," unpublished manuscript, University of Kansas, November, 1977.

## CAPITAL MARKET IMPERFECTIONS

In this section we discuss each of the imperfections shown in Table 14-1 and the qualitative implications for the firm's financing and investment decisions.

### Trading Costs

In real markets securities transactions usually involve some costs incurred by investors in the form of fees paid to the broker or dealer actually performing the transactions. Costless transactions are confined to the rare direct sale of securities from one investor to another. The costs are in the form of fees paid to the securities broker executing the transaction and may be 8% to 10% of the transaction for small amounts. Large volumes result in small percentage costs. With the advent of negotiated commissions in 1975 on transactions through the organized exchanges, commissions on sales over $0.5 million average less than ½%.[7] For securities traded "over the counter," investor costs result from the differences (spreads) between purchase prices (ask) and selling prices (bid) charged by securities dealers. Spreads typically range between 5% and 10% of the bid price for stocks, with much lower spreads for bonds. Spreads are also dependent on the volume transacted.[8]

Even though trading costs may be material for a given investor, especially one making relatively small transactions, they do not appear to affect firm financial decisions in any systematic fashion. For example, if the firm chooses a debt-equity ratio that provides a risk-return combination different from that preferred by an investor, the investor must incur some trading costs to shift into a more preferred position. If the investor prefers less debt, he or she can sell the firm's shares and buy the firm's bonds to unlever the position. This operation is not cost-free, and this investor would prefer the firm to maintain the "right" debt-equity ratio. However, the market includes many types of investors with differing preferences. Any given debt-equity ratio is likely to appeal to someone, and it is not clear whether trading costs alone would induce the firm to choose any particular debt-equity ratio. That is, it is unlikely that trading costs alone imply an optimal (firm or share value maximizing) financial structure since any particular structure may appeal to some "clientele."[9]

[7] Robert O. Edmister, Management of Commission Costs in Institutional Equity Portfolios, *Journal of Contemporary Business*, vol. 6, pp. 45–57, summer 1977.

[8] S. M. Tinic and R. R. West, Competition and the Pricing of Dealer Service in the Over-the-Counter Stock Market, *Journal of Financial and Quantitative Analysis*, vol. 7, pp. 1707–1728, June 1972.

[9] With many investor groups preferring different financing policies, and many firms with each of these policies, security prices in equilibrium will imply no incentive for a particular firm to prefer any one of these financial policies over the others. That is, market prices will adjust so that, at equilibrium, a particular set of financial policies is prevalent among firms in a given business risk class (with a given distribution of earnings before interest and taxes); each of these policies appeals to some significant segment of the investing community and there is no incentive, at equilibrium, for a firm to switch from one policy to another.

Dividend policy is affected by trading costs in a similar fashion. Investors who desire dividends from the firm for consumption would prefer the firm to finance investments externally and pay higher dividends. If the firm finances with internal funds, paying low or no dividends, these investors will need to sell some of their stock, thereby incurring trading costs. Alternatively, those investors who do not wish to use dividends for consumption would prefer that the firm finance investments internally and pay low or no dividends. Any dividends received by this group of investors will be reinvested with associated trading costs. Here again the existence of diverse preferences in the market suggests that any given dividend policy will be preferred by some investors and there may be no given policy that maximizes value.[10]

Trading costs affect firm diversification in a more systematic way than they do financing. Purchasing a relatively large amount of stock in a small number of firms will result in lower trading costs than purchasing small amounts of stock in a larger number of firms. Yet the latter policy is one which reduces the desirability of diversification by the firm. If investors tend to be relatively undiversified because diversification by them is too expensive, then the firm should consider diversification benefits [2(*c*) above] in evaluating investments. However, we also observe that an entire industry—mutual funds—has developed providing diversification benefits to small investors at almost the same costs as they would incur by investing the same amount of money in a single security. Therefore, it is not clear that trading costs alone are sufficient to make firm investment diversification relevant.

## Limitations on Personal Borrowing

The existence of transaction costs and restrictions on the amount of funds available to investors in financing personal investment (e.g., margin requirements) implies that at least some investors may prefer that the firm borrow to create the financial leverage that the investor cannot create on a personal basis. This implies an advantage for debt financing even in the no-corporate-tax case. In theory, limitations on non-business-firm borrowing (i.e., limitations on borrowing by all arbitragers, including financial firms) may invalidate the VAP and therefore is a rate effect with serious implications for firm financial decisions. However, it is not clear how empirically significant such limitations are. We simply do not know whether they are material. Furthermore, it should be noted that it is not necessary to have totally unrestricted borrowing for the VAP to hold. The costs involved may be immaterial (and therefore not significantly inhibit arbitrage), or they may be material only for small investors, thereby leaving large investors (including financial firms such as mutual funds, banks, and savings and loan institutions) and firms free to arbitrage among securities and thereby enforce the VAP.

[10] See the preceding footnote.

## Personal Taxes

We examine the impact of personal taxes in some depth in Chap. 15. Here we wish only to point out that the tax structure is not neutral with respect to firm decisions and that tax rates vary substantially among investors. Tax structure varies from country to country; in the United States two aspects of the tax structure are of particular importance. First, the rates applying to capital gains and losses (difference between purchase cost and selling price of an asset) are less than the rates applying to dividend and interest income for most individual investors. Second, capital gains taxes are levied only when the gains are realized by selling the asset. The result is to create a preference for capital gains over dividends from stock ownership on the part of individual investors. This preference implies that firms should use internal funds to finance investment rather than paying dividends and financing with external sources. The tax structure appears to produce a systematic and material effect on firm financial decisions. However, this effect may not actually exist because there are substantial differences among investors. A very large investor group owning common stock is not taxed—pension funds. These investors may prefer dividend income because of certain laws governing their operations. Other investors are in low tax brackets—retired people, for example—and may depend on dividend income. Furthermore, under present United States laws, the first $100 of dividend income is not taxed. Thus investors owning small amounts of stock would also prefer dividends. Given the wide variation among investors' tax situations, it is impossible to say a priori whether any particular policy should be pursued. Moreover, countries differ in their tax structures; therefore, arguments applying to the United States system will not necessarily apply elsewhere. This may be of special significance to multinational corporations whose securities are traded in several countries.

We observed earlier, in discussing trading costs, that such costs would be incurred by investors when changes in firm policies forced investors to undertake security transactions. A similar argument applies to personal tax effects. Thus, even if the choice of financing policies is not affected directly by these two imperfections, consistency in the policies that are chosen is highly desirable.

## The Clientele Effect

In imperfect markets for any given set of financial policies adopted by the firm, there are likely to be investors who prefer that policy. These investors will become the firm's stockholders. Hence each firm will tend to attract a "clientele" of shareholders who prefer the policies of the firms they have invested in. A firm that does not maintain any particular policy increases uncertainty for investors, and its securities will be relatively unattractive to *all* investors since it is "unreliable." The clear implication of this argument is that firms should establish and maintain a particular set of financial policies, making few changes over time and only after careful consideration. This is the clientele effect.

Suppose a firm with an established set of policies decides to change. Its current shareholders, who preferred the original policies (that is why they bought that firm's securities), are likely to be unhappy with the new policies and may sell their interests in the firm to investors who prefer the new policies. Both buyers and sellers are subject to trading costs on the transactions. Hence the value of the firm may fall at least temporarily unless the demand for the new policies is quite high (as would be true if there were a shortage of firms providing the new policies relative to the number of investors who prefer them). Consequently, the firm should not change policies without carefully evaluating the impact of the change.

Suppose a firm is inconsistent in its policies. Current and prospective investors in the firm's securities know that its current policy is subject to unpredictable changes. When the changes occur, there will be a turnover in clientele, resulting in added trading costs and perhaps capital gains taxes for investors. A firm with inconsistent policies will probably not be valued as highly as it would be if it maintained almost any reasonable policy, since inconsistency increases the likelihood of a desire by investors to sell the company's securities and incur transaction costs and taxes.

We do not mean to imply here that investors hold shares in only one firm. Diversification by investors among firms is still desirable; however, the portfolio of each investor will depend on the policies of the firms included in it. Such diversification is one reason that no particular policy is likely to command a premium in the market. From the viewpoint of a diversified investor, it is the total result from the portfolio that is of concern. By including an appropriate mix of firms with various policies, a preferred total "policy" from the portfolio can be established. The only policies that might command premiums are extreme ones such as firms that pay no dividends or firms that pay out all earnings as dividends. *If* there is a relative shortage of such extreme policies, they might command premiums. A portfolio having an intermediate average policy can be obtained by blending more extreme ones; but a portfolio having an extreme policy can only be composed of firms with such extreme policies. Therefore, firms with intermediate "middle of the road" policies are unlikely to sell at premiums (even if there are very few such firms). Diversification by investors also lends support to the need for consistency. If a firm changes its policies, its shareholders may be forced to rearrange their total portfolios, which could lead to appreciable trading costs and capital gains taxes.

## Information Access and Cost

Information is not generally cost-free and all investors do not have equal access to information. Also, management is apt to have different information than investors and is likely to have better information regarding the firm and its prospects than that available to investors. Empirically, there is little evidence that differences in information among investors is a problem for large, publicly held firms (see footnote 5 on page 369). The cost of information and differential access between management and investors does have some important consequences regarding external financing which we discuss below in the section on agency costs. One additional implication has to do with dividend policy.

If the level of dividends paid is used by investors as an index of the soundness of the firm or as an indication of management's views regarding the future, then dividend policy can affect share prices. Dividend payments in this case become a signal to investors, and in a world of imperfect information, the use of dividends to provide information is reasonable. If imperfections in information did not exist, there would be no reason for expectations to change as a result of changes in dividends, and dividend policy would remain irrelevant in the absence of other imperfections. However, it should be clear that despite any short-term impacts on stock prices due to dividend signals, the long-term value of the firm will be based on actual and anticipated performance. A dividend change that does not reflect a real change in the prospects for the firm can have only a temporary impact on share values. The effect will persist only so long as the fundamental condition of the firm remains hidden from investors. Therefore, information imperfections are apt to affect firm values only in the short run. Both good and bad news circulates quickly in the market.[11]

## Issue Costs

Flotation or issue costs are expenses incurred by the firm when issuing new securities. Some data on the magnitude of these costs are shown in Table 14-2. The existence of issue costs favors internal over external financing since these costs can be avoided if internal funds are used to finance investments. There are differences in issue costs among the various types of securities. Generally, the less risky the security, the lower the cost of issuing it. Thus debt financing of a given dollar amount is normally cheaper in terms of issue costs than stock financing. There are also economies of scale in issuing securities. Issue costs as a percentage of the amount of the issue decline as the size of the issue increases for each type of security. Therefore, small frequent issues will be more costly than large infrequent issues. This provides an incentive for management to plan financing needs well in advance and to issue securities relatively infrequently.

## Costs of Financial Distress

The impact of financial distress costs on firm financing is discussed in Chap. 15; here we are concerned with the concept. Financial distress costs here refer to the added costs (legal and accounting fees, increased production and financing costs, reduced sales, etc.) arising because the firm cannot meet its obligations to

[11] There have been cases of fraudulent activities by management which remained hidden for appreciable periods of time. Examples are Equity Funding Corporation and U.S. National Bank. We trust and hope these are rare exceptions, but it is unfortunately true that there are large incentives for management to conceal bad news.

**table 14-2 Issue Costs as a Percentage of Amount Issued**

| *Amount[a] issued* | *Common stock* | *Preferred stock* | *Debt[b]* |
|---|---|---|---|
| $ 0–$ 0.49 | 23.6% | [c] | 14.2%[d] |
| $ 0.5–$ 0.99 | 20.1 | [c] | 10.0[d] |
| $ 1.0–$ 1.99 | 16.5 | 11.7%[d] | 17.0[d] |
| $ 2.0–$ 4.99 | 11.9 | [c] | 6.2 |
| $ 5.0–$ 9.99 | 8.7 | 2.5 | 3.1 |
| $10.0–$19.99 | 6.6 | 1.8 | 1.9 |
| $20.0–$49.99 | 5.0 | 1.7 | 1.4 |
| $50.0–$99.99 | 4.2 | 1.6 | 1.2 |
| Over $100 | 3.2 | 2.4[d] | 1.0 |

[a] In millions.
[b] Nonconvertible debt only.
[c] No issues in this size range.
[d] Based on three or fewer issues.
*Source:* "Cost of Flotation of Registered Issues 1971–1972," Securities and Exchange Commission, December 1974.

creditors without altering its operating or external financing activities. As discussed below, a mild form of financial distress exists if the firm cannot make its debt payments without curtailing investment or resroting to external financing (e.g., stock sales). The most serious case of financial distress is bankruptcy (takeover of the firm by its creditors). Note that financial distress does *not* imply financial distress costs since no such costs would arise in perfect capital markets in which creditors could costlessly (no legal or accounting costs, etc.) press their claims (e.g., take over the firm) without affecting the firm's operations; but, even with no financial distress costs, debt can be risky since the bankrupt firm may be worth less than the amount owed on the debt.

In Chap. 8 we showed that (in the absence of taxes) the issuance of risky debt did not affect the value of the firm. In Chap. 11 we argued that under more general assumptions this conclusion still holds. However, we explicitly assumed in both chapters that there were no costs associated with financial distress. Such costs do exist and their existence forces us to modify our conclusions about the use of debt financing.

There are several possible types of costs arising from financial distress. They include lawyers' and accountants' fees, lost sales, higher costs of production, reduced output, foregone or delayed investments, higher financing costs, and general disruption of firm activities. The most obvious and probably least significant are the direct expenses (legal fees, trustee expenses, filing fees, etc.) associated with bankruptcy. As noted above, bankruptcy is a legal concept. If the firm is unable to pay its creditors the amount promised to them, the firm may be forced into bankruptcy. Bankruptcy proceedings result in a variety of direct expenses largely associated with the professional services required from lawyers and accountants. An increased probability of bankruptcy provides an increase in the expected cost (probability of the event times the cost associated with the event). Hence, in the absence of any benefit from debt, this factor alone would be sufficient to discourage its use. However, the magnitude of these costs is difficult to determine. Whether they are sufficient even at very high levels of debt to offset the tax advantage is unknown.[12]

Bankruptcy is the extreme case of financial distress; however, all the costs of financial distress noted above may occur in milder conditions of financial distress as well as in bankruptcy. Whenever the firm has problems in meeting its current debt service requirements (principal and interest payments), the firm's customers may begin to worry about its reliability as a supplier and begin purchasing from other firms. The firm's employees (including its management) may begin seeking other jobs to protect against loss of employment. Furthermore, management is forced to spend time negotiating with creditors and lawyers, reducing the time available to fulfill normal responsibilities. Creditors may restrict operating policies of the firm, thereby reducing the firm's profitability. The firm may be forced to issue new shares in place of debt, which it would not do otherwise. The firm may find it generally difficult to finance its investments; therefore, profitable opportunities must be forgone. All these would be detrimental to the firm's value. Consequently, high levels of debt that increase the chance of financial distress (even if bankruptcy is virtually impossible) could be disadvantageous. Note that these arguments implicitly assume a variety of imperfections other than financial distress costs. If capital markets were perfect there would be no need for the firm to modify its policies, since funds could always be obtained for profitable opportunities. It is the presence of other imperfections that creates the possibility of this type of cost to financial distress.

## Agency Costs

Agency costs, as we define them, arise from efforts by creditors of the firm to ensure that the firm honors its contractual obligations.[13] These costs result from the following:

[12] A study of J. Warner, Bankruptcy Costs: Some Evidence, listed in the Suggested Readings at the end of this chapter, indicates that direct bankruptcy expenses such as legal fees tend to be less than 1% of the value of the firm, when the value is measured well before bankruptcy occurs; *expected* bankruptcy costs of a going enterprise will therefore be far less than 1% of value (since the probability of bankruptcy is well below unity).

[13] Agency costs have been extensively analyzed by M. Jensen and W. Meckling, Theory of the Firm: Managerial Behavior, Agency Costs, and Ownership Structure, *Journal of Financial Economics,* vol. 3, pp. 305–360, October 1976. Our treatment differs from theirs in significant ways. First, they include as agency costs some types of the following: information costs, costs of financial distress, issue costs, and costs of managing the firm. We treat these separately. Second, the bulk of their analysis is concerned with owner-managed firms where the owner-manager maximizes his or her personal utility. We treat professionally managed firms and are concerned only with policies that benefit the firm's stockholders. Third, they are very much interested in the potential conflicts between new shareholders and existing shareholders. We focus on the firm-creditor relationship, which is only a part of their total work. Despite these differences, our development is based on their work, which we consider to be one of the major research papers of the past decade.

1. Attempts by creditors to modify or control firm decisions.
2. The failure to make some investments due to the pricing of debt contracts.

The primary approach used by creditors to control firm decisions is the inclusion of restrictive covenants or requirements in the debt contract. Limits may be placed on new investment, disposal of assets, dividends, managerial salaries, etc. Failure to abide by such covenants generally results in the entire amount of the debt's becoming payable on demand. In many instances, this means that creditors would take over effective control of the company, which may impose costs on the firm and its shareholders by restricting management in decisions.[14]

The losses due to pricing debt contracts are conceptually more difficult. Creditors have reason to price debt contracts to account for the possibility that management, acting in the interests of the shareholders, will adopt more risky investments if debt financing is used than they would if equity were used. Debt provides an incentive to take risks because the owners reap all the rewards if the results turn out well but creditors bear a large part of the costs if the results are poor. Given this observation, creditors will require a higher promised interest rate to compensate for their added risk. This in turn induces management to undertake more risky investments in order to achieve high enough returns to pay the creditors.

The result of agency costs of this type is to make debt financing relatively undesirable in the absence of tax effects. Therefore, agency costs plus costs of financial distress must be balanced against the tax benefits from debt in financing decisions. We develop these issues in more detail in Chap. 15.

Two additional comments are appropriate. First, agency costs are intrinsically related to risky debt. If the firm issues riskless debt, there are no agency costs. Second, agency costs of the sort discussed here strictly apply only when other market imperfections are present. These costs arise from market imperfections such as (1), (2), (4), (6), and (9) in Table 14-1. Otherwise, in perfect markets there will be no need for creditors to overprice their loans or to place restrictions on management since they always have the option of purchasing the firm's stock and forcing policy changes that maximize the total value of the firm. Outsiders would also have this option. We discuss this issue in Chap. 17. Even though it seems unrealistic to discuss this possibility, the basic point still holds. Agency costs, by themselves, are irrelevant in perfect markets, but see the footnote on page 13 for an alternative definition of these costs.

### Asset Indivisibilities

The fact that most (but not all) financial assets are not perfectly divisible in "small" units, say \$1, is an imperfection whose significance depends very

[14] For an illustration of the potential costs, see J. Van Horne, A Linear Programming Approach to Evaluating Restrictions under a Bond Indenture or Loan Agreement, *Journal of Financial and Quantitative Analysis,* vol. 1, pp. 68–83, June 1966.

much on the particular problem. If we are concerned with the portfolio decisions of an investor with only a few thousand dollars to place in risky assets, then the fact that a single share of IBM stock (the smallest unit) sells for $200 to $300 is relevant. Similarly, corporate bonds normally sell in units of $1,000 par value with normal market prices, per bond of $900 to $1100. It is very difficult for an investor with $5,000 to obtain a diversified portfolio of corporate bonds directly. However, in a broader context, such problems really matter very little. The small investor can always buy shares in a mutual fund. For large investors, such indivisibilities are not important since they are small relative to their total portfolios. Perfect divisibility is often assumed for analytical convenience and, theoretically, indivisibilities could create significant rate effects. However, it should be noted that the VAP holds as long as arbitragers in the market do not face indivisibilities more stringent than do firms, that is, as long as arbitragers can duplicate any stream that could be offered by the firm. Thus, for example, if bonds cannot be offered by firms in denominations of less than one thousand dollars (institutional constraints creating this indivisibility), as long as arbitragers are able to issue bonds in denominations of one thousand dollars the arbitragers can duplicate what the firm can do and it does not matter in which of the possible (given the indivisibilities) forms the firm offers its income stream to the market. Arbitragers will always convert the firm's income stream into the form most desired by investors, given whatever indivisibility constraints exist. As a closing point, it is worth mentioning that indivisibilities observed in practice do not appear to be material and we believe that any rate effects produced by them are probably quite small.

## Limited Markets

A rather serious imperfection which narrows the applicability of perfect-market-based decision rules is the limited markets for many firm securities. Consider the problems in buying or selling stock in a small local company with six stockholders and an (approximate) market value of $100,000. To buy the stock, you have to convince one of the six people to sell. If you are one of the six, how do you propose to find a buyer? Markets for this size of firm are not "competitive" or "efficient" in any meaningful sense.

There is a similar problem which arises for large firms. Suppose you are a stockholder in Giant Manufacturing and Giant has just borrowed $100 million from Bank of America. You feel this debt makes the stock too risky, and having read Chap. 11, you decide to neutralize the risk by owning some of the debt. How do you convince the bank to sell you a piece of the loan? An alternative to owning part of the bank loan would be to purchase an identical debt instrument available in the market, but such an identical substitute may not exist in limited markets. Thus, an investor may find it very difficult to neutralize the impact of a privately held debt issue.

To the extent that limited markets exist, the value-additivity principle may not apply. Essentially such markets do not provide opportunities for arbitrage, and therefore some other argument must be made if the VAP is to hold.

In general, with limited markets, management faces the full-blown investment-financing problem and there is very little help that finance theory currently provides in the way of a solution. This is one imperfection we shall not examine further.

## FINANCING STRATEGIES IN USE

Given the number of potential and observed imperfections in the capital markets, it is worthwhile considering some of the financing strategies in actual use. One of the more striking divergences of "real world" finance from the theory is the number of different types of securities and financing methods employed by firms.

The theory developed to this point has been concerned with only three financing methods: (1) debt of no particular maturity, (2) new shares of common stock, and (3) retained earnings (internal funds). If we examine actual financing practices, we find all kinds of financial instruments being employed—negotiated loans of various maturities with differing types of repayment plans, short-term marketable debt (commercial paper), intermediate term notes, and bonds of maturities from 10 to 40 years. Some bonds are perpetual and others convert into common stock. Firms issue mortgage bonds, debentures, subordinated debentures, and capital notes. They issue a variety of types of preferred stock and even different classes of common stock. They issue warrants and rights and stock dividends. One might well ask how this incredible array of financing methods squares with the theory.

The existence of many types of claims in the market is not inconsistent with theory. Of course, with completely perfect markets with homogeneous expectations, e.g., given assumptions A.1 to A.8 in Table 11-1 on page 280, the firm will be virtually all debt (assuming the presence of corporate taxes) and the wide array of security types seen in practice would not exist. However, if we introduce heterogeneous expectations, personal tax biases (e.g., in favor of capital gains) and financial distress costs, different kinds of securities will best meet the preferences of different investors. In such a world, either the firm will offer the securities preferred by investors or arbitragers will convert the firm's income stream into the form preferred by investors (if the firm has not offered its income in the form—i.e., using the security types—investors like most). If transaction costs of arbitrage are large, then firms will likely provide the desired variety of securities to investors since this will minimize costs. We will now consider some of the alternative security forms that are made available to the market both by the firms themselves and by arbitragers (i.e., by financial intermediaries who own financial assets and simultaneously issue financial assets).

## Preferred Stock

Preferred stock is sometimes described as "a bond with a tax disadvantage." If this description is true, why would firms ever issue preferred stock? The fact that few firms (with the exception of utilities) have issued preferred stock in recent years may lend support to the view that this security can safely be ignored in modern financial policy.[15] In terms of the perfect-market theory, there is no advantage to preferred stock. The dividends paid on preferred stock are not tax-deductible; therefore, the results applicable to the no-tax case would hold.

When capital markets are subject to imperfections, we can no longer be certain that preferred stock offers no advantages. From Table 14-2 we see that although preferred stock is more expensive than bonds in terms of issue costs, it is less expensive than common stock. Hence issue costs alone would suggest the use of preferred stock rather than new common. Continuing along this line of reasoning we note that our earlier arguments suggested there may be a limit to (or an optimal amount of) debt for the firm. Suppose the firm is in a situation where new common shares are superior to debt. Would the firm in this situation be better off issuing preferred rather than common stock? Personal tax considerations suggest that common stock would be more highly valued than preferred stock because of the favorable tax treatment of capital gains. However, many institutional investors may prefer preferred stock since only 15% of the dividends on stock (common or preferred) received by a corporation are taxable to that corporation; capital gains do not receive this special treatment. Also, pension funds (which are not taxed) may prefer preferred stock to common stock paying little or no dividends. The evidence suggests that corporate management may indeed view preferred stock as "a bond with a tax disadvantage."[16]

## Debt Maturity

Given that the firm is planning to finance in part with debt, the question of the maturity structure of debt arises. The traditional answer to this question is "finance long-term needs with long-term sources and short-term needs with

[15] *Convertible* preferred is often issued in conjunction with mergers and acquisitions; however, the reasons for this are too complicated to discuss here. Also, the corporate tax disadvantage of preferred stock relative to bonds does not exist for utilities due to rate regulation.

[16] For an argument opposing this view see Donaldson, In Defense of Preferred Stock (listed in the Suggested Readings at the end of this chapter).

short-term sources.'' The emphasis in the traditional answer is on the use of the funds provided. The traditional approach implicitly assumes that the debt itself is temporary in the sense that after the need has passed, the debt will be retired. Seasonal investments in inventory and accounts receivable are considered to be most appropriately financed with short-term loans. Investments in plant and equipment are financed with long-term debt. When the assets financed have been sold or their productive services have been exhausted, the debt is presumably retired. This policy minimizes the interest cost of financing short-term investments and minimizes the financing risk of long-term investments (since refinancing the same asset will not be needed).

Short-term financing may also be considered appropriate as interim financing, that is, as a means of financing long-term investment before issuing longer-maturity securities. The short-term debt is paid off from the proceeds of the longer-term issue, which in some cases may be common stock. This procedure serves to reduce the frequency of long-term security issues, thereby saving on issue costs since issue costs tend to have a fixed component.

Many firms have had *both* short-term and long-term debt outstanding for a considerable period. This policy is counter to the traditional prescription. One might ask why such a policy is desirable and what determines the appropriate mix of short-term and long-term debt. One explanation might be that a portion of such a firm's assets are subject to unpredictable reductions, especially working assets.[17] If, as appears to be the case, short-term debt can be issued or paid off with low transaction costs as compared to long-term debt, then it may make sense to finance in this manner. An additional factor that must of course be present is a difference between the costs of borrowed funds and the rate at which the firm can invest the temporary cash balances that would result from a reduction in the working assets of the firm. Otherwise, the firm could borrow long-term and invest temporary cash balances instead of reducing debt. In other words, two conditions can hold in order for unpredictable reductions in working assets to cause the firm to hold on the average both short-term and long-term debt. The cost of adjusting short-term debt must be less than the cost of adjusting long-term debt; and the rate at which the firm can invest temporary cash must be less than the rate at which it can borrow long-term.

Another explanation could be the existence of ''normal backwardization'' of interest rates.[18] In other words, if short-term rates are generally less than long-term rates, firms may trade off lower interest costs with refinancing risks and costs. In any case, the issue of debt maturity has not been well developed; little more can be provided as a guide to policy.

[17] ''Working assets'' refers to current assets excluding temporary cash holdings and securities investments not needed in the operations of the firm.

[18] The reader is referred to the debate on the term structure of interest rates. For a basic explanation of the issues see James C. Van Horne, ''Financial Market Rates and Flows,'' chap. 4, Prentice-Hall, Inc., Englewood Cliffs, New Jersey, 1978.

## Negotiated Debt

The debt maturity question brings into view another area of financing strategy that is of some interest—the use of negotiated or "privately placed" debt as compared to public issues of marketable debt.[19] It is possible, at least in theory, for firms to issue marketable debt of any maturity, yet in practice few companies issue short-term marketable debt (commercial paper) and many firms do not issue marketable bonds. Instead, firms borrow from financial institutions, negotiating the terms and interest rates directly with the lender. Why? The answer would appear to lie in the existence of information costs and issue costs. Firms may find it advantageous to deal directly with the lender so that the lender can be made privy to information which would be expensive to the firm to provide to the market. Some of the cost of providing information is included in the issue costs of public issues. In addition there may be information about the operations of the firm that management would prefer to conceal from the firm's competitors. By dealing directly with the lender, the lender can achieve a better appraisal of the prospects of the firm than the firm could (or would be willing to) make public. Moreover, the terms of the agreement can be established to suit the preferences of both parties as opposed to having to anticipate the desires of the market in general. Finally, the close communication between borrower and lender on a continuing basis reduces uncertainty on the part of the lender. In risky situations the cost of the debt may therefore be much less than would otherwise be true.

In short, negotiated loans can be and are widely used by small firms for which information is not already widely available and which may be appreciably risky. Large firms use negotiated loans to increase the flexibility of the terms of the agreement, to reduce direct costs, and to avoid making public information that would be of benefit to their competitors.

## Convertible Bonds

Issuing bonds that can be converted into common stock does not seem very reasonable in the context of the theory, given perfect markets. If the firm wished to issue common stock, then what conceivable advantage would there be to issuing debt that might or might not be converted? On the other hand, if the firm wished to issue debt, then it surely would not like to see that debt turn into equity. We shall argue that there are two factors which create an incentive to use convertible bonds. First, and probably less important, is the fact that issue costs for convertible bonds are somewhat less than for common stock. Hence, if the firm were interested in issuing stock, it might issue convertible bonds to save on issue costs, expecting the securities to convert shortly. More

[19] A discussion of the issues, and considerable data on public vs. privately placed bond issues, has been developed by A. Cohan, "Yields on Corporate Debt Directly Placed," National Bureau of Economic Research, New York, 1967.

interesting and more important to financing strategy is the concept of a convertible bond as a delayed equity issue.

Given heterogeneous expectations and securities issue costs, there may be good reason for management to issue convertibles. Suppose that management has investment opportunities available that it believes will be highly profitable. The market is less optimistic about the investments, resulting in a current stock price that management feels is unrealistically low. Also assume that management wants in the long run to finance the new investments with equity, but, due to the depressed stock price, is considering short term financing with debt and then retirement of the debt and issuance of new stock when the market comes to realize how profitable the firm's investments are (at which time the price of the stock will be realistically priced). In this situation, the firm could issue straight debt, then at a later date retire the debt and issue stock. However, it might be more desirable from the firm's standpoint to simply issue convertible debt which will be converted when the stock's price rises. That is, the transaction costs of using convertibles which will become stock when the stock price rises provide a low-cost way to utilize debt financing in the short run and equity financing in the long run.

An alternative scenario for the issuance of convertibles can be based either on general conditions in the capital markets or on the particular condition of the firm. Suppose management wishes to finance with new shares but believes that the market price of its shares is too low, either because of general market conditions or because of pessimism regarding the firm's overall operations (instead of a failure to recognize profitable opportunities). In this situation, as before, management is "betting" that its opinion is superior to that of the market. However, it should be noted that in this case there is less cause for management to believe it knows more than the market.

## OVERVIEW OF CHAPTERS 15, 16, AND 17

In Chap. 15 we formally examine the consequences of most of the imperfections shown in Table 14-1 for the major financing decisions of the firm—the choices among debt, external equity, and internal funds. As should be clear from our discussion here, the financing decision is not irrelevant to the owners of the firm. Given that financing decisions do matter, the latter part of Chap. 15 considers the implications for firm investment decisions. A general procedure for evaluating investments in the presence of imperfections is described.

Chapter 16 concerns some special financial issues that are especially important under imperfect capital markets—mergers and leasing. We show that in perfect markets, business combinations via merger or acquisition provide net benefits to the shareholders only if there are cash flow benefits that result from the combination. However, in imperfect markets, firm diversification considerations become important. In Chap. 16 we treat these issues in depth. Leasing is a method of acquiring the use of assets without purchasing them.

Thus leasing can be considered a means of financing the asset. We show that with perfect product and capital markets and with identical tax brackets for all asset users and lessors, leasing offers no advantage over debt financing. We then provide a general method of evaluating the lease alternative which can be used in practice.

Throughout we have assumed in our discussions and sometimes proved that maximizing the total value of the firm's securities is consistent with shareholder wealth maximization. Our decision rules have focused on firm value maximization. In Chap. 17 we examine the circumstances under which this consistency of objectives breaks down. Chapter 17 is devoted to the topic of firm objectives and the assumptions required to ensure that shareholders will be better off from decisions made in the pursuit of given objectives. Thus this chapter is concerned with the foundations of the theory of finance.

## SUGGESTED READINGS

Donaldson, Gordon: In Defense of Preferred Stock, *Harvard Business Review,* vol. 40, pp. 123–136, July-August 1962.

Durand, David: The Cost of Capital, Corporation Finance, and the Theory of Investment: Comment, *American Economic Review,* vol. 49, pp. 639–655, September 1959, reprinted in Archer, Stephen H. and Charles A. D'Ambrosio, "The Theory of Business Finance," 2d ed., The Macmillan Company, New York, 1976.

Modigliani, Franco and Merton H. Miller: The Cost of Capital, Corporation Finance and the Theory of Investment: Reply, *American Economic Review,* vol. 49, pp. 655–669. September 1959, reprinted in Archer and D'Ambrosio, *ibid.*

Robichek, Alexander A. and Stewart C. Myers: Problems in the Theory of Optimal Capital Structure, *Journal of Financial and Quantitative Analysis,* vol. 1, pp. 1–35, June 1966.

Scanlon, John J.: Bell System Financial Policies, *Financial Management,* vol. 51, pp. 16–26, Summer 1972.

Warner, Jerold B.: Bankruptcy Costs: Some Evidence, *Journal of Finance,* vol. 32, pp. 333–347, May 1977.

CHAPTER

# FIFTEEN

# FINANCING AND INVESTMENT DECISIONS WITH IMPERFECT MARKETS

In Chap. 14 we presented many of the major departures from the perfect-market assumptions and discussed their general impact on individual and firm financial decisions. This chapter is devoted to a more rigorous treatment of firm financial decisions with the perfect-markets assumptions relaxed. Specifically, we shall consider the financing and investment decisions of the firm when the following "imperfections" are present:

1. Investor trading costs and limitations on personal borrowing
2. Costs of issuing securities and paying dividends
3. Costs of financial distress
4. Personal taxes
5. Agency costs
6. Costly information

We first consider financing decisions given investment decisions. That is, we look at the problem of financing any given capital budget. This assumption permits us to examine the impact of imperfections on financing decisions in isolation. We discuss only the three basic financing alternatives here—internal funds, debt, and common stock. Financial instruments such as preferred stock and convertible debt and more elaborate financing strategies were discussed in Chap. 14 and will not be analyzed further here. In the last sections of the chapter we look at the investment problem and interactions between investment and financing decisions. The investment and financing decisions of the firm are, in general, interdependent, and we explore the nature and consequences of such interdependencies for management decisions.

**table 15-1 Perfect-Market Assumptions**

A.1. Costless capital markets: No capital market transaction costs, no government restrictions which interfere with capital market transactions, and transaction-costless infinite divisibility of financial assets.

A.2. Neutral personal taxes: There are no personal taxes or the effective tax rates on interest, dividends, and capital gains (realized or unrealized) are equal.*

A.3. Competitive markets: There are many perfect substitutes for all securities of a firm at any point in time and they can be acquired at the same market price regardless of a given firm's behavior or a given investor's behavior.†

A.4. Equal access: Investors and firms can borrow, lend, and issue claims on the same terms.

A.5. Homogeneous expectations: Everyone has the same expectations.

A.6. No information costs: Firms and individuals have available the same information, and this information is acquirable at a zero cost.

A.7. No bankruptcy costs: Firms and individuals incur no bankruptcy costs or costs of financial distress (legal costs, accounting costs, etc.), although financial distress or bankruptcy can occur.‡

A.8. Salability of tax losses: Firms and individuals can sell tax losses in the market.§

* Assumption A.2 would hold if capital gains were taxed as they accumulate (when the asset's price changes and not when the gains are realized by a sale) and at the same tax rate as ordinary income (dividends and interest); A.2 would also hold for certain capital-gain rates if the gains were taxed when realized and the capital-gains tax rate depended on the holding period.

† Assumption A.3 implies that the firm cannot affect the structure of interest rates in the market by its actions.

‡ The crucial aspect of this assumption is that the existence of contractual financial obligations (e.g., debt or lease) does not affect the pretax cash flow of the firm (see Chap. 14).

§ A loss of $L$ can be sold for $\tau L$, where $\tau$ is the tax bracket of the seller of the loss.

In the course of our development we shall need to be quite precise as to what assumptions we are or are not making. Table 15-1 is a list of assumptions which, taken as a whole, constitute "perfect markets" for our purposes. We shall be referring to these assumptions by number throughout this chapter.

In the next two sections we examine the firm's debt policy and dividend policy for a given investment policy (the exception is in considering agency costs). Debt policy concerns the relative proportions of debt and equity in the firm's financial structure. Dividend policy relates to the proportion of firm investment that is financed internally rather than with the sale of new shares. In the third and last section we examine the interrelationships between the financing and investment decisions.

## FINANCING DECISIONS—DEBT POLICY

Take as given a firm with a stock of real assets $A_0$ plus investment opportunities with initial outlay $I_0$ which together provide an expected future pretax cash stream of $\tilde{\mathbf{X}}$. The firm is assumed to have "excess cash" of amount $Q_0$ available for investment, dividends, or retirement of existing debt. The amount $Q_0$ is net of any time 0 contractual payments to creditors, taxes on current income, cash needed to support the operations of the firm, etc. We assume that investment outlays $I_0$ have been determined to be desirable for the firm to undertake; how their desirability may be determined is discussed later in the chapter.

Management's primary problem in the situation just outlined is to determine how to raise $I_0$. The choices are stock, debt, internal funds, or some combination of the three. In general, this decision cannot be made without also considering the present financial structure of the firm and future financing requirements. In perfect markets in the absence of corporate taxes, we know that the decision is irrelevant; that is, regardless of present circumstances and future expectations it simply does not matter what choice of financing management makes. With corporate taxes and perfect markets, tax deductibility of interest on debt provides an advantage to debt. Indeed in the tax case not only should $I_0$ be entirely financed with debt, but enough additional debt should be issued to ensure that no corporate income taxes need ever be paid on the income produced by present assets $A_0$ and investments $I_0$. The additional funds raised through debt issues are to be paid as a dividend to present stockholders.[1] This financing decision is rarely observed in practice. When we do find close approximations, such schemes are considered "tax avoidance" and are normally challenged by the Internal Revenue Service!

However, limits imposed by the IRS are not a problem for the vast majority of firms. We simply do not observe debt usage of a magnitude that is consistent with the prescriptions of the perfect-markets theory with taxes. Indeed normal business practice is to finance the majority of investment outlays with internal funds, most of the remaining needs with debt, and only a very small proportion, on average, with stock issues. Of course, these relationships are true only for the average firm over time. Some firms in any given year will be financing primarily with stock and others with debt. Given this general observation, one of our primary objectives in this chapter will be to examine imperfections that may help to explain why firms do not use more debt.

In considering firm financing decisions, the immediate question arises as to what factors encourage firms to employ equity financing and thereby sacrifice the advantage of interest tax deductibility. Four causes of this phenomenon have been suggested: the costs of financial distress, flotation costs, personal tax biases in favor of capital-gains income, and agency costs. Let us examine each of the four factors in turn.

## Financial-Distress Costs

As a firm increases the proportion of its financing that is from debt sources (increases its debt-equity ratio), it also increases the probability of incurring

[1] The objective of this perfect-markets policy is to keep the value of the shares at a minimum and to therefore keep the debt-equity ratio near unity.

financial distress or even bankruptcy as a result of an inability to meet creditor claims. Financial distress can mean disruption of the company's business and resultant decreased net returns (e.g., suppliers or customers may be unwilling to deal with a firm in obvious financial difficulty, or the terms of such dealing may be less favorable). The actual bankruptcy of a firm (the takeover of the firm by creditors) will mean added costs for investors in the form of lost revenues or increased operating costs, and added accounting and legal costs as creditors take over. What this can mean is that borrowing, although it produces the advantage of interest tax deductibility, also increases the chances of incurring financial-distress costs. The optimal level of borrowing is that level at which the marginal disadvantage (in terms of firm value) of the increased chance of financial distress just offsets the marginal interest tax deductibility advantage.

Defining $\tilde{F}$ as the cost of financial distress ($\tilde{F}$ is assumed to be tax-deductible), we can define the returns to shareholders and bondholders $\tilde{\mathbf{Y}}$ as

$$\tilde{\mathbf{Y}}^S + \tilde{\mathbf{Y}}^B \equiv \tilde{\mathbf{Y}} = \tilde{\mathbf{X}} - \tilde{\mathbf{I}} - \tilde{\mathbf{F}} - \tau(\tilde{\mathbf{X}} - \widetilde{\mathbf{DP}} - \tilde{\mathbf{R}} - \tilde{\mathbf{F}}) \tag{15-1}$$

where

$$\tilde{\mathbf{F}} = f(\tilde{\mathbf{X}},\tilde{\mathbf{R}},\tilde{\mathbf{P}}) \tag{15-2}$$

where $\tilde{\mathbf{P}}$ is defined as principal payments made on the debt. As the level of debt $B$ and the amount of promised interest and principal payments increase for any given $\tilde{\mathbf{X}}$ distribution, there is a greater likelihood of financial distress and the probability of a positive $\tilde{\mathbf{F}}$ increases. Similarly, for any given level of debt, the smaller $\tilde{\mathbf{X}}$ is (the more to the left the distribution of $\tilde{\mathbf{X}}$ is), the greater the

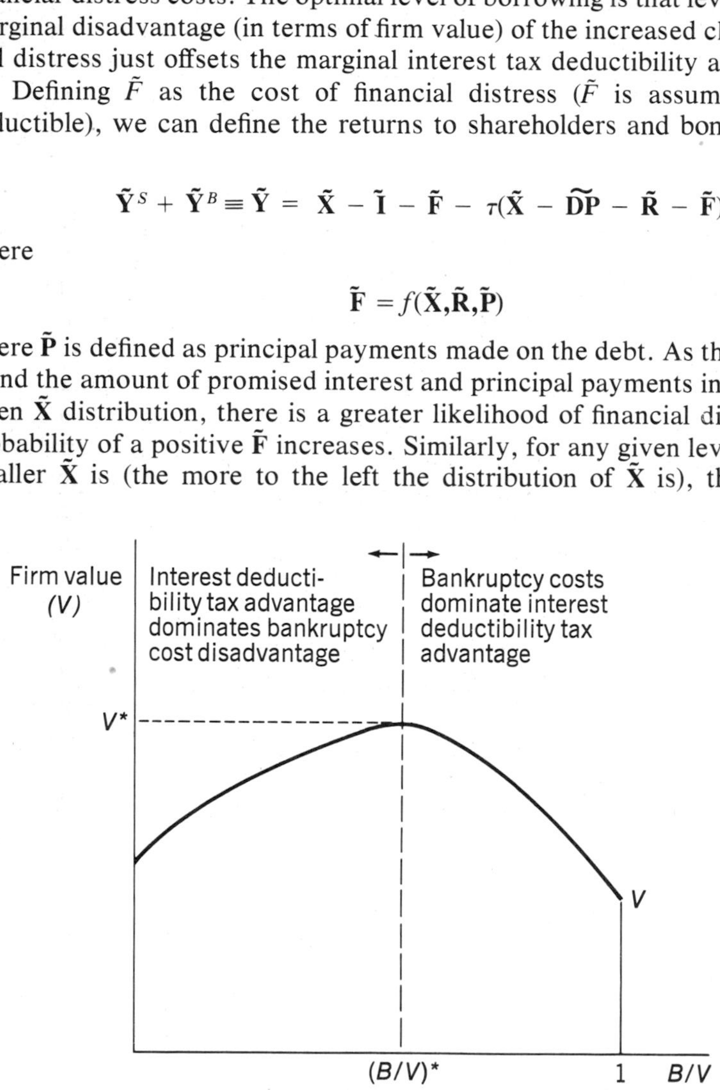


**figure 15-1**

probability of incurring financial distress. More debt or a smaller $\tilde{\mathbf{X}}$ means a higher expected cost of financial distress. But greater debt and greater interest due also means that the firm's interest tax shield is larger [$\tau\tilde{\mathbf{R}}(2) > \tau\tilde{\mathbf{R}}(1)$ if $\tilde{\mathbf{R}}(2) > \tilde{\mathbf{R}}(1)$]. The optimal level of debt is that which produces the most valuable $\tilde{\mathbf{Y}}$ in (15-1), where $\tilde{\mathbf{F}}$ rises and $\tau\tilde{\mathbf{R}}$ rises as debt increases in (15-1). Figure 15-1 illustrates the optimal debt level.

Note that financial-distress costs include not only the explicit legal and accounting costs of bankruptcy but also the other costs of financial distress, such as lost business and increased costs due to financial problems with creditors. Empirical research suggests that explicit bankruptcy costs alone are insufficient to account for the very large use of equity financing by most business.[2] The magnitude of the other costs have yet to be established, but they would have to be quite substantial to limit debt usage to the levels found in practice.

## Flotation Costs

Two aspects of flotation costs influence the choice between debt and equity. First, since the flotation costs of issuing debt securities are much less than the cost of issuing the same dollar amount of stock (see Table 14-2), debt financing is more advantageous than stock financing even in the absence of any tax benefits from the use of debt. Second, the presence of flotation costs on debt issues and the absence of such costs with internal financing means that, from a flotation-cost standpoint, internal equity sources will be preferred to debt issues. Thus, under the assumption of taxless (no corporate or personal taxes) perfect markets, flotation-cost considerations encourage the firm to finance investment exclusively with internal funds to the extent that these funds are available. Once internal sources have been exhausted, debt financing is the preferred source of financing and stock will never be issued.

The combination of financial-distress costs and flotation costs would limit debt financing at extreme levels of debt. Thus one would expect only very highly levered firms which have exhausted internal funds to use common stock. The corporate tax advantages of debt support the conclusion that common stock would rarely be issued; however, the choice between internal equity and debt is less clear since the tax effect may be sufficiently large to offset flotation costs and costs of financial distress. In this case we would expect to find firms borrowing money while simultaneously paying dividends, that is, internal financing being restricted in order that debt may be expanded. Indeed this combination of policies is often found in practice. However, here again, flotation costs and costs of financial distress do not appear large enough to explain why firms limit their use of debt to rather low levels nor can they explain why some firms use virtually no debt at all. One explanation is the existence of a *personal* tax bias in favor of equity securities. This is our next topic.

[2] See Jerold B. Warner, Bankruptcy, Absolute Priority, and the Pricing of Risky Debt Claims, *Journal of Financial Economics*, vol. 4, no. 3, pp. 239–276, May 1977.

## Personal Tax Biases

Recall that in Chap. 11 we assumed that the personal tax system does not favor one kind of personal income over another; i.e., the same effective tax rate was assumed to apply to dividends, capital gains, and interest income on debt. We found in Chap. 11 that, with no personal tax biases in favor of stock income relative to income from debt, the capital structure that maximizes firm value is made up of virtually all debt. The reason for this was shown to be that debt interest is tax-deductible at the corporate level but equity income is not. Thus a dollar of earnings before interest and corporate taxes which is paid out as interest will completely avoid the corporate income tax, whereas this is not the case for income to stockholders, whether retained by the firm or paid out as dividends. Corporate equity income is taxed at the corporate level. It was assumed in Chap. 11 that both debt and equity income were taxed at the same effective rate at the personal level. Obviously, therefore, since debt income is taxed only once (at the personal level) whereas equity income is taxed twice (at the corporate level and again at the personal level), a strong incentive existed in favor of the use of debt. Indeed, with assumptions A.1 to A.8 (which includes the existence of no personal tax biases under A.2), a firm will increase its use of debt relative to equity as long as the Internal Revenue Service allows the firm to deduct the additional debt interest in computing corporate taxable income.

Now drop assumption A.2; that is, let us introduce personal tax biases in favor of equity income but retain assumptions A.1 and A.3 to A.8. We shall assume that the tax rate on capital gains from stock is less than the tax rate on dividends and interest. This means that even though the *corporate* income tax favors debt over equity financing, this advantage to debt can be canceled out by the lower *personal* tax rate on equity income in the form of capital gains. Whether this cancellation effect occurs depends on investors' tax rates.

If the investors in the firm's securities have low personal tax brackets, they will be better off (from a tax standpoint) if the firm finances with debt since the corporate tax advantage from debt financing will outweigh the personal tax disadvantage of debt financing relative to equity financing. On the other hand, if investors in the firm's securities have high personal tax brackets, then the corporate tax advantage of debt may be outweighed by the personal tax disadvantage of debt (i.e., debt interest will be taxed at the high tax rate and capital gains at a low tax rate, especially if the stock is not sold for a long time). Those who prefer stock income may have such a strong preference for that type of income that it might behoove firms to issue stock rather than to finance with debt even though it means paying a corporate tax on the equity income.

We shall begin our analysis by first considering the financing problem from the perspective of a firm's management. Given existing capital market conditions we determine relationships that indicate the relative advantages of debt over internal financing and debt over new stock issues. We show that debt may or may not be the preferred means of financing depending on the circumstances of the firm and the marginal personal tax rates embodied in the prices of securities. Then we consider the implications of our analysis for market equilibrium.

**The firm's financing decision.** Assume that capital markets are perfect except for the existence of personal tax biases (we assume A.1 and A.3 to A.8). Income from securities is taxed at rates which may differ among investors. In a tax system with increasing marginal tax rates on income, $\tau_I$ is the marginal income tax rate on ordinary (dividends and interest) income for investors in the market. That is, $\tau_I$ is the marginal tax rate of the *marginal* purchasers of income streams that are taxed as ordinary (not capital gain) income. Capital gains (appreciation in securities prices) are also taxed. For simplicity we assume that the capital-gains tax is paid when the price appreciation occurs (not when the securities are sold as in the present United States tax system). However, this assumption is not necessary for our results.[3] Capital losses result in tax credits computed at the capital-gains rate. The capital-gains tax rate for any given investor is assumed less than the tax rate on ordinary income for that investor. The capital-gains tax rate for marginal investors is $\tau_G$. Both $\tau_G$ and $\tau_I$ are implied by current securities prices.[4] The tax rate on corporate income may differ among firms. For the firm being analyzed, that rate is $\tau$. Tax rates $\tau_I$, $\tau_G$, and $\tau$ are assumed to be given and constant over time. Interest on debt issued by the firm is deductible from corporate income in determining taxable income, but dividends are not deductible. Since we are assuming transaction-costless capital markets, the value-additivity principle can be applied in the analysis.

[3] It is sufficient that there exists an implied marginal tax rate on capital gains that reflects the expectations of marginal investors in the market as to when the gains will be realized. See also the first footnote under Table 15-1.

[4] Rates $\tau_I$ and $\tau_G$ are the marginal tax rates that are implied by the values of income streams in the market, where such values are determined by the marginal investors for each type of income stream. Thus let $\tilde{\mathbf{Y}}_I^f = \tilde{\mathbf{Y}}_I$ but assume that $\tilde{\mathbf{Y}}_I^f$ is not subject to a personal income tax; therefore, $V[\tilde{\mathbf{Y}}_I^f]$ is the value of $\tilde{\mathbf{Y}}_I$ if $\tilde{\mathbf{Y}}_I$ were not taxable. Defining $V[\tilde{\mathbf{Y}}_I]$ as the market value of $\tilde{\mathbf{Y}}_I$, it follows that

$$V[\tilde{\mathbf{Y}}_I] = V[(1 - \tau_I)\,\tilde{\mathbf{Y}}_I^f] = (1 - \tau_I)\,V[\tilde{\mathbf{Y}}_I^f]$$

and therefore,

$$\tau_I = \frac{V[\tilde{\mathbf{Y}}_I^f] - V[\tilde{\mathbf{Y}}_I]}{V[\tilde{\mathbf{Y}}_I^f]} \qquad (a)$$

Similarly, if $V[\tilde{\mathbf{Y}}_G]$ is the market value of $\tilde{\mathbf{Y}}_G$, $\tilde{\mathbf{Y}}_G^f = \tilde{\mathbf{Y}}_G$, but $\tilde{\mathbf{Y}}_G^f$ is not subject to personal taxes, then

$$V[\tilde{\mathbf{Y}}_G] = V[(1 - \tau_G)\tilde{\mathbf{Y}}_G^f] = (1 - \tau_G)V[\tilde{\mathbf{Y}}_G^f]$$

and therefore,

$$\tau_G = \frac{V[\tilde{\mathbf{Y}}_G^f] - V[\tilde{\mathbf{Y}}_G]}{V[\tilde{\mathbf{Y}}_G^f]} \qquad (b)$$

Throughout, we are assuming a given investment policy by the firm; only financing policy is under consideration here.[5]

The objective of management is to maximize the value of the shares owned by current shareholders, $S_0^{o*}$. $S_0^{o*}$ is the value of the firm's old shares (not including any new shares issued at time 0) immediately before they go ex-dividend; i.e., $S_0^{o*}$ is the *cum*-dividend value of the old shares. Define $S_0^o$ as the *ex-dividend* value of the old shares, where the shares go ex-dividend in a negligible period of time after $S_0^{o*}$ is measured in the analysis to follow. Investors will pay for the cum-dividend shares $S_0^{o*}$, and this must equal the after-tax amount they will have one moment later when the stock goes *ex-dividend;* that is (keeping in mind the assumption that taxes on capital gains are taxed as they accrue),

$$S_0^{o*} = (1 - \tau_I)D_0 + S_0^o - \tau_G(S_0^o - S_0^{o*})$$

and rearranging terms

$$S_0^{o*} = \frac{(1 - \tau_I)D_0 + (1 - \tau_G)S_0^o}{(1 - \tau_G)} \tag{15-3}$$

In comparing various policies, we can compare their relative effects on the numerator of the right-hand side of (15-3), since maximizing $S_0^{o*}$ (the objective) is consistent with maximizing the expression in the numerator; this expression equals $(1 - \tau_G)S_0^{o*}$, and the change in $(1 - \tau_G)S_0^{o*}$, which is signified here as $\Delta$, equals

$$\Delta = (1 - \tau_I)\Delta D_0 + (1 - \tau_G)\Delta S_0^o \tag{15-4}$$

where $\Delta D_0$ is the change in time 0 dividends and $\Delta S_0^o$ is the change in ex-dividend value of the "old" shares (shares that were outstanding prior to any time 0 issues of new stock) resulting from the policy. The best policy is that which produces the largest $\Delta$.

Given the possibility of issuing new stock, we need to know how such issues affect $\Delta S_0^o$. The *ex-dividend* value of *all* stock $S_0$ after issuing new stock $S_0^N$ is the sum of the values of new and old stock

$$S_0 = S_0^o + S_0^N$$

Thus

$$S_0^o = S_0 - S_0^N$$

$$\Delta S_0^o = \Delta S_0 - \Delta S_0^N \tag{15-5}$$

[5] We assume in this section that a distribution by the firm of its bonds to its shareholders may result in ordinary income for the shareholders. Also, we assume that the firm may not be able to repurchase its own shares without shareholders treating the payment as a dividend for tax purposes. Both these assumptions are consistent with the existing United States tax code. An implication is that, under assumptions A.1 and A.3 to A.8, a firm may find it in the best interests of shareholders to pay cash dividends to its shareholders even though such dividends are taxed as ordinary income.

Substituting for $\Delta S_0^O$ in (15-4) using (15-5) we arrive at

$$\Delta = (1 - \tau_I)\Delta D_0 + (1 - \tau_G)(\Delta S_0 - \Delta S_0^N) \tag{15-6}$$

We now examine two cases using (15-6). In case I we compare debt financing with internal financing. In this case new stock issues are not affected by the debt issue. This case also corresponds to a rearrangement of capital structure by issuing debt in excess of investment needs and paying out the proceeds as dividends. Case II compares debt with new stock. Here we assume current dividends are unaffected and that increases in debt result in less new stock being issued. This case also corresponds to a capital-structure change via debt issue and repurchase of stock. However, in both cases, the most difficult problem is to determine how the total value of stock changes as a result of issuing debt. That is, we must determine $\Delta S_0$ for a given $\Delta B_0$. We attack this problem first.

Issuing debt and paying out larger dividends (relative to using internal financing and paying out lower dividends) necessarily reduces the ex-dividend value of the stock given present and future investment policies. This is so because the interest and principal payments required to service the debt reduce the cash flow of the firm that is available for future investment and dividends. Given investment policy, the future debt service requirements must either reduce future dividends or be financed with new securities issues or some combination of the two. New securities issues in future periods reduce the capital gains on the stock in those periods. Thus the impact of a time 0 debt issue is to reduce future dividends and capital gains and therefore the time 0 value of the stock. We examine this problem in the text assuming perpetual debt (interest payments only). Footnotes provide the more general case and show that the perpetual-debt assumption is a reasonable approximation in many instances.

The value of the stock at time 0 after financing has occurred, $S_0$, is the value of the after tax-stream of dividends $\tilde{\mathbf{D}}$ and capital gains $\tilde{\mathbf{G}}$ expected to be earned from the stock. The applicable tax rates are the implied rates in the market, $\tau_I$ and $\tau_G$; thus

$$S_0 = V[(1 - \tau_I)\tilde{\mathbf{D}} + (1 - \tau_G)\tilde{\mathbf{G}}] \tag{15-7}$$

The change in $S_0$, $\Delta S_0$, due to a debt issue of $\Delta B_0$ is therefore

$$\Delta S_0 = V[(1 - \tau_I)\,\Delta\tilde{\mathbf{D}} + (1 - \tau_G)\,\Delta\tilde{\mathbf{G}}] \tag{15-8}$$

where $\Delta\tilde{\mathbf{D}}$ and $\Delta\tilde{\mathbf{G}}$ are the changes in the streams of dividends and capital gains resulting from the additional time 0 debt. A debt issue $\Delta B_0$ produces a net cash drain on the firm of $(1 - \tau)\,\Delta\tilde{\mathbf{R}}$ assuming that the debt is perpetual, that interest payments $\Delta\tilde{\mathbf{R}}$ are tax-deductible, and that tax credits (or sales of tax losses) are always available in the event of any losses.[6]

[6] With principal payments, $\Delta\tilde{\mathbf{P}}$, the net cash drain is $(1 - \tau)\,\Delta\tilde{\mathbf{R}} + \Delta\tilde{\mathbf{P}}$.

At the extremes, the debt service requirement may be met entirely either by reducing dividends by amount $\Delta\tilde{\mathbf{D}} = -(1 - \tau)\,\Delta\tilde{\mathbf{R}}$ or by issuing new stock.[7] If new stock is issued, from Eq. (15-5) above we know that stock issues of amount $\Delta\tilde{S}_0^N = (1 - \tau)\,\Delta\tilde{\mathbf{R}}$ would produce a corresponding reduction in capital gains $\Delta\tilde{\mathbf{G}} = -(1 - \tau)\,\Delta\tilde{\mathbf{R}}$. Suppose the entire impact of the debt service is borne by dividend reductions, then

$$\Delta\tilde{\mathbf{G}} = 0$$

$$\Delta\tilde{\mathbf{D}} = -(1 - \tau)\,\Delta\tilde{\mathbf{R}}$$

and, using (15-8),

$$\begin{aligned}(\Delta S_0)_D &= V[-(1 - \tau_I)(1 - \tau)\,\Delta\tilde{\mathbf{R}}] \\ &= -(1 - \tau_I)(1 - \tau)V[\Delta\tilde{\mathbf{R}}] \end{aligned} \tag{15-9}$$

On the other hand, if the debt service falls dollar for dollar on capital gains, then

$$\Delta\tilde{\mathbf{G}} = -(1 - \tau)\,\Delta\tilde{\mathbf{R}}$$

$$\Delta\tilde{\mathbf{D}} = 0$$

and, using (15-8),

$$\begin{aligned}(\Delta S_0)_G &= V[-(1 - \tau_G)(1 - \tau)\,\Delta\tilde{\mathbf{R}}] \\ &= -(1 - \tau_G)(1 - \tau)V[\Delta\tilde{\mathbf{R}}] \end{aligned} \tag{15-10}$$

Now suppose that debt service can be financed by some combination of reduced dividends and reduced capital gains (due to security sales by the firm); in this case we can express $\Delta S_0$ as a weighted average of (15-9) and (15-10):

$$\Delta S_0 = \alpha_D(\Delta S_0)_D + \alpha_G(\Delta S_0)_G \tag{15-11}$$

where $0 \le \alpha_D \le 1.0$ and $0 \le \alpha_G \le 1.0$. The quantities $\alpha_D$ and $\alpha_G$ depend on many aspects of the firm's future financial circumstances. For example, a firm which is expected to pay dividends in all future periods might have $\alpha_D$ close to 1.0 and $\alpha_G$ close to zero. A firm which is expected to require substantial amounts of external financing and to pay no dividends for a long time would have $\alpha_D$ close to zero and $\alpha_G$ close to 1.0. Generally, the more risky the firm is, the greater are the firm's future investment opportunities, and the greater are the firm's debt service requirements, the higher will be $\alpha_G$ relative to $\alpha_D$ since the firm will be more likely to be forced to issue securities to meet debt service requirements.[8]

[7] There are intermediate possibilities including issuing debt. Our analysis provides for the possibility of such intermediate cases, as shown later.

[8] A more complete discussion of the significance of $\alpha_D$ and $\alpha_G$ and the empirical implications of the resulting model are in C. W. Haley, "Taxes and Corporate Financial Decisions," University of Washington, 1978 (unpublished manuscript).

Substituting for $(\Delta S_0)_D$ and $(\Delta S_0)_G$ from (15-9) and (15-10) into (15-11):

$$\Delta S_0 = -[\alpha_D(1-\tau_I) + \alpha_G(1-\tau_G)]\,(1-\tau)\,V[\Delta\tilde{\mathbf{R}}] \tag{15-12}$$

We now need to specify $V[\Delta\tilde{\mathbf{R}}]$. We can do this by observing that the value of the debt issued, $\Delta B_0$, must be the value of the after-tax stream received by investors:

$$\begin{aligned}\Delta B_0 &= V[(1-\tau_I)\,\Delta\tilde{\mathbf{R}}] \\ &= (1-\tau_I)V[\Delta\tilde{\mathbf{R}}]\end{aligned} \tag{15-13}$$

Solving (15-13) for $V[\Delta\tilde{\mathbf{R}}]$ and substituting the result into (15-12) we obtain[9]

$$\begin{aligned}\Delta S_0 &= -[\alpha_D(1-\tau_I) + \alpha_G(1-\tau_G)](1-\tau)\,\frac{\Delta B_0}{(1-\tau_I)} \\ &= -\left[\alpha_D + \alpha_G\left(\frac{1-\tau_G}{1-\tau_I}\right)\right](1-\tau)\,\Delta B_0\end{aligned} \tag{15-14}$$

Equation (15-14) expresses the change in the value of the firm's stock as a function of the amount of debt issued. Since $\alpha_D$, $\alpha_G$, $(1-\tau_G)$, $(1-\tau_I)$, and $(1-\tau)$ are all positive numbers, the stock value decreases because of the debt. The magnitude of the decrease depends critically on the tax rates $\tau_G$, $\tau_I$, and $\tau$ and on whether the burden of debt service will be borne primarily by a reduction in future dividends ($\alpha_D > \alpha_G$) or by a reduction in future capital gains ($\alpha_G > \alpha_D$). Note that for $\tau_G < \tau_I$, the coefficient of $\alpha_G$ [i.e., $(1-\tau_G)/(1-\tau_I)$] is greater than 1.0; in this case, increasing $\alpha_G$ implies a greater loss in stock value for any given amount of debt.

[9] With principal payments $\Delta\tilde{\mathbf{P}}$, the following changes occur in the equations:
(15-9) becomes

$$(\Delta S_0)_D = -(1-\tau_I)\,[(1-\tau)\,V[\Delta\tilde{\mathbf{R}}] + V[\Delta\tilde{\mathbf{P}}]] \tag{15-9'}$$

(15-10) becomes

$$(\Delta S_0)_G = -(1-\tau_G)\,[(1-\tau)\,V[\Delta\tilde{\mathbf{R}}] + V[\Delta\tilde{\mathbf{P}}]] \tag{15-10'}$$

(15-13) becomes

$$\Delta B_0 = (1-\tau_I)\,V[\Delta\tilde{\mathbf{R}}] + V[\Delta\tilde{\mathbf{P}}] \tag{15-13'}$$

Solving (15-13') for $V[\Delta\tilde{\mathbf{R}}]$ and defining $p = V[\Delta\tilde{\mathbf{P}}]/\Delta B_0$ we have

$$V[\Delta\tilde{\mathbf{R}}] = \frac{(1-p)\Delta B_0}{(1-\tau_I)} \quad . \tag{i}$$

Equation (i) is then used to substitute for $V[\Delta\tilde{\mathbf{R}}]$ in (15-9') and (15-10') or the equivalent to (15-11) to obtain the more general version of (15-14)

$$\Delta S_0 = -\left[\alpha_D + \alpha_G\left(\frac{1-\tau_G}{1-\tau_I}\right)\right][(1-\tau) + p(\tau-\tau_I)]\,\Delta B_0^N \tag{15-21'}$$

For perpetual debt $p = 0$; for bonds with all principal to be paid with certainty in 30 years and an interest rate of 8% per year $p = 0.1$. Since $p(\tau-\tau_I)$ will generally be small relative to $(1-\tau)$ we can neglect it as an approximation for long-term debt. However, depending on the tax rates, the approximation could be rather poor for short-term debt.

Given $\Delta S_0$ from (15-14) we are now able to compare debt with alternative means of financing. We first consider debt versus internal financing, case I.

**Case I.** In case I we assume that additional time 0 debt results in an increase in time 0 dividends. The alternative to issuing debt is not paying as high a dividend and financing investment with internal funds. Formally, issuing debt rather than using internal funds for investment produces

$$\Delta D_0 = \Delta B_0$$

$$\Delta S_0^N = 0$$

Using the above and (15-14), $\Delta$ in Eq. (15-6) becomes

$$\begin{aligned}\Delta &= (1 - \tau_I)\,\Delta D_0 + (1 - \tau_G)(\Delta S_0 - \Delta S_0^N)\\ &= (1 - \tau_I)\,\Delta B_0 + (1 - \tau_G)\left[-\left[\alpha_D + \alpha_G\left(\frac{1 - \tau_G}{1 - \tau_I}\right)\right](1 - \tau)\,\Delta B_0\right]\\ &= \left\{(1 - \tau_I) - (1 - \tau_G)(1 - \tau)\left[\alpha_D + \alpha_G\left(\frac{1 - \tau_G}{1 - \tau_I}\right)\right]\right\}\Delta B_0\end{aligned} \tag{15-15}$$

Define the quantity within the braces as $\phi$; therefore,

$$\Delta = \phi \Delta B_0 \tag{15-16}$$

It follows that:

(1) $\phi > 0$ implies debt financing is preferred to internal financing (issue debt and pay dividends)
(2) $\phi = 0$ implies shareholders would be indifferent between debt and internal financing
(3) $\phi < 0$ implies internal financing is preferred to debt

(1), (2), or (3) is possible depending on the magnitudes of the components.

Before analyzing $\phi$ and its magnitude, we develop the parallel result for the choice between debt and stock, case II.

**Case II.** In case II we assume that additional time 0 debt results in less new stock being issued at time 0; thus the alternative to issuing debt is issuing stock. Current dividends are assumed to be given (may be zero) and therefore to be unaffected by the debt issue. Formally, issuing debt rather than issuing new stock produces

$$\Delta D_0 = 0$$

$$\Delta S_0^N = -\Delta B_0$$

From (15-6), (15-14), and the assumed impact of debt on stock issues and dividends, we obtain an expression in case II comparable with (15-15) for case I.

$$\Delta = \left\{(1 - \tau_G) - (1 - \tau_G)(1 - \tau)\left[\alpha_D + \alpha_G\left(\frac{1 - \tau_G}{1 - \tau_I}\right)\right]\right\}\Delta B_0 \tag{15-17}$$

Equation (15-17) is identical to (15-15) except for the use of $\tau_G$ instead of $\tau_I$ in the first term within the braces. When a dividend is paid, the after-tax impact on $\Delta$ per dollar paid is $(1 - \tau_I)$ in case I. In case II a reduction in stock issues increases $\Delta$ by $(1 - \tau_G)$ per dollar of reduction. Define the quantity in braces in (15-17) as $\psi$; therefore,

$$\Delta = \psi \Delta B_0 \tag{15-18}$$

Then we have:

(4) $\psi > 0$ implies debt is preferred to stock
(5) $\psi = 0$ implies shareholders are indifferent between debt and stock
(6) $\psi < 0$ implies stock is preferred to debt

Again, either (4), (5), or (6) is possible depending on the magnitudes of the quantities in $\psi$.

If we subtract $\phi$ from $\psi$ we obtain

$$\begin{aligned} \psi - \phi &= (1 - \tau_G) - (1 - \tau_I) \\ &= \tau_I - \tau_G \end{aligned} \tag{15-19}$$

The difference $(\psi - \phi)$ in (15-19) indicates the advantage of debt over external equity financing (new stock) relative to the advantage of debt over internal equity financing. If $(\psi - \phi)$ is positive, internal financing is superior to external financing. If the implied tax rate on capital gains $(\tau_G)$ were less than the implied tax rate on ordinary income $(\tau_I)$, $\psi$ would be greater than $\phi$, and internal financing would be preferred to external equity financing. This is consistent with our findings on pages 412 to 415 that lower tax rates on capital gains for all investors favor internal financing over stock issues. With $t_G < \tau_I$, we can see also that if condition (1) holds $(\phi > 0)$ then condition (4) must hold $(\psi > 0)$; and if condition (6) holds $(\psi < 0)$ then condition (3) must hold $(\phi < 0)$. Several intermediate cases are also possible.

Let us examine an extreme possibility—that debt is the most desirable method of financing [both condition (1) and condition (4) hold]. To ensure that debt will be preferable in all cases, it is sufficient that $\phi > 0$, $\tau_G < \tau_I$, and $\alpha_G = 1.0$; that is, debt is preferred to internal financing (so it must also be preferred to external equity financing) and the entire impact of debt service falls on future capital gains dollar for dollar. From (15-15)

$$\phi = (1 - \tau_I) - (1 - \tau_G)(1 - \tau)\left[\alpha_D + \alpha_G\left(\frac{1 - \tau_G}{1 - \tau_I}\right)\right] > 0$$

Setting $\alpha_D = 0$, $\alpha_G = 1.0$, we have

$$(1 - \tau_I) - (1 - \tau_G)(1 - \tau)\left(\frac{1 - \tau_G}{1 - \tau_I}\right) > 0$$

$$(1 - \tau_I)^2 > (1 - \tau_G)^2(1 - \tau)$$

$$(1 - \tau_I) > (1 - \tau_G)\sqrt{1 - \tau}$$

$$\tau_I < 1 - (1 - \tau_G)\sqrt{1 - \tau} \tag{15-20}$$

The table below shows some representative values for the left side of (15-20) for different values of $\tau_G$ and $\tau$. These values are the highest tax rates on ordinary income ($\tau_I$) that marginal investors could have to ensure that debt financing is preferred over equity under the assumption that $\alpha_D = 0$ and $\alpha_G = 1.0$.

| $\tau$ \ $\tau_G$ | 0% | 10% | 30% |
|---|---|---|---|
| 20% | 11% | 20% | 38% |
| 48% | 28% | 35% | 50% |

Under United States tax laws, these are not unrealistic rates. Some studies have estimated $\tau_I$ to be roughly 32%. An investor with this marginal tax rate on ordinary income would normally have a capital-gains tax rate of 16%. Allowing for a lower value due to the deferral of capital-gains taxes, a 10% value of $\tau_G$ would be reasonable. If values for $\tau_I$ of 32% and $\tau_G$ of 10% are approximately correct, then debt would have a modest advantage over internal financing for corporations taxed at 48% (large firms), but corporations taxed at 20% (small firms) should use internal financing rather than debt.

Regardless of the precise situation in the capital markets, it should be clear that the introduction of differences in the taxation of dividends and capital gains reduces and may eliminate entirely the advantage of debt produced by corporate taxes alone. Depending on the prospects for the firm and the marginal tax rates in the market, debt may or may not be the preferred method of financing. The major theoretical issue to be resolved is the determination of the marginal tax rates in equilibrium.

**Market equilibrium with personal taxes—certainty case.**[10] The above analysis showed that the best financing policy of a firm depends on the market's implied tax rates $\tau_I$ and $\tau_G$, i.e., on the relative market valuations placed by investors on ordinary and capital-gain income streams. It was not explained, however, what the equilibrium valuations will be and what is implied for firm financial decisions. To develop an understanding of the equilibrium process, we shall first consider a simple certainty model which illustrates the general problem. Appendix 15A provides the uncertainty case analog. In the next section we shall discuss equilibrium with personal taxes under uncertainty and consider the financial-policy implications of the equilibrium results.

Assume a world of certainty. The firm will invest $I_0$ (which is to be determined) at time 0 and will receive a level perpetual pretax return of $X_t = X$, $t = 1, \ldots, \infty$. Stream $X_t$ will be paid out either as a level debt stream $Y_t^B = Y^B$, $t = 1, \ldots, \infty$ or as a level equity stream $Y_t^S = Y^S$, $t = 1, \ldots, \infty$; $Y_t^B$ is tax-deductible at the corporate level but $Y_t^S$ is not. Define the value of the firm, of its stock, and of its bonds as $V$, $S$, and $B$, respectively, and let $P_S$ and $P_B$ be

[10] This section on debt policy under certainty is based on Harry DeAngelo and Ronald W. Masulis, "Optimal Capital Structure Under Corporate and Personal Taxation," U.C.L.A. Working Paper, 1977.

the market value per dollar of equity (dividend) stream and debt stream paid by the firm. That is,

$$S = P_S Y^S \tag{15-21}$$

$$B = P_B Y^B \tag{15-22}$$

where

$$\begin{aligned} Y^S &= X - \text{Taxes} - Y^B \\ &= X - \tau(X - Y^B) - Y^B \\ &= (1 - \tau)(X - Y^B) \end{aligned} \tag{15-23}$$

The objective of the firm is to set $I_0$ and its debt-equity ratio so as to maximize its net present value, $V - I_0$. That is, the firm's problem is to maximize $V$ with respect to $Y^B$ and $I_0$; stated in equation form,

$$\begin{aligned} \underset{I_0, Y^B}{\text{Maximize}} \{S + B - I_0\} &= \underset{I_0, Y^B}{\text{maximize}} \{P_S[(1 - \tau)(X - Y^B)] + P_B Y^B - I_0\} \\ &= \underset{I_0, Y^B}{\text{maximize}} \{[P_B - P_S(1 - \tau)]Y^B \\ &\qquad + P_S(1 - \tau)X - I_0\} \end{aligned} \tag{15-24a}$$

subject to

$$I_0 \geq 0$$

$$0 \leq Y^B \leq X \tag{15-24b}$$

Define the term in brackets in (15-24$a$) as $\pi$, i.e.,

$$\pi = P_B - P_S(1 - \tau) \tag{15-25}$$

From (15-24$a$) it is clear that to achieve (15-24$a$) [i.e., to maximize the expression in braces in (15-24$a$)] the firm will use *all* debt (will maximize $Y^B$, and therefore set $Y^B = X$) if $\pi > 0$, will use all equity ($Y^B = 0$) if $\pi < 0$, and will be indifferent concerning the level of $Y^B$ (be indifferent concerning the debt-equity ratio) if $\pi = 0$. Since $\pi$ is the same for all firms in the economy, all firms will behave in this way. We can state this in the form of the following rule:

> If $\pi > 0$, all firms will issue only debt claims; if $\pi < 0$, all firms will issue only equity claims, and if $\pi = 0$, all firms will be indifferent between debt and equity claims (both can be issued) (15-26)

Now let us look at investor i whose problem is to maximize utility $U^i(C_0^i, Y^{\tau i})$, where $C_0^i$ is i's current consumption and $Y^{\tau i}$ is i's after-personal-tax income per period at $t = 1, \ldots, T$ ($T$ = time horizon for i), i.e., by assumption $Y_t^{\tau i} = Y^{\tau i}$, all $t$. Individual i's wealth is $W^i$ and all $W^i$ will be allocated to $C_0^i$ or to acquiring $Y_t^{\tau i}$ (future consumption). Define $\tau_S^i$ and $\tau_I^i$ as i's personal tax rates on equity (dividend) and debt (interest) income, respectively. Assume that the tax rate on dividends is less than the tax rate on interest income.[11] It follows that

[11] Under United States tax law, the personal tax rate on the first \$100 of dividends income is zero.

$$Y^{\tau i} = (1 - \tau_S^i)\, Y^{Si} + (1 - \tau_I^i)\, Y^{Bi} \tag{15-27}$$

where $Y^{Si}$ and $Y^{Bi}$ are the equity and debt dollars per period, respectively, received by i from i's investments. The problem of i is to maximize $U^i(C_0^i, Y^{\tau i})$; in equation form, i's problem is

$$\underset{C_0^i, Y_1^{\tau}}{\text{Maximize}}\ U^i(C_0^i, Y^{\tau i}) = \underset{C_0^i, Y_1^S, Y_1^B}{\text{maximize}}\ U^i[C_0^i, (1 - \tau_S^i) Y^{Si} + (1 - \tau_I^i) Y^{Bi}] \tag{15-28a}$$

subject to

$$C_0^i + P_B Y^{Bi} + P_S Y^{Si} = W^i$$

$$C_0^i \geq 0,\ Y^{Si} \geq 0,\ Y^{Bi} \geq 0 \tag{15-28b}$$

where we assume that $U^i$ increases with a rise in $C_0^i$ or in $Y^{\tau i}$ (i.e., $(\partial U^i / \partial C_0^i) > 0$, $(\partial U^i / \partial Y^{\tau i}) > 0$). Now observe that for any $C_0^i$, i will allocate $(W^i - C_0^i)$ between $Y^{Si}$ and $Y^{Bi}$ so as to maximize $Y^{\tau i}$, i.e., so as to get the maximum after-tax income for the $(W^i - C_0^i)$ invested in securities. From (15-28*b*), we know that

$$P_B Y^{Bi} + P_S Y^{Si} = W^i - C_0^i \tag{15-29}$$

and for any given $C_0^i$ and $W^i$,

$$P_B \Delta Y^{Bi} + P_S \Delta Y^{Si} = 0$$

or

$$\Delta Y^{Si} = -(P_B / P_S)\, \Delta Y^{Bi} \tag{15-30}$$

Relation (15-30) shows the tradeoff between $Y^{Bi}$ and $Y^{Si}$ that is provided to i by the market. Using (15-27), we also know that

$$\Delta Y^{\tau i} = (1 - \tau_S^i)\, \Delta Y^{Si} + (1 - \tau_I^i)\, \Delta Y^{Bi} \tag{15-31}$$

and substituting (15-30) into (15-31) we find that

$$\begin{aligned} \Delta Y^{\tau i} &= (1 - \tau_S^i) \left( -\frac{P_B}{P_S}\, \Delta Y^{Bi} \right) + (1 - \tau_I^i)\, \Delta Y^{Bi} \\ &= \left[ (1 - \tau_I^i) - \frac{P_B}{P_S} (1 - \tau_S^i) \right] \Delta Y^{Bi} \end{aligned} \tag{15-32}$$

$Y^{\tau i}$ rises with $Y^{Bi}$ if the bracketed expression in (15-32) is positive; that is,

$$\text{i prefers debt income (prefers } Y^{Bi}\text{) if } \frac{1 - \tau_I^i}{P_B} > \frac{1 - \tau_S^i}{P_S} \tag{15-33}$$

The left-hand side of (15-33) is the amount of *after*-personal-tax income from a dollar of $Y^{Bi}$ divided by the cost of a dollar of $Y^{Bi}$; clearly, if this amount exceeds the right-hand side of (15-33) (which equals the amount of after-personal-tax income from a dollar of $Y^{Si}$ divided by the cost of a dollar of $Y^{Si}$), debt is a better investment for i. Similarly, $Y^{\tau i}$ falls with a rise in $Y^{Bi}$ if the bracketed expression in (15-32) is negative; that is, i prefers no debt income (prefers $Y^{Si}$) if $$\frac{1-\tau_I^i}{P_B} < \frac{1-\tau_S^i}{P_S} \tag{15-34}$$

And $Y^{\tau i}$ does not change with $Y^{Bi}$ if the bracketed expression is zero; that is,

i is indifferent between debt and equity income ($Y^{Bi}$ and $Y^{Si}$) if $$\frac{1-\tau_I^i}{P_B} = \frac{1-\tau_S^i}{P_S} \tag{15-35}$$

Now assume the existence of some investors $j$ for whom

$$(1-\tau_I^j) > (1-\tau_S^j)(1-\tau) \tag{15-36}$$

and some investors $k$ for whom

$$(1-\tau_I^k) < (1-\tau_S^k)(1-\tau) \tag{15-37}$$

Any investor $j$ will prefer that the firm make available (issue) equity securities if (15-34) holds; using (15-34) and (15-36), this means that $j$ will prefer that the firm issue equity if

$$\frac{(1-\tau_S^j)(1-\tau)}{P_B} < \frac{(1-\tau_I^j)}{P_B} < \frac{1-\tau_S^j}{P_S} \tag{15-38}$$

which implies that [using the leftmost and rightmost terms in (15-38)]

$$\frac{1-\tau}{P_B} < \frac{1}{P_S}$$

which in turn implies that $j$ prefers equity if

$$P_B - P_S(1-\tau) \equiv \pi > 0 \tag{15-39}$$

All $j$ investors prefer equity to debt if $P_B$ and $P_S$ are at levels satisfying (15-39); that is, $j$ investors will pay a price for equity that exceeds any $P_S$ satisfying (15-39).[12] But, with $\pi > 0$, although investors $j$ prefer equity, by (15-26), no firm will issue any equity (note that $P_S$ is the price that firms *would get* for the equity *if* it were issued). This means that any $P_B$ and $P_S$ satisfying (15-39) in a market with no equity available cannot be in equilibrium. Investors $j$ will offer up to $P_S = [P_B/(1-\tau)]$ (i.e., up to that $P_S$ which makes $j$ indifferent between debt and equity, which means a $P_S$ making $\pi = 0$), and this will mean that on issues of equity firms *can get* $P_S = P_B/(1-\tau)$; that is, relative prices will be such that $\pi = 0$. $P_S$ and $P_B$ therefore cannot, at equilibrium, imply that $\pi > 0$.

Using a similar argument, all $k$ investors will *prefer debt* income [using (15-33) and (15-37)] if

$$\frac{(1-\tau_S^k)(1-\tau)}{P_B} > \frac{1-\tau_I^k}{P_B} > \frac{1-\tau_S^k}{P_S} \tag{15-40}$$

[12] We make the assumption here that these investors $j$ [satisfying (15-36)] and investors $k$ [satisfying (15-37)] will choose to hold either bonds or stock or both (depending on their prices), i.e., will not refuse to hold either bonds or stock because they are overpriced relative to consumption. Any persons with tax brackets satisfying (15-36) or (15-37) who do not satisfy this assumption are excluded from the category "investor" for the purposes here.

which implies that [using the leftmost and rightmost terms in (15-40)] $k$ prefers debt income if

$$P_B - P_S(1 - \tau) \equiv \pi < 0$$

But, by (15-26), if $\pi < 0$, firms will issue no debt and, as before, this cannot be an equilibrium. Prices will adjust so that $\pi < 0$ no longer holds.

Thus $\pi > 0$ and $\pi < 0$ cannot hold at equilibrium if there are $j$- and $k$-type investors in the market [as defined by (15-36) and (15-37)]. *At equilibrium, $\pi = 0$; i.e., at equilibrium, using (15-26), firms will issue both debt and equity claims and firms will be indifferent between debt and equity financing as long as type-j and type-k investors exist in the market.*[13] That is, at equilibrium a firm's value will be independent of its debt-equity ratio.

Observe that there is a clientele effect since with $\pi = 0$ at equilibrium, $j$ investors will prefer debt income (will buy bonds) and $k$ investors will prefer equity income (will buy stock). To see this, the reader can simply assume a $j$ investor satisfying (15-36), let $\pi = P_B - P_S(1 - \tau) = 0$ (equilibrium), and it follows that (15-34) must hold for investor $j$; for a $k$ investor, assume (15-37) and $\pi = 0$, and it follows that (15-33) must hold for investor $k$. Only marginal investors, $m$, for whom $(1 - \tau_I^m) = (1 - \tau_S^m)(1 - \tau)$, will be indifferent between debt and equity [(15-35) will be satisfied for investors $m$, given that $\pi = 0$].

**Market equilibrium with personal taxes—general uncertainty case.** In this section we shall consider the implications of the preceding section for firm financial policies assuming uncertainty. Although we have examined only debt policy and not dividend policy up to this point, our discussion here also relates to the dividend decision. The dividend policy question is treated in greater detail later on pages 412 to 415.

The point of the certainty example of the previous section was that if investors vary sufficiently in their personal tax rates, then the firm's value will be independent of its debt level. Appendix 15A shows that the same conclusion holds with uncertainty. A related and useful principle that applies under assumptions A.1 and A.3 to A.8 is that the firm's value is independent of its financial structure and dividend policies as long as the policies adopted imply that the firm will generate dividends, capital gains, and debt returns with risk return properties (probability distributions) identical to those already available in the marketplace. To clarify this point, assume that there is a large number of firms with identically distributed $\tilde{X}_t$ and $\tilde{I}_t$, all $t$.[14] Each firm will select a financial structure and provide a stream of returns to investors in the form of dividends

[13] Notice that, with corporate tax rate $\tau$ equals to 46%, (15-36) would hold for any $\tau_S^j \geq 0$ as long as $\tau_I^j < 46\%$; this includes a majority of investors. For "high" tax bracket investors $k$ ($\tau_I^k >$ 46%), (15-37) will be satisfied if the *effective* tax rate on equity income is very low; for example, if $\tau_I^k = 60\%$ and $\tau_S^k = 25\%$, (15-37) is satisfied. On effective tax rates, see footnote 19, p. 413.

[14] The firms may differ by a scale factor, that is, $(X_t^a - I_t^a) = \gamma(X_t^b - I_t^b)$, any $\gamma > 0$, for any firms $a$ and $b$ in the same risk class.

($D$), interest ($R$), and/or capital gains ($G$). Those firms that pay large dividends and generate low capital gains on their stock will attract low-tax-bracket stockholders, and the opposite is true for firms paying low dividends and large capital gains. Firms that are highly levered will sell their bonds to investors who do not benefit a great deal from the lower tax rate on capital gains on stock, for example, investors in low tax brackets. No firm will purposely select a financing policy that is not preferred by investors, and with diverse investors, more than one kind of financing policy will exist among firms at equilibrium. Each of these prevailing capital structure–dividend policy strategies must produce the same firm value at equilibrium, or firms will switch to the policy that generates the highest value. The point here is that with differing investors it is unlikely that one unique policy will dominate all others; instead, there will be a number of policies that will be adopted by various firms. The number of firms adopting a particular policy will depend on how many investors prefer that policy. The greater the level of investment in the economy by high-tax-bracket investors relative to low-tax-bracket investors, the more firms will tend to adopt high-tax-bracket financial policies, i.e., to use equity financing and to pay low dividends on the firm's stock. The opposite financial policies will be more popular if the market is dominated by low-tax-bracket investors. However, whether high- or low-tax-bracket investors predominate, both types of investors exist, and consequently securities and the implied firm financial policies will exist in the economy so that both types of investors are satisfied.

To clarify the concept that each firm in the economy is likely to have a wide variety of equally desirable financial structure–dividend policies from which to choose, let us look at the firm in any particular risk class [all firms in the same risk class have identical distributions of $(\tilde{\mathbf{X}} - \tilde{\mathbf{I}})$, except for a scale factor]. Assume $n$ firms in the risk class and assume that at equilibrium they adopt financial structure–dividend policies $P_1, \ldots, P_m$, $m \leq n$. Each policy $P$ defines the amount of expected dividends, capital gains, and debt interest the firm provides to investors in the firm's securities. Since the system is, by assumption, at equilibrium, it must be that firm values $V_1 = V_2 = \ldots = V_n$ where $V_i$ is the value of firm i ($V_i = S_i + B_i$). These values must be equal since if the equality did not hold, e.g., if $V_1$ were higher than $V_2, \ldots, V_n$, the other firms would change to the policy of firm 1 (say $P_1$) so as to maximize value; but the existence of a motivation to switch to $P_1$ implies that equilibrium has not been attained. Therefore, if more than one $P$ exists for the $n$ firms at equilibrium, all the $P$'s must imply the same total firm value. Given the existence of such an equilibrium, it remains to be explained in what sense a specific firm's value is independent of which of the existing $P$ it chooses. That is, if firm i switches from say $P_1$ to $P_2$, will not equilibrium be disturbed? To see how equilibrium is maintained even if a firm alters its financial policy by switching from one $P$ to a different $P$, assume that the system is at equilibrium and firm i is following policy $P_1$. Let firm i switch from $P_1$ to $P_2$. Equilibrium will be disturbed since there will be an oversupply of securities generating returns provided under $P_2$ and insufficient returns generated under $P_1$. The result will be a rise in the market price of securities provided under $P_1$ and a fall in the price of securities provided under $P_2$; this change in security prices will encourage firms adopting $P_2$ to switch to $P_1$ and this switch will occur until the old equilibrium is reestablished. The point is that given the tax brackets of investors in the market and given the existence of many firms in each of the various risk classes in the economy, an equilibrium set of $P$ (and their associated security types) is implied. If a particular firm changes its financial policy so as to appeal to a different group of investors, other firms will tend to make the appropriate adjustment in their financial policies until equilibrium is established.

In the above discussion of this section, it was not proved that more than one financial policy (more than one $P$) is desirable for any risk class of firm or, indeed, for all firms in the economy. It was instead assumed that investors' tax brackets were sufficiently diverse that more than one financial policy was necessary in order to satisfy existing demand for various types of income streams (dividends, capital gains, and interest). It was argued that if more than one financial policy is demanded at equilibrium, all such policies must imply the same total firm value or equilibrium could not hold. Given the fact that all financial policies $P$ adopted by firms in a given risk class imply the same value for any firm within that risk class, it followed that a particular firm would be indifferent in selecting from among those prevalent policies. Any switching by a particular firm from one policy $P$ to another policy $P$ would elicit compensatory policy changes by other firms until equilibrium prevailed in the market. For this analysis to be of interest, it remains to be shown that more than one financial policy will exist at equilibrium for a given risk class in an economy with a tax structure such as that which actually exists. This issue is dealt with in Appendix 15A. In that appendix, it is shown that under simplified but somewhat realistic assumptions concerning the tax structure, firms will be indifferent to the financial structure (debt-equity ratio) that is adopted (i.e., *all* possible debt-equity policies provide the same value). Although this is not done in the present volume, a similar exercise could be developed to demonstrate that a sufficiently wide diversity of tax brackets among investors will imply that the firm will be indifferent with regard to the dividend policy that it selects.[15]

[15] If the personal tax rate on dividends were identical to that on debt interest and if share repurchases by the firm (treasury stock) and payments of the firm's bonds to shareholders could not result in ordinary income taxes being levied on such transactions (see the footnote on p. 392), in otherwise perfect markets (assumptions A.1 and A.3 to A.8 holding) no firm would pay cash dividends; all cash payouts would be on debt securities and stock would be issued only for those seeking capital gains. The reason is that anyone desiring a payout security would be able to get more after taxes (after corporate and personal taxes) on a bond since the firm would not have to pay any corporate taxes on the debt interest. However, in actuality, the above-mentioned tax factors do exist and, furthermore, the first $100 of dividends are not taxed whereas this is not so for debt interest; these conditions are sufficient to motivate some firms to pay dividends (the stock being bought by high-tax-bracket investors). Of course, in general, whether or not dividends are justified from a tax standpoint will depend on the tax structure, and for some structures, no dividends would be warranted at all (from a tax standpoint). In the next section on dividend policy it is shown that, under the currently existing tax system, if assumptions A.1 and A.3 to A.8 hold, firms will generally

## Agency Costs and Debt Policy

In Chap. 14 we mentioned the possibility that the firm may have to pass up profitable investments or be forced to abide by costly restrictions due to the existence of debt. The losses imposed on the firm through debt contracts were called agency costs. We shall now consider the nature and effects of agency costs on the firm's financing decisions. Such costs incurred by the firm can reduce any tax advantages of debt. Furthermore, when information is costly and not completely accessible to creditors and when securities cannot be purchased freely at the going market price (assumptions A.1, A.3, and A.6 do not hold), creditors may limit the amount they are willing to lend to the firm. The result is that the level of debt used by the firm, even in the absence of flotation costs and costs of financial distress, will be much less than 100% of the firm's value.

The investor in a firm's stock or bonds is acquiring a claim against two income streams: the income stream generated by the firm's assets currently in place (past investments made by the firm) and the income stream generated by investments the firm is expected to make in the future. The total value of the firm's outstanding securities can therefore be thought of as the sum of the value of the present claims against these two streams. However, almost all future investments are discretionary. They are expected "options" that are not contracted for currently and may or may not be undertaken by management depending on conditions that exist at the time the investment option is available. If management acts in the best interests of the *shareholders,* only those investments that are desirable from the *shareholders'* point of view will be undertaken. But here lies a problem. As we shall see, investments that are desirable from the owners' standpoint may not be those which maximize firm value (values of shares and bonds), and vice versa. The result is that the set of investments that maximizes the firm's total value is not the same as the set that maximizes share values, and it is share-value maximization that dictates the choice of investments (since management represents shareholders). There may be investments which raise firm value but lower share values (and raise bond values) and are therefore rejected by the firm. Such forgone investments represent opportunity losses for a levered firm and constitute "errors of omission." Further there may be investments which lower firm value but raise share values (and lower bond values) and are therefore adopted. Undertaking these investments constitutes an "error of commission," since firm value is diminished by the investments. Thus, from an economic standpoint, investment decisions by a levered firm may be inefficient because of errors of omission or commission. Moreover, as the level of debt increases, the degree of inefficiency may increase and can result in creditors' limiting the amount of money they will lend to the firm to

---

not sell new shares in order to pay larger dividends to current shareholders; equivalently, firms will not sell shares to finance investment if the firm can finance the investment internally (i.e., if it can reduce current dividends to finance investment).

well below the point at which the debt would be 100% of the total value of the firm.[16]

To illustrate the problem, assume a firm which will liquidate one period hence (at time 1). Assume no taxes. The firm can invest today amount $I_0$ in a project or set of projects which will pay off at time 1. The investment of $I_0$ will be made by reducing current (time 0) dividends ($Y_0^S$) by $I_0$ (i.e., shareholders make the sacrifice in financing the investment). The firm has risky debt outstanding at time 0 which requires a payment at time 1 of $\hat{Y}_1^B = 100$. The time 1 firm net cash flow, including cash from liquidating the firm's assets, is signified as $\tilde{X}_1$. The payment to shareholders (a liquidating dividend) at time 1 is $Y_1^S$; thus $\tilde{X}_1 = \tilde{Y}_1^B + \tilde{Y}_1^S$. It is assumed that two possible states can occur at time 1, state *a* and state *b*; the probabilities of the states are equal (each is .5). As stated in Tables 15-2 and 15-3, without any investment $I_0 = 0$ and $Y_0^S = 100$; if state *a* obtains at time 1, $\tilde{X}_1 = 120$, $\tilde{Y}_1^S = 20$, and $\tilde{Y}_1^B = 100$, and, if state *b* obtains at time 1, $\tilde{X}_1 = 60$, $\tilde{Y}_1^S = 0$, and $\tilde{Y}_1^B = 60$ (since creditors have prior claim to $\tilde{X}_1$ up to the 100 owed at time 1 on the firm's debt). Thus, using a bar over a variable to indicate an expected amount, with *no* investment, $\overline{X}_1 = 90$, $\overline{Y}_1^S = 10$, and $\overline{Y}_1^B = 80$.

Investment *J*, which is described in Tables 15-2 and 15-4, raises $\bar{y}_1^S$ by only 10 even though it costs shareholders 20 at time 0. Investment *J* would therefore be rejected by shareholders and rejected by the firm. However, note that bond holders benefit from investment *J* since $\overline{Y}_1^B$ increases by 20 (and bondholders have invested nothing). Expected time 1 total returns from the investment ($\Delta\overline{X}_1 = \Delta\overline{Y}_1^S + \Delta\overline{Y}_1^B$) are 30, which means that the investment is highly attractive from a *total* return standpoint, even though it is rejected by shareholders. The reason that the investment is rejected is that most of the benefits from the

[16] The exact effect of increased debt on the efficiency of firm investment depends on the time-state payoffs of the firm's investments. For the situation in which an investment's returns are known with certainty when the investment is adopted (in which case investment efficiency is lower the greater the level of risky firm debt), see Myers, Determinants of Corporate Borrowing, listed in the Suggested Readings at the end of this chapter.

**table 15-2 Firm Variables with an Investment (*J*) Which Has a High Total Payoff, Hurts Shareholders but Benefits Bondholders**

| | *If no new investment* | | | *With investment J* | | |
|---|---|---|---|---|---|---|
| | | *Time 1* | | | *Time 1* | |
| | *Time 0* | *State a* | *State b* | *Time 0* | *State a* | *State b* |
| $I_0$ | 0 | | | 20 | | |
| $Y_0^S$ | 100 | | | 80 | | |
| $\tilde{X}_1$ | | 120 | 60 | | 140 | 100 |
| $\tilde{Y}_1^S$ | | 20 | 0 | | 40 | 0 |
| $\tilde{Y}_1^B$ | | 100 | 60 | | 100 | 100 |

**table 15-3 Firm Variables with an Investment (*K*) Which Has a Low Total Payoff, Benefits Shareholders but Hurts Bondholders**

| | *If no investment* | | | *With investment K* | | |
|---|---|---|---|---|---|---|
| | | *Time 1* | | | *Time 1* | |
| | *Time 0* | *State a* | *State b* | *Time 0* | *State a* | *State b* |
| $I_0$ | 0 | | | 20 | | |
| $Y_0^S$ | 100 | | | 80 | | |
| $\tilde{X}_1$ | | 120 | 60 | | 190 | 10 |
| $\tilde{Y}_1^S$ | | 20 | 0 | | 90 | 0 |
| $\tilde{Y}_1^B$ | | 100 | 60 | | 100 | 10 |

investment are captured by the bondholders, and it is the benefits received by the shareholders that are relevant to the company's management in selecting investments. Observe that if the firm had no debt, then $\Delta\overline{Y}_1^S = \Delta\overline{X}_1 = 30$ and the investment would be accepted if the discount rate $k_S$ were less than 50% [implying that $NPV = \Delta\overline{Y}_1^S/(1 + k_S) - I_0 > 0$]. It is the presence of the risky debt that has encouraged the firm to reject investment *J*.

Now consider investment *K*, which is described by Tables 15-3 and 15-4. Shareholders will probably have the firm adopt the investment since it raises $\overline{Y}_1^S$ by 35 even though the time 0 outlay required is only 20 (it would be accepted if $k_S < 75\%$). But bondholders are significantly worse off as a result of the investment ($\overline{Y}_1^B$ falls by 25). In terms of expected total returns, the investment is not attractive ($\Delta\overline{X}_1 = 10$ on an investment of $I_0 = 20$, an expected loss of 50%). If the firm were all equity, investment *K* would not be adopted; with the risky debt, the investment is adopted because losses from the investment (in state *b*) can be imposed on the bondholders.

The above illustration reveals the nature of the problem. Specifically, as long as firms ignore the gains and losses imposed on bondholders and select

**table 15-4 Comparison of Investments *J* and *K***

| | *Investment J* | *Investment K* |
|---|---|---|
| Initial outlay $I_0$ (sacrifice by shareholders) | 20 | 20 |
| Expected time 1 total return from investment $(\Delta\overline{X}_1)^a$ | 30 | 10 |
| Expected time 1 return to shareholders $(\Delta\overline{Y}_1^S)^b$ | 10 | 35 |
| Expected time 1 return to bondholders $(\Delta\overline{Y}_1^B)^c$ | 20 | −25 |

[a] The expected time 1 total return from the investment equals the increase in the expected level of $X_1$ due to the investment; using the Table 15-2 data, for investment *J*, this equals $[.5(140) + .5(100)] - [.5(120) + .5(60)] = 30$, the probabilities of states *a* and *b* are each .5. Similarly for investment *K* using the Table 15-3 data.

[b] The expected time 1 return to shareholders from the investment is the increase in $\overline{Y}_1^S$ due to the investment; from Table 15-2, for investment *J* this equals $[.5(40) + .5(0)] - [.5(20) + .5(0)] = 10$. Similarly for investment *K* using the Table 15-3 data.

[c] The expected time 1 return to bondholders from the investment is the rise in $\overline{Y}_1^B$ due to the investment; from Table 15-2, for investment *J*, this equals $[.5(100) + .5(100)] - [.5(100) + .5(60)] = 20$. Similarly for investment *K* using the Table 15-3 data.

investments solely in terms of the investments' net benefits to shareholders, the investments chosen by a firm with debt will not in general be those which maximize the welfare of shareholders and bondholders combined; indeed, investments which raise firm value $V$ $(= S + B)$ may be rejected (investment $J$ above) and investments which lower firm value may be adopted (investment $K$ above).

As the firm's debt-equity ratio increases, the investments adopted may tend more and more to deviate from those that maximize the joint interests of stockholders and bondholders (investment becomes "less efficient"). This will occur if more debt means that a greater share of the gains and losses on any set of investments would be absorbed by the bondholders but are ignored in selecting investments. These gains and losses of bondholders are part of the joint bondholder-stockholder gains and losses but are not taken into account if investment policy is based solely on the net benefits to shareholders.[17]

An interesting implication of the above concept is that, because firm investment policy tends to become less and less efficient as the debt-equity ratio rises, creditors may limit the credit they extend regardless of the interest rate the firm is willing to promise on any additional debt. This is because it is possible for the expected total dollar payments to the lenders (principal plus interest) actually to *decrease* if the amount lent *increases*. This can happen because the greater debt causes the firm to change its investment policy as a result of its higher debt-equity ratio and thereby reduce its ability to pay off creditors. To illustrate this possibility, assume a firm with no assets other than an investment opportunity that can be adopted one period hence (at time 1); the investment will require outlay $I_1$ at time 1 and will be all equity-financed. The firm currently has securities outstanding. We shall see how the type of securities (debt and equity) will affect the decision to invest at time 1. The \$100 investment at time 1, if made, will yield $\tilde{X}$ per year beginning at time 2 and we shall know at time 1 what $\tilde{X}$ will be; $\tilde{X}$ depends on the state of the world at time 1 and this will not be known until time 1. Five states are possible at time 1, and the $\tilde{X}$ associated with each state is shown in Table 15-5. Thus, for example, if state 1 occurs at time 1, the investment is sure to perpetually pay \$15 per period (before interest) beginning at time 2. Assume that the discount rate used by shareholders at time 1 to discount the expected returns to them, $\overline{Y}^S$, is 10%; therefore, investment $I_1$ will be made at time 1 only if $\tilde{Y}^S \geq .10I_1 = \$10$. If the investment is made, annual return $\tilde{Y}^S$ equals $\tilde{X}$ less interest paid to creditors, where this annual interest is signified as $\tilde{R}$ (assume perpetual debt, with the interest payable beginning at time 2). Define $\hat{R}$ as the annual interest promised on any debt outstanding at time 0, where $\hat{R}$ is promised to begin at time 2. Table 15-6 shows the level of expected annual interest per period (beginning at time 2) for each level of promised interest on debt outstanding at time 0. The data in Table 15-5 are used to generate Table 15-6. First observe that if $\hat{R} \leq \$5$, regard-

[17] See the preceding footnote.

**table 15-5 Firm Returns in Different States**

| *States* | *Probability* | $\tilde{X}$ |
|---|---|---|
| 1 | .05 | $15 |
| 2 | .05 | 16 |
| 3 | .3 | 17 |
| 4 | .4 | 18 |
| 5 | .2 | 19 |

less of which state occurs $I_1$ will be made since shareholders will receive the $10 necessary to motivate their spending $I_1$ ($\tilde{Y}^S = \tilde{X} - \hat{R}$, and with $\hat{R} \leq \$5$, $\tilde{Y}^S$ is at least $10 in every state). But, with $\hat{R} > \$5$, there are some states in which $I_1$ will not be made. Thus, for example, if $\hat{R} = \$6$, then at time 1 the shareholders will not adopt the investment if state 1 occurs. This is so because, with state 1, $\tilde{X} = \$15$, and, if the investment $I_1$ of $100 were made, $\tilde{Y}^S = \tilde{X} - \hat{R} = \$9$; but $9 is less than the $10 annual return adequate to motivate the stockholders to make the $100 investment. With $\hat{R} = \$6$, only if states 2, 3, 4, or 5 occur will the investment be made; the probability at time 0 that one of these states will occur is .95 (see Table 15-5), and the *expected* interest with $\hat{R} = \$6$ is therefore $5.70 (= .95 × $6). Similar reasoning applies to all the other data in Table 15-6. Observe that as $\hat{R}$ increases from $7 to $8 the expected interest on the debt actually *decreases*; this means that as the time 0 promised debt payments rise, the value of that debt (the *value* of the expected debt payments) actually falls.[18] The reason is that the greater promised debt payments encourage the firm to adopt a different investment strategy which reduces the expected payment that bondholders will receive.

In the above discussion corporate taxes were ignored. The introduction of such taxes does not alter the conclusion that investment policy may be inefficient (will not maximize the joint interests of shareholders and bondholders)

[18] As $\hat{R}$ increases from $7 to $8, the return per dollar of amount lent remains the same or decreases in every state.

**table 15-6 Expected Return to Bondholders with Different Debt Levels**

| *Promised debt interest* $\hat{R}$ *(1)* | *Minimal level of* $\tilde{X}$ *for investment* $I_1$ *to be made by stockholders (2)* | *Probability that investment* $I_1$ *will be made (3)* | *Expected interest paid on debt [(1) X (3)] (4)* |
|---|---|---|---|
| ≤$ 5 | 15 | 1.0 | $\hat{R}$ |
| 6 | 16 | .95 | $5.70 |
| 7 | 17 | .90 | 6.30 |
| 8 | 18 | .60 | 4.80 |
| 9 | 19 | .20 | 1.80 |
| 10 | 20 | 0 | 0 |

and that greater debt relative to equity tends to increase this inefficiency. The corporate tax deductibility of interest does encourage the use of debt beyond the level that would be desirable with no such tax subsidy. But it remains true that there may be a limit on the amount of debt the firm can incur because, beyond that limit, added lending will actually imply a smaller value of the creditors' claim against the firm (of the firm's bonds).

It should be pointed out that the effects described do not imply that management seeks out ways to impose losses on bondholders. Rather, management seeks investments that maximize share values and in doing so losses may be imposed on existing bondholders. But notice also that when a firm issues debt, those purchasing the firm's bonds will take into account the possibility that the firm will adopt investments that reduce the expected return on those bonds. Rational bondholders will ask the question, "What investments will shareholders select to maximize the value of the shares to the shareholders, and what do those investments imply about the returns on the bonds?" Assuming that the market operates in this way, the *proceeds* the firm receives for its bonds will reflect the future losses that an inefficient investment policy will inflict on bondholders. That is, the present value of such reductions in the expected future returns to bondholders will be deducted from what current bondholders will pay for the company's bonds. But this means that shareholders will be the ones to suffer from the inefficient investment policy (since bondholders will pay less for the bonds). An implication is that, in the absence of a compensating benefit to the firm from issuing risky debt (e.g., the tax deductibility of debt interest), no firm will issue such debt. Given that there are corporate tax advantages to debt, why then do shareholders not promise to adopt an efficient ($V$-maximizing) investment policy in the future? Because there is no way for bondholders to effectively enforce that promise. *Once the bonds are sold,* it always behooves the firm (the shareholders) to adopt the *share* value maximizing strategy, since the proceeds from the bonds have already been received. Bondbuyers will operate under the assumption that the firm will serve shareholders and will accordingly set the price they are willing to pay for the bonds. The bonds will therefore have a lower value than would be the case if an efficient investment policy were assured.

It is true that creditors can and do impose constraints on the firm's investment (and other) policies by stipulating provisions in this regard in the bond agreement. The purpose of the restrictions is to encourage the firm to adopt policies that protect the *bondholders'* interests. Unfortunately, the restrictions may create new inefficiencies by preventing the firm from adopting policies that would increase firm value. For example, creditors might force the firm to maintain investments in current assets which would protect creditors in liquidation but which would not be maintained by an all-equity firm since they are in excess of normal operating needs. Moreover, even if the restrictions were completely effective (which they will not be in practice) and did not impose additional costs on the firm, they would not prevent errors of omission since creditors cannot force management to undertake all investments that would maximize firm value.

To further clarify the issue, define the investment policy of maximizing firm value (maximizing the joint interests of shareholders and bondholders) as $P_V$, and define $B_V$ as the bond proceeds from issuing bonds if bondbuyers expect $P_V$ to be followed in the future (after the bonds are issued). Define $P_S$ as the share-value-maximizing investment policy, and define $B_S$ as the bond proceeds if bond buyers expect $P_S$ to be followed in the future. We know from the above discussion that $B_S < B_V$. We also know that for any given bond proceeds (regardless of what is received for the bonds), it is always in the interests of shareholders (by definition) to pursue $P_S$.

A ranking of the combinations of bond proceeds and investment policies in terms of the benefits to shareholders (in terms of which maximize shareholder wealth) is shown in Table 15-7. The table indicates which combinations of $P$ and $B$ most benefit shareholders when the $(P,B)$ combination chosen applies to the firm currently and in all future periods.

Table 15-7 indicates that shareholders would most prefer $(P_S,B_V)$, which is reasonable since $(P_S,B_V)$ means that the firm receives a top price for its bonds and then proceeds to ignore the interests of bondholders and chooses investments that maximize the wealth of shareholders. But $(P_S,B_V)$ is not achievable in practice. Even if the firm promises to follow $P_V$ when it issues its bonds, bondholders know that they cannot compel the firm to follow $P_V$; bondholders will generally assume that the firm will follow $P_S$ since management represents shareholders. Furthermore, if the firm issues bonds and then proceeds to follow $P_S$, in the future all *new* bond issues will sell for $B_S$ since the company has revealed its intentions. Similarly, $(P_V,B_V)$ will not be achievable as long as bondholders expect the firm to follow $P_S$. Even if the firm follows $P_V$, it is very difficult for bondholders to know that the firm is in fact following $P_V$ rather than

**table 15-7 Shareholder Preferences Concerning Investment Policy-Bonds Proceeds Combinations**

| | $P$ | $B$ |
|---|---|---|
| Most benefit to shareholders when policy is adopted ↑ | | |
| | $P_S$ | $B_V$ |
| | $P_V$ | $B_V$ |
| | $P_S$ | $B_S$ |
| | $P_V$ | $B_S$ |
| ↓ Least benefit to shareholders when policy is adopted | | |

$P_S$, since information on specific firm investment decisions is not readily available. And even if investors do believe that $P_V$ has been followed, there is no guarantee that $P_V$ will be followed in the future. Bond buyers will therefore tend to assume that $P_S$ (or something between $P_S$ and $P_V$) will be pursued in the future. Thus, although $(P_S,B_V)$ and $(P_V,B_V)$ are preferred by shareholders, they are probably not attainable as long as bondholders cannot guarantee that $P_V$ is followed.

To clarify the ranking of $(P_V,B_V)$ over $(P_S,B_S)$ in Table 15-7, assume that at time 0 the firm is being established and shareholders can choose between $(P_V,B_V)$ and $(P_S,B_S)$. In this case, $(P_V,B_V)$ is preferred to $(P_S,B_S)$. This is so because shareholders own the entire firm and are ''selling'' to bondholders, for $B_0$, part of the firm's returns. Therefore, shareholders have $S_0$ in stock plus $B_0$ in bond proceeds; since $S_0 + B_0$ is maximized under $(P_V,B_V)$ (by definition), this combination maximizes shareholder wealth. We can conclude that if a firm at a specific point in time, signified time 0, is deciding on a particular future policy $[(P_V,B_V)$ or $(P_S,B_S)]$ which is to be pursued from then on, and if at that moment it has either riskless debt or no debt outstanding (i.e., it decides on the policy and announces it before any risky debt is issued), then shareholder wealth *at time t* is greater with $(P_V,B_V)$ than with $(P_S,B_S)$.

As a final note, we did not specify at the beginning of this section what assumptions were or were not being made. It is sufficient for the above effects to make any assumptions that render it very costly or impossible for bondholders to control the firm's investment policy. As explained in Chap. 17 (pages 477 to 483), there will not be investment errors of omission or commission if all debt is riskless in all circumstances; or if capital markets are transactionless (A.1) and competitive (A.3), personal taxes are neutral (A.2), and investor expectations are homogeneous (A.5); or if shareholders and bondholders are the same people and each investor owns the same proportion of the firm's shares as that investor owns of the firm's bonds. Perhaps other assumptions exist which will ensure an efficient investment policy. But in actuality, it is probably unlikely that such assumptions fully apply, and consequently investment inefficiency is probably a not infrequent phenomenon. In any case, it should be clear that the existence of investment inefficiencies of the sort described above means that no firm would issue risky debt in the absence of corporate tax benefits, or some other kinds of benefits, from debt financing.

## DIVIDEND POLICY: INTERNAL VS. EXTERNAL EQUITY FINANCING

Under the existing tax code, dividends and income from debt securities (e.g., bonds) are taxed as ordinary income, and long-term capital gains (if an asset is held over one year) are taxed at a preferential rate that is approximately half the rate on ordinary income. Furthermore, the capital gain is not taxed until the gain is realized in cash through sale of the stock. This means that the tax can be deferred for many years (until sale).[19] What impact does this have on the firm's choice between internal and external financing, i.e., between financing investments through the reduction in dividends and through selling new securities? The answer is that the personal tax structure favors internal relative to external financing. Of course, we also know that the corporate tax favors debt relative to equity financing. Therefore, the tax system as a whole encourages firms to use internal equity financing of investment relative to external equity financing. That is, the tax system encourages the firm *not* to pay a larger dividend by selling additional new shares of stock.[20] Let us compare internal equity financing and external equity financing under the assumption that markets are perfect except that there is a personal tax bias in favor of capital-gain income (i.e., we assume A.1 and A.3 to A.8). We shall show that any investor i owning proportion $\alpha_i$ of the stock of a firm when dividends are paid (if any are paid) will always prefer that the firm finance its investments internally rather than with external equity even though it means a lower current dividend.

Assume that for investor i capital gains are taxed at rate $\tau_G^i$, and dividends and bond income (interest) are taxed at rate $\tau_D^i$, where $\tau_G^i < \tau_D^i$. For stockholder i owning proportion $\alpha_i$ of the firm's stock, a change in the firm's current dividend of $\Delta D_0$ produces $(1 - \tau_D^i)\alpha_i \, \Delta D_0$ of after-tax returns and a share-price appreciation (capital gain) of $\Delta S_0^o$ produces an after-tax current return of $(1 - \tau_G^i)\alpha_i \, \Delta S_0^o$ where the $o$ superscript refers to current or "old" shares (as opposed to any new shares issued at time 0) and the 0 subscript refers to time 0 (now); shareholder i will therefore prefer a dollar of capital gain [which produces $\$(1 - \tau_G^i)$ in after-tax return] to an added dollar of dividend (which produces $\$(1 - \tau_D^i)$ in after-tax return). Assume that the firm has a new investment costing $I_0$ and will finance the investment by either selling new shares worth $S^N$ (external financ-

[19] Because of the ability to defer the tax on capital gains, the effective tax rate on a capital gain is less than the tax rate applicable to gains when realized. Rate $\tau_G^i$ in this section is the effective tax rate on a gain. The "effective tax rate" $\tau_G$ on a capital gain occurring at time $t$ but not realized (shares not sold) until time $t + j$ is

$$\tau_G = \frac{\tau'_G}{(1 + k)^j}$$

where $k$ is the discount rate and $\tau'_G$ is the actual tax rate on the capital gain when it is realized at time $t + j$ (we drop superscript i for notational simplicity).

[20] The fundamental point is that the tax system encourages a firm not to pay dividends and simultaneously sell shares; from a tax standpoint, it would be better to pay no dividends and reduce the amount of new shares sold. This means that if a firm has internally generated funds in amount $H$ which it can use to finance investment or to pay out in dividends, it is better that the firm invest the $H$ (finance internally) rather than pay the $H$ out as dividends and finance the investment by selling new shares (external equity financing). Note that we are assuming here that, at the margin, the dividends to a shareholder will be subject to a higher tax rate than would a like dollar amount of capital gains. This is only an approximation since the first one hundred dollars of dividends to a shareholder (total dividends from *all* shares in United States corporations owned by the shareholder) are not taxed under the Federal Income Tax. In theory, this \$100 exemption could be sufficient to motivate some firms in the economy to pay dividends even though the firms must issue new shares to do so.

ing), reducing dividends ($\Delta D_0 < 0$), or some combination of both (we assume that no new debt will be issued to finance investment). Therefore,

$$S^N - \Delta D_0 = I_0 \tag{15-42}$$

where there are, by assumption, no flotation costs in selling the new shares. Thus, from (15-42)

$$\Delta D_0 = S^N - I_0 \tag{15-43}$$

The impact of the investment on the after-tax wealth of any investor i who owns shares of the stock when $D_0$ is paid is signified as $\Delta W_i$, where

$$\Delta W_i = (1 - \tau_D^i)\alpha_i \,\Delta D_0 + (1 - \tau_G^i)\alpha_i \,\Delta S_0^o \tag{15-44}$$

Note that the total value of the firm *after* investment and financing has occurred, $V_0$, is independent of the choice of equity financing since the assets of the firm and the total value of the firm's shares and bonds are unaffected. All that is affected is who owns the firm's shares; the greater $S^N$ is, the more of the firm's shares will be owned by new shareholders and the less by current shareholders. Assume that the new investment does not change the value of the firm's bonds. Define $S_0^o$, $B_0^o$, and $V_0$ as values of the old shares (ex-dividend $D_0$ value), old bonds, and firm ($V_0 = S_0^o + B_0^o + S^N$) under the investment and financing policy that is adopted and define $S_0^{o\prime}$, $B_0^{o\prime}$, and $V_0'$ as these values if the new investment is *not* adopted. Note that, by assumption, $B_0^o = B_0^{o\prime}$. Therefore,

$$V_0 = S_0^o + B_0^o + S^N \tag{15-45}$$

$$V_0' = S_0^{o\prime} + B_0^{o\prime} \tag{15-46}$$

Using (15-45) and (15-46) to solve for $S_0^o$ and $S_0^{o\prime}$, respectively, we find that the change in old shares' value due to the new investment, $\Delta S_0^o$, is

$$\begin{aligned}\Delta S_0^o &= S_0^o - S_0^{o\prime}\\ &= V_0 - V_0' - S^N\\ &= \Delta V_0 - S^N\end{aligned} \tag{15-47}$$

Substituting $\Delta D_0$ of (15-43) and $\Delta S_0^o$ of (15-47) into (15-44), we find that

$$\begin{aligned}\Delta W_i &= (1 - \tau_D^i)\alpha_i \,\Delta D_0 + (1 - \tau_G^i)\alpha_i \,\Delta S_0^o\\ &= (1 - \tau_D^i)\alpha_i(S^N - I_0) + (1 - \tau_G^i)\alpha_i(\Delta V_0 - S^N)\\ &= \alpha_i\{(\tau_G^i - \tau_D^i)S^N + [(1 - \tau_G^i)\,\Delta V_0 - (1 - \tau_D^i)I_0]\}\end{aligned} \tag{15-48}$$

$\Delta V_0$ and $I_0$ are independent of whether the investment is financed internally or externally. Since $\tau_G^i < \tau_D^i$, it is clear that $\Delta W_i$ in (15-48) is maximized by setting $S^N = 0$, i.e., by financing internally [letting $-\Delta D_0 = I_0$ in (15-48)].

The above analysis tells us that, in the absence of other factors which encourage investors to prefer dividends to capital gains, all investors will prefer internal equity financing to external equity financing. Investors will be willing to pay more for the stock of a firm which finances investment with internal rather than with external equity funds; i.e., investors prefer that the firm not sell additional new shares in order to pay larger dividends. This means that the present market value of the stock of a firm which is expected to finance internally in the future rather than issue new stock will be higher than the value obtained if the firm were expected to finance externally in order to pay higher dividends. Thus, under the present assumptions, dividends should be paid only to the extent that funds are not needed for investment.[21] Notice that if we introduce *flotation costs* into the analysis, the above conclusion is strengthened since flotation costs are imposed by the firm only with external financing when new securities are sold and not with internal financing. Similarly, the costs of paying dividends (accounting, postage, clerical, etc.) also tend to discourage the payment of dividends if the funds can be used for investment purposes.

Are there other factors which might compensate for the tax and flotation-cost advantage of internal over external equity financing? The answer is yes. There are two major reasons that a firm might wish to maintain its dividend and finance an investment with external equity rather than to finance internally, and both these reasons relate to *imperfect markets*:

(*a*) Investor transaction costs (A.1 does not hold): The investors in the firm may need funds for current consumption and prefer a dividend to a capital gain if large transaction costs are involved in selling shares of stock to raise the needed funds. For some investors, these transaction costs (including the time spent calling the broker) may outweigh the tax advantage of a capital gain relative to a dividend of an equal amount.

(*b*) Information costs (A.6 does not hold): A dividend is a way of conveying information to the market concerning management's earnings expectations for the company. A dividend cut may suggest declining fortunes to investors in the market, and this can cause at least a temporary depression in the value of the firm's securities, which can hurt the security holders (if they wish to sell).

Empirical work strongly suggests that firms are very reluctant to cut the dollar dividends per share paid and will usually do so only in the face of a long-term decline in company earnings. It is not clear, however, whether it is (*a*) or (*b*), or some other factor(s), that is the primary cause of this reluctance.[22]

## AN OVERVIEW OF FINANCING POLICY IN IMPERFECT MARKETS

Taking each imperfection individually, i.e., assuming that the other imperfections do not exist, we found that financial-distress costs and agency costs

[21] That is, the firm should not sell additional new shares in order to pay a larger current dividend. See the preceding footnote.

[22] Note that the above discussion relates to firm's selling additional shares to finance dividend payments (or, equivalently, to finance investment which could have been financed by the funds used to pay dividends). Factors (*a*) and (*b*) could also, of course, motivate a firm with excess funds (a firm not selling new shares) to pay dividends; also see the footnote on p. 404 for tax factors that can motivate a firm with excess funds to pay dividends.

discourage the use of debt; flotation costs encourage internal financing over external financing and are biased in favor of debt relative to external equity. Personal tax effects were more complex. We found that: (*a*) assuming A.1 and A.3 to A.8, if capital gains are taxed more favorably than are dividends and interest, and if investors vary sufficiently in terms of tax brackets, the firm's value may be independent of its debt-equity ratio and therefore independent of whether the firm use *external* equity financing or debt financing of investment; and (*b*) with A.1 and A.3 to A.8 and with capital gains taxed more favorably than dividends, internal financing of investment is necessarily preferred over external equity financing of investment; i.e., the firm will never sell new shares in order to pay a higher current dividend. An implication of (*a*) and (*b*) is that with A.1 and A.3 to A.8, a capital-gains personal tax bias, and a wide range of investor tax brackets, internal financing is preferred to debt financing as well as to external equity financing. We also noted that, with A.1 and A.3 to A.8, any firm i can change to a financing policy used by other firms in the same risk class at equilibrium and firm i's value will not change.

Examining the implications of personal and corporate taxes, agency costs, costs of financial distress, and flotation costs simultaneously, a more complex picture emerges. Flotation costs and personal tax considerations clearly imply that internal financing of investment is preferred over common stock. These imperfections encourage the firm not to sell additional shares of stock to pay larger dividends. Since there will always be a limit on the internal funds available, common stock may be issued when internal funds are not sufficient to finance investment. The desirability of debt financing relative to the two equity sources is less clear if the presence of these various imperfections is assumed. Suppose there is no net tax advantage to debt relative to new common stock (i.e., $\psi = 0$ on page 397). Tax considerations alone would cause the firm to prefer internal financing over debt (i.e., $\phi < 0$ on page 396) and be indifferent between debt and stock. Agency costs and costs of financial distress impose a penalty on the use of debt, however, which may be offset by the lower flotation costs associated with debt compared with common stock as shown in Table 14-2. Thus, in the absence of tax incentives favoring debt over stock, debt financing may or may not be preferred over common stock depending on the relative costs of the two methods of financing to the firm.

Suppose now that tax incentives alone favor debt over equity (both $\phi$ and $\psi$ are positive). In this case firms that are able to issue low-risk debt that therefore involves low agency costs and low costs of financial distress are likely to prefer debt strongly over stock. However, flotation costs favor internal financing, so that even if debt has tax benefits relative to internal funds ($\phi > 0$), it is not necessarily true that debt will be favored over internal financing.

Given the tax structure and the marginal tax rates embodied in security prices and given the circumstances of the firm (including the amount of outstanding debt), the riskiness of income streams produced by the firm's present assets, the characteristics of expected future investment opportunities, and the costs of issuing securities, the financial manager must devise the best means of

financing the firm's current capital budget. Different managements may reach different conclusions on the appropriate financing package for their firms.

One implication of the analysis has not yet been explored—the dynamics of the system. Wealth positions, tax laws, expectations regarding future investment opportunities, etc., change. These changes in the structure of the economy and the circumstances of individual firms change the magnitudes of tax incentives and the costs of debt. Financial policies that were optimal yesterday may not be so today. The financial manager must be aware of events affecting the market and the firm. Financing policy in this world is neither irrelevant nor stable. There will be times when debt issues are relatively attractive and times when they are not. The financial managers' job is not as simple as the perfect-markets theory suggests, and financial theorists have yet to provide adequate decision models that deal effectively with imperfections. The models presented here illustrate the issues but do not provide solutions. There is much work yet to be done in this area.

## THE INTERDEPENDENCE OF INVESTMENT AND FINANCING DECISIONS

Under the perfect-market assumptions A.1 to A.8 in Table 15-1, investment and financing decisions are completely independent. Each investment is financed with debt (to the extent that interest is tax-deductible) and each investment project is assessed independently. Stochastic relationships between investments are irrelevant and only economic interdependencies matter (see pages 308 to 311. In a world in which some of assumptions A.1 to A.8 do not apply, two new considerations become important:

1. Financing of investment becomes relevant; different investments with different risk properties may require different financing.
2. The statistical relationship between investments is important. This can occur either (*a*) because the incremental firm returns (cash flows) of a project depend on their correlation with the returns from other firm projects (e.g., if bankruptcy costs depend on the variability of total firm cash flow), or (*b*) because investors cannot diversify themselves and the firm is trying to create the most desirable package (portfolio) of assets for investors. With (*a*), the VAP still holds but with (*b*) the VAP does not hold.[23]

[23] With (*a*), the incremental cash flow of an investment is valued by itself (by the VAP) to determine the desirability of an investment and its impact on firm value; but that incremental cash flow includes the impact of the investment on bankruptcy costs, where that impact depends on how the investment affects the variability of firm cash flow. The effect on variability in turn depends on the correlation of the investment's returns and the returns from other firm investments. With (*b*), investors cannot costlessly diversify and conduct arbitrage and therefore the VAP no longer strictly holds; in this case, the firm must choose that portfolio of assets and method of financing that produces the most desirable stream of returns to investors.

We shall consider both 1 and 2 above. First, we examine the consequences of dropping assumption A.1; that is, we no longer assume that investors can arbitrage or costlessly buy and sell assets in the market. We shall retain assumptions A.2 to A.8 but point out that, although financing policy is relevant in this case, projects can still be assessed individually and without regard to statistical interdependencies.[24]

## Irrelevancy Of Firm Diversification: The Value-Maximization Theorem

Assume A.2 through A.8 on page 386, and assume that firms can costlessly change their financial structures; also assume that assets are infinitely divisible. Investors in the market cannot perform arbitrage and the M-M theorem and the VAP do not hold; this might occur because of government restrictions (e.g., margin requirements) or transaction costs faced by individuals in the market. It has been shown elsewhere that, under the above assumptions, diversification considerations are irrelevant to firm investment decisions even though financing decisions are relevant, i.e., even though the value of each cash flow of the firm *is* dependent on how it is divided into parts (i.e., into debt and/or equity streams of various distributions).[25] The value of a cash flow is dependent upon its division into parts because, by assumption, investors in the market cannot arbitrage and convert streams themselves; to maximize firm value, the firm must offer its income stream in the form that is preferred by investors since they themselves cannot convert the firm's income stream into the form that they prefer. The VAP does not hold.

Since the value of the firm is assumed to be dependent on how the firm divides its returns into debt and equity streams, an optimal capital structure is assumed to exist. Management will seek to divide its returns into the set of debt and equity streams which maximizes firm value. Assume for the moment that there are no firm taxes; the firm-tax case will be considered later. Under assumptions 1 and 2 above, any firm can divide the total cash flow it pays to

[24] For studies of project evaluation and capital budgeting techniques used in practice, see T. Klammer: Empirical Evidence of the Adoption of Sophisticated Capital Budgeting Techniques, *Journal of Business*, pp. 387–397, vol. 45, October 1972; and L. D. Schall, G. L. Sundem, and W. R. Geijsbeek, Jr.: Survey and Analysis of Capital Budgeting Methods, *Journal of Finance*, vol. 33, pp. 281–287, March 1978.

[25] See Schall, Firm Financial Structure and Investment (listed in the Suggested Readings at the end of this chapter). The proof of the value-maximization theorem used here appears in Schall's paper as a proof of Proposition II for the no-tax case and of Proposition III for the tax case. However, both propositions can be represented as a single proposition applicable to after-tax streams. The division into two propositions is appropriate assuming the inability of the firm to sell its tax losses or to obtain a rebate from the government on past taxes paid. Under the assumptions here, such tax losses are recoverable by the firm and the value-maximization theorem as a single proposition is applicable with or without taxes and with risky or riskless debt.

investors, $\tilde{\mathbf{Y}}_T$, into any number of separate equity and debt streams ($\tilde{\mathbf{Y}}_1 \ldots \tilde{\mathbf{Y}}_n$) in making $\tilde{\mathbf{Y}}_T$ available to the market, and can do so with no transaction costs, where $\tilde{\mathbf{Y}}_T = \Sigma_{i=1}^{n} \tilde{\mathbf{Y}}_i$. Define the total market value of the stream into which $\tilde{\mathbf{Y}}_T$ is divided as $V_T$, that is, $V_T = \Sigma_i V_i$, where $V_i$ is the market value of $\tilde{\mathbf{Y}}_i$. The division of $\tilde{\mathbf{Y}}_T$ may involve dividing the firm into several distinct firms, each providing productive services to the others and each with its own equity and debt issues. No such productive services may even be involved, as in the case of a conglomerate firm. The division of $\tilde{\mathbf{Y}}_T$ may also involve its separation into various equity and debt claims, of varying priority, of the single firm. Such a division of $\tilde{\mathbf{Y}}_T$ into smaller streams may raise the total value of $\tilde{\mathbf{Y}}_T$ by providing investors in the market with a greater variety of income distributions from which to choose. Management will divide $\tilde{\mathbf{Y}}_T$ so as to maximize $V_T$. Define the maximum value that $\tilde{\mathbf{Y}}_T$ can achieve as $V_T^*$ and define the maximum value that any stream $\tilde{\mathbf{Y}}_g$ can achieve (by appropriately dividing $\tilde{\mathbf{Y}}_g$ into debt and equity streams) as $V_g^*$. The following principle (referred to as the value-maximization theorem or VMT) can be shown to hold: for *any* set of streams ($\tilde{\mathbf{Y}}_1 \ldots \tilde{\mathbf{Y}}_m$) for which $\Sigma_{g=1}^{m} \tilde{\mathbf{Y}}_g = \tilde{\mathbf{Y}}_T$, it follows that $\Sigma_{g=1}^{m} V_g^* = V_T^*$. The VMT states that the maximum value of a given stream $\tilde{\mathbf{Y}}_T$ is equal to the sum of the maximum values of *any* set of streams that sum to $\tilde{\mathbf{Y}}_T$.

Although the VMT is not proved here, two examples may help to clarify the theorem.[26] Assume two firms with total cash flows of $\tilde{\mathbf{Y}}_1$ and $\tilde{\mathbf{Y}}_2$. Firm 1 will divide $\tilde{\mathbf{Y}}_1$ into debt and equity streams paid to investors in the market in such a fashion that $V_1$ is maximized, i.e., so that $V_1 = V_1^*$. Similarly, firm 2 will divide $\tilde{\mathbf{Y}}_2$ so that $V_2$ is maximized, i.e., so that $V_2 = V_2^*$. Now assume that firm 1 and firm 2 merge with no real economies into a new firm, firm $T$, with a total cash flow to stockholders and bondholders of firm $T$ equal to the sum of the cash flows of firm 1 and firm 2; thus, $\tilde{\mathbf{Y}}_T = \tilde{\mathbf{Y}}_1 + \tilde{\mathbf{Y}}_2$. Let firm $T$ now divide $\tilde{\mathbf{Y}}_T$ into a set of debt and equity streams that maximizes $V_T$; therefore, $V_T = V_T^*$. Firm $T$ can provide the market with a *greater* variety of types of income streams than could firm 1 and firm 2 together (before merger); this is so because firm $T$ can combine some $\tilde{\mathbf{Y}}_1$ and some $\tilde{\mathbf{Y}}_2$ to create a new type of stream that was not available when firm 1 and firm 2 were separate. Recall that investors themselves are also limited in what they can do in terms of reconstituting streams, since markets are imperfect. Therefore, neither firm 1 nor firm 2 nor the investors themselves could create some of the streams that firm $T$ is able, after merger, to create by mixing parts of $\tilde{\mathbf{Y}}_1$ and $\tilde{\mathbf{Y}}_2$. Notice also that firm $T$ *can* provide the market with *any* stream that firm 1 and firm 2 individually before merger could provide to the market. This is so because $\tilde{\mathbf{Y}}_T = \tilde{\mathbf{Y}}_1 + \tilde{\mathbf{Y}}_2$ can be divided into any set of streams into which $\tilde{\mathbf{Y}}_1$ and $\tilde{\mathbf{Y}}_2$ were divided before merger; this is simply so because $\tilde{\mathbf{Y}}_T = \tilde{\mathbf{Y}}_1 + \tilde{\mathbf{Y}}_2$. It therefore follows that firm $T$ can provide investors with any set of streams that firm 1 and firm 2 could provide before merger and

[26] For a proof of the value-maximization theorem, see Schall, *op. cit.* Also see the preceding footnote.

also can provide some added types of streams impossible without merger. This would seem to imply that $V_T^*$ might be greater than $(V_1^* + V_2^*)$. That is, since the assortment of cash-flow alternatives that firm $T$ can provide to investors includes all those possible with firm 1 and firm 2 plus additional alternatives, the best division of $\tilde{\mathbf{Y}}_T$ (producing $V_T^*$) might be better (have greater value to investors) than the best division of $\tilde{\mathbf{Y}}_1$ and $\tilde{\mathbf{Y}}_2$ separately. The VMT states that this is *not* so. That is, the best that firm $T$ can do in terms of maximizing the total value of the streams is no better than the best that firm 1 and firm 2 can do individually. That is, if $\tilde{\mathbf{Y}}_T = \tilde{\mathbf{Y}}_1 + \tilde{\mathbf{Y}}_2$ then $V_T^* = V_1^* + V_2^*$.

Notice that the preceding example implies that the stochastic relationship of $\tilde{\mathbf{Y}}_1$ and $\tilde{\mathbf{Y}}_2$ is *irrelevant* with regard to the maximum total value that the two streams can attain when combined and then divided into debt and equity streams. This maximum total value is the maximum value of $\tilde{\mathbf{Y}}_1$ plus the maximum value of $\tilde{\mathbf{Y}}_2$; this is so regardless of the statistical relationship of $\tilde{\mathbf{Y}}_1$ and $\tilde{\mathbf{Y}}_2$.

The second example concerns a firm making an investment. Assume that the firm's cash flow to investors is $\tilde{\mathbf{Y}}'$ and that if it adopts a particular investment budget its cash flow will rise to $\tilde{\mathbf{Y}}$; the incremental cash flow from the investment budget is designated $\Delta\tilde{\mathbf{Y}}$, where $\Delta\tilde{\mathbf{Y}} = \tilde{\mathbf{Y}} - \tilde{\mathbf{Y}}'$, or $\tilde{\mathbf{Y}} = \tilde{\mathbf{Y}}' + \Delta\tilde{\mathbf{Y}}$. If the firm makes no investment, it has an optimal capital structure that involves dividing $\tilde{\mathbf{Y}}'$ into the set of debt and equity streams which produces a total firm value $V'^*$. If the firm adopts the investment budget, it will so divide $\tilde{\mathbf{Y}} = \tilde{\mathbf{Y}}' + \Delta\tilde{\mathbf{Y}}$ that the total firm value is maximized and equals $V^*$. If stream $\Delta\tilde{\mathbf{Y}}$ were available as a single stream to be appropriately divided into the debt and equity streams that maximize the value of $\Delta\tilde{\mathbf{Y}}$, then such a maximum value could be designated as $V_{\Delta Y}^*$. The VMT states that $V^* = V'^* + V_{\Delta Y}^*$. That is, the increase in the firm's value from the investment budget equals

$$V^* - V'^* = V_{\Delta Y}^* \tag{15-49}$$

Equation (15-49) implies that the increase in firm value from the investment is dependent only upon stream $\Delta\tilde{\mathbf{Y}}$; it equals the maximum value that stream $\Delta\tilde{\mathbf{Y}}$ could achieve by appropriately dividing $\Delta\tilde{\mathbf{Y}}$ into debt and equity streams. Since this depends only upon $\Delta\tilde{\mathbf{Y}}$ and not upon $\tilde{\mathbf{Y}}'$, it follows that the stochastic relationship of $\Delta\tilde{\mathbf{Y}}$ to $\tilde{\mathbf{Y}}'$ is irrelevant.

It also follows from the preceding discussion that the added value of a stream to the firm can be ascertained by examining only that marginal stream. If the firm optimally (i.e., to maximize firm value) divides its total cash flow both before and after investment, the maximum achievable (by appropriately dividing the firm cash-flow stream) increase in firm value due to that investment is merely dependent upon the incremental stream produced by the investment and what that incremental value would be when the incremental stream is divided so as to maximize its value. *The stochastic relationship between* $\Delta\tilde{\mathbf{Y}}$ *and* $\tilde{\mathbf{Y}}'$ *is irrelevant with regard to the effect on firm value of adding* $\Delta\tilde{\mathbf{Y}}$.

To derive an investment strategy, first observe that the optimal investment budget is the one which will

$$\max[\Delta V^* - I_0] \tag{15-50}$$

Criterion (15-50) follows exactly as criterion (12-10) followed for the perfect-market case. The only difference is that in contrast to the perfect-market case, financial structure is relevant here with imperfect capital markets. Therefore, the change in firm value from investment is the *maximum* postinvestment firm value $V^*$ less the *maximum* zero-investment firm value $V'^*$; that is,

$$\Delta V^* = V^* - V'^* \tag{15-51}$$

Maximum postinvestment firm value $V^*$ is achieved by appropriately dividing postinvestment cash flow $\tilde{\mathbf{Y}}$ into debt and equity streams, i.e., by achieving the optimal capital structure; similarly, $V'^*$ would be achieved by optimally dividing zero-investment cash flow $\tilde{\mathbf{Y}}'$ into debt and equity streams. By (15-49), however, $\Delta V^*$ is the value of the marginal stream generated by the investment budget; from (15-49) and (15-51) we know that $\Delta V^* = V^*_{\Delta Y}$, and substituting this into criterion (15-50), the firm objective is to

$$\max[V^*_{\Delta Y} - I_0] \tag{15-52}$$

As in Chap. 12, the cash flow from a project will be defined as $\tilde{\mathbf{Z}}$. The discussion here will parallel that on pages 312 to 316 since the consequences of the value, maximization theorem for investment analysis are similar to those of the value-additivity principle. Those pages should be reread since much of that discussion holds here and will not be repeated.

As in deriving expression (12-14), note that the addition of a project $Z$ to the capital budget will add a new budget outlay of $I_{Z0}$ to total outlay $I_0$ and add a new stream $\tilde{\mathbf{Z}}$ to $\Delta\tilde{\mathbf{Y}}$; the new capital budget outlay and cash flow with project $Z$ are $(I_0 + I_{Z0})$ and $(\Delta\tilde{\mathbf{Y}} + \tilde{\mathbf{Z}})$, respectively. By the VMT, the maximum value of $(\Delta\tilde{\mathbf{Y}} + \tilde{\mathbf{Z}})$ equals $(V^*_{\Delta Y} + V^*_Z)$; that is, the maximum value of the total new stream equals the sum of the maximum values that the individual streams could achieve by their appropriate division into debt and equity streams. Thus, project $Z$ raises the maximum value of the stream from the investment budget by $V^*_Z$ and raises capital outlays at time 0 by $I_{Z0}$. Since it is the difference between the incremental value and the investment outlay that we wish to maximize [criterion (15-52)], it follows that project $Z$ should be undertaken if and only if

$$[(V^*_{\Delta Y} + V^*_Z) - (I_0 + I_{Z0})] > V^*_{\Delta Y} - I_0$$

or

$$V^*_Z - I_{Z0} > 0 \tag{15-53}$$

The criterion stated in (15-53) is similar to criterion (12-14). The difference is that $V^*_Z$ is not a given value independent of how $\tilde{\mathbf{Z}}$ is divided into debt and equity streams (whereas such independence held in Chap. 12 with no-tax perfect markets). The value $V^*_Z$ is the maximum value that stream $\tilde{\mathbf{Z}}$ could achieve by its division into debt and equity streams in being made available to investors in the market. Thus, if a stream of the form of $\tilde{\mathbf{Z}}$ had a maximum total value if divided into stock and bond streams $\tilde{\mathbf{Z}}^{S*}$ and $\tilde{\mathbf{Z}}^{B*}$ with values $S^*_Z$ and $B^*_Z$, respectively, then $V^*_Z = S^*_Z + B^*_Z$ in criterion (15-53).

The discussion following criterion (12-14) applies here except that $V_Z^*$ instead of $V_Z$ is now appropriate since the division of $\tilde{\mathbf{Z}}$ into debt and equity streams is now relevant. The advantages of being able to disregard stochastic relationships apply here just as with perfect markets. Furthermore, as explained for the perfect-markets case, the returns from a given project may depend upon which firm adopts the project. It is the $\tilde{\mathbf{Z}}$ received by the firm evaluating the investment that the firm uses in determining the desirability of the project for that firm.

In place of criterion (12-15) for perfect markets, the choice among mutually exclusive alternatives should be based on the criterion that

$$[V_{Z_i}^* - I_{Z_i0}] \qquad \text{is maximum} \tag{15-54}$$

and the alternative should be adopted if and only if

$$V_{Z_i}^* - I_{Z_i0} \geq 0 \tag{15-55}$$

The procedure for investment analysis is similar to that prescribed for perfect markets on page 315, but the method of financing is now relevant.

1. Define the total set of investment opportunities available to the firm.
2. Divide the opportunities into the *maximum* number of projects achievable. Any two opportunities that are *economically* dependent must be included in the same project; thus, an opportunity is economically independent of all opportunities not within the same project. All opportunities are within some project; it is possible for a project to comprise only one opportunity.
3. For each project defined in (2) above:
   (*a*) Define every possible combination of opportunities within that project. Each combination is referred to as an "alternative." One of the alternatives is to accept none of the opportunities in the project (to reject the project). The other alternatives contain one or more opportunities.
   (*b*) For each alternative determined in (3*a*) above, determine the maximum value that a stream generated by that alternative could have if appropriately divided into debt and equity streams. Select and adopt the alternative i with the highest maximum value less initial cost. That is, for project $Z$, select and adopt the alternative i with the

   $$\max[V_{Z_i}^* - I_{Z_i0}]$$

   where $V_{Z_i}^*$ is the maximum market value that stream $\tilde{\mathbf{Z}}_i$ from alternative i could attain, and $I_{Z_i0}$ is the current (time 0) outlay associated with alternative i. The alternative of accepting none of the opportunities has a $[V_Z^* - I_{Z0}]$ of zero; this will be the alternative that is adopted if every other alternative in the project has a negative $[V_Z^* - I_{Z0}]$.

It should be noted here that the division of any project alternative cash flow $\tilde{\mathbf{Z}}_i$ into debt and equity streams which maximize $V_{Z_i}$ (make $V_{Z_i} = V_{Z_i}^*$) is not necessarily the division of $\tilde{\mathbf{Z}}$ that will occur if the alternative i is adopted. All that is argued here is that the value $V^*_{\tilde{Z}_i}$ is the incremental value of $\tilde{\mathbf{Z}}$ to the firm assuming that the firm adopts alternative i and then divides firm total postinvestment cash flow so as to maximize total firm value. That is, the maximum postinvestment firm value $V^*$ of the firm's total postinvestment cash flow $\tilde{\mathbf{Y}}$ will equal the sum of the maximum achievable values of the individual cash flows (from past and present projects) comprising $\tilde{\mathbf{Y}}$; this is so by the VMT. Thus the firm should follow the three-step procedure outlined above and, after determining the optimal capital budget, decide what optimal financing should be.

As explained above, $V^*_{\tilde{Z}}$ is the maximum value of $\tilde{\mathbf{Z}}$ and equals the sum of the values of the individual stream into which $\tilde{\mathbf{Z}}$ would have to be divided so that $V_Z = V^*_{\tilde{Z}}$. Thus, if to produce its maximum value $\tilde{\mathbf{Z}}$ would have to be divided into equity and debt streams $\tilde{\mathbf{Z}}^{S*}$ and $\tilde{\mathbf{Z}}^{B*}$ with values $S^*_{\tilde{Z}}$ and $B^*_{\tilde{Z}}$, then $V^*_{\tilde{Z}} = S^*_{\tilde{Z}} + B^*_{\tilde{Z}}$. As a simplified example to illustrate these results, assume that $\tilde{\mathbf{Z}}$ is a perpetual stream which has a constant mean over time. Using the discount-rate–expected-return model it follows that

$$V^*_{\tilde{Z}} = S^*_{\tilde{Z}} + B^*_{\tilde{Z}} = \frac{\bar{Z}^{S*}}{k^*_S} + \frac{\bar{Z}^{B*}}{k^*_B} \tag{15-56}$$

where $k^*_S$ and $k^*_B$ are the capitalization rates on the expected values of stock and bond streams $\tilde{\mathbf{Z}}^{S*}$ and $\tilde{\mathbf{Z}}^{B*}$ into which $\tilde{\mathbf{Z}}$ is divided so as to make $V_Z = V^*_{\tilde{Z}}$.

Each alternative associated with any given project has a particular cash flow; each cash flow implies a particular division into debt and equity streams that would be necessary for that alternative's cash flow to have a maximum value. Therefore, each alternative would have its own $\bar{Z}^{B*}$, $\bar{Z}^{S*}$, $k^*_B$, and $k^*_S$ in Eq. (15-56), assuming that all cash flows are level perpetuities. As described above, the alternative with the highest $(V^*_{\tilde{Z}_i} - I_{Z_i 0})$ is the "best" alternative associated with a particular project and is accepted if and only if its $(V^*_{\tilde{Z}_i} - I_{Z_i 0})$ is positive.

Some additional interpretation of what is going on may be helpful. Suppose the firm is considering a project which involves entry into a new industry for that firm. The new industry may be related to the firm's present activities (an automobile manufacturer considering producing steel) or not. The firm should estimate the incremental income it will derive from entering the industry. The value it imputes to this income will depend in part on the *optimal financing policy for firms in the industry it is planning to enter* but not on what its own present financing policy is. That is, to determine the value of the incremental stream to the firm, the firm must determine the value such a stream would have if it were optimally financed (optimally divided into debt and equity streams). If a discount rate is applied to the project, it should essentially be the cost of capital of optimally financed firms in that new industry.[27] This is the practical implication of (15-54) and (15-55).

[27] This has also been suggested by Wilbur G. Lewellen, "The Cost of Capital," pp. 104–106, Wadsworth Publishing Company, Inc., Belmont, Calif., 1969, but under different assumptions.

**table 15-8**

| *Type* | *Initial outlay* ($I_{Z0}$) | *Mean annual cash income* ($\bar{X}_Z$) | *Mean annual capital outlay* ($\bar{I}_Z$) |
|---|---|---|---|
| *A* | 1,000 | 200 | 50 |
| *B* | 400 | 100 | 40 |

It was assumed above that there were no taxes. If firm taxes are introduced, and if it is assumed that tax losses can be sold in the market, then it can be shown that the VMT implies the same project-selection approach as described for the no-tax case.[28] The maximum value of the stream from each alternative associated with a project is determined assuming the existence of taxes. The maximum value is the price investors would pay for the set of after-tax streams which could be provided to the market by that alternative. The only difference between the no-tax and tax cases is that the cash flows valued by investors are after-firm tax cash flows in the latter case.

An illustration of the application of these principles will now be presented, first assuming no taxes and then assuming the presence of firm taxes. Only a choice between two alternatives associated with a project will be illustrated. The reader should be able to generalize the example to projects with more alternatives using the steps in the three-step project evaluation procedure outlined earlier (see page 422).

Assume that the firm is evaluating two opportunities—to purchase one type *A* computer and to purchase one type *B* computer (referred to simply as *A* and *B*). Suppose that *A* and *B* are economically independent of all other investment opportunities of the firm; therefore, *A* and *B* constitute a project. The alternatives (possible combinations of opportunities) to be examined are *A* alone and *B* alone; *A* and *B* together has been rejected as being obviously unprofitable.

Assume for simplicity that all streams from the alternatives are perpetuities having constant means over time and that investors discount expected returns to compute values. Let the data in Table 15-8 apply to the alternatives.

Considering the no-tax case first, recall that an optimal debt-equity ratio is

[28] Recall that we are making assumption A.8, which states that if a firm experiences a loss of $L$ in a period, it can sell that loss to another firm for the amount $\tau L$, where $\tau$ is the corporate tax rate.

**table 15-9**

| | $\bar{Z} = (\bar{X}_Z - \bar{I}_Z)$ | $\bar{R}^*$ | $\bar{D}^*$ | $k_B^*$ | $k_S^*$ | $B^* = \bar{R}^*/k_B^*$ | $S^* = \bar{D}^*/k_S^*$ | $V^* = B^* + S^*$ | $V^* - I_{Z0}$ |
|---|---|---|---|---|---|---|---|---|---|
| *A* | 150 | 20 | 130 | .067 | .125 | 300 | 1,040 | 1,340 | 340 |
| *B* | 60 | 30 | 30 | .05 | .10 | 600 | 300 | 900 | 500 |

**table 15-10**

| | $\overline{DP}$ | $\bar{Z}$ [See eq. (15-57)] | $\bar{R}^*$ | $\bar{D}^*$ | $k_B^*$ | $k_S^*$ | $B_Z = \bar{R}^*/k_B^*$ | $S_Z = \bar{D}^*/k_S^*$ | $V_Z^* = B_Z^* + S_Z^*$ | $V_Z^* - I_{Z0}$ |
|---|---|---|---|---|---|---|---|---|---|---|
| $A$ | 100 | 120 | 40 | 80 | .10 | .20 | 400 | 400 | 800 | −200 |
| $B$ | 60 | 65 | 34 | 6 | .08 | .167 | 425 | 40 | 485 | 85 |

assumed. Assume that the value-maximizing level of expected interest per period paid on debt per period is designated as $\bar{R}^*$.[29] The value-maximizing stock cash flow per period has an expected value of $\bar{D}^*$.[30] These and the other relevant statistics for the example are stated in Table 15-9.

The value-maximizing division (into $\tilde{R}$ and $\tilde{D}$) of the cash flow from each alternative provides an $\bar{R}$ and $\bar{D}$ of 20 and 130 for $A$ and 30 and 30 for $B$; the discount rates on each of these streams are designated as $k_B^*$ and $k_S^*$. Alternative $B$ has the higher maximum value less cost and is therefore the better alternative by step (3$b$). Since the $(V_Z^* - I_{Z0}) > 0$ for $B$, $B$ and the project are accepted.

Assuming taxes, the expected cash flow from each alternative becomes

$$\bar{Z} = \bar{X} - \bar{I} - \overline{\text{Tax}}_t = (1 - \tau)\bar{X} - \bar{I} + \tau(\bar{R} + \overline{DP}) \qquad (15\text{-}57)$$

where $\tau$ is the tax rate and $\overline{\text{Tax}}_t = \tau(\bar{X}_t - \bar{R}_t - DP_t)$ for any period $t$.[31] Some value-maximizing division of the streams from the alternatives will exist. Assume that the relevant statistics are as represented in Table 15-10. It is assumed in Table 15-10 that the data in Table 15-8 apply and that the tax rate $\tau$ equals 50%. Note that the total after-tax expected cash flow $\bar{Z}$ in (15-57) is divided between $\bar{R}$ and $\bar{D}$, that is, $\bar{Z} = \bar{R} + \bar{D}$.

From Table 15-10 it follows that alternative $B$ is preferred to alternative $A$ since the former has a higher $(V_Z^* - I_{Z0})$; indeed, $A$ is unacceptable whether or not $B$ is available since its $(V_Z^* - I_{Z0})$ is negative. By step (3$b$) it follows that alternative $B$ and the project are accepted.

## Source And Importance Of Statistical Interrelationships

In perfect markets, we recall from Chap. 12 that statistical relationships between the cash flows from different investments did not matter. We also just

[29] Recall from earlier discussion that expected interest will be less than promised interest on firm debt if there is any probability of default.

[30] It is assumed in this example that the financial structure which would maximize the value of stream $\tilde{Z}$ is a current issue of debt yielding an expected stream $\bar{R}$ per period and an issue of stock yielding an expected return $\bar{D}$ per period. It is assumed that no further issuance of stock or debt and no treasury stock or bond purchases in later (after time 0) periods would be associated with the value-maximizing capital structure associated with $\tilde{Z}$.

[31] For a discussion of the effects of taxes on cash flow, see chap. 9, pp. 215 and 216.

showed above that with A.2 through A.8, the ability of firms to costlessly change their financial structures, and the infinite divisibility of assets, the value-maximization theorem holds and therefore statistical interdependencies between investments are irrelevant. We now ask, when and why might statistical relationships matter? Assume that A.1, A.2, A.4 and A.5 or A.6 hold and therefore that the VAP holds. The VAP means that an incremental cash flow from a new investment determines that investment's value in the market; that incremental stream $\tilde{\mathbf{Z}}$, has a value to the firm equal to its value as an individual stream in the market. Net value to the firm is $V[\tilde{\mathbf{Z}}] - I_{Z0}$, just as with perfect markets in Chap. 12.[32] In perfect markets $\tilde{\mathbf{Z}}$ equaled

$$\tilde{\mathbf{Z}}(\text{perfect markets}) = \tilde{\mathbf{X}}_Z - \tilde{\mathbf{I}}_Z - \tau(\tilde{\mathbf{X}}_Z - \widetilde{\mathbf{DP}}_Z - \tilde{\mathbf{R}}_Z) \qquad (15\text{-}58)$$

and the value of $\tilde{\mathbf{Z}}$, $\tilde{\mathrm{V}}_Z$, was independent of the stochastic relationship of $\tilde{\mathbf{Z}}$ and other firm cash flow. With imperfections (i.e., dropping A.3, A.6, A.7, or A.8), $\tilde{\mathbf{Z}}$ may not equal (15-58). For example, if we introduce costs of financial distress $\tilde{\mathbf{F}}$ (see pages 387 to 389), $\tilde{\mathbf{Z}}$ becomes

$$\tilde{\mathbf{Z}} = \tilde{\mathbf{X}}_Z - \tilde{\mathbf{I}}_Z - \tilde{\mathbf{F}}_Z - \tau(\tilde{\mathbf{X}}_Z - \widetilde{\mathbf{DP}}_Z - \tilde{\mathbf{R}}_Z - \tilde{\mathbf{F}}_Z) \qquad (15\text{-}59)$$

where $\tilde{\mathbf{F}}_Z$ (the incremental effect of project $Z$ on the firm's $\tilde{\mathbf{F}}$) in (15-59) for project $Z$ is likely to depend on the correlation coefficient of the cash flows from the project and the cash flows from other firm projects. The reason is that the incremental impact $\tilde{\mathbf{F}}_Z$ of project $Z$ on the firm's total cost of financial distress, $\tilde{\mathbf{F}}$, depends on project $Z$'s effect on the variability of total firm cash flow and on total firm principal and interest ($\tilde{\mathbf{R}}$) payments. But this depends on the correlation of project $Z$'s cash flows with other firm cash flows and on the level of firm debt associated with other firm assets. That is, $\tilde{\mathbf{F}}_Z$ cannot be independently determined without looking at the returns and debt associated with other firm assets. But, once $\tilde{\mathbf{F}}_Z$ is determined, the value of $\tilde{\mathbf{Z}}$ in (15-59) is simply its value

[32] The VAP states that the equilibrium value of an income stream is independent of how the firm offers that stream to the market since arbitragers will always convert the stream into the form investors prefer. For the VAP to hold only assumptions A.1, A.2, A.4 and A.5 or A.6 are necessary. Defining the firm's cash flow without project Z as $\tilde{\mathbf{Y}}'$, the incremental cash flow from project $Z$ as $\tilde{\mathbf{Z}}$, and the post-investment total firm cash flow with project Z as $\tilde{\mathbf{Y}} = \tilde{\mathbf{Y}}' + \tilde{\mathbf{Z}}$, it follows using the VAP that, *at the equilibrium after project Z is adopted,* firm value $= V = V[\tilde{\mathbf{Y}}] = V[\tilde{\mathbf{Y}}' + \tilde{\mathbf{Z}}] = V[\tilde{\mathbf{Y}}'] + V[\tilde{\mathbf{Z}}]$. But note that for the change in firm value due to project Z (firm value with project $Z$ minus firm value without project $Z$) to be $V[\tilde{\mathbf{Z}}] = V[\tilde{\mathbf{Y}}] - V[\tilde{\mathbf{Y}}']$ using *post* $\tilde{\mathbf{Z}}$ equilibrium valuations (as defined in the previous sentence), it must be that $V[\tilde{\mathbf{Y}}']$ (the value that the market places on an individual stream with the distribution of $\tilde{\mathbf{Y}}'$) is the same whether or not the firm makes $\tilde{\mathbf{Z}}$ available to the market (i.e., whether or not the firm adopts project $Z$). For $V[\tilde{\mathbf{Y}}']$ to be the same with and without $\tilde{\mathbf{Z}}$, $\tilde{\mathbf{Z}}$ must have an insignificant effect on the value the market places on a stream of the distribution of $\tilde{\mathbf{Y}}'$, $V[\tilde{\mathbf{Y}}']$. In actual situations this is very likely since $\tilde{\mathbf{Z}}$ will be an insignificant part of the total income of the economy; sufficient (but not necessary) for this result would be that $\tilde{\mathbf{Z}}$ has many substitutes (streams with identical probability distributions except for a possible scale factor) in the market.

as an individual stream in the market (assuming that the VAP holds).[33] That is, using the VAP, the project's net present value is still $V[\tilde{\mathbf{Z}}] - I_{Z0}$, where $\tilde{\mathbf{Z}}$ is shown by (15-59).

If we also drop assumption A.8 and assume that losses are not tax-deductible, then Eq. (15-58) is not correct because the tax term is no longer $\tau(\tilde{\mathbf{X}} - \widetilde{\mathbf{DP}} - \tilde{\mathbf{R}})$ if the amount $(\tilde{\mathbf{X}} - \widetilde{\mathbf{DP}} - \tilde{\mathbf{R}})$ is negative (a tax loss). Equation (15-58) assumes that if $(\tilde{\mathbf{X}} - \widetilde{\mathbf{DP}} - \tilde{\mathbf{R}})$ is negative, then there is a tax rebate of amount $\tau(\tilde{\mathbf{X}} - \widetilde{\mathbf{DP}} - \tilde{\mathbf{R}})$, or the loss can be sold to another firm for $\tau(\tilde{\mathbf{X}} - \widetilde{\mathbf{DP}} - \tilde{\mathbf{R}})$ [either option produces a positive amount $\tau\left|(\tilde{\mathbf{X}} - \widetilde{\mathbf{DP}} - \tilde{\mathbf{R}})\right|$ in Eq. (15-58)]. But losses in reality cannot simply be sold; they can normally be carried back 3 years or forward 7 years. A carry-forward is not as good as getting a tax rebate or selling the loss in the market.[34] To deal with this problem, we again have to consider the relationship of project $Z$'s cash flows to other firm cash flows since the likelihood of not getting an immediate rebate on a loss on project $Z$ will depend on the size of losses on other assets during the period.[35] To determine the actual incremental tax effect of project $Z$, signified $\widetilde{\mathrm{Tax}}_Z$, we would have to examine the magnitude of the returns from the other firm assets. We would then have (assuming financial distress costs $\tilde{\mathbf{F}}$)

$$\tilde{\mathbf{Z}} = \tilde{\mathbf{X}}_Z - \tilde{\mathbf{I}}_Z - \tilde{\mathbf{F}}_Z - \widetilde{\mathbf{Tax}}_Z \tag{15-60}$$

Cash flow $\tilde{\mathbf{Z}}$ would then be evaluated as an individual stream (using the discount rate appropriate to the risk of $\tilde{\mathbf{Z}}$) to compute $V_Z$; $V_Z - I_{Z0}$ would be the net value of project $Z$ to the firm. Note that we have used the VAP here since the VAP does not require assumption A.8.

Flotation costs on new securities would be another reason to consider project interdependencies, this time of the $\tilde{\mathbf{I}}_Z$ on all new projects. Defining $\tilde{\mathbf{C}}_Z$ as the flotation cost incurred by externally financing project $Z$, the magnitude of $\tilde{\mathbf{C}}_Z$ could not be ascertained unless we know whether project $Z$ can be financed internally ($\tilde{\mathbf{C}}_Z = 0$) or, if not, how many other projects are being financed externally. If, for example, $I_{Z0} = \$100{,}000$ and the firm has \$500,000 in

[33] If the VAP did not hold, then even if we determine $\tilde{\mathbf{Z}}$ in (15-59), we could not use $\tilde{\mathbf{Z}}$ to determine $V_Z$. As explained later, we would have to determine the value of the entire firm with and without project $Z$, the difference being $\Delta V$ associated with project $Z$.

[34] A potential reduction in future income taxes using a carry-forward is not as valuable as a carry-back because of the time value of money and the uncertainty of generating future taxable income against which to use the carry-forward. To illustrate carry-backs and carry-forwards, if a firm loses \$1 million in 1980 but had at least \$1 million of taxed profits in 1977, the firm could cancel the \$1 million 1980 loss against \$1 million 1977 profit and get a rebate in 1980 of the 1977 taxes paid on the \$1 million in 1977 profits. If the 1977 profits were less than \$1 million, say \$400,000, the remaining \$600,000 of the 1980 loss could be cancelled against 1978 profits, then 1979 profits, and if still not used up, the remaining portion of the loss could be carried forward (up to 1987).

[35] For example, if the loss on project $Z$ is \$1 million and profits in the previous 3 years were \$1.5 million, there would be a carry-back and immediate tax rebate $\tau$ \$1,000,000 due to project $Z$'s loss as long as current losses on other firm projects did not exceed \$.5 million; if other projects are currently losing \$1.5 million or more, project $Z$ will generate no marginal carry-back and $Z$'s loss will have to be carried forward. See the preceding footnote on carry-backs and carry-forwards.

firm-held funds to internally finance an investment, then, if $\tilde{\mathbf{C}}_Z = C_{Z0}\ (\tilde{C}_{Zt} = 0, t > 0)$:

$C_{Z0} = 0$ if all other firm investments do not use up more than \$400,000 of the \$500,000 in internal funds.

$C_{Z0} > 0$ if the other projects use up more than \$400,000 of the internal funds; $C_{Z0}$'s magnitude will depend on the magnitude of total firm investment and on how the other investments are financed; this is so because there are economies of scale in financing and $Z$'s marginal impact on financing costs depends on the total capital budget.

Since $C_{Z0} > 0$, $\tilde{\mathbf{Z}}$ becomes

$$\tilde{\mathbf{Z}} = \tilde{\mathbf{X}}_Z - \dot{\mathbf{I}}_Z - \check{\mathbf{T}}\mathbf{ax}_Z - \tilde{\mathbf{C}}_Z \tag{15-61}$$

where $\tilde{\mathbf{C}}_Z = (C_{Z0}, 0, \ldots, 0)$, and where $C_{Z0}$ is relevant in determining taxes if it is tax-deductible. Using the VAP, the $\tilde{\mathbf{Z}}$ of (15-61) can be valued as an individual stream using the appropriate discount rate for that stream's degree of riskiness to compute the value of $\tilde{\mathbf{Z}}$, $V_Z$, and therefore to compute $V_Z - I_{Z0}$.

## An Algorithm For Evaluating Financial Decisions

One approach for evaluating financial decisions when interdependencies (either financing and investment interdependencies or other cash-flow interdependencies) are important is mathematical programming. To outline such an approach, assume that the firm has an array of investments that it can undertake.[36] Its problem is to make the choice of investments and to select a financing plan over some planning period $T$, i.e., to choose financing at $t = 0,1,2, \ldots, T$. The financing plan will specify for each point in time $t$, $t = 0,1,2, \ldots, T$, the level of firm debt, the cash dividends, and the proceeds from issuing new securities.

Assume the following definitions:

$x_j$ = proportion of project $j$ accepted, $j = 1, \ldots, m$

$B_t$ = expected debt outstanding at $t$

$D_t$ = expected cash dividends at $t$

$S_t^N$ = expected proceeds from issuing new stock at $t$

$N_t = X_t - I_t - \tau(X_t - DP_t)$ = expected net after tax cash inflow in $t$ ignoring the debt effect on taxes ($N_t < 0$ if a net outflow)

$K_t$ = firm debt capacity at $t$, i.e., the expected maximum attainable level of $B_t$; $K_t$ depends on the firm's choice of assets and $\partial K_t/\partial x_j > 0$ in most cases (more assets implies a greater debt capacity)

$k_B$ = interest rate on debt (assumed constant over time for simplicity)

[36] For the derivation of the approach described here, see S. C. Myers, Interactions of Corporate Financing and Investment Decisions—Implications for Capital Budgeting, listed in the Suggested Readings at the end of this chapter.

We have deleted the bars over the expected magnitudes for notational simplicity. The objective here is to maximize the current value of the firm, $V_0$. Current decisions will change $V_0$, and we wish to choose that set of investments and financing methods that produce the greatest positive change in $V_0$; i.e., we wish to maximize $\Delta V_0$. For convenience, let $v$ signify $\Delta V$, where $v$ depends on the $K_t$, $B_t$, $D_t$, and $S_t^N$. We seek to maximize $v$ subject to the following constraints:

$$\gamma_j = x_j - 1 \leq 0 \qquad j = 1. \;.\; .\, m \tag{15-62a}$$

$$\gamma_t^B = B_t - K_t \leq 0 \qquad t = 1, \;.\; .\; .\; , T \tag{15-62b}$$

$$\gamma_t^N = -N_t - \{B_t - B_{t-1}[1 + (1 - \tau)k_B]\} + D_t - S_t^N = 0 \tag{15-62c}$$

where

$$x_j \geq 0, B_t \geq 0, D_t \geq 0, \text{ and } S_t^N \geq 0 \tag{15-63}$$

Constraint (15-62$a$) states that we cannot adopt more than 100% of a particular project (i.e., $x_j \leq 1$). Constraint (15-62$b$) states that debt in any period, $B_t$, cannot exceed the debt limit $K_t$. Skipping (15-62$c$) for a moment, constraint (15-63) restricts all variables to be nonnegative.

Constraint (15-62$c$) needs clarification. The constraint is derived from the definitions of the terms and from the cash inflow (source) = cash outflow (use) accounting identity. To see this, let us define cash sources and uses and then set sources equal to uses:

$$\overbrace{X_t + (B_t - B_{t-1}) + S_t^N}^{\text{Sources}} = \overbrace{I_t + \tau(X_t - DP_t - k_B B_{t-1}) + k_B B_{t-1} + D_t}^{\text{Uses}} \tag{15-64}$$

where $(B_t - B_{t-1})$ is the increase in debt during period $t$ which thereby provides an inflow of borrowed funds [if $B_t - B_{t-1} < 0$, then put $(B_{t-1} - B_t)$ on the Uses side of the equation, since this means that $(B_{t-1} - B_t)$ of the $B_{t-1}$ debt is repaid]; $k_B B_{t-1} = R_t$ = interest paid at time $t$ on debt incurred at time $t - 1$; and $\tau(X_t - DP_t - k_B B_{t-1})$ = taxes. Subtract sources from uses in (15-32), rearrange terms, use the definition for $N_t$, and we get constraint (15-62$c$):

$$\begin{aligned} &\text{Uses} - \text{Sources} \\ &\quad = [I_t + \tau(X_t - DP_t - k_B B_{t-1}) + k_B B_{t-1} + D_t] - [X_t + (B_t - B_{t-1}) + S_t^N] \\ &\quad = -N_t - \{B_t - B_{t-1}[1 + (1 - \tau)k_B]\} + D_t - S_t^N = 0 \end{aligned}$$

which is constraint (15-62$c$).

We shall use the Kuhn-Tucker conditions to solve the problem of maximizing $v$ subject to constraints (15-62$a$) through (15-63). The symbols $\lambda_j$, $\lambda_t^B$, and $\lambda_t^N$ represent the "shadow prices" associated with constraints (15-62$a$), (15-62$b$), and (15-62$c$), respectively; these shadow prices indicate the marginal change in $v$ (i.e., in $\Delta V$) due to a small relaxation (increase) in the constraint (e.g., $\lambda_j$ = the increase in $v$ due to a very small increase in the unity constraint—that is, how much $v$ would increase if we could adopt slightly more than 100% of the project; and $\lambda_t^B$ = the increase in $v$ if the debt constraint were slightly increased above $K_t$). The $\lambda$ are zero or positive (this is discussed further below). The expression $\partial v/\partial x_j$ is the partial derivative of $v$ due to a change in $x_j$ holding constant all other variables—$B_t$, $D_t$, $S_t^N$, all $t$—in the system; and similarly for all other partial derivatives.

The solution to the problem is that level of all variables (the $x_j$, $j = 1, \ldots, m$ and the $B_t$, $D_t$, and $S_t^N$, $t = 1, \ldots, T$) satisfying the inequalities stated below. That is, we are maximizing with respect to the $x_j$, $B_t$, $D_t$, and $S_t^N$.[37] For each investment $j$,

$$\frac{\partial v}{\partial x_j} + \sum_{t=0}^{T} \left[ \lambda_t^B \frac{\partial K_t}{\partial x_j} + \lambda_t^N \frac{\partial N_t}{\partial x_j} \right] - \lambda_j \leq 0 \tag{15-65a}$$

For expected debt in each period, $B_t$,

$$\frac{\partial v}{\partial B_t} - \lambda_t^B - \lambda_t^N - \left[ 1 + (1 - \tau)k_B \right] \lambda_{t+1}^N \leq 0 \tag{15-65b}$$

For expected dividends in each period,

$$\frac{\partial v}{\partial D_t} - \lambda_t^N \leq 0 \tag{15-65c}$$

For expected new shares issued in each period

$$\frac{\partial v}{\partial S_t^N} + \lambda_t^N \leq 0 \tag{15-65d}$$

There are $m$ inequalities like (15-65$a$) (since by assumption there are $m$ investments and therefore $m$ $x_j$'s); and there are $T + 1$ (one for each point in time, $0, 1, \ldots, T$) of each of relations (15-65$b$), (15-65$c$), and (15-65$d$). Each inequality is a necessary condition for an optimum.

The properties of the optimal solution are:

1. If a decision variable is positive in the optimal solution, then the relation for that variable is an equality. Thus, for example, if $B_3 > 0$ at the optimum then (15-65$b$) for $B_3$ will be an equality (=0).
2. A $\lambda$ is positive if the constraint associated with that $\lambda$ is "binding," i.e., if relaxing the constraint a little bit produces a rise in $v$. If a decision variable is zero in the optimal solution then its $\lambda$ is zero; e.g., if $B_3 = 0$ optimally, then $\lambda_3^B = 0$ at the optimum. If a decision variable is positive at the optimum but is not so positive that it presses against the constraint (i.e., the constraint is not binding and does not matter), its $\lambda$ is zero at the optimum (a zero shadow price to the constraint); e.g., if $0 < B_3 < K_3$ at the optimum, $\lambda_3^B = 0$. If the decision variable is positive *and* it presses against the constraint (the con-

[37] In deriving the solutions (15-65$a$) through (15-65$d$) using the Kuhn-Tucker conditions, note that $\partial \gamma_j/\partial x_j = 1$, $\partial \gamma_t^B/\partial B_t = 1$, and $(\partial \gamma_t^N/\partial B_t) = -1$; also, $\partial \gamma_t^N/\partial x_j = -\partial N_t/\partial x_j$.

straint is binding and therefore $v$ would rise if we could loosen the contraint), then its $\lambda$ is positive (a positive shadow price to the constraint); e.g., if $B_3 = K_3$ at the optimum, then $\lambda_3^B > 0$.[38]

Relation (15-65*a*) is of interest because it indicates the marginal value of a project, taking into account its interactions with financing [reflected in the $\lambda_t^B(\partial K_t/\partial x_j)$ and $\lambda_t^N(\partial N_t/\partial x_j)$]. Define the terms left of the $\lambda_j$ in (15-65*a*) as the adjusted present value (APV) of project $j$ where

$$\text{APV}_j = \frac{\partial v}{\partial x_j} + \sum_{t=0}^{T} \left[ \lambda_t^B \frac{\partial K_t}{\partial x_j} + \lambda_t^N \frac{\partial N_t}{\partial x_j} \right] \tag{15-66}$$

The $\text{APV}_j$ is the *marginal (incremental) increase* in $v$ due to an incremental (small) change in $x_j$ *if we take into account all the interactions between the project and financing decisions*. Term $(\partial v/\partial x_j)$ is the marginal impact of an increase in project $j$ ignoring debt and dividend policy effects. Term $(\partial K_t/\partial x_j)$ is the marginal impact of $j$ on firm debt capacity $K_t$, and $\lambda_t^B$ is the change in $v$ due to the change in debt capacity, and $\lambda_t^B(\partial K_t/\partial x_j)$ is therefore the change in $v$ due to an increase in $x_j$ via the impact of $x_j$'s increase on debt capacity. Similarly, $\lambda_t^N(\partial N_t/\partial x_j)$ is the change in $v$ due to the marginal impact of project $j$ on the terms in constraint (15-62*c*).

From optimal solution properties 1 and 2 discussed above, we know that (15-66) is an equality if $x_j > 0$ (some or all of the project is desirable) and $\lambda_j > 0$ if $x_j = 1$ [if constraint (15-62*a*) is binding]; that is, we shall want to expand the investment if

$$\text{APV}_j = \lambda_j > 0 \tag{15-67}$$

From 1 and 2, it follows that if $\lambda_j > 0$, then $x_j = 1$ (accept project). If $x_j = 1$, $\lambda_j \geq 0$, but most likely $\lambda_j > 0$ and we would benefit from expanding the investment.[39] If $0 < x_j < 1$ (partially accept project $j$), then $\lambda_j = 0$ and $\text{APV}_j = 0$ (marginal expansion of project produces zero gain). If $x_j = 0$ (project $j$ rejected) then $\lambda_j = 0$ and $\text{APV}_j \leq 0$.[40]

The magnitudes of the terms in (15-66) will depend on the particular circumstances. For example, if dividend policy were irrelevant in the sense that $\partial v/\partial D_t = \partial v/\partial S_t^N = 0$, then it follows from (15-65*c*) and (15-65*d*) that $\lambda_t^N = 0$, all $t$, and (15-66) would reduce to

$$\text{APV}_j = \frac{\partial v}{\partial x_j} + \sum_{t=0}^{T} \lambda_t^B \frac{\partial K_t}{\partial x_j} \tag{15-68}$$

On the other hand, if dividend policy were relevant (e.g., because selling new shares involves flotation costs or because of the personal tax bias in favor of

[38] It is possible but very unlikely that a variable equals the constraint but the constraint is not binding, i.e., with $\lambda = 0$ (e.g., $B_3 = K_3$ and $\lambda_3^B = 0$; or $x_j = 1$ and $\lambda_j = 0$).

[39] See the preceding footnote.

[40] With $x_j = 0$ and $\lambda_j = 0$, it is possible but unlikely that $\text{APV}_j = 0$.

capital gains over dividends), then $\lambda_t^N \neq 0$ and we would use the complete $\mathrm{APV}_j$ equation (15-66).

Similarly, if debt were not a favored form of financing at the margin (firm indifferent between small changes in debt and equity), $\lambda_t^B = 0$ in (15-66) and the first $\Sigma$ term in (15-66) would drop out.

**Decentralized capital budgeting.** An issue that has received frequent attention—largely because of its important practical implications—is the firm's ability to make investment and financing decisions separately. It is clear from (15-66) that this is possible only if $\mathrm{APV}_j$ can be computed by the investment analyst without obtaining information concerning that project $j$'s financing from the party making the financing decision. This is referred to as decentralization because it allows the choice of investments to be made by division managers or department personnel even though the funds to finance the investments are derived from the pool of funds obtained to finance the entire enterprise (separate bonds and shares of stock are not issued for each project). There are three situations that allow the investment analyst to determine a project's desirability without the need to communicate with someone in the firm on how each project is to be financed (i.e., on what each project will do to the level of debt and equity of the firm):

1. If financing policy is irrelevant, e.g., if there were no corporate taxes and perfect-market assumptions A.1 to A.8 (page 386) hold. In this case $\lambda_t^B = 0$ and $\lambda_t^N = 0$ in (15-66) and $\mathrm{APV}_j = (\partial v/\partial x_j)$. The net present value of an entire project $j$ is simply $V_j - I_{j0} = V[\tilde{\mathbf{X}}_j - \tilde{\mathbf{I}}_j] - I_{j0}$, where future capital outlays on the project $\tilde{\mathbf{I}}_j = (\tilde{I}_{j1}, \tilde{I}_{j2}, \ldots, \tilde{I}_{jT})$.
2. If in (15-66) the parameters $\lambda_t^B$, $\partial K_t/\partial x_j$, $\lambda_t^N$, and $\partial N_t/\partial x_j$ were the same for all projects $j$. In this case, $\mathrm{APV}_j$ could be computed by the investment analyst simply using those parameter values. This condition is not likely to hold except as an approximation for small investments in the same risk class as is the firm (therefore not affecting the firm's risk class and optimal method of financing).
3. If a general guideline for determining terms $\lambda_t^B$, $\partial K_t/\partial x_j$, $\lambda_t^N$, and $\partial N_t/\partial x_j$ for each project exists which the capital budgeting analyst can use in assessing each project. This is discussed below.

Situation 1 is simply the M-M no-corporate-tax case. Situation 2 requires that terms $\lambda_t^B$, $\partial K_t/\partial x_j$, $\lambda_t^N$, and $\partial N_t/\partial x_j$ be constant regardless of the size of the capital budget and regardless of the risk of the project. This is not likely. For example, a riskier project $A$ may have a lower $(\partial K_t/\partial x_j)$ than would lower risk project $B$. Or the $\lambda_t^N$ may depend on the size of the capital budget (this is the case if flotation costs on external financing vary with the amount of new securities sold). The important point is that at best the terms in the summation ($\Sigma$'s) in (15-66) are only approximately constant.

A case sufficient for situation 3 is the perfect-markets (M-M) corporate tax case with virtually all firm securities being debt securities (to maximize interest tax deductibility). In this case of virtually no stock and perfect markets, dividend policy is irrelevant ($\lambda_t^N = 0$) and all firm cash flow is paid out as interest on debt. From page 325, the net cash flow on project $j$ is $\widetilde{\mathbf{NCF}}_j$, where

$$\widetilde{\mathbf{NCF}}_j = \tilde{\mathbf{X}}_j - \tilde{\mathbf{I}}_j - \tau(\tilde{\mathbf{X}}_j - \widetilde{\mathbf{DP}}_j - \tilde{\mathbf{R}}_j) \tag{15-69}$$

$\widetilde{\mathbf{NCF}}_j$ is all paid out to bondholders, i.e., $\widetilde{\mathbf{NCF}}_j = \tilde{\mathbf{R}}_j$; setting $\tilde{\mathbf{R}}_j$ equal to (15-69)

$$\tilde{\mathbf{R}}_j = \tilde{\mathbf{X}}_j - \mathbf{I}_j - \tau(\tilde{\mathbf{X}}_j - \widetilde{\mathbf{DP}}_j - \tilde{\mathbf{R}}_j)$$

which, solving for $\tilde{\mathbf{R}}_j$,

$$\tilde{\mathbf{R}}_j = \frac{(1 - \tau)\tilde{\mathbf{X}}_j - \tilde{\mathbf{I}}_j + \tau\widetilde{\mathbf{DP}}_j}{1 - \tau} \tag{15-70}$$

The value of project $j$ equals the value of its $\widetilde{\mathbf{NCF}}$ less its initial cost. If $\widetilde{\mathbf{NCF}}_j$ begins one period (of any time length) after the investment $I_{j0}$, the net present value of $j$ equals

$$\begin{aligned} V_j - I_{j0} &= V[\tilde{\mathbf{R}}_j] - I_{j0} \\ &= V\left[\frac{(1 - \tau)\tilde{\mathbf{X}}_j - \tilde{\mathbf{I}}_j + \tau\widetilde{\mathbf{DP}}_j}{1 - \tau}\right] - I_{j0} \end{aligned} \tag{15-71}$$

where $\tilde{\mathbf{I}}_j = (\tilde{I}_{j1}, \tilde{I}_{j2}, \ldots, \tilde{I}_{j\infty})$ = future firm investment necessitated by project $j$. $\tilde{\mathbf{R}}_j$ for a project can be computed by the capital budgeting analyst, its risk assessed, and the resulting $\bar{R}_{jt}$ discounted using the appropriate risk-adjusted discount rate. That is, using bars to signify expected amounts,

$$V_j - I_{j0} = \sum_{t=1}^{\infty} \frac{\bar{R}_{jt}}{(1 + k_{Bt})^t} - I_{j0} \tag{15-72}$$

where expected interest $\bar{R}_{jt}$ in (15-72) equals

$$\bar{R}_{jt} = \frac{(1 - \tau)\bar{X}_{jt} - \bar{I}_{jt} + \tau\overline{DP}_{jt}}{1 - \tau} \tag{15-73}$$

and $k_{Bt}$ is the risk-adjusted discount rate. Thus the capital budgeting analyst needs no special financing information for each project regardless of its size and risk. Knowledge that all investments are entirely debt-financed means that the investment analyst can simply compute $\bar{R}_{jt}$ and use the proper $k_{Bt}$ for all $t$. Total decentralization is possible as in the no-corporate-tax case [in which case the capital budgeting analyst determines the risk-adjusted rate to discount $(\bar{X}_{jt} - \bar{I}_{jt})$].

## SUMMARY

Whereas in perfect markets (assumptions A.1 to A.8) both the financing and investment policies of the firm conform to rather straightforward guidelines, these policy areas become significantly more complex when the perfect-market assumptions are relaxed. Among the imperfections considered here are investor transaction costs, costs of issuing new securities and paying dividends, costs of financial distress, personal taxes, agency costs, and information-acquisition costs. The greater are expected financial distress costs as a function of debt; the less will be the firm's optimal debt-equity ratio. The presence of flotation costs encourages the use of internal relative to external financing and favors the use of debt relative to external equity. Personal income taxes are biased in favor of equity income and motivate firms to finance to a substantial extent with equity funds. This personal tax bias has an effect on the debt-equity choice that is opposite to that of the corporate income tax which favors debt. At any given point in time, the optimal (share-value-maximizing) financing strategy for a firm depends on how the market values interest, dividend, and capital-gain income. If we assume A.1 and A.3 to A.8, it can be shown that, under some tax structures, at equilibrium both debt and equity financing will be employed in the economy but, for any individual firm, debt and equity securities will be so priced that firm value will be independent of the firm's debt-equity ratio. Because bondholders cannot compel the firm to adopt specific investments, firms which maximize share values may not adopt the set of investments which maximizes the value of the entire firm (shares plus bonds). The firm's investments in such cases are "inefficient," and this inefficiency can increase as the level of firm risky debt increases, with creditors refusing to advance further credit beyond some limit of debt. Beyond that limit, the expected return to creditors may actually fall as promised principal and interest payments to creditors rise because the greater promised payments mean a less efficient investment policy. The possibility of inefficient investments discourages the use of risky debt, and it will not be in the shareholders' interests to issue risky debt unless there are compensating advantages, such as tax benefits from the debt.

In a world of imperfections, a firm will determine its financing and investment simultaneously. Under certain conditions, the value-maximization theorem holds and statistical dependencies among investments can be ignored; i.e., diversification effects of investments are irrelevant. In general, however, the existence of imperfections necessitates taking into account statistical interdependencies among investments.

APPENDIX

# FIFTEEN A

## THE IRRELEVANCE OF FINANCIAL STRUCTURE WITH PERSONAL AND CORPORATE TAXES[41]

Let us assume A.1 and A.3 through A.8. Thus we have a world of personal tax biases (A.2 does not hold), which we assume to favor equity financing. We shall show that if for some, but not necessarily all investors, the *personal* tax bias in favor of equity financing offsets the *corporate* tax bias in favor of debt, then the firm will be indifferent with regard to its capital structure. A state-preference approach will be used in the analysis because it most clearly identifies the economic process that is involved. We shall examine the supply of debt and equity securities and the demand for those securities and show that equilibrium prices must imply no firm advantage to issuing debt or equity securities. It is important to keep in mind the assumptions we are making here, particularly the lack of bankruptcy costs. We are assuming "perfect markets" except for the existence of a *personal* tax bias in favor of equity income.

We shall assume that all debt payments are tax-deductible to the firm and taxable to the bondholder and that all firm net income (net of interest on debt) is taxable to the firm (at corporate tax rate $\tau$) and is also taxable to the stockholder. Also, to simplify the discussion, we make no distinction between the personal tax rates on dividends and capital gains. We also assume competitive capital markets; i.e., no single investor or firm is significant enough to alter

[41] This appendix is based on Harry DeAngelo and Ronald W. Masulis, "Optimal Capital Structure Under Corporate and Personal Taxation," U.C.L.A. Working Paper, 1977.

state claim prices in the economy. It will be shown that the firm is indifferent with regard to its debt-equity ratio. Using arguments similar to those below, it can also be shown that the firm is indifferent between having outstanding in period $t$ any of security types $1, \ldots, q$ (e.g., debt, common stock, preferred stock, warrants, convertible bonds) as long as there are some investors in the marketplace who, because of their personal tax brackets, prefer security types $1, \ldots, q$. That is, each security has its own "clientele" and is as attractive to the firm as a means of financing as any other security type which has a "clientele."

Assume that now is time 0, and that the firm is being established. The problem of the firm is to determine its financial structure and its investments. The company will raise capital by issuing shares and bonds and will adopt the financing-investment decision which provides the greatest net present value. Expression $(s,t)$ signifies state $s$ at time $t$. Thus "dividends in $(s,t)$" means "dividends occurring at time $t$ if state $s$ occurs at time $t$," etc. Assume the following definitions:

$\tau$ = the corporate tax rate (assumed the same for all firms)

$\tau_S^i$ = the personal tax rate of investor i on income from stock

$\tau_B^i$ = the personal tax rate of investor i on income from bonds

$v_S(s,t)$ = the current price of a security that generates one dollar of dividend (stock) income in $(s,t)$

$v_B(s,t)$ = the current price of a security that generates one dollar of interest (bond) income in $(s,t)$

$S_0$ = current value of the firm's stock

$B_0$ = current value of the firm's debt

$I(s,t)$ = the firm's investment in $(s,t)$

$I_0$ = the firm's current investment which is made by current shareholders or bondholders who provide the initial capital to finance the firm

$X(s,t)$ = the firm's revenues less expenses in $(s,t)$; $X(s,t)$ depends on $I(s,j)$, all $s$, all $j < t$, i.e., $X(s,t)$ depends on investment before time $t$

$DP(s,t)$ = the firm's depreciation for tax purposes in $(s,t)$

$Y^B(s,t)$ = payments by the firm to bondholders in $(s,t)$; all of $Y^B(s,t)$ is assumed to be tax-deductible

$Y^S(s,t)$ = the firm's stock returns net of corporate taxes but before personal taxes on stock income in $(s,t)$; assume initially that all of $\hat{Y}^S(s,t)$ is paid out as a dividend in $(s,t)$ and taxed as personal income (more on this later)

Beginning with the supply of debt and equity securities to the market, it follows from the above definitions that

$$Y^S(s,t) = X(s,t) - I(s,t) - Y^B(s,t) - \tau[X(s,t) - DP(s,t) - Y^B(s,t)] \quad (15A\text{-}1)$$

The market values of the firm's debt and equity are

$$S_0 = \sum_{s,t} v_S(s,t)\hat{Y}^S(s,t) \quad (15A\text{-}2)$$

$$B_0 = \sum_{s,t} v_B(s,t) Y^B(s,t) \tag{15A-3}$$

At time 0 the firm sets $I_0$ and contractually arranges debt payments $Y^B(s,t)$, all $s,t$, so as to maximize its net present value [for any given $I_0$ there is an implied set of $X(s,t)$ and $I(s,t)$, all $s,t$; all investors agree on what the $X(s,t)$ and $I(s,t)$ are]. Thus, using (15A-2) and (15A-3), the problem at time 0 is

$$\underset{I_0, Y^B(s,t)}{\text{Maximize}} \left\{ \sum_{s,t} v_S(s,t) \hat{Y}^S(s,t) + \sum_{s,t} v_B(s,t) Y^B(s,t) - I_0 \right\} \tag{15A-4a}$$

Substituting $Y^S(s,t)$ of Eq. (15A-1) into (15A-4$a$), we find that the firm's goal is to

$$\begin{aligned} \underset{I_0, Y^B(s,t)}{\text{Maximize}} \Bigg\{ & \sum_{s,t} [v_B(s,t) - v_S(s,t)(1 - \tau)] Y^B(s,t) \\ & + \sum_{s,t} v_S(s,t)[(1 - \tau)X(s,t) - I(s,t) + \tau DP(s,t)] - I_0 \Bigg\} \end{aligned} \tag{15A-4b}$$

subject to

$$I_0 \geq 0 \tag{15A-4c}$$

$$0 \leq Y^B(s,t) \leq X(s,t) + \frac{1}{1 - \tau}[\tau DP(s,t) - I(s,t)] \qquad \text{all } s,t \tag{15A-4d}$$

where (15A-4$d$) is simply the constraints $Y^B(s,t) \geq 0$ and $Y^S(s,t) \geq 0$ combined into a single constraint.

In the above analysis, the firm has complete flexibility in designing its capital structure. For example, it can issue separate claims to stock and bond income in each $(s,t)$. The firm can also issue only equity [$Y^B(s,t) = 0$, all $s,t$]; or only risk-free debt in $t$, $Y^B(s,t) = Y_t^B \leq$ [minimum $\{x(s,t)[1/(1 - \tau)][\tau DP(s,t) - I(s,t)]\}$ for all $s$]; or risky debt in some or all $t$; or only debt, in which case, $Y^B(s,t) = X(s,t) + [1/(1 - \tau)][\tau DP(s,t) - I(s,t)]$ all $s,t$.

Define the following term:

$$\pi(s,t) = v_B(s,t) - (1 - \tau)v_S(s,t) \tag{15A-5}$$

Term $\pi(s,t)$ in (15A-5) equals the *current market price* of a dollar of debt returns in $(s,t)$ less the product of $(1 - \tau)$ and the current market price of a dollar of equity returns in $(s,t)$. $\pi(s,t)$ is a market relationship faced by all firms in the economy.

From (15A-4$b$), we have the following conclusions:

(i) If $\pi(s,t)$ is positive, the firm will issue only debt payoffs for $(s,t)$ since (15A-4$b$) increases as $Y^B(s,t)$ increases in this case; and the firm will issue only equity payoffs for $(s,t)$ if $\pi(s,t) < 0$, since, with $\pi(s,t) < 0$, (15A-4$b$) is maximized if $Y^B(s,t) = 0$. Only if $\pi(s,t) = 0$ is the firm indifferent between issuing debt and equity for $(s,t)$.

Since (i) applies to *every* firm in the economy, the following is true:

(ii) The aggregate (economy's) supply of $(s,t)$ *equity* claims will be zero if $\pi(s,t) > 0$; the aggregate supply of $(s,t)$ *debt* claims will be zero if $\pi(s,t) < 0$; therefore, both $(s,t)$ equity and $(s,t)$ debt claims can exist simultaneously only if $\pi(s,t) = 0$.

We shall now show that if $\pi(s,t) > 0$, there will be an aggregate demand (preference by some investors) for equity claims even though by (ii) firms issue no $(s,t)$ equity claims. This investor demand will drive up $(s,t)$ equity prices until firms are willing to issue equity claims [i.e., drive up $(s,t)$ equity prices so that $\pi(s,t) \leq 0$]. But we shall also show that if $\pi(s,t) < 0$, there will be a demand for $(s,t)$ debt claims even though by (ii) there will be no debt claims in the economy. Equilibrium in the $(s,t)$ debt market will obtain only if $\pi(s,t) \geq 0$. Therefore, for there to be equilibrium in both the $(s,t)$ equity and $(s,t)$ debt markets $\pi(s,t) = 0$ must hold. But, by (i) this means that at equilibrium, firms are indifferent between issuing debt and equity claims.

Assume any individual i with utility function $U^i(C^i, Y^{\tau i}(s,t))$, all $s,t$, where $C^i$ is units of current consumption and $Y^{\tau i}(s,t)$ is the net of personal tax income of i in $(s,t)$. $W^i$ is i's wealth, the price of current consumption is defined as 1, and $\tau_B^i$ and $\tau_S^i$ are i's tax rates on debt and stock income, respectively. Investor i's problem is:

$$\underset{C^i, Y^{Bi}(s,t), Y^{Si}(s,t)}{\text{Maximize}} \quad U^i(C^i, Y^{\tau i}(s,t)) \tag{15A-6$a$}$$

subject to

$$C^i + \sum_{s,t} v_B(s,t) Y^{Bi}(s,t) + \sum_{s,t} v_S(s,t) Y^{Si}(s,t) \leq W^i \tag{15A-6$b$}$$

$$Y^{\tau i}(s,t) = (1 - \tau_B^i) Y^{Bi}(s,t) + (1 - \tau_S^i) Y^{Si}(s,t) \qquad \text{all } s,t \tag{15A-6$c$}$$

$$C^i \geq 0, \; Y^{Bi}(s,t) \geq 0, \; Y^{Si}(s,t) \geq 0 \qquad \text{all } s,t \tag{15A-6$d$}$$

where $Y^{Si}(s,t)$ and $Y^{Bi}(s,t)$ are the pre-personal-tax stock and debt income received by i in $(s,t)$.

If, for individual i, the after-personal-tax return per dollar of $(s,t)$ equity investment exceeds the after-personal-tax return per dollar of $(s,t)$ debt claim, that is, if

$$\frac{1 - \tau_S^i}{v_S(s,t)} > \frac{1 - \tau_B^i}{v_B(s,t)} \tag{15A-7$a$}$$

then i will prefer $(s,t)$ equity to $(s,t)$ debt, i.e., will want only $(s,t)$ equity. If the reverse inequality holds, that is, if

$$\frac{1 - \tau_S^i}{v_S(s,t)} < \frac{1 - \tau_B^i}{v_B(s,t)} \tag{15A-7$b$}$$

then i will demand only $(s,t)$ debt. If $(1 - \tau_S^i)/v_S(s,t) = (1 - \tau_B^i)/v_B(s,t)$, then $(s,t)$ equity and $(s,t)$ debt are perfect substitutes for individual i, i.e., i will be indifferent between the two types of claims.

Define as marginal investors $m$ those investors with tax rates that satisfy

$$1 - \tau_B^m = (1 - \tau_S^m)(1 - \tau) \tag{15A-8}$$

Using (15A-5) and (15A-8), it follows that for investors $m$

$$\frac{1 - \tau_B^m}{v_B(s,t)} \gtreqless \frac{1 - \tau_S^m}{v_S(s,t)} \qquad \text{as } \pi(s,t) \lesseqgtr 0 \tag{15A-9}$$

But (15A-9) implies that investors $m$ will prefer $(s,t)$ debt claims if $\pi(s,t) < 0$, even though by (ii) no such claims will exist in the market; and by (15A-9), investors $m$ will prefer $(s,t)$ equity claims if $\pi(s,t) > 0$, even though by (ii) no such claims will exist in the market. As explained above, these are disequilibrium situations and equilibrium can exist only if $\pi(s,t) = 0$, which, by (i), means that firms are indifferent between issuing $(s,t)$ debt and $(s,t)$ equity claims.

To see that the existence of investors $m$ implies that $\pi(s,t) = 0$ must hold, assume that $\pi(s,t) < 0$ and no firm is issuing debt claims [by (ii)]. As long as $\pi(s,t) < 0$, investors $m$ will be willing to pay *more* for $(s,t)$ bonds [a bond that pays one dollar in $(s,t)$] than their going price [by (15A-19)], and this will drive up the $(s,t)$ bond prices until $\pi(s,t) = 0$, at which point investors $m$ are indifferent between $(s,t)$ bonds and $(s,t)$ stocks.[42] Thus, if $\pi(s,t) = -\gamma$, any $\gamma > 0$, then using (15A-5), the price of an $(s,t)$ bond payment is

$$v_B(s,t) = v_S(s,t)(1 - \tau) - \gamma \tag{15A-10a}$$

But, investors $m$ are, by (15A-9), *willing to pay* for the $(s,t)$ bond payment the price $v_B(s,t)'$ where

$$v_B(s,t)' = v_S(s,t)(1 - \tau) \tag{15A-10b}$$

Since (15A-10$b$) > (15A-10$a$), bond prices must rise [i.e., the price that a firm could get for its bonds if it issued the bonds; keep in mind no $(s,t)$ bonds are issued as long as $\pi(s,t) < 0$]. The bond prices will continue to rise until (15A-10$b$) holds. Using similar reasoning, if $\pi(s,t) > 0$, marginal investors will demand equity streams even though none is issued; equilibrium will obtain only when $\pi(s,t) = 0$.[43]

[42] We are making the implicit assumption here that there are some investors $m$ who will choose to hold either bonds or stock or both (depending on their prices); i.e., not all investors satisfying (15A-8) will refuse to buy either bonds or stock because they both are overpriced relative to current consumption. The same assumption is made below for investors $j$ for whom $(1 - \tau_B^j) > (1 - \tau_S^j)(1 - \tau)$ and investors $k$ for whom $(1 - \tau_B^k) < (1 - \tau_S^k)(1 - \tau)$; that is, there are some investors $j$ and $k$ who will *not* refuse to hold either stock or bonds.

[43] To see that (15A-10$b$) holds, observe that using (15A-7$b$) and the discussion following that equation, investor i will be willing to buy $(s,t)$ bonds as long as

$$\frac{1 - \tau_S^i}{v_S(s,t)} \leq \frac{1 - \tau_B^i}{v_B(s,t)} \tag{a}$$

that is, as long as [rearranging ($a$)]

$$v_B(s,t) \leq \left[\frac{(1 - \tau_B^i)}{(1 - \tau_S^i)}\right] v_S(s,t) \tag{b}$$

If the equality holds in ($b$), investor i is indifferent between $(s,t)$ stocks and bonds. That is, investor i will pay for an $(s,t)$ bond up to $v_B(s,t)'$, where

Also notice [using relations like (15A-7*a*) and (15A-9)] that *all* investors $j$ with tax rates such that $(1 - \tau_B^j) > (1 - \tau_S^j)(1 - \tau)$ will demand $(s,t)$ equity claims if $\pi(s,t) > 0$, but by (ii) no such equity claims will exist; and all investors $k$ for whom $(1 - \tau_B^k) < (1 - \tau_S^k)(1 - \tau)$ will demand debt claims if $\pi(s,t) < 0$, but by (ii) no such claims will exist in the market. It follows that if $\pi(s,t) > 0$, the price of equity claims will rise until $\pi(s,t) \leq 0$ so that such claims emerge; and if $\pi(s,t) < 0$, the price of debt claims will rise until $\pi(s,t) \geq 0$. Thus, only if $\pi(s,t) = 0$ can there be equilibrium. Notice that for this process there does not have to exist an investor $m$ satisfying (15A-8).

Thus, at equilibrium, $\pi(s,t) = 0$ for all $s,t$; i.e., at equilibrium,

$$v_B(s,t) = v_S(s,t)(1 - \tau) \tag{15A-11}$$

Using inequalities such as (15A-7*a*) and (15A-7*b*), it follows that all investors $j$ with tax rates such that $(1 - \tau_B^j) > (1 - \tau_S^j)(1 - \tau)$ will demand $(s,t)$ equity claims and all investors $k$ for whom $(1 - \tau_B^k) < (1 - \tau_S^k)(1 - \tau)$ will demand $(s,t)$ equity claims. Investors $m$ for whom $(1 - \tau_B^m) = (1 - \tau_S^m)(1 - \tau)$ will be indifferent between $(s,t)$ equity and $(s,t)$ debt claims. This phenomenon can be referred to as a "clientele effect," with firms issuing debt attracting a different clientele than those issuing equity.

## SUGGESTED READINGS


Altman, Edward I.: Corporate Bankruptcy Potential, Stockholder Returns, and Share Valuation, *Journal of Finance,* vol. 24, pp. 887–900, December 1969.

Elton, Edwin J.: Capital Rationing and External Discount Rates, *Journal of Finance,* vol. 25, pp. 573–584, June 1970.

Haley, Charles W. and Lawrence D. Schall: A Note on Investment Policy with Imperfect Capital Markets, *Journal of Finance,* vol. 27, pp. 93–96, March 1972.

Kim, E. Han: A Mean-Variance Theory of Optimal Capital Structure and Corporate Debt Capacity, *Journal of Finance,* vol. 33, no. 1, pp. 45–64, March 1978.

Miller, Merton: Debt and Taxes, *Journal of Finance,* vol. 32, no. 2, pp. 261–276, May 1977.

Myers, Stewart C.: Interactions of Corporate Financing and Investment Decisions—Implications for Capital Budgeting, *Journal of Finance,* vol. 29, no. 1, pp. 1–25, March 1974.

———: Determinants of Corporate Borrowing, *Journal of Financial Economics,* vol. 5, November 1977.

Pye, Gordon: Present Values for Imperfect Capital Markets, *Journal of Business,* vol. 39, January 1966.

Schall, Lawrence D. Firm Financial Structure and Investment, *Journal of Financial and Quantitative Analysis,* vol. 6, no. 3, pp. 925–942, June 1971.


---

$$v_B(s,t)' = \frac{1 - \tau_B^i}{1 - \tau_S^i} v_S(s,t) \tag{c}$$

For investors $m$, i.e., if $i = m$, then (15A-8) holds and substituting (15A-8) into (*c*) we have

$$v_B(s,t)' = v_S(s,t)(1 - \tau) \tag{d}$$

That is, investors $m$ will pay up to (*d*) for an $(s,t)$ bond payment.

Scott, James H., Jr.: Bankruptcy, Secured Debt, and Optimal Capital Structure, *Journal of Finance,* vol. 32, pp. 1–19, March 1977.

Stapleton, R. C. and M. G. Subrahmanyam: Market Imperfections, Capital Market Equilibrium and Corporation Finance, *Journal of Finance,* vol. 32, pp. 307–319, May 1977.

Stiglitz, Joseph E.: Some Aspects of the Pure Theory of Corporate Finance: Bankruptcies and Takeovers, *Bell Journal of Economics and Management Science,* pp. 458–482, autumn, 1972.

Van Horne, James C.: Capital Budgeting Decisions Involving Combinations of Risky Investments, *Management Science,* vol. 13, pp. 384–393, October 1966.

Warner, Jerold B.: Bankruptcy, Absolute Priority, and the Pricing of Risky Debt Claims, *Journal of Financial Economics,* vol. 4, pp. 239–276, 1977.

Weingartner, H. Martin: Capital Rationing: *n* Authors in Search of a Plot, *Journal of Finance,* vol. 32, no. 5, pp. 1403–1432, December 1977.

CHAPTER

# SIXTEEN

# SPECIAL TOPICS: MERGERS AND LEASING

All firms are confronted with the questions of which assets to acquire (investment policy) and of how the firm should be financed (the debt-equity choice). In this chapter we examine two issues that are faced by many, but not all, firms—mergers and leasing. Merger and acquisition policy (whether to merge with, or acquire, another firm) can be viewed as both an investment problem and a financial structure problem: a merger involves adding the assets of another firm to existing assets (an investment decision) and also involves superseding the previously distinct entities with their own shares and debt outstanding with a single firm with its stocks and bonds. The first section of the chapter considers the consequences of a merger under various sets of assumptions concerning capital markets, taxes, expectations, and firm bankruptcy costs.

The second section of the chapter deals with leasing, an increasingly popular method of acquiring assets. We shall discuss both the asset market equilibrium when leasing is an alternative and the algorithm a firm uses in deciding whether or not to lease an asset.

## MERGER POLICY

In technical terms, a *merger* involves the acquisition of one firm by another, with the former company surviving (for example, $A$ acquires $B$, with $A$ surviving), whereas a *consolidation* involves two firms combining to form a new firm ($A$ and $B$ consolidate into new firm $C$). We shall refer to both these arrangements as a merger since the issues involved are essentially the same from a financial theory standpoint. We are interested here in the impact of a merger on firm cash flow, share values, bond values, and total firm values. This impact will depend on the nature of the economic system that we are assuming. We begin by stating a set of assumptions about the system and then we examine merger policy under various subsets of those assumptions. We assume throughout this chapter that investors prefer more consumption to less and that management acts in the interests of shareholders. Other assumptions that will be used are (these are the perfect-market assumptions listed on page 280):

A.1. Costless markets: No capital market transaction costs, no government constraints on transactions, and financial assets are infinitely divisible at no cost.
A.2. No personal tax biases: Either there are no personal taxes or the effective tax rates on interest, dividends, and capital gains (realized or unrealized) are equal.
A.3. Competitive markets: There are many perfect substitutes for all securities of a firm at any point in time and they can be acquired at the same market price regardless of a given firm's behavior or a given investor's behavior. This assumption implies that a firm cannot create a new type of security (one that is different from all others currently available in the market) and cannot affect the structure of interest rates in the market.
A.4. Equal access: Investors and firms can borrow, lend, and issue claims on the same terms.
A.5. Homogeneous expectations: Everyone has the same expectations.
A.6. No information costs: Firms and individuals have available the same information, and this information is acquirable at a zero cost.
A.7. No financial distress costs: Firms and individuals incur no costs of financial distress, although financial distress can occur (see Chap. 14).
A.8. Salability of tax losses: Firms and individuals can sell tax losses in the market.

## The Idealized Case

Assume A.1 to A.8. Under these assumptions, the value-additivity principle (VAP) holds.[1] An implication of the VAP is that a merger will not benefit shareholders unless there are cash-flow benefits. If the new cash flow after the merger of two (or more) firms is expected to be greater than the sum of their separate premerger cash flows, then there is a benefit from the combination. Otherwise, there is not. The point is that the justification for the merger or acquisition of firms in perfect markets *must* come from real benefits in terms of total cash-flow gains. Firm diversification per se (i.e., with no cash-flow benefits) will not benefit shareholders. This conclusion follows from value additivity. Thus, assume for firms $G$ and $H$ merging into firm $T$ that the resulting cash flow, $\tilde{\mathbf{Y}}_T$, is simply the sum of the cash flows from $G$ and $H$. We then have

$$\tilde{\mathbf{Y}}_T = \tilde{\mathbf{Y}}_G + \tilde{\mathbf{Y}}_H \tag{16-1}$$

[1] Actually, only A.1, A.2, A.4, and either A.5 or A.6 are required for the VAP.

$\tilde{\mathbf{Y}}$ in general is defined as

$$\tilde{\mathbf{Y}} = \tilde{\mathbf{X}} - \mathbf{I} - \tau(\tilde{\mathbf{X}} - \widetilde{\mathbf{DP}} - \tilde{\mathbf{R}}) \tag{16-2}$$

where $\tilde{\mathbf{X}}$, $\tilde{\mathbf{I}}$, $\tau$, $\widetilde{\mathbf{DP}}$, and $\tilde{\mathbf{R}}$ are cash income less expenses, cash investment, the corporate tax rate, depreciation for tax purposes, and interest payments, respectively. Using (16-1) and the VAP, it follows that

$$V_T = V_G + V_H \tag{16-3}$$

The cash-flow streams ($\tilde{\mathbf{Y}}_T$, $\tilde{\mathbf{Y}}_G$, and $\tilde{\mathbf{Y}}_H$) defined by (16-2) are those received by investors in the market and, with taxes, are the net of firm-tax cash flow. Notice that (16-3) holds regardless of the stochastic relationship of $\tilde{\mathbf{Y}}_G$ and $\tilde{\mathbf{Y}}_H$ provided (16-1) is true. For example, $\tilde{\mathbf{Y}}_G$ and $\tilde{\mathbf{Y}}_H$ may be highly negatively correlated, resulting in a much lower variance for $\tilde{\mathbf{Y}}_T$ than was true for either of $\tilde{\mathbf{Y}}_G$ and $\tilde{\mathbf{Y}}_H$. The reduction in variance does not matter—there is still no net benefit from the merger. A benefit would arise only if $V_T > (V_G + V_H)$, the benefit equaling $V_T = (V_G + V_H)$. Equation (16-3) indicates that this benefit is zero if (16-1) holds. Diversification effects are therefore irrelevant in determining the desirability of a merger.[2]

Diversification considerations should also be ignored if a merger involves real economies. Only the real economies are significant. For example, assume that firms $G$ and $H$ merge into firm $T$ and that, because of production economies, the cash flow generated by the new firm exceeds the sum of the cash flows that would have been generated by firms $G$ and $H$ had they not merged. That is, assume that

$$\tilde{\mathbf{Y}}_T = \tilde{\mathbf{Y}}_G + \tilde{\mathbf{Y}}_H + \tilde{\mathbf{Y}}_M \tag{16-4}$$

where, using (16-2), and signifying the benefit stream as $\tilde{\mathbf{Y}}_M$,

$$\begin{aligned}
\tilde{\mathbf{Y}}_M &= \tilde{\mathbf{Y}}_T - \tilde{\mathbf{Y}}_G - \tilde{\mathbf{Y}}_H \\
&= [\tilde{\mathbf{X}}_T - \tilde{\mathbf{I}}_T - \tau(\tilde{\mathbf{X}}_T - \widetilde{\mathbf{DP}}_T - \tilde{\mathbf{R}}_T)] \\
&\qquad - [\tilde{\mathbf{X}}_G - \tilde{\mathbf{I}}_G - \tau(\tilde{\mathbf{X}}_T - \widetilde{\mathbf{DP}}_G - \tilde{\mathbf{R}}_G)] \\
&\qquad\qquad - [\tilde{\mathbf{X}}_H - \tilde{\mathbf{I}}_H - \tau(\tilde{\mathbf{X}}_H - \widetilde{\mathbf{DP}}_H - \tilde{\mathbf{R}}_H)] \\
&= (1 - \tau)(\tilde{\mathbf{X}}_T - \tilde{\mathbf{X}}_G - \tilde{\mathbf{X}}_H) - (\tilde{\mathbf{I}}_T - \tilde{\mathbf{I}}_G - \tilde{\mathbf{I}}_H) \\
&\qquad + \tau(\widetilde{\mathbf{DP}}_T - \widetilde{\mathbf{DP}}_G - \widetilde{\mathbf{DP}}_H) + \tau(\tilde{\mathbf{R}}_T - \tilde{\mathbf{R}}_G - \tilde{\mathbf{R}}_H)
\end{aligned} \tag{16-5}$$

If a merger results in an $\tilde{\mathbf{X}}_T = \tilde{\mathbf{X}}_G + \tilde{\mathbf{X}}_H$, $\tilde{\mathbf{I}}_T = \tilde{\mathbf{I}}_G + \tilde{\mathbf{I}}_H$, and $\widetilde{\mathbf{DP}}_T = \widetilde{\mathbf{DP}}_G + \widetilde{\mathbf{DP}}_H$, i.e., if there are no changes in operations, then under present assumptions A.1 to A.8, $\tilde{\mathbf{R}}_T = \tilde{\mathbf{R}}_G + \tilde{\mathbf{R}}_H$ and, using (16-5), $\tilde{\mathbf{Y}}_M = 0$.[3] In this case there are no benefits from the merger. But a merger can also lead to a $\tilde{\mathbf{Y}}_M > 0$, i.e., to

[2] See the merger example at the end of the text discussion of the value-addivity principle in Chap. 9, p. 207.

[3] Recall from Chap. 11 that the firm will, under assumptions A.1 to A.8, be financed virtually entirely with debt. If the merger does not change total $\tilde{\mathbf{X}}$, $\tilde{\mathbf{I}}$, or $\widetilde{\mathbf{DP}}$ in each period, then the firms will have the same total debt capacity whether or not merged and will be virtually financed 100% with debt. This implies that $\tilde{\mathbf{R}}_T = \tilde{\mathbf{R}}_G + \tilde{\mathbf{R}}_H$.

"synergies." Such synergies could result from production cost reductions, a more effective sales program, an improved market position (for example, the gaining of an oligopolistic or monopolistic position in the firm's product market), or lower costs of financial management of the company. We refer to these benefits as "operating synergies" because they directly affect the operating terms in (16-5)—$\tilde{\mathbf{X}}$, $\tilde{\mathbf{I}}$, and $\widetilde{\mathbf{DP}}$—rather than financing methods or costs [in (16-5), represented by $\tilde{\mathbf{R}}$]. Thus, in (16-5), $\tilde{\mathbf{Y}}_M > 0$ could occur because $\tilde{\mathbf{X}}_T > \tilde{\mathbf{X}}_G + \tilde{\mathbf{X}}_H$ if firm $T$ produces the products more cheaply (lower expenses) or sells the product more effectively (higher revenues); or because $\tilde{\mathbf{I}}_T < \tilde{\mathbf{I}}_G + \tilde{\mathbf{I}}_H$ if firm $T$ can acquire capital equipment more cheaply. It might also be that $\tilde{\mathbf{X}}_T > \tilde{\mathbf{X}}_G + \tilde{\mathbf{X}}_H$ and $\tilde{\mathbf{I}}_T > \tilde{\mathbf{I}}_G + \tilde{\mathbf{I}}_H$ with $\tilde{\mathbf{Y}}_M > 0$ because the merged firm $T$ will embark on a capital expansion program that will raise $\tilde{\mathbf{X}}$ more than it raises $\tilde{\mathbf{I}}$ (highly profitable investment); in this case firm $T$ will be larger than the total of firms $G$ and $H$, will have more debt, and therefore $\tilde{\mathbf{R}}_T > \tilde{\mathbf{R}}_G + \tilde{\mathbf{R}}_H$.

With $\tilde{\mathbf{Y}}_M > 0$ in (16-4) and (16-5) it follows using the VAP that

$$V_T = V_G + V_H + V_M \tag{16-6}$$

The benefit from the merger equals $V_T - (V_G + V_H) = V_M$ from (16-6). Quantity $V_M$ is the value that stream $\tilde{\mathbf{Y}}_M$ would have as an individual stream in the market.[4] This value is completely unrelated to the stochastic relationship of $\tilde{\mathbf{Y}}_M$ to $\tilde{\mathbf{Y}}_G$ or to $\tilde{\mathbf{Y}}_H$ and is unrelated to the stochastic relationship of $\tilde{\mathbf{Y}}_G$ to $\tilde{\mathbf{Y}}_H$. That is, the added value or benefit $V_M$ depends *only* upon how the market would value a stream of the distribution of $\tilde{\mathbf{Y}}_M$. This point is made particularly clear if one notes that if firm $G$ were to merge with firm $K$ to form firm $S$ (rather than to merge with firm $H$ to form firm $T$ as above), and if the incremental cash flow were $\tilde{\mathbf{Y}}_M$ as with a merger of $G$ with $H$, the benefit from the merger would be the same even though $\tilde{\mathbf{Y}}_H$ and $\tilde{\mathbf{Y}}_K$ have completely different distributions. That is, if

$$\tilde{\mathbf{Y}}_S = \tilde{\mathbf{Y}}_G + \tilde{\mathbf{Y}}_K + \tilde{\mathbf{Y}}_M \tag{16-7}$$

then, by the VAP

$$V_S = V_G + V_K + V_M \tag{16-8}$$

and the benefit from the merger is the same as before, that is, equals $V_S - (V_G + V_K) = V_M$. Thus $V_M$ is still the net gain from the merger since this gain depends not upon any of the stochastic relationships but only upon the distribution of $\tilde{\mathbf{Y}}_M$.

[4] The condition $\tilde{\mathbf{Y}}_M > 0$ on vector $\tilde{\mathbf{Y}}_M$ means that $\tilde{Y}_{Mt} \geq 0$ for all $t$ and $\tilde{Y}_{Mt} > 0$ for some $t$. The condition $\tilde{\mathbf{Y}}_M > 0$ is sufficient but not necessary for $V_M > 0$, that is, for benefits. As with any cash-flow stream, a positive market value does not require that the stream have a zero probability of a negative level in all periods. For $V_M > 0$, the stream need only have a sufficiently high probability of various positive magnitudes in some or all future periods. Note also that if there are disbenefits from a merger, i.e., if many or all the elements of $\tilde{\mathbf{Y}}_M$ are negative, then $V_M < 0$. Value $V_M$ would then equal the amount one would have to pay other investors to assume ownership of $\tilde{\mathbf{Y}}_M$, that is, to assume the obligations to meet the outflows represented by a negative $\tilde{\mathbf{Y}}_M$.

## Financial Distress Costs and Merger Benefits

Let us now drop assumption A.7 and assume the presence of financial distress costs. We continue to assume A.1 to A.6 and A.8. The VAP still holds as in the previous section. Except for (16-2) and (16-5), relations (16-1) to (16-8) still apply. With financial distress costs, $\tilde{\mathbf{F}}$, (16-9) replaces (16-2), and (16-10) replaces (16-5). A merger can affect cash flow by altering the magnitude or probability of financial distress costs. To see how this can happen, let us look at $\tilde{\mathbf{Y}}$, the total cash flow to the firm's security holders:

$$\tilde{\mathbf{Y}} = \tilde{\mathbf{X}} - \tilde{\mathbf{I}} - \tilde{\mathbf{F}} - \tau(\tilde{\mathbf{X}} - \widetilde{\mathbf{DP}} - \tilde{\mathbf{R}} - \tilde{\mathbf{F}}) \tag{16-9}$$

where $\tilde{\mathbf{X}}$, $\tilde{\mathbf{I}}$, $\tilde{\mathbf{R}}$, and $\widetilde{\mathbf{DP}}$ were defined earlier and $\tilde{\mathbf{F}}$ is costs of financial distress. $\tilde{\mathbf{F}}$ includes accounting and legal fees and any business disruption costs due to conditions of financial distress as discussed in Chap. 14.

A merger can reduce expected total $\tilde{\mathbf{F}}$ by reducing the uncertainty of total firm cash flow (because the merger involves diversification). Thus for any given total debt (i.e., total amount of promised payments to creditors in each period), there is less chance of financial distress. The result is lower expected financial distress costs (a smaller expected $\tilde{\mathbf{F}}$) and a larger expected $\tilde{\mathbf{Y}}$ in (16-9).[5]

If the merger reduces the variability (uncertainty) of firm cash flow, the newly merged firm may wish to raise its total debt above the total debt of the unmerged firms before the merger because of the reduced risk of financial distress; this greater debt will raise $\tilde{\mathbf{R}}$ and lower corporate taxes. Of course, this will raise expected $\tilde{\mathbf{F}}$ above the level the merged firm would have if it kept the total debt at the premerger level. The merged firm will set its debt at that level which maximizes firm value, and this level of debt will often be higher than the total debt of the premerger firms.[6]

We can represent the above discussion in terms of Eq. (16-9). Assume that firms $A$ and $B$ merge into firm $C$. The net gain from operating synergies, reduced financial distress costs, and reduced corporate taxes if leverage is increased above the premerger level (increase in $\tilde{\mathbf{R}}$) can be shown as follows:

$$\begin{aligned}
\tilde{\mathbf{Y}}_M = \tilde{\mathbf{Y}}_C - \tilde{\mathbf{Y}}_A - \tilde{\mathbf{Y}}_B &= [\tilde{\mathbf{X}}_C - \tilde{\mathbf{I}}_C - \tilde{\mathbf{F}}_C - \tau(\tilde{\mathbf{X}}_C - \widetilde{\mathbf{DP}}_C - \tilde{\mathbf{R}}_C - \tilde{\mathbf{F}}_C)] \\
&\quad - [\tilde{\mathbf{X}}_A - \tilde{\mathbf{I}}_A - \tilde{\mathbf{F}}_A - \tau(\tilde{\mathbf{X}}_A - \widetilde{\mathbf{DP}}_A - \tilde{\mathbf{R}}_A - \tilde{\mathbf{F}}_A)] \\
&\quad - [\tilde{\mathbf{X}}_B - \tilde{\mathbf{I}}_B - \tilde{\mathbf{F}}_B - \tau(\tilde{\mathbf{X}}_B - \widetilde{\mathbf{DP}}_B - \tilde{\mathbf{R}}_B - \tilde{\mathbf{F}}_B)] \\
&= (1 - \tau)(\tilde{\mathbf{X}}_C - \tilde{\mathbf{X}}_A - \tilde{\mathbf{X}}_B) - (\tilde{\mathbf{I}}_C - \tilde{\mathbf{I}}_A - \tilde{\mathbf{I}}_B) \\
&\quad + \tau(\widetilde{\mathbf{DP}}_C - \widetilde{\mathbf{DP}}_A - \widetilde{\mathbf{DP}}_B) + \tau(\tilde{\mathbf{R}}_C - \tilde{\mathbf{R}}_A - \tilde{\mathbf{R}}_B) \\
&\quad + (1 - \tau)(\tilde{\mathbf{F}}_A + \tilde{\mathbf{F}}_B - \tilde{\mathbf{F}}_C)
\end{aligned} \tag{16-10}$$

[5] Expected financial distress costs = [probability of financial distress] × [financial distress costs] ≡ [P(F)][F]. Merger reduces P(F) by diversification, i.e., by lowering the variability of firm cash flows when the cash flows of the merged firms are not perfectly correlated. For a more complete discussion of bankruptcy costs and mergers, see Higgins and Schall, Corporate Bankruptcy and Conglomerate Merger, noted in the Suggested Readings at the end of this chapter.

[6] Given assumptions A.1 to A.6 and A.8, the only reason to be less than 100% debt financed is the existence of financial distress costs or the nondeductibility of interest for tax purposes of interest beyond some level.

Table 16-1 illustrates a very simple one-period case in which the merger of firms $A$ and $B$ into firm $C$ results in a decline in the uncertainty (variance) of $\tilde{\mathbf{X}}$. The result is that the postmerger firm $C$ has less probability of financial distress than had either of premerger firms $A$ and $B$ assuming that firm $C$ has promised debt payments equal to the sum of the debt payments of firms $A$ and $B$. This will normally imply lower expected financial distress costs with merger.[7] Firm $C$ may want to expand its debt above the total premerger level to increase its interest tax shield advantage.

## The Deductibility of Tax Losses

There is another benefit that can arise from merger if we drop assumption A.8 and instead assume the nonsalability of tax losses.[8] This is so regardless of which of assumptions A.1 to A.7 we retain. If losses are not salable in the market, then a merger allows a firm with substantial losses to benefit immediately from the loss (by canceling the loss against the profits of a profitable firm with which the losing firm has merged). A business loss can be carried back 3 years or forward 7 years.[9] The amount of a current period loss that can be carried back for immediate tax credits is limited to the taxable income earned (if any) in the previous 3 years. If previous taxable income is less than the current loss, part (or all) of the loss must be carried forward (which means waiting for

[7] Reduction of variance of $\tilde{\mathbf{X}}$ will reduce financial distress risk for any level of debt if the distribution of $\tilde{\mathbf{X}}$ is symmetrical. Also, it is not necessary that the merger reduce the variance of total cash flow below that of either merger partner for the probability of financial distress to decline for a given level of total debt. Diversification can occur even if the correlation coefficient of $\tilde{\mathbf{X}}_A$ and $\tilde{\mathbf{X}}_B$ (or the covariance of $\tilde{\mathbf{X}}_A$ and $\tilde{\mathbf{X}}_B$) is positive.

[8] Note that eqs. (16-2) and (16-5) assume that tax losses produce an immediate tax rebate in amount $\tau(\tilde{\mathbf{X}} - \widetilde{\mathbf{DP}} - \tilde{\mathbf{R}})$, where $(\tilde{\mathbf{X}} - \widetilde{\mathbf{DP}} - \tilde{\mathbf{R}})$ is the tax loss [and, in Eqs. (16-9) and (16-10), the tax loss of $(\tilde{\mathbf{X}} - \widetilde{\mathbf{DP}} - \tilde{\mathbf{R}} - \tilde{\mathbf{F}})$ produces an immediate rebate of $\tau(\tilde{\mathbf{X}} - \widetilde{\mathbf{DP}} - \tilde{\mathbf{R}} - \tilde{\mathbf{F}})$]. That is, eqs. (16-2), (16-5), (16-9), and (16-10) assume A.8.

[9] See discussion of tax carry-forwards and tax carry-backs on p. 427.

**table 16-1 Effect of Merger on the Distribution of $\tilde{X}$**

*Assumptions:*

$\tilde{I} = \widetilde{DP} = 0$

$\tilde{Y} = \tilde{X} - \tilde{F} - \tau(\tilde{X} - \tilde{R} - \tilde{F})$

Firms $A$ and $B$ are merged into firm $C$

| *Firm A* | *Firm B* | *Firm C* |
|---|---|---|
| $E[\tilde{X}_A] = 100$ | $E[\tilde{X}_B] = 80$ | $E[\tilde{X}_C] = 180$ |
| $\text{var}[\tilde{X}_A] = 64$ | $\text{var}[\tilde{X}_B] = 50$ | $\text{var}[\tilde{X}_C] = 44^a$ |
| $\text{cov}[\tilde{X}_A,\tilde{X}_B] = -35$ | | |

[a] $\text{var}[\tilde{X}_C] = \text{var}[\tilde{X}_A] + \text{var}[\tilde{X}_B] + 2\,\text{cov}[\tilde{X}_A,\tilde{X}_B] = 64 + 50 - 70 = 44.$

the tax benefit, implying a lower present value of the tax benefit). If the losses continue for 7 more years or if they exceed the income generated in those years, some of the losses produce no tax benefits at all.[10] If tax losses were salable, the losing firm could always sell a loss in the year incurred for the benefit it produces to the buyers of the loss. But we are assuming now that tax loss sales are not possible, and that an ongoing firm can gain a tax benefit from a loss only by carrying it back or forward or by merging. By merging a losing firm with a profitable firm, the losses of the former each year are canceled against that year's profits of the more profitable merger partner, producing an immediate tax benefit; the benefit is the reduced taxes paid by the profitable firm.

It should be noted that we have discussed only one aspect of business taxation, one that can produce benefits from the merger. Other tax effects may make a merger undesirable; i.e., the merger could produce a tax disadvantage rather than a benefit by increasing the marginal tax rate on firm income, for example.

The tax benefit (or loss) from a merger should be included with the other merger benefits to produce a $\tilde{\mathbf{Y}}_M$ that incorporates all merger gains. We then use Eqs. (16-7) and (16-8) to determine $V_M$, the value of the merger gain. The merger should be consummated only if $V_M$ is positive.

## Share Values, Bond Values, and Merger Benefits[11]

We now examine the impact of the merger of two firms, one or both of which have outstanding risky debt before the merger. The primary point of this section is that firms that merge should always retire risky premerger debt before the merger occurs if they can retire the debt by paying it off at the premerger market price of the debt (retiring the debt "without penalty").[12] The reason is that *not* retiring debt means that the merger will result in a windfall gain to bondholders and an equal windfall loss to shareholders because the merger improves the risk position and returns of the outstanding bonds and diminishes the returns to shareholders. That is, the total value (shares plus bonds) of the firms is the same with or without the merger, but unless the premerger bonds are retired before the merger, the value of the firms' shares will generally fall and the value of firms' bonds rises with merger. This occurs if the merger of firms produces a cash-flow diversification effect which lowers the chance that the

[10] For example, if the firm loses \$1 million per year for 10 years (in years 1 to 10), the losses in years 4 and 5 cannot be carried forward or back. Or, if a firm loses \$1 million in 1980 and has profits in years 1977 to 1979 and in 1981 to 1985 which total less than \$1 million, some of the 1980 loss will produce no tax benefits.

[11] This section is based on Higgins and Schall, Corporate Bankruptcy and Conglomerate Merger, listed in the Suggested Readings at the end of this chapter.

[12] See the next footnote.

firm will not have sufficient resources to meet debt obligations. The result will be a windfall gain to bondholders that can be avoided only if the premerger bonds are retired before the merger.

To explain the concept, assume A.1, A.2, and A.4 to A.8; we drop A.3. Without A.3, the merging firms may not be able to buy up the premerger debt at its market price; we also assume that the firm cannot call the debt at its market price and therefore the premerger debt can be retired before the merger only at a price above the debt's premerger market value (at a penalty).[13] We shall assume

[13] As discussed in chap. 17, without A.3, maximizing firm value and maximizing share value may be inconsistent objectives, and, indeed, market value maximization and utility maximization may not be consistent. The purpose of the present discussion is to show that merger can raise bond values and lower share values even though firm value ($S + B$) is unchanged; this can lower shareholder utility. To see how this can arise, assume firms $i = 1, \ldots, n$ merge into firm $T$. Retiring the premerger debt without penalty here means retirement at a price no greater than the premerger market value of the bonds, $\Sigma_{i=1}^{n} B_i$. With assumption A.3, this is always possible (since A.3 implies that markets are competitive and no firm can affect the price of any type of security). But, by dropping A.3, the firm may have to pay more than the current market price for the bonds. If the firm pays $\Sigma_{i=1}^{n} B_i$ for the bonds (using firm cash, or, for example, a short-term bank loan), merges, and then resissues new bonds in amount $B_T = \Sigma_{i=1}^{n} B_i$, we find the change in shareholder wealth $\Delta W$ is zero, since (defining $S$ and $V$ as share values and total firm value, where $V = S + B$)

$$
\begin{aligned}
\Delta W = \Delta S &= S_T - \sum_{i=1}^{n} S_i \\
&= [V_T - B_T] - \left[\sum_{i=1}^{n} V_i - \sum_{i=1}^{n} B_i\right] \\
&= \left[V_T - \sum_{i=1}^{n} V_i\right] - \left[B_T - \sum_{i=1}^{n} B_i\right] \\
&= 0 - 0 = 0
\end{aligned}
$$

If the bond market price is below call price, purchase by the firm of its debt will generally involve an average price above market price. This is so since market price is determined by the marginal seller, and only in the unlikely case of an infinitely elastic reserve demand schedule for the bonds, i.e., if all bondholders are willing to sell at the same price, will no payment above market price be required in repurchasing the bonds. It follows, using an argument similar to that above, that if $\Sigma_{i=1}^{m} B_i + P$ (capital) is paid for the old debt, where $P$ is a premium, then $P$ must come from issuing new shares or curtailing dividends (assuming $B_T = \Sigma B_i$) and

$$
\begin{aligned}
\Delta W = \Delta S - P = S_T &- \sum_{i=1}^{n} S_i - P \\
&= \left[V_T - \sum_{i=1}^{n} V_i\right] - \left[B_T - \sum_{i=1}^{n} B_i\right] - P \\
&= 0 - 0 - P = -P
\end{aligned}
$$

If $P$ is deductible for corporate tax purposes, then $\Delta W = -(1 - \tau)P$. $P$ is deductible to the extent that the price paid for the bonds exceeds the bonds' adjusted book value (face value plus unamortized premium or less unamortized discount).

that there are no corporate taxes ($\tau = 0$), that $\tilde{\mathbf{I}} = \tilde{\mathbf{F}} = 0$, and that the merger of firms $G$ and $H$ into firm $K$ is *nonsynergistic* (a "conglomerate merger," i.e., $\tilde{\mathbf{Y}}_M = 0$). Thus,

$$\tilde{\mathbf{X}}_K = \tilde{\mathbf{X}}_G + \tilde{\mathbf{X}}_H \tag{16-11}$$

In this simple case, the total cash flow to bondholders and to stockholders is $\tilde{\mathbf{Y}} = \tilde{\mathbf{X}}$, $\tilde{\mathbf{Y}} = \tilde{\mathbf{Y}}^S + \tilde{\mathbf{Y}}^B$, defining $\tilde{\mathbf{Y}}^S$ and $\tilde{\mathbf{Y}}^B$ as payments to the stockholders and bondholders. Assume also that when the firm merges, the old bonds of firm $G$ and firm $H$ remain outstanding because the firms find it too expensive to retire the bonds.[14] Thus, using (16-11)

$$\tilde{\mathbf{Y}}_K = \tilde{\mathbf{Y}}_G + \tilde{\mathbf{Y}}_H = (\tilde{\mathbf{Y}}_G^S + \tilde{\mathbf{Y}}_G^B) + (\tilde{\mathbf{Y}}_H^S + \tilde{\mathbf{Y}}_H^B) \tag{16-12}$$

Equation (16-12) states that the total return of the firm is unaffected by the merger. Using the VAP, it follows using (16-12) that

$$V_K = V_G + V_H = (S_G + B_G) + (S_H + B_H) \tag{16-13}$$

Equation (16-13) states that the value of firm $K$, $V_K$, must equal the sum of the values of firms $G$ and $H$ since, by (16-12), the total returns of firm $K$ ($\tilde{\mathbf{Y}}_K$) equal the total returns of firms $G$ and $H$ ($\tilde{\mathbf{Y}}_G + \tilde{\mathbf{Y}}_H$). But it is important to note that we have said *nothing* about the relative magnitudes of $\tilde{\mathbf{Y}}_K^S$ and ($\tilde{\mathbf{Y}}_G^S + \tilde{\mathbf{Y}}_H^S$) or of $\tilde{\mathbf{Y}}_K^B$ and ($\tilde{\mathbf{Y}}_G^B + \tilde{\mathbf{Y}}_H^B$); and therefore we have said nothing about the relative magnitudes of $S_K$ and ($S_G + S_H$) or of $B_K$ and ($B_G + B_H$). We only know from (16-13) that *in the aggregate* bondholders and stockholders *combined* are no better and no worse off (total market value $V$ of these holdings are unchanged) as a consequence of the merger. We do not yet know whether shareholders alone are better or worse off (i.e., whether $S_K$ exceeds, equals, or is less than $S_G + S_H$), or if bondholders alone are better or worse off (i.e., whether $B_K$ exceeds, equals, or is less than $B_G + B_H$). As we shall see, bondholders are almost certainly better off ($B_K > B_G + B_H$), and shareholders almost certainly worse off ($S_K < S_G + S_H$). The explanation for this is based on the concept of corporate "coinsurance." As long as the income streams of the premerger firms imply that one firm can become insolvent (and bankrupt) when the other firm has a positive equity position, merger will produce a corporate coinsurance effect. If the firms are separate, the creditors of the bankrupt firm will sustain a loss. However, if the two firms are merged, the cash flows of the solvent firm which are in excess of its own debt needs are available to service the debt requirement of the other firm. The merged firms thus provide each other with a form of corporate coinsurance which reduces the bankruptcy risk to the creditors of the merged firm. As a result, bond prices will rise with merger, and since the coinsurance is in effect provided by the equity shareholders, stock prices will fall.

[14] That is, firm $G$ must pay significantly more than $B_G$ for its bonds and firm $H$ must pay significantly more than $B_H$ for its bonds. This can occur if the firm must pay more than the market price to induce some of the bondholders to sell their bonds and if the call price on the bonds is significantly above market price. See the preceding footnote.

To clarify the above points, assume first the firms' premerger bonds are not retired and therefore remain outstanding after merger. Assume that promised interest and principal on debt is the same before and after merger; that is, assume $\hat{\mathbf{Y}}_K^B = \hat{\mathbf{Y}}_G^B + \hat{\mathbf{Y}}_H^B$, where $\hat{\mathbf{Y}}^B$ is the promised payment on the debt. We define $\tilde{\mathbf{Y}}_i^B$ as the actual payment (not promised payment) on the debt; if $\tilde{Y}_{it}^B < \hat{Y}_{it}^B$ for firm i in any period $t$, there is default on the debt.

By reducing bankruptcy risk, merger can produce a superior bond stream if the total promised debt stream $\hat{\mathbf{Y}}^B$ is the same after merger as it was before. That is, for a conglomerate merger of firms $G$ and $H$ into firm $K$, it is easily shown that, if $\hat{\mathbf{Y}}_K^B = \hat{\mathbf{Y}}_G^B + \hat{\mathbf{Y}}_H^B$, then

$$\tilde{\mathbf{Y}}_K^B \geq \tilde{\mathbf{Y}}_G^B + \tilde{\mathbf{Y}}_H^B \qquad \text{for all possible outcomes of } \tilde{\mathbf{X}}_K, \tilde{\mathbf{X}}_G \text{ and } \tilde{\mathbf{X}}_H \text{ with the inequality for one or more possible outcomes of } \tilde{\mathbf{X}}_K, \tilde{\mathbf{X}}_G, \text{ and } \tilde{\mathbf{X}}_H \tag{16-14}$$

Relation (16-14) follows if, without merger, it is possible that firm i suffers insolvency and default in some period ($\tilde{Y}_{it}^B < \hat{Y}_{it}^B$) and firm $j$ has a positive equity position in the same period, any i, $j = G$ or $H$, i $\neq j$.[15] As will be illustrated later using an example, this is so because of the diversification effect on firm returns which results in a greater probability that a given level of debt obligation will be met (the corporate coinsurance effects noted earlier). However, since stockholder returns $\tilde{\mathbf{Y}}^S$ equal total firm returns $\tilde{\mathbf{Y}}$ less bond returns $\tilde{\mathbf{Y}}^B$, substituting relation (16-14) into Eq. (16-12), it follows that

$$\tilde{\mathbf{Y}}_K^S \leq \tilde{\mathbf{Y}}_G^S + \tilde{\mathbf{Y}}_H^S \qquad \text{for all possible outcomes of } \tilde{\mathbf{X}}_K, \tilde{\mathbf{X}}_G \text{ and } \tilde{\mathbf{X}}_H\text{, with the inequality for one or more possible outcomes of } \tilde{\mathbf{X}}_K, \tilde{\mathbf{X}}_G, \text{ and } \tilde{\mathbf{X}}_H \tag{16-15}$$

Relations (16-14) and (16-15) state that the premerger distribution of stock payments must dominate the postmerger distribution of stock payments if postmerger bond payments statistically dominate premerger bond payments.[16] This implies that in perfect markets bond values will rise due to the merger and stock values will fall.[17] Since by Eq. (16-13) total firm value (stock plus bonds) is unaffected by the merger, the fall in share values equals the rise in bond values.

Using (16-14) and (16-15), the VAP implies that[18]

$$B_K > B_G + B_H \tag{16-16}$$

[15] Relation (16-14) means that $\tilde{Y}_{Kt}^B \geq \tilde{Y}_{Gt}^B + \tilde{Y}_{Ht}^B$ for all $t$ and for all states of the world with the inequality for some states of the world in some $t$. That is, $\tilde{Y}_{Kt}^B$ is never less than, and, in some $t$, can exceed $\tilde{Y}_{Gt}^B + \tilde{Y}_{Ht}^B$.

[16] Relation (16-15) means that $\tilde{Y}_{Kt}^S \leq \tilde{Y}_{Gt}^S + \tilde{Y}_{Ht}^S$ for all $t$ and for all states of the world with the inequality for some $t$ and some states of the world. That is, $\tilde{Y}_{Kt}^S$ never exceeds and, in some $t$, can be less than $\tilde{Y}_{Gt}^S + \tilde{Y}_{Ht}^S$.

[17] The VAP implies that, with perfect markets, statistical dominance produces greater value. That is, if $\tilde{\mathbf{Y}}_A = \tilde{\mathbf{Y}}_B + \tilde{\mathbf{Y}}_Q \geq \tilde{\mathbf{Y}}_B$, with the inequality for some set of states and time periods, then by the VAP it follows that $V_A = V_B + V_Q$ where the value of $\tilde{\mathbf{Y}}_Q$ is $V_Q$ and $V_Q > 0$.

[18] See the preceding footnote.

and

$$S_K < S_G + S_H \tag{16-17}$$

Thus, by (16-17), shareholders suffer a loss due to the merger.

The only way shareholders can avoid this windfall loss is to call or purchase all the outstanding debt of the unmerged firms without penalty before the merger. New debt can then be issued for the merged firm. Since this new debt will reflect the reduced bankruptcy risk to creditors, it should carry a lower interest rate, and thereby increase the income stream to equity. If in this manner the shareholders are successful in eliminating the windfall gain to creditors, shareholders will be unaffected by conglomerate merger.[19]

If the bonds outstanding before merger are called with prepayment penalty $P$, then shareholders are worse off and bondholder wealth is enhanced by the amount $P$.[20] Thus, if existing debt cannot be called or cannot be called without penalty, the implication for share price maximizing firms is apparent. In the absence of corporate taxes and bankruptcy costs, conglomerate merger can only reduce equity values.

The question arises as to whether the decline in the share values really means that shareholders are worse off; i.e., is share value a proper measure of shareholder utility or welfare?[21] The answer is that the merger results in a necessarily inferior stream for shareholders in the sense that $(\tilde{\mathbf{Y}}_G^S + \tilde{\mathbf{Y}}_H^S)$ *completely dominates* $\tilde{\mathbf{Y}}_K^S$, which means that the shareholders' returns in *all* cases are no greater—and in some cases are less—after the merger than before. The VAP ensures that the dominant stream $(\tilde{\mathbf{Y}}_G + \tilde{\mathbf{Y}}_H)$ is worth more. In addition, the assumptions of this section ensure that investors prefer the dominant stream because the dominant stream provides no less consumption in all states and periods and more consumption in some states and periods.

In the above discussion we did not show why relation (16-14) holds but simply said that it does, leaving an explanation of why for later. We shall now use a single-period illustration to show how a completely dominant stream for bondholders arises as a result of the merger and why the premerger stock stream completely dominates the postmerger stock stream. To show why bond income improves and stock income suffers as a consequence of the merger,

[19] Unfortunately for shareholders, with bondholder knowledge of the possible merger and its coinsurance effects, the market value of the bonds will rise before the merger unless the firm can call the bonds at their before-merger announcement value. In the discussion of this section, when we refer to premerger value we mean before the merger announcement.

[20] See the footnote on p. 449 on the prepayment penalty.

[21] See chap. 17 on the use of share values as a measure of shareholder welfare. In this section on share values, bond values, and merger benefits, we have dropped A.3, and therefore we are *not* assuming conditions that are sufficient to imply in general that market value and utility are always positively related; i.e., current share value maximization and shareholder utility maximization are not always consistent goals. However, the assumption that investors prefer an income stream that provides more income in some periods and no less in all others is sufficient to ensure that a *dominant stream* is preferred (and is worth more by the VAP).

consider a one-period world in which firms i, i = 1,2, each raise $B_i$ of debt and $S_i$ of equity at the start of the period and invest the funds to earn a random return at the end of the period. Assume that the face value of this debt, $\hat{B}_i$, equals the market value, $B_i$. Defining $\tilde{Y}_i$, $\tilde{Y}_i^B$, and $\tilde{Y}_i^S$ as total end of period cash flow to the firm, to bondholders, and to stockholders, respectively, bankruptcy occurs in this single-period world whenever the firm's end-of-period cash flow is insufficient to meet its interest and principal obligations; that is, whenever $\tilde{Y}_i < \hat{B}_i(1 + r_i)$, where $r_i$ is the contractual (coupon) interest rate on the bonds. Assuming the information given in Table 16-2, the contractual cash flow promised the creditors of firm 1 is $B_1(1 + r_1) = 110$. Since $\tilde{Y}_i = 80$, firm 1 alone (unmerged) is bankrupt. However, since $B_2(1 + r_2) = 220$ and $\tilde{Y}_2 = 330$, firm 2 has a cash flow in excess of its debt service needs. As separate firms, this excess goes to the shareholders of firm 2; however, if the firms are merged, 30 of the excess goes to the bondholders of firm 1. Because of the coinsurance effect just illustrated, promised bond payments are less risky, bonds will rise in value with merger, and the stock will decline in value. But, since $\tilde{Y}_T = \tilde{Y}_1 + \tilde{Y}_2$, the VAP still guarantees that total firm value will be unaffected by the merger under perfect-market assumptions; i.e., $V_T = V_1 + V_2 = 200 + 400 = 600$, where firm value $V = S + B$.

The above discussion and illustration assumed that corporate taxes are zero. If corporate taxes were introduced, no change in the main conclusions would result.[22] To summarize these conclusions, we have shown that if the merged firms do not retire their premerger *risky debt,* then the merger will result in an increase in the wealth of the bondholders due to the debt coinsurance effect discussed above and a corresponding loss to shareholders. It therefore behooves the firm to retire the premerger debt if this can be done without penalty (i.e., without paying more than the premerger market price of the debt). If the premerger debt remains outstanding and there are no synergistic benefits (production synergies, reduced bankruptcy costs, tax savings) from the merger, shareholder wealth will fall and firm value will remain unchanged by the

[22] See Higgins and Schall, *op. cit.,* for a discussion of the tax case. Higgins and Schall show in their appendix that if the firm's objective is to minimize corporate taxes, then except under very unusual circumstances (if the firm's total assets at the time of a bankruptcy are not even worth as much as one period's interest payments on firm debt) the firm will not default on its interest payments but may default on its principal payments to creditors; this implies that corporate taxes and total after-tax cash flow paid by the firm to investors (shareholders and creditors) are the same with and without bankruptcy (assuming zero bankruptcy costs). If it were assumed that the firm did not seek to minimize corporate taxes or that firm assets could be less than interest or debt at the time of default, then the total cash flow from bankruptcy could be greater with merger than without, since merger would (via corporate coinsurance) ordinarily raise the expected level of interest payments. The probability that default on firm debt will occur only after firm assets were reduced to less than the interest due in a single period is ordinarily insignificant; therefore, if corporate-tax minimization is sought by the firm (i.e., if management attempts to maximize the after-corporate-tax funds available to shareholders), interest payments will be the same with and without merger (for a given total promised debt stream), and the expected after-tax cash flow to bondholders and stockholders will be unaffected by merger; i.e., the Higgins-Schall results will hold.

**table 16-2 Numerical Example of Corporate Coinsurance**

| | *Assume* | *Return to investors* |
|---|---|---|
| Firm 1 unmerged | $\hat{B}_1 = B_1 = 100$ | $\tilde{Y}_1^B = 80$ |
| | $r_1 = 10\%$ | |
| | $S_1 = 100$ | $\tilde{Y}_1^S = 0$ |
| | $\tilde{Y}_1 = 80^a$ | |
| Firm 2 unmerged | $\hat{B}_2 = B_2 = 200$ | $\tilde{Y}_2^B = 220$ |
| | $r_2 = 10\%$ | |
| | $S_2 = 200$ | $\tilde{Y}_2^S = 80$ |
| | $\tilde{Y}_2 = 300$ | |
| Firm $T$ | $\hat{B}_T = \hat{B}_1 + \hat{B}_2 = 300$ | $\tilde{Y}_T^B = 330$ |
| | $r_T = 10\%$ | |
| | $B_T > B_1 + B_2 = 300^b$ | |
| | $S_T < S_1 + S_2 = 300$ | $\tilde{Y}_T^S = 50$ |
| | $\tilde{Y}_T = \tilde{Y}_1 + \tilde{Y}_2 = 380$ | |

[a] Since $\tilde{Y}_1 = 80 < B_1(1 + r_1) = 110$, firm 1 experiences bankruptcy.
[b] The decreased risk associated with the bonds if the firms are merged is reflected in a lower *market* discount rate on the bonds; i.e., $k_T < r_T = r_1 = r_2 = k_1 = k_2 = 10\%$, where $r$ and $k$ are the contractual (coupon) and market rates, respectively; therefore, $B_T = (1 + r_T)\hat{B}_T/(1 + k_T) = (1.1)\,300/(1 + k_T) > 300$.

merger. If there are such synergistic benefits, the coinsurance effect loss will tend to offset the synergy gain.

It is important to keep in mind that the above does not imply that all mergers reduce shareholder wealth. If a merger produces synergistic benefits (assumed above to be zero only to simplify the discussion), then these benefits may outweigh the coinsurance wealth-transfer effect (from shareholders to bondholders). Also keep in mind that the wealth transfer occurs only if the premerger debt of one or both of the merged firms is risky; if all debt is riskless, there is no wealth transfer at all and the value of the premerger debt equals the value of the postmerger debt.

## Relaxing More Assumptions

We found above that benefits from merger can arise from operating synergies (the *only* possible benefits assuming A.1 to A.8) and from reduced financial distress and tax costs. We also observed that bondholders owning risky premerger firm debt will gain from the merger; and this gain is expropriated from stockholders unless the firm acts to prevent it. If the debt cannot be retired or called at its premerger market value (A.3 does not hold) the stockholders lose unless the merger produces compensating benefits, e.g., operating synergies or reductions in taxes or in financial distress costs.

This section briefly examines the merger benefits to shareholders that can arise if we relax assumptions A.1 to A.6. Without A.1, investors can no longer costlessly diversify (combine income streams), which suggests that a company may benefit shareholders by creating "portfolios" of firms through merger. In actuality, this is not likely to produce significant benefits since transaction costs are not great and, in addition, firms incur transaction costs themselves when they conduct mergers. There may therefore be no benefit from firms providing diversification for investors.[23]

Relaxing A.2, A.5, or A.6 will produce no particular advantage or disadvantage to mergers in general. Without A.2, the value of the firm's shares is a function of its anticipated future dividend policy. But, as we recall from Chaps. 14 and 15, dividend and investment policies are interrelated in a world of imperfections. A merger may consequently result in an advantage (or a disadvantage) to shareholders depending on the dividend and investment policy changes that the merger produces. Similarly, without A.5 (i.e., if expectations are heterogeneous) and A.6 (if information is not equally distributed), the effects of a merger on share values will depend upon investor expectations regarding the merger's effect on earnings and dividends, which in turn will depend on available information, on how it is distributed among investors, and on how it is interpreted by those investors.

## LEASING

In recent years, leasing has become a very popular method of acquiring assets. Under a lease, the user of the asset (the lessee) pays the owner of the asset (the lessor) a periodic payment for the right to use the asset. The lease payment is tax-deductible to the lessee, and the lessor is allowed to deduct depreciation and interest on debt used by the lessor to purchase the asset. The lease rental is taxable income to the lessor.

[23] With significant market imperfections (e.g., prohibitive transaction costs of conducting arbitrage), the VAP may not apply and a merger may even produce a disadvantage to shareholders if they do not want to own the same proportions of all the merged firms. For example, assume that two firms, $A$ and $B$, merge into firm $C$. Without merger, an investor can own fraction $\alpha_A$ of the shares of firm $A$ and $\alpha_B$ of the shares of firm $B$, $0 \leq \alpha_A \leq 1$ and $0 \leq \alpha_B \leq 1$, where $\alpha_A$ need not equal $\alpha_B$. But, with the merger, the investor can buy only some fraction $\alpha_C$ of firm $C$, and not differing proportions of the two firms that now make up firm $C$; if the merger is a conglomerate merger of two all-equity firms and $\tilde{\mathbf{Y}}_C^S = \tilde{\mathbf{Y}}_A^S + \tilde{\mathbf{Y}}_B^S$, then the investor can own income stream $\alpha_C \tilde{\mathbf{Y}}_C^S = \alpha_C \tilde{\mathbf{Y}}_A^S + \alpha_C \tilde{\mathbf{Y}}_B^S$, whereas without the merger the investor could own $\alpha_A \tilde{\mathbf{Y}}_A^S$ and $\alpha_B \tilde{\mathbf{Y}}_B^S$, where $\alpha_A$ could differ from $\alpha_B$. The merger has reduced the range of choices for investors and the result, even with the above conglomerate merger, can consequently mean that

$$V_C < V_A + V_B$$

The value of firm $C$ is less than the sum of the values of firms $A$ and $B$ because $\tilde{\mathbf{Y}}_C$ is not as good as having $\tilde{\mathbf{Y}}_A$ and $\tilde{\mathbf{Y}}_B$ as separate streams, therefore providing more investor investment options (since $\alpha_A \neq \alpha_B$ is possible).

In this section we examine two issues: the nature of the benefits that arise when leasing is an option for asset users and, second, the algorithm that should be used by a firm in determining whether or not to lease an asset.

Before proceeding, we shall define certain terms that are used below. Note that we signify the user with an "e" and the lessor with an "r".

$V[\ \ ]$ = the value of the term in brackets.
$\tau_r, \tau_e$ = the tax brackets of the lessor and the asset user, respectively.
$\tilde{L}_t$ = the lease rental paid at time $t$.
$I_0$ = the purchase price of the asset.
$\tilde{X}_t$ = cash revenues less cash expenses associated with the asset if it is leased; $\tilde{X}_t$ = cash revenues − cash expenses (including $\tilde{Q}_t^e$).
$\widetilde{DP}_t$ = depreciation on the asset.
$\tilde{Q}_t^r, \tilde{Q}_t^e$ = the maintenance costs (e.g., property taxes, upkeep) on the asset that are covered by the lessor and lessee, respectively; $\tilde{Q}_t = \tilde{Q}_t^r + \tilde{Q}_t^e$ = total maintenance costs.
$n$ = economic life of the asset.
$\tilde{H}_n$ = salvage value of the asset at time $n$.
$\tilde{K}_n$ = book value of the asset at time $n$.
$\tilde{R}_t$ = the change in the interest paid by the firm at time $t$ if the asset is purchased (relative to not obtaining the asset at all).
$\tilde{R}_t'$ = the change in the interest paid by the firm at time $t$ if the asset is leased (relative to not obtaining the asset at all).
$\tilde{Z}_t$ = after firm-tax cash flow (before debt interest deduction) generated by the new asset at time $t$.
$\tilde{G}_t$ = the part of $\tilde{Z}_t$ that is independent of the method of financing the purchase.
$k$ = risk-adjusted discount rate.

The meaning of the above terms will become clearer when they are used in the analysis.

In the discussion below we assume for simplicity that $n$ is known, where $n$ is the economic life of the asset from the standpoint of the user (the user will either lease the asset for $n$ periods or sell it at time $n$ if it is purchased at time 0).

## The Benefits of Leasing[24]

To identify the source of any benefits from leasing, we shall first show that *no* benefits accrue from leasing under certain simplifying assumptions. This will help in identifying what assumptions must be made for any benefits to accrue. We shall establish the following proposition:

[24] This section is based on Lewellen, Long, and McConnell, Asset Leasing in Competitive Markets, listed in the Suggested Readings at the end of this chapter.

**Proposition.** Asset users are indifferent between the lease and purchase of an asset if the following assumptions hold:

1. Assumptions A.1 to A.8 (see page 443).
2. All lessors and users are identical in the following respects:
   (*a*) Tax brackets, i.e.,

$$\tau_r = \tau_e \equiv \tau$$

   (*b*) Price paid for the asset if purchased ($I_0$).
   (*c*) Depreciation pattern used on the asset.
   (*d*) Salvage value expected to be received on the asset.
   (*e*) In acquiring the asset, the lessor borrows the same amount on the asset and pays the same interest rate on the debt as would the user if the user acquired the asset. (This assumption must follow given A.1 to A.8, and is stated here only to highlight it.)
3. *Total* maintenance cost $\tilde{Q}_t$ on the asset is the same whether the user purchases the asset (user pays all maintenance costs) or the user leases the asset (with any division of the maintenance cost between user and lessor), that is,

$$\tilde{Q}_t^r + \tilde{Q}_t^e = \tilde{Q}_t \qquad (16\text{-}18)$$

4. Asset markets are competitive (there are many asset sellers, users, lessors, and lessees) and there are no costs to running a leasing company (except the cost of acquiring the assets to lease).

**Proof.** Assume that the asset has a useful life to the user of $n$ periods, at the end of which the user would sell the asset at time $n$ for $\tilde{H}_n$ if it is purchased by the user; the present value of the asset to the lessor at time $n$ is also $\tilde{H}_n$ (by assumption 2*d*). The lessor is willing to lease the asset only if the net present value of doing so is nonnegative, that is, if[25]

$$\begin{aligned}\text{NPV (lessor)} &= V[\tilde{\mathbf{L}} - \tau(\tilde{\mathbf{L}} - \widetilde{\mathbf{DP}} - \tilde{\mathbf{R}}) + \tilde{H}_n - \tilde{I}_0] \\ &= V[(1-\tau)\tilde{\mathbf{L}}] + V[\tau\widetilde{\mathbf{DP}}] + V[\tau\tilde{\mathbf{R}}] + V[\tilde{H}_n] - I_0 \geq 0 \qquad (16\text{-}19)\end{aligned}$$

where the stream can be broken up into its component parts [second equality in (16-19)] using the VAP, and where $\tilde{\mathbf{L}}$, $\widetilde{\mathbf{DP}}$, and $\tilde{\mathbf{R}}$ are vectors.[26] At equilibrium, with competitive leasing markets, lessors will compete so as to just earn a zero

[25] Only for simplicity, in the proof we shall assume that $\tilde{Q}_t = 0$. The proof is identical with $\tilde{Q}_t > 0$ except additional terms in eqs. (16-19) through (16-23) must be added to reflect the $\tilde{Q}_t^r$ and $\tilde{Q}_t^e$.

[26] Thus $\tilde{\mathbf{L}} = (\tilde{L}_1, \tilde{L}_2, \ldots, L_n)$, $\widetilde{\mathbf{DP}} = (\widetilde{DP}_1, \widetilde{DP}_2, \ldots, \widetilde{DP}_n)$, and $\tilde{\mathbf{R}} = (\tilde{R}_1, \tilde{R}_2, \ldots, \tilde{R}_n)$. Using a discounting model, (16-19) would equal

$$\begin{aligned}\text{NPV(lessor)} &= \sum_{t=1}^{n} \frac{\overline{L}_t - \tau(\overline{L}_t - \overline{DP}_t - \overline{R}_t)}{(1+k_1)^t} + \frac{\overline{H}_n}{(1+k)^n} - I_0 \\ &= \sum_{t=1}^{n} \frac{\overline{L}_t(1-\tau)}{(1+k_L)^t} + \sum_{t=1}^{n} \frac{\tau\overline{DP}_t}{(1+k_D)^t} + \frac{\tau\overline{R}_t}{(1+k_R)^t} + \frac{\overline{H}_n}{(1+k_H)^n} - I_0 \geq 0\end{aligned}$$

*net* present value at the margin on assets leased; i.e., (16-19) will be zero. Setting NPV (lessor) in (16-19) equal to zero and rearranging terms, we find that

$$I_0 = V[(1 - \tau)\tilde{\mathbf{L}}] + V[\tau\widetilde{\mathbf{DP}}] + V[\tau\tilde{\mathbf{R}}] + V[\tilde{H}_n] \tag{16-20}$$

We shall now show that (16-20) implies that lease and purchase are equally desirable to the user of the asset. If the user *purchases* the asset, its net present value to the user equals

$$\begin{aligned} \text{NPV (user with purchase)} \\ &= V[\tilde{\mathbf{X}} - \tau(\tilde{\mathbf{X}} - \widetilde{\mathbf{DP}} - \tilde{\mathbf{R}}) + \tilde{H}_n - I_0 \\ &= V[(1 - \tau)\tilde{\mathbf{X}}] + V[\tau\widetilde{\mathbf{DP}}] + V[\tau\tilde{\mathbf{R}}] + V[\tilde{H}_n] - I_0 \end{aligned} \tag{16-21}$$

If the user *leases* the asset, its net present value to the user is

$$\begin{aligned} \text{NPV (user with lease)} &= V[\tilde{\mathbf{X}} - \tilde{\mathbf{L}} - \tau(\tilde{\mathbf{X}} - \tilde{\mathbf{L}})] \\ &= V[(1 - \tau)\tilde{\mathbf{X}}] - V[(1 - \tau)\tilde{\mathbf{L}}] \end{aligned} \tag{16-22}$$

Substitute the right-hand side of (16-20) for $I_0$ in (16-21) and note that by assumption 2*e*, $\tilde{\mathbf{R}}$ in (16-19) is equal to $\tilde{\mathbf{R}}$ in (16-21). The result is

$$\begin{aligned} \text{NPV(user with purchase)} &= \{V[(1 - \tau)\tilde{\mathbf{X}}] + V[\tau\widetilde{\mathbf{DP}}] + V[\tau\tilde{\mathbf{R}}] + V[\tilde{H}_n]\} \\ &\quad - \{V[(1 - \tau)\tilde{\mathbf{L}}] + V[\tau\widetilde{\mathbf{DP}}] + V[\tau\tilde{\mathbf{R}}] + V[\tilde{H}_n]\} \\ &= V[(1 - \tau)\tilde{\mathbf{X}}] - V[(1 - \tau)\tilde{\mathbf{L}}] \\ &= \text{NPV (user with lease)} \end{aligned} \tag{16-23}$$

Relation (16-23) states that the rental payment $\tilde{\mathbf{L}}$ that satisfies (16-20) [makes equality (16-20) hold]—which is the rental set by lessors in a competitive market—makes leasing and purchase have the same NPV to the user of the asset; i.e., the user is indifferent between the two options. This proves the proposition.

What is the rationale behind the above proposition? It is simply that under assumptions 1 through 4, a leasing firm is nothing more than an intermediary which obtains a rental that is just sufficient to cover the after-tax cost of owning the asset. But, under the assumptions, the after-tax cost to the lessor of owning the asset is exactly the same as the after-tax cost to the lessee of owning the asset. Therefore, the present value of the rental needed to cover the lessor's ownership costs equals the present value of the ownership costs to the user with purchase by the user. The user will consequently be indifferent between leasing or purchasing the asset.

The obvious question is, Why then do leasing firms exist? The answer is that assumptions 1 through 4 do not generally hold, and leasing may arise for such reasons as:

(*a*) Lessors and users have different tax brackets, which may produce tax advantages from leasing.

(*b*) The lessor may be able to find another use for the asset more easily (with lower search costs) when the current user no longer needs the asset. This may arise because the lessor is in the business of finding users for the asset. Using the notation here, $\tilde{H}_n$ for the lessor is higher than $\tilde{H}_n$ for the user (if the user purchases the asset) in this case.

(*c*) A lessor in the business of marketing the particular type of asset may be able to maintain the asset more cheaply than could a user; this may mean that the lessor can charge a rental (including a charge to cover the maintenance costs) that has a present value less than the present value of the purchase and maintenance costs to the user if the user purchased the asset.

It should be noted that the benefits under (*b*) and (*c*) do not require that lessors exist. For example, to achieve the benefits of (*b*), firms which can efficiently find users of used assets could simply act as used asset dealers rather than lessors; a user could purchase the assets it uses and resell them to used asset dealers. Similarly, to gain the benefits of (*c*), firms which can cheaply maintain assets need not be lessors but may simply provide maintenance services to asset owner-users. However, the tax benefits of (*a*) can be achieved only with leasing.

## The Lease-or-Purchase Decision[27]

We noted in the previous section that lease and purchase of an asset is a matter of indifference under certain assumptions. However, these assumptions may not apply, in which case the choice between lease and purchase can be important. In this section, we retain assumptions A.1 to A.8 (general assumption 1 on p. 443), but we drop assumptions 2, 3, and 4. In this case, lease or purchase can produce advantages because of tax and cost differentials between user-purchasers and lessors. Our concern here is the method a user employs in analyzing whether to lease an asset, purchase that asset, or do neither (i.e., not acquire the asset at all). We shall ignore the investment tax credit in the analysis, since its inclusion does not change any of the basic results.[28]

It is important to understand that assumptions A.1 to A.8 are sufficient to imply the value-additivity principle (which requires perfection only in the *capi-*

[27] This section is based on Schall, The Lease or Buy and Asset Acquisition Decisions, noted in the Suggested Readings at the end of this chapter. In the appendix to that article it is shown that eq. (16-24), which is the basis of the lease-or-buy analysis, applies with leasing as well as purchase; the equation is simply stated here without proof.

[28] If the investment tax credit (signified $C_0$) is considered, it is included in eq. (16-28*b*) as a reduction in the cost of the asset. That is, (16-28*b*) becomes

$$\delta W(P) = V[\tilde{\mathbf{G}}] + V[\tau\tilde{\mathbf{R}}] - I_0 + C_0$$

The tax credit can be passed on by the lessor to the lessee, in which case eq. (16-26*b*) would become

$$\delta W(L) = V[(1-\tau)\tilde{\mathbf{X}}] - V[(1-\tau)\tilde{\mathbf{L}}] + C_0$$

On the optimal strategy concerning whether the lessor or lessee should take the credit and on the market equilibrium implications of the credit, see L. Schall and G. Sundem, "The Investment Tax Credit and the Leasing Industry," working paper, University of Washington, 1978.

*tal* markets) but are not sufficient to ensure that leasing and purchase are a matter of indifference. If we do not have, in addition to A.1 to A.8, assumptions 2, 3, and 4 on page 457, leasing or purchase can produce advantages because of user and lessor differentials in tax brackets, asset maintenance or acquisition costs, etc. Thus tax differences or productive *asset* market imperfections and differentials can imply that either leasing or purchase is preferable for the productive asset user.

As explained in Chap. 12, assuming A.1 to A.8, the *change* in the wealth of the firm's shareholders due to acquiring a particular new asset (whether by lease or purchase) can be expressed as $\delta W$, where[29]

$$\delta W = V[\tilde{\mathbf{Z}}] - I_0 \tag{16-24}$$

where $\tilde{\mathbf{Z}}$ is the incremental after-tax stream from the asset and $I_0$ is the initial outlay required to obtain the asset. If the asset is purchased, $I_0$ is the purchase price of the asset. If the asset is leased, $I_0 = 0$, since there is no purchase price (stream $\tilde{\mathbf{Z}}$ is net of after-tax rental payments, as explained below). The firm's objective is to maximize $W$ (shareholder wealth), which means that in acquiring the particular asset under consideration, it will prefer the method of acquisition (lease or purchase) which produces the largest $\delta W$; furthermore, it will acquire the asset only if that best method of acquisition produces a positive $\delta W$. Let us look at $\tilde{\mathbf{Z}}$ and at $\delta W$ for lease and for purchase of the asset.

*Lease*:

$$\begin{aligned} \tilde{Z}(L)_t &= \tilde{X}_t - \tilde{L}_t - \tilde{\text{Tax}}_t \\ &= (1 - \tau)(\tilde{X}_t - \tilde{L}_t) \qquad t = 1, \ldots, n \end{aligned} \tag{16-25}$$

where $\tilde{\text{Tax}}_t = \tau(\tilde{X}_t - \tilde{L}_t)$. Under a lease, $I_0 = 0$ in Eq. (16-24). Using vector notation, $\tilde{\mathbf{Z}}(L) = (1 - \tau)(\tilde{\mathbf{X}} - \tilde{\mathbf{L}})$. Thus,

$$\delta W(L) = V[(1 - \tau)(\tilde{\mathbf{X}} - \tilde{\mathbf{L}})] \tag{16-26a}$$

where $\delta W(L)$ is the change in the shareholders' wealth if the asset is leased and where $V[\ ]$ is the value of the stream in the brackets. But $(1 - \tau)(\tilde{\mathbf{X}} - \tilde{\mathbf{L}}) = (1 - \tau)\tilde{\mathbf{X}} - (1 - \tau)\tilde{\mathbf{L}}$, and therefore, using the VAP, it follows that $\delta W(L)$ can also be expressed as

$$\delta W(L) = V[(1 - \tau)\tilde{\mathbf{X}}] - V[(1 - \tau)\tilde{\mathbf{L}}] \tag{16-26b}$$

[29] The discussion on p. 305 uses $\Delta W$ instead of $\delta W$ since $\Delta W$ refers to the change in shareholder wealth due to the entire capital budget for the period (i.e., is due to the acquisition of many assets). Here we are examining a single asset. Thus,

$$\Delta W = \sum_{i=1}^{n} \delta W_i$$

if the firm acquires $n$ assets in the period. Equation (16-24) holds with lease or with purchase of the asset (see text discussion below and see footnote 27 on p. 459).

*Purchase:*

$$\tilde{Z}(P)_t = \tilde{G}_t + \tau\tilde{R}_t \qquad t = 1, \ldots, n \tag{16-27}$$

where for $t = 1, \ldots, n = 1$

$$\widetilde{\text{Tax}}_t = \tau(\tilde{X}_t - \tilde{Q}_t^{\text{e}} - \widetilde{DP}_t - \tilde{R}_t)$$
$$\tilde{G}_t = (1 - \tau)(\tilde{X}_t - \tilde{Q}_t^{\text{e}}) + \tau\widetilde{DP}_t$$

and, for $t = n$,

$$\widetilde{\text{Tax}}_n = \tau(\tilde{X}_n - \tilde{Q}_n^{\text{e}} - \widetilde{DP}_n - \tilde{R}_n) + \tau_g(\tilde{H}_n - \tilde{K}_n)$$
$$\tilde{G}_n = (1 - \tau)(\tilde{X}_t - \tilde{Q}_t^{\text{e}}) + \tau\widetilde{DP}_t + \tilde{H}_n - \tau_g(\tilde{H}_n - \tilde{K}_n)$$

where $\tau_g$ is the tax rate on the gain (or loss) of amount $(\tilde{H}_n - \tilde{K}_n)$ on selling the asset at time $n$. Using vector notation, $\tilde{\mathbf{Z}}(P) = \tilde{\mathbf{G}} + \tau\tilde{\mathbf{R}}$ and therefore

$$\delta W(P) = V[\tilde{\mathbf{G}} + \tau\tilde{\mathbf{R}}] - I_0 \tag{16-28a}$$

which, using the VAP, also equals

$$\delta W(P) = V[\tilde{\mathbf{G}}] + V[\tau\tilde{\mathbf{R}}] - I_0 \tag{16-28b}$$

If purchase includes no debt, then $\tilde{\mathbf{R}} = 0$. In perfect markets (A.1 to A.8 assumed), and if all interest is tax-deductible, the asset will be virtually 100% debt financed (see Chap. 11). If all interest is not tax-deductible, the asset may be less than 100% debt financed. In any case, $\overline{R}_t$ is the added expected interest payment of the firm due to acquiring the asset, assuming optimal behavior on the part of the firm.[30]

The user of the asset must make two decisions: whether the asset should be acquired and, second, how the acquisition should be financed if the asset is acquired. The proper approach is to compute $\delta W(L)$ and $\delta W(P)$, select the larger of the two since it is better, and adopt the associated method of acquisition (lease or purchase) only if that higher $\delta W$ is positive. For example, if

[30] Under the tax code, there are limits (although not very stringent) on the proportion of debt financing with interest still tax-deductible. Therefore, even with assumptions A.1 to A.8, a firm might not be 100% debt financed. $\tilde{R}_t$ in (16-27) is the tax-deductible added interest due to acquiring the asset by purchase. Also, although we are here assuming A.1 to A.8 (p. 443), essentially the same analysis applies as long as A.1, A.2, A.4, and either A.5 or A.6 are retained (which are sufficient for the VAP) although, without A.7 and A.8, the cash flows will have to take into account both tax effects due to nonsalability of tax losses and financial distress costs. With financial distress costs, the asset might not be financed entirely with debt even if all debt interest is tax-deductible.

If the firm operates with less than 100% debt plus lease financing (i.e., finances in some given proportion with equity), the leasing of an asset may cause the firm to reduce its level of debt on other assets. This is ignored in eqs. (16-26a) and (16-26b), and to take account of that effect, (16-25) would become

$$\tilde{Z}(L)_t = (1 - \tau)(\tilde{X}_t - \tilde{L}_t) + \tau\tilde{R}_t'$$

where $\tilde{R}_t'$ is the change in the interest on firm debt if the asset is leased. This is discussed in greater detail in the next section.

$\delta W(L) = \$100$ and $\delta W(P) = \$80$, the asset should be leased; if $\delta W(L) = -\$30$ and $\delta W(P) = \$20$, the asset should be purchased; if $\delta W(L) = -\$10$ and $\delta W(P) = -\$5$, the asset should not be acquired at all.

To use Eqs. (16-26*a*) [or (16-26*b*)] and (16-28*a*) [or (16-28*b*)], we need a method of valuing income streams. We can use the risk-adjusted discount rate approach. Thus, using a bar over a variable to indicate the expected amount,

*Lease:*

$$\delta W(L) = \sum_{t=1}^{n} \frac{(1-\tau)(\bar{X}_t - \bar{L}_t)}{(1+k')^t} \tag{16-29a}$$

$$= \sum_{t=1}^{n} \frac{(1-\tau)\bar{X}_t}{(1+k_X)^t} - \sum_{t=1}^{n} \frac{(1-\tau)\bar{L}_t}{(1+k_L)^t} \tag{16-29b}$$

*Purchase:*

$$\delta W(P) = \sum_{t=1}^{n} \frac{\bar{G}_t + \tau\bar{R}_t}{(1+k'')^t} - I_0 \tag{16-30a}$$

$$= \sum_{t=1}^{n} \frac{\bar{G}_t}{(1+k_G)^t} + \sum_{t=1}^{n} \frac{\tau\bar{R}_t}{(1+k_R)^t} - I_0 \tag{16-30b}$$

where (16-29*a*), (16-29*b*), (16-30*a*), and (16-30*b*) correspond to (equal), respectively, (16-26*a*), (16-26*b*), (16-28*a*), and (16-28*b*). Either (16-29*a*) or (16-29*b*) may be used for lease and either (16-30*a*) or (16-30*b*) may be used for purchase. The discount rates $k'$, $k_X$, $k_L$, $k''$, $k_G$, and $k_R$ are the risk-adjusted discount rates applied by the market to streams with the risk properties (distributions) possessed by $(1-\tau)(\tilde{\mathbf{X}} - \tilde{\mathbf{L}})$, $(1-\tau)\tilde{\mathbf{X}}$, $(1-\tau)\tilde{\mathbf{L}}$, $\tilde{\mathbf{G}} + \tau\tilde{\mathbf{R}}$, $\tilde{\mathbf{G}}$, and $\tau\tilde{\mathbf{R}}$, respectively. These various discount rates are likely to differ from one another in magnitude, since the streams will generally have different distributions; e.g., $k' \neq k''$, $k_X \neq k_G$, and even $k_L$ may differ from $k_R$. It is also probable that each discount rate will be different for different assets of the firm, since not all firm assets are of the same risk. Each summation in Eqs. (16-29*a*) through (16-30*b*) is the value the associated stream would have in the market as an individual stream. An important concept highlighted here is that each income stream in (16-29*a*) through (16-30*b*) should be discounted at the rate that is appropriate given the risk of that particular stream; and the rates can differ from project to project.

A second and critical point revealed in the above analysis is that it is ordinarily improper to separate the choice of financing methods from the decision of whether or not to acquire the asset. The desirability of obtaining the asset may depend on the choice of financing. The asset may be profitable under one financing approach, e.g., lease, but unprofitable under the other financing approach, e.g., purchase. The correct method of analysis is to compute $\delta W$ under each available financing approach and to choose the approach with the highest $\delta W$; acquire the asset using the superior financing approach (the one with the highest $\delta W$) only if that highest $\delta W$ is positive.

Tables 16-3 and 16-4 provide a numerical illustration of the above method. The firm has a tax rate of 40% and can purchase an asset with a 5-year life for

**table 16-3 Computation of Cash Flows for Purchase and Lease**

| Year | After-tax cash flow with leasing | After-tax added operating cost with purchase | Tax savings on depreciation | Salvage value net of taxes | Operating cash flow with purchase of asset | Tax savings on interest on loan | After-tax lease rental |
|---|---|---|---|---|---|---|---|
| | $[(1-\tau)\overline{X}_t]$ | $[(1-\tau)\overline{Q}_t^e]$ | $[\tau\overline{DP}_t]$ | $[\overline{H}_n - \tau_g(\overline{H}_n - \overline{K}_n)]$ | $[\overline{G}_t]$[a] | $[\tau\overline{R}_t]$ | $[(1-\tau)\overline{L}_t]$ |
| (1) | (2) | (3) | (4) | (5) | (6) | (7) | (8) |
| 1 | .6 (1000) | .6 (200) | .4 (800) | | 800 | .4 (160) | .6 (800) |
| 2 | .6 (1000) | .6 (200) | .4 (700) | | 760 | .4 (160) | .6 (800) |
| 3 | .6 (1000) | .6 (200) | .4 (600) | | 720 | .4 (160) | .6 (800) |
| 4 | .6 (1000) | .6 (200) | .4 (500) | | 680 | .4 (160) | .6 (800) |
| 5 | .6 (1000) | .6 (200) | .4 (400) | 100 | 740 | .4 (160) | .6 (800) |

[a] $\overline{G}_t = (1-\tau)(\overline{X}_t - \overline{Q}_t^e) + \tau\overline{DP}_t = (2) - (3) + (4)$, for $t = 1, \ldots, n-1$; and
$\overline{G}_n = (1-\tau)(\overline{X}_n - \overline{Q}_n^e) + \tau\overline{DP}_n + \overline{H}_n - \tau_g(\overline{H}_n - \overline{K}_n) = (2) - (3) + (4) + (5)$.

**table 16-4 Computation of $\delta W(L)$ and $\delta W(P)$ Using Equations (16-29b) and (16-30b) Applied to the Data in Table 16-4**

*Discount rates assumed:* $k_X = 12\%$, $k_L = 8\%$, $k_G = 10\%$, $k_R = 8\%$

$\delta W(L)$ = [value of $(1-\tau)\bar{X}_t$ at 12%] − [value of $(1-\tau)\bar{L}_t$ at 8%]
= \$600(3.6048) − \$480(3.9927) = \$246

$\delta W(P)$ = [value of $\bar{G}_t$ at 10%] − [value of $\tau\bar{R}_t$ at 8%] − [cost of asset]
= [\$800(.9091) + \$760(.8264) + \$720(.7513) + \$680(.6830) + \$740(.6209)] + [\$64(3.9927)] −\$2,500 = \$576

Conclusion Purchase is preferred to lease because $\delta W(P)$ = \$576 > \$246 = $\delta W(L)$; and purchase is desirable because $\delta W(P)$ = \$576 > 0.

\$2,500; it has an expected net of tax salvage value of \$100 at the end of the 5 years (but salvage value for depreciation calculation is zero) and will be depreciated on a sum-of-years'-digits basis. The purchase, if made, will be with 80% debt (\$2,000) with expected interest payments of \$160 per year and the principal due at the end of the 5 years.[31] The operating costs with purchase in excess of those that would have to be incurred with lease are \$200 per year. If the asset is leased, the annual expected lease rental is \$800. All annual amounts are assumed to occur at the end of the period (at time 1, time 2, . . . , time 5, where the purchase or lease decision is made at time 0). The computations indicate that purchase is superior since $\delta W(P) > \delta W(L)$ and the purchase should be made since $\delta W(P)$ = \$576 > 0.

## Leasing and Debt Capacity

In the preceding section we simply assumed that $\tilde{R}_t$ in (16-27) could be estimated and the problem solved in the manner described above.[32] In this section, the determination of $\tilde{R}_t$ is examined in greater detail.

Let us restate Eq. (16-29) as (16-31) below:

$$\delta W(L) = \sum_{t=1}^{n} \frac{(1-\tau)\bar{X}_t}{(1+k_X)^t} - \sum_{t=1}^{n} \frac{(1-\tau)\bar{L}_t}{(1+k_L)^t} + \sum \frac{\tau\bar{R}'_t}{(1+k_R)^t} \qquad (16\text{-}31)$$

[31] In the statement of the problem we refer to the "expected" interest payments of the debt $\bar{R}_t$ and the "expected" lease payments $\bar{L}_t$. Only if $\tilde{R}_t$ and $\tilde{L}_t$ are riskless will these expected amounts equal the contractually promised amounts $\hat{R}_t$ and $\hat{L}_t$ (if $\tilde{R}_t$ and $\tilde{L}_t$ are not riskless, then $\bar{R}_t < \hat{R}_t$ and $\bar{L}_t < \hat{L}_t$). We could just as well use promised streams $\hat{R}_t$ and $\hat{L}_t$ in eqs. (16-29$a$) to (16-30$b$), in which case the discount rates would have to be adjusted; thus, for example, in (16-29$b$), $k_L < \hat{k}_L$ and in (16-30$b$), $k_R < \hat{k}_R$, where $\hat{k}_L$ would be the rate for discounting $\hat{L}_t$ in (16-29$b$) if $\hat{L}_t$ were substituted for $\bar{L}_t$ in (16-29$b$) and where $\hat{k}_R$ would be the rate for discounting $\hat{R}_t$ if $\hat{R}_t$ were substituted for $\bar{R}_t$ in (16-30$b$). Note also that if we used $\hat{L}_t$ in (16-29$a$) we would use a lower $k'$ and if we use $\hat{R}_t$ in (16-30$a$) we would use a larger $k''$.

[32] And, as discussed in the footnote on p. 461, if a lease changes firm debt we assumed that $\tilde{R}'_t$ could also be estimated.

where $\bar{R}'_t$ is the change in expected interest paid by the firm due to the leasing of the asset.[33] $\bar{R}'_t$ would be negative if the firm reduces its debt associated with other assets because of leasing the asset under consideration. The firm might do this because a lease is similar to 100% debt financing and if less than 100% of debt and lease financing is sought (if the firm wants a certain proportion of equity financing), the adoption of a lease on one asset may mean a reduced amount of debt financing on other firm assets which are purchased. $\bar{R}'_t$ could also be positive if the firm leases an asset which is extremely profitable and the lease payments are very small, in which case the firm might borrow against the asset's net cash flow in excess of the lease payments.

Equation (16-30*b*) still applies to purchase of the asset, where $\bar{R}_t$ is the expected change in firm interest due to acquiring the asset. To highlight the issues at hand, assume that the asset's expected actual salvage value and its salvage value for tax purposes are zero (i.e., $H = K = 0$), and assume that $Q_t = 0$. We also continue to ignore the investment tax credit.

Let us subtract (16-30*b*) from (16-31) to get the net advantage of leasing relative to purchase of the asset (signified $NAL_0$) as of time 0 (when the decision is made whether to lease or purchase):

$$\begin{aligned} NAL_0 &\equiv \delta W(L) - \delta W(P) \\ &= I_0 - \sum_{t=1}^{n} \frac{(1-\tau)\bar{L}_t}{(1+k_L)^t} \\ &\quad - \sum_{t=1}^{n} \frac{\tau \overline{DP}_t}{(1+k_{DP})^t} + \sum_{t=1}^{n} \frac{\tau \bar{R}'_t}{(1+k_{R'})^t} - \sum \frac{\tau \bar{R}_t}{(1+k_R)^t} \end{aligned} \qquad (16\text{-}32)$$

$NAL_0$ in Eq. (16-32) is the net advantage to the user of leasing the asset rather than purchasing it.

How do we use (16-32)? $NAL_0$ alone does not indicate whether the asset should be acquired but only whether leasing or purchase is better *if* it is acquired. For example, if $NAL_0 > 0$, leasing is preferred to purchase, but $\delta W(L)$ may still be negative. Regardless of the magnitude of $NAL_0$, either $\delta W(L)$ or $\delta W(P)$ must still be computed *if* it is not known whether the asset should be acquired. We can summarize how the $NAL_0$ equation (16-32) can be used, noting, however, that the approach in the preceding section [computing $\delta W(L)$ and $\delta W(P)$] is still completely valid:

*A*. If it is *not* known whether the asset should be acquired, then compute $NAL_0$ of (16-32) and:
   (i) If $NAL_0 > 0$, compute $\delta W(L)$ and lease the asset if $\delta W(L) > 0$ [if $\delta W(L) < 0$, do not acquire the asset at all and if $\delta W(L) = 0$, we are indifferent about acquiring the asset].

[33] See footnote 31 on p. 464.

(ii) If $NAL_0 < 0$, compute $\delta W(P)$ and purchase the asset if $\delta W(P) > 0$ [if $\delta W(P) < 0$, do not acquire the asset at all and if $\delta W(P) = 0$, we are indifferent about acquiring the asset].

(iii) If $NAL_0 = 0$, do either (i) or (ii) above.

*B*. If we know without formal analysis that the asset should be acquired and the only decision is how to finance the acquisition (lease or purchase), then simply compute $NAL_0$ of (16-32) and lease if $NAL_0 > 0$, and purchase if $NAL_0 < 0$ (indifference if $NAL_0 = 0$).

Approach *A* above is no better and no worse than the approach of the previous section since it in effect interrelates the investment and financing decisions by including one of steps (i) or (ii). Approach *B* is appropriate and is more direct than separate computations of $\delta W(L)$ and $\delta W(P)$ if the asset's desirability is so obvious that only the financing decision need be made. In any case, *A* and *B* will produce the same result as did the method described earlier involving separate computations of $\delta W(L)$ and $\delta W(P)$.[34]

Notice that (16-32) is in terms of $\bar{R}'_t$ and $\bar{R}_t$, both of which must be estimated if $NAL_0$ is to be determined. As shown elsewhere, under certain assumptions (16-32) can be represented as[35]

$$NAL_0 = I_0 - \sum_{t=1}^{n} \frac{(1 - \tau)\bar{L}_t + \tau \overline{DP}_t}{(1 + k^*)^t} \tag{16-33}$$

where $k^* = (1 - \tau)k_R$. To derive (16-33), it is sufficient to assume A.1 to A.8 plus the assumptions that the expected depreciation ($\overline{DP}_t$), lease payments ($\bar{L}_t$), and debt interest ($\bar{R}'_t$ and $\bar{R}_t$) should all be discounted at rate $k_R$ (all are of the same risk as the debt interest), and the asset has no salvage value.[36] Relation (16-33) is based on the idea that the amount of firm debt not incurred because of the lease rather than the purchase of an asset [and therefore $\bar{R}'_t$ and $\bar{R}_t$ in (16-32)] depends on the size of the lease obligation, i.e., on the lease payments $\tilde{L}_t, t = 1, \ldots, n$. The greater the lease obligation on a particular asset, the less borrowing the firm can afford to do. For example, assume that a company obtains an asset which will generate a particular annual net cash flow before lease payments or taxes (*EBLT*). If the lease payments $\tilde{L}_t$ were extremely small, the firm could easily borrow against the remaining net cash flow (net of lease payments) of the asset (and use the borrowing proceeds either to retire some of its shares, to pay larger dividends or to buy another asset). But if the lease payments on the asset are very large and absorb a great deal of the cash flow (*EBLT*), then the firm could borrow far less against the net of lease payment cash flow. The point

[34] We are assuming that $\tilde{R}'_t$ is properly taken into account if it is nonzero; see footnote 30 on p. 461.

[35] See Myers, Dill and Bautista, Valuation of Financial Lease Contracts, listed in the Suggested Readings at the end of this chapter.

[36] If different discount rates are appropriate, then an equation similar to but more complicated than (16-33) would apply.

is that $\bar{R}'_t$ in (16-32) is dependent on the $\tilde{L}_t$. This interdependency is used to derive (16-33).

To illustrate (16-33), assume that a firm can purchase an asset with a 4-year life for \$2,200. The depreciation on the asset would be straight-line (\$500 per year). The company can also lease the asset for \$700 per year. Rate $k_R = 8\%$, $\tau = 50\%$ and therefore $k^* = (1 - \tau)k_R = 4\%$. Thus,

$$\begin{aligned} NAL_0 &= \$2{,}200 - \sum_{t=1}^{4} \frac{(1 - .5)\$700 + (.5)\$500}{(1.04)^t} \\ &= \$2{,}200 - \$600(3.63) \\ &= \$22 \end{aligned}$$

Since $NAL_0$ is positive, leasing is preferred to purchase of the asset. If we know without any formal analysis that the asset should be acquired, the above analysis indicates that the asset should be leased. But, if we do not yet know if the asset is acceptable, we do not know whether leasing is good (but only that it is superior to purchase). To establish whether the asset should be acquired, we must have an estimate of the benefits generated by the asset; with this estimate, and an estimate of $\bar{R}'_t$ in (16-31), we can determine $\delta W(L)$. The asset should be leased only if $\delta W(L)$ is positive (or zero). If $\delta W(L)$ is negative, the asset should not be acquired at all.

## SUGGESTED READINGS

Alberts, William W. and Joel E. Segall (eds.): "The Corporate Merger," 2d ed., The University of Chicago Press, Chicago, 1975.

Haugen, Robert A. and Terrence C. Langetieg: An Empirical Test for Synergism in Merger, *Journal of Finance,* vol. 30, pp. 1003–1114, September 1975.

Higgins, Robert C. and Lawrence D. Schall: Corporate Bankruptcy and Conglomerate Merger, *Journal of Finance,* vol. 30, no. 1, pp. 93–111, March 1975.

Lewellen, Wilbur G., Michael S. Long, and John J. McConnell: Asset Leasing in Competitive Capital Markets, *Journal of Finance,* vol. 31, no. 3, pp. 787–798, June 1976.

Mason, R. Hal and Maurice B. Goudzwaard, Performance of Conglomerate Firms: A Portfolio Approach, *Journal of Finance,* vol. 31, no. 1, pp. 39–48, March 1976.

Miller, Merton H. and Charles W. Upton: Leasing, Buying, and the Cost of Capital Services, *Journal of Finance,* vol. 31, no. 3, pp. 761–786, June 1976.

Mueller, Dennis C.: A Theory of Conglomerate Mergers, *Quarterly Journal of Economics,* vol. 83, pp. 643–659, November 1969.

Myers, Stewart C., David A. Dill, and Alberto J. Bautista, Valuation of Financial Lease Contracts, *Journal of Finance,* vol. 31, no. 3, pp. 799–820, June 1976.

Schall, Lawrence D.: The Lease or Buy and Asset Acquisition Decisions, *Journal of Finance,* vol. 39, no. 4, pp. 1203–1214, September 1974.

CHAPTER

# SEVENTEEN

# FIRM OBJECTIVES WITH IMPERFECT MARKETS

Throughout this book we have evaluated the financial decisions of business firms in terms of their impact on the market value of the ownership interest in the firm; that is, we have taken the objective of the firm to be the maximization of the market value of the firm's common stock.[1] In perfect capital markets (i.e., with assumptions A.1 to A.8 below, which were made in Chaps. 10 to 13), share-value maximization is consistent with the broader objective of maximizing the welfare of individual shareholders. Each shareholder agrees that share-value maximization is the appropriate objective. Also, in perfect markets, an alternative objective can be used—maximization of the market value of *all* the firm's securities (stocks *and* bonds). This objective of total firm-value maximization is completely consistent with maximization of share values under the perfect-market assumptions. However, in imperfect markets, it may be that

[1] Actually, the objective that has been assumed has been the maximization of current (old) shareholder wealth in the firm, which equals $D_0$, the current dividend, plus $S_0^0$, the ex-dividend value of the firm's old shares; but this is equal to the *cum*-dividend value of the old shares, and *it is the* cum-*dividend value that we use to define share value in this chapter.* Also, the reader may be confused concerning the apparent contradiction between the perfect-market goal of share-value maximization stated here and the fact that with A.1 to A.8 and the tax-deductibility of corporate debt interest, the firm's capitalization should be virtually *all* debt (virtually zero stock value), or at least should be debt to the extent that interest is tax-deductible (see chap. 11). However, there is no contradiction. When a firm decision is made, if there is any stock in the capital structure (i.e., any ownership position at all, which there must be), in perfect markets the proper decision at that point in time is that which maximizes the *cum*-dividend value of the shares outstanding at the time the decision is made. In perfect markets, the financing decision which maximizes the market value of those shares is to use debt to the maximum degree possible.

neither maximizing share value nor maximizing total firm value maximizes shareholders' utility.

In this chapter we consider the following related issues:

I. What criterion is appropriate for individual shareholders in evaluating the firm's performance? That is, what is it that shareholders want maximized (or minimized)?
II. Are the shareholders of a firm unanimous in their preferences concerning firm policy options? Under what conditions will they all agree on what the firm should do?
III. Is the maximization of a firm's total value consistent with the maximization of the firm's stock value? Under what conditions will the joint interests of shareholders and bondholders combined coincide with the interests of shareholders alone?

Except where otherwise noted, in examining the idealized "perfect markets case" in Chaps. 10 through 13, we made the following assumptions:

A.1. Costless capital markets: No capital market transaction costs, no government restrictions which interfere with capital market transactions, and transaction costless infinite divisibility of financial assets.
A.2. Neutral personal taxes: There are no personal taxes or the effective tax rates on interest, dividends and capital gains (realized or unrealized) are equal.[2]
A.3. Competitive markets: There are many perfect substitutes for all securities of a firm at any point in time, and they can be acquired at the same market price regardless of a given firm's behavior or a given investor's behavior.[3]
A.4. Equal access: Investors and firms can borrow, lend, and issue claims on the same terms.
A.5. Homogeneous expectations: Everyone has the same expectations.
A.6. No information costs: Firms and individuals have available the same information, and this information is acquirable at a zero cost.
A.7. No financial distress costs: Firms and individuals incur no financial distress costs (legal costs, accounting costs, etc.), although financial distress can occur.
A.8. Salability of tax losses: Firms and individuals can sell tax losses in the market.[4]

An assumption that is not included above but which is made throughout this book is that all investors are rational and all prefer more consumption to less. This means that if income stream $\tilde{\mathbf{Y}}_A$ necessarily provides at least as much

[2] Assumption A.2 implies that capital gains are taxed as they accumulate (when the asset's price changes) and not when they are realized by a sale, or that the capital-gains tax rate depends on the holding period.

[3] Assumption A.3 implies that a firm cannot create a new type of security (one that is different from any already available in the market and issued by another firm). In addition the firm is a "price taker," i.e., it cannot affect the structure of interest rates in the market by its actions.

[4] A loss of $L$ can be sold for $\tau L$, where $\tau$ is the tax bracket of the seller of the loss.

in all time periods as does $\tilde{\mathbf{Y}}_B$ and provides more consumption in one or more periods ($\tilde{\mathbf{Y}}_A$ dominates $\tilde{\mathbf{Y}}_B$), then $\tilde{\mathbf{Y}}_A$ is preferred to $\tilde{\mathbf{Y}}_B$.

Note that A.3 and A.5 are separate assumptions. A.5 does not imply A.3, since even with homogeneous expectations there need not be substitutes for all assets and securities. Furthermore, A.3 does not imply A.5, since it is possible that even though investors have heterogeneous expectations, each observes substitutes for each asset, with all substitutes for any particular asset having the same price. With heterogeneous expectations there are two alternative versions of A.3 or two ways in which A.3 can hold.

1. All investors have the same view as to which assets are substitutes for one another, but they have different expectations concerning the distributions of returns from each asset; e.g., all agree that streams $\tilde{\mathbf{Y}}_A$ and $\tilde{\mathbf{Y}}_B$ of firms $A$ and $B$ are perfect substitutes, where $V_A = V_B$ (equal market values), but investors may disagree on the probability distributions of $\tilde{\mathbf{Y}}_A$ and $\tilde{\mathbf{Y}}_B$.
2. Investors disagree on which assets are substitutes. Thus investor i may regard $\tilde{\mathbf{Y}}_A$ and $\tilde{\mathbf{Y}}_B$ as substitutes and $V_A = V_B$, while investor $j$ regards $\tilde{\mathbf{Y}}_A$ and $\tilde{\mathbf{Y}}_C$ (but not $\tilde{\mathbf{Y}}_A$ and $\tilde{\mathbf{Y}}_B$) as substitutes, and $V_A = V_C$. Notice that if investor $j$ regards $\tilde{\mathbf{Y}}_B$ as inferior to $\tilde{\mathbf{Y}}_A$ and $\tilde{\mathbf{Y}}_C$, investor $j$ will not hold asset $B$ since $V_B = V_A = V_C$.

If A.1 through A.8 hold, then current share-value maximization is the goal of shareholders, shareholders are unanimous (they all prefer the policy that maximizes current share values), and firm value and share-value maximization are consistent objectives. It should be noted, however, that assumptions A.1 through A.8 are clearly quite restrictive, and in fact none strictly holds in the real world. We shall now relate these assumptions to issues I through III and examine the consequences when some of the assumptions are relaxed.

## I. THE SHAREHOLDER'S OBJECTIVE AND SHARE VALUE

A share of stock provides monetary returns to the stockholder in the form of dividends, and the dollar proceeds when the stock is eventually sold. Given any two alternative streams of returns from a share of stock, the shareholder will either prefer one of the two or be indifferent between the two. The investor's ultimate criterion in assessing income streams may be the maximization of expected utility of lifetime consumption (the criterion under quite general assumptions—see Chap. 9) or some other utility-maximization criterion. The issue of interest here is whether or not there is some characteristic of the income stream to shareholders that management can use to assess alternative policies in terms of their desirability to shareholders, for example, the market value of that stream (i.e., the market value of the firm's shares). In this section we observe that, under certain conditions, maximization of current share values

is consistent with shareholder utility maximization; however, in general, share-value maximization is at best only approximately consistent with shareholder utility maximization.

In perfect markets under conditions of *certainty* the ability to convert a given income stream into other streams with the same present value makes the present value of the stream equal to the market value and makes the present value (and market value) an index of individual preference. The time patterns of incomes provided by different assets are irrelevant so long as each stream can be converted through market transactions into any other stream with the same present value. This is so regardless of the consumption preferences of the individual. Therefore, if management wishes to act in the best interests of the firm's shareholders, maximization of the current market value of the firm's shares is consistent with that overall objective.

With *uncertainty*, however, investors do not know their own future consumption preferences nor do they know future asset prices and payments (except for riskless assets). In determining the most desirable portfolio of assets to hold, the investor must consider the possibilities for all three of these variables (preferences, prices, and payments). There is no guarantee that maximizing current market value is in the best interests of all shareholders. Some may prefer a course of action by management that would result in a higher future value but lower current value than some alternative. A careful examination of the problem is needed.

The current market value of any asset is the highest current price the owner can receive for the set of possible future returns from that asset (the cash payments over any given holding period and the price at the end of the period). The "wealth" of an individual at any point in time is the market value of the income streams he or she owns. The question arises as to whether it can be said that the cash-flow stream provided by asset $A$ ($\tilde{\mathbf{Y}}_A$) is preferred by all individuals to the stream provided by asset $B$ ($\tilde{\mathbf{Y}}_B$) if the market value of $A$ ($V_A$) is greater than the market value of $B$ ($V_B$). The answer is: "only under particular conditions." Asset $A$ will be preferred to asset $B$ only if the best stream obtainable by either owning $\tilde{\mathbf{Y}}_A$ or transforming $\tilde{\mathbf{Y}}_A$ into another stream is preferred to the best stream obtainable by owning or transforming $\tilde{\mathbf{Y}}_B$. Transforming a stream is accomplished by undertaking such market transactions as borrowing against the asset, or selling part or all of an asset, and using the proceeds to acquire another asset or to consume.

There are two conditions under which the opportunities provided by stream $\tilde{\mathbf{Y}}_A$ are preferred by the investor to the opportunities provided by stream $\tilde{\mathbf{Y}}_B$ if $V_A > V_B$:

1. If $\tilde{\mathbf{Y}}_A$ itself (to hold and not transform) is preferred by the investor to any stream obtainable by holding or transforming $\tilde{\mathbf{Y}}_B$.
2. If the most desirable stream that can be obtained by transforming $\tilde{\mathbf{Y}}_A$ is preferred by the investor to the most desirable stream that can be obtained by holding or transforming $\tilde{\mathbf{Y}}_B$.

Condition 1 merely states that so long as current market value reflects the preferences of the investor, then $\tilde{Y}_A$ must be preferred to $\tilde{Y}_B$ if $V_A > V_B$. This is tautological. However, note that market value may *not* reflect the preferences of *all* investors, since a higher market value only implies that the stream is preferred as an asset to hold by *some* investors. This is similar to any good; if an orange sells for more than an apple, it does not follow that everyone prefers oranges to apples. The reason, therefore, for stating condition 1 is to note that it is a condition which *may* hold in the market for all investors but not necessarily so. It must hold for some investors, however.

Condition 2 implies that the investor can transform $\tilde{Y}_A$ and necessarily be better off than the best alternative provided by $\tilde{Y}_B$. Thus, if there is some stream in the market $\tilde{Y}_C$ preferred to the best stream obtainable by holding or transforming $\tilde{Y}_B$, where $V_C = V_A$, then the investor can sell $\tilde{Y}_A$ for $V_A$ and obtain $\tilde{Y}_C$. Clearly, this is better than having $\tilde{Y}_B$, since $\tilde{Y}_C$ is preferred to all alternatives provided by $\tilde{Y}_B$ by assumption.

If both $\tilde{Y}_A$ and $\tilde{Y}_B$ are readily available in the market (or other streams viewed as identical to them are available) at prices $V_A$ and $V_B$, condition 2 must hold. An investor owning $\tilde{Y}_A$ but preferring $\tilde{Y}_B$ could sell $\tilde{Y}_A$ and purchase $\tilde{Y}_B$. This transaction would provide him or her with $\tilde{Y}_B$ plus a current cash gain of $(V_A - V_B)$; in other words, with a new stream $\tilde{Y}_C$ ($\tilde{Y}_C = \text{cash} + \tilde{Y}_B$), which is clearly preferable to $\tilde{Y}_B$ alone. To put it another way, if you offered the choice between the two streams to an investor as a gift, the investor should always take $\tilde{Y}_A$ even though he or she would prefer $\tilde{Y}_B$, since $\tilde{Y}_A$ can be converted into $\tilde{Y}_B$ plus some cash. Therefore, if streams equivalent to $\tilde{Y}_A$ and $\tilde{Y}_B$ are obtainable in the market, the condition $V_A > V_B$ implies that $\tilde{Y}_A$ is preferred (to either hold or transform) to $\tilde{Y}_B$.

But what if streams viewed as identical to $\tilde{Y}_A$ and $\tilde{Y}_B$ are not already available in the market and an investor must choose between receiving stream $\tilde{Y}_A$ and receiving stream $\tilde{Y}_B$? This could occur if a firm had to select between one investment and another or between one financial structure and another, with firm return $\tilde{Y}_A$ resulting from one choice and $\tilde{Y}_B$ from the other. It might be that no other asset in the market currently provides a stream identical to $\tilde{Y}_A$ or $\tilde{Y}_B$. In such a case, would an investor in the firm prefer firm stream $\tilde{Y}_A$ or $\tilde{Y}_B$, assuming that $V_A > V_B$; that is, assuming that the current market value which $\tilde{Y}_A$ would attain exceeds the current market value which $\tilde{Y}_B$ would attain? Is current market value a correct index of investor preference in this case? It is, but only if condition 1 or condition 2 holds for the investor. That is, the opportunities provided by owning $\tilde{Y}_A$ must be preferred to those provided by owning $\tilde{Y}_B$; this may not be the case.

An example may help to illustrate the situation in which streams identical to $\tilde{Y}_A$ and $\tilde{Y}_B$ do not already exist in the market. Assume a firm that has two investment opportunities, one which will imply a firm cash flow of $\tilde{Y}_A$ and the other a cash flow $\tilde{Y}_B$. Assume that the market value of the firm in the two cases would be $V_A$ and $V_B$, where $V_A > V_B$. Does it follow that *all* the firm's owners prefer that $A$ be adopted? No, it does not unless condition 1 or condition 2 holds for all owners. If all the owners of the firm prefer the stream $\tilde{\mathbf{Y}}_A$ to any opportunity provided by $\tilde{\mathbf{Y}}_B$—condition 1—then clearly $A$ is preferred to $B$. If 1 is not satisfied, 2 may hold for each owner. A current owner of firm $A$ shares could then transform his or her part of $\tilde{\mathbf{Y}}_A$ by selling the firm $A$ shares and purchasing some preferred income stream in the market. However, condition 2 may be unsatisfied for some or all owners. There may be no stream obtainable in the market for the proceeds from selling his or her shares that an owner views as good as the best stream obtainable by holding or transforming his or her part of $\tilde{\mathbf{Y}}_B$. Some or all of the firm's owners may consequently prefer that the firm adopt $B$ rather than $A$ even though $V_A > V_B$.

The result of the preceding is that current share-value maximization by the firm is consistent with the preferences of *all* its owners only if condition 1 or condition 2 holds for all of them. It may be that such conditions do not prevail. This is particularly so with heterogeneous expectations. For example, the owners (and management) of a firm may feel that a particular project will yield immense returns (and firm value) in the *future*. The market in general, however, may disagree, for example, if the project is viewed as far more risky by outsiders than by the firm's insiders. Adopting another investment that is perhaps more conservative in the eyes of outsiders may increase the firm's *current* market value but not the happiness of the firm's owners. The owners may be willing to face a temporarily (they hope) lower market value for their firm and adopt the "riskier" project; this is so since, even with the higher current value under a more conservative investment policy, they feel they would not be able to obtain a more desirable stream (e.g., by selling their shares and purchasing another stream) than that from the risky project.

The consequence of this discussion is that whether market-value maximization is an appropriate goal in general depends on the market opportunities of the shareholders. Even though we cannot be sure that market value is an appropriate index of preference for all investors, we usually assume that it is and that the objective of management in making financial decisions is to maximize the current market value of the firm's shares. Although this assumption has the limitations just discussed, it is an assumption that is generally accepted (implicitly) throughout most of the financial literature. It may have wide validity, and in any case, it is immensely useful from an analytical standpoint.

We shall now demonstrate that assumptions A.1, A.2, and A.3 are sufficient for current share-value maximization to be the preferred goal of all the firm's shareholders. An identical argument applies to all investors in assets other than stock (e.g., bonds) to show that investors prefer asset-value maximization (e.g., bond-value maximization).

**Theorem 1.** With assumptions A.1, A.2, and A.3, all shareholders prefer the firm policy that maximizes the current market value of the firm's shares.

To prove Theorem 1, assume that investor i owns $\alpha_i$ of the shares of the firm. Suppose that the firm is considering alternative policies $A$ and $B$. The values of investor i's shares under the alternative policies are $\alpha_i S_A$ and $\alpha_i S_B$, and they imply income streams (dividends and proceeds from stock sales) to i of $\tilde{\mathbf{Y}}_{A\mathrm{i}}$ and $\tilde{\mathbf{Y}}_{B\mathrm{i}}$ (which depend on i's expectations). Assume that $S_A > S_B$; we must show that investor i necessarily prefers $A$ to $B$ in order to prove the theorem. If $A$ is adopted, i can sell out for $\alpha_\mathrm{i} S_A$ and, by A.3, buy a substitute for $\tilde{\mathbf{Y}}_{B\mathrm{i}}$, say $\tilde{\mathbf{Y}}_{C\mathrm{i}}$, for $\alpha_\mathrm{i} S_B < \alpha_\mathrm{i} S_A$ (note: $S_A > S_B$ by assumption). Investor i will end up with $\alpha_\mathrm{i}(S_A - S_B)$ in cash plus $\tilde{\mathbf{Y}}_{C\mathrm{i}}$, which is superior to $\tilde{\mathbf{Y}}_{B\mathrm{i}}$ by itself (what i would have if policy $B$ were adopted). Therefore, $A$ is preferred to $B$ by i as long as $S_A > S_B$. This establishes Theorem 1.

Theorem 1 is based on the idea that each shareholder prefers the firm policy that maximizes the value of the firm's shares because the maximum share value provides the widest choice of income stream opportunities. With a higher share value, the shareholder can acquire anything that could be acquired if the shares were worth less and can acquire even more. Therefore, policies which generate higher share values are preferred by all shareholders.

Note that Theorem 1 really tells us two things. First, assuming A.1 to A.3, all shareholders prefer the policy that maximizes current share values. Second, assuming A.1 to A.3, all shareholders are *unanimous*; i.e., there is a unique policy (or set of equivalently good policies all of which achieve a maximum $S$) that satisfies all shareholders (since all prefer that policy which maximizes $S$).

Although A.1, A.2, and A.3 are sufficient for Theorem 1, they are not strictly necessary in that transaction costs and taxes may be positive provided that, for policies $A$ and $B$ in Theorem 1, the added taxes and/or transaction costs involved in switching from the firm's shares to a substitute stream for $\tilde{\mathbf{Y}}_{B\mathrm{i}}$ impose a present value of cost to investor i less than $\alpha_\mathrm{i}(V_A - V_B)$. That is, small transaction costs and tax effects do not negate the theorem and we can relax A.1 and A.2. We can formalize this in an additional assumption:

> A.9. For investor i's sale of security $M$ and purchase of perfect substitute security $N$ with part or all of the proceeds of the sale ($V_M \geq V_N$),
>
> $$V_M - V_N \geq \mathrm{Tax_i} + \mathrm{Tr_i} \tag{17-1}$$
>
> where $\mathrm{Tax_i}$ and $\mathrm{Tr_i}$ are the *added* present and future tax and transaction cost burdens imposed on i expressed in terms of their current dollar equivalents (number of current dollars equivalent to those cost burdens in the view of i).

A proof identical to that for Theorem 1 implies that i prefers policy $A$ to policy $B$ if $S_A > S_B$ if assumptions A.3 and A.9 hold. Note that A.1 and A.2 imply A.9 (since $\mathrm{Tax_i} + \mathrm{Tr_i} = 0$ under A.1 and A.2) but not vice versa. Assumption A.9 is less restrictive than A.1 and A.2 taken together. Using assumptions A.3 and A.9, we find as in the earlier proof of Theorem 1 that shareholders prefer that share values be maximized since this provides the widest range of income-stream opportunities. As before, with higher share values the stockholders can acquire anything that could be acquired if share values were lower, and in addition, they can obtain something extra. Greater share values mean an expanded set of income-stream opportunities for shareholders and are therefore preferred by shareholders.

It should be noted that while A.9 may hold in some tax and transaction cost environments, it is unlikely to hold in many others. For example, in a period of rising security prices and assuming that capital gains taxes are levied when the securities are sold (as is the case in actuality), $\text{Tax}_i$ in (17-1) may be substantial and for many investors (17-1) might not hold for some or all securities.

## II. UNANIMITY

We just explained that A.3 and A.9 are sufficient to ensure that the firm's shareholders are unanimous in their preferences concerning firm policy alternatives. The same assumptions—A.3 and A.9—imply that bondholders prefer the firm policy that maximizes the current market value of the firm's bonds (Theorem 1 applies to bonds as well as stocks; simply substitute the words bondholders and bonds for shareholders and shares, respectively, in the statement of the theorem). It also follows from the preceding section that, in general, shareholders (or bondholders) *may* disagree concerning firm policy if A.3 and A.9 do not hold. Note that when the firm maximizes current share values, assumptions A.3 and A.9 ensure market opportunities for shareholders which allow them to attain through market operations the stream that they would prefer the firm to generate. These opportunities make shareholders unanimous in preferring the current market value maximization of their stock. It is interesting to explore whether there is a single fundamental condition which will ensure unanimity. The answer is that there is. We will now examine the condition necessary for unanimity among the shareholders of a given firm. We later explain that the same principles apply to bondholders, and to stockholders and bondholders together. Assume the following definitions:

$\tilde{\mathbf{Y}}_{pi}$ = the stream (net of transaction costs and taxes) of returns to investor i (as anticipated by i) if investor i continues to hold fraction $\alpha_i$ of the firm's stock until some future date given that the firm pursues policy $p$.

$\tilde{\mathbf{Y}}^*_{pi}$ = the stream (net of transaction costs and taxes) most desirable to i that can be obtained by i if firm policy $p$ is adopted. This stream may result either from i's holding $\alpha_i$ of the firm's stock or from i's transforming the stock (e.g., by selling or borrowing against the stock and buying another security).

We shall use the term "transform" to signify the sale, trade, or other market conversion of a security. For example, a stockholder transforms shares by selling them and buying a different security (transforms them into another asset).

*For there to be unanimity there must exist a policy* w *such that*

$$\tilde{\mathbf{Y}}^*_{wi} \; PI \; \tilde{\mathbf{Y}}^*_{pi} \qquad \text{all policies } p \neq w, \text{ all stockholders i} \tag{17-2}$$

where $\tilde{\mathbf{Y}}^*_{wi} \; PI \; \tilde{\mathbf{Y}}^*_{pi}$ means that investor i prefers or is indifferent to $\tilde{\mathbf{Y}}^*_{wi}$ relative to $\tilde{\mathbf{Y}}^*_{pi}$. Relation (17-2) states that there exists a policy $w$ which provides all shareholders with after-tax, after-transaction cost holding or transformation opportunities which are no worse than the opportunities provided by any other policy $p$; i.e., all investors agree on the policy or set of policies that are best. But transformation opportunities depend on the availability of substitutes for the alternative return streams that the firm can provide to shareholders. It is easily shown that without assumptions A.1 and A.9, there must be constraints on investors' utility functions, wealth levels, and expectations (i.e., on *all* three) for unanimity to be assured; that is, if A.1 and A.9 do not hold, then *without constraints on investors' utility functions, wealth levels, and expectations,* it is possible for there to be, for stockholders i and $j$ in a firm, two firm policies $A$ and $B$ for which $i$ prefers $\tilde{\mathbf{Y}}^*_{Bi}$ to $\tilde{\mathbf{Y}}^*_{Ai}$ (signified $\tilde{\mathbf{Y}}^*_{Bi} P \tilde{\mathbf{Y}}^*_{Ai}$), whereas $j$ prefers $\tilde{\mathbf{Y}}^*_{Aj}$ (i.e., $\tilde{\mathbf{Y}}^*_{Aj} P \tilde{\mathbf{Y}}^*_{Bj}$). Thus there may be one firm policy that investor i regards as superior and another policy that investor $j$ regards as superior; i.e., there is no dominant firm policy or set of firm policies that all investors agree is best.

An important question is, what condition must hold in order that a policy, say $A$, can be unanimously agreed upon as best by i and $j$? The answer is that there must be equally good or superior alternatives in the market for the firm's streams and they must be available at a sufficiently low price to make transformation by i or $j$ superior to holding shares in the firm.[5] To see this, assume that i and $j$ above agree that $A$ is the best policy for the firm to pursue. For this to be so, i must know of some way to transform $\tilde{\mathbf{Y}}_{Ai}$ into another stream, say $\tilde{\mathbf{Y}}_{Ci}$ (e.g., by selling the firm's shares and buying the shares of another firm which provide returns $\tilde{\mathbf{Y}}_{Ci}$), where $\tilde{\mathbf{Y}}_{Ci}$ is as desirable as $\tilde{\mathbf{Y}}_{Bi}$ (recall that $\tilde{\mathbf{Y}}_{Bi} P \tilde{\mathbf{Y}}_{Ai}$) but does not sell for more than $V[\tilde{\mathbf{Y}}_{Ai}]$, the market value of $\tilde{\mathbf{Y}}_{Ai}$. This can be done only if there exists a $\tilde{\mathbf{Y}}_{Ci}$ as good as $\tilde{\mathbf{Y}}_{Bi}$ which has a price $V[\tilde{\mathbf{Y}}_{Ci}] \leq V[\tilde{\mathbf{Y}}_{Ai}]$ (since i sells his or her shares in the firm for $V[\tilde{\mathbf{Y}}_{Ai}]$ in order to buy $\tilde{\mathbf{Y}}_{Ci}$ for $V[\tilde{\mathbf{Y}}_{Ci}]$). It is clear that a market opportunity must exist for i to transform the shares of the firm into an alternative to $\tilde{\mathbf{Y}}_{Bi}$ that i feels is at least as good as $\tilde{\mathbf{Y}}_{Bi}$, and for a price that does not involve a net loss to i (i.e., a price no greater than the value of i's shares in the firm).

It should be kept in mind that, for unanimity in general, substitutes for the firm's securities not only must exist but must be obtainable at a price which, when taxes and transactions costs are netted out, is sufficiently low that all shareholders can rearrange their portfolios and be better off under the same policy. With homogeneous expectations and negligible transaction costs and taxes, assumption A.3 is likely to at least be approximately satisfied and share-value maximization is a valid goal and unanimity will likely hold. But, in actuality, expectations are often diverse and tax effects and even transaction costs are frequently significant; in such cases, substitutes with sufficiently low prices may not exist and consequently unanimity among shareholders may be absent.

[5] A general statement of the proposition is: If there are no constraints on investor utility functions, wealth levels, and expectations, for unanimity among shareholders to exist in general, for each shareholder there must exist in the market the capability to create a perfect substitute for every stream the firm can provide to its shareholders, the substitute must sell at a price equal to the price of the firm's stream generated to the shareholder under the unanimously preferred policy.

The above discussion focused on shareholder unanimity. The same concepts apply to bondholders as a group and to bondholders and stockholders as a single group. Thus, bondholders are unanimous only if there exists a policy $w$ satisfying (17-2) for all bondholders (the policy $w$ unanimously preferred by bondholders may differ from the policy $w$ unanimously preferred by shareholders, as discussed in the next section below). We can also say that for all shareholders and bondholders to be unanimous (as a single group) there must be some single policy $w$ which satisfies (17-2) both shareholders and bondholders. In general, there can be unanimity among all shareholders and bondholders, among shareholders but not bondholders, among bondholders but not shareholders, or no unanimity at all. The reason that we focus most sharply on shareholder unanimity is that it is shareholders who select management (indirectly through a board of directors) and it is the interests of shareholders that firm policy is meant to serve.

## III. SHARE VALUE AND FIRM VALUE

We have shown that share-value maximization is a valid firm objective (i.e., maximizes shareholder utility) under certain conditions. The question arises whether firm-value maximization (maximization of the total market value of the firm's stocks *and* bonds) is consistent with share-value maximization or with maximum benefit to the shareholders. Is it possible, for example, that a policy $A$ will maximize firm value but that alternative policy $B$ will maximize share value? The answer is yes, which means that share-value and firm-value maximization are not necessarily consistent goals.

Any lack of consistency poses problems both in theory and in practice. First, criteria for optimal financing policies become more difficult to specify. We must consider the implications of any given financing policy both for share values and for bond values now and in the long run. A financing decision which appears to be desirable in the short run from the viewpoint of the shareholders may result in capital losses for the firm's bondholders. In the long run bondholders will seek to protect themselves against such actions by imposing constraints on the firm. These constraints may impose future costs on the firm. To the extent that such costs are anticipated by present investors, share values may actually decrease as a result of what initially appeared to be a decision that was beneficial to the stockholders. We discussed some of these issues at the beginning of Chap. 12 and also in Chap. 15.

A second problem area is in criteria for firm investment decisions. Our previous analysis focused almost entirely on firm-value maximizing investment decisions.[6] If maximum firm value is not consistent with maximum share value, then investment decisions based on the former may result in the stockholders'

[6] In our previous analysis, we made assumptions that implied that firm-value maximization and share-value maximization were always consistent objectives.

being worse off from the investment decision. Not only must our investment criteria be revised to consider the impact on share value, but also the criteria themselves become more complex and less easy to apply in practice. In particular, the investment rules which result may be less easily applied by lower levels of management so that optimal decentralized investment decisions may not be possible. Large firms virtually cannot operate without some decentralization, and management may be forced into a choice between inaccurate decentralized investment criteria or costly centralized procedures. Thus the consistency between firm-value maximization and share-value maximization is an important issue for business finance.

A final problem area concerns the impact of firm decisions on society. Although we do not consider the issue in this book, total firm-value maximization is important in the theory of social welfare. If firms pursue policies that do not maximize total value, then society is likely to be benefited less by those policies than by alternative policies that do maximize total value. Consequently the issue has broad, theoretical importance.

There are two principal causes for divergences between policies that maximize firm value and those that maximize share value:

1. *The firm adopts investments which change the risk of the firm's outstanding bonds*. For example, the firm's low risk bonds may become much more risky if the company undertakes a new and very risky activity. Thus the investment may produce a $\Delta S > 0$ and a $\Delta B < 0$ which could imply a $\Delta V = \Delta S + \Delta B < 0$. Or the firm's previously high-risk bonds may become less risky if the company expands its asset base or shifts from high-risk to low-risk activities. In this case we could have a $\Delta S < 0$, $\Delta B > 0$, and a $\Delta V = \Delta S + \Delta B > 0$.
2. *The firm issues new bonds which are not of a lower priority than the old bonds*. This will lower the value of the old bonds (since their position is now riskier) and produce a benefit to the shareholders. Assume A.1, A.2, A.4, A.5 or A.6, A.7, and A.8 and that there are no corporate taxes; therefore, the firm's total value (stock plus bonds) is independent of its debt-equity ratio.[7] Assume that the firm issues new bonds of value $B^N$ and pays the proceeds to shareholders as a dividend. The assets and total income of the firm do not change and therefore firm value does not change. Define $V^*$, $B^{O*}$, and $S^{O*}$ as the value of the firm, of the old bonds, and of the shares before the new bonds are sold and $V^{**}$, $B^{O**}$, and $S^{O**}$ as the values after the new bonds are sold (let $S^{O**}$ be the ex-dividend value). The net benefit (if any) to shareholders from issuing new bonds and paying out the proceeds to shareholders is determined as follows:

$$V^* = S^{O*} + B^{O*} \tag{17-3}$$

$$V^{**} = S^{O**} + B^{O**} + B^N \tag{17-4}$$

[7] See chap. 11, pp. 284 to 286.

where

$$V^* = V^{**} \tag{17-5}$$

Shareholders get $S^{O**}$ plus dividend $D_0$ where

$$D_0 = B^N \tag{17-6}$$

The shareholders' net benefit from the sale of new bonds and dividend payments is [using (17-3) to (17-6)]

$$\begin{aligned} \text{Net benefit to shareholders} &= (S^{o**} + D_0) - S^{o*} \\ &= (V^{**} - B^{o**} - B^N + D_0) - (V^* - B^{o*}) \\ &= (V^{**} - V^*) + (B^{o*} - B^{o**}) \\ &= B^{o*} - B^{o**} \end{aligned} \tag{17-7}$$

Equation (17-7) shows that the shareholders will only benefit from issuing the new bonds if the value of the old bonds falls, i.e., if $B^{O*} - B^{O**} > 0$. If the new bonds have the same priority as the old bonds, the value of the old bonds will fall and the shareholders will benefit.[8] In this case shareholders benefit even though firm value remains unchanged [since (17-7) is positive but (17-5) holds]. Indeed, in general, a policy could reduce $V$ and reduce $B^O$ (because of nonsubordination of new debt) and shareholders benefit.

The most important implication of the above discussion is that if the objective of the firm is to maximize share values, it is not generally correct to look at firm value as a guide. Policies that maximize share value $S$ may not maximize firm value $V$, and vice versa.[9]

The question that immediately follows is whether there are conditions under which the policy that maximizes $V$ also maximizes $S$. Keep in mind that maximizing $V$ means maximizing the joint wealth of the shareholders and bondholders, i.e., maximizing the total value of the net returns from the firm's

[8] To see why the issuance of new bonds that are not subordinated to the old bonds will increase the risk of the old bonds (assuming no investments by the firm that neutralize this effect), assume that the firm sells new bonds $B^N$ and uses the proceeds to acquire some of the firm's stock. Assume that the promised interest on the old bonds is \$100,000 and on the new bonds is \$50,000. The assets and income (EBIT) of the firm are unaffected. If the new bonds are subordinated to the old bonds, the old bonds are unaffected since they still have first priority to the firm's unchanged EBIT (the first \$100,000 goes to the old bonds). But, if the new bonds are *not* subordinated to the old bonds, the old bonds must share the priority position with the new bonds. Thus, if the firm has an EBIT of \$100,000, \$66,667 goes to the old bonds and \$33,333 goes to the new bonds (with subordination, all of the \$100,000 would have gone to the old bonds).

[9] When we refer to investment and financing (1 and 2 above) policies that affect old bond values and thereby create a discrepancy between share-value and bond-value maximization, we do not necessarily mean that the impact on the value of the old bonds occurs when the investment or financing policy is adopted. The market may have already anticipated 1 or 2 before 1 or 2 occurred and consequently may have placed a lower value on the old bonds. The point made here is that 1 or 2 or the expectation of 1 or 2 can cause a fall in the value of the old bonds and a corresponding increase in the value of shares.

assets. Maximizing $S$ and $V$ are consistent under either one of the following assumptions:

> A. *All debt is riskless.* If debt is riskless, the value of outstanding bonds will not change as a result of firm decisions so that maximum $S$ is always achieved at maximum $V$.
> B. *Capital markets have no transaction costs (A.1) and are competitive (A.3), personal taxes are neutral (A.2), and investor expectations are homogeneous (A.5).*

Under case $B$ we need to consider two possibilities: (1) that the firm is pursuing policies that maximize the firm's total value ($V = S + B$), and (2) that the firm is not pursuing policies that maximize the firm's total value. Let $V_s$, $S_s$, and $B_s$ be the values with any policy other than the firm-value maximizing policy and let $V_v$, $S_v$, and $B_v$ be the values with the total value ($V$) maximizing policy. Suppose that the firm is presently pursuing policy $S$, where, since policy $v$ maximizes $V$, it follows that

$$V_s < V_v \tag{17-8}$$

Consistent with (17-8) would be $S_s < S_v$ and $B_s < B_v$. We now show that it is in the interests of the shareholders for the firm to change policies so as to maximize $V$, i.e., achieve $V_v$. Note that, under assumption A.3, the firm could borrow $B_s$ on a short-term basis, purchase all bonds outstanding for $B_s$, change its policies to those that maximize $V$, and then issue new bonds in amount $B_s$ to pay off the short-term debt.[10] The stockholders now own all the firm's stock which is worth $S_v = V_v - B_s$. The change in stockholder wealth is therefore

$$S_v - S_s = (V_v - B_s) - S_s = V_v - V_s > 0 \tag{17-9}$$

Thus share values increase by shifting from policy $s$ to policy $v$ and performing the appropriate bond transaction; i.e., policy $v$ is best. That is, if the firm is pursuing any policy other than $v$, it can raise $S$ by adopting $v$ and performing the proper bond transactions.

Notice that if management does not perform these transactions there is an incentive for others—the bondholders or outsider investors or other firms—to buy up the stock at a price of $S_s$ (and the bonds at $B_s$ in the case of outsiders) and force a change in firm policy to policy $v$. Thus, whether management, bondholders, or outsiders take the initiative, the firm should pursue policies that maximize its total value.

Assumptions A.1, A.2, A.3, and A.5 also imply the possibility of side payments between shareholders and bondholders which will lead to the adoption of firm policies that always maximize $V$. Assume again policies $s$ and $v$ and that the values of the bonds are $B_s$ and $B_v$ under those policies, respectively. First assume that $B_v > B_s$. Bondholders would pay shareholders (or the firm)

[10] We ignore interest on the short-term debt since with A.1, A.2, A.3, and A.5, the transaction can be virtually instantaneous, implying negligible interest.

$(B_v - B_s)$ in side payments to encourage the firm to adopt *v* rather than *s*. For purposes of this discussion of side payments, note that we are defining $B$, $S$, and $V$ as values of the currently outstanding (old) bonds and shares and total firm value, respectively, one moment *after* the side payments are made. That is, for example, $S_v$ does not include the value of side payment $(B_v - B_s)$ in the case where $B_v > B_s$. Thus the shareholders' wealth gain from adopting *v* over *s* is the following amount:

Gain to shareholders from adopting policy *v* over policy *s*

$$\begin{aligned} &= \text{(change in share value)} + \text{(side payment)} \\ &= (S_v - S_s) + (B_v - B_s) \\ &= V_v - V_s > 0 \end{aligned} \qquad (17\text{-}10)$$

Thus, shareholder wealth maximization dictates adopting *v* if $B_v > B_s$. Now assume that $B_v < B_s$, in which case bondholders would pay shareholders $(B_s - B_v)$ *not* to adopt policy *v*. By adopting *v* over *s* the shareholders' net gain equals:

Gain to shareholders from adopting policy *v* over policy *s*

$$\begin{aligned} &= \text{(change in share value)} - \text{(loss of side payment)} \\ &= (S_v - S_s) - (B_s - B_v) \\ &= V_v - V_s > 0 \end{aligned} \qquad (17\text{-}11)$$

Again, shareholder wealth maximization dictates adopting firm-value maximizing policy *v*.

As a side point, there is another situation which implies that firm-value maximization will be the *shareholders'* goal even though firm-value maximization and share-value maximization are *not* necessarily consistent. This is the case (which we shall refer to as case *C*) in which, at the time the firm policy is being made, shareholders and bondholders are the same people, with each shareholder owning the same proportion of the firm's bonds as the shareholders own of the firm's stocks (e.g., shareholder i owns 10% of the firm's shares and 10% of the firm's bonds, *j* owns 5% of the stock and 5% of the bonds, etc.). When case *C* holds, a policy which maximizes the total value of the firm's securities will be preferred over other policies by the shareholders (who are also the bondholders). Of course, this policy may not result in maximum share values, but this is not important since bond values will be great enough to compensate for the lower share values (if *V* is maximized) and the benefits from the higher bond values go to the shareholders.

If none of cases *A*, *B*, and *C* holds, share-value and firm-value maximization may conflict and maximization of total firm value may result in the firm's adopting policies that are not in the best interests of the shareholders. How likely is this? For many companies, the debt is of such low risk that it is relatively insensitive to financing and investment decisions; i.e., case *A* approximately holds. The market value of the debt therefore does not change for normal financial decisions made by these firms. The low risk of the debt is often due in part to the use of restrictions in the debt contracts which prevent management from taking actions that would benefit the shareholders at the expense of the firm's creditors. "Me first" rules that require the subordination of new debt to existing debt or the pledging of specific assets to serve as collateral for the debt keep new financing from appreciably increasing the risk of the existing debt. The result is that for many companies the debt can be considered sufficiently riskless that total-value maximization is a reasonable objective for the firm.

Case *C* requires investors to own both the stock and the bonds of the firm when the firm's policies are set. In practice this is rare. However, one of the implications of the single-period perfect-markets model of Chaps. 7 and 8 was precisely this result. Recall that investors, under the assumptions of that model, would hold a proportionate share of all risky assets—the market portfolio. We might consider what assumptions were sufficient to permit investors to hold proportionate shares of the firm's stock and bonds. These assumptions are A.1 through A.5, the existence of a riskless asset, a single-period framework, and all assets tradable in the marketplace (including human capital). Since this set of assumptions is not very realistic, it is not surprising that we find very few investors holding the market portfolio.

Case *B* is also not too likely to hold. Usually the transactions costs (violation of A.1) and the existence of a noninfinite elasticity of demand for the firm's securities (violation of A.3) mean that buying up all the firm's bonds (or stock or both) is far more costly than simply the current market value ($S_s$ and $B_s$ in the above discussion).[11] The potential gain from such activity ($V_v - V_s$) is usually too small relative to the costs to justify the action. Thus, for firms with risky debt, maximization of $V$ may not be in the best interests of the shareholders.

Let us review and restate the issues in a somewhat different way. If management pursues policies that maximize the total value of the firm's securities, under some circumstances those policies may result in lower values for the firm's shares but higher values for the firm's debt (bonds). If the shareholders can capture the potential benefits accruing to the bondholders, then total-value maximization is consistent with share-value and shareholder-*wealth* maximization; otherwise it may not be.[12]

## SUMMARY

We have seen that shareholders will all agree that those firm policies which maximize share values are best if capital market transactions are costless (A.1),

[11] A less than infinite elasticity of demand means that there is not a large number of substitutes in the market for the firm's stock and bonds. The result is that as one buys up the firm's shares (or bonds), the price will tend to rise since it takes a higher and higher price to induce less willing shareholders to sell their stock. With many perfect substitutes in the market (assumption A.3) a shareholder will be willing to sell out for only slightly more than the going market value $S^*$, say $S^* + \delta$ (small $\delta$), since a perfect substitute for the stock is available elsewhere at price $S^*$.

[12] See the footnote on p. 468 on why share-value and shareholder-wealth maximization are the same.

personal taxes are neutral (A.2), and capital markets are competitive with perfect substitutes available for all streams (A.3). (We can substitute A.9 for A.1 and A.2.)

Assumptions A.1, A.2, and A.3 (or A.3 and A.9) are sufficient to ensure that shareholders are unanimous, i.e., all prefer the same policies; however, there are other assumptions which also produce unanimity. For all individual stockholders to agree, perfect substitutes must be available for any streams that may be preferred over the ones that maximize share value and those substitute streams must be obtainable at a price which is no greater than the maximum share value achieved by the firm.

We found that share-value maximization is consistent with firm-value maximization if either firm debt is riskless or if assumptions A.1, A.2, A.3, and A.5 hold. It was also observed that shareholders will prefer firm-value maximization over share-value maximization if they own the firm's debt as well as equity; however, this is highly unlikely in actuality.

## SUGGESTED READINGS

Fama, E. F. and M. H. Miller: "The Theory of Finance," Chap. 4, Holt, Rinehart and Winston, Inc., New York, 1972.

Grossman, S. J. and J. E. Stiglitz: On Value Maximization and Alternative Objectives of the Firm, *Journal of Finance,* vol. 32, pp. 389–402, May 1977.

Jensen, M. C. and W. H. Meckling: Theory of the Firm: Managerial Behavior, Agency Costs and Ownership Structure, *Journal of Financial Economics,* vol. 3, pp. 305–360, October, 1976.

Kim, E. Han, J. J. McConnell, and P. R. Greenwood: Capital Structure Rearrangements and Me-First Rules in an Efficient Capital Market, *Journal of Finance,* vol. 32, no. 3, pp. 789–810, June 1977.

Milne, F.: Choice over Asset Economies: Default Risk and Corporate Leverage, *Journal of Financial Economics,* vol. 2, pp. 165–185, June 1975.

# BIBLIOGRAPHY


Alberts, William W.: The Profitability of Conglomerate Investment Mergers: Sources and Prospects, *University of Washington Business Review,* Winter 1970, pp. 13–27.

——— and Joel E. Segall (eds.): "The Corporate Merger," 2d ed., University of Chicago, 1975.

Altman, Edward I.: Corporate Bankruptcy Potential, Stockholders Returns, and Share Valuation, *Journal of Finance,* vol. 24, pp. 887–900, December 1969.

———: Financial Ratios, Discriminant Analysis and the Prediction of Corporate Bankruptcy, *Journal of Finance,* vol. 23, pp. 589–609, September 1968.

Ang, James: Weighted Average vs. True Cost of Capital, *Financial Management,* vol. 2, pp. 56–60, Autumn 1973.

Archer, Stephen H. and LeRoy G. Faerber: Firm Size and the Cost of Equity Capital, *Journal of Finance,* vol. 21, pp. 69–84, March 1966.

Arditti, Fred D.: Risk and the Required Return on Equity, *Journal of Finance,* vol. 22, pp. 19–36, March 1967.

———: The Weighted Average Cost of Capital: Some Questions on Its Definition, Interpretation, and Use, *Journal of Finance,* vol. 28, pp. 1001–1008, September 1973.

——— and John M. Pinkerton: The Valuation and the Cost of Capital of the Levered Firm with Growth Opportunities, *Journal of Finance,* vol. 33, no. 1, pp. 65–73, March 1978.

Arrow, Kenneth: "Essays in the Theory of Risk-Bearing," Markham Publishing Co., Chicago, Ill., 1971.

———: The Role of Securities in the Optimal Allocation of Risk Bearing, *Review of Economic Studies,* vol. 31, pp. 91–96, April 1964.

Azzi, C.: Conglomerate Mergers, Default Risk, and Homemade Mutual Funds, *American Economic Review,* vol. 68, no. 1, pp. 161–172, March 1978.

Bailey, Martin J.: Formal Criteria for Investment Decisions, *Journal of Political Economy,* vol. 67, October 1959.

Banz, Rolf W. and Merton H. Miller: Prices for State-Contingent Claims: Some Estimates and Applications, *Journal of Business,* vol. 51, October 1978.

Barges, Alexander: "The Effect of Capital Structure on the Cost of Capital," Prentice-Hall, Inc., Englewood Cliffs, N.J., 1963.

Baumol, William J.: "Business Behavior, Value and Growth," The Macmillan Company, New York, 1959.

———: On Dividend Policy and Market Imperfection, *Journal of Business,* vol. 36, pp. 112–115, January 1963.

———: The Transactions Demand for Cash: An Inventory Theoretic Approach, *Quarterly Journal of Economics,* vol. 65, pp. 542–556, November 1952.

——— and Burton G. Malkiel: The Firm's Optimal Debt-Equity Combination and the Cost of Capital, *Quarterly Journal of Economics,* vol. 81, pp. 547–578, November 1967.

———, ———, and Richard E. Quandt: The Valuation of Convertible Securities, *Quarterly Journal of Economics,* vol. 80, pp. 48–59, February 1966.

———, and ———: Investment and Discount Rates under Capital Rationing—A Programming Approach, *Economic Journal,* vol. 75, pp. 317–329, June 1965.

Baxter, Nevins D.: Leverage, Risk of Ruin, and the Cost of Capital, *Journal of Finance,* vol. 22, pp. 395–404, September 1967.

———: Marketability, Default Risk, and Yields on Money-Market Instruments, *Journal of Financial and Quantitative Analysis,* vol. 3, pp. 75–85, March 1968.

Beaver, William H.: Market Prices, Financial Ratios, and the Prediction of Failure, *Journal of Accounting Research,* vol. 6, pp. 179–192, Autumn 1968.

Ben-Zion, Uri and Michael Balch: Corporate Financial Theory under Uncertainty: A Comment, *Quarterly Journal of Economics,* vol. 87, no. 2, pp. 290–295, May 1973.

Benishay, Haskel: Variability in Earnings-Price Ratios of Corporate Equities, *American Economic Review,* vol. 51, pp. 81–94, March 1961.

Beranek, William: "Analysis for Financial Decisions," Richard D. Irwin, Inc., Homewood, Ill., 1963.

———: The Cost of Capital, Capital Budgeting, and the Maximization of Shareholder Wealth, *Journal of Financial and Quantitative Analysis,* vol. 10, no. 1, pp. 1–20, March 1975.

Bernhard, Richard H.: Mathematical Programming Models for Capital Budgeting—A Survey, Generalization, and Critique, *Journal of Financial and Quantitative Analysis,* vol. 4, pp. 111–158, June 1969.

Bernoulli, Daniel: Exposition of a New Theory on the Measurement of Risk, *Econometrica,* vol. 22, pp. 23–36, January 1954.

Bierman, Harold, Jr.: The Bond Refunding Decision as a Markov Process, *Management Science,* vol. 12, pp. 545–551, August 1966.

———: Risk and the Addition of Debt to the Capital Structure, *Journal of Financial and Quantitative Analysis,* vol. 3, pp. 415–423, December 1968.

——— and Richard West: The Acquisition of Common Stock by the Corporate Issuer, *Journal of Finance,* vol. 21, pp. 687–696, December 1966.

Black, Fischer: Capital Market Equilibrium with Restricted Borrowing, *Journal of Business,* vol. 45, no. 3, pp. 444–455, July 1972.

———: Fact and Fantasy in the Use of Options, *Financial Analysts Journal,* vol. 31, pp. 36–72, July–August 1975.

———: The Pricing of Commodity Contracts, *Journal of Financial Economics,* vol. 3, nos. 1–2, pp. 167–179, January/March 1976.

——— and John C. Cox: Valuing Corporate Securities: Some Effects of Bond Indenture Provisions, *Journal of Finance,* vol. 31, no. 2, pp. 351–367, May 1976.

——— and Myron Scholes: The Effects of Dividend Yield and Dividend Policy on Common Stock Prices, *Journal of Financial Economics,* vol. 1, no. 1, pp. 1–22, May 1974.

——— and ———: The Pricing of Options and Corporate Liabilities, *Journal of Political Economy,* vol. 81, pp. 637–654, May–June 1973.

——— and ———: The Valuation of Option Contracts and a Test of Market Efficiency, *Journal of Finance,* vol. 27, pp. 399–417, May 1972.

Blume, Marshall E.: Portfolio Theory: A Step toward Its Practical Application, *Journal of Business,* vol. 43, pp. 152–173, April 1970.

——— and Irwin Friend: A New Look at the Capital Asset Pricing Model, *Journal of Finance,* vol. 28, no. 1, pp. 19–33, March 1973.

Bodenhorn, Diran: A Cash Flow Concept of Profit, *Journal of Finance,* vol. 19, pp. 16–31, March 1964.

———: On the Problem of Capital Budgeting, *Journal of Finance,* vol. 14, pp. 473–492, December 1959.

Boness, A. James: A Pedagogic Note on the Cost of Capital, *Journal of Finance,* vol. 19, pp. 99–106, March 1964.

Borch, Karl: "The Economics of Uncertainty," Princeton University Press, Princeton, N.J., 1968.

Bower, Richard S. and Dorothy H. Bower: Risk and the Valuation of Common Stock, *Journal of Political Economy,* vol. 77, pp. 349–362, May–June 1969.

Brealey, Richard A.: "An Introduction to Risk and Return from Common Stocks," The M.I.T. Press, Cambridge, Mass., 1969.

Breeden, Douglas T. and Robert H. Litzenberger: Prices of State-Contingent Claims Implicit in Option Prices, *Journal of Business,* vol. 51, October 1978.

Brennan, Michael J.: An Approach to the Valuation of Uncertain Income Streams, *Journal of Finance,* vol. 28, pp. 661–674, June 1973.

———: A New Look at the Weighted Average Cost of Capital, *Journal of Business Finance,* vol. 5, pp. 24–30, Winter 1973.

———: Capital Market Equilibrium with Divergent Borrowing and Lending Rates, *Journal of Financial and Quantitative Analysis,* vol. 6, pp. 1197–1208, December 1971.

Brewer, D. E. and J. Michaelson: The Cost of Capital, Corporation Finance, and the Theory of Investment: Comment, *American Economic Review,* vol. 55, pp. 516–524, June 1965.

Brigham, Eugene F.: An Analysis of Convertible Debentures: Theory and Some Empirical Evidence, *Journal of Finance,* vol. 21, pp. 35–54, March 1966.

——— and Myron J. Gordon: Leverage, Dividend Policy, and the Cost of Capital, *Journal of Finance,* vol. 23, pp. 85–104, March 1968.

Brittain, John A.: "Corporate Dividend Policy," The Brookings Institution, Washington, 1966.

Carleton, Willard T.: Linear Programming and Capital Budgeting Models: A New Interpretation, *Journal of Finance,* vol. 24, pp. 825–833, December 1969.

Carleton, Willard T., Charles L. Dick, Jr., and David H. Downes: Financial Policy Models: Theory and Practice, *Journal of Financial and Quantitative Analysis,* vol. 8, no. 5, pp. 691–710, December 1973.

Chen, Andrew H. and James A. Boness: Effects of Uncertain Inflation on the Investment and Financing Decisions of a Firm, *Journal of Finance,* vol. 30, no. 2, pp. 469–483, May 1975.

———, E. H. Kim, and S. J. Kon: Cash Demand, Liquidation Costs, and Capital Market Equilibrium under Uncertainty, *Journal of Financial Economics,* vol. 2, no. 3, pp. 293–308, September 1975.

———, ———, and ———: Cash Demand, Liquidation Costs, and Capital Market Equilibrium under Uncertainty: Reply, *Journal of Financial Economics,* vol. 3, no. 3, pp. 297–298, June 1976.

Cheng, P. L. and M. K. Deets: Statistical Biases and Security Rates of Return, *Journal of Financial and Quantitative Analysis,* vol. 6, pp. 977–994, June 1971.

Cohan, Avery B.: "Private Placements and Public Offerings: Market Shares Since 1935," School of Business Administration, University of North Carolina Press, Chapel Hill, N.C., 1961.

———: "Yields on Corporate Debt Directly Placed," National Bureau of Economic Research, New York, 1967.

Cohen, Dalman J. and Edwin J. Elton: Inter-temporal Portfolio Analysis Based upon Simulation of Joint Returns, *Management Science,* vol. 14, pp. 5–18, September 1967.

Conard, J. W.: "An Introduction to the Theory of Interest," University of California Press, Berkeley, 1959.

Constantinides, G. M.: Comment on Chen, Kim and Kon, *Journal of Financial Economics,* vol. 3, no. 3, pp. 295–296, June 1976.

Cord, Joel: A Method for Allocating Funds to Investment Projects When Returns Are Subject to Uncertainty, *Management Science,* vol. 10, pp. 335–341, January 1964.

Cox, John and Stephen Ross: A Survey of Some New Results in Financial Option Pricing Theory, *Journal of Finance,* vol. 31, no. 2, pp. 383–402, May 1976.

——— and ———: The Valuation of Options for Alternative Stochastic Processes, *Journal of Financial Economics,* vol. 3, nos. 1–2, pp. 145–166, January/March 1976.

Dann, Larry, David Mayers, and Robert J. Raab, Jr.: Trading Rules, Large Blocks and the Speed of Price Adjustment, *Journal of Financial Economics,* vol. 4, no. 1, pp. 3–22, January 1977.

Darling, Paul G.: The Influence of Expectations and Liquidity on Dividend Policy, *Journal of Political Economy,* vol. 65, pp. 209–224, June 1957.

DeAngelo, H.: "Three Essays in Financial Economics," Ph.D. dissertation, U.C.L.A., 1977.

——— and Ronald W. Masulis: Optimal Capital Structures Under Corporate and Personal Taxation, working paper, U.C.L.A., 1977.

Debreu, G.: "The Theory of Value," John Wiley & Sons, Inc., New York, 1959.

Dhrymes, Phoebus J. and Mordecai Kurz: On the Dividend Policy of Electric Utilities, *Review of Economics and Statistics,* vol. 46, pp. 76–81, February 1964.

Diamond, Peter: A Stock Market in a General Equilibrium Model, *American Economic Review,* vol. 57, pp. 759–776, September 1967.

———: Welfare Analysis of Imperfect Information Equilibria, *Bell Journal of Economics and Management Science,* vol. 9, no. 1, pp. 82–105, Spring 1978.

Dobrovolsky, S. P.: Economics of Corporate Internal and External Financing, *Journal of Finance,* vol. 13, pp. 35–47, March 1958.

Donaldson, Gordon: "Corporate Debt Capacity," Division of Research, Harvard Business School, Boston, 1961.

———: In Defense of Preferred Stock, *Harvard Business Review,* vol. 40, pp. 123–136, July–August 1962.

Dudley, Carlton L., Jr.: A Note on Reinvestment Assumptions in Choosing between Net Present Value and Internal Rate of Return, *Journal of Finance,* vol. 27, no. 4, pp. 907–915, September 1972.

Durand, David: The Cost of Capital, Corporation Finance, and the Theory of Investment: Comment, *American Economic Review,* vol. 49, pp. 639–655, September 1959.

Ekern, Steinar: On the Theory of the Firm in an Economy with Incomplete Markets: An Addendum, *Bell Journal of Economics and Management Science,* vol. 6, no. 1, pp. 388–393, Spring 1975.

——— and R. Wilson: On the Theory of the Firm in an Economy with Incomplete Markets, *Bell Journal of Economics and Management Science,* vol. 5, no. 1, pp. 171–180, Spring 1974.

Ellsburg, D.: Classic and Current Notions of "Measurable Utility", *Economic Journal,* vol. 64, pp. 528–556, September 1954.

Elton, Edwin J.: Capital Rationing and External Discount Rates, *Journal of Finance,* vol. 25, pp. 573–584, June 1970.

———: The Effect of Share Repurchases on the Value of the Firm, *Journal of Finance,* vol. 23, pp. 135–150, March 1968.

——— and Martin J. Gruber: Asset Selection with Changing Capital Structure, *Journal of Financial and Quantitative Analysis,* vol. 8, pp. 459–474, June 1973.

——— and ———: Marginal Stockholder Tax Rates and the Clientele Effect, *Review of Economics and Statistics,* February 1970.

Fama, Eugene F.: The Behavior of Stock Market Prices, *Journal of Business,* vol. 38, pp. 34–105, January 1965.

———: The Effects of a Firm's Investment and Financing Decisions, *American Economic Review,* vol. 68, no. 3, pp. 272–284, June 1978.

———: The Effects of a Firm's Investment and Financing Decisions on the Welfare of Its Securityholders, unpublished manuscript, University of Chicago, 1977.

———: Efficient Capital Markets: A Review of Theory and Empirical Work, *Journal of Finance,* vol. 35, pp. 383–417, May 1970.

———: The Empirical Relationships between the Dividend and Investment Decisions of Firms, *American Economic Review,* vol. 64, no. 3, pp. 304–318, June 1974.

———: Multiperiod Consumption-Investment Decisions, *American Economic Review,* vol. 60, pp. 163–174, March 1970.

———: Risk Adjusted Discount Rates and Capital Budgeting under Uncertainty, *Journal of Financial Economics,* vol. 5, no. 1, pp. 3–24, August 1977.

———: Risk, Return, and Equilibrium: Some Clarifying Comments, *Journal of Finance,* vol. 23, pp. 29–40, March 1968.

——— and Harvey Babiak: Dividend Policy: An Empirical Analysis, *Journal of the American Statistical Association,* vol. 63, pp. 1132–1161, December 1968.

———, Lawrence Fisher, Michael Jensen, and Richard Roll: The Adjustment of Stock Prices to New Information, *International Economic Review,* vol. 10, pp. 1–21, February 1969.

——— and James D. MacBeth: Risk, Return, and Equilibrium: Empirical Tests, *Journal of Political Economy,* vol. 81, no. 3, pp. 607–636, May/June 1973.

——— and Merton H. Miller: "The Theory of Finance," Holt, Rinehart and Winston, Inc., New York, 1972.

——— and G. William Schwert: Asset Returns and Inflation, *Journal of Financial Economics,* vol. 5, no. 2, pp. 115–146, November 1977.

——— and ———: Human Capital and Capital Market Equilibrium, *Journal of Financial Economics,* vol. 4, no. 1, pp. 95–125, January 1977.

Farrar, Donald E. and Lee L. Selwyn: Taxes, Corporate Financial Policy and Return to Investors, *National Tax Journal,* vol. 20, pp. 444–454, 1967.

Feldstein, M. S.: Mean-Variance Analysis in the Theory of Liquidity Preference and Portfolio Selection, *Review of Economic Studies,* January 1969.

Fischer, Stanley: The Demand for Index Bonds, *Journal of Political Economy,* vol. 83, no. 3, pp. 509–534, June 1975.

Fishburn, Peter C.: Utility Theory, *Management Science,* vol. 14, pp. 335–378, January 1968.

Fisher, Donald E. and Glenn A. Wilt, Jr.: Nonconvertible Preferred Stock as a Financing Instrument, 1950–1965, *Journal of Finance,* vol. 23, pp. 611–624, September 1968.

Fisher, Irving: "The Theory of Interest," Augustus M. Kelley, Publishers, New York, 1965 (reprinted from the 1930 edition).

Fisher, Lawrence: Determinants of Risk Premiums on Corporate Bonds, *Journal of Political Economy,* vol. 57, pp. 217–237, June 1959.

Friedman, Milton and Leonard J. Savage: The Utility Analysis of Choices Involving Risk, *Journal of Political Economy,* vol. 56, pp. 279–304, August 1948.

Friend, Irwin and Marshall E. Blume: The Demand for Risky Assets, *American Economic Review,* vol. 65, no. 5, pp. 900–922, December 1975.

——— and Marshall Puckett: Dividends and Stock Prices, *American Economic Review,* vol. 54, pp. 656–682, September 1964.

———, Randolph Westerfield, and Michael Granito: New Evidence on the Capital Asset Pricing Model, *Journal of Finance,* vol. 33, no. 3, pp. 903–916, June 1978.

Galai, D. and R. W. Masulis: The Option Pricing Model and the Risk Factor of Stock, *Journal of Financial Economics,* vol. 3, no. 1/2, pp. 53–81, January/March 1976.

Gordon, Myron J.: A General Solution to the Buy or Lease Decision: A Pedagogical Note, *Journal of Finance,* vol. 29, no. 1, pp. 245–250, March 1974.

———: Optimal Investment and Dividend Policy, *Journal of Finance,* vol. 18, pp. 264–272, May 1963.

———: Towards a Theory of Financial Distress, *Journal of Finance,* vol. 26, pp. 347–356, May 1971.

Grossman, S. J. and J. E. Stiglitz: On Value Maximization and Alternative Objectives of the Firm, *Journal of Finance,* vol. 32, no. 1, pp. 389–402, May 1977.

Hakansson, Nils H.: Friedman-Savage Utility Functions Consistent with Risk Aversion, *Quarterly Journal of Economics,* vol. 84, no. 3, pp. 472–487, August 1970.

———: On the Dividend Capitalization Model under Uncertainty, *Journal of Financial and Quantitative Analysis,* vol. 4, pp. 65–87, March 1969.

———: Optimal Investment and Consumption Strategies under Risk for a Class of Utility Functions, *Econometrica,* vol. 38, pp. 587–607, September 1970.

Haley, C. W.: Comment on the Valuation of Risk Assets . . . , *Review of Economics and Statistics,* pp. 220–221, May 1969.

———: A Note on the Cost of Debt, *Journal of Financial and Quantitative Analysis,* vol. 1, pp. 72–93, December 1966.

———: Taxes, the Cost of Capital, and the Firm's Investment Decision, *Journal of Finance,* pp. 901–918, September 1971.

——— and Lawrence D. Schall: A Note on Investment Policy with Imperfect Capital Markets, *Journal of Finance,* vol. 27, pp. 93–96, March 1972.

——— and ———: Problems with the Concept of the Cost of Capital, *Journal of Financial and Quantitative Analysis,* vol. 13, pp. 847–880, December 1978.

Hamada, Robert S.: Investment Decisions with a Mean-Variance Approach, *Quarterly Journal of Economics,* vol. 85, no. 4, pp. 667–683, November 1971.

———: Portfolio Analysis, Market Equilibrium and Corporation Finance, *Journal of Finance,* vol. 24, pp. 13–31, March 1969.

Hanoch, G. and H. Levy: The Efficiency Analysis of Choices Involving Risk, *Review of Economic Studies,* July 1969.

Haugen, Robert A. and Terence C. Langetieg: An Empirical Test for Synergism in Merger, *Journal of Finance,* vol. 30, no. 4, pp. 1003–1014, September 1975.

——— and Lemma W. Senbet: The Insignificance of Bankruptcy Costs to the Theory of Optimal Capital Structure, *Journal of Finance,* vol. 33, no. 2, pp. 383–393, May 1978.

Heins, A. James and Case M. Sprenkle: A Comment on the Modigliani-Miller Cost of Capital Thesis, *American Economic Review,* vol. 59, pp. 590–592, September 1969.

Hertz, D. B.: Risk Analysis in Capital Investment, *Harvard Business Review,* vol. 42, pp. 95–106, January–February 1964.

Hespos, Richard F. and Paul A. Strassmann: Stochastic Decision Trees for the Analysis of Investment Decisions, *Management Science,* vol. 11, pp. 224–259, August 1965.

Hicks, J. R.: "Value and Capital," 2d ed., Oxford University Press, Oxford, 1946.

Higgins, Robert C.: The Corporate Dividend-Savings Decision, *Journal of Financial and Quantitative Analysis,* March 1972.

———: Dividend Policy and Increasing Discount Rates: A Clarification, *Journal of Financial and Quantitative Analysis,* vol. 7, pp. 1157–1162, June 1972.

———: Growth, Dividend Policy, and the Cost of Capital to the Electric Utility Industry, *Journal of Finance,* vol. 29, no. 4, pp. 1189–1201, September 1974.

——— and Lawrence D. Schall: Corporate Bankruptcy and Conglomerate Merger, *Journal of Finance,* vol. 30, no. 1, pp. 93–111, March 1975.

Hillier, F. S.: The Derivation of Probabilistic Information for the Evaluation of Risky Investments, *Management Science,* April 1963.

Hirshleifer, Jack: Investment Decision under Uncertainty: Applications of the State-Preference Approach, *Quarterly Journal of Economics,* vol. 80, pp. 252–277, May 1966.

———: Investment Decision under Uncertainty: Choice-Theoretic Approaches, *Quarterly Journal of Economics,* vol. 79, pp. 509–536, November 1965.

———: "Investment, Interest and Capital," Prentice-Hall, Inc., Englewood Cliffs, N.J., 1970.

———: On the Theory of Optimal Investment Decision, *Journal of Political Economy,* August 1958.

Hite, Gailen L.: Leverage, Output Effects, and the M-M Theorems, *Journal of Financial Economics,* vol. 4, no. 2, pp. 177–202, March 1977.

Hogarty, Thomas F.: The Profitability of Corporate Mergers, *Journal of Business,* vol. 43, pp. 317–327, July 1970.

Ibbotson, Roger G. and Rex A. Sinquefield: Stocks, Bonds, Bills, and Inflation: Simulations of the Future (1976–2000), *Journal of Business,* vol. 49, pp. 313–338, July 1976.

——— and ———: Stocks, Bonds, Bills, and Inflation: Year-by-Year Historical Returns (1926–1974), *Journal of Business,* vol. 49, no. 1, pp. 11–47, January 1976.

Ingersoll, Jon E.: A Contingent-Claims Valuation of Convertible Securities, *Journal of Financial Economics,* vol. 4, pp. 289–322, 1977.

———: A Theoretical and Empirical Investigation of the Dual Purpose Funds: An Application of Contingent-Claims Analysis, *Journal of Financial Economics,* vol. 3, no. 1/2, pp. 83–124, January/March 1976.

Jaedicke, Robert K. and Robert T. Sprouse: "Accounting Flows: Income, Funds, and Cash," Prentice-Hall, Inc., Englewood Cliffs, N.J., 1965.

Jaffe, Jeffrey F.: Corporate Taxes, Inflation, the Rate of Interest and the Return to Equity, *Journal of Financial and Quantitative Analysis,* vol. 13, no. 1, pp. 55–64, March 1978.

Jen, Frank C. and James E. Wert: The Deferred Call Provision and Corporate Bond Yields, *Journal of Financial and Quantitative Analysis,* vol. 3, pp. 157–169, June 1968.

———: The Effect of Call Risk on Corporate Bond Yields, *Journal of Finance,* vol. 22, pp. 637–651, December 1967.

Jensen, Michael C.: Capital Markets: Theory and Evidence, *Bell Journal of Economics and Management Science,* vol. 3, no. 2, pp. 357–398, Autumn 1972.

———: Risk, the Pricing of Capital Assets, and the Evaluation of Investment Portfolios, *Journal of Business,* vol. 42, pp. 167–247, April 1969.

———: "Studies in the Theory of Capital Markets," Frederick A. Praeger, Inc., New York, 1972.

——— and John B. Long, Jr.: Corporate Investment under Uncertainty and Pareto Optimality in the Capital Markets, *Bell Journal of Economics and Management Science,* vol. 3, no. 1, pp. 151–174, Spring 1972.

——— and William H. Meckling: Theory of the Firm: Managerial Behavior, Agency Costs and Ownership Structure, *Journal of Financial Economics,* vol. 3, no. 4, pp. 305–360, October 1976.

Johnson, Keith B.: Stock Splits and Price Changes, *Journal of Finance,* vol. 21, pp. 675–686, December 1966.

Johnson, Ramon E.: Term Structures of Corporate Bond Yields as a Function of Risk of Default, *Journal of Finance,* vol. 22, pp. 313–345, May 1967.

Jorgenson, Dale W.: Econometric Studies of Investment Behavior: A Survey, *Journal of Economic Literature,* vol. 9, pp. 1111–1147, December 1971.

Keenan, Michael: Models of Equity Valuation: The Great SERM Bubble, *Journal of Finance,* vol. 25, pp. 243–273, May 1970.

Kim, E. Han: A Mean-Variance Theory of Optimal Capital Structure and Corporate Debt Capacity, *Journal of Finance,* vol. 33, no. 1, pp. 45–64, March 1978.

——— and John J. McConnell: Corporate Merger and the Co-Insurance of Corporate Debt, *Journal of Finance,* vol. 32, no. 2, pp. 349–365, May 1977.

———, John J. McConnell, and Paul R. Greenwood: Capital Structure Rearrangements and Me-First Rules in an Efficient Capital Market, *Journal of Finance,* vol. 32, no. 3, pp. 789–810, June 1977.

King, Benjamin F.: Market and Industry Factors in Stock Price Behavior, *Journal of Business,* vol. 39, pp. 139–190, January 1966.

Kraus, Alan: The Bond Refunding Decision in an Efficient Market, *Journal of Financial and Quantitative Analysis,* vol. 8, no. 5, pp. 793–806, December 1973.

——— and Robert Litzenberger: A State-Preference Model of Optimal Financial Leverage, *Journal of Finance,* vol. 28, no. 4, pp. 911–922, September 1973.

Krouse, Clement G.: Optimal Financing and Capital Structure Programs for the Firm, *Journal of Finance,* vol. 27, no. 5, pp. 1057–1072, December 1972.

——— and Wayne Y. Lee: Optimal Equity Financing of the Corporation, *Journal of Financial and Quantitative Analysis,* vol. 8, no. 4, pp. 539–564, September 1973.

Kruizenga, Richard: Introduction to the Option Contract, in P. Cootner (ed.), "The Random Character of Stock Prices" pp. 377–391, The M.I.T. Press, Boston, 1964.

Larner, Robert J.: "Management Control and the Large Corporation," Dunellen Publishing Co., New York, 1970.

Laudadio, Leonard: Size of Bank, Size of Borrower, and the Rate of Interest, *Journal of Finance,* vol. 18, pp. 20–28, March 1963.

Lerner, Eugene M.: Capital Budgeting and Financial Management, in Alexander A. Robichek (ed.), "Financial Research and Managerial Decisions," John Wiley & Sons, Inc., New York, 1967.

——— and Willard T. Carleton: Financing Decisions of the Firm, *Journal of Finance,* vol. 21, pp. 202–214, May 1966.

——— and ———: The Integration of Capital Budgeting and Stock Valuation, *American Economic Review,* vol. 54, pp. 683–702, September 1964.

Levy, Haim and Yoram Kroll: Stochastic Dominance with Riskless Assets, *Journal of Financial and Quantitative Analysis,* vol. 11, no. 5, pp. 743–778, December 1976.

——— and Marshall Sarnat: Diversification, Portfolio Analysis, and the Uneasy Case for Conglomerate Mergers, *Journal of Finance,* vol. 25, pp. 795–802, September 1970.

Lewellen, Wilbur G.: "The Cost of Capital," Wadsworth Publishing Company, Inc., Belmont, Calif., 1969.

———, Michael S. Long, and John J. McConnell: Asset Leasing in Competitive Capital Markets, *Journal of Finance,* vol. 31, no. 3, pp. 787–798, June 1976.

——— and George A. Racette: Convertible Debt Financing, *Journal of Financial and Quantitative Analysis,* vol. 8, no. 5, pp. 777–792, December 1973.

Linke, Charles M. and Moon K. Kim: More on the Weighted Average Cost of Capital, *Journal of Financial and Quantitative Analysis,* vol. 9, pp. 1069–1081, December 1974.

Lintner, John: The Aggregation of Investors' Judgments and Preferences in Purely Competitive Security Markets, *Journal of Financial and Quantitative Analysis,* vol. 4, pp. 347–400, December 1969.

———: The Cost of Capital and Optimal Financing of Corporate Growth, *Journal of Finance,* vol. 18, May 1963.

———: Distribution of Income of Corporations among Dividends, Retained Earnings, and Taxes, *American Economic Review,* vol. 46, pp. 97–113, May 1956.

———: Dividends, Earnings, Leverage, Stock Prices and the Supply of Capital to Corporations, *Review of Economics and Statistics,* vol. 44, pp. 243–269, August 1962.

———: Expectations, Mergers, and Equilibrium in Purely Competitive Security Markets, *American Economic Review,* vol. 61, no. 2, pp. 101–111, May 1971.

———: The Valuation of Risk Assets and the Selection of Risky Investments in Stock Portfolios and Capital Budgets, *Review of Economics and Statistics,* vol. 47, pp. 13–37, February 1965.

Litzenberger, Robert H. and Howard B. Sosin: The Theory of Recapitalizations and the Evidence of Dual Purpose Funds, *Journal of Finance,* vol. 32, no. 5, pp. 1433–1455, December 1977.

Lloyd-Davies, Peter R.: Optimal Financial Policy in Imperfect Markets, *Journal of Financial and Quantitative Analysis,* vol. 10, no. 3, pp. 457–482, September 1975.

Long, Michael S. and George A. Racette: Stochastic Demand, Output and the Cost of Capital, *Journal of Finance,* vol. 29, no. 2, pp. 499–506, May 1974.

Luce, R. D. and Howard Raiffa: "Games and Decisions," John Wiley & Sons, Inc., New York, 1957.

Lutz, Frederick and Vera Lutz: "The Theory of Investment of the Firm," Princeton University Press, Princeton, N.J., 1951.

Machol, Robert E. and Eugene M. Lerner: Risk, Ruin, and Investment Analysis, *Journal of Financial and Quantitative Analysis,* vol. 4, pp. 473–492, December 1969.

Malkiel, Burton G.: Equity Yields, Growth, and the Structure of Share Prices, *American Economic Review,* vol. 53, pp. 1004–1031, December 1963.

——— and John G. Cragg: Expectations and the Structure of Share Prices, *American Economic Review,* vol. 60, pp. 601–617, September 1970.

Mandelbrot, Benoit: The Variation of Certain Speculative Prices, *Journal of Business,* vol. 36, pp. 394–419, October 1963.

———: Forecasts of Future Prices, Unbiased Markets, and Martingale Models, *Journal of Business,* vol. 39 (Special Supplement), pp. 242–255, January 1966.

Mandelker, Gershon: Risk and Return: The Case of Merging Firms, *Journal of Financial Economics,* vol. 1, no. 4, pp. 303–336, December 1974.

Mao, James C. T.: The Internal Rate of Return as a Ranking Criterion, *Engineering Economist,* vol. 11, pp. 1–13, Winter 1966.

———: Survey of Capital Budgeting: Theory and Practice, *Journal of Finance,* vol. 25, pp. 349–360, May 1970.

——— and John F. Helliwell: Investment Decisions under Uncertainty: Theory and Practice, *Journal of Finance,* vol. 24, pp. 323–338, May 1969.

Markowitz, Harry: Portfolio Selection, *Journal of Finance,* vol. 7, pp. 77–91, March 1952.

———: "Portfolio Selection," Wiley, New York, 1959.

Mason, R. Hal and Maurice B. Goudzwaard: Performance of Conglomerate Firms: A Portfolio Approach, *Journal of Finance,* vol. 31, no. 1, pp. 39–48, March 1976.

Masse, Pierre: "Optimal Investment Decisions," Prentice-Hall, Inc., Englewood Cliffs, N.J., 1962.

Mayshar, Joram: Investors' Time Horizon and the Inefficiency of Capital Markets, *Quarterly Journal of Economics,* vol. 92, no. 2, pp. 187–208, May 1978.

McConnell, John J.: Valuation of a Mortgage Company's Servicing Portfolio, *Journal of Financial and Quantitative Analysis,* vol. 11, pp. 433–453, September, 1976.

Melicher, Ronald W. and David F. Rush: Evidence on the Acquisition-Related Performance of Conglomerate Firms, *Journal of Finance,* vol. 29, no. 1, pp. 141–149, March 1974.

Merton, Robert C.: An Intertemporal Capital Asset Pricing Model, *Econometrica,* vol. 41, pp. 867–887, September 1973.

———: Lifetime Portfolio Selection under Uncertainty: The Continuous-Time Case, *Review of Economics and Statistics,* vol. 50, pp. 247–257, August 1969.

———: On the Pricing of Corporate Debt: The Risk Structure of Interest Rates, *Journal of Finance,* vol. 29, no. 2, pp. 449–470, May 1974.

———: On the Pricing of Contingent Claims and the Modigliani-Miller Theorem, *Journal of Financial Economics,* vol. 5, no. 2, pp. 241–250, November 1977.

———: Optimum Consumption and Portfolio Rules in a Continuous Time Model, *Journal of Economic Theory,* December 1971, pp. 373–413.

———: Option Pricing When Underlying Stock Returns Are Discontinuous, *Journal of Financial Economics,* vol. 3, January/March 1976.

———: Theory of Finance from the Perspective of Continuous Time, *Journal of Financial and Quantitative Analysis,* vol. 10, pp. 659–674, November 1975.

———: Theory of Rational Option Pricing, *Bell Journal of Economics and Management Science,* vol. 4, pp. 141–183, Spring 1973.

Miller, Edward M.: Risk, Uncertainty, and Divergence of Opinion, *Journal of Finance,* vol. 32, no. 4, pp. 1151–1168, September 1977.

Miller, Merton H.: Debt and Taxes, *Journal of Finance,* vol. 32, no. 2, pp. 261–276, May 1977.

———: The Demand for Money by Firms: Extension of Analytic Results, *Journal of Finance,* vol. 23, pp. 735–759, December 1968.

——— and Franco Modigliani: Dividend Policy, Growth and the Valuation of Shares, *Journal of Business,* vol. 34, pp. 411–432, October 1961.

——— and ———: Some Estimates of the Cost of Capital to the Electric Utility Industry, *American Economic Review,* vol. 56, pp. 334–391, June 1966.

——— and Daniel Orr: A Model of the Demand for Money by Firms, *Quarterly Journal of Economics,* vol. 80, pp. 413–435, August 1966.

——— and Charles W. Upton: Leasing, Buying and the Cost of Capital Services, *Journal of Finance,* vol. 31, no. 3, pp. 761–786, June 1976.

Milne, F.: Choice over Asset Economies: Default Risk and Corporate Leverage, *Journal of Financial Economics,* vol. 2, no. 2, pp. 165–186, June 1975.

Moag, Joseph S. and Eugene M. Lerner: Capital Budgeting Decisions under Imperfect Market Conditions— A Systems Framework, *Journal of Finance,* vol. 24, pp. 613–621, September 1969.

Modigliani, Franco and M. H. Miller: The Cost of Capital, Corporation Finance, and the Theory of Investment, *American Economic Review,* vol. 48, pp. 261–297, June 1958.

——— and ———: The Cost of Capital, Corporation Finance, and the Theory of Investment: Reply, *American Economic Review,* vol. 49, pp. 655–669, September 1959.

——— and ———: Reply to Heins and Sprenkle, *American Economic Review,* vol. 59, pp. 592–595, September 1969.

——— and ———: Taxes and the Cost of Capital: A Correction, *American Economic Review,* vol. 53, pp. 433–443, June 1963.

Mossin, Jan: Equilibrium in a Capital Asset Market, *Econometrica,* vol. 34, pp. 768–783.

———: Optimal Mutliperiod Portfolio Policies, *Journal of Business,* vol. 41, pp. 215–229, April 1968.

———: Security Pricing and Investment Criteria in Competitive Markets, *American Economic Review,* vol. 59, pp. 749–756, December 1969.

Mueller, Dennis C.: A Theory of Conglomerate Mergers, *Quarterly Journal of Economics,* vol. 83, pp. 643–659, November 1969.

Myers, Stewart C.: A Note on Linear Programming and Capital Budgeting, *Journal of Finance,* vol. 27, pp. 89–92, March 1972.

———: Determinants of Corporate Borrowing, *Journal of Financial Economics,* vol. 5, no. 2, pp. 147–176, November 1977.

———: Interactions of Corporate Financing and Investment Decisions—Implications for Capital Budgeting, *Journal of Finance,* vol. 29, no. 1, pp. 1–25, March 1974.

———: Procedures for Capital Budgeting under Uncertainty, *Industrial Management Review,* vol. 9, pp. 1–15, Spring 1968.

———: A Time-State Preference Model of Security Valuation, *Journal of Financial and Quantitative Analysis,* vol. 3, pp. 1–34, March 1968.

———, David A. Dill, and Alberto J. Bautista: Valuation of Financial Lease Contracts, *Journal of Finance,* vol. 31, no. 3, pp. 799–820, June 1976.

——— and Gerald A. Pogue: A Programming Approach to Corporate Financial Management, *Journal of Finance,* vol. 29, no. 2, pp. 579–599, May 1974.

——— and Stuart M. Turnbull: Capital Budgeting and the Capital Asset Pricing Model: Good News and Bad News, *Journal of Finance,* vol. 32, no. 2, pp. 321–332, May 1977.

Nantell, Timothy J. and C. Robert Carlson: The Cost of Capital as a Weighted Average, *Journal of Finance,* vol. 30, pp. 1343–1355, December 1975.

Naslund, Bertil and Andrew Whinston: A Model of Multi-period Investment under Uncertainty, *Management Science,* vol. 9, pp. 184–200, January 1962.

Nelson, Charles R.: Inflation and Capital Budgeting, *Journal of Finance,* vol. 31, no. 3, pp. 923–931, June 1976.

Pettit, R. Richardson: Dividend Announcements, Security Performance, and Capital Market Efficiency, *Journal of Finance,* vol. 27, no. 5. pp. 993–1008, December 1972.

Pinches, George E.: Financing with Convertible Preferred Stock, 1960–1967, *Journal of Finance,* vol. 25, pp. 53–63, March 1970.

Pratt, J.: Risk Aversion in the Small and in the Large, *Econometrica,* vol. 32, pp. 122–136, January–April 1964.

Pye, Gordon: Capital Gains Taxation, Dividends, and Capital Budgeting, *Quarterly Journal of Economics,* vol. 86, no. 2, pp. 226–242, May 1972.

———: Present Values for Imperfect Capital Markets, *Journal of Business,* vol. 39, January 1966.

———: The Value of the Call Option on a Bond, *Journal of Political Economy,* vol. 74, pp. 200–205, April 1966.

———: The Value of Call Deferment on a Bond: Some Empirical Results, *Journal of Finance,* vol. 22, pp. 623–636, December 1967.

Raiffa, Howard: "Decision Analysis," Addison-Wesley Publishing Company, Inc., Reading, Mass., 1968.

Reilly, Raymond R. and William E. Wecker: On the Weighted Average Cost of Capital, *Journal of Financial and Quantitative Analysis*, vol. 8, pp. 123–126, January 1973.

Resek, Robert W.: Multidimensional Risk and the Modigliani-Miller Hypothesis, *Journal of Finance*, vol. 25, pp. 47–52, March 1970.

Robichek, Alexander A.: Risk and the Value of Securities, *Journal of Financial and Quantitative Analysis*, vol. 4, pp. 513–538, December 1969.

——— and S. C. Myers: Conceptual Problems in the Use of Risk-Adjusted Discount Rates, *Journal of Finance*, December 1966, pp. 727–730.

——— and ———: "Optimal Financing Decisions," Prentice-Hall, Inc., Englewood Cliffs, N.J., 1965.

——— and ———: Problems in the Theory of Optimal Capital Structure, *Journal of Financial and Quantitative Analysis*, vol. 1, pp. 1–35, June 1966.

——— and ———: Valuation of the Firm: Effects of Uncertainty in a Market Context, *Journal of Finance*, vol. 21, pp. 215–227, May 1966.

———, D. Teichroew, and J. M. Jones: Optimal Short Term Financing Decision, *Management Science*, vol. 12, pp. 1–36, September 1965.

——— and James C. Van Horne: Abandonment Value and Capital Budgeting, *Journal of Finance*, vol. 22, pp. 577–589, December 1967.

Roll, Richard: A Critique of the Asset Pricing Theory's Tests; Part I: On Past and Potential Testability of the Theory, *Journal of Financial Economics*, vol. 4, no. 2, pp. 129–176, March 1977.

Ross, Stephen: The Current Status of the Capital Asset Pricing Model, *Journal of Finance*, vol. 33, no. 3, pp. 885–902, June 1978.

———: The Determination of Financial Structure: The Incentive-Signalling Approach, *Bell Journal of Economics and Management Science*, vol. 8, no. 1, pp. 23–40, Spring 1977.

———: Options and Efficiency, *Quarterly Journal of Economics*, vol. 90, no. 1, pp. 75–89, February 1976.

Rubinstein, Mark E.: A Comparative Statics Analysis of Risk Premiums, *Journal of Business*, vol. 46, no. 4, pp. 605–615, October 1973.

———: Corporate Financial Policy in Segmented Securities Markets, *Journal of Financial and Quantitative Analysis*, vol. 8, no. 5, pp. 749–762, December 1973.

———: A Mean-Variance Synthesis of Corporate Financial Theory, *Journal of Finance*, vol. 28, no. 1, pp. 167–181, March 1973.

———: Securities Market Efficiency in an Arrow-Debreu Economy, *American Economic Review*, vol. 65, no. 5, pp. 812–824, December 1975.

———: The Valuation of Uncertain Income Streams and the Pricing of Options, *Bell Journal of Economics and Management Science*, vol. 7, no. 2, pp. 407–425, Autumn 1976.

Sametz, Arnold W.: Trends in the Volume and Composition of Equity Finance, *Journal of Finance*, vol. 19, pp. 450–469, September 1964.

Samuelson, Paul A.: Lifetime Portfolio Selection by Dynamic Stochastic Programming, *Review of Economics and Statistics*, vol. 50, pp. 239–246, August 1969.

———: Proof That Properly Anticipated Prices Fluctuate Randomly, *Industrial Management Review*, vol. 6, pp. 41–49, Spring 1965.

———: Proof That Properly Discounted Present Values of Assets Vibrate Randomly, *Bell Journal of Economics and Management Science*, vol. 4, no. 2, pp. 369–374, Autumn 1973.

———: Some Aspects of the Pure Theory of Capital, *Quarterly Journal of Economics*, vol. 51, pp. 469–496, May 1937.

——— and Robert C. Merton: A Complete Model of Warrant Pricing That Maximizes Utility, *Industrial Management Review*, vol. 10, pp. 17–46, Winter 1969.

Sarnat, Marshall: A Note on the Implications of Quadratic Utility for Portfolio Theory, *Journal of Financial and Quantitative Analysis*, vol. 9, no. 4, pp. 687–690, September 1974.

——— and Haim Levy: The Relationship of Rules of Thumb to the Internal Rate of Return: A Restatement and Generalization, *Journal of Finance*, vol. 24, pp. 479–489, June 1969.

Schall, Lawrence D.: Asset Valuation, Firm Investment, and Firm Diversification, *Journal of Business,* vol. 45, no. 1, pp. 11–28, January 1972.

———: Firm Financial Structure and Investment, *Journal of Financial and Quantitative Analysis,* vol. 6, no. 3, pp. 925–942, June 1971.

———: The Lease or Buy and Asset Acquisition Decisions, *Journal of Finance,* vol. 39, no. 4, pp. 1203–1214, September 1974.

———, Lowell R. Bassett, and Roger LeRoy Miller: The Value of Stock Options, *Insurance Counsel Journal,* July 1971, pp. 433–445.

———, Gary L. Sundem, and William R. Geijsbeek Jr.: "Survey and Analysis of Capital Budgeting Methods," *Journal of Finance,* vol. 33, no. 1., pp. 281–287, March 1978.

Schlaifer, Robert: "Analysis of Decisions under Uncertainty," McGraw-Hill Book Company, New York, 1969.

———: "Probability and Statistics for Business Decisions," McGraw-Hill Book Company, New York, 1959.

Schwab, Bernhard and Peter Lusztig: A Comparative Analysis of the Net Present Value and the Benefit-Cost Ratios as Measures of the Economic Desirability of Investments, *Journal of Finance,* vol. 24, pp. 507–516, June 1969.

Schwartz, Eli: Theory of the Capital Structure of the Firm, *Journal of Finance,* vol. 14, pp. 18–39, March 1959.

——— and Richard Aronson: Some Surrogate Evidence in Support of the Concept of Optimal Financial Structure, *Journal of Finance,* vol. 22, pp. 10–18, March 1967.

Scott, James H., Jr.: A Theory of Optimal Capital Structure, *Bell Journal of Economics and Management Science,* vol. 7, no. 1, pp. 33–54, Spring 1976.

———: Bankruptcy, Secured Debt, and Optimal Capital Structure, *Journal of Finance,* vol. 32, no. 1, pp. 1–19, March 1977.

———: On the Theory of Conglomerate Mergers, *Journal of Finance,* vol. 32, no. 4, pp. 1235–1250, September 1977.

Shadrack, Frederick C., Jr.: Demand and Supply in the Commercial Paper Market, *Journal of Finance,* vol. 25, pp. 837–852, September 1970.

Sharpe, William F.: Capital Asset Prices: A Theory of Market Equilibrium under Conditions of Risk, *Journal of Finance,* vol. 19, pp. 425–442, September 1964.

———: "Portfolio Theory and Capital Markets," McGraw-Hill Book Company, New York, 1970.

Smith, C. W., Jr.: Option Pricing: A Review, *Journal of Financial Economics,* vol. 3, pp. 3–51, January/March 1976.

Smith, Vernon L.: Corporate Financial Theory under Uncertainty, *Quarterly Journal of Economics,* vol. 84, no. 3, pp. 451–471, August 1970.

———: Default Risk, Scale, and the Homemade Leverage Theorem, *American Economic Review,* vol. 62, no. 1, pp. 66–76, March 1972.

Soldofsky, Robert M.: The Size and Maturity of Direct Placement Loans, *Journal of Finance,* vol. 15, pp. 32–44, March 1960.

Solomon, Ezra: Alternative Rate of Return Concepts and Their Implications for Utility Regulations, *Bell Journal of Economics and Management Science,* vol. 1, pp. 65–81, Spring 1970.

———: Leverage and the Cost of Capital, *Journal of Finance,* vol. 17, pp. 273–279, May 1963.

———: "The Theory of Financial Management," Columbia University Press, New York, 1963.

Sprenkle, Case M.: The Uselessness of Transactions Demand Models, *Journal of Finance,* vol. 24, pp. 835–848, December 1969.

Stapleton, Richard C.: Portfolio Analysis, Stock Valuation and Capital Budgeting Decision Rules for Risky Projects, *Journal of Finance,* vol. 26, pp. 95–118, March 1971.

——— and M. G. Subrahmanyam: Market Imperfections, Capital Market Equilibrium, and Corporation Finance, *Journal of Finance,* vol. 32, no. 2, pp. 307–319, May 1977.

Stigler, G.: Imperfections in the Capital Markets, *Journal of Political Economy,* vol. 24, pp. 287–292, June 1967.

Stiglitz, J. E.: A Re-examination of the Modigliani-Miller Theorem, *American Economic Review,* vol. 59, pp. 784–793, December 1969.

———: On the Irrelevance of Corporate Financial Policy, *American Economic Review,* vol. 64, no. 6, pp. 851–866, December 1974.

———: Some Aspects of the Pure Theory of Corporate Finance: Bankruptcies and Take-overs, *Bell Journal of Economics and Management Science,* vol. 3, no. 2, pp. 458–482, Autumn 1972.

———: Taxation, Corporate Financial Policy, and the Cost of Capital, *Journal of Public Economics,* vol. 2, pp. 1–34, February 1973.

Sundem, Gary L.: Evaluating Capital Budgeting Models in Simulated Environments, *Journal of Finance,* vol. 30, no. 4, pp. 977–992, September 1975.

Teichroew, D., A. A. Robichek, and M. Montalbano: An Analysis of Criteria for Investment and Financing Decisions under Certainty, *Management Science,* November 1965.

———, ———, and ———: Mathematical Analysis of Returns under Certainty, *Management Science,* pp. 395–403, January 1965.

Terborgh, George: "Dynamic Equipment Policy," McGraw-Hill Book Company, New York, 1949.

Theil, Henri: On the Use of Information Theory Concepts in the Analysis of Financial Statements, *Management Science,* vol. 15, pp. 459–480, May 1969.

Tinsley, P. A.: Capital Structure, Precautionary Balances, and Valuation of the Firm: The Problem of Financial Risk, *Journal of Financial and Quantitative Analysis,* vol. 5, pp. 33–62, March 1970.

Tobin, James: Liquidity Preference as Behavior toward Risk, *Review of Economic Studies,* vol. 26, pp. 65–86, February 1958.

———: The Theory of Portfolio Selection, in F. H. Hahn and F. P. R. Brechling (eds.), "The Theory of Interest Rates," chap. 1, Macmillan & Co., Ltd., London, 1965.

Tuttle, D. L. and R. H. Litzenberger: Leverage, Diversification and Capital Market Effects on a Risk Adjusted Capital Budgeting Framework, *Journal of Finance,* vol. 23, pp. 427–443, June 1968.

Van Horne, James C.: A Note on Biases in Capital Budgeting Introduced by Inflation, *Journal of Financial and Quantitative Analysis,* vol. 6, March 1971.

———: Capital Budgeting Decisions Involving Combinations of Risky Investments, *Management Science,* vol. 13, pp. 84–92, October 1966.

———: Implied Fixed Costs of Long-term Debt Issues, *Journal of Financial and Quantitative Analysis,* vol. 8, no. 5, pp. 821–834, December 1973.

———: Interest Rate Risk and the Term Structure of Interest Rates, *Journal of Political Economy,* vol. 73, pp. 344–351, August 1965.

———: New Listings and Their Price Behavior, *Journal of Finance,* vol. 25, pp. 783–794, September 1970.

———: Optimal Initiation of Bankruptcy Proceedings, *Journal of Finance,* vol. 31, no. 3, pp. 897–910, June 1976.

Vickers, Douglas: The Cost of Capital and the Structure of the Firm, *Journal of Finance,* vol. 25, pp. 35–46, March 1970.

———: "The Theory of the Firm: Production, Capital, and Finance," McGraw-Hill Book Company, New York, 1968.

Von Neumann, J. and O. Morgenstern: "Theory of Games and Economic Behavior," 2d ed., Princeton University Press, Princeton, N.J., 1947.

Wallingford, Buckner A., II: Intertemporal Approach to the Optimization of Dividend Policy with Predetermined Investments, *Journal of Finance,* vol. 27, pp. 627–635, June 1972.

Walter, James E.: Dividend Policies and Common Stock Prices, *Journal of Finance,* vol. 11, pp. 29–41, March 1956.

———: Dividend Policy: Its Influence on the Value of the Enterprise, *Journal of Finance,* vol. 18, May 1963.

Warner, Jerold B.: Bankruptcy, Absolute Priority, and the Pricing of Risky Debt Claims, *Journal of Financial Economics,* vol. 4, no. 3, pp. 239–276, May 1977.

Weil, Roman L., Jr., Joel E. Segall, and David Green, Jr.: Premiums on Convertible Bonds, *Journal of Finance,* vol. 23, pp. 445–463, June 1968.

Weingartner, H. Martin: Capital Rationing: *n* Authors in Search of a Plot, *Journal of Finance,* vol. 32, no. 5, pp. 1403–1432, December 1977.

———: The Excess Present Value Index—A Theoretical Basis and Critique, *Journal of Accounting Research,* vol. 1, pp. 213–224, Autumn 1963.

———: The Generalized Rate of Return, *Journal of Financial and Quantitative Analysis,* vol. 1, pp. 1–29, September 1966.

———: "Mathematical Programming and the Analysis of Capital Budgeting Problems," Markham Publishing Co., Chicago, 1967.

———: Optimal Timing of Bond Refunding, *Management Science,* vol. 13, pp. 511–524, March 1967.

West, Richard R. and Harold Bierman, Jr.: Corporate Dividend Policy and Preemptive Security Issues, *Journal of Business,* vol. 42, pp. 71–75, January 1968.

Weston, J. Fred: A Test of Cost of Capital Propositions, *Southern Economic Journal,* vol. 30, pp. 105–112, October 1963.

——— and Surendra K. Mansinghka: Tests of the Efficiency of Conglomerate Firms, *Journal of Finance,* vol. 26, pp. 919–936, September 1971.

———, Keith V. Smith, and Ronald E. Shrieves: Conglomerate Performance Using the Capital Asset Pricing Model, *Review of Economics and Statistics,* pp. 357–363, November 1972.

Whitmore, G. A.: Market Demand Curve for Common Stock and the Maximization of Market Value, *Journal of Financial and Quantitative Analysis,* vol. 5, pp. 105–114, March 1970.

Williams, Joseph T.: Capital Asset Prices with Heterogeneous Beliefs, *Journal of Financial Economics,* vol. 5, no. 2, pp. 219–240, November 1977.

Williamson, Oliver E.: Managerial Discretion and Business Behavior, *American Economic Review,* vol. 53, pp. 1032–1057, December 1963.

Winkler, Robert L.: "An Introduction to Bayesian Inference and Decision," Holt, Rinehart and Winston, Inc., New York, 1972.

Wippern, Ronald F.: Financial Structure and the Value of the Firm, *Journal of Finance,* vol. 20, pp. 615–634, December 1966.

Wood, J. H.: Expectations and the Demand for Bonds, *American Economic Review,* pp. 522–530, September 1969.

# INDEX

# INDEX